# INVESTMENTS

## SPOT
## AND
## DERIVATIVES MARKETS

# INVESTMENTS

## SPOT
## AND
## DERIVATIVES MARKETS

**Keith Cuthbertson**
**and**
**Dirk Nitzsche**

JOHN WILEY & SONS, LTD

Chichester • New York • Weinheim • Brisbane • Singapore • Toronto

*Other Wiley Editorial Offices*

John Wiley & Sons, Inc., 605 Third Avenue,
New York, NY 10158-0012, USA

WILEY-VCH Verlag GmbH, Pappelallee 3,
D-69469 Weinheim, Germany

John Wiley & Sons Australia, Ltd, 33 Park Road, Milton,
Queensland 4064, Australia

John Wiley & Sons (Asia) Pte, Ltd, 2 Clementi Loop #02-01,
Jin Xing Distripark, Singapore 129809

John Wiley & Sons (Canada), Ltd, 22 Worcester Road,
Rexdale, Ontario M9W 1L1, Canada

***Library of Congress Cataloguing-in-Publication Data***

Cuthbertson, Keith.
 Investments : spot and derivatives markets / Keith Cuthbertson and Dirk Nitzsche.
   p. cm.
 Includes bibliographical references and index.
 ISBN 0-471-49583-2 (alk. paper)
 1. Derivative securities. 2. Investment analysis. I. Nitzsche, Dirk. II. Title.

 HG6024.A3 C883 2001
 332.6–dc21                                                   00-067211

***British Library Cataloguing in Publication Data***

A catalogue record for this book is available from the British Libary

ISBN 0 471 49583 2

Typeset in 10/12pt Times from the author's disks by Keytec Typesetting Ltd, Bridport, Dorset UK
Printed and bound in Great Britain by Bookcraft (Bath) Ltd, Midsomer Norton
This book is printed in acid-free paper responsibly manufactured from sustainable forestry, in which at least two trees are planted for each one used for paper production.

**To Alfred Stanley and Flossy**
*Keith Cuthbertson*


**To Mum and Dad**
*Dirk Nitzsche*


'Show me the money! Show me the money!'
(spoken by rookie football player to his agent, the eponymous Jerry McGuire,
United Artists, 1996)

# Contents

## INVESTMENTS: SPOT AND DERIVATIVES MARKETS

# PART 2: BASIC CONCEPTS

# PART 3: MONEY AND FIXED INCOME MARKETS

## PART 4: PORTFOLIO THEORY AND CAPITAL STRUCTURE

# PART 5: EQUITY MARKETS

# PART 6: THE FOREX MARKET

# PART 7: DERIVATIVE SECURITIES

# Preface

You may remember the rookie football player in the movie *Jerry McGuire* screaming 'Show me the money! Show me the money!' at his eponymous agent (played by Tom Cruise). Well this phrase certainly sums up a key motivation for this book, although as the reader will discover, the methods needed to make money and then protect its value can involve quite subtle strategies. Sure, you can make and lose (usually other people's) money in financial centres such as London, New York, Tokyo and Hong Kong without having much technical knowledge. But the majority of well paid jobs today in banking and finance, particularly as you rise up the corporate ladder, require a clear understanding of basic theoretical ideas and how these translate into real world decisions. One only has to think of the losses of Orange County, Metallgesellschaft, Nick Leeson of Barings, Long Term Capital Management and many others to realise that some financial decisions are rather complex and may involve risking vast sums of money. Clearly the impact of monetary and exchange rate policies, together with technological innovation (e.g. the move to electronic trading, sometimes via the internet), is also important in setting the framework in which investors, corporate treasurers and strategists operate.

The material in this book has been tried and tested on students taking MBA and MSc finance courses, primarily at Imperial College Management School, and professional courses for those working in the financial sector. Our 'customers' at the Management School are a mixture of social science and natural science students and are therefore somewhat heterogeneous in their academic backgrounds. They pay 'serious money' and for the most part are not interested in theories solely for their elegance but for their applicability to problems and issues found in 'the real world'. Keat's dictum in *Ode on a Grecian Urn* that 'Beauty is Truth, Truth Beauty-that is all ye know on earth and all ye need to know' has not been embraced 100% by the finance students we have met. Of course, as instructors we do emphasise 'elegance' wherever possible and, although we don't 'Show them the money', we do show them ways to get the money (legally) and then to protect it.

So, we always demonstrate the practical relevance of any theoretical concepts we use, and this is the basic philosophy behind this text and our companion volume *Financial Engineering: Derivatives and Risk Management*.

## AIMS

A key aim of the book is to take basic concepts from finance and economics and to demonstrate how these can be used to understand real world practical issues facing individual investors, firms, governments and regulators. The book covers three broad themes:

- **Behaviour in financial markets**—including the pricing of risky assets and alternative investment strategies.
- **Decisions in corporate finance**—such as raising capital (including an analysis of callable bonds, convertibles, warrants and stock options), the valuation of firms and investment projects, creating shareholder value, capital structure, dividend policy, mergers and acquisitions, hedging business and financial risk.
- **Public policy issues**—including the impact of monetary policy, the choice of exchange rate policy, 'excess volatility' in financial markets, internet day trading, hedge funds and the role of derivatives and finally, policy issues in international finance, including EMU.

The book is aimed at final year undergraduates in finance, business studies/management and core courses for MBA and MSc finance students and those undertaking professional qualifications in the finance sector. No prior knowledge of math or stats is assumed beyond that in a first-year undergraduate 'quants for business studies' course, and two separate revision chapters on these topics are included.

After completing a one or two-semester course based on this text, the student can then deepen her knowledge of financial markets by reading our companion text *Financial Engineering: Derivatives and Risk Management*.

# MARKET NICHE

There are many texts with the title of either *Investments* or *Corporate Finance*. Our view is that at an introductory level it is a mistake to compartmentalise to this extent, since the same basic concepts can be applied to these two broad areas and it is important that students recognise this fact. For example, mean–variance portfolio theory provides one possible method of asset allocation for 'the investor'. However (with a few additional assumptions) the same basic ideas also give the CAPM and hence provide a risk adjusted discount rate for an (all equity) firm, as discussed in corporate finance texts. Discounted present value (DPV) and arbitrage arguments can be used by investors to price equities and bonds. Similarly, these concepts are also central in establishing the famous Modigliani–Miller theorem on capital structure, found in corporate finance texts. Options can be used by investors to obtain leverage on their speculative investments, but the same theoretical ideas are used to aid corporate strategy decisions (i.e. real options) and to value companies themselves (e.g. pricing internet stocks) for floatation and takeover decisions. Of course, both investors and corporates use derivatives to hedge commodities, stocks, bonds, FX and interest rate risk, so these ideas are common to both participants. If the student has worked hard to master the basic concepts in finance, it seems wasteful not to demonstrate their practical use both in understanding investments and analysing corporate finance issues, in a single text.

So, this text uses ideas from both economics and finance and its coverage is therefore wider than more traditional texts that have the title *Investments*. Sure, we cover the 'standard topics' but we also have something of a market niche in the following.

## THE BIG PICTURE

We include issues that place investments and corporate finance decisions in their wider context. For example, we include a discussion of the role of independent Central Banks in setting monetary policy and its implications for the real economy, business risk and hence for asset prices. Theories of the spot exchange rate allow us to examine their implications for policy issues such as the appropriate exchange rate regime, entry into a common currency (EMU), and the importance of international portfolio diversification and arguments surrounding a 'New International Financial Architecture'. The hedging of business and financial risk using a wide variety of derivatives is also examined in some detail.

## NON-TRADITIONAL APPROACHES

Here we include noise trader models and 'behavioural finance', stock market predictability, chaos theory, anomalies, volatility and bubbles. We also examine the behaviour of chartists, momentum traders and the use of technical analysis, candlestick charts and more technical methods such as artificial neural networks for predicting asset prices.

## PRACTICAL DETAILS

Practical aspects used 'On the Street' are highlighted. These include market structure and conventions such as short selling, 'haircuts' and margins, bid–ask spreads, price quotes and interpreting information in the financial press, such as the *Financial Times* and *Wall Street Journal*. We emphasise the limitations of 'textbook' portfolio allocation and therefore include a discussion of the home bias problem, hedging foreign currency receipts, model error and sensitivity analysis. Speculative strategies in stock, bond and spot FX markets are also examined, as is the use of FX swaps for hedging forward deals. Practical corporate finance issues include project evaluation methods which take account of working capital, depreciation and 'tax shields' and the valuation of companies (including internet stocks) using NPV, EVA, real options, etc. Actual capital structure decisions (e.g. Eurotunnel restructuring) and mergers and takeovers (e.g. Time Warner and AOL) are used to demonstrate the limitations of some theoretical approaches.

# ACCESSIBLE STYLE

The motivation for the theoretical concepts presented is based on practical issues. Linking intuitive arguments to simple math and stats is also viewed as of paramount importance. Separate chapters in basic math and stats are provided, and any complex derivations are relegated to appendices so as not to interfere with the flow of the argument in the text.

Given the heterogeneous academic backgrounds of students on many MBA and MSc finance courses, we do not shy away from occasionally using contemporary analogies to reinforce theoretical ideas. Take, for example, Mr Vincent Vega in the opening shot of the film *Pulp Fiction*, where he is talking to his partner Jules about his recent trip to Amsterdam. Are you aware that in discussing the relative merits of a BigMac in L.A. and a BigMac in Amsterdam, Vincent was imparting important information on the difficulties in testing purchasing power parity? (Although the primary aim of his visit seems to have been a mixture of international portfolio diversification and risky arbitrage, with illegal substances.) You will meet more of these analogies in the text (and even more if you attend our lectures).

## TOPIC BOXES

Separate 'boxes' highlight the following three broad objectives:

- **Linking theoretical ideas to 'real world' issues**—such as debt rescheduling, mergers and acquisitions, international asset allocation, valuation of internet stocks.
- **Public policy issues**—such as the Maastricht conditions for entry into 'Euroland', excess volatility in financial markets, monetary policy, new international financial architecture, hedge funds and LTCM, the merger of AOL and Time Warner.
- **Finance can be fun**—this includes a mini 'soap opera' of the amorous relationship between Barbie and Ken and how derivatives can help the course of true love. The BigMac Index, Bowie Bonds, electronic day trading and 'Float and Sink?' also fall under this heading.

## STUDENT LEARNING

### TEXT

Includes learning objectives, 'summary' boxes, 'topic' boxes, worked examples, end of chapter exercises, glossary of terms, technical appendices, lists of symbols, further reading, equation listing. Logical sequence of material and clear layout, two colours.

### WILEY WEB SITE http://www.wiley.co.uk/cuthbertson

(i) Download Excel 'hands-on' software reproducing the tables in the text and answers to selected questions. These Excel files are 'cell based' so the student can clearly see the methods used and directly relate these to material in the text (e.g. pricing a bond using spot rates, calculating the yield to maturity, forward rates, etc.). Interactive user inputs and graphical results also aid comprehension (e.g. price yield relationship for bonds, Black–Scholes equation for the option price–stock price relationship).

(ii) Excel software where the interactive user input is based on specific Visual Basic programs.

(iii) Gauss programs. Gauss code closely matches the algebra used in the text and the user can amend the source code. It gives very quick results and high quality graphical output for numerical problems (e.g. NPV, forward rates, duration, Black–Scholes, portfolio allocation, forward rates, yield curves). Students can purchase Gauss Lite for around USD 40 from Aptech Systems (www.aptech.com). The Gauss programming language is very similar to other languages (e.g. Visual Basic, C++) and can easily handle both complex statistical/econometric problems and numerical finance problems, so the student will learn generic skills.

(iv) Web links to other sites with free Gauss and Excel software.
(v) Useful linked web sites for further financial information on a wide variety of topic areas (e.g. futures and options exchanges, Central Banks, financial regulators, internet share dealers and general investment information services).
(vi) Download additional self-test questions, quizzes (with answers), selected reading and additional 'topic boxes' on matters of current debate.

## LECTURER'S MATERIAL

**WILEY WEB SITE** `http://www.wiley.co.uk/cuthbertson`

Download:
(i) All figures and tables in the text (for use in Word or Powerpoint).
(ii) A 'full' set of Powerpoint slides for complete lectures, which can then be customised.
(iii) Answers to end of chapter exercises from the text plus additional questions and answers.
(iv) 'Topic box' updates on key issues plus selected additional reading for students.

---

**INVESTMENTS: SUGGESTED COURSE STRUCTURE**
**(One or Two Semesters)**

---

ONE SEMESTER COURSE
TWO SEMESTER COURSE (ADDITIONAL MATERIAL = **)

| | |
|---|---|
| Chapter 1 | Markets, Firms and Investors |
| Chapter 2** | The Business Environment |
| Chapter 3** | Investment Appraisal |
| Chapter 6 | Money Markets |
| Chapter 7 | Bond Markets |
| Chapter 8** | Forward Rates, Yield Curves and the Term Structure |
| Chapter 9** | Bond Market Strategies |
| Chapter 10 | Portfolio Theory and Asset Returns |
| Chapter 12 | Equity Finance and Stock Valuation |
| Chapter 13** | Efficient Markets and Predictability |
| Chapter 14** | Anomalies, Noise Traders and Chaos |
| Chapter 15 | The Foreign Exchange Market |
| Chapter 16** | Spot FX: Fundamentals and Noise Traders |
| Chapter 17** | Technical Trading Rules |
| Chapter 18** | International Portfolio Diversification |
| Chapter 19 | Derivative Securities: An Overview |
| Chapter 20 | Futures Markets |
| Chapter 21 | Options Markets |

Selected elements from Chapter 4 'Financial Arithmetic' and Chapter 5 'Basic Statistics' could be included if the students do not have prior math and stats, or they could be used for self-study. Clearly, a one-semester course can only cover 'traditional' basic concepts, but the accompanying 'topic boxes' provide interesting practical examples. In addition, the Excel software (on the web pages) provides interactive 'hands-on' experience, while links to other web sites provide further 'real world' issues as a basis for projects and coursework.

A two-semester course can go much deeper into the non-traditional or 'behavioural finance' aspects that are often excluded from basic texts on investments (e.g. noise traders, technical trading rules, chaos, neural networks, etc.). The issues surrounding international portfolio diversification, the home bias problem and hedge funds can also be analysed, along with monetary and exchange rate policy and issues arising from currency unions such as EMU.

---

**CORPORATE FINANCE: SUGGESTED COURSE STRUCTURE**
**(One Semester)**

---

Chapter 1   Markets, Firms and Investors
*Box 1.1: Loan Sales*
*Box 1.2: Bowie Bonds*
*Box 1.3: Russian Eurobond Issues*
*Box 1.4: Warrants versus Convertibles*

Chapter 3   Investment Appraisal
*Box 3.1: Project Finance*
*Box 3.2: Time Warner and AOL: Synergies?*

Chapter 6   Money Markets
*Box 6.1: CDs: Market Conventions*
*Box 6.2: Orange County (Repos and Leverage)*

Chapter 7   Bond Markets
*Box 7.1: Auctions and Tenders*
*Box 7.2: Convertible Bonds*

Chapter 10   Portfolio Theory and Asset Returns
*Box 10.1: Asset Allocation in Practice*

Chapter 11   Valuing Firms: Capital Structure and the Cost of Capital
*Box 11.1: Is EVA Popular?*
*Box 11.2: Eurotunnel Restructuring*

Chapter 12   Equity Finance and Stock Valuation
*Box 12.1: Valuation of Internet and Biotechnology Stocks*
*Box 12.2: Uses for 'Betas'*

Chapter 13    Efficient Markets and Predictability
*Box 13.1: Float and Sink?*

Chapter 15    The Foreign Exchange Market
*Box 15.1: Maastricht Criteria and EMU*
*Box 15.2: BigMac Index*

Chapter 19    Derivative Securities: An Overview
*Box 19.1: Swaps: Ken and Barbie*

Chapter 20    Futures Markets
*Box 20.1: Hedging with Forwards and Futures: Ken and Barbie*

Chapter 21    Options Markets
*Box 21.1: Options: Ken and Barbie, the Finale*

Above, we have included the list of topic boxes to demonstrate the wide range of issues that can be analysed in a one-semester course in corporate finance, and of course all the software and other web material is available to the student. Note that mergers and acquisitions are mainly dealt with in Chapter 3 'Investment Appraisal', with some discussion of the real options approach in Chapter 21. Chapter 11 on valuation, capital structure and dividend policy is rather substantial and would probably take up two lectures, with the material in Chapter 13 on efficient markets and Chapter 15 on the FX market being used selectively (see detailed contents list).

Topics which are not included above but do come under the heading of corporate finance include cash and credit management, financial planning and leasing. But these topics do not use any interesting new concepts and generally we find they do not enthuse the students (or us). So, we have omitted these from the text. Further analysis of the use of real options in corporate finance can be found in our companion text *Financial Engineering: Derivatives and Risk Management*.

# ACKNOWLEDGEMENTS

This book and its companion text *Financial Engineering: Derivatives and Risk Management* seem to have had a rather longer gestation period than the birth cycle of a consecutive sequence of half a dozen pregnant elephants. Thanks go to the many people with whom we have discussed the issues in the book and the best methods for presentation, particularly our colleagues in the finance section at the Management School at Imperial College. Our thanks must also go to students and finance practitioners who have given us comments on the material. In particular, 'demanding' students on several MBA finance courses and the MSc (Finance) at the Management School at Imperial College and the students who 'drifted over' from the MSc (Mathematics and Finance) run by the Mathematics Department at Imperial. Other comments from MSc students at City University Business School, students on the DEA at Bordeaux, in the Economics Departments at UNAM, Mexico City and the Freie University, Berlin, where Cuthbertson was Bundesbank Visiting Professor, have also been most useful. The material has also been 'tested' on practitioners in the City of London (not forgetting the Inland Revenue, who helpfully did not tax the fee at source). The typing of the many redrafts has been cheerfully and competently undertaken by Brenda Munoz and Yvonne Doyle. Finally, our thanks to Sam Whittaker, the commissioning editor at John Wiley, who oversaw the birth of this (and our companion text) while herself in the process of giving birth, but thankfully over a much shorter time scale.

# PART 1

# OVERVIEW AND BASIC CONCEPTS

# CHAPTER 1

# Markets, Firms and Investors

**LEARNING OBJECTIVES**

- To present some of the terminology used across many different financial instruments and markets.
- To discuss the main **financial instruments**, who issues them and the functions they perform.
- To analyse the main **forms of ownership** and how **corporate control** is exercised between shareholders, directors and managers.
- How **mergers and takeovers** provide a method of changing corporate control.
- To examine the main decisions facing investors and the role played by **arbitrageurs, speculators and hedgers** in the trading process.

Finance is the antithesis of Polonius' advice to his son, in Shakespeare's *Hamlet*, of 'neither a borrower nor a lender be'. Individuals benefit from consuming goods and services, which are primarily produced by firms but also by the government sector (e.g. education, health and transport facilities in many countries). To produce 'goods', firms and the government often have to finance additional current and capital investment expenditures by borrowing funds. Financial markets and institutions facilitate the flow of funds between surplus and deficit units.

The *existing* stock of financial assets (e.g. stocks and bonds) is far larger than the flow of new funds onto the market, and this stock of assets represents accumulated past savings. Individuals and financial institutions trade these 'existing' assets in the hope that they either increase the return on their portfolio of asset holdings or reduce the riskiness of their portfolio.

Just as there are a wide variety of goods to purchase, there are also a wide variety of methods of borrowing and lending money, to suit the preferences of different individuals and institutions. When you 'walk around' alternative supermarkets, department stores and the internet there is a bewildering array of merchandise. Some sellers try as far as possible to cater for the 'mass market' (e.g. Marks and Spencer), others cater for more idiosyncratic tastes and styles (e.g. John-Paul Gaultier), while some sell rather shoddy goods (there are no examples we can name here, because of possible litigation, but you will have your favourites). Brand names and reputation effect can be important when selling goods. Similarly, the markets for funds cater both for the relatively homogeneous 'mass market' but also try to tailor 'products' to individual requirements.

'Brand names' like the London Stock Exchange, NASDAQ (North American Securities Dealers Automated Quotations) and the Chicago Board of Trade, as well as financial intermediaries like Merrill Lynch, Morgan Stanley (Dean Witter), Citibank, Salomon Bros, Goldman Sachs, etc. are a key element in the process of transferring funds between different 'players' in the financial marketplace. There are even financial products which are on a par with 'shoddy goods', and junk bonds or bonds of certain emerging economies come to mind here. But that's not to say that these do not provide 'value for money', that is they may be 'high risk' but this may also entail high average returns.

In this chapter we begin by presenting an overview of the main markets and instruments used for raising new funds and in trading existing financial 'claims'. In Section 1.2 we then look more closely at the different forms of ownership and control and how they relate to equity and debt holders. We conclude Section 1.2 with an overview of the market for corporate control via mergers and takeovers. In Section 1.3 we examine more closely the types of traders in the market and the types of 'deals' in which they are engaged.

Most of the issues discussed in this opening chapter will be reconsidered in greater depth in subsequent chapters. However, there is still quite a lot of new terminology to digest. If this becomes too overwhelming you should at this point 'skim read' this material, returning to it when you forget particular definitions. Nevertheless, we think it is useful to try and take in some of the 'big picture' before getting immersed in the fine details of the plethora of financial instruments available in today's modern economies.

# 1.1 MARKETS AND INSTRUMENTS

Financial markets facilitate the exchange of financial instruments such as stocks, bills and bonds, foreign exchange, futures, options and swaps. These assets are the means by which 'claims' on cash flows are transferred from one party to another. Frequently, financial assets involve delayed receipts or payments and they therefore also transfer funds across time (e.g. if you purchase a bond today you hand over cash but the payouts from the bond occur over many future periods). Trading may take place face-to-face as, for example, pit-trading in futures and options on the Chicago Mercantile Exchange (CME) (and until 1999 on the London International Financial Futures Exchange, LIFFE). Trading in some markets takes place via telephone or telex with the aid of computers to track prices (e.g. the foreign exchange or FX market). There is also a general move towards settling transactions using only computers (i.e. non-paper transactions), for example, as reflected in the London Stock Exchange new CREST system for automated settlements.

Financial instruments are generally referred to as **securities**. Securities differ in the timing of payments, whether they can be readily sold prior to maturity in a secondary liquid market (e.g. via the stock exchange) and in the legal obligations associated with each security (e.g. bondholders must be paid before equity holders). Many securities are *readily negotiable claims*. They entitle the owner to a claim on future payments from the issuer of the security (usually a firm or governments). *Readily negotiable* means that the owner of the security may sell it quickly and with low transactions costs—then the market is said to be *liquid*. The London Stock Exchange has an automated quotation system (SEAQ) which gives continuous screen prices. However, even in highly competitive financial markets, the price at which an investor can purchase an instrument (the **offer price**) will differ from that at which the same instrument could be sold (the **bid price**). The difference between the two is called the **bid–ask spread**. A small bid–ask spread is the hallmark of a highly competitive market.

The **tick size** is the minimum price movement allowed on a particular asset. For example, the tick size for most coupon paying government bonds is 1/32 of 1% (of the par value). The **tick value** represents the cash value of 1 tick. Clearly this depends on the size of the deal being quoted. For example, on $100,000 held in government bonds, the tick value is $31.25 = $100,000(1/3200)]. Changes in interest rates are generally discussed in terms of **basis points**. A rise in interest rates from 5% to 6% is a change of 100 basis points (bp), hence 1 bp is equivalent to 0.01%. Different markets (e.g. for FX, futures and options) have different tick sizes and tick values. These concepts provide a useful shorthand for market participants who might for example state that 'government bond prices have just risen 4 ticks'.

**Market makers** hold a portfolio of securities which they stand ready to buy or sell at quoted prices, this is known as **'a book'**. The bid–ask spread allows market makers to make a profit, as they buy instruments at a lower price than they sell them. If a market is highly competitive, with many buyers and sellers, and widely-disseminated information on bid and offer prices, the bid–ask spread will be reduced to that level which just allows traders to make a profit. On SEAQ the **touch** is the difference between the highest bid and the lowest offer price and on SEAQ these are displayed in a 'yellow strip' on the screen. Whereas market makers trade on their 'own account' and hold positions in various securities, a **broker** acts as a middle man between two investors (usually referred to as counterparties—see Figure 1.1). The broker brings the buyer and seller together (e.g. this could be two different market makers or a private or institutional investor and a market maker). The broker does not hold 'a book' but charges a commission for transacting the deal between the two counterparties.

Some financial 'deals', rather than taking place on an organised exchange where prices are continuously quoted (e.g. the New York Stock Exchange), are instead negotiated directly between two (or more) parties. For example, this applies to the market for bank term loans and deposits between large companies and the banks and in the market for forward foreign exchange. Trading often takes place over the telephone (and telex) between the two counterparties. These transactions are said to take place in **over-the-counter (OTC) markets**.

Financial instruments derive their value purely on the basis of the future performance of the issuer. A financial instrument has no intrinsic value—it is usually a piece of paper or an entry in a register. In an extreme case, if the issuer ceases to make payments on the

## FIGURE 1.1: Brokers and dealers

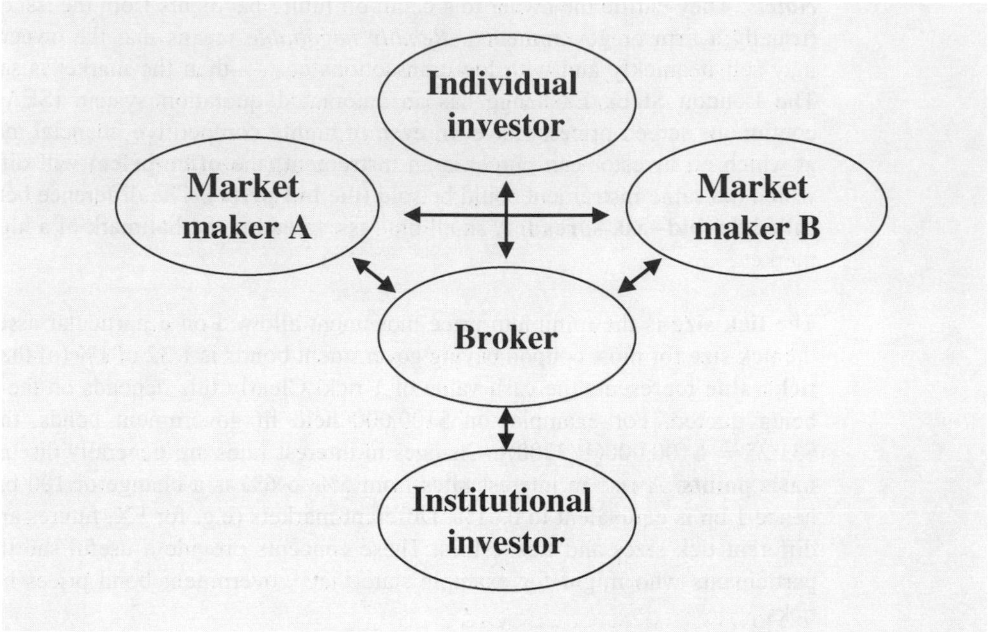

instrument (i.e. the issuer *defaults*), the instrument may be worthless, or its value may suddenly become a small fraction of that were the issuer not to have defaulted. The main financial markets, securities traded and the motives for their issuance are discussed next.

## GOVERNMENT SECURITIES MARKET

Central governments issue securities for two reasons. First, short-term *Treasury bills* are issued to cover temporary shortfalls in the government's net receipts. For example, a government purchasing department may have to pay its suppliers of stationery next week, but in this particular week tax receipts may be unusually low. It may therefore obtain the finance required by issuing Treasury bills. Second, medium and long-term bonds are issued to raise funds to cover any excess of long-term planned government spending over forecasted tax revenue (i.e. the government's budget deficit or public sector borrowing requirement, PSBR).

Traditionally, governments used to alter the quantity of money in circulation by buying and selling T-bills from the private sector. This is still possible but it is now often accomplished by using the repo market (see below). Government securities have several common characteristics. First, they are generally regarded as being free from default risk. This makes them a safer investment than most other instruments, and so allows governments to offer lower yields, reducing the cost of debt finance to the taxpayer. Usually new issues of T-bills and T-bonds are by public auction, with the securities allotted on the basis of the highest prices in the (sealed) bids. There are usually very active secondary markets in these instruments (in industrialised nations).

Medium and long-term bonds pay out fixed amounts known as *coupon* payments, usually paid semi-annually, as well as a lump sum at redemption. Finally, government securities may be **bearer securities**, in which case whoever currently holds the security is deemed to be the owner, or there may be a **central register** of owners to whom interest payments (and eventually the redemption value) are made. The main instruments issued by the UK Government (Debt Management Office) and the US Government (through the Federal Reserve Bank) are as follows.

## UK GOVERNMENT SECURITIES
- **Treasury bills**—Short-term securities used in money market operations. T-bills are offered for tender on the last business day of each week, normally have a maturity of 91 or 182 days, and are pure discount bearer instruments.
- **Gilts**—Long-term UK government bonds are called gilt-edged stock, or just gilts. They are issued on a broadly monthly basis for maturities of up to 30 years.
- **Eurobonds**—The UK Government may issue bonds in London, denominated in currencies other than sterling. The funds raised are added to the government's foreign exchange reserves, rather than used to finance the borrowing requirement.

## US GOVERNMENT SECURITIES
- **Treasury bills**—As in the UK, these are short-term securities, with maturities of 13 weeks, 26 weeks and 1 year. Again, they are pure discount bearer instruments. 13-week and 26-week TBs are issued by auction every Monday.
- **Treasury notes**—Treasury notes have a maturity of between 1 and 7 years, and the holder receives a series of coupon payments.
- **Treasury bonds**—Treasury bonds are generally issued for the purpose of long-term finance at maturities between 7 and 30 years. Coupon payments are usually made semi-annually.

## OTHER PUBLIC-SECTOR SECURITIES
In the UK, local authorities and public corporations (companies) also issue debt, denominated in both sterling and foreign currencies. In the US, bonds issued by states, counties, cities and towns are called *municipal bonds*. These public-sector securities are not perceived as being free from default risk, nor are the markets for them as deep or as liquid as those for central government debt. Consequently they tend to offer higher yields than central government debt.

For long term borrowing, some local governments (municipalities) and central governments also use the syndicated bank loan market (i.e. an OTC transaction involving several banks) or the Eurobond market.

The technical details of the relationship between bond prices and yields on government bonds and further details of these important markets are discussed in Chapter 7. In Chapter 8 we look at a related issue, namely the relationship between yields on bonds of different maturities, which is referred to as the **term structure of interest rates**. In turn, this leads to the concept of forward rates which can be used to price forward rate agreements and futures contracts. In Chapter 9 we investigate how you can hedge future cash flows (e.g. pension payments) using bonds: this is known as **portfolio immunisation**.

## MONEY MARKET

The money market refers to a loosely connected set of institutions that deal in short-term securities (usually with a maturity of less than 1 year). These money market instruments include those issued by the public sector (e.g. Treasury bills, Local Authority bills) and by the private sector (e.g. commercial bills/paper, trade bills, certificates of deposit, CDs). Bills are usually **discount instruments**. This means that the holder of the bill does not receive any interest payments: the bill derives its value wholly from the fact that it is redeemed at an amount greater than its selling price.

The **commercial paper** market is very large in the US where large corporates very often borrow money by issuing commercial paper rather than using bank loans. On the other hand, if corporates have a short-term cash surplus which they do not need for 3 months, they may place this on deposit in a bank and receive a certificate of deposit (which can either be 'cashed in' at maturity or sold in the secondary market). A **certificate of deposit (CD)** is a 'piece of paper' giving the terms (i.e. amount, interest rate and time to maturity) on which a corporate has placed funds on deposit, for say 6 months in a particular bank. In this respect it is like a (fixed) term deposit. However, with a CD, if the corporate finds itself in need of cash it can sell the CD to a third party (at a discount) before the 6 months are up and hence obtain cash immediately.

Market makers hold an inventory of these assets and stand ready to buy and sell them (usually over the telephone) at prices that are continuously quoted and updated on the dealers' screens. At the core of the market in the US are the 'money market banks' (i.e. large banks in New York), government securities dealers, commercial paper dealers and money brokers (who specialise in finding short-term money for borrowers and placing it with lenders). Until fairly recently only the Discount Houses could deal with the Bank of England in buying and selling UK T-bills, but this 'special relationship' became defunct with the development of the repo market (in bills and bonds) in 1997, so the UK market now operates in a similar way to the US market. We deal with the relationship between the Central Bank, which sets the 'official' interest rate, and its impact on other interest rates and asset prices in Chapter 2, when discussing monetary policy and the flow of funds.

## REPURCHASE AGREEMENTS

A widely used method of borrowing cash (used particularly by market makers) is to undertake a **repurchase agreement** or **repo**. A repo, or more accurately a 'sale and repurchase agreement' is a form of collateralised borrowing. Suppose you own a government bond but wish to borrow cash over the next 7 days. You can enter an agreement to sell the bond to M's A for $100 today and *simultaneously agree* to buy it back in 7 days time for $100.2. You receive $100 cash (now) and the counterparty M's A receives $100.2 (in 7 days)—an interest rate of 0.2% over 7 days (or $10.43\% = 0.2 \times 365/7$, expressed as a simple annual rate). M's A has provided a collateralised loan since she holds the bond and could sell it if you default on the repo. Central Banks often use repos in their open market operations (see below) rather than outright purchases/sales of bonds, when trying to influence interest rates. Repos can be as short as over 1 day and there are very active markets in maturities up to 3 months. Note that if you undertake a repo, the counterparty is said to undertake a **reverse repo** and the counterparty will therefore be *lending* money. Further details of assets traded in the money market and the methods used to determine their prices and yields are the subject of Chapter 6.

## CORPORATE SECURITIES

A limited company is a firm owned by two or more shareholders who have limited liability, (i.e. their responsibility for covering the firm's losses does not reach beyond the capital they have invested in the firm). In return for their capital investment, shareholders are entitled to a portion of the company's earnings, in accordance with their proportionate shareholding. Firms issue equity and debt (corporate bonds) to raise finance for investment projects.

### PRIMARY (NEW ISSUES) AND SECONDARY MARKETS

The initial sale of securities (equities and bonds) takes place in the **primary market** and there are two main vehicles: initial public offerings and private placements. Most **initial public offerings (IPOs)** or **unseasoned new issues** are *underwritten* by a syndicate of merchant banks (for a fee of around 1.5–2% of the value underwritten, which is sometimes paid in the form of share warrants—see below). In a **firm commitment**, the underwriter buys the securities from the corporation at an agreed price and then hopes to sell them on to other investors at a higher price (thus earning a 'spread' on the deal). The advantage to the corporation is the guaranteed fixed price, with the underwriter taking the risk that 'other investors' may be willing to pay less for the shares.

IPOs have been a feature of the sell off of publicly owned industries in many industrial countries and emerging market economies. For example, in the UK, the privatisation of British Telecom, British Airways, British Gas and Railtrack. In some large public offerings by government the lead banks will run 'roadshows' where they inform institutional investors of prospects for the industry. In the case of the sale of the UK Government's remaining 40% stake of £4bn in the UK's large power generators, National Power and PowerGen, in 1995 the lead banks were Barclays, DeZoete Wedd (BZW) and Kleinwort Benson who acted as 'bookrunners'. They obtained bids from institutional investors worldwide who were asked to state how much they would purchase at particular prices and whether the bids were firm or indicative. (Retail investors were also allocated a proportion of the shares on a tapering scale if they were oversubscribed, that is if someone bid for 10,000 shares and another person 500 at the offer price then the latter might receive his bid in full and the former might only receive 2000, or even zero shares.) For the institutional bids, computers are used to 'construct' a demand curve for the offer and display other information such as the geographical distribution of potential sales, demand by type of customer (e.g. banks, corporates, pension funds, hedge funds), etc. In contrast, the Czech Republic in the 1990s used a voucher scheme to enable individuals to obtain shares in newly privatised industries. In many developing countries the privatisation of banks and power generation has involved IPOs. Of course, many companies whose shares are not initially traded eventually come to market via an IPO, such as Richard Branson's *Virgin* company, Anita Roddick's *Body Shop* and recently 'dot.com' companies such as *Lastminute.com*.

The alternative to a firm commitment deal is for the underwriter to agree to act as an agent and merely try and sell the shares at the offer price in a **best efforts** deal. Here, the underwriter does not buy the shares outright and hence incurs no underwriting risk. Usually, if the shares cannot be sold at the offer price they are withdrawn.

Sometimes the underwriter has a **green-shoe provision** whereby she can purchase additional shares from the company (say up to 15% of the initial issue) at the offer price, over a fixed period of time (e.g. for 30 days after the floatation). If the issue is oversubscribed and the post-issue market price goes above the offer price the underwriter can make additional profits by buying shares from the company and selling them in the open market.

Because of the relatively high transactions costs of public offerings (and evidence of economies of scale), they are used only for large floatations. For smaller firms 'going public' **private placements** are often used. Here, debt or equity is sold to large institutions such as pension funds, insurance companies and mutual funds, on the basis of private negotiations. Sometimes a new issue is a mix of IPO and private placement.

It is rather difficult to set a 'fair price' for a new issue. If the offer price is too high then the issue will be unsuccessful and may be withdrawn, while if the offer price is too low this will hurt the existing shareholders, since less funds will be raised (than otherwise) and their equity stake has been diluted (i.e. a given level of future earnings is now 'spread' over more shareholders). Empirical work shows that (in the US) on average IPOs are oversubscribed and the initial rise in the price of shares immediately after an IPO is in excess of 15%.

So IPOs are underpriced on average. Why is this? It may be because of the *winner's curse*. If Mr Average decides to 'blindly' apply for 1000 shares in every IPO, the underpricing does not in fact imply that he will earn the average return of over 15%. This is because the 'smart money' will apply for (say) twice as many shares as Mr Average, if they believe the share is genuinely underpriced. Then the 'smart money' will be allocated twice as many shares as Mr Average, if they are allocated on a pro-rata basis. If the 'smart money' think an IPO is overpriced then they will apply for no shares and Mr Average will receive his full allotment of 1000 'duff' shares, on which he will lose money. This is the winner's curse. To counteract the winner's curse and attract the average investor, underwriters will tend to underprice IPOs on average.

After securities are originally sold they are said to trade in the **secondary market**, either in an auction market or a dealer market. An **auction market** provides continuously updated prices to all participants either on the floor of an exchange or via computers. Most stocks of large corporations are bought and sold in auction markets. **Dealer markets** involve dealers getting in touch with each other on a bilateral basis usually over the telephone (or 'wires').

## CORPORATE EQUITY MARKET

The largest equity market in Europe is the London Stock Exchange (LSE) and in the US it is the New York Stock Exchange (NYSE). A firm that wishes its equity to be traded on these markets must apply to be listed, and must satisfy certain criteria (e.g. minimum bounds are placed on market capitalisation, yearly turnover, pre-tax profits and the proportion of shares in public hands). Because a full listing is expensive, some companies are listed on a **'second market'** where the listing requirements are less onerous. In the UK the second market is called the Alternative Investment Market (AIM) and, like the Paris second market, there are around 300 firms listed. In all countries the differences between the listed and secondary market are to be found in the required levels of disclosure of company information, the amount of capital raised by public stockholding and the membership costs. For example, on the London and Paris second markets the amount of shares required to be held in 'outside hands' is 10% rather than the 25% for a full listing. Thus these 'second markets' impose less stringent regulations on companies wishing to have their shares traded, and are often viewed as a starting point for new firms aiming eventually for a full listing. Secondary market shares are regarded as being more risky than fully listed shares.

There are a plethora of 'new' markets emerging for selling shares, including the Euro.NM which is an alliance of 'second markets' in France, Germany, Belgium and Holland, which have a common electronic platform and shares listed. There is also a consortium of US and European banks which have set up a new pan-European market called EASDAQ (modelled on NASDAQ). There are also active OTC markets such as the Hors Cote in Paris and the huge NASDAQ market in the US. Challenges to traditional markets are also appearing from broker and dealing systems on the internet such as Charles Schwab, E*Trade, Merrill Lynch's and Barclays internet, which act as catalysts for alliances and mergers amongst the existing stock exchanges. For example, the merger between the American Stock Exchange and NASDAQ, and the planned merger of the London Stock Exchange and Deutsche Börse (Frankfurt) in 2001 to create 'iX', which has been complicated by the hostile bid for the LSE (market value at around £900m) by Sweden's OM Group.

There is also competition between **order driven dealing systems** (i.e. where buyers and sellers are matched, often electronically), which predominate in most European centres, whereas the NYSE and NASDAQ have **quote driven systems** (i.e. market makers quote firm bid and ask prices). In London most shares are traded on the quote driven SEAQ (Stock Exchange Automated Quotations), but there is also an order driven system (SETS—Stock Exchange Electronic Trading System) for the FTSE100 and Eurotop30 shares.

## STOCK EXCHANGE LISTING

If a company wishes to widen its share ownership and raise additional finance then it may seek a listing on a stock exchange. The broad requirements for a listing are:

- a minimum amount of the firm's shares must be available for purchase/sale on the exchange (e.g. on the London Stock Exchange, the figure is 25% and in the Alternative Investment Market, AIM, it is 10%);
- the company must provide detailed financial information (e.g. on company assets, profits, etc.), both past data (e.g. over the last 3 years) and then on a periodic basis (e.g. annually).

The US stock exchange has particularly onerous reporting disclosures and hence an alternative for UK firms wishing to attract US investors is the issue of **American depository receipts (ADRs)**. Here a US bank (e.g. Morgan Trust Guarantee) acts as an intermediary and purchases and holds UK company sterling denominated shares (listed on the London Stock Exchange). The bank then sells US investors *dollar denominated* 'receipts' each of which are 'backed' by a fixed number of UK company shares. These 'receipts' or ADRs are traded (in USDs) rather than the UK shares themselves. The US investor has the same rights as a UK investor (but not the rights of an owner of US listed shares) and the sponsoring bank collects the sterling dividends, converts them to USDs and passes them on to the holder of the ADRs. There are about 2000 ADR programmes outstanding, worth around $400bn. This idea has been extended to **global depository receipts (GDRs)** which allow shares to be traded on exchanges outside the US, and has been particularly useful in allowing 'emerging markets shares' to trade on developed exchanges (e.g. in London, Paris).

It has become more common in recent years for multinational firms to be listed on more than one exchange, in order to attract a wider investment clientele.

In general, there are two types of shares issued: ordinary and preference shares. **Ordinary shareholders** (in the US, **'common stock'**) are the owners of the firm with a residual claim on 'earnings' (i.e. profits, after tax and payment of interest on debt). Such 'earnings' are either retained or distributed as dividends to shareholders. Ordinary shares carry voting rights at the AGM of the company. In the UK, **preference shares** (or preferred stock in the US and participation certificates in the rest of Europe) have some characteristics of ordinary shares and some characteristics of debt instruments. In particular, holders have a claim on dividends which takes 'preference' over ordinary shareholders, but they usually do not carry voting rights. A corporation can raise additional capital by selling additional shares on the open market or by selling more shares to its *existing shareholders*—the latter is known as a **rights issue**. Further discussion on the above issues, on the pricing of equity and speculation using equities can be found in Chapter 12.

In recent years in the UK and US, the supply of corporate equity has been reduced by **share repurchases**, whereby the company buys back a proportion of shares from each shareholder. Repurchases are often used when the company has accumulated a large amount of retained earnings (capital) but has no investment projects which it thinks can earn more than the market return. Assuming that the repurchase does not affect expectations of the firm's future profits, repurchases raise earnings per share and the share price (for the same reason that a split reduces the price), so that investors receive a return in the form of a capital gain rather than dividend income. Other countries tend to have legal limits on the amount of its own shares that a company can buy back, but these restrictions are gradually being eased.

**Share warrants** are not actually 'shares' but they are *an option* to buy a stated number of company shares over a certain period in the future, at a price fixed today. In fact, warrants are often initially 'attached' to ordinary *bonds* which are issued by private placement, but sometimes warrants are attached to bonds issued in an IPO. Usually, the warrants can be 'detached' and sold separately in the secondary market. Because bonds with warrants attached have an embedded long-term option to purchase the company's shares, these bonds can be issued at lower yields than conventional bonds. (Occasionally, companies also issue warrants on bonds—the warrant can be used in the future to purchase a particular bond of the company at a fixed price.) Sometimes, warrants are issued on their own (i.e. not attached to a bond issue) and these were a very popular form of raising finance for Japanese firms in the 1980s. Also, sometimes an institution will issue warrants on another company, such as Salomon Bros issuing warrants on Eurotunnel shares. This is often called the *covered warrants* market because Salomon's must cover its position by being ready to purchase Eurotunnel shares. Warrants are also sometimes offered by institutions on a 'basket' of different shares. Whether the warrants are attached to bonds or sold separately, they provide additional 'cash' for the issuer. Also, separate warrants are sometimes issued either to pay for underwriting services or are given to managers of the firm and they are then known as **share options**.

You will exercise the warrant when the share price rises above the strike price, at which point you hand over cash (or occasionally you surrender the bond) and receive the company's shares. Exercise of the warrant therefore involves 'share dilution' for existing shareholders and it alters the cash flow of the company, as the latter has more shares outstanding and an additional cash inflow. A bond issued with warrants attached allows the investor to 'get a piece of the action' should the company do well and its profits and hence share price increase, whilst also allowing the investor to receive the coupon payments on the bond. In addition, the initial warrant holder can 'detach' the warrant and sell it in the open market at any time she wishes.

## CORPORATE DEBT

Firms can borrow in their domestic or foreign currency using bank term loans with anything from 1 to 20 years to maturity. In general bank loans to corporates are non-marketable, and the bank has the loans on its books until maturity (or default). The 'corporate interest rate' charged by the bank $r_{corp}$ will comprise the risk free rate $r$ plus a risk premium $rp$, to reflect the riskiness of the borrower. In addition there may be a loan origination fee $f$ (e.g. 1/8 of 1% of the principal), giving a 'basic return' of $f + r_{corp}$. In the US companies often have to hold part of the loan proceeds (e.g. $b = 0.1$ or 10%) as 'compensating balances', which are held as non-interest bearing demand deposits. The return to the bank ($= r_{bank}$) on \$1 of corporate loans is therefore given by:

$$1 + r_{bank} = 1 + \frac{f + r_{corp}}{1 - b}$$

For $b = 0.1$ this means that the return to the bank is increased by a factor of $1/0.9 = 1.11$, because the bank can on-lend these compensating balances to other customers. There is one further complication. If the Central Bank has a reserve requirement of $R = 0.1$ (10%) on deposits then only 90% ($= 1 - R$) of these compensating balances can actually be on-lent, hence the return to the bank is:

$$1 + r_{bank} = 1 + \frac{f + r_{corp}}{1 - b(1 - R)}$$

Thus the return to the bank is only $1/(1 - 0.1 \times 0.9) = 1.0989$ higher than $f + r_{corp}$.

In certain industrialised countries, most notably the US, there is a secondary market in buying and selling 'bundles' of corporate bank loans. This is not a large or highly liquid market but it does provide a valuable function for altering a bank's loan liabilities—see Box 1.1. (Another alternative here is 'securitisation'—see below.)

## Box 1.1    LOAN SALES

In some well-developed financial systems there is a secondary market in buying and selling bank loans. Note that this is different from securitisation, since the loans are directly sold by a bank to another counterparty (e.g. another bank, an insurance company or hedge fund); no new 'securities' are created and sold. The loan sales market is most active in the US and grew tremendously in the 1980s as highly leveraged transactions (HLT) using bank loans were used to finance leveraged buyouts (LBOs) and mergers and acquisitions.

A HLT is one where financing results in a high level of debt relative to equity. The banks then had highly risky loans on their balance sheets (which were also sometimes highly concentrated geographically and within sectors, such as oil loans in Texas). After the regulatory changes of 1988 (i.e. the 'Basle Accord'), these banks (and Savings and Loan Associations) in the US had to hold capital (i.e. broadly share capital plus retained profits) equal to 8% of their loan value outstanding, which they considered as a form of tax. However, if these loans are sold **without recourse** to a counterparty, then the default risk is transferred to the counterparty and the capital charge on the banks removed.

The HLT loans may be non-distressed (i.e. bid price exceeds 80 cents per $1 of loans) or distressed (i.e. price less then 80 cents per $1 of loans or the borrower is in default). The main sellers of these loans are large money centres and investment banks (e.g. Merrill Lynch, First Boston, Goldman Sachs) whose corporate finance departments may have originated the HLT loans in the first place. Another source of loan sales is the US Resolution Trust Corporation, which is a government agency set up in 1989 to restructure 'problem' savings banks. The selling bank may continue to collect the interest payments on the loans (for a fee) and may have earned an initial origination fee for setting up the initial loan agreements.

The buyers of loan sales are the large banks who speculate on the change in market value of such loans, as the credit default risk of the constituent companies alters over time. So-called **vulture funds** and hedge funds also purchase these HLT loan 'bundles', sometimes to influence the outcome of any restructuring deal. These HLT loans, in the secondary market, are rather like trading in *illiquid* junk bonds. The illiquidity arises because it can often take up to 3 months to complete a loan sale and many deals fall through before completion because of legal problems (or because the market price moves below the initial offered price in the loan sale deal). Clearly this market is less liquid than if the loans were fully securitised.

Often bank loans to large corporates (or governments) will be **syndicated loans** which are arranged by a lead bank, and the loan will be underwritten by a syndicate of banks. The syndicated banks may well get other banks to take a portion of their loan commitment. The interest payments could be at a fixed interest rate or at a floating rate (e.g. at the 6-month London Interbank Offer Rate (LIBOR) plus a 0.5% premium for default risk).

**Eurodollars** are US dollars deposited in a bank outside the US, for example in Barclays in London, or in Crédit Agricole in Paris. These time deposits can be on-lent in the form of USD term loans to companies, with most maturities in the range 3–10 years. These are the **Eurocurrency markets** and are direct competitors with the domestic loan markets.

Euromarkets interest rates are usually floating (e.g. based on the Eurodollar LIBOR rate, set in the London Interbank Market).

An alternative to an OTC bank loan is to issue corporate bonds, either in the home or a foreign currency. Just as with a bank term loan, by issuing bonds a corporate obtains a large amount of cash 'up front' (e.g. to spend on real investment projects) in return for a promise to pay a stream of cash flows ('the coupons') in the future, until the maturity date of the bond (when the principal will also be repaid). The coupon payments can either be fixed or vary with some reference interest rate (i.e. 'floating'). Bonds therefore allow a transfer of cash (and hence purchasing power) between two parties and allow the borrower to pay back the loan (plus interest) over time. Without this mechanism the investment project might not be possible. Corporate bond issues are mainly undertaken by large multinationals in their respective domestic markets (and currencies), but smaller 'firms' are now tapping these markets (see Box 1.2). The US has by far the most active corporate bond market, whereas firms in Europe and Japan tend to mainly use bank term loans as a source of long-term debt finance.

| Box 1.2 | **BOWIE BONDS** |
| --- | --- |

Would you like to own a piece of David Bowie or even Rod Stewart? This may not be literally possible but you can certainly own a claim on the royalties of their back catalogue of songs. Towards the end of the 1990s, David Bowie and Rod Stewart did exactly this. You could purchase a 'Bowie Bond' (and hence hand over cash to Bowie) in return for a promise to receive a portion of their future song royalties. These bonds carry credit counterparty or default risk because David or Rod's old hits may go out of fashion and future sales revenues might not cover the promised future coupon payments on the bond.

Merrill Lynch has recently been involved in extending this idea and trying to get funding via bond issues for collectives of artists, people having intellectual property rights (e.g. inventors of computer games) or other media assets (e.g. book publishers). For example, Cecci Gori, an Italian film company (which made *Il Postino*) acquired the rights to show a back catalogue of Hollywood films in Italy. Merrill's separated the credit risk on future film revenues from the credit risk of the overall company and hence was able to sell these 'movie bonds' at a high price (low yield).

So, if you have a good idea you need to develop (e.g. for a new computer game or film) don't sell the intellectual property rights to a large company, find someone who will issue bonds against a proportion of the future revenues.

Some bond issues involve foreign currencies. **Eurobonds** or **international bonds** are bonds denominated in a different currency from the countries in which they were issued. This is the meaning of 'Euro', and it has nothing to do with Europe per se. They are often issued simultaneously in the bond markets of several different countries and most have maturities between 3 and 25 years. For example, a US firm issuing bonds in London, Paris and Singapore, denominated either in yen or in USDs, would be classified as Eurobond (or international bond) issues. Eurobonds are also issued by governments, international organisations like the International Bank for Reconstruction and Development, the finance arm of the World Bank, in Washington, DC.

New issues are usually sold via a syndicate of banks (minimum about $100m) to institutional investors, large corporations and other banks, but some are issued by private placement. New issues are usually underwritten on a firm commitment basis. Most Eurobonds are listed on the London (and Luxembourg) Stock Exchange and there is a secondary market operated mainly OTC between banks by telephone and computers (rather than on an exchange) under the auspices of the International Securities Markets Association, ISMA. Eurobonds are credit rated and nearly all new issues have a high credit rating (i.e. there is not a large 'Euro' junk bond market).

Eurobonds pay interest gross and are bearer instruments (and are therefore attractive to thieves—as anyone who has seen the opening scenes of the film *Heat* with Al Pacino and Robert deNiro will know). Tax is not deducted at source and they are unsecured. The issuer may face exchange rate risk, since a home currency depreciation means that more home currency is required to pay back one unit of foreign interest payments. However, if the firm's products are sold for foreign currency (e.g. oil which is priced in US dollars) then the exchange rate risk of a Eurobond issue in USDs is reduced. However, some major financial disasters have been partly the result of defaults on Eurobond issues, for example the Latin American debt crises of the 1980s and the Russian 'melt down' of 1998 (see Box 1.3). Although most Eurobonds are 'floaters' they can be issued with fixed coupons, and as zeros, convertibles and mortgage-backed bonds.

## Box 1.3    RUSSIAN EUROBOND ISSUES

In 1996, it looked as if the Russian economy was over the worst. 'The worst' had been extremely bad, as output had fallen dramatically after the move from communist central planning to privatisation and a more market-orientated economy. The distribution of income became much more unequal as only relatively few benefited from the market economy while others (e.g. pensioners, ordinary workers and government employees) saw their savings rendered worthless by rampant inflation and devaluation and many became unemployed.

Nevertheless, in 1996 the Russian Government made its first Eurodollar bond issue since the revolution of 1917. About 45% of the $1bn issue was taken up by US investors, 30% in Asia and about 25% in Europe. The yield was about 340–350 bp above US Treasuries (to reflect the higher credit risk involved in lending to Boris Yeltsin's government rather than to Bill Clinton's). Hence, in 1996, investors had faith in Russia's ability to use this finance wisely. Foreign investors were attracted by a risk premium of around 350 bp above US Treasuries.

Municipalities in Russia (e.g. the cities of Moscow and St. Petersburg) and large Russian oil (e.g. Lukoil) and gas (e.g. Gasprom) companies also considered raising funds via Eurobond issues. Unfortunately, all did not go well for the Russian economy as in 1998 the Russian Government defaulted on its *rouble denominated* debt and froze Western investors' accounts in which these bonds were held. The value of these bonds fell sharply. (Note that Russia did not default on its debt denominated in foreign currency.) There were therefore worries that the Russian bond default could lead to financial difficulties for Western banks that had invested heavily in Russian bonds (and would receive less foreign currency given the rouble devaluation) and that this might lead to a systemic crisis.

However, by 2000 things were looking up a little. After the crisis of 1998, oil prices rose sharply from their $10 a barrel low point (Russia is a large oil exporter), the devaluation of the rouble of over 80% against the US dollar led to a rise in exports and tax receipts. Russia negotiated a write-off of more than a third of its $32bn debt with the 'London Club' (of banks) and swapped the rest for long-dated, low-interest Eurobonds. It was also looking for a similar deal from its other European creditors who are owed in the region of $40bn. Perhaps it will not be long before Russia returns to the international bond market.

Clearly, some companies borrow in foreign currency because they have subsidiaries in these foreign countries. But why would Abbey National, a UK bank dealing predominantly in UK sterling mortgages, issue Eurobonds denominated in Swiss francs? This brings us to the world of swaps, which we deal with briefly below and in later chapters. It may be that Abbey National can borrow in Swiss francs at a lower rate than in sterling. However, it can then go to a swap dealer and first it can swap the principal amount in Swiss francs and receive sterling from the swap dealer which it on-lends as mortgages to UK residents. (They also agree to swap the principal amounts at the end of the deal, so Abbey National can redeem the Swiss franc bonds.) In the swap, Abbey National also agrees to receive Swiss francs say every 6 months in return for paying sterling to the swap dealer every 6 months. It can then use the sterling from its mortgage receipts to pay the swap dealer, and use the swap dealer's Swiss franc receipts to pay the coupons on its Eurobond issue. The Eurobond issue plus the swap is equivalent to Abbey National having a debt in sterling! It is not surprising therefore that about 70% of Eurobond issues are followed by a swap transaction.

**Foreign bonds** are bonds issued by foreign borrowers in a particular country's domestic market. For example, if a UK company issues bonds denominated in USDs *in New York* then these are foreign bonds, known as **Yankee bonds** (and must be registered with the SEC under the 1933 Securities Act) and would probably be listed on the NYSE. If the UK company issued yen denominated bonds in Tokyo, they would be known as **Samurai bonds**. There are also **bulldogs** in the UK, **matadors** in Spain and **kangaroos** in Australia. The bonds are domestic bonds in the local currency and it is only the issuer who is foreign. Foreign bonds are registered, which makes them less attractive to people trying to delay or avoid tax payments on coupon receipts.

All bonds have specific legal clauses which restrict the behaviour of the issuer (e.g. must keep a minimum ratio of profits to interest payments—so-called 'interest cover') and determine the order in which the debtors will be paid, in the event of bankruptcy. These conditions are often referred to as **bond indentures**. Often the bond indenture will be made out to a corporate trustee whose job it is to act on behalf of the bondholders and see that promises in the indentures are kept by the company.

The payments on some bonds are 'backed' by specific tangible assets of the firm (e.g. mortgage bonds in the US are backed by specific real estate), so if the firm goes bankrupt, these 'secured' bondholders can sell off these assets for cash. (Such bonds are generically referred to as 'senior secured debt'.) However, most bonds are only payable out of the 'general assets' of the firm and in the US these bonds are called **debentures**. So a debenture in the US is really unsecured debt (i.e. not tied to specific assets of the company). The terminology here differs between different countries and, for example, in the UK debentures are a little different from in the US. In the UK, a **debenture** or **secured loan stock** is simply the legal document which indicates a right to receive coupon payments and repayment of principal. A **'fixed-charge debenture'** is backed by specific assets (e.g. buildings and fixed assets like the rolling stock of railroad companies), while a **'floating-charge debenture'** is only secured on the general assets of the firm. So in the UK 'a debenture' could be either secured or unsecured. **Unsecured loan stock** is a bond where the holder will only receive payments after the debenture holders.

**Subordinated debt** is the lowest form of debt in terms of repayment if the firm goes bankrupt (i.e. it is junior debt). It ranks below US bond/debenture holders and often after some general creditors but above equity holders claims. It is therefore close to being equity, but the subordinated debt holders do not have voting rights.

Rather than concentrating on the 'name' given to the bond, the key issues are (i) whether the payments on the bond are secured on specific assets or not and (ii) what is the order in which the different bondholders will be paid, if default occurs. The latter is usually very difficult to ascertain ex-ante and when a firm enters bankruptcy proceedings it can take many years to 'work out' who will receive what, and in what order the creditors will be paid. It is usually a messy business involving expensive corporate insolvency lawyers and practitioners.

There are many variants on the 'plain vanilla' corporate bonds discussed above and we briefly mention these below—more details are provided in Chapter 7. **Debt convertibles** (**convertible bonds** or, **convertible loan stock**) are bonds which are 'convertible' into ordinary shares of the same firm, at the choice of the bondholder, after a period of time. The shares are 'paid for' by surrendering the bonds. They are therefore useful in financing 'new high-risk, high-growth firms' since they give the bondholder a valuable 'option' to share in the future profits of the company, if the bonds are converted to equity. Convertibles will usually carry a lower coupon because of the benefit of the in-built option to convert to ordinary shares (i.e. the convertible bondholder has written a call option on the bond, which is held by the issuer). The similarities and differences between warrants and convertibles are summarised in Box 1.4.

| Box 1.4 | WARRANTS VERSUS CONVERTIBLES |
|---------|------------------------------|

The main similarities and differences between warrants and convertibles are:

- Both are ways of issuing debt finance which also gives the holder the option of obtaining an equity stake in the firm at a later date.
- Most convertibles are issued publicly while warrants are often issued through private placements.
- Most warrants are 'detachable' and some warrants are issued without initially being 'attached' to bonds at all (e.g. executive stock options).
- Warrants are exercised for cash, while convertibles usually involve an exchange of bonds for equity. Warrants and convertibles therefore give rise to different cash flows and changes in debt-to-equity ratios for the company.

**Exchangeable bonds** are like convertibles except the bonds are exchanged for the shares of another company.

A **callable bond** is one where the issuer (i.e. the company) has the option to redeem the bond at a known fixed value (usually its par value), at certain times in the future, prior to the maturity date. The company may wish to call the bond if the market price rises above the call price and, if it does, the holder of the bond is deprived of this capital gain. Clearly, call provisions provide a disincentive for investors to buy the bonds, consequently, callable bonds offer higher yields when issued than those on conventional bonds. Usually, there is a specific period of time (e.g. first 3 years after issue) within which the company cannot call the bond, and sometimes there may be a set of prices at which the bond can be called at specific times in the future.

A **floating rate note (FRN)** is a bond on which the coupon payments $C are linked to a short-term interest rate such as 3 or 6-month LIBOR. FRNs are particularly popular in the Euromarkets.

Some companies also raise finance by issuing **deep-discount bonds**. These are zero coupon bonds and they are attractive to institutions like pension funds which have a known *nominal* payment (e.g. a pension lump sum) at a specific date in the future. A 'zero' then provides a perfect hedge.

From the above we can infer that the 'mass market' is in plain vanilla corporate bonds with either fixed or floating rate coupons. But clearly there are many specialist debt securities which can be tailored to meet the requirements of specific investors. There are also 'investment boutiques' which will combine existing securities (including equity, bonds and options) to provide the investor with a particular desired risk–return trade off. This is often referred to as **structured finance**.

### Mezzanine finance and junk bonds
**Mezzanine finance** is a catch-all term for hybrid debt instruments that rank for payment below 'conventional' debt but above equity—it is often also referred to as **subordinated, high-yield, low-grade** or **junk bonds**.

Since the early 1980s, it has become common for firms to make initial offerings of bonds graded below investment grade (i.e. usually those ranked below BBB by S&P and below Baa for Moody's). These were often issued in the 1980s in the US as a source of finance for management buyouts (MBOs, for example, the $25bn takeover of RJR Nabisco) or raising cash for takeovers (i.e. leveraged buyouts, LBOs). Interest payments on such debt are predetermined and either fixed or floating (e.g. linked to LIBOR). These bonds have a high risk of default and hence carry a correspondingly high yield. They have come to be known as **junk bonds**.

There is a contentious debate on whether a portfolio of junk bonds does earn a return that compensates for the risks involved. There have been surprisingly few actual defaults on junk bonds, although if default were unlikely they would, of course, not offer such a high yield. They appear to be useful speculative instruments for investors who wish to increase their risk exposure, and for companies who wish to avoid the ownership and control implications of issuing equity. Some junk bonds arise from 'fallen angels'. If a company starts out with a high credit rating, performs poorly and then experiences a downgrade in its rating to below triple-B, this would be referred to as a **fallen angel**.

Because high coupon bonds are risky, in some LBOs they are issued with **deferred coupon payments** (e.g. for 3–7 years) or are **step-up bonds**, where the coupon starts low and increases over time, or **extendable reset bonds**, where the coupon is periodically reset so the bond trades at a predetermined price (e.g. if the credit spread over Treasuries increases, then the coupon will be raised to reflect this, so that the bond will still trade near par).

The junk bond 'king' of the 1980s was Michael Milken who worked for the investment bank Drexel Burnham Lambert and who was able to persuade large institutional investors to purchase junk bonds which were then used for MBOs or takeovers. The debt-to-equity ratio of such financial deals could be higher than 10 to 1, so the firms were very highly geared and some inevitably failed. Once a year Drexels held a lavish party which colloquially became known as the 'Predator's Ball'. Milken was in fact sent to jail for fraud (and paid about $600m in fines) and Drexels went bankrupt in 1990. However, after a hiatus in the early 1990s the junk bond market again recovered with annual amounts raised in excess of $40bn p.a.

## BOND RATINGS AND SPREADS

The corporate bond market in the UK is not large and firms rely more on retained earnings and bank loans for investment finance. However, the US corporate bond market is much more active. As a consequence, the US market has developed **bond rating agencies**, which study the quality (in terms of default risk) of corporate (and indeed municipal and government) bonds and give them a rating. The classifications used are shown in Tables 1.1a and b, while Figure 1.2 gives the relative yields one might expect as the company's Standard & Poor's credit ratings change.

The starting point for AAA rated at 6% is purely arbitrary since all rates move up and down with changes in inflation, so it is the spreads (e.g. the difference between yields on BBB and AAA bonds) which measure the relative riskiness of two corporate bonds. The spreads over US Treasuries for 20-year corporate bonds are around 50 bp on average. For various ratings the average spreads are AAA (7 bp), AA (23 bp), A (50 bp), BBB (124 bp), while for junk

## TABLE 1.1a: Standard & Poor's corporate bond ratings

| AAA | Debt rated 'AAA' has the highest rating assigned by Standard & Poor. Capacity to pay interest and repay principal is extremely strong. |
|---|---|
| AA | Debt rated 'AA' has a very strong capacity to pay interest and repay principal and differs from the higher rated issues only in a small degree. |
| A | Debt rated 'A' has a strong capacity to pay interest and repay principal although it is somewhat more susceptible to the adverse effects of changes in circumstances and economic conditions than debt in higher rated categories. |
| BBB | Debt rated 'BBB' is regarded as having an adequate capacity to pay interest and repay principal. Whereas it normally exhibits adequate protection parameters, adverse economic conditions or changing circumstances are more likely to lead to a weakened capacity to pay interest and repay principal for debt in this category than in higher rated categories. |
| BB, B, CCC, CC, C | Debt rated 'BB', 'B', 'CCC', 'CC' and 'C' is regarded, on balance, as predominantly speculative with respect to capacity to pay interest and repay principal in accordance with the terms of the obligation. 'BB' indicates the lowest degree of speculation and 'C' the highest degree of speculation. While such debt will likely have some quality and protective characteristics, these are outweighed by large uncertainties or major risk exposures to adverse conditions. |
| C1 | The rating 'C1' is reserved for income bonds on which no interest is being paid. |
| D | Debt rated 'D' is in payment default. |

Source: *Standard & Poor's Bond Guide*, June 1992, p. 10. Reproduced by permission of The McGraw-Hill Companies

bonds the spread varies enormously over the business cycle from around 300 bp to over 850 bp, with an average over the last 20 years of around 400 bp. The positive relation between risk and return is clear to see in Figure 1.2, with yields rising from a baseline of 6.07% on the highest investment grade bonds to a level above 12% on speculative (junk) bonds.

Eurobonds or international bonds (see above) also have ratings and this is reflected in their yields. This can be seen in Figure 1.3 (from the *Financial Times*) by, for example, looking down the 'bid yield' column for say the Canadian dollar 'C$'. We see that yields rise as the credit rating falls.

## TABLE 1.1b: Moody's corporate bond ratings

| | |
|---|---|
| **Aaa** | Bonds which are rated 'Aaa' are judged to be of the best quality. They carry the smallest degree of investment risk and are generally referred to as 'gilt edge'. Interest payments are protected by a large or an exceptionally stable margin and principal is secure. While the various protective elements are likely to change, such changes as can be visualised are most unlikely to impair the fundamentally strong position of such issues. |
| **Aa** | Bonds which are rated 'Aa' are judged to be of high quality by all standards. Together with the 'Aaa' group they comprise what are generally known as high-grade bonds. They are rated lower than the best bonds because margins of protection may not be as large as in 'Aaa' securities or fluctuation of protective elements may be of greater amplitude or there may be other elements present which make the long-term risks appear somewhat larger than in 'Aaa' securities. |
| **A** | Bonds which are rated 'A' possess many favourable investment attributes and are to be considered as upper medium grade obligations. Factors giving security to principal and interest are considered adequate but elements may be present which suggest a susceptibility to impairment at some time in the future. |
| **Baa** | Bonds which are rated 'Baa' are considered as medium grade obligations, i.e. they are nether highly protected nor poorly secured. Interest payments and principal security appear adequate for the present but certain protective elements may be lacking or may be characteristically unreliable over any great length of time. Such bonds lack outstanding investment characteristics and in fact have speculative characteristics as well. |
| **Ba** | Bonds which are rated 'Ba' are judged to have speculative elements; their future cannot be considered as well assured. Often the protection of interest and principal payments may be very moderate and thereby not well safeguarded during other good and bad times over the future. Uncertainty of position characterises bonds in this class. |
| **B** | Bonds which are rated 'B' generally lack characteristics of the desired investment. Assurance of interest and principal payments or of maintenance of other terms of the contract over any long period of time may be small. |
| **Caa** | Bonds which are rated 'Caa' are of poor standing. Such issues may be in default or there may be present elements of danger with respect to principal or interest. |
| **Ca** | Bonds which are rated 'Ca' represent obligations which are speculative in a high degree. Such issues are often in default or have other marked shortcomings. |
| **C** | Bonds which are rated 'C' are the lowest rated class of bonds and issues so rated can be regarded as having extremely poor prospects of ever attaining any real investment standing. |

Source: *Moody's Bond Record*, June 1992, p. 3

## FIGURE 1.2: Yields on corporate bonds

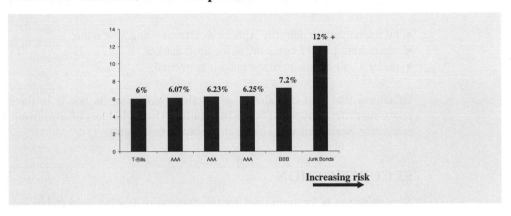

## FIGURE 1.3: Bond yields and credit ratings (*Financial Times*). Reproduced with permission

### INTERNATIONAL BONDS

| Oct 3 | Red date | Coupon | S&P* Rating | Moody's Rating | Bid price | Bid yield | Day's chge yield | Mth's chge yield | Spread vs Govts |
|---|---|---|---|---|---|---|---|---|---|
| **$** | | | | | | | | | |
| IBRD | 06/10 | 7.125 | AAA | Aaa | 102.2063 | 6.80 | -0.02 | -0.05 | +0.96 |
| Wal-Mart | 08/09 | 6.875 | AA | Aa2 | 100.2472 | 6.84 | -0.03 | -0.09 | +1.01 |
| Ford | 06/10 | 7.875 | A | A2 | 102.3276 | 7.53 | -0.02 | -0.05 | +1.69 |
| Viacom | 07/10 | 7.700 | BBB+ | Baa1 | 102.0272 | 7.40 | -0.03 | -0.08 | +1.56 |
| **C$** | | | | | | | | | |
| Inter Am Dev Bk | 06/09 | 5.625 | AAA | Aaa | 95.7680 | 6.26 | -0.02 | +0.07 | +0.47 |
| JP Morgan | 03/04 | 6.875 | A+ | A2 | 99.7793 | 6.93 | -0.02 | -0.02 | +1.08 |
| Province of BC | 06/03 | 7.750 | AA- | Aa2 | 104.4319 | 5.94 | -0.02 | -0.09 | +0.22 |
| Deutsche B FRN | 09/02 | 5.875 | AA | Aa3 | 99.3198 | 6.26 | -0.01 | -0.04 | +0.56 |
| **£** | | | | | | | | | |
| EIB | 12/09 | 5.500 | AAA | Aaa | 95.8000 | 6.11 | +0.01 | -0.21 | +0.88 |
| GUS | 07/09 | 6.375 | A- | A2 | 93.1100 | 7.47 | -0.06 | -0.38 | +2.24 |
| Gallaher | 05/09 | 6.625 | BBB+ | Baa2 | 96.1609 | 7.23 | -0.02 | -0.59 | +2.00 |
| Halifax | 04/08 | 6.375 | AA | Aa1 | 99.2100 | 6.50 | +0.02 | -0.17 | +1.07 |
| **SFR** | | | | | | | | | |
| EIB | 01/08 | 3.750 | AAA | Aaa | 97.5950 | 4.14 | -0.01 | +0.07 | +0.28 |
| Italy (REP) | 07/10 | 3.125 | AA | Aa3 | 91.7140 | 4.17 | -0.03 | +0.05 | +0.28 |
| Hydro-Quebec | 05/01 | 6.750 | A+ | A2 | 101.2301 | 4.61 | +0.01 | -0.09 | +1.06 |
| Gen Elect. | 07/09 | 3.125 | AAA | Aaa | 92.4414 | 4.17 | -0.02 | +0.09 | +0.29 |
| **YEN** | | | | | | | | | |
| IBRD (World Bk) | 03/02 | 5.250 | AAA | Aaa | 106.9100 | 0.48 | - | +0.14 | -0.10 |
| Spain (Kingdom) | 03/02 | 5.750 | AA+ | Aa2 | 107.6630 | 0.48 | -0.01 | - | -0.10 |
| KFW Int | 03/10 | 1.750 | AAA | Aaa | 99.2000 | 1.84 | - | - | +0.02 |
| Procter & Gamble | 06/10 | 2.000 | AA | Aa2 | 98.2000 | 2.21 | +0.01 | +0.14 | +0.39 |
| **A$** | | | | | | | | | |
| IBRD (World Bk) | 02/08 | 6.000 | AAA | Aaa | 95.5397 | 6.78 | - | -0.04 | +0.62 |
| Queensland Trsy | 06/05 | 6.500 | AAA | Aaa | 100.4124 | 6.39 | - | -0.09 | +0.25 |
| S. Aus Gov Fin | 06/03 | 7.750 | AA+ | Aa2 | 102.5626 | 6.67 | +0.01 | -0.11 | +0.52 |
| Quebec, Provn of | 10/02 | 9.500 | A+ | A2 | 103.8433 | 7.35 | +0.01 | -0.11 | +1.17 |

London closing.
*Standard & Poor's. Yields: Local market standard/Annualised basis.

Source: Interactive Data/FT Information

Finally note that there are three ways in which the supply of corporate bonds may be reduced, if *the firm wishes* to reduce its leverage (i.e. its debt-to-equity ratio):

- by repayment on maturity without a corresponding new issue;
- repurchased by the company in the open market;
- under a call provision or the bond is converted.

Of course, the firm can always recapitalise by buying its bonds in the open market and reissuing different types of bonds (or equity). Also, if holders of convertible bonds choose to convert to equity this will change the debt-to-equity ratio.

## SECURITISATION

*Securitisation* is the term used for the practice of issuing marketable securities backed by non-marketable loans. For example, suppose that a bank has made a series of mortgage loans to firms in a particular industry. Mortgages are long-term, non-marketable loans, so the bank has taken on a large amount of exposure to this industry. One way of reducing this exposure would be to create a separate legal entity known as a *special purpose vehicle (SPV)*, into which the mortgages are placed and therefore are 'off balance sheet' for the bank. The SPV then issues securities to investors entitling them to the stream of income paid out of the mortgage interest payments. These are **mortgage-backed securities (MBS)**. Thus the default risk on the mortgages is spread amongst a number of investors, rather than just the bank. The bank continues to collect the interest payments and repayments of principal on the mortgages, on behalf of the new owners. Usually the MBS are marketable and highly liquid. From the investors' point of view, purchasing such securities provides them with a higher yield than government bonds, allows them to take on exposure to the (mortgage) loans sector which may otherwise have been too costly, and is more liquid than direct lending.

In general, tradeable securities that are supported by a pool of loans, for example, corporate loans (National Westminster bank), car loans (VW, General Motors), credit card receivables (most large banks), record royalties (Bowie and Rod Stewart), telephone call charges (Telemex, Mexico) and sales of football season tickets (Lazio, Real Madrid), are termed *asset-backed securities* **(ABS)**. Although the first ABS issues were made in the US during the 1970s, it is only recently that they have caught on in other countries.

## UNIT TRUSTS AND MUTUAL FUNDS

*Unit trusts* or *mutual funds* as they are known in the US are firms whose assets comprise shares of other companies or portfolios of bonds. A mutual fund therefore owns a portfolio of financial assets, and issues its own shares against this portfolio. Since each share of a fund is a claim on income from a number of different securities, mutual funds allow investors to hold a diversified portfolio, something they may otherwise be unable to afford.

Mutual funds may be *open-end* or *closed-end* funds. With an **open-end fund**, the managers of the fund agree to repurchase an investor's shareholding at a price equal to the market value of the underlying securities (called the *net asset value*, *NAV*). Accrued dividend income and capital gains are accredited to shareholders in the form of additional shares (or 'units').

With a **closed-end fund** (i.e. **investment trusts** in the UK) however, the managers have no obligation to repurchase an investor's shares. Instead, the shares of closed-end funds are quoted on a stock exchange and traded in the open market. Closed-end funds generally pay out dividends and capital gains from the underlying portfolio directly to shareholders. Because closed-end funds can be sold 'separately', yet the constituent shares are also quoted on the stock exchange, the value of the closed-end fund (i.e. its selling price) can differ from the net asset value of the underlying shares. Often closed-end funds sell for much less than their net asset value and this 'discount' is considered to be irrational (i.e. cannot be accounted for by management fees, bid–ask spreads, etc.) and is referred to under the general term of 'stock market anomaly'.

## DERIVATIVE SECURITIES

Under this heading we have forwards, futures, options and swaps. Forwards, futures and options are 'contracts' whose value depends on the value of some other underlying asset. The forward market in foreign currency is the most active forward market. In a forward contract you fix the price for delivery at a specific time in the future (e.g. 1.5 dollars per pound sterling, in 6 months time on a principal of £1m). Today, no money changes hands but in 6 months time one party to the deal will receive $1.5m in exchange for £1m. The forward contract 'locks in' a delivery price for a future date and, as such, the forward contract removes any exchange risk. Forward contracts usually result in delivery of the underlying asset (in this case foreign currency) and are OTC instruments.

A futures contract is very similar to a forward contract except that futures contracts are traded on an exchange and you can 'close out' or 'reverse' your initial deal and hence get out of the contract very easily (all it takes is a telephone call). Futures contracts are 'written' on a wide variety of 'assets', for example on agricultural products (e.g. corn, live hogs), on commodities (such as oil, gold and silver) and on financial assets such as foreign exchange, stock indices, T-bonds and interest rates. For example, consider a sterling interest rate **futures contract** on 3-month LIBOR, where the futures contract matures in 2 months time. This gives the owner of the futures contract the right to 'lock in' a fixed borrowing rate, beginning in 2 months time, and lasting for a further 3 months. The current market value of the futures contract depends on the rate of interest expected to prevail in 3 months time.

Futures contracts can also be used for speculation. For example, if you are long a futures contract on the S&P500 stock index and the latter rises then so will the futures price. The holder of the futures contract can then sell the contract at a higher price than she bought it, and receive the difference in cash (from the person who took the opposite side of the deal). When a futures contract is entered into, the buyer only has to place a small amount of cash with the futures exchange (e.g. 5% of the value of the stock index), as a 'good faith' deposit so that she does not renege on the terms of the contract. (This is known as a **margin payment**.) Hence the investor gains leverage, since she only uses a small amount of her own funds, yet she will reap substantial financial gains if the S&P500 rises.

A **call option** on AT&T shares, for example, gives the owner of the option the right (but not the obligation) to purchase a fixed number of AT&T shares for a fixed price, at a designated time in the future. The value of the option contract depends on the movement of the underlying stock price of AT&T. To purchase an option you have to pay an option premium, but this is a small fraction of the value of the assets (e.g. stocks) underlying the option contract. Therefore, the investor again obtains 'leverage'. One of the key differences between futures and options is that with options you can 'walk away from the contract'. So, if the option increases in value you can benefit from the upside but if it falls in value the most you can lose is the option premium. Hence, the option provides insurance and the 'insurance premium' is the option premium you pay at the outset.

A **swap** is an agreement between two parties to exchange a series of cash flows in the future. For example, a firm can negotiate an interest rate swap contract whereby it agrees to pay interest at a floating rate in return for receiving fixed rate payments, every 6 months for the next 5 years. Or, it might agree to pay US dollars in return for receiving French francs. Swaps are like a series of forward contracts and are extremely useful in hedging interest rate and exchange rate risk for a series of periodic cash flows, over a long horizon.

Forwards, futures, options and swaps are extremely useful instruments for hedging (i.e. reducing the risk of an existing portfolio position), as well as for speculation. Futures and options are traded in auction markets, but there is also a large over-the-counter (OTC) market in options, while the forward market for foreign exchange and swaps consists of purely OTC transactions. Swaps are usually between large banks or corporations, with a swap dealer acting as an intermediary.

## NON-MARKETABLE AND OVER-THE-COUNTER TRANSACTIONS

A 'non-marketable instrument' is one that is not traded in the secondary market. It is usually a financial agreement between two (or more) parties with the arrangement being held to maturity of the contract (e.g. a term loan or deposit in a bank). They are usually OTC agreements. A bank term loan to a firm is a non-marketable (OTC) instrument since neither the bank nor the firm can (in general) *easily* shift this specific contract to other parties. Clearly, this 'non-marketability' is a matter of degree. In fact there is a secondary market in 'bundles' of bank loans in the US and bank loans can also be securitised (see above), but these possibilities are quite costly and cannot be accomplished quickly. Similarly, a firm may place funds in a term deposit with a bank and the firm cannot usually sell this asset to another firm. (However, note that deposits known as CDs are marketable.) The terms of a non-marketable contract may be implicit or explicit. For example, a firm who supplies goods to another firm may not receive immediate payment. This then constitutes a loan (implicit) from one firm to the other, known as *trade credit*.

A *financial letter of credit* from a bank to a firm allows the firm to borrow (up to a certain limit) from the bank at times determined by the firm. Similarly a firm may have an arrangement to draw-down further funds from an existing bank loan—this is known as a *loan commitment*. Both the letter of credit and the loan commitment are known as *off balance sheet items* because they do not appear on the bank's balance sheet until they are activated at some time in the future.

**Business angels** are wealthy individuals who come together to provide start-up finance for small companies (e.g. 'dot.com' companies, spin-outs from scientific inventions). They will often provide a mixture of debt (i.e. loans) and equity finance. When the company is ready to come to market or wishes to expand its operations then **venture capital** firms may become involved. These are usually independent organisations who obtain funds from a variety of sources (banks, life assurance and pension funds, wealthy private investors—some of whom are 'dumb dentists', who join the bandwagon) and on-lend them to unquoted companies which promise high returns but with concomitant high risks (e.g. biotechnology, computer software and internet firms—the 'dot-coms'). Large banks such as Citicorp, Chemical, Goldman Sachs will often set up venture capital subsidiaries. Generally there will be some equity participation (or an option to convert debt to equity) by the venture capital company. The finance is usually medium term (5–10 years) and there is generally direct and active involvement by the venture capitalists with the strategic management decisions of the company. Initially any share capital will be largely illiquid until the 'new' company becomes established. Venture capital is usually used either to finance potentially high-growth companies, or in refinancing, or in the rescue of ailing companies by, for example, a management buy out.

Non-marketable instruments provide a problem for financial institutions because if they are falling in value (e.g. the firm with an outstanding loan is heading towards liquidation) they cannot be easily sold off. Clearly, they are also a problem for the regulatory authorities who must assess changes in creditworthiness of financial institutions and ensure that they have sufficient capital to absorb losses, without going bankrupt. Such non-marketable assets therefore involve **credit risk**. The Basle Committee of Central Bankers has imposed risk capital provisions on G10 banks to cover credit risk and recently new alternatives have been suggested (e.g. J.P. Morgan's 'CreditMetrics'—these issues are discussed in depth in Cuthbertson and Nitzsche, 2001).

All of the above instruments are OTC transactions between two (or more) parties and the 'price' is not continuously quoted but negotiated at the outset of the contract. The other 'large' OTC markets include the syndicated loans market, Eurobonds and foreign bond issues, the market for **forward foreign exchange** and **swaps markets**. Also note that although many transactions in options involve standardised contracts that are traded on an exchange, there is also a very substantial OTC market.

## 1.2 FIRMS: OWNERSHIP AND CONTROL

The purpose of setting up a firm is usually taken to be the creation of value. By this we mean that the owners raise 'cash' by various means and use this to buy materials, capital equipment and labour. The aim is to use these inputs to produce *future* cash flows which exceed the cash used to finance the firm. This area is known as **investment appraisal** and uses the concepts of **discounted present value (DPV)**, and **internal rate of return**, which are explored in detail in Chapter 3. Valuation of the firm is clearly important in deciding whether to mount a takeover bid (see below), and the DPV technique can also be useful here.

A firm's *fixed assets* have a long physical life, and include *tangible assets* such as buildings and machinery (see Figure 1.4) and *intangible assets* such as patents, goodwill and the quality of management. *Current assets* usually have a life of less than 1 year (e.g. work in progress, unsold output, inventories). **Short-term debt** is a *current liability* and usually must be repaid within the year (e.g. bank loans, commercial bills). **Long-term debt** may be marketable (e.g. corporate bonds) or non-marketable (e.g. long-term bank loans). *Shareholder equity* represents the residual claim on the firm's assets:

[1.1]    **Shareholder equity = total assets − (current liabilities + long-term debt)**

In addition, the cash flow 'gap' between the flow of current assets (inventories) and current liabilities (i.e. short-term debts) gives rise to a **change in working capital**. Any negative net cash flow needs to be financed by borrowing or the firm may face a liquidity crisis. A financial manager is responsible for all aspects of finance in the firm. Some key issues for the financial manager, discussed in this book, are:

- how best to finance working capital and how to hedge the risks involved when the firm has a net position in certain assets or liabilities (e.g. variable rate bank deposits or loans, T-bills, equity and bonds of other firms, as well as foreign assets/liabilities);
- how to raise funds to finance the new investment activities of the firm;
- how to decide on the best capital investment projects;
- how to choose the appropriate debt-to-equity mix to maximise the value of the firm;
- merger, takeover and disinvestment decisions.

The hedging of a firm's (or individual's) financial assets, such as stocks, bonds and foreign exchange, or liabilities, such as bank loans in a foreign currency or with a variable interest rate, is analysed in Chapter 15 on the forward market and in Chapters 19–21 on derivative securities, that is futures, options and swaps.

Raising finance through corporate bonds and equity is the subject of Chapters 7 and 12,

## FIGURE 1.4: Simplified balance sheet

| (1) **Current Assets** (e.g. inventories, receivables) | (1) **Liabilities** (e.g. accounts payable) |
|---|---|
| (2) **Fixed Assets** (2a) Tangibles (e.g. plant and machinery) (2b) Intangibles (e.g. goodwill) | (2) **Long-Term debt** (e.g. bank loans, bonds outstanding) |
| | (3) **Shareholder equity** (e.g. ordinary and preference shares) |
| **Total Assets** = 1 + 2a + 2b | **Total Liabilities** = 1 + 2 + 3 |
| Note that net working capital = current assets - current liabilities | |

respectively, while decisions on fixed investment using DPV and other techniques are dealt with in Chapter 3. DPV can either be used to assess an individual investment project (e.g. to build a new factory) or to value the whole firm. When valuing the whole firm, the discount rate we use is a weighted average of the cost of equity finance and the cost of debt finance, known as the **weighted average cost of capital**. A key issue in corporate finance which is explored in Chapter 11 is whether one can lower the cost of capital by changing the mix of debt and equity finance, and thereby increase the value of the firm. This is the famous Modigliani–Miller proposition.

We now turn to the issue of how control of the firm is divided between managers, directors, bondholders and shareholders. Answers to these questions depend in part on the legal structure of the firm and we consider the three main forms of ownership below. The three main forms of ownership are sole proprietor, partnership and limited company (or corporation), with the latter form accounting for most of the output (GDP) produced in developed industrial economies.

## OWNERSHIP OF FIRMS

### SOLE PROPRIETOR

The owner of the firm is a single individual who has unlimited liability for the firm's debts. The firm is not subject to corporation tax but the individual owner is subject to income tax. The ability to raise finance is limited to the owner's initial wealth, the future profits she can plough back into the business and any bank loans she can obtain.

### PARTNERSHIP

The most commonly known partnerships involve the professions such as lawyers, architects and accountants. Whenever two or more persons combine for the purpose of conducting business, a partnership is created. The profits of the partnership are subject to income tax and both profits and tax are usually 'shared' on a pro-rata basis. Some partners may be designated as having limited liability (i.e. limited partnership), but there is always a subset of the partners who must have unlimited liability (i.e. general partnership). New partners are allowed to enter and old partners leave. The agreement usually includes terms and conditions for the distribution of assets upon dissolution. The limited partners generally do not participate in managing the business. Equity contributions are limited to the funds provided by the partners.

### LIMITED COMPANY OR CORPORATION

A limited company or corporation is owned by the shareholders. If the company goes bankrupt, personal assets of the 'share owners' may not be taken to pay off any of the company's residual debts. The corporation therefore has limited liability and is subject to corporation tax.

In principal the shareholders control the management, although in practice this direct link is usually rather weak, being exercised by voting (at the AGM) on specific issues, including the election of directors, who then appoint managers to run the day-to-day affairs of the company. However, this control mechanism is enhanced if the managers also hold shares (or deferred share options) in the company, since their remuneration then depends directly on the value of the firm's shares.

The shareholders can also indirectly influence the managers' behaviour, since if managers are thought to be underperforming the shareholders can sell their shares which will depress the share price and encourage a takeover bid. The incumbent management may then find themselves out of a job. Hence the managers have an 'indirect' incentive to maximise the value of the firm and this works in the interests of existing stockholders. The management–shareholder relationship comes under the heading of *corporate governance*, while the takeover literature is often referred to as the *market for corporate control*. In the corporation there is a separation of ownership and control. The shareholders act as **principals** and appoint the directors who then appoint managers as their **agents**. This can give rise to conflicts of interest known as **principal–agent problems**.

**In the UK** setting up a limited company is usually done via the Company Formation Agency. A certificate of incorporation is issued by the Registrar of Companies based at Companies House. The 'Memorandum and Articles of Association' set out the rights and obligations of the firm and corporations must file accounts annually with Companies House (which are publicly available). **In the US** the procedure is similar. A **registration statement** by the corporation must be lodged with the **Securities and Exchange Commission SEC**, a prospectus issued to potential new shareholders and for an IPO, an advertisement known as a **tombstone** will appear in the press with basic details of the new share offer and the institutions involved. In the US each state has its own laws which must be adhered to (e.g. Nevada has relatively lax laws on setting up corporations to provide 'gambling services').

In the UK a *public limited company* (plc) is a corporation whose shares have a listing on the stock exchange. The requirements for listing are detailed and rigorous but then shares in the company can be freely traded. A *private liability company* is a corporation whose shares are not freely transferable.

A 'plc' or corporation is owned by the shareholders who have limited liability. The latter makes it easier to raise finance in large amounts by issuing shares, because the purchaser of the shares will only lose her initial investment (and not her other personal assets). Hence limited liability plus an active secondary market in shares facilitates the raising of large amounts of cash. This is the major advantage of a corporation over a partnership. A corporation can raise long-term funds from three main sources: (i) retained earnings, (ii) non-marketable debt (e.g. bank loans) and marketable debt (e.g. corporate bonds) and (iii) equity capital (e.g. ordinary shares).

To set up a company, start-up capital is needed and for a limited liability company this initially consists of a mixture of bank loans and an equity issue (sometimes limited to the firm's directors). The funds raised are then used to provide plant and machinery, and pay wages and other costs. Once profits (earnings) accrue these are initially distributed to debt holders (interest income) and the remainder are either retained or distributed to shareholders as dividends. Debt holders have a legal right to be repaid and can place the firm into liquidation (receivership in the UK) if debt interest payments are not forthcoming. However, debt holders (usually) do not have voting rights on company policy.

# THE MARKET FOR CORPORATE CONTROL

A firm can expand its activities by raising finance by stock or debt issues, but in so doing it opens itself to scrutiny by potential investors (e.g. pension funds, banks, venture capitalists, etc.). It can also use retained earnings to finance its expansion, which involves far less scrutiny of the managers by the incumbent shareholders. However, another way in which the 'market' disciplines managers is via mergers and takeovers. The idea here is that efficient 'new' managers replace 'inefficient' incumbent managers—this is the **market for corporate control**. How does this take place and why is this process often subject to some form of regulation?

**Merger activity** is usually financed either by 'cash acquisitions' or from shareholders in the target firm receiving shares in the acquiring firm (i.e. effectively the 'new' merged firm). The acquirer must gain over 50% of the target's shares and in so doing the share price of the target will be bid up (i.e. the bid premium).

The funds in a cash acquisition come from retained earnings, rights issues (by the acquirer) or from new debt finance (e.g. bank loans, bond issues—including sometimes junk bonds). A 'cash offer' provides certainty to the shareholders of the target firm and does not dilute the equity base of the acquirer in the new merged firm (i.e. the acquirer will own 100% of the merged firm). The disadvantage for the target shareholders is that because the price is bid up in the merger process (by 30–50% on average), they are subject to capital gains tax (since the gains are realised).

What happens when the acquirer offers its shares to the target? Suppose at the end of the bid process the acquiring firm is worth $100m and the target firm $50m on the stock market. Then the acquirer might offer one 'new' share for two of the target's shares. Because the capital gain (i.e. the bid premium) on the target's shares is not realised, then there is no capital gains tax liability (at the time of the merger). Also, the acquiring firm does not have to deplete its cash resources (or increase its debt level), although its original shareholders will see their equity stake diluted because the target shareholders now own part of the merged firm.

In the UK at the end of the 1990s, about 60% of the value of merger activity comprised 'cash acquisitions', 33% by offering shares in the acquirer (to the target shareholders) and about 2% by the issue of preference shares and loan stock (i.e. bonds) to the target shareholders. In the US, particularly in the 1980s, the proportion of mergers financed by junk bonds was much higher than in the UK.

The details of the merger process are different in different countries, but the broad procedures are similar. We will illustrate the issues using the UK system based on the **City Code on Takeovers and Mergers** which is administered by the **Takeover Panel**. The UK system is 'self-regulatory' rather than statutory and has as its aim 'the fair and equal treatment for all shareholders'. This implies (inter alia) the following.

- Information must be given to all shareholders on the terms of any merger offer.
- The acquirer must present any claims about the benefits of the merger with 'due care and consideration' and the financial aspects must be certified by independent accountants.

- The target management must act in the best interest of the shareholders (and not in their own interest).
- The acquirer must not artificially inflate its own share price by getting 'friendly parties' to buy its shares (and hence have to swap less of its now 'higher priced' shares for each share in the target firm). This was a big issue in the Guinness hostile takeover of Distillers for which Ernest Saunders, the Chief Executive of Guinness, was prosecuted.
- The bid process should not be unduly dragged out.

To facilitate an orderly merger process the Takeover Panel requires that a 3% holding in any company is disclosed (whether or not a merger is in the offing) so that a potential target can prepare a defence. If an acquirer has more than a 30% stake in a company then the Takeover Panel usually insists the acquirer makes a formal bid for all the shares in the target firm (the 30% also includes so-called 'concert parties', where a group of firms each buys a stake in the target with a view to one of them instigating a takeover in the future). The acquirer (whether friendly or hostile) has to provide a formal bid document to the target's board who then must immediately inform their shareholders and send the bid document to them within 28 days. The target's board has 14 days to respond to the offer document. They may suggest that their shareholders reject the offer (e.g. 'derisory offer', 'totally unacceptable'). The bid then becomes a hostile one rather than a friendly one. There are then attacks and counter-attacks and revised offers are likely to be made by the acquirer (e.g. offering a higher share price to the target shareholders). If no other bidders enter the race, then there is a maximum of 60 days from the initial offer document for the target shareholders to vote on the revised offer. If the offer is rejected then the acquirer cannot launch another bid for a year. If a second bidder emerges during the process then it has a maximum of 60 days to present its offer and then both firms' offers must be voted on by this date.

There are many 'game theory' elements in the bid process of a hostile takeover and the public relations machine is used by both sides (usually at great expense) to present their respective cases. Other defensive tactics used in a hostile takeover include:

- **White Knight**—get a friendly company to make a bid;
- **Pac Man**—make a counterbid for the bidder;
- **Poison Pills**—increase the acquirer's costs should the bid be successful (e.g. target shareholders are given bonus cash payments if the bid is successful);
- **Crown Jewels defence**—target sells off most profitable parts of the business.

The 'market for corporate control' is, about 90% of the time, via friendly mergers and only about 10% are hostile takeovers. Of course, mergers are not the only way a firm can grow. Most firms grow organically by investment in their own profitable projects or sometimes by strategic alliances (e.g. amongst airlines in the late 1990s) which allow firms to tap new markets. Also, do not forget that firms sometimes divest themselves of assets (i.e. their subsidiary firms) in order to concentrate on their 'core business' (e.g. UK banks and building societies in the 1980s purchased estate agency businesses but these were not successful and the banks sold them off in the 1990s)—small can also be profitable!

# 1.3  INVESTORS AND TRADERS

Investors save in the form of financial assets such as bank and building society deposits (Savings and Loan Associations in the US) and by directly purchasing equities, government and corporate debt. Much long-term saving is invested via life assurance and pension funds (LAPF) and these investment portfolios are often managed by large investment management companies (e.g. Mercury Asset Management, Fidelity, Schroder Investment Management, etc.), many of which are subsidiaries of commercial and merchant banks.

Because firms (domestic and foreign) issue a wide variety of securities, (stocks and bonds), and governments also issue many different bonds, then investors face a problem of exactly how much of each asset to hold in their portfolio. To determine this asset allocation they will consider expected returns and the riskiness of the portfolio. Investors therefore need to forecast the expected returns on each of the assets, their riskiness and the correlations between the individual asset returns. For example, for the US one can see from Figure 1.5 that **equity price movements** in different industrial sectors have different characteristics. The Entertainment (and Media) sector has a high average return and high volatility, compared to say the Oil sector. The positive correlation between returns in the Chemical and Automobile sectors appears to be reasonably high whereas the correlation between returns in the Entertainment and Oil sectors appears to be rather low.

The **NASDAQ index** gives a high weighting to 'new economy' stocks (e.g. media, IT, dot.coms, etc.), whereas the S&P500 gives a high weighting to 'old economy' stocks (e.g. textiles, engineering, chemicals). We see from Figure 1.6 that these two indices have moved very differently, with the 'high-tech' NASDAQ index having a higher return and considerably higher volatility than the S&P500.

---

## FIGURE 1.5: US industrial sectors

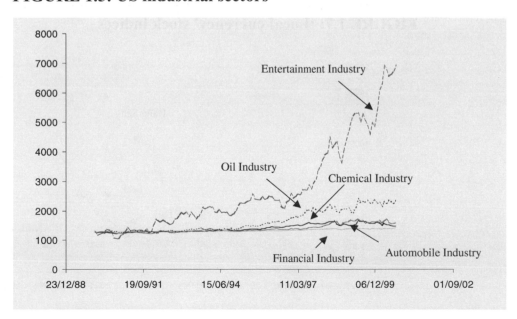

## FIGURE 1.6: US stock markets (S&P500 and NASDAQ)

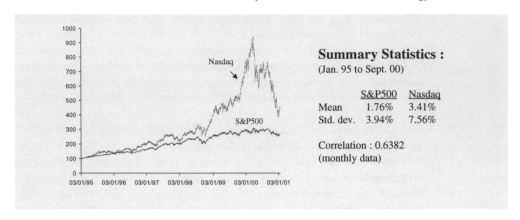

Summary Statistics :
(Jan. 95 to Sept. 00)

|  | S&P500 | Nasdaq |
|---|---|---|
| Mean | 1.76% | 3.41% |
| Std. dev. | 3.94% | 7.56% |

Correlation : 0.6382
(monthly data)

Holding **foreign assets** presents additional difficulties because the return to say a US investor who holds assets in the UK will depend not only on the return on the FTSE100 (say) but also on the USD–sterling exchange rate. Stock market price indices for a number of countries are given in Figure 1.7. Once again we see considerable differences in the average rate of return to investing in these countries and in the volatility of returns. Investing *solely* in the Japanese Nikkei at the beginning of 1990 would have earned a *negative* return (in yen) by the end of 1999, whereas the Hong Kong Hang Seng index shows a relatively high average return (in Hong Kong dollars), of around 16.5% p.a. [= ln(11,000/2500)/9— see Chapter 4], albeit at a 'cost' in terms of the high volatility in returns. The S&P500 (15% p.a.), FTSE100 (9% p.a.) and the (German) DAX (9% p.a.) indices all give a reasonable return over the longer term, with relatively moderate volatility. The positive correlation between the (monthly) returns on the latter three indices seems reasonably high and there is

## FIGURE 1.7: 'Local currency' stock indices

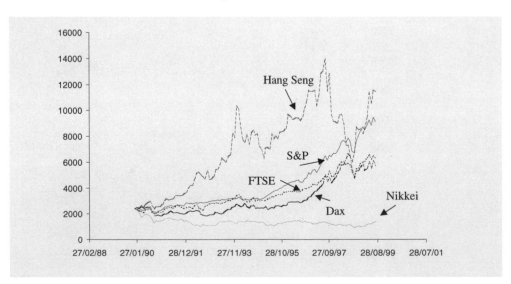

a relatively low correlation between returns on these three indices and the return on the Nikkei. However, these are all 'local currency' returns and a US investor would also be interested in movements in the USD exchange rate against these countries' currencies, since exchange rate movements determine the return in USDs.

By way of an extreme (although not unrealistic) example, suppose a US investor held assets in the emerging economies of Indonesia, Thailand and Malaysia at the beginning of 1996 (Figure 1.7). In 1996 these countries linked their exchange rates to the US dollar, under a fixed currency peg.

In the spring of 1997, foreign investors for whatever reason (still largely unclear) decided to sell the assets they held in these Asian countries. These currencies came under speculative attack, as foreign investors liquidated their SE Asian assets and sold the local currency receipts and purchased USDs. This put downward pressure on their exchange rates as international banks were faced with an increased demand for USDs and were being asked to purchase large amounts of Thai baht, Indonesian rupiah and Malaysian ringgit. Hence, international banks had mismatched FX 'books' and did not wish to be left holding devalued currencies. To maintain the fixed exchange rate against the USD, the Central Banks of these Asian countries had to step in and use their foreign exchange reserves (i.e. USDs) to pay out USDs *at the official exchange rate* in exchange for their own currencies. Because they quickly began to run out of foreign exchange reserves, they were forced to abandon the official fixed rate and these Asian currencies fell sharply in value against the USD. Indeed it is evident from Figure 1.8 that the rupiah fell by over 60% in the space of a few months, while the ringgit and baht initially fell by about 50%. This was followed by some 'bounce back' in the baht and the ringgit with the latter declaring a new lower fixed rate against the USD (see the horizontal line in Figure 1.8). Thus although a US investor might earn a positive return in terms of 'local currency' assets, this could be wiped out by a fall in the foreign currency against the USD.

## FIGURE 1.8: Asian crises: spot FX rates

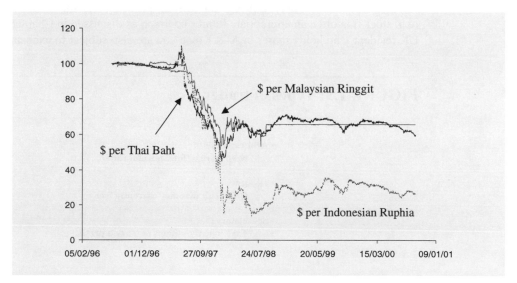

The above issues touch on the difficulties in forecasting stock returns on domestic and world stock markets, a recurring theme in this book. They are also important for asset allocation where you are trying to balance risks against return: this comes under the heading of **portfolio theory**. As we see in Chapter 10, volatility of the returns on individual stocks and the correlations between these returns are crucial elements in determining how to allocate your wealth between different risky assets. When we consider (in Chapter 18) choosing foreign as well as domestic assets then the 'returns' and risk due to changes in the exchange rate are important. In Chapter 15 on foreign exchange we learn that these exchange rate risks can be removed (hedged) by using the forward market for foreign exchange. However, somewhat paradoxically it is not always optimal to hedge all of your foreign assets.

## ARBITRAGE, HEDGING AND SPECULATION

The decisions facing the individual investor come under the broad headings of asset pricing and portfolio theory, which are a key feature of this book.

Asset prices are often determined by **arbitrage**, that is setting the price of an asset equal to its true, correct or fundamental value (see Figure 1.9). Put another way, two identical assets (e.g. shares of AT&T) cannot simultaneously sell for two different prices on two different stock exchanges. Arbitrage is an important concept in finance, particularly in the pricing of derivative securities such as forwards, futures, options and swaps.

Some investors may wish to offset the riskiness of their existing portfolio of assets which is known as **hedging**. For example, if you hold 100 shares of AT&T this is highly risky since AT&T's share price can move up or down by a large amount. However, suppose you can find another (mystery) asset 'F' whose return has a perfect negative correlation with the return on AT&T. (This means that every time the AT&T share price goes up, then F's price goes down). Hence if you hold *both assets* the gain on one is offset by the loss on the other and you have reduced the riskiness of your initial asset holding of AT&T shares. As we shall see, the mystery 'asset F' used to hedge an existing position in some other (underlying) asset (e.g. stocks) is often an appropriate futures contract, as discussed in Chapter 20. If you are a UK resident who holds shares in AT&T then you are also subject to exchange rate risk. You

## FIGURE 1.9: Types of trader

• **Arbitrageurs :**
      **Keep price = 'fundamental value'**

• **Hedgers :**
      **Offset risk that they currently face**

• **Speculators :**
      **Take 'open' positions to make a profit**

can hedge this risk by using foreign currency forward contracts (or FX futures contracts), as discussed in Chapters 15 and 21.

Another form of hedging is to ensure that the initial portfolio of 100 AT&T shares does not fall below a certain minimum value but you can also benefit from any increase in the value of the shares. This is a form of insurance. So-called call and put options can be used to 'engineer' insurance. Not surprisingly this branch of finance is often referred to as **financial engineering**. However, call and put options can also be used for speculation, by paying a relatively low price equal to the call or put premium. You may remember that Long Term Capital Management (LTCM) and Nick Leeson of Barings fame used options for speculation. These aspects are discussed in Chapters 19 and 21.

Finally, the investor may wish to take a pure gamble with all or part of her portfolio: this is **speculation**. Buying shares in the hope that their price will rise in the future or selling a share and hoping to buy it back at a lower price in the future are forms of speculation. Any marketable financial asset can provide a vehicle for speculation including bonds, foreign currency, futures and options. Although speculative activity is often frowned upon by 'outsiders', nevertheless as we shall see, speculators provide funds to enable hedging activity to take place (which is usually applauded by 'outsiders'). Forecasts of future returns on financial assets can be taken on the basis of forecasts of 'fundamentals', and by that we mean variables that a rational agent would consider important. For example, a forecast of higher dividends (because the company has just announced a lucrative new product) might lead you to forecast a rise in its share price. On the other hand some traders might forecast returns based purely on the past behaviour of returns (e.g. 'buy after a rise of more than 2% on any one day') and these are referred to in the academic literature as 'noise traders'. If all investors are 'rational' then this implies that it is impossible to forecast asset returns and hence make 'excess profits', without taking on excessive risk. This is the efficient markets hypothesis which is discussed in detail in Chapter 13. Models which analyse noise trader behaviour are the subject of Chapter 14 and the actual practical methods used by noise traders such as chartism, candlesticks, neural networks, etc. are discussed in Chapter 17.

## CASH AND MARGIN ACCOUNTS

Investors with a large amount of capital and a high credit rating are able to purchase securities via a broker, either via a cash account or a margin account.

**Cash account**:    This is like a normal bank account but it is held with the broker. Positive (negative) flows occur when the investor buys (sells) securities. It must always have a positive balance.

**Margin account**:    This is like a bank account with an overdraft limit. If the overdraft is taken up the broker charges the investor interest. A portfolio of securities owned by the investor is usually held with the broker as collateral (against default).

A margin account allows the investor **leverage**, that is to increase the return (or losses) on a security purchase, relative to that obtained when only 'own funds' are used. For example purchasing 100 shares at $2 per share and selling them at $2.5 gives a return of:

**[1.2]**  $\text{Return} = \dfrac{250 - 200}{200} = 25\%$

Suppose the investor now purchased the securities using an **initial margin** of 70% (and hence borrowing 30% of the funds at 10% interest). The return is calculated as follows:

| | |
|---|---|
| Own funds used | $= 0.7(200) = \$140$ |
| Amount borrowed | $= 0.3(200) = \$60$ |
| Sale proceeds | $= 100(2.5) = \$250$ |
| Interest on loan | $= 0.10(60) = \$6$ |

**[1.3]**  $\text{Leveraged return} = \dfrac{\text{profit}}{\text{'own funds'}} = \dfrac{250 - (140 + 60 + 6)}{140} = 31.4\%$

Hence the leveraged purchase using the margin account has increased the return (on 'own fund' capital) from 25% to 31.4%. However, if prices fall then the leveraged transaction will cause a larger *negative* percentage return. The initial margin $m_0$ (%) is the proportion of the total outlay that is provided by the investor's own funds (i.e. the investor's equity):

**[1.4]**  $m_0 = \dfrac{\text{value of investor's equity}}{\text{value of investor's equity} + \text{loan}} = \dfrac{V_0}{V_0 + L_0}$

Clearly the initial margin is $m_0 = 140/(140 + 60) = 0.7$ (70%). To minimise default risk, the broker will insist on a *maintenance margin*, whereby the investor pays more 'own funds' into the margin account if the share price falls. For example, if the *maintenance margin (m)* is set at 60% then from equation [1.4] we see that when the investor's equity falls to $V_m = mL_0/(1 - m) = 0.6(60)/(1 - 0.6) = \$90$ a *margin call* for extra funds will be initiated. This represents a fall in the value of investor's equity of $50 (= 140 - 90 = V_0 - V_m)$. Suppose the share price fell from $2 to $1.2 which represents a loss in *market value* of $80 ($0.8 \times 100$). Hence the margin call would be $30 (= \$80 - \$50)$. The payment of a maintenance margin is a form of *marking to market* and is also used (in a slightly different way) in futures markets.

As we shall see there are other ways to obtain leverage, most notably by investing in futures or options. With futures, you can gain exposure to the market (e.g. stock market) of say $100m by paying only a relatively small margin payment of say $5m (i.e. around 5%). Similarly, for options, if you purchase a call option on shares you only pay a relatively small option premium of around 3% of the value of the shares in the option contract. But if share prices rise you reap the whole of the benefit of the increase in value of all the shares in the option contract.

## 'LONG', 'SHORT' AND SHORT SELLING

If an investor purchases a security (e.g. equities) she is said to **go long** (in the security) and if she sells a security *she owns* she is said to **go short**. However, if she sells a security *that she does not own* she makes a **short sale**.

Suppose the investor thinks a particular share will fall in price in the future but she does not own the share. She may be able to make a profit by short selling. Initially, she borrows the share from her broker for an agreed time period. Suppose she sells it in the market for $100. If the price actually does fall to say $90, then she can repurchase it at a lower price and return the share to the broker, thus pocketing the difference of $10. The short sale is like a bank loan to the investor and in principal involves 'infinite leverage' because the investor uses no own funds. The short seller has to pay any dividends due to the broker for the benefit of the broker's 'other client' who really owns the share. Of course, if the share price rises the investor who has sold short will make a loss (which can increase without limit). Short selling is risky for the investor and the broker, so the latter usually insists that say 50% of the proceeds from the short sale have to be deposited as an initial margin (and further margin calls are made if the share price subsequently rises). However, if the price subsequently falls the investor can withdraw cash from her margin account. For most investors there are limits on the extent they can engage in short selling.

The calculation of the rate of return from short selling is usually based on the initial receipts. For example suppose you short sell 100 shares at $2 per share and buy them back at $1.50. Assume the $200 raised earns interest of 10% (=$20) and the dividends paid out to the broker are $0.1 per share (= $10 on 100 shares). The return would be calculated as:

[1.5] $$\text{Return} = \frac{\text{net cash inflow}}{\text{proceeds from short sale}} = \frac{200 - 150 + 20 - 10}{200} = \frac{60}{200} = 30\%$$

## TYPES OF ORDER

There any many different types of buy or sell orders that the investor can give to her broker and some are listed below.

**Market order:** An instruction to immediately buy at the lowest offer price and sell at the highest bid price.

**Limit order:** For example a *buy limit order* is an instruction to purchase 1000 shares of XYZ but only if the price is below (or falls below) say $5.

**Stop order:** An instruction to buy or sell as soon as the price passes a particular level. A stop loss order (or **'sell stop order'**) for 1000 shares at $5 implies that the shares are to be sold as soon as the price drops below $5. A **buy stop order** is the purchase of 1000 shares if the price rises above $5.

**Stop limit order:** This might be an instruction to 'sell 1000 shares at $5, stop $4.95 limit'. Hence the order will be executed if the share price falls below $5 but does *not* fall below $4.95.

**Fill-or-kill order:** This is an instruction that is cancelled if it cannot be executed immediately.

**Open order:** (**good-till-cancelled**) This is an order which remains 'operative' until it is either executed or cancelled.

# 1.4 SUMMARY

This chapter has provided an introductory overview of some key market participants and the financial instruments they use to achieve their goals. This provides an introduction to the key issues that will be examined in the rest of the book. The main points are as follows.

- Domestic and foreign firms and governments issue a wide variety of **equity and debt instruments** to bridge the gap between receipts and expenditures and to finance new capital projects.
- Some financial instruments are sold in 'standardised form' in a continuous auction market (e.g. government bonds, equities, futures and options) but many are individually negotiated and sold **'over-the-counter' (OTC)** (e.g. bank term loans and deposits, forward foreign exchange, swaps and some options).
- Large corporations raise long-term external finance from internal funds (i.e. **retained profits**) and from external sources such as **corporate debt** (e.g. bank loans and from issuing corporate bonds) and from new **equity issues**. A key difference between the latter two sources of finance is that only the debtholders can institute bankruptcy proceedings and only the equity holders have voting rights in major company decisions.
- Smaller firms raise funds internally, from bank loans, from **business angels** and from **venture capitalists** (who usually take some form of equity stake and often sit on the board of directors).
- The value of **derivative securities** such as forwards, futures and options depends on the value of the underlying asset (e.g. stocks, foreign exchange) in the derivative contract.
- **Forward contracts** (e.g. on foreign exchange) 'lock in' a price for future delivery and usually forward contracts are held to maturity and 'delivery' takes place. Futures are also useful hedging instruments but can also be used for speculation. **Futures** can be used to 'lock in' a known buying or selling price for the underlying asset in the futures contract (e.g. corn). But because they can be easily 'closed out' they can be used for speculation: simply buy the futures for $100 and then 'close out' (i.e. sell the same contract) at $110 and you will have made $10 cash profit.
- **Options** provide 'insurance' in the form of a maximum purchase price (or minimum selling price) in the future, but also allow the holder to 'walk away' from the contract, if this is advantageous. **Swaps** can be used to convert one kind of periodic cash flow (e.g. floating rate payments) to a different type of cash flow (e.g. fixed rate payments).
- The **market for corporate control** largely takes place via mergers and takeovers, although some firms also take a strategic decision to divest themselves of part of their business.
- There are many hybrid securities, two of the most common being **convertible bonds** and **warrants**. Both allow 'small' firms to issue debt at lower yields than on conventional debt since the convertible or warrant holders have the right (but not the obligation) to obtaining an equity stake in the firm, at some time in the future.

> Convertibles and warrants are like conventional securities but they also contain 'embedded options'.
> - Individuals and financial intermediaries hold a wide variety of non-marketable and marketable assets for **arbitrage, hedging and speculation**. They usually buy and sell financial instruments via a broker who will then pass on the orders to a market maker who holds an inventory of securities (i.e. holds a 'book').

## END OF CHAPTER EXERCISES

**Q1** What are the 'bid–ask spread', tick size and tick value?

**Q2** Do market makers and brokers have different functions?

**Q3** How do bonds differ from equity (stocks)?

**Q4** In what way is a repo comparable to a visit to pawnbrokers?

**Q5** A firm is undertaking a '1 for 4' rights issue. The current share price is $3 and you hold 100 shares. The ex-rights price is $2.8. How much could you obtain for the 'rights' you have acquired?

**Q6** If you start a 'high-tech' firm, what are the likely sources of finance as the firm becomes successful?

**Q7** What are the main types of bond issued by governments and firms? Why would they choose a particular mix of bonds for financing and what risks are involved?

# 2

# The Business Environment

## LEARNING OBJECTIVES

- To examine the main **financial flows** in the economy and to see how markets (e.g. stock and bond markets) and financial intermediaries channel these funds between surplus and deficit units.
- To discuss ways in which the **monetary policy** influences asset values, short and long term interest rates and hence the exchange rate and the real economy (e.g. National Income) and inflation.
- To discuss the rationale behind **Central Bank independence** in the operation of monetary policy.
- To distinguish between **nominal and real rates** of interest. To decompose the return on an asset into a risk free (nominal return) plus a return to compensate for expected inflation: this is the **Fisher equation**.
- To analyse the main **sources of risk** which are market risk, inflation risk, liquidity risk and default (or credit) risk. These give rise to the **risk premium** on financial asset returns (e.g. equity returns).
- To examine why the average return on stocks is so much higher (over a run of years) than the average return on risk free assets (e.g. T-bills). This is sometimes referred to as the '**equity premium puzzle**'.

We have already examined some key financial instruments and briefly outlined their use by firms, individuals and government. Financial transactions between these three sectors are substantial, some of which take place because investors wish to switch between assets within their existing portfolios (we might call these 'information traders') and some because investors' cash balances change with normal day-to-day business transactions (we might call these 'liquidity traders'). Sometimes these financial transactions take place directly between the borrowers and lenders (e.g. a share floatation) and others occur indirectly using financial intermediaries. Pivotal in the flow of funds are the government and the monetary authorities (Central Bank). The government sector alters cash flows to the private sector (i.e. firms and individuals) because of changes in government expenditure and taxation. The Central Bank, when conducting monetary policy, alters interest rates and this alters cash flows directly (e.g. interest on bank loans) and indirectly via its effect on the exchange rate, price competitiveness and net trade flows. The latter then influence the general business environment in which firms operate, in particular the overall level of demand and the inflation rate.

# 2.1 FLOW OF FUNDS AND FINANCIAL INTERMEDIATION

It is difficult to capture the complexity of the flow of funds since all sectors interact with each other. First consider the personal sector. Some of the savings of the personal sector (i.e. households + small businesses) are placed in bank deposits and are then channelled to the company (corporate) sector in the form of bank loans. In addition, non-bank financial intermediaries (i.e. the life assurance and pension funds, LAPF) take the **contractual savings** of the personal sector and purchase corporate bonds, equity and government bonds via the capital markets (e.g. stock exchange or as OTC transactions). Most of these funds will be used to purchase *existing* shares and bonds but some will be for purchases of 'new issues' and hence provide additional finance for fixed investment of companies (e.g. in plant, machinery and buildings).

The interaction between the public sector (i.e. central government + municipal authorities + public corporations) and the banking sector usually takes place via the Central Bank and the money market. This mainly involves the purchase and sale of Treasury bills and government bonds (using repos) and is elaborated upon below when discussing monetary policy. The overseas sector (i.e. foreign investors) places deposits and takes out loans from domestic banks in both domestic and foreign currencies. As far as foreign currencies are concerned most banks attempt to keep a 'matched book', that is outstanding foreign currency deposits equal outstanding foreign currency loans. Foreigners also invest in UK stocks and bonds via the capital market, as well as undertaking direct investment (e.g. setting up a subsidiary in the UK).

The flow of funds refers to the exchange of assets (and debts) between various sectors of the economy, a *stylised version* of which is shown in Table 2.1 for the UK. (For an actual flow of funds matrix for the UK, see *Financial Statistics*.) The main surplus unit with funds to on-lend is the **personal sector**, which invariably has positive nominal saving (i.e. income less consumer spending):

**Saving = income − consumers' expenditure**

Savings can be used to purchase new capital assets (e.g. new housing) and what is left is available for adding to financial assets or reducing financial liabilities and is referred to as the financial surplus of the personal sector:

**Financial surplus = saving − new (physical) investment**

Simplifying somewhat, these surplus funds are borrowed by the public sector and the (non-financial) company sector. This is shown in Table 2.1 (row 1) where the personal sector surplus of £2500 mainly goes to the public sector (£2600) and the company sector (£700). The figures in row 1 should sum to zero (ignoring the residual error). Broadly speaking, the public sector has to borrow when tax receipts fall short of government expenditure, that is, when the authorities have a budget deficit (or public sector borrowing requirement, PSBR in the UK). The (non-financial) **corporate** or **company sector** is often a net borrower because its retained profits are usually insufficient to finance its real investment plans.

If any sector has a net inflow of funds then it can either purchase additional assets or reduce

## TABLE 2.1: Stylised flow of funds

| | | | Sectors | | | | |
|---|---|---|---|---|---|---|---|
| Assets/liabilities | 1. Personal | 2. Corporate[1] | 3. Monetary[2] | 4. Financial[3] | 5. Public[4] | 6. Overseas | 7. Sum of rows = residual error |
| 1. Finance surplus | 2500 | −700 | 700 | 100 | −2600 | 500 | 500 |
| **Increase in assets (+) and liabilities (−)** | | | | | | | |
| 2. Cash | 100 | 100 | −200 | 0 | 0 | 0 | 0 |
| 3. Bank deposits | 1000 | 1000 | −2300 | 300 | 0 | 200 | 200 |
| 4. Building society deposits | 2000 | 0 | 0 | −2000 | 0 | 0 | 0 |
| 5. LAPF[5] | 2000 | 0 | 0 | −2000 | 0 | 0 | 0 |
| 6. Treasury bills | 200 | 200 | 100 | 0 | −500 | 0 | 0 |
| 7. Commercial bills | 200 | −1000 | 200 | 600 | 0 | 0 | 0 |

*continued overleaf*

## TABLE 2.1: (Continued)

| Assets/liabilities | | 1. Personal | 2. Corporate[1] | 3. Monetary[2] | Sectors 4. Financial[3] | 5. Public[4] | 6. Overseas | 7. Sum of rows = residual error |
|---|---|---|---|---|---|---|---|---|
| 8. | Government bonds | 800 | 200 | 0 | 1000 | −2000 | 100 | 100 |
| 9. | Company securities (equities) | 300 | 400 | 0 | −700 | 0 | 300 | 300 |
| 10. | Bank loans | −1700 | −1500 | 2700 | 500 | 0 | −100 | −100 |
| 11. | Building society mortgages | −2000 | 0 | 0 | 2000 | 0 | 0 | 0 |
| 12. | Sum of columns | 2900 | −600 | 500 | 400 | 500 | 500 | 700 |
| 13. | Balancing item[6] | −400 | −100 | 200 | −300 | 0 | 0 | 0 |

Notes: 1. The corporate sector is basically non-financial firms
2. The monetary sector consists of commercial and investment banks and transactions of the Central Bank
3. The 'financial sector' are financial institutions that are not classified by the authorities as 'banks' or LAPF (e.g. building societies, mutual funds)
4. The public sector consists of central government, municipalities and public corporations
5. LAPF = life assurance and pension funds
6. The balancing item represents the error between data gathered on asset holdings and data gathered from the (national) income−expenditure accounts

its outstanding liabilities. Hence the surplus of £2500 for the personal sector leads to changes in financial assets and liabilities shown in Table 2.1 (column 1). For example, the net inflow of funds of £2500 was used to add to bank deposits (£1000), building society deposits (£2000) and pension contributions (£2000). These and other purchases of assets exceeded the net inflow of £2500 and the difference was made up by borrowing additional bank advances (£1700) and building society mortgages (£2000). Looking down each column indicates how the particular financial surplus/deficit resulted in changes in assets or liabilities. The public sector, for example, had a deficit of £2600 (row 1, column 5) which was financed by issuing £500 of Treasury bills and £2000 of government bonds. By looking across any row we can see how each change in financial assets/liabilities is distributed across each sector. For example, government bonds (row 8) are issued by the public sector (−£2000, row 8, column 5) and taken up by the personal sector (£800, row 8, column 1), company sector (£200, row 8, column 2), 'other financial institutions' (£1000) and the overseas sector (£100). (There is also a measurement or 'residual' error of £100.)

Note that if a particular sector is in surplus that does not mean to say it has no outstanding debts, merely that its increase in assets outweighs the increase in its liabilities. For example, the personal sector, even though it has a net surplus of £2500, may take out additional bank loans (£1700) or house mortgages (£2000) (see Table 2.1, column 1). Also within a particular sector, one group may lend to another as, for example, when one person's building society deposit is on-lent to another person taking out a new mortgage. It follows that a 'surplus unit' provides a *net flow* of funds to deficit units.

The **overseas sector** surplus of £500 might arise because UK imports (of goods and services) exceed UK exports by £500. In other words the UK's **current account deficit** is £500. To pay for the excess of imports (over exports) UK firms will write cheques to overseas firms, usually in foreign currency. Hence the UK current account deficit could give rise to an increase in foreign currency bank deposits (held in UK banks)—see the £200 entry (row 2, column 6). However, the overseas sector can undertake purchases and sales of UK assets without any underlying current account transactions. For example, looking down column 6 we see that the overseas sector purchased £300 of UK company securities financed partly by borrowing bank advances from UK banks (of £100).

The financial flows with the overseas sector are collectively known as the **capital account**. With a perfectly flexible exchange rate and no government intervention in the FX market, the overseas sector must obtain 'finance' for its purchases/sales of UK assets (on the capital account) from other UK residents or financial institutions. It is these transactions that lead to changes in the UK exchange rate as foreign residents buy or sell sterling to invest in UK assets (this argument also applies to UK residents who wish to purchase foreign assets). Hence, in general terms the **sterling spot exchange rate** responds to the forces of supply and demand for sterling (and other currencies).

At certain times, particularly when the overseas sector is selling large quantities of sterling assets and putting downward pressure on the sterling exchange rate, the Central Bank will step in and purchase sterling (and sell the foreign currency) at the prevailing exchange rate. This is an attempt by the Central Bank to 'hold' the exchange rate at its current level and of course leads to a fall in its foreign exchange reserves. (The latter is also an entry in the flow of funds matrix but we have excluded it from Table 2.1 for simplicity.) For example, the

Exchange Rate Mechanism (ERM) of the European Monetary System in the 1980s and 1990s was an attempt to keep exchange rates within designated bands. This was to be achieved by co-ordination of macroeconomic policies and gradual 'convergence' of these economies, in the longer term. However, in the short term the Central Banks of the member states could intervene to support a temporarily weak currency by co-ordinated purchases of the weaker currency. This was not always successful (e.g. the large devaluation of sterling and the Italian lira around Black Wednesday in September 1992). At the end of 1999, there was also co-ordinated intervention to help support the euro, which since its introduction in January 1999 had fallen continuously for around 2 years.

A substantial part of this book is devoted to analysing the key relationships in the foreign exchange market, in an attempt to understand the debate between those who favour fixed or floating exchange rates and the economic arguments for the move to a common currency, the euro within Europe. This analysis will cover such issues as the determination of spot and forward rates, including exchange rate overshooting. The role of chartists and other forecasting schemes (e.g. candlesticks, momentum models) are also examined, as well as the use of swaps, futures and options in hedging exchange rate risk.

## FINANCIAL INTERMEDIARIES

The major portion of the funds from individuals to the government and corporate sectors are channelled via financial intermediaries such as banks, building societies, life assurance and pension funds (LAPF) and finance houses. Why have financial intermediaries taken up this role in preference to direct lending from persons to deficit units? The main reasons involve transactions, search and information costs, and risk spreading.

Specialist firms can more easily assess the creditworthiness of borrowers (e.g. for bank loans), and a diversified loan portfolio has less credit (default) risk. There are economies of scale in buying and selling financial assets (and property). Also, by taking advantage of 'the law of large numbers' they can hold less low-yield 'cash balances' and pass on this cost saving in the form of lower interest rates to borrowers or higher interest rates to depositors. For example, the daily *net* flow of cash out of a large commercial bank is much less than the 'over-the-counter' *gross* flow because a large number of both surplus and deficit units use the same branch on any one day. In contrast, a small operator would have to hold a high level of 'cash reserves'. This is part of the reason why financial intermediaries can engage in **asset transformation**. That is, they borrow 'short' (usually at variable interest rates) and lend 'long' (often at fixed interest rates). They can then hedge this 'mismatch' of fixed and floating interest rates by using swaps, futures and options.

Portfolio diversification means that, if one invests in a wide range of 'risky' assets (i.e. each with a variable market price), then the 'risk' on the whole portfolio is much less than if you held just a few assets. This tends to lead to financial intermediaries 'pooling' the funds of many individuals to purchase a diversified portfolio of assets (e.g. money market mutual funds, equity mutual funds and the development of large financial intermediaries). This is not, of course, to deny that there are some relatively small direct transactions between surplus and deficit units, such as purchases of shares by individuals (e.g. over the internet).

Most financial institutions will hold a wide range of assets and liabilities of differing maturities and liquidity. All we can do here is highlight the key activities of the various sectors, which will enable us to determine the main source of possible changes in particular interest rates. Members of the personal sector on-lend via building society deposits to other members of the personal sector in the form of new mortgages for house purchase. The building society (Savings and Loan Association, S&L in the US) itself will hold a small amount of precautionary liquid assets including cash, bank deposits and Treasury bills (T-bills). Similarly, the personal sector holds a substantial amount in bank deposits, some of which are on-lent as bank loans to households and corporates. A large proportion of a firm's external investment finance comes from bank advances.

The LAPF are key protagonists in financial markets. They take funds mainly from the personal sector in the form of life assurance and other policies as well as occupational pension payments. As these are long-term liabilities from the point of view of the LAPF, a large proportion are invested in T-bonds and, to a lesser extent equities, property and foreign assets. In this way they can match the maturity date of future pension payments to the redemption date of their assets. However, they can and do rely on portfolio diversification to spread their risks, and also hold a relatively small cushion of liquid assets. These funds will be invested and managed on behalf of the LAPF by investment management companies which are often subsidiaries of large banks (e.g. HSBC, Barclays, Morgan Stanley, Citibank, Merrill Lynch). The build-up of foreign financial assets held by the LAPF in the UK proceeded apace after the abolition of the United Kingdom exchange controls in 1979. However, in many countries the proportion of funds one can invest in domestic equities and foreign assets is limited by law to a relatively low figure, but these restrictions are gradually being eased in Europe, the US and even in Japan. Fund managers will actively trade with a proportion of the funds in their domestic and foreign portfolio and hence have an important influence on domestic interest rates, security prices and the exchange rate.

## 2.2 MONEY MARKET AND OPEN MARKET OPERATIONS

The banking system takes in deposits from the personal and company sectors and on-lends a small proportion of these funds to the government by its purchase of new issues of T-bills and government bonds. However, the main part of its assets consists of loans to persons and companies. The banks have a special position in the financial system because their liabilities (i.e. current and deposit accounts) constitute the (main part of the) money supply, a variable the authorities often seek to monitor and occasionally use as the target of policy (Figure 2.1).

The way the Central Bank actually influences interest rates and the money supply differs somewhat from the normal textbook description, but we will begin with the latter. The textbook account has the Central Bank buying (and selling) assets from the (non-bank) private sector, usually Treasury bills or government bonds—this is an *open market operation* (**OMO**). (In actual fact in developed economies these are not outright purchases/sales but so-called repurchase agreements, repos.) For example, if the Central Bank purchases government bonds from the private sector, it will tend to push up bond prices and (as we shall see) this implies a fall in the yield (interest rate) on bonds. As well as a fall in

## FIGURE 2.1: Money market: institutions and instruments

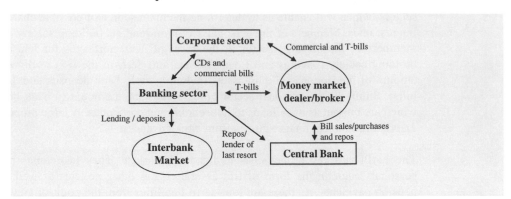

interest rates the OMO also leads to an increase in the money supply. This comes about because the private sector receives a cheque (from its bond sale) which is 'signed' by the Central Bank. When this cheque is presented to a commercial bank the private sector's deposits (i.e. the money supply) increase. But the cheque itself becomes an asset of the commercial bank which, when presented to the Central Bank, constitutes an increase in **'base money'** (or cash reserves) held with the Central Bank by the commercial bank. This increase in base money ('reserves') might also lead to a further expansion of bank loans which, when spent, become someone's bank deposit (thus leading to a further rise in the money supply). In practice, the way the Monetary Policy Committee (MPC) of the Bank of England (or the Board of Governors of the Federal Reserve System in the US) influences (or sets) interest rates is a little different from the textbook description and is described in Box 2.1.

## Box 2.1   MONETARY POLICY COMMITTEE: SETTING THE OFFICIAL RATE

In practice, Central Banks usually keep the commercial banks and the money market short of funds. In any one day the Central Bank estimates the inflows (i.e. tax receipts plus receipts from bond sales) and outflows of funds (i.e. government expenditure plus interest payments on bonds plus redemptions) between the Central Bank and the commercial banks/money market. Broadly speaking, if tax receipts exceed government expenditure plus net bond sales, the Central Bank will be a net recipient of funds and the commercial banks will be losing base money (i.e. cash reserves held at the Central Bank). The Central Bank can then choose to relieve this cash shortage either at the prevailing market interest rate or at a higher rate of its choosing.

If government expenditure exceeds tax receipts then the Central Bank may step in and sell bonds to 'mop up' any excess cash. The Central Bank always makes sure that at the start of each day the private sector is due to pay money to it, and hence there is a cash shortage in the money market (see Figure 2.1). The Central Bank can buy and sell (usually using 2-week repos) a wide variety of short-term instruments such as T-bills, commercial bills and eligible bank bills to ensure a shortage. In the UK, the daily 'shortage' in the market will be announced, as say £1200m at 9.45 a.m. made up of:

| | |
|---|---|
| T-bills and maturing outright purchases | −£600m |
| Maturing bills and gilt repos | −£300m |
| Bank/Exchequer transactions | −£100m |
| Rise in note circulation | −£50m |
| Bankers' balances below target | −£50m |
| Maturing settlement bank late repo facility | −£100m |

Again, the Bank can then choose to relieve this shortage (at say 2 p.m.) either at the existing interest rate or at a higher rate, announced by the MPC. (The higher rate would have been decided at the MPC's monthly meeting at the end of the previous day and announced the next day at 12 noon to the market.) By about 4.20 p.m. the Bank of England will have relieved the banks' cash shortage (e.g. by purchasing T-bills in a repo) at say the 'official' interest rate announced by the MPC. If there are any remaining banks short of cash at 4.20 p.m. then the Bank deals directly with the settlement banks, whose accounts at the Bank are credited at the end of the day. As we see below any new rate set by the MPC will very quickly be reflected in other short-term interest rates. The key to controlling interest rates is therefore the fact that the Central Bank controls the level of 'base money'.

If a commercial bank is short of reserve assets it can initially obtain additional cash from other banks who have surplus funds. This is the **interbank market** with loans having maturities from overnight up to 1 year (but with most transactions in the up to 3 months maturity range). The interest rates on these loans/deposits in the UK and Europe are appropriate LIBOR and LIBID rates—the **London Interbank 'Offer' and 'Bid' Rates**. In the US, the equivalent rate is the **Federal Funds Rate**. In an OMO the aim of the Central Bank is to create a shortage of (cash) reserves for the banking system *as a whole*, so that after the redistribution of cash reserves from surplus to deficit banks, there is an overall cash shortage.

Historically, in the United Kingdom there were a unique set of institutions known as the **Discount Houses** which acted as intermediaries between the banks and the Bank of England. Instead of the Bank of England directly buying and selling bills from the banks, thus directly altering their base money, it did it in an indirect manner. The banks lent money to the Discount Houses and the latter purchased bills from the Bank of England. Conversely, if the banks required cash they 'called in' their loans from the Discount Houses (naturally, known as 'call loans'), and the Discount Houses had to sell T-bills to obtain the cash required. For historic reasons the Discount Houses were an intermediary between the Bank and the commercial banks. The introduction of the repo market in the UK in 1997 meant that the 'special position' held by the Discount Houses has now disappeared and has been replaced by the repo market.

## ASSET RETURNS: A FIRST LOOK

As we shall see there are many alternative ways of measuring 'the return' on different assets. Here, our discussion will be kept at a fairly intuitive and simple level. Consider the return on a Treasury bill *if you have a 3-month investment horizon*. Suppose you purchase the T-bill today for $98 and it has a face (or par or maturity) value of $100. A T-bill is a liability of the government and is therefore free of default (credit) risk. If the T-bill has exactly 3 months to maturity there is no market risk since the investor knows she will receive $100. The **risk free** or 'safe' return on this investment over 3 months is:

[2.1] $$r = [(\$100 - \$98)/\$98]100 = 2.04\% \text{ (per quarter)}$$

This is the ***nominal return r***. However, we can decompose this nominal return into a real return '$rr$' and the expected rate of inflation $\pi$. If you initially have $1.0, a nominal return of 2.04% p.q. implies you will receive $1.024 ($= 1 + r$) in 3 months. However, if the initial price level of consumer goods is 1 and inflation equals 1% p.q., then your $1.024 will only purchase 1.0103 ($= 1.024/1.01$) extra consumer goods. Hence the *exact* real return ($1 + rr$) is:

[2.2] $$(1 + \text{real return}) = \frac{(1 + \text{nominal return})}{(1 + \text{inflation rate})}$$

$$(1 + rr) = \frac{(1 + r)}{(1 + \pi)}$$

which gives $rr = 1.03\%$. An approximation to equation [2.2], using $(1 + rr)(1 + \pi) \approx 1 + rr + \pi$ (if we ignore the relatively 'small' value of '$rr.\pi$') is:

---

**FISHER EQUATION**

**Nominal (risk free) return = real return + expected inflation**

[2.3] $$r = rr + \pi$$

$$(2.04\%) = (1.04\%) + (1\%)$$

---

If expected inflation is 1% p.q. then interest receipts of 2.04% will only purchase (approximately) 1.04% ($= 2.04\% - 1\%$) additional 'real goods'. For example, suppose our representative basket of goods is contained in a Sak's Hamper which initially cost $100. If we begin with $100 then initially we can purchase one Sak's Hamper. If we do not purchase the hamper but invest the $100 then at the end of 3 months we have earned $2.04 interest. However the Sak's Hamper now costs $101, so we can only purchase $1.04 ($= \$102.04 - \$101$) Sak's Hampers. The real return on our investment is 1.04% per quarter. Equation [2.3] is known as the ***Fisher equation***. The real rate of interest is a 'real reward' for postponing consumption of the Sak's Hamper for 3 months, the technical term for which is known as the ***pure rate of time preference***.

Now let us consider the (expected) **holding period return HPR** on a risky asset such as corporate bonds or equity. The HPR on a risky asset is defined as the capital gain (i.e. percentage price rise) plus any cash payments from the asset (e.g. dividends as a proportion of the price). We can *decompose* this HPR into risk free (nominal) return plus a compensation for any 'risk' attached to the asset (which is a liability of the private sector). The latter is referred to as the **risk premium** *rp*:

**Risky return = risk free rate + risk premium**

[2.4]    $$HPR = r + rp$$

What are the types of risks that give rise to this risk premium? Some of them are:

- **Market risk**—the selling price in 3 months time is uncertain, as may be the dividend payment;
- **Inflation risk**—actual inflation may turn out to be different from what was initially *expected*;
- **Default (credit) risk**—the company may go bankrupt which severely reduces any future payouts to bond and stockholders;
- **Liquidity risk**—the asset might trade in a 'thin' market implying a large fall in price if it is to be sold quickly.

A corporate bond or equity of a large company will be subject to the first three risks, and bonds and equity of small companies may also suffer from liquidity risk. Portfolio theory deals with models of market risk and this is thoroughly covered in later chapters. Credit risk is crucial in the pricing of corporate bonds, in assessing changes in the default probability of firms and the consequent likely losses of financial institutions that hold assets subject to credit risk (e.g. bank loans). In Europe and the US regulators have imposed capital requirements on banks and securities houses, for both market and credit risk, in an attempt to reduce the probability of insolvency of these financial intermediaries (see Cuthbertson and Nitzsche, 2001).

Suppose we can calculate the risk premium on equity which is say 2% (per quarter) and that the safe rate is $r = 1\%$. It follows from equation [2.4] that the required (holding period) return on equity is 3% per quarter. Hence what equation [2.4] implies is that, on average, the return on equity should exceed that on a risk free asset. (Of course, the average return on a safe asset should also exceed the expected rate of inflation, equation [2.4], in order to give the investor in the safe asset a positive *real* return for tying his money up, and as a 'reward' for deferring consumption from 'today' to 'tomorrow'.)

Note that until we have an economic model of what determines the risk premium, equation [2.4] is merely an intuitive way of 'apportioning' the return on a risky asset. For example, if when averaged over say a 10-year period, the annual return on equity is 12% p.a. and the (average) nominal safe rate $r = 4.0\%$ p.a., then we can calculate the average risk premium as 8% p.a. But if our economic model of the risk premium indicates that it should have a value of 4% p.a. then this implies a 'theoretical' return on equity of only 8% (= 4% + 4%), hence:

> **If the observed average return on equity is higher than that predicted by economic models of the risk premium. This is known as the *equity premium puzzle*.**

It is also the case that returns on risky assets are in part predictable and hence you may earn excess (risk adjusted) profits from a number of alternative equity investment strategies. Predictability in asset returns is often referred to as a ***stock market anomaly*** and it is a refutation of the so-called ***efficient markets hypothesis***. These aspects are discussed in Chapters 13 and 14.

If we assume that the required *real* return on assets is fairly constant at 3% per annum then market determined changes in the *absolute* (nominal) return on risk free assets mainly depend on expected inflation. *Relative* rates of return (e.g. on equity versus bonds) will depend on the risk premium attached to these assets. Hence highly liquid assets such as bank deposits tend to earn a relatively low rate of interest. Marketable assets such as government bonds (gilts in the UK, T-bonds in the US) earn a higher average return because their market price, if sold before the redemption date, is uncertain. Finally, debentures and equity, which have highly volatile market prices depending upon the actual and expected profitability of particular companies, earn an even higher average return. Hence the differential between the returns on government bonds, corporate bonds and equities reflects the different perceived risk characteristics of these assets.

The reader must obviously be aware of the high degree of volatility in financial markets as interest rates, bond and equity prices, and exchange rates can undergo very substantial changes over short periods. One question that arises is whether such movements are the result of actions by rational agents based on economic fundamentals or whether they are heavily influenced by caprice and herding behaviour. There is evidence to support the view that some financial markets, and stock markets in particular, are excessively volatile and this may be due to fads or speculative bubbles. Certainly, it is difficult to see what major changes in economic fundamentals could have occurred in the week of 19th October 1987 to cause the world's stock markets to crash by over 30%. Evidence and new theoretical models are beginning to appear in the literature that suggest herding behaviour could play a major role in determining fluctuations in financial markets in particular periods. If correct, and asset prices are not based on economic fundamentals, then there is a possible rationale for government intervention in the market. The latter has always been a hotly debated issue in the market for foreign exchange, where governments have sometimes tried to influence exchange rates by intervention, 'gambling' with their foreign exchange reserves. For example, the Plaza and Louvre Agreements of the late 1980s tried to stabilise the US dollar. The Exchange Rate Mechanism ERM, of the 1980s and 1990s was an attempt to limit movements in European exchange rates (which culminated in some countries moving to a common currency, the euro). However, there will always be some volatility in speculative asset markets which is due to entirely rational behaviour, because the arrival of new information or 'news' leads investors to reappraise the future cash flows from their assets (e.g. dividends). Much of this book is about why asset prices are so volatile and, how one can minimise or remove such risk.

Now let us turn to the issue of how the interest rate on government long-term bonds is determined. Such bonds carry (little or) no default and liquidity risk and, if held to maturity, no market risk (since they are sold at their known redemption value at maturity). However, there is some inflation risk because the *purchasing power* of the future periodic (coupon) payments on the bond is uncertain. As we see in Chapter 8, the return (interest rate) on a long maturity bond is a weighted average of the rates of return (interest rates) on short-term bonds, plus an inflation risk premium, *rp*. For example:

[2.5] $$R_{2t} = (1/2)(r_t + r_{t+1}^e) + rp$$

where $R_{2t}$ is the current interest rate on a 2-year maturity bond
$r_t$ is the current interest rate on a 1-year bond
$r_{t+1}^e$ is the interest rate on a 1-year bond *expected to prevail* between the end of year 1 and the end of year 2.

The relationship in equation [2.5] is known as the ***term structure of interest rates*** and if we assume the inflation risk premium is zero, then equation [2.5] is known as the *pure expectations hypothesis*. Essentially, it says that current long rates will rise (fall) with a rise in current short rates $r_t$ *as long as* expected future short rates $r_{t+1}^e$ either remain unchanged or also increase. The term structure is the subject of Chapter 8, but this brief introduction will be useful in understanding the transmission mechanisms of monetary policy. If the Central Bank raises short-term interest rates then this may signal that it feels the economy is overheating and hence interest rates in the future will also be higher, because of higher expected inflation rates in the future. In this case long rates will also rise when the Central Bank raises short rates. However, if a rise in short rates by the Bank is taken as a signal that the Bank is putting strong downward pressure on future inflation, then current long rates may actually *fall*. Hence the effect of the Central Bank's change in short rates has an ambiguous effect on long rates. This is one source of uncertainty in the monetary policy transmission mechanism.

# 2.3 MONETARY POLICY AND THE BUSINESS ENVIRONMENT

Above, we discussed how the Central Bank determines the 'official' (repo) interest rate. In this section we investigate how a rise in this official rate spreads to other interest rates (e.g. on corporate bonds), how it alters asset values (e.g. equity prices) and cash flows (e.g. company profits) and other key 'prices' like the exchange rate. The change in the official interest rate also influences expectations and confidence about the future course of the economy, and this can have a direct impact on real expenditures on investment and consumers' expenditure. Changes in real expenditures influence total demand in the economy and hence wage and price inflation. How we arrived at the current consensus on monetary (and fiscal) policy is briefly outlined in Box 2.2.

**Box 2.2**  **MONETARY POLICY: THE LONG AND WINDING ROAD**

In Western economies in the 1950s and 1960s governments altered fiscal policy to try and change the level of unemployment in the economy. This **Keynesian policy** was known as 'fine tuning', but in the high inflation period of the 1970s the policy became discredited for two reasons, one practical the other 'theoretical'. The practical reason was that it was thought that governments got the timing wrong so that by the time an expansionary fiscal policy increased real output (GNP), the economy was itself automatically in an upturn and the activist fiscal policy merely fuelled additional inflation.

In the 1950s and 1960s monetary policy was largely irrelevant. One view was that the economy was like a brick on a table top, attached to which was a piece of elastic. If you pushed on the elastic, nothing happened—this was like trying to get the economy out of a recession by lower interest rates. Fiscal policy was akin to kicking the brick which was much more efficacious, if occasionally painful. When the economy was in a boom period then trying to reduce aggregate demand by raising interest rates was like pulling on the elastic. For a long time nothing happened and then the brick shot across the table and hit you in the eye. The analogy implied that monetary policy had 'long and variable lags' (and lags that were more variable than those for fiscal instruments like tax changes).

The theoretical reason for the atrophy of activist fiscal policy was the view that in the long term, the level of real output was independent of the level of aggregate *demand* and was determined *solely* by **supply side factors**, such as the rate of technological innovation and the productivity of the labour force. This idea was embodied in the 'long run' **vertical Phillips** curve, whereby increases in aggregate demand (e.g. from an expansionary fiscal policy) eventually just resulted in higher inflation and no change in real output.

At the end of the 1970s the money supply (rather than interest rates) became the focus of monetary policy. (This was particularly true for the UK 1979–84 and the US 1979–82.) Although 'money' could affect 'real demand', output and employment in the short run, it had no effect in the long run (see 'the supply side' above). However, the money supply did influence inflation in the long run. These two tenets describe the long run **neutrality of money**. Indeed, the proposition was that 'inflation is always and everywhere a monetary phenomenon' (Milton Friedman). Control the money supply and you can control inflation (and the exchange rate in an open economy).

Another theoretical strand in the 1980s was the **rational expectations revolution**. This was the view that economic agents were forward looking. No harm in that. But in its extreme form one assumed that firms' and individuals' spending plans today, were based on a forecast of the future and that any *forecasting errors made were purely random* (around zero). That is, there are no systematic forecast errors. You will forecast (say) next month's inflation incorrectly and in a month's time you will forecast wrongly again. However, over a run of months your 'overpredictions' will exactly offset your underpredictions, giving you a zero forecast error, on average. This rational expectations view, when combined with the assumption that wages and prices were 'flexible', plus the supply side idea, became known as the **new classical** approach.

In policy terms it implied that governments who wished to reduce inflation should lower the rate of growth of the money supply and inflation would fall, *with little or no adverse impact on real output and unemployment.* Experiments in controlling the money supply are generally now viewed to have been a failure, in that the cost, in terms of lost output, of reducing inflation was very severe. The policy in the UK also spawned some nice catchphrases. The money supply itself was very difficult to define and measure (e.g. do you include building society deposits as well as bank deposits?) and the Bank of England could not seem to hit the target figure for its rate of growth. Oscar Wilde had described foxhunting (a popular 'sport' amongst the rich in the UK, Prince Charles is an advocate) as 'the unspeakable in pursuit of the uneatable'. Therefore one 'detached' Tory politician (John Biffen) at the time Margaret Thatcher was pursuing a monetary control regime described the money supply as 'the unmeasurable in pursuit of the uncontrollable'. Also, Charles Goodhart (a former chief economic adviser at the Bank of England and latterly on the MPC of the Bank of England) cited **Goodhart's Law**, namely that as soon as you try and control an economic variable like the money supply, it no longer measures what it used to measure.

The view that counter-cyclical fiscal policy is harmful and cannot be used to affect the level of real output in the long run is now firmly entrenched. However, it is probably the case that if there were a severe and prolonged 'cyclical' recession then an expansionary fiscal policy would be used (e.g. Japan at the end of the 1990s). In general, however, the 'supply side' idea remains intact and it implies that over the longer term the budget deficit (as a proportion of output/GNP) should be broadly constant, implying that government debt grows in line with the underlying rate of growth of output).

The view that expectations are important (which was always the case) remains, but the rational expectations assumption has fallen by the wayside as far as policy is concerned and the emphasis has moved to how people's expectations change when they have rather limited information about the economy. The money supply as a target variable has also been dropped and instead we have seen the adoption of an explicit inflation target. Also there had been a move towards monetary policy being determined by *independent* Central Banks who set interest rates to meet the inflation target (e.g. in New Zealand, the US, the UK and in the euro area).

The move to an independent Central Bank (rather than interest rates being set by the Finance Minister and politicians) arises for two main reasons. First, on an empirical level, it was noted that if you constructed a (subjective) index of bank independence for countries and the average rate of inflation in these countries (over say 1960 to 1990), there was a negative relationship. Countries like Germany, the US, Switzerland, Canada and Australia which had a high level of independence had relatively low rates of inflation (3–6%), whereas countries like Greece, New Zealand, Spain, Italy and the UK which had less 'independence' had relatively high average rates of inflation (7–11%). The 'index of independence' depends on such items as (i) appointment and dismissal procedures for the Governor, (ii) objectives of Central Bank policy, (iii) limitations on lender of last resort, (iv) transparency in setting monetary policy targets (e.g. Cukierman, 1992) and are somewhat subjective. Clearly there are a whole host of reasons other than Central Bank independence why particular countries might have low average inflation (e.g. less susceptible to imported inflation due to overshooting in the exchange rate, more flexible labour markets, etc.).

The second (and perhaps less important) reason was the 'theoretical' **time inconsistency problem** (Barro and Gordon, 1983). Governments could pre-commit to a low inflation policy but before an election there is a great temptation to abandon this policy to gain electoral advantage. If the government expands the economy (e.g. by lowering interest rates) then there will be a rise in output and incomes in the short run—this is the short run Phillips curve. This will win votes at the election. However, inflation will follow later and this will 'destroy' the new jobs, so after the election all you get is higher inflation and no extra jobs (and output)—this is the 'supply side' again. Hence the government's anti-inflation policy is 'time inconsistent' because it has an incentive to renege on the policy before the election. Independent members of the MPC of a Central Bank are not elected and therefore do not have an incentive to renege on the anti-inflation stance. Hence, their pronouncements on a low inflation policy will have **more credibility** than those of elected officials, and this in itself may lead the private sector to set lower prices. Of course, the move to independence of Central Banks in setting interest rates also reflects the general feeling against 'big government' and that 'the economy is too important to be left to politicians'.

An independent Central Bank can set its interest rate by using its discretion or it can use a **'monetary rule'**. One of the favoured rules is the so-called **Taylor rule** (named after the US Professor John Taylor) whereby the interest rate is increased either:

(i) if output is above its long run 'sustainable' ('natural') level (sometimes called the 'output gap'); or

(ii) the inflation rate is above its target level.

This is part of the wider **rules versus discretion** debate in public policy. (It also appears for example in the US in the form of limitations on the budget deficit, a variant of which can be found in the Maastricht Treaty setting the guidelines for entry into the euro zone). There are variants on the basic Taylor rule but essentially 'rules' are there because 'monetary policy is too important even to be left to independent experts'—it must be determined by a computer, based on a 'consensus' model of the economy (presumably built by independent experts!).

> The **transmission mechanisms** of monetary policy work via:
> - Interest rates and other asset returns (e.g. equity returns).
> - Asset prices (e.g. equity values) and cash flows (e.g. profits).
> - Expectations and confidence.
> - The exchange rate.

## INTEREST RATES AND REAL EXPENDITURE

Movements in interest rates have a direct and important impact upon the firm. First and most obvious, actual changes and expected future movements in interest rates influence a firm's *real investment decisions.* This applies to longer term projects such as expansion of an existing plant, the purchase of new machinery or a new vehicle fleet as well as short-term investment, such as deciding what quantity of stocks of raw materials or finished goods to hold.

In principle, *real* **investment** should respond to changes in *real* interest rates, that is, the nominal percentage interest rate less the expected rate of price inflation. If inflation is expected to be 10% p.a. over the life of the investment project and the cost of borrowing is 12% p.a., then the investment project should be just as profitable as when $r = 3\%$ p.a. and inflation is 1% p.a. because the real interest rate is 2% in both cases. The use of discounted present value (DPV) in analysing the impact of interest rates on the profitability of real investment decisions is discussed in Chapter 3. When the Bank raises short-term rates it hopes that it is taken as a signal that inflation will be lower in the future and hence results in a rise in real short-term rates. Note that after a *rise in* short rates, if the nominal long rate *falls* (see above) then as long as expectations of future inflation fall more than nominal long rates, *real long-term rates* will rise. (Got it? If not read it slowly again.) However, because fixed investment depends on long rates, and the impact of monetary policy on the latter is ambiguous, then this channel of monetary policy is subject to considerable uncertainty.

Because of the low transactions costs of bank lending (which is now available on a longer term basis of up to 20 years as well as short-term overdrafts) and issuing commercial bills and corporate bonds, these 'outside' sources of finance are used quite frequently for the finance of inventory and fixed investment. But note that even if a firm uses retained profits as a source of finance for fixed investment, the cost of such funds is not zero, but the interest the firm could make by investing the funds elsewhere (e.g. in a corporate bond). Therefore the interest cost is still relevant to its investment decisions.

Changes in interest rates may also influence a firm's cash flow position and hence its fixed investment. If a firm has a high level of **income gearing** (i.e. net interest payments on short-term liabilities as a proportion of cash flow or profits), then a rise in interest rates will increase interest payments. If a cushion of liquid assets is not readily available, the firm may experience cash flow problems and may decide to cut back on employees and real investment.

It is perhaps also worth noting that some firms expand by takeovers. They borrow funds in order to purchase the shares of 'target' firms whose shares they believe are undervalued (i.e. relative to the PV of profits under the current management). However, this is not an expansion in aggregate investment in the economy, but merely a change in ownership and control. However, it could lead to higher aggregate investment after the merger/takeover.

A rise in interest rates is usually accompanied by a fall in the price of bonds, equity and real estate property. To the extent that firms hold equity and bonds of other firms, their financial wealth will fall. Also, as the value of their fixed assets (e.g. factories, office buildings) falls, it may be more difficult to raise additional bank loans for fixed investment, because they have less collateral to pledge against these loans. (This is sometimes known as the 'credit channel'.) Banks may also be reluctant to lend if the existing loans on their books have fallen in value (and hence they are required by the regulator to hold more capital—this is a type of **'credit crunch'**; see Cuthbertson and Nitzsche, 2001 on credit risk and the Basle capital requirements). Hence real investment may fall because of these asset price effects.

A rise in interest rates affects consumers in a broadly similar way to that for firms. It directly raises the cost of borrowing on consumer durables, it lowers financial wealth (in bonds, stocks) and most importantly it lowers the market value of housing wealth. In the UK, which has variable rate housing loans, a rise in interest rates also leads to a fall in income for mortgage holders and a rise in income for holders of building society deposits. The net effect depends on how this change in income affects debtors and creditors. Hence, a rise in interest rates is likely to reduce consumers' expenditure and investment in new housing.

The effect on expectations and consumer confidence is difficult to assess since it depends on firms and individuals forecasting the likely effect of a change in monetary policy on future cash flows (e.g. sales revenues and costs for firms and income from employment for individuals). However, a rise in interest rates is likely to depress expectations about future incomes and hence lead to a postponement of real expenditure on investment and consumption.

The interest rate–exchange rate link is subject to much controversy. One argument is that if there is an unexpected rise in domestic interest rates then this will encourage inward portfolio investment in domestic bank deposits, bonds and equities. In turn this leads to an increased demand for the domestic currency on the foreign exchange market and hence the domestic currency appreciates. Some models incorporate a large appreciation in the short term, with a gradual falling back to some long non-equilibrium level. This is known as *exchange rate overshooting* and is discussed in Chapter 16. The exchange rate assumption used by the MPC of the Bank of England in its 'central projection' used to be that sterling would move in line with the domestic–foreign interest rate differential—this is the **uncovered interest parity** assumption—see Chapter 15. Since November 1999 the (effective) exchange rate is assumed to be an average of a constant (nominal) rate and a path related to interest differentials. These assumptions reflect the fact that *any* exchange rate assumption could be extremely wide of the mark.

If the price of exports (in the domestic currency) is fairly stable in the short term, then an appreciation of the domestic currency will make exports (price) uncompetitive on world markets. Hence exports will fall, and unemployment will rise, putting downward pressure on wage and price inflation (i.e. the short run Phillips curve). The appreciation of the domestic currency has a direct effect in lowering the cost of imported goods (in terms of the domestic currency). These imported goods are either consumption goods or goods used as inputs (e.g. coal, steel, oil) to the production process and hence this tends to lower domestic inflation. In addition, the lower domestic price of imported goods (e.g. cars, machine tools) tends to switch demand to foreign suppliers which puts downward pressure on domestic prices as they compete for customers. The interest rate–exchange rate link is a powerful influence on the real economy and is the subject of Chapters 15 and 16. Unfortunately it is one of the least understood linkages in the monetary transmission mechanism. The Central Bank has great difficulty in knowing what precise effect (if any) a rise in domestic interest rates will have on the future path of the exchange rate. An (unanticipated) rise in interest rates could lead to either a rise, fall or no change in the exchange rate in practice, although on balance one might generally see a rise. Clearly the interest rate–exchange rate nexus is much more important for very 'open' economies (i.e. ones where a relatively large proportion of output, say 20%, is traded).

Investors who hold foreign financial assets will also see a change in their wealth after a change in the exchange rate, unless these changes in portfolio value are hedged using FX forwards, futures, swaps or options (see later chapters). This revaluation of foreign assets is only of major importance if domestic residents hold large amounts of foreign assets (e.g. 'dollarisation' in certain countries).

## TRANSMISSION MECHANISM

If the Central Bank raises its 'official' short-term rate then this will be immediately followed by a rise in interest rate on wholesale and term deposits. This will then require a rise in rates on bank advances in order that the bank earns a positive spread on lending out funds. People now have an incentive to switch funds out of low-yield building society (Savings and Loan Association) deposits and T-bills into high-yield bank deposits. To counter this loss of business, the building societies will quickly raise both their deposit and mortgage advance rates. As T-bills are sold their price will fall and their interest rate rise. The higher return on T-bills might encourage people to switch out of debentures and equity. This leads to a *fall* in current equity prices and (with unchanged future dividends) a rise in the return on equity. Thus we see that a whole chain of interest rate increases and rise in equity and bond returns has followed the initial rise in rates engineered by the Central Bank's open market operation. We noted above that there is an ambiguous effect on long-term interest rates, but let us assume these also increase. Hence the rise in official rates tends to have a *ripple effect* on other interest rates within the system which triggers off the effects described earlier and is intended to reduce the rate of inflation. But it is widely recognised that the transmission mechanisms have 'long and variable lags', so do we have a good idea about the quantitative impact of all these effects? The Bank of England (2000) published some estimates for the UK economy recently, based on simulations of (one of) the Bank's macroeconomic models. The two alternative simulations assume:

(1) Government (consumption) expenditure is held fixed in *money* terms and interest rates are set to achieve a price-level target.
(2) Government (consumption) expenditure is fixed *as a proportion of GDP* and there is a monetary policy 'rule' whereby interest rates are altered depending on the 'output gap' and the deviation of inflation from its target level.

The results are shown in Figures 2.2a and b for a 'shock' to official interest rates of +1% (higher than the base run) that lasts for 1 year. GDP (Figure 2.2a) falls quite quickly, by about 0.20% in scenario 1 and 0.25% in scenario 2, by the end of the year and then returns to its initial level after 3 years. The inflation rate (Figure 2.2b) hardly changes in the first year but then falls by 0.2 percentage points in scenario 1 and 0.4 percentage points in scenario 2. However, because the 'shock' here is temporary one cannot extrapolate the results to infer how much interest rates would have to be raised to achieve any given

**FIGURE 2.2: Effect on (a) GDP and (b) inflation rate of a 'shock' to official interest rates (Bank of England, 2000) Source: 'The Transmission Mechanism of Monetary Policy', Monetary Policy Committee, Bank of England (1999) Reproduced with permission of the Bank of England**

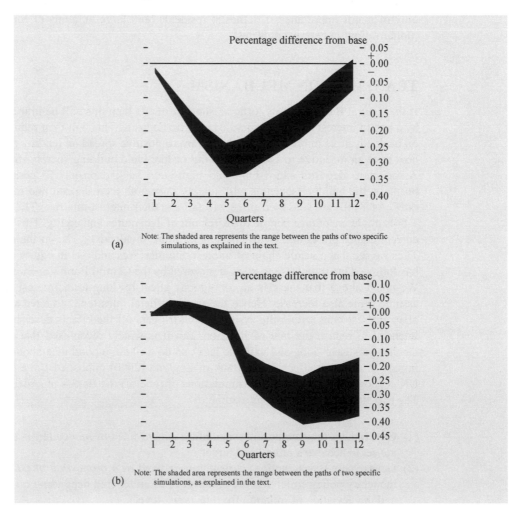

Note: The shaded area represents the range between the paths of two specific simulations, as explained in the text.

(a)

Note: The shaded area represents the range between the paths of two specific simulations, as explained in the text.

(b)

reduction in inflation. (Even the Bank does not believe in that degree of transparency—presumably because it believes the private sector would misinterpret the nuances and caveats of such a simulation.)

This then is the macroeconomic environment faced by firms and individuals and this is why the meetings of the MPC of the Central Bank are keenly watched by both financial market participants and managers of corporates.

## 2.4 SUMMARY

This chapter has shown how savings and investment give rise to financial surpluses and deficits. The deficit units are usually the government and company sectors with the personal (household) sector usually in surplus. We then had a preliminary look at why different assets might have different returns. Next we examined how the business environment faced by firms and individuals is affected by the monetary policy actions of the Central Bank. The main points to emerge from this chapter are the following.

- **Financial intermediaries** and the **capital markets** channel funds from surplus to deficit units (i.e. 'flow of funds') thus allowing production and consumption to be changed, independently of immediate revenue inflows (e.g. from personal income and retained profits).
- Financial intermediaries take advantage of **portfolio diversification**, **specialisation** and low information and **transaction costs** in efficiently channelling funds between surplus and deficit units.
- Financial flows (particularly capital flows) between domestic and foreign residents have an effect on the exchange rate.
- The **monetary authorities** have a direct influence on interest rates via **open market operations** (usually in the **repo market**) and hence an indirect effect on the level of output in the short run and the rate of inflation in the long run. This is the **transmission mechanism** of monetary policy which works via interest rates, asset prices, expectation/confidence effects and the exchange rate.
- There has been a move in recent years for interest rates to be set by **independent Central Banks**, rather than by Finance Ministers (who are subject to influence from the political process). This is partly the result of the so-called **time inconsistency problem**.
- **Returns on risky assets** such as stocks can be thought of as being determined by a risk free rate plus a **risk premium**. The latter arises because of the volatility of market prices and other sources of risk, such as credit and liquidity risk. Much of finance theory is concerned with finding an appropriate measure for the risk premium.
- The **real return** on an asset is the nominal return less the expected rate of inflation.

# END OF CHAPTER EXERCISES

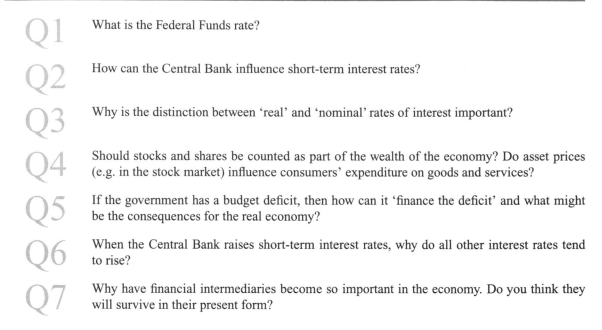

**Q1**  What is the Federal Funds rate?

**Q2**  How can the Central Bank influence short-term interest rates?

**Q3**  Why is the distinction between 'real' and 'nominal' rates of interest important?

**Q4**  Should stocks and shares be counted as part of the wealth of the economy? Do asset prices (e.g. in the stock market) influence consumers' expenditure on goods and services?

**Q5**  If the government has a budget deficit, then how can it 'finance the deficit' and what might be the consequences for the real economy?

**Q6**  When the Central Bank raises short-term interest rates, why do all other interest rates tend to rise?

**Q7**  Why have financial intermediaries become so important in the economy. Do you think they will survive in their present form?

# PART 2

# BASIC CONCEPTS

3

# Investment Appraisal

## LEARNING OBJECTIVES

- To understand **compound interest** and its 'mirror image', **discounting**.
- To learn why and how we evaluate capital investment projects using either **discounted present value (DPV)** or the **internal rate of return (IRR)** criterion.
- To examine the relative merits of DPV, IRR and other decision criteria (e.g. payback period, discounted payback, profitability index) for choosing between alternative investment projects.
- To show how **decision trees** and **scenario analysis** can be used in DPV calculations when there is uncertainty about future cash flows.
- To discuss a number of practical issues in applying the DPV technique such as **mutually exclusive projects**, **capital rationing**, **real versus nominal cash flows**, the treatment of **taxation**, **depreciation** and **working capital**.
- To briefly discuss alternative **sources of finance** for investment projects and the **weighted average cost of capital**.

In this Chapter we illustrate the use of compounding, discounted present value (DPV) and the internal rate of return (IRR). Using simple arithmetic examples we consider the correct method of evaluating the profitability of investing in a business enterprise (i.e. a physical investment project). It is shown that when the discounted present value equals the capital cost of the project DPV = KC or, IRR = cost of borrowing, 'the investment project earns just enough profits to cover the repayment of interest and principal on the loan'. When evaluating an investment project, a businesswoman will consider the latter statement but in finance theory this is most conveniently expressed in terms of the concepts of DPV and IRR.

## 3.1 COMPOUNDING AND DISCOUNTED PRESENT VALUE

Suppose the annual interest rate is 10% (equivalent to $r = 0.1$) *and is expected to remain constant*. You have $A = \$1000$ to invest, today. What is the terminal value (TV) of $1000 in 2 years time? *At the end of the 1st year we have:*

[3.1]     $TV_1 = A + rA = (1 + r)A = (1.1)\$1000 = \$1100$

If we now reinvest the \$1000 initial capital **and** the first year's interest receipts (of $rA = \$100$) then *at the end of the 2nd year we have*:

[3.2]     $TV_2 = $ (interest earned on initial capital) $+$ (interest-on-interest)

$$= (1 + r)A + (1 + r)rA = (1 + r)^2 A$$

$$= (1.1)\$1000 + (1.1)(0.1)\$1000 = (1.1)^2\$1000 = \$1210$$

Hence compounding takes account of receipts of interest-on-interest. In general the **terminal value after *n* years** of an initial investment of \$$A$ is:

[3.3]     $TV_n = A(1 + r)^n$

## DISCOUNTING

Discounting is the exact opposite of compounding. Suppose someone offers you the prospect of \$1210 payable with certainty after 2 years. How much are you prepared to give her as a loan today, if the interest rate is 10% p.a. ($r = 0.1$)? The answer of course is \$1000, since if you had \$1000 today you could invest it and have \$1210 in 2 years time. We then say that the *discounted present value* **(DPV)** of \$1210 (payable in 2 years time) is \$1000 (today). The term *discounted cash flow* **(DCF)** is also used and in general the method is known as the **present value PV technique**. The amount payable in 2 years is reduced (discounted) to an equivalent amount today. Hence, if $V_2 = \$1210$ then the DPV is:

[3.4]     $DPV = \dfrac{V_2}{(1 + r)^2} = \dfrac{\$1210}{(1.1)^2}$

Put another way, \$1000 today (i.e. the DPV) is equivalent to \$1210 in 2 years time. In the capital markets, if you can promise certain delivery of \$1210 in 2 years time, someone will lend you \$1000 today. Now suppose I offer to pay you \$1100 ($= V_1$) in 1 years time and \$1210 ($= V_2$) in 2 years time. How much are you prepared to give me as a loan *today* in exchange for these two certain future payments? The answer is that you will give me \$2000 *today*, because:

[3.5]     $DPV = \dfrac{V_1}{(1 + r)} + \dfrac{V_2}{(1 + r)^2} = \dfrac{\$1100}{(1.1)} + \dfrac{\$1210}{(1.1)^2} = \$2000$

The important principle here is that if the interest rate (i.e. opportunity cost of the money) is positive, then amounts of money that accrue at different points of time in the future must be measured/compared **at a specific point in time**. The PV concept takes this 'specific point' as *today*, but in principle it could be any single specific point in time, for example, the terminal date at the end of the second year.

# 3.2 INVESTMENT APPRAISAL: 'VITO'S DELI'

As we shall see the concept of DPV is widely used to evaluate all types of investment decisions such as physical investment in plant and machinery (capital investment), investment in stocks and bonds and in the pricing of futures and options.

## NET PRESENT VALUE

PV is probably the most widely used concept in finance. Suppose we consider a physical investment project, namely buying a New York deli called 'Vito's Deli'. Suppose forecast sales revenues less input costs (e.g. wages and materials), known as free (or net) cash flows, are $CF_1 = \$1100$ *at the end* of year 1 and $CF_2 = \$1210$ at the end of year 2. At the end of year 2 you know with certainty that your Deli will be 'torched' by a rival (e.g. the 'Bucconi Brothers') and as you have no insurance it will then have zero value (see Figure 3.1). Note that the cash flows $CF_1$ and $CF_2$ are the same as used above. Suppose the capital (or 'investment') cost of purchasing the Deli today is $KC = \$2100$ and the interest rate is 10% ($r = 0.1$). The interest rate is the 'opportunity cost' of the use of your 'own funds', since we assume the best alternative use of your 'own funds' is to invest them in a bank account at the rate $r$. (Equally, we could also have assumed that the $2100 was a loan from the bank and the same analysis as below would apply.) Is the Deli business the correct investment decision (i.e. the one that maximises your return)?

### Calculation A:

| | | |
|---|---|---|
| Total cash flows (undiscounted) | = | $2310 |
| Capital cost (today) | = | −$2100 |
| Crude profit | = | $210 |

This crude calculation suggests we should invest in the Deli business since the 'profit is positive'.

## FIGURE 3.1: Cash flows for Vito's Deli

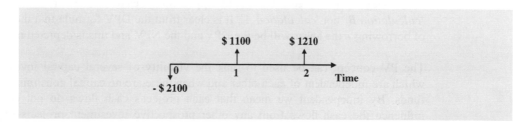

### Calculation B:

| | |
|---|---|
| DPV (cash flows) | = $2000 |
| Capital cost (today) | = −$2100 |
| Net profit (on DPV basis) | = −$100 |

Here, using the DPV formula (calculation B), we have DPV = $2000 and with a capital cost KC = $2100, the net present value NPV = DPV − KC = −$100. Hence in this case:

[3.6]     **DPV (cash flows) < capital cost KC**

or

[3.7]     **Net present value NPV = DPV − KC < 0**

It looks as though we should **not** invest in the project, which is the correct answer. The reason why the PV approach (equation [3.6]) is correct is most easily seen by compounding to the terminal date, 2 years hence, and taking account of the **opportunity cost** of the funds used to invest in the Deli. The next best (here the only) alternative use for your initial funds of $2100 is placing them on deposit at the bank which pays an annual rate of interest $r$. This yields a terminal value TV of:

### End of year 2 (bank):

[3.8]     **TV(bank)** = $2100(1 + r)^2 = $2100(1.1)^2 = $2541

If you invest in 'Vito's Deli', your $1100 revenues received at the end of year 1 can be invested at $r$ to give $1100(1 + r) = $1100(1.1) = $1210 at the end of year 2. This can be (directly) added to your cash flow at the end of year 2 (= $1210) since both are measured *at the same time period*. Hence investing in 'Vito's Deli' gives a terminal value as follows.

### End of year 2 (Vito's):

[3.9]     **TV(Vito's)** = $1210 + $1210 = $2420

Clearly, the terminal value of 'Vito's Deli' ($2420) is less than the terminal value of investing in the bank ($2541). Hence you should **not** invest in 'Vito's Deli'. The DPV or NPV investment rule (equations [3.6] and [3.7]) is equivalent to comparing terminal values, that is if DPV(Vito's) < KC then this implies that TV(Vito's) < TV(bank). The above also stresses the fact that even if you are given your initial outlay of $2100 (by 'Uncle Paulie') the money is not 'free'. It has an **opportunity cost** and the relevant calculation is *'calculation B'* not *'calculation A'*. It is clear from the DPV formula that the higher the cost of borrowing $r$ the lower will be the DPV and the NPV, and this is depicted in Figure 3.2.

The PV concept can be used to rank the viability of several capital investment projects which are independent of each other and when there are no capital constraints on borrowing funds. By independent we mean that each project's cash flows do not depend upon or influence the cash flows from any other prospective investment projects (e.g. setting up

## FIGURE 3.2: NPV and the discount rate

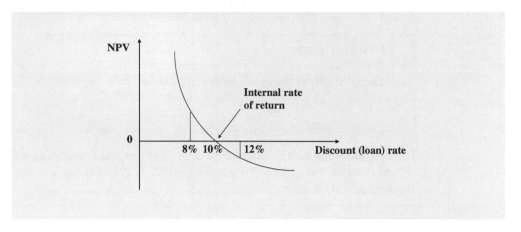

'delis' in towns that are geographically far apart). At any point in time, the firm is faced with one discount (loan) rate and can use this to calculate the NPV for each individual project. We can now think of ranking these NPVs from highest to lowest. Hence:

> **When funds are available, invest in all projects for which the NPV is positive**

However, note that if there is a capital constraint on finance, then the NPV criterion is misleading (see 'performance index' below).

## VALUATION OF THE WHOLE FIRM

The PV approach can be used to value the whole firm. Here we merely aggregate the free cash flows and capital costs from all the firm's current and planned projects and find their total NPV. Equivalently we could simply sum the NPVs of each individual project. It can be shown that:

> **If managers invest in all positive NPV projects then this maximises the value of the firm and maximises the returns to shareholders**

The PV approach is one way stock analysts try and calculate the value of the firm. Suppose by summing the NPVs of all the divisions of the firm they find that the NPV of the firm is $V_{firm} = \$100m$. If this is an all equity firm and there are $N = 10m$ shares outstanding then the 'fair value' of these shares is $V_s = \$10$ per share ($= 100/10$). If the shares are currently trading at $P = \$9$ then the analyst might recommend purchasing this undervalued share and hence making a capital gain when the rest of the market corrects the undervaluation. This issue is explored in detail in Chapter 12. If the firm in question is 'levered' and hence is financed by a mix of debt and equity then:

---

**LEVERED FIRM**

Value of equity = value of the firm − value of debt

$$V_s = V_{firm} − V_{debt}$$

---

Hence to calculate the fair value of the equity and hence the 'fair' stock price we need to be able to calculate the value of the outstanding debt (e.g. bonds, bank loans) of the firm. This is the subject of Chapter 7.

## INTERNAL RATE OF RETURN

The internal rate of return (IRR) provides an equivalent way of evaluating physical investment projects, as the DPV criterion. Consider an investment project with a capital cost (today) of KC = $2000 and (net) revenues accruing in the future of $CF_1$ = $1100 and $CF_2$ = $1210. Now assume for the moment that the cost of the funds to finance this project are unknown, but we will call this unknown value $y$ (% p.a., expressed as a decimal). The PV of the future cash flows is:

[3.10] $$\frac{CF_1}{(1 + y)} + \frac{CF_2}{(1 + y)^2} = \frac{\$1100}{(1 + y)} + \frac{\$1210}{(1 + y)^2}$$

Now **equate** the known capital cost KC = $2000 with the DPV of future receipts:

[3.11] $$\$2000 = \frac{\$1100}{(1 + y)} + \frac{\$1210}{(1 + y)^2}$$

The (constant) value of $y$ that satisfies equation [3.11] is $y = 0.10$ (or 10% p.a.) and is called the IRR of the investment project (see Figure 3.2). It is that constant rate of return $y$ that just allows the project to 'break even', where 'break even' here means that DPV (receipts) = capital cost. The basic investment rule is then:

---

**Invest in the project if IRR ⩾ opportunity cost of the funds (the loan rate = $r$)**

---

Hence if the cost of borrowing $r = 10\%$ p.a., the IRR of $y = 10\%$ suggests it is just worthwhile to invest in the Deli. Note also that for $r = 10\%$ the DPV of this project is $2000 which just equals the capital cost of $2000 and hence the NPV = 0. The DPV rule also indicates that the Deli investment is just viable for $r = 10\%$. Hence, our two investment rules give equivalent decisions. They are, invest in the project if:

**[3.12a]**     $DPV \geqslant KC$

or

**[3.12b]**     $IRR \geqslant r$

If DPV > KC or IRR > r then this implies that at the end of the investment period (i.e. terminal date) you will have more 'cash' if you invest in a physical investment project such as Vito's Deli rather than investing your own funds in a bank deposit (i.e. the next best alternative use for the funds). Or, if the capital cost is financed by a bank loan, you will be able to pay off the principal and interest and still have some cash remaining in 2 years time.

Let us examine the DPV and IRR rules and interpret them in a language more frequently used by business persons. The 'bottom line' for an investment project from a business perspective is that the cash flows generated at least pay off the initial capital (cash) outlay and any interest on this capital (or opportunity cost of the own funds used). We now demonstrate using a simple example that:

> **If DPV = KC or if the IRR just equals the opportunity cost of the funds (e.g. bank lending rate $r$), then the investment project will just pay back the principal and the interest on the loan**

For example, if $KC = \$1528$ and $CF_1 = CF_2 = \$1000$ then the IRR using equation [3.11] is easily found to be $y = 0.2$ (or 20%). If we let the bank loan rate $r = 0.2$, then the DPV equals \$1528 which just equals the capital cost. Given the cash flows $CF_1$ and $CF_2$ the sequence of payments is given in Table 3.1.

At the end of year 1 the loan outstanding has increased to \$1833.6 ($= \$1528(1.2)$), part of which is paid off with receipts of \$1000, leaving an outstanding loan of \$833.6. At the end of year 2 this accrues to \$1000 which can be wholly paid off with the \$1000 received at the end of year 2. Note however that the above simple analysis side-steps some of the problems

---

## TABLE 3.1: Cash flow for investment with DPV = 0 or IRR = cost of borrowing

|  | End of 1st year | End of 2nd year |
|---|---|---|
| **Loan outstanding (including interest)** | (1.2) $1528 = $1833.60 | (1.2) $833.6 = $1000.32 |
| **Receipts** | −$1000 | −$1000 |
| **Amount owing** | = $833.6 | = $0.32 (= 0) |

that can arise when using the IRR concept and it is not always the case that DPV and IRR rules give identical decisions in the ranking of investment projects.

## 3.3 PROBLEMS AND REFINEMENTS

Generally speaking businessmen prefer to talk in terms of IRR. Hence they can say that 'project A is expected to earn an IRR of 10% which is 3% over borrowing costs'. However, the PV method is the one that nearly always gives unambiguously correct investment decisions. As we see below, in certain circumstances the IRR investment rule given above has to be amended, otherwise it may indicate the wrong project choice.

### DIFFERENT CASH FLOW PROFILES

Consider the cash flows from the three projects A, B and C shown in Table 3.2. Project A has a 'normal' or 'regular' pattern of cash flows, namely an initial investment outlay of $-\$100$ and receipts (in 1 year) of $150.

The NPV is negatively related to the bank loan rate (i.e. the discount rate) and the IRR is 50% (Figure 3.3). The NPV rule indicates that the project should be implemented for any discount rate $r$ below 50% and the IRR rule gives the same investment decision rule (i.e. invest in the project if $y\ (=50\%) > r$, the cost of borrowing).

Consider the cash flows for project B, a Rolling Stones Concert. Here, ticket sales before the concert result in an inflow of $100 and the cash outflow of equipment and salaries of $150 takes place after 1 year. The graph of the NPV against the discount rate is positive, as in Figure 3.4 and the IRR is again $y = 50\%$.

---

### TABLE 3.2: Different cash flow profiles

| | |
|---|---|
| **Project A** | $(-100, 150)$ |
| **Project B** | $(100, -150)$ |
| **Project C** | $(-100, 245, -150)$ |
| | |
| **Project A** | 'normal' |
| **Project B** | 'Rolling Stones Concert' |
| **Project C** | 'open-cast mining' |
| | |
| **NPV gives correct decision for A, B, C** | |
| **IRR gives wrong decision for B and C** | |

## FIGURE 3.3: Project A: normal cash flows

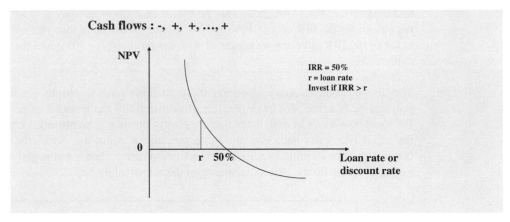

Cash flows : -, +, +, ..., +

IRR = 50%
r = loan rate
Invest if IRR > r

## FIGURE 3.4: Project B: Rolling Stones concert

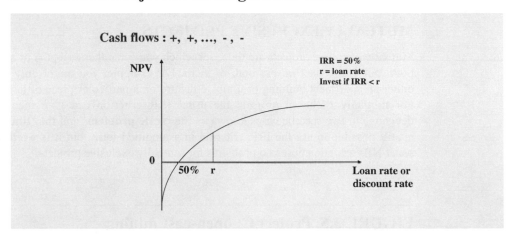

Cash flows : +, +, ..., -, -

IRR = 50%
r = loan rate
Invest if IRR < r

The NPV becomes more positive as the loan rate increases (above 50%). Hence the NPV rule indicates that a loan rate *greater than 50%* implies that project B should be implemented since then the NPV > 0. However, somewhat paradoxically, the latter implies a reversal of the usual IRR rule: for this project to go ahead we require IRR < discount (loan) rate $r$. The paradox is resolved by noting that the cash inflow (at $t = 0$) from project B of $100 is equivalent to borrowing $100 with an implicit cost equal to the IRR of 50%. If the *actual cost* of borrowing from the bank is greater than 50%, then it pays to get your $100 today, by undertaking project B. Hence you invest in project B if $y < r$.

Cash flows from project C could be due to an investment in open-cast mining, where there are large initial capital costs, followed by positive receipts from the sale of the minerals and a final negative cash flow due to the cost of returning the site back to its original state. The

NPV–discount rate relationship is shown in Figure 3.5 with a positive NPV for discount rates between 20 and 25%, and therefore on the basis of the NPV rule, project C should be undertaken for $20\% < r < 25\%$. This profile of cash flows, namely $\{-, +, -\}$, gives multiple values for the IRR of $y = 10\%$ or 30%. Clearly if the bank loan rate equals say 14% one value of the IRR indicates we go ahead with the project ($y = 30\%$) and the other ($y = 10\%$) that we do not.

The above problems apply whenever the cash flows have the same qualitative form as in projects A, B and C. For example, if a project initially has a *series* of negative cash flows followed by a *series* of cash flows that are always positive (like project A), then the NPV and the usual IRR rules both give the same investment decisions. Similarly, a *series* of cash flows which are all initially negative, then some positive, then some negative again may give multiple values for the IRR. A summary of the above might be:

**Use NPV and not IRR when cash flows are irregular**

## MUTUALLY EXCLUSIVE PROJECTS

Mutually exclusive projects are those for which you can either accept A or accept B or reject both, but you cannot *accept* both of them. For example, you might only be able to build either an apartment building or a movie theatre on a particular piece of land (but not both). For mutually exclusive projects the usual IRR criterion can give incorrect investment decisions in two specific cases known as the **'scale problem'** and the **'timing problem'**. It is still possible to use the IRR criterion in a modified form, but it is worth noting that the usual NPV criterion poses no problems for mutually exclusive projects.

## FIGURE 3.5: Project C: open-cast mining

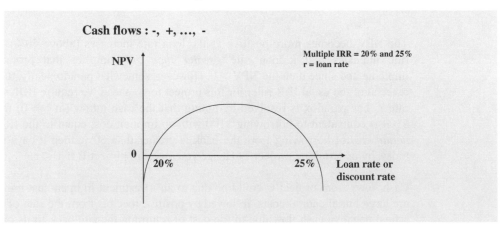

## SCALE PROBLEM

To illustrate this issue consider the NPV and IRR from the two 'projects' in Table 3.3.

For project A, the businesswoman pays out $10 now and receives $15 at $t + 1$. The NPV for $r = 10\%$ is $3.64 and the IRR is 50%. Project B involves an outlay of $80 and a payout at $t + 1$ of $110, giving an NPV of $20 but an IRR of only 37.5%. The projects are mutually exclusive so you can choose only one of them. Intuition (and the NPV criterion) would suggest you choose project B since it has a larger NPV of $20 which exceeds that of project A of $3.64. However, the IRR criterion indicates you should choose project A with an IRR of 50% rather than project B with an IRR of only 37.5%. Which is correct? It turns out that the NPV criterion gives the correct investment choice primarily because the IRR ignores the issue of the scale of the two projects. After all, 50% of almost nothing is nearly nothing while 37.5% of a lot is quite a lot. In these circumstances the problem is in part caused by the mutually exclusive nature of the projects (i.e. only one at best can be implemented). The IRR rule (i.e. invest if IRR > cost of borrowing) can be shown to give a similar investment decision to the NPV rule providing we consider the **incremental IRR** relative to the cost of borrowing. The incremental cash flows are those in moving from the smaller to the larger project (see Table 3.4):

> **Incremental cash flows = cash flow of B − cash flow of A**

The incremental IRR is calculated from:

## TABLE 3.3: Scale problem

|  | Cash flow at $t = 0$ ($) | Cash flow at $t + 1$ ($) | NPV ($) ($r = 10\%$) | IRR (%) |
|---|---|---|---|---|
| **Project A** | −10 | 15 | 3.64 | 50 |
| **Project B** | −80 | 110 | 20 | 37.5 |

## TABLE 3.4: Incremental cash flows

|  | Cash flow at $t = 0$ (L − S) | Cash flow at $t + 1$ hour (L − S) |
|---|---|---|
| **Incremental cash flow** | L − S = −80 − (−10) = **−70** | L − S = 110−15 = **95** |

Note: L = large, S = small

[3.13]  $$0 = -70 + \frac{105}{(1 + IRR)}$$

Hence IRR = 35.7%. The incremental IRR in moving from the smaller to the larger project is 35.7% which exceeds the discount (loan) rate $r = 10\%$, hence the *incremental* IRR rule gives the same investment decision as the standard NPV criterion. Notice also that the **incremental NPV** using $r = 10\%$ equals $-70 + 95/(1.1) = 16.36 > 0$ which also indicates that you should move from project A onto project B. In summary, mutually exclusive projects can be handled by any of the following equivalent decision rules.

- Choose the project with the largest NPV.
- Choose the 'larger' project B if the incremental IRR exceeds the discount (loan) rate.
- Choose the 'larger' project B if the *incremental* NPV is positive.

TIMING PROBLEM

Suppose a firm can use a plot of land to either build a warehouse which earns considerable revenue in the early years (project E, Table 3.5) or build a deli which earns most of its revenues in later years (project L, Table 3.5). The **timing problem for these mutually exclusive projects** can be illustrated by considering project E whose positive cash flows in the early years of the project are larger than those of project L, while in later years the relative size of the cash flows is reversed (see Table 3.5). The NPVs of the two projects are shown in Figure 3.6.

For a discount rate less than 8.71%, $NPV_L > NPV_E$ but project E has a higher IRR (= 33.15%) than project L (= 18.36%). Hence the two criteria give conflicting investment decisions. Once again the usual NPV criterion turns out to be correct, although calculation of the incremental IRR (or the incremental NPV) will also result in 'correct' investment decisions (as outlined above).

SUMMARY OF NPV AND IRR

Overall then our conclusions on investment decision rules are:

- NPV and IRR give identical decisions for independent projects with 'normal cash flows' (i.e. of the form $\{-, -, \ldots, +, +\}$, with only one sign change).

## TABLE 3.5: Timing problem with mutually exclusive projects

|  |  |  |  |  | NPV | | | |
|---|---|---|---|---|---|---|---|---|
| **Year** | 0 | 1 | 2 | 3 | 0% | 10% | 15% | IRR |
| **Project E** | −10,000 | 12,000 | 1000 | 1000 | 4000 | 2486.85 | 1848.44 | 33.15% |
| **Project L** | −10,000 | 1000 | 1000 | 14,000 | 6000 | 2253.94 | 830.94 | 18.37% |

## FIGURE 3.6: Mutually exclusive projects—timing problem

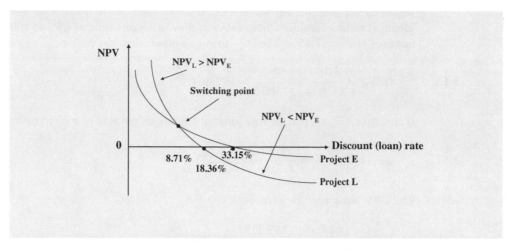

- For cash flows which change sign more than once, for example $\{-, -, +, +, -, -\}$, the IRR gives multiple solutions and cannot be used. Use NPV.
- For mutually exclusive projects use the standard NPV criterion or the incremental IRR criterion.

## REAL VERSUS NOMINAL

Cash flows and discount rates can be measured either in nominal terms or real terms. In the DPV formula the rule is very straightforward, namely:

> **The same value for the DPV ensues if:**
> **Nominal cash flows are discounted at the nominal rate**
> **or**
> **Real cash flows are discounted at the real interest rate**

Suppose the inflation rate is $\pi = 5\%$ p.a. and the real rate $rr = 3\%$ p.a. Then the nominal rate of interest is given by:

[3.14]  $(1 + \text{nominal rate}) = (1 + \text{real rate})(1 + \text{inflation rate})$

$(1 + r) = (1 + rr)(1 + \pi)$

$1.0815 = (1.03)(1.05)$

If \$1 invested for a year earns 8.15% but inflation is 5%, you can only purchase 3% more 'goods' (i.e. Sak's Hampers) at the end of the year. Note that an approximation to equation [3.16] if we ignore the '$rr.\pi$' term is:

[3.15]     $r = rr + \pi$

which is the relationship we discussed in Chapter 2. To show that each method gives identical results consider a nominal cash flow in 1 years time of $CF = \$100$, discounted at a nominal rate $r = 8.15\%$. The DPV using *nominal variables* is:

[3.16]     $$DPV_N = \frac{CF}{(1 + r)} = \frac{\$100}{1.0815} = \$92.464$$

If inflation $\pi = 5\%$ p.a. the real value of CF dollars payable in $n = 1$ years time is:

[3.17]     $$CF_r = \frac{CF}{(1 + \pi)^n} = \frac{\$100}{(1.05)^1} = \$95.238$$

The DPV using *real variables* is:

[3.18]     $$DPV_r = \frac{CF_r}{(1 + rr)} = \frac{\$95.238}{1.03} = \$92.464$$

Hence the DPV is the same in both cases. (This is easy to see algebraically by substituting for $CF_r$ and $rr$ in equation [3.18] using equations [3.17] and [3.14].)

## TIMING OF CAPITAL EXPENDITURES

In practice, the capital costs of an investment project may take place over several years. But this provides no additional problems because we either discount 'net cash flows' $(CF_i - KC_i)$ in each year or discount the net revenues $(R - C)_i$ and the capital costs $KC_i$ *separately*.

A very different issue arises when we consider the possibility that the investment project could be started at any time in the next 5 years. (For simplicity, and without loss, we assume the project is worthless if not started within 5 years.) By delaying the start of the project you forgo the revenues you would otherwise earn in the early years. On the other hand you also delay the capital costs. What is the optimal start date for the project (assuming it has a positive NPV at $t = 0$)?

When net cash flow and investment costs are known with certainty, this is a simple problem. We merely work out the NPV for each 'start period' $t = 0, 1, 2, 3$, etc. For example, assuming we start the project in year 3, this has NPV *in year 3* of $NPV_3$. Hence for each 'start date' for the project we have a set of NPVs labelled $NPV_t$ (for $t = 0, 1, 2, 3, 4, 5$). These NPVs at $t$ can be discounted back to $t = 0$, to give a set of values $NPV_{0,t}$ which stands for 'NPV at $t = 0$, assuming the project is started at $t$', hence:

$NPV_{0,t} = NPV_t/(1 + r)^t$

We then choose that year ($t$) to commence the project which gives the highest $NPV_{0,t}$. Let's see what is really happening with the above procedure. Intuitively, we start the project 'later' if the growth rate of $NPV_t$, that is $g_t = (NPV_t/NPV_{t-1}) - 1$ is higher than the discount rate *r*. By delaying, the percentage increase in the NPV of the cash flows exceeds the cost of borrowing. So, if the increase in $NPV_t$ in years 1, 2, 3, 4, 5 is $g_t = 11\%, 12\%, 11\%, 12\%, 9\%$ and the (risk adjusted) discount rate is 10% then the optimal investment date is to start in year 4, since after that date the increase in NPV of 9% by waiting a further year does not exceed the cost of borrowing. In this case, it will be found that $NPV_{0,4}$ takes the largest value.

## UNCERTAINTY AND RISK

There may be a great deal of uncertainty concerning the future cash flows from a capital investment project. One way of dealing with this is the use of **decision trees**. For example, consider the following simple one-period case. Suppose there is a 75% chance of a cash inflow of $V_U = \$100$ (i.e. economy is 'up') and a 25% chance of $V_D = \$40$ (i.e. economy is 'down') at the end of year 1. We could use the expected cash flow $V^e$ in the DPV calculation where:

$$V^e = 0.75 V_U + 0.25 V_D = \$85 \qquad \text{and hence} \qquad NPV = -KC + V^e/(1+r)$$

The problem with decision trees is that they can quickly become very complicated. For example, if we have only two possible states of the economy in any one year of U or D then by the second year we have 4 ($= 2^2$) possible outcomes (i.e. UU, UD, DU and DD). After 10 years we have 1024 ($= 2^{10}$) possible outcomes, for which we need estimates of probabilities and cash flows! Not only that, suppose at $t = 1$ we have the possibility of selling the factory for a known abandonment value $AV_1 = \$50$ (Figure 3.7). To find the NPV of the project when abandonment is possible we have to work back through the tree, starting at $t = 2$, since our decision of whether to invest today depends on whether we abandon at $t = 1$ or

## FIGURE 3.7: Decision tree: abandonment possible

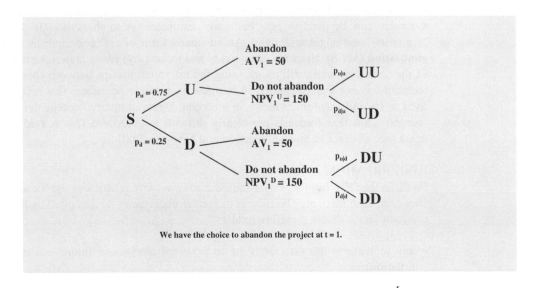

We have the choice to abandon the project at t = 1.

not (Figure 3.7). Suppose on the U-branch we use the expected present value approach above to calculate the NPV *at* $t = 1$ of the expected cash flows for the outcomes UU and UD using the conditional probabilities $p_{u|u}$, $p_{d|u}$. Suppose we find NPV(not abandon)$_1^U = 150 > AV_1 = 50$. We then take NPV(not abandon)$_1^U = 150$ as our value at $t = 1$ on the U-path. It is more likely that we would abandon on the D-path since the expected value at $t = 1$ of the cash flows at $t = 2$ on the DU and DD nodes is likely to be low. If NPV(not abandon)$_1^D = 40 < AV_1 = 50$ then we take $AV_1 = 50$ as our value for the D-path. Hence the NPV at $t = 0$, when we take account of the abandonment option is:

$$NPV = -KC + [0.75 NPV(\text{not abandon})_1^U + 0.25 AV_1]/(1 + r)$$

and if this were greater than zero we would go ahead with the project at $t = 0$. (See Kellogg and Chames, 2000 for a user friendly account of valuation of a biotechnology company using decision trees). Because decision trees quickly become very complex, another method of valuing investment projects where outcomes are very uncertain and there are possibilities for expansion or abandonment of the project is **real options theory** (see Cuthbertson and Nitzsche, 2001).

There are other methods we could use to get a feel for the impact of uncertainty on the NPV of the project. For example, we could use **sensitivity analysis**. Here we calculate several different values for the NPV based on a variety of *independent* assumptions, taken one at a time. We have our 'central NPV' calculation (NPV$_c$ = $10m say) and we then alter one forecast (e.g. assume lower sales volume) while keeping all other factors the same. If our 'new NPV' is very different from the 'central NPV' (e.g. NPV$_n$ = −$1m) then we may wish to go back and do more market research and refine our analysis of this crucial assumption. The difficulty here is that in reality, the assumption of a lower sales volume in a recession is likely to be accompanied both by lower output prices and lower input costs (e.g. wages). That is, these three variables are positively correlated. The variables in the sensitivity analysis are not really independent and hence the latter technique may give highly mis-leading results. We really therefore need to consider these interdependencies in any simulation we undertake: the technique is then often referred to as **scenario analysis**. Clearly, getting these 'correlations' right is rather difficult, although past data on the variables can be used to get 'ball-park' estimates. Also there is a limit to how many 'scenarios' one might undertake. An advanced form of scenario analysis is **Monte Carlo simulation (MCS)** where we can quickly and (relatively) easily undertake many simulations of the variables, while still maintaining the interrelationships between them. However, this technique is not widely applied in business investment decisions. But recently it has been used to try and value investments in biotechnology and internet companies, where possible 'central' cash flow forecasts are clearly difficult to ascertain. This is **real options theory** again (see Chapter 11 and Cuthbertson and Nitzsche, 2001).

## RISK PREMIUM

So far in the DPV formula we have used a *constant* safe rate of interest for all future periods. However, cash flows may be subject to greater uncertainty than implied by the safe rate. The discount factor should therefore reflect:

- any increase in the safe rate (due to expected changes in future real rates or expected inflation);

- a risk premium to reflect the fact that the firm's revenues and costs are uncertain. The latter adjustment is much debated in academia using such principles as the capital asset pricing model (which is covered in later chapters), the weighted average cost of capital, WACC (see Chapter 11) and real options theory (see Cuthbertson and Nitzsche, 2001).

## OTHER INVESTMENT DECISION RULES

### PAYBACK PERIOD

The **payback period** is the number of years it takes for the (undiscounted) future receipts to exceed the initial capital outlay, which for the cash flows in Table 3.6 is 2 years. A judgement is then made as to whether this period is reasonable given the uncertainty attached to future cash flows. The payback period is quite often used in conjunction with a full NPV calculation, since it provides a useful simple 'yardstick' with which to compare the NPV figure (which is likely to have a larger degree of uncertainty than the payback period). Sometimes the cash flows are discounted before the payback period is calculated. For example, in Table 3.6 the discounted cash flows are $435, $378 and $348 for years 1–3, respectively. Hence the **discounted payback period** given a capital cost of $1000 is between 2 and 3 years.

The problem with the payback methods is that they ignore the contribution of 'distant' cash flows (which accrue after the payback period), to the value of the investment project. If the payback method had been used, the Channel Tunnel between England and France would no doubt never have been built. (Some would also argue that even on a NPV calculation the project was not viable.)

### RETURN ON CAPITAL EMPLOYED

The **return on capital employed (ROC)** is also referred to as the **return on investment (ROI)** and the **accounting rate of return (ARR)**. The return on capital employed is:

$$ROC = \text{'profits'}/\text{capital investment undertaken}$$

## TABLE 3.6: Investment appraisal: other methods

|     | Year 0 | Year 1 | Year 2 | Year 3 | Year 4 |
| --- | --- | --- | --- | --- | --- |
| **FV** | −1000 | 500 | 500 | 700 | 0 |
| *d* | 1 | 0.8696 | 0.7561 | 0.4972 | – |
| **PV** | −1000 | 435 | 378 | 348 | – |

**NPV = 161**

**Payback period = 2 years**

**Discounted payback = 2–3 years**

The ROC can be applied to a particular project or division of a (non-financial) firm or to the firm as a whole. (The allied concept applied to financial firms like banks is 'RAROC'—see Cuthbertson and Nitzsche, 2001.) The difficulty lies in the measurement of 'profits' and 'capital investment'. First, profits can be measured in many different ways (see below) and there is then the question of whether we use current profits, an average of past profits or an estimate of forecast profits over the next few years. Similarly if investment takes place over a number of years, precisely what figure do we use? Although widely quoted as a 'rule of thumb' figure and as a point of comparison between firms in a particular sector or for a single firm over time, the ROC ignores the time value of money and should be interpreted with caution.

## PROFITABILITY INDEX

If we take discounting into account, the PV approach may be reinterpreted in terms of a rate of return on capital and this is known as the **profitability index (PI)**:

$$\textbf{Profitability index} = \frac{\text{DPV (cash flows)}}{\text{capital cost}} = \frac{\text{DPV (cash flows)}}{\text{KC}}$$

For example, suppose DPV = \$120m and the initial capital outlay for the project is KC = \$100m at $t = 0$. The NPV = \$20m which implies we proceed with the project. The value of PI = \$120m/\$100m = 1.20, which is interpreted as a 20% 'return'. It is easy to see that NPV = DPV(CF) − KC > 0 is equivalent to PI > 1. Indeed, both criteria give identical investment decisions when ranking *independent* projects. If capital costs accrue over several years then the denominator is the PV of the capital costs. For mutually exclusive projects the PI index may give the wrong investment decision because of the scale problem, but this can be corrected by seeing if the incremental PI index exceeds unity.

## CAPITAL RATIONING

There is one area where the NPV rule gives incorrect results and this is when a firm does not have enough funds to undertake all projects with NPV > 0. When the firm is subject to *capital rationing* independent projects must be ranked by the PI index and implemented from the highest to lowest (but with all PI > 1) until the capital constraint is reached. Intuitively the PI index works in this case because it measures 'bang per buck' since the present value of receipts is scaled by the capital cost of the project. The NPV rule breaks down because the NPV of one large project using all the capital funds available may be exceeded by the sum of the NPVs of two other projects (each of which used half the capital available), even though each taken separately has a lower NPV than the large project.

# 3.4 FINANCING AND INVESTMENT DECISIONS

The cash flows in our PV calculation take no account of the source of financing. If debt finance is used then there is a cash inflow at $t = 0$ (e.g. from a bank loan or bond issue) and a series of interest payments (and repayment of principal) giving rise to periodic cash outflows, however:

> **In calculating a project's (or firm's) PV we ignore any cash flows arising from debt finance because we wish to keep the financing decision separate from the investment decision**

Below, we outline a fairly straightforward method of adjusting our PV calculations for debt finance which involves the 'weighted average cost of capital', WACC. In applying this method we do not adjust cash flows (i.e. the numerator in the PV calculation), instead we adjust the discount rate (i.e. the denominator). Because the interrelationship between debt finance and project appraisal is quite complex, we postpone detailed discussion until Chapter 11.

To undertake our NPV calculation we need to know the cost of borrowed funds ('the cost of capital' to the firm). In our analysis above we simply assumed borrowing from a bank at a fixed known interest rate. In reality, as we saw in Chapter 1, there are many alternative sources of finance (e.g. banks, bonds, debentures, preference shares, ordinary shares), each of which have a different cost. We can think of the 'overall cost of finance' as a weighted average of all these different sources of finance (with the weights in proportion to the different sources of funds used). This is known as the **'weighted average cost of capital' (WACC)**.

A key question in corporate finance is whether the WACC rises as the company takes on more debt finance relative to its equity finance. At first blush one would think that the WACC would (eventually) rise as the level of debt rose to say 90% of the value of the firm, because of the increased risk of bankruptcy. But as we shall see in Chapter 11, the so-called Modigliani–Miller theorem implies that (under certain restrictive assumptions) the WACC does not change as the debt-to-equity ratio is increased. However, at this point, we do not take a position on *whether in the real world* the 'mix' of finance alters the cost of capital, hence the discount rate in PV calculations and the value of the firm. Indeed this is a highly contentious issue in corporate finance. It has not been made any easier by the increasing importance for some companies of 'new' sources of finance such as venture capital, junk bonds and 'project finance'. The latter is used to finance very large scale investment projects and is an attempt to reduce the risk of such huge projects to any individual firm (see Box 3.1).

## Box 3.1    PROJECT FINANCE

Some large investment projects are financed via a separate legal entity set up by the parent company, to build and operate a specific project (e.g. hydroelectric dam, oil pipeline, ports, roads and power plant). The key feature of project finance is that the payments on the loans are dependent on the cash flows from the project and not on the general profits of the parent firm. Hence, it is important that lenders are aware of the details of any DPV calculations, since their future interest receipts are dependent on the assumptions behind these calculations.

In practice, there is a whole spectrum of risk sharing. For example, the parent company may agree to underwrite *some* of the project (e.g. until completion of the project), while the lenders can only obtain payments based on the future success of the project (e.g. from the operating revenues). The advantages/disadvantages of project finance include:

(i) transferring (some) risk from the parent company onto other lenders;

(ii) for the parent company, project finance usually does not appear in its accounts (i.e. it is an off balance sheet item) and hence does not directly increase its gearing ratio (leverage);

(iii) if several companies are involved in the project, it may simplify the legal arrangements, since security for repayments of the loan are linked to the cash flows from the project and not from the separate firms;

(iv) the cost of loans for project finance may be up to 100 bp (1%) above LIBOR, whereas the parent company's general borrowing might cost no more than 20 bp above LIBOR. This is because of the increased risk to the lenders of project finance—the risk is specific to the project. Legal costs are also usually substantial because of the complexity of the arrangements between the different partners in the project (e.g. construction companies, governments, suppliers of funds).

# 3.5 INVESTMENT APPRAISAL IN PRACTICE

So far we have largely concentrated on the broad principles of PV and investment appraisal. Evaluating investment projects which are similar to those that have previously taken place (e.g. to expand your hamburger chain, to decide whether to replace existing machinery this year or next year) is relatively straightforward since the estimates of cash flows should not be subject to great uncertainty. However, even here there are measurement problems in moving from accounting figures to a measure of 'free cash flows' from a project (or for the firm as a whole). Very often accounting conventions mean that 'accounting figures' such as reported profits do not represent actual cash flows, but are based on rules and conventions that differ across countries. Also we need to take account of taxes, depreciation and working capital in our analysis. At the risk of turning into accountants we deal briefly with these issues in turn and conclude with a set of stylised accounts.

## TAXES, DEPRECIATION AND WORKING CAPITAL

So far, we have only considered *forecasts* of sales revenues ($R$) and 'input' costs ($C$) (e.g. labour, materials, lighting, heating, apportionment of overheads). To be more precise, **earnings before interest, tax and depreciation (EBITD)** is defined as:

$$\text{EBITD} = \text{sales revenues} - \text{input costs} = R - C$$

**Depreciation ($D$)** in principle represents the 'wearing out' of (fixed) capital equipment. The simplest form of depreciation is **straight-line depreciation**. For example, if the capital cost at $t = 0$ is KC = \$10,000, the life of the project is taken to be $n = 5$ years and scrap value is estimated as SV = \$1000, then the *constant* (dollar) depreciation per annum is:

$$D = \frac{KC - SV}{n} = \frac{9000}{5} = \$1800 \text{ p.a.}$$

In the 'income–expenditure' (or 'profit and loss') accounts of a firm it is customary to report earnings after deduction of depreciation. This is thought to give a clearer picture about the contribution of profits/earnings to the value of the firm, than deducting *actual expenditure* on fixed capital (investments), since the latter are 'lumpy'. For example, above we have total expenditure of \$1000 but depreciation 'spreads' this figure out over a 5-year period, giving a 'smoother' series for reported annual profits in any single year. We return to this issue below.

In determining free cash flow we require *actual* expenditures on fixed investment. Therefore as we shall see, the accountant's figures for 'depreciation' are irrelevant since they do not involve actual cash flows and they are *only important to the extent that they reduce taxable income*. The tax authorities in most countries allow depreciation to be deducted from earnings before calculating corporate tax liabilities. After-tax operating cash flow (earnings) and tax payments $T$ are therefore:

$$\text{After-tax operating CF } = R - C - T$$

$$\text{Tax } T = t(R - C - D)$$

where $t$ = corporate tax rate (e.g. $t = 0.35$). It follows that:

---

**After-tax operating CF = after-tax net revenue + depreciation tax shield**

$$= (R - C)(1 - t) + tD$$

---

Hence an addition to cash flow is provided by the **'depreciation tax shield'** (*tD*). The higher is depreciation, the higher are after-tax cash flows. However in practice, the rate at which machines, land and buildings are assumed to depreciate for tax purposes is set by the tax authorities (i.e. there is a difference between 'economic depreciation' and depreciation as expressed in the tax code).

In practice, the tax authorities usually allow **accelerated depreciation** and set a schedule showing how a particular piece of capital equipment (e.g. buildings) can be 'written down'. For example in the US, an asset deemed to have a life of $n = 5$ years can be 'written down' in each year according to the following percentages: $z_i = 20\%$, 30%, 19.2%, 11.52%, 11.52% and 5.76%. (There are six values here because the IRS in the US assumes you purchase mid-year.) The annual dollar depreciation and tax shield are:

$$D_i = z_i(KC) \qquad \text{Tax Shield (year } i) = t(z_i KC)$$

After-tax cash flow (earnings) is:

$$\text{After-tax operating CF} = R - C - T \equiv \text{EBITD} - T$$

Often in practice, to calculate the PV we use the 'after-tax cash flows' for each year and discount these 'net' figures back to $t = 0$, using the WACC. In this case we are assuming that the receipts from the tax shield are as uncertain as the cash flows from the project itself. However, if we assume that the tax code is unlikely to change and the firm can carry forward losses (i.e. if taxable profits are negative in any year, it can still obtain the benefit of the tax shield in later years) then annual taxes $T$ should be discounted at the risk free rate $r$, while the operating revenues $R - C$ are discounted using the WACC. Which discount rates to use is a controversial issue in corporate finance which is explored further in Chapter 11.

If we calculate the PV of the 5-year tax shield separately using r, then:

$$\text{PV(tax shield)} = t \sum_{i=1}^{5} z_i(\text{KC})/(1 + r)^i = t(\text{KC}) \left[ \sum_{i=1}^{5} z_i/(1 + r)^i \right]$$

The term in square brackets can be found in 'tax tables', giving for example a value of 0.7733 for the present value (per dollar of capital cost) for $n = 5$ and $r = 10\%$. Hence, the PV of the tax shield for KC = \$10,000 is:

$$\text{PV(tax shield)} = 0.35(10,000)0.7733 = \$2706$$

**Working capital** is rather a 'slippery' concept for non-accountants. In project appraisal it provides a correction for the fact that revenues and costs are forecast or 'smoothed' figures and may not reflect the best estimate of future cash flows. This is because there can be 'leads and lags' in actually receiving or paying out cash amounts. For example, if customers delay payment for goods received then the accountant's forecast sales revenue in a particular year will overstate the actual cash inflow. Working capital is the net investment in short-term assets required to undertake the project. In fact it is the *change* in working capital $\Delta$WC that is important in accurately calculating future cash flows. Working capital is:

> **Working capital (WC) = inventory level + accounts receivable − accounts payable**
> **Increase in WC = increase in inventories + increase in accounts receivable − increase in accounts payable**

The actual cash flows accruing to the project (or whole firm) will not equal the forecast of revenues and costs prepared by the various divisions (e.g. marketing, production engineering) and a better estimate of future cash flows to use in our PV calculations is:

$$\text{CF(after tax)} = (R - C - T) - \Delta\text{WC}$$

where $\Delta$WC = *increase* in working capital. Changes in WC (from year to year say) arise because:

(i) If customers are slow to pay for goods then **'accounts receivable'** will increase and so will $\Delta$WC, hence the actual cash inflow will be less than the *forecast* revenues. For example 'accounts receivable' in year 1 will increase if we assume $100 of expected sales of $1000 (in year 1) will be sold on credit. Hence actual cash flow will be $900 (= $1000 − $100). Note that if this $100 cash is received in year 2, then accounts receivable will fall by $100 in year 2 and cash flow will increase.

(ii) If the firm undertaking an investment project expects to get credit from its suppliers of $100, then this is an increase in **'accounts payable'** (i.e. what you owe). So $\Delta$WC will fall and cash flow will increase, because actual cash payments are less than the forecast value for input costs, $C$.

(iii) If it is thought prudent in the planning process for some output to be added to inventory to avoid a stockout (e.g. unsold cars held at the factory) then this will be entered as an **'increase in inventories'**. Hence, $\Delta$WC rises and actual cash inflow falls (below its forecast value).

In general, the change in working capital is positive in the early years of a project (as customers are allowed goods on credit and planned inventories rise) and hence reduces cash flows. But in later years, as inventories are sold off and customers' debts are paid off, then $\Delta$WC is negative thus adding to cash flows. We now bring all of the above elements together to calculate the free cash flow for an investment project (or for the firm as a whole) and hence its PV.

## STYLISED ACCOUNTS FOR FREE CASH FLOW

Tables 3.7–3.10 give a stylised example of how to determine free cash flows from an individual investment project or the value of the firm as a whole (i.e. assuming the cash flow figures are aggregated across all projects currently being undertaken or planned by the firm). We assume a 5-year horizon for simplicity.

Table 3.7 shows the capital account *as set out by the firm's accountants*. The firm is planning to invest KC = $1000. The accountant uses straight-line depreciation over 5 years, with zero scrap value, giving depreciation of $200 per year (row 2). Hence the year-end book value of fixed assets (row 4) declines to zero by year 5. The *level of* working capital is shown in row 5 and total book value of capital in row 6. The *change in* working capital from year to year is shown in row 7. We will assume that 'economic depreciation' (i.e. the actual rate at which the economic value of the fixed capital declines) is also the method used in the 'tax books'. Therefore the forecast levels of corporate tax $T = t(R − C − D)$ are given in row 5 of Table 3.8.

Having transferred our tax figures to Table 3.9 (row 4) and our figures for the increase in working capital ($\Delta$WC) to row 6, we are in a position to calculate the free cash flow CF to use in our PV calculation. Earnings before interest, tax and depreciation EBITD = $R − C$ are shown in row 3. 'After-tax operating cash flows' are shown in row 4, from which we deduct the increase in working capital ($\Delta$WC, row 6) and the *actual* cash expenditures on

## TABLE 3.7: Capital account

| | Year 0 | Year 1 | Year 2 | Year 3 | Year 4 | Year 5 |
|---|---|---|---|---|---|---|
| **1. Capital cost KC** | 1000 | | | | | |
| **2. Depreciation[1] (= KC − SV)/n** | | 200 | 200 | 200 | 200 | 200 |
| **3. Accumulated depreciation (= 'sum of depreciation')** | | 200 | 400 | 600 | 800 | 1000 |
| **4. Year-end book value (= 4 − 3)** | 1000 | 800 | 600 | 400 | 200 | 0 |
| **5. Working capital WC** | 0 | 400 | 500 | 600 | 500 | 200 |
| **6. Total book value (= 4 + 5)** | 1000 | 1200 | 1100 | 1000 | 700 | 200 |
| **7. Change in working capital $\Delta$WC (= $WC_t - WC_{t-1}$)[2]** | | 400 | 100 | 100 | (100) | (300) |

Notes: 1. Total capital cost is KC = $1000. Scrap value SV = 0 at $n$ = 5 years
Hence $D = (KC - SV)/5 = 200$ per year (straight-line depreciation)
2. Parentheses indicate a negative number

## Table 3.8: Depreciation and tax

| | Year 1 | Year 2 | Year 3 | Year 4 | Year 5 |
|---|---|---|---|---|---|
| **1. Sales R** | 1000 | 1500 | 2000 | 2500 | 3000 |
| **2. Labour + materials cost, C** | 600 | 900 | 1200 | 1500 | 1800 |
| **3. EBITD[1] (= 1 − 2)** | 400 | 600 | 800 | 1000 | 1200 |
| **4. Depreciation D** | 200 | 200 | 200 | 200 | 200 |
| **5. Earnings after depreciation = R−C−D (= 3 − 4)** | 200 | 400 | 600 | 800 | 1000 |
| **6. Tax[2] = 0.30(R − C − D)** | 60 | 120 | 180 | 240 | 300 |

Notes: 1. EBITD = earnings before interest, tax and depreciation. Accounting profits (before tax) reported in the 'income–expenditure' (or 'profit–loss') account would be (EBITD − D)
2. Corporate tax rate is assumed to be $t$ = 0.30 (30%)

fixed investment. Note that in Table 3.7 the accountant assumed that total fixed investment of $1000 took place in year 0 and then she used straight-line depreciation (of $200 p.a.) to obtain the 'book value' of investment. In Table 3.9 we are interested in *actual* cash flows in each year, so it is the projected *expenditures* on fixed investment which are relevant (i.e. $600 in year 1 and $400 in year 2).

## Table 3.9: Calculating free cash flow

| | | Year 1 | Year 2 | Year 3 | Year 4 | Year 5 |
|---|---|---|---|---|---|---|
| 1. | Sales[1] $R$ | 1000 | 1500 | 2000 | 2500 | 3000 |
| 2. | Labour + material cost[1] | 600 | 900 | 1200 | 1500 | 1800 |
| 3. | Earnings before interest, tax and depreciation EBITD (= 1 − 2) | 400 | 600 | 800 | 1000 | 1200 |
| 4. | Tax[1] $T$ | 60 | 120 | 180 | 240 | 300 |
| 5. | After-tax operating cash flow (= 3 − 4) | **340** | **480** | **620** | **760** | **900** |
| 6. | Increase in working capital[2] $\Delta$WC | 400 | 100 | 100 | (100) | (300) |
| 7. | Capital cost KC (investment expenditure)[3] | 600 | 400 | 0 | 0 | 0 |
| 8. | Operating cash flow (after tax) (= 5 − 6 − 7) | **(660)** | **(20)** | **520** | **860** | **1200** |
| 9. | Cash flow from non-operating assets | 50 | 0 | 0 | 100 | 0 |
| 10. | Interest income from assets | 10 | 15 | 20 | 15 | 10 |
| 11. | Decrease (increase) in marketable securities | 0 | (10) | 20 | 15 | (10) |
| 12. | Free cash flow[4] CF (= 8 + 9 + 10 + 11)[5] | **(600)** | **(15)** | **560** | **990** | **1200** |

Notes: 1. Figures are from Table 3.8
2. An increase in working capital is a cash outflow. Figures are from Table 3.7 (row 7)
3. These are the actual cash expenditures on investment in each year and they sum to the total capital cost KC (in Table 3.7)
4. Cash flow available to investors (i.e. debt and equity holders)
5. Parentheses indicate a negative number

The **cash flow from non-operating assets** (Table 3.9, row 9) might, for example, include receipts from the sale of a subsidiary or factory. 'Sales of assets' owned by firms include disposals of subsidiaries which occur when large companies decide to concentrate on their 'core competences' (to use the business strategy jargon). Firms also purchase other firms in mergers and takeovers, some of which are cash purchases (rather than issuing shares of the predator to the shareholders of the firm being taken over), but this would be counted as 'investment expenditure' from which the firm would expect to receive additional free cash flows in the future. Firms often hold shares in other companies and any sales (purchases) of these shares would be a cash inflow (outflow).

Interest income (Table 3.9, row 10) arises from financial assets held by the firm (e.g. income from government bonds) and row 11 gives the change in the market value of any financial

## TABLE 3.10: Use of free cash flow of the firm

|  | Year 1 | Year 2 | Year 3 | Year 4 | Year 5 |
|---|---|---|---|---|---|
| **1. Free cash flow** | −600 | −15 | 560 | 990 | 1200 |
| **(Table 3.9, row 12)** | | | | | |
| **FINANCING (USE OF FREE CASH FLOWS)** | | | | | |
| **2. Interest paid to debt holders** | 30 | 30 | 30 | 30 | 30 |
| **3. Dividends paid** | 100 | 105 | 110 | 115 | 120 |
| **4. Share repurchases** | 100 | 100 | 100 | 100 | 100 |
| **5. (Increase) decrease in net debt** | (830) | (250) | 320 | 745 | 950 |
| **Total financing (= 2 + 3 + 4 + 5)** | −600 | −15 | 560 | 990 | 1200 |

assets held. Free cash flow CF is shown in row 12 and these are the figures that would be used to calculate the NPV of the project (or firm as a whole).

If we are calculating the value of the whole firm, then we might also want to consider how the free cash flow will be used. An illustration is given in Table 3.10. Basically any free cash flow can be used either to pay dividends to shareholders and interest income to debt holders or to retire (i.e. buy back) outstanding shares or pay back the principal on debt (i.e. bond-holders, bank loans, etc.). A negative free cash flow requires external finance such as an increased net debt (e.g. bank loans) shown for year 1 in row 5 of Table 3.10.

It is also perhaps worth noting that 'reported profits' in the income–expenditure account can be retrieved from Table 3.8, although different accounting procedures would give somewhat different values for 'profits'. A 'reasonable' estimate of reported 'gross profits' would be EBITD so:

Profits (before interest, tax and depreciation) $\equiv$ EBITD

whereas 'accounting profit' would be recorded net of economic depreciation:

'Accounting profit' $=$ EBITD $-$ (economic) depreciation

Note that actual capital expenditures (row 7, Table 3.9) would not appear in the income–expenditure accounts but in some version of the reported, 'capital account'.

A couple of final points. If we are dealing with the PV of an investment project then only the *incremental* **costs** should be included in the calculation of free CF. Hence, if the project uses no resources from head office (e.g. marketing, sales, legal expertise, R&D) then these should not be included in the costs of this project (of course, they should be included in the costs attributable to the *whole firm's* cash flow). Only incremental overhead costs (e.g. extra administrative staff) should be included.

Costs should be measured in terms of what economists call **opportunity costs**. For example, if the investment project uses a factory building that is already owned by the firm, then its cost is not zero but the income the building could earn 'in its next best alternative use'. This might be the rental income obtainable from another firm, if the building could be leased in the open market.

If the project reduces the firm's cash flow from other areas (e.g. introducing a new soft drink reduces sales of the firm's existing soft drinks range) then this lost revenue must be deducted from the sales figures for the project.

Finally, genuinely **sunk costs** must not be deducted from the cash flows of the project. For example, if we are at the point of deciding whether to take an invention to market (e.g. a new civil aircraft) then past R&D expenditures are irrelevant to this decision. They are 'sunk costs' because they remain unchanged whether or not we go ahead with construction and sales of the new aircraft. (Of course, these R&D costs were relevant in deciding *a few years ago* whether to start the R&D programme, to develop a new type of aircraft.)

## CONTINUING VALUE

Suppose we are using PV techniques to value the *whole firm*. While we might be able to forecast *annual* free cash flows for each of the next 5 (or 10) years, this becomes extremely difficult as we extend the time horizon. One commonly used approach is to undertake a detailed year-by-year cash flow analysis for say the first 5 years and then estimate the continuing value of the firm.

The **continuing value (CV)** assumes a *constant* growth rate of cash flows (e.g. $g = 0.03$ or 3% p.a.) and, assuming we use the WACC as the discount rate, it can be shown (see Chapter 4):

[3.19] $$\text{CV (at } t = 5) = \frac{\text{CF}_{t+1}}{\text{WACC} - g}$$

[3.20] $$\text{CV (at } t = 0) = \frac{\text{CV(at } t = 5)}{(1 + \text{WACC})^5}$$

Note that CV depends on a forecast of cash flows in year 6 and a forecast of $g$. The above formula for CV can be 'broken down' into what corporate strategy aficionados call the **'value drivers'** of the firm, which are (i) the 'incremental return on invested capital', (ii) the WACC and (iii) the growth rate of cash flows. This involves the following. First assume a fixed constant proportion of after-tax (operating) 'profits' $\Pi$ are reinvested each year so that:

[3.21] Investment ratio, $\text{IR} = I/\Pi$

where $I$ = fixed investment. For example, we might assume that after year 5 the firm 'retains' 40% of its (after-tax) profits and uses these funds for fixed investment. The (free) cash flow in year 6 would then be 60% of forecast profits in year 6:

[3.22]     $CF_6 = \Pi_6(1 - IR)$

The above equation implies that CF grows at the same rate as $\Pi$. We now set up the following *identity*:

[3.23]     $g = \dfrac{\Pi_{t+1} - \Pi_t}{\Pi_t} \equiv \dfrac{\Pi_{t+1} - \Pi_t}{I_t}\left(\dfrac{I_t}{\Pi_t}\right) = IROC \times IR$

where the *incremental* return on capital (investment) is defined as:

[3.24]     $IROC = (\Pi_{t+1} - \Pi_t)/I_t$

and is assumed to be constant (after year 5). Substituting for IR from equation [3.23] in equation [3.22] and then substituting for $CF_6$ in equation [3.19] we obtain:

[3.25]     $CV(\text{at } t = 5) = \dfrac{\Pi_6}{IROC} \times \dfrac{(IROC - g)}{(WACC - g)}$

Hence the continuing value CV depends on the 'value drivers' IROC, WACC and $g$. If the IROC exceeds the WACC then equation [3.25] implies that 'growth' adds value and is beneficial for the shareholders. (The converse also applies.) **Value management** (another piece of strategy jargon) requires managers to 'add value' by raising either the IROC or the growth rate of profits (earnings) or lowering the WACC (ceteris paribus). Of course, it must be recognised that these three 'drivers' are not independent of each other. For example, it is relatively easy to raise the growth rate of cash flows by investing much more capital (e.g. new outlets for McDonalds). But if this leads to a fall in IROC (as the incremental McDonalds outlets earn less profit than their predecessors) then value may not increase. At best therefore equation [3.25] has to be handled with care as a guide to business strategy. However, it does provide some insights into what is generating this continuing value. The total value of the firm is then given by:

$V_{\text{firm}}(\text{at } t = 0) = NPV(\text{CF in years 1 to 5}) + CV(\text{at } t = 0)$

Above we have detailed how the 'PV method' can be used to value the firm as a 'stand-alone' entity. We now consider how the PV approach might be applied in calculating the benefits of a merger or takeover.

## MERGERS AND ACQUISITIONS

Sometimes the application of PV comes up against severe measurement problems. This occurs when the 'project' is rather unique or 'one off' as occurs for example when valuing internet (i.e. dot.com companies) or biotechnology and other new 'high-tech' firms, which have a limited track record—we deal with this issue in Chapter 11 and also in Cuthbertson and Nitzsche (2001). Similarly difficult valuation problems arise when applying the PV approach to value mergers as we shall see below.

Mergers (or acquisitions or takeovers) occur when two (or more) firms join together to form a single unit. Merger activity often comes in waves, so for example in the UK there have been high levels of merger activity in 1986–89, in 1995–98 and another 'wave' looks likely to continue in 2000. The 'big deals' usually take up many column inches in the financial press, for example the pharmaceutical merger between Glaxo and Wellcome, the takeover of Forte by Granada (at about $60bn) in the leisure industry and in 2000 the 'media' merger of AOL–Time Warner (over $200bn) and the many mergers taking place in the financial sector at the turn of the millennium. Mergers are an example of the 'market for corporate control', the idea being that the merger should 'add value'. In principle, the gains from a merger are given by:

$$\text{Gain} = \text{NPV}_{A+B} - (\text{NPV}_A + \text{NPV}_B) - \text{transactions costs}$$

The merger adds value if the NPV of the *joint firm* $A + B$ has greater value than the individual firms taken as separate entities (after taking account of transactions costs, such as those due to investment bankers, underwriters and lawyers fees). Why might the value of the joint firm be greater than the sum of the parts, and can we use NPV to measure these gains? Another key issue is who acquires the gains—society in general, the acquiring firm, or the target firm? We discuss these issues below.

Cash flows (profits) of a merged firm might be higher because of additional revenues or lower costs. These might arise because of economies of scale resulting in lower marketing and distribution costs, lower costs in the provision of central services and lower labour costs. The merger might open up a new customer base (e.g. in a merger between two banks) or result in the acquisition of technical skills (e.g. the R&D knowledge base of Glaxo and Wellcome, the internet knowledge of AOL gained by Time Warner). Genuine real resource gains (i.e. producing or selling goods and services at a lower unit cost) are what are important for society in general. However, a merger might also result in financial gains which are important to the companies concerned, such as a lower tax bill (e.g. if one firm has high investment grants or tax breaks on investment expenditure). Note that a (conglomerate) merger which produces a less *variable* earnings stream is an inefficient way of reducing shareholder risk, since it is much easier for shareholders to change the composition of their own portfolios.

In the NPV calculation we could take (and often do) the NPV of A and B *separately,* simply as the market value of the shares of A and B prior to the merger. However, calculating the NPV of the merged firm involves a wide range of very uncertain calculations and this becomes even more difficult if much of the value of the combined firm comes from (i) an increased 'knowledge base' (e.g. in biochemical or internet firms) or from (ii) reputation, or brand names, (e.g. in advertising or media firms) or from (iii) integration of management 'cultures' or 'synergies'—two key buzzwords in the 'management speak' used in this area. It is fairly obvious that scenario analysis will have to be used in conjunction with any NPV calculations, given the wide range of possible assumptions one could make.

Another practical problem is what discount factor to use when calculating the $\text{NPV}_{A+B}$. If the merger involves **horizontal integration** (i.e. when firms A and B are in the same industry), as with the pharmaceutical companies Glaxo and Wellcome, then one could reasonably assume that the merger was scale enhancing and use the WACC for the combined company. However, for a merger involving **vertical integration** (i.e. a merger between firms in different stages of the production process), say between an oil producer and a refinery industry, the cost of capital for the two firms is likely to be very different and the appropriate cost of capital for the merged company will depend on how these two disparate 'businesses' are expected to grow within the merged firm. The appropriate choice of discount rate for a conglomerate merger (i.e. a merger of two very disparate firms) is even more acute. (An alternative procedure known as 'adjusted present value' may be useful in these difficult cases—see Chapter 11.)

Empirical evidence on whether, ex-post, particular mergers have been successful is very mixed. This is primarily because, although we know what happens to the NPV of the profits of the merged firm (and other measures such as the rate of return on capital, etc.), we cannot precisely say what would have happened *if it had not* merged. The only 'handle' we can get on the latter is to look at the performance of a 'control group' of firms in that sector which did not merge (but the latter is clearly not identical to what would have happened to A and B had they not merged). What evidence there is suggests that *on average* the real resource gain to society from mergers is probably positive (but not very positive and subject to large margins of error). However, there are clear financial gains made by the directors of the acquiring firm (e.g. higher salaries, stock options and 'status') and by the shareholders of the target firm (since they receive a bid premium of, on average, a 30–50% increase in the value of their shares, immediately after a successful takeover). The directors of the acquired firm usually lose out (e.g. they are sacked but sometimes given a 'golden parachute' payout), as do the shareholders of the acquiring firm (whose share price tends to rise less or, at best, at the same rate as similar non-merged firms in the sector). Often the ordinary employees of both firms suffer since many mergers are undertaken to achieve lower costs through economies of scale (e.g. in bank mergers and retail mergers, the number of outlets or branches is reduced).

In practice, acquiring firms often do undertake some kind of scenario analysis using NPV, to work out the value of the merged firm, but they are fully aware that the analysis is subject to a wide margin of error. However, the latter is better than a wild guess or hunch about the advantages of a merger. Nevertheless, it is probably true that some mergers take place to achieve specific managerial goals, rather than being undertaken solely in the interests of the shareholders (this is the principal–agent problem again). One of the key ideas here is due to Jensen (1968) who argues that 'free cash flow' is the immediate trigger for merger activity. If a firm has undertaken all projects with NPV > 0, yet it still has positive cash flows, then this surplus should be distributed (in dividend payments) to shareholders. This maximises shareholder wealth because the latter can now purchase shares in companies that have not exhausted their projects with NPV > 0. However, it is Jensen's view that instead, managers use this free cash flow for merger acquisitions. This is because the managers want to 'empire build' and earn higher salaries as well as enjoying the 'thrill of the chase' in the merger process. Indeed, they may have a genuine yet misguided view that they have superior managerial qualities that can add value in the target firm. In the words of Tom Wolfe's 1980s novel *Bonfire of the Vanities* such people believe they are 'Masters of the Universe' or they are Gordon Gekko types (as played by Michael Douglas in *Wall Street*), who believe that 'lunch is for wimps'.

One of the most difficult attributes to value in a merger is the extra flexibility the merged firm might have to exploit future opportunities, and this is even more acute in industries subject to rapid technological innovation. For example, in 1997 Cable and Wireless Communications (CWC), formed from a merger of Nynex CableComms, Bell Cablemedia, Videotron and Mercury Communications, was to be floated but with most City estimates of the DPV of the merged group ranging from £4.5bn to £6bn. The merged group would have access to a national network of cable customers. However, the difficulties lie in estimating the future customer base. The latter involves a careful analysis of such factors as 'penetration rates' relative to the number of homes 'passed' (i.e. the number of homes paying to take the service compared with the number that could potentially take it). Also important is the 'churn rate', that is the number of customers who fail to renew their subscriptions which can be around 30% in the UK. The latter was an issue for ONdigital in 2000, a digital TV venture owned by Carlton Communications and Granada Media which had provided free 'set top boxes' for TVs if the subscriber took out a 12-month subscription. They are relying on the setting up of high-speed internet access via the TV to reduce the churn rate.

Another interesting example is the AOL–Time Warner merger. AOL, an internet provider, now owns 55% of Time Warner which produces and distributes movies, cable TV and magazines. Both companies presumably see that together they have 'an option' to expand into the new media technologies. In the merger AOL provides additional customers plus its internet technology and expertise while Time Warner has currently an operable (broad band) delivery system (i.e. cable). Time Warner can also offer AOL extensive 'high-quality', tried and tested media products (e.g. Batman movies, TV series, toys, etc.). Each firm could have grown organically (e.g. AOL manufacturing its own media content and Time Warner its own internet technology) but they believe the merger will accomplish this at lower cost and risk — see Box 3.2.

## Box 3.2    TIME WARNER AND AOL: SYNERGIES?

In 2000, Time Warner was viewed as an 'old media' company involved in cable TV, movies and magazines while America OnLine (AOL) is 'new media', working via the internet. The sales of Time Warner at around $26bn were about five times larger than those of AOL at $5bn. So how could Time Warner hand over 55% of the merged company to AOL? Surely the NPV of Time Warner is far greater than that of AOL, even if the discount rate for AOL is much lower than that for Time Warner (which is unlikely given the high risk attached to AOL's revenues). The answer must lie in the NPV of the *merged* company. Both AOL and Time Warner must believe that the $NPV_{A+B}$ is greater than each NPV taken separately.

The market capitalisation of AOL (in 2000) was around $160bn while that of Time Warner was about $80bn. Hence the combined company was then *currently* worth $240bn of which AOL's shareholders owned 55%, equal to $132bn. So it looks as if AOL shareholders were worth $160bn before the merger and only $132bn immediately after the merger, a loss of $28bn in value, implying that AOL was offering its shares at about a 17% discount. This is fine as long as the merged company is expected to have higher returns in the future than AOL would have had if it did not merge. What are the possible synergies in this merger which will enable higher future revenues (or lower costs) for the merged firm?

First, Time Warner can provide advertising via its cable TV and print media for the output of AOL and the internet services it provides. This is not uncommon, for example CBS paid for its investment in *Sportsline* with 'free' advertising. Time Warner can also offer AOL immediate access to its new cable facilities (which take digital signals) so that high-quality videos can be delivered via the internet. Finally, Time Warner has an inventory of high-quality media products (e.g. Batman series, feature films, CNN news) that AOL can market via the internet. Almost 75% of AOL's internet customers stay within AOL's 'walled garden' of content and AOL also has 40% of the total US web market. This American internet market is large and has the potential to develop into a 'world market' as more countries embrace the internet.

Of course, Time Warner could itself have tried to exploit the internet and indeed it did, but the strategy was a failure. Also, AOL could have tried to produce 'quality media content', but this is a time consuming and expensive process and requires expertise which AOL did not have. So, in this fast moving media market the two companies believe that their marriage of technologies and expertise will generate additional revenues via a wider market for their complementary products. In short, they hope to establish a quality 'internet media brand' which can respond flexibly to future developments. However, while NPV is a useful way of thinking about the key issues involved, it definitely does not provide a definitive solution.

Another major issue in some mergers is regulatory concerns about the possible reduction of competition. The US regulatory body, the Federal Trade Commission (FTC), expressed concern that Time Warner might refuse its 'popular content' to other cable networks unless they favoured AOL as the internet service provider (ISP). (This is a similar issue to the Paramount Pictures case of 1948 when the Supreme Court forced the film studios to divest themselves of the movie theatres they also owned.) The FTC is pushing for open access to other ISPs, while Time Warner has concluded a financial deal for access by Juno Online Services (the US third largest ISP), but Earthlink (the second largest ISP after AOL) has claimed that the revenue split for access to Time Warner material would not be profitable for them. The debate continues at the time of writing.

In addition, Warner Music, a subsidiary of Time Warner, is negotiating a separate merger with EMI which will create the world's largest music business. Also AOL Europe is a 50:50 joint venture between AOL and the German group Bertelsmann, which is a rival to EMI in the music business. Also, AOL France is a joint venture between AOL and Vivendi and the latter may merge with Seagram, the owner of Universal Music. The European Commission is worried that these mergers will stifle competition in the music industry. The EC could insist on AOL divesting itself of some of these interests (e.g. Bertelsmann and Vivendi) as well as extracting a commitment from Time Warner that it will make its 'content' available on on-line systems other than AOL and that it will make its music content compatible with several types of software players. The EU's advisory committee on mergers under the auspices of the competition commissioner Mario Monti was insisting on EMI disposing of its interests in Virgin (recorded music) and Warner disposing of Chappell (music publishing) before it clears the merger. This $20bn merger was in fact dramatically called off the day the EC committee was to meet because of fears the EC would block it. However, a revised deal is likely to be put together in the near future, which meets the regulator's fears. These uncertainties make the NPV calculation of a merger exceptionally difficult.

As noted above there is a branch of finance called **real options theory** which suggests that the PV of a merger is not just the discounted cash flows from the 'best guess' of what the merged firm's future profits will be. Instead the merger is also seen as giving the merged firm greater opportunities to take advantage of *possible* future developments (e.g. to quickly expand should a particular new technology provide rapid and efficient access to a worldwide consumer base). These possible future developments of the merged firm have a value today, even though you do not know for certain today that any particular course of action in the future will be worthwhile. According to real options theory these strategic possibilities provide an added 'option value' which should be added to the 'conventional NPV' to give the 'true' NPV of the proposed merger (see Cuthbertson and Nitzsche, 2001).

# 3.6 SUMMARY

- Cash flows which accrue at different points in time cannot be directly compared: they must be discounted. Hence cash flows are worth less today, the further into the future they are received. This is the concept of **discounted present value (DPV)**.
- Capital investment projects can be compared using either the **net present value (NPV)** concept or the **internal rate of return (IRR)**. These two methods give identical decision rules for independent projects and when there are no capital constraints.
- In general the NPV approach is more straightforward than the IRR approach when **cash flows are uneven**, or for **mutually exclusive projects**.
- In practice, calculation of cash flows requires consideration of **depreciation** and **taxation**, **changes in working capital** and using **real or nominal variables**.
- When there are many sources of finance available, the appropriate discount rate to use in the NPV calculation is the **weighted average cost of capital (WACC)**. Whether or not the WACC can be lowered by a judicious mix of alternative sources of finance, is a much debated topic in corporate finance (which is discussed further in Chapter 11).
- **Uncertainty** can be dealt with by using expected values and decision trees. However, in practice it is not always easy to apply NPV to particular strategies (e.g. to calculate the potential gains in a merger) and here **scenario analysis** is a useful complementary approach. Even then, the degree of uncertainty may still be very large because of measurement problems, but at least NPV provides a useful framework for analysing alternative possible outcomes for an investment project.

# END OF CHAPTER EXERCISES

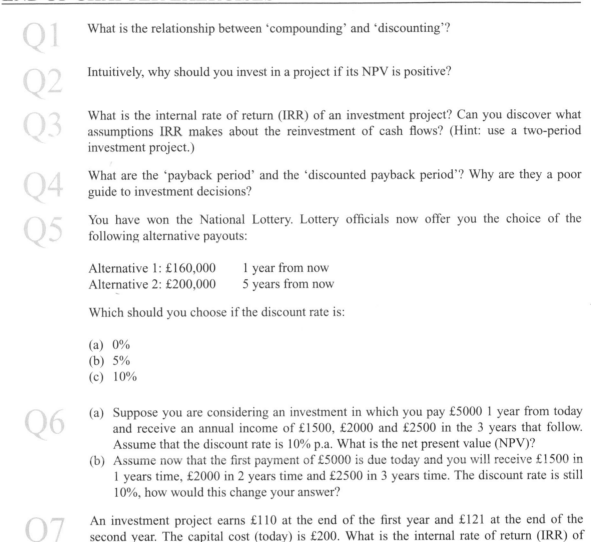

Q1   What is the relationship between 'compounding' and 'discounting'?

Q2   Intuitively, why should you invest in a project if its NPV is positive?

Q3   What is the internal rate of return (IRR) of an investment project? Can you discover what assumptions IRR makes about the reinvestment of cash flows? (Hint: use a two-period investment project.)

Q4   What are the 'payback period' and the 'discounted payback period'? Why are they a poor guide to investment decisions?

Q5   You have won the National Lottery. Lottery officials now offer you the choice of the following alternative payouts:

Alternative 1: £160,000    1 year from now
Alternative 2: £200,000    5 years from now

Which should you choose if the discount rate is:

(a)  0%
(b)  5%
(c)  10%

Q6   (a) Suppose you are considering an investment in which you pay £5000 1 year from today and receive an annual income of £1500, £2000 and £2500 in the 3 years that follow. Assume that the discount rate is 10% p.a. What is the net present value (NPV)?
(b) Assume now that the first payment of £5000 is due today and you will receive £1500 in 1 years time, £2000 in 2 years time and £2500 in 3 years time. The discount rate is still 10%, how would this change your answer?

Q7   An investment project earns £110 at the end of the first year and £121 at the end of the second year. The capital cost (today) is £200. What is the internal rate of return (IRR) of the project? If the cost of capital (i.e. cost of borrowing) is 12% should you invest in the project? Briefly explain the intuition behind your answer.

# 4

# Financial Arithmetic

This chapter provides an overview of the algebra and arithmetic calculations needed to understand basic concepts in finance. It is here for reference purposes. If your basic math is weak and you read this chapter in one go, then you are likely to end up with a severe headache. So use the material in this chapter as a useful reference point and when these concepts appear in later chapters, return to it.

## 4.1 DISCOUNTING AND COMPOUNDING

It is useful at this point to group together the general formulae used in calculating terminal value (TV) and discounted present value (DPV). These formulae will be used throughout the book in calculating the 'price' and 'rate of return' on financial assets.

### TERMINAL VALUE (CONSTANT INTEREST RATE)

The terminal value $TV_n$ is the future value of $\$Z$ invested today at a constant annual interest rate $r$, compounded for $n$ years. Then:

[4.1] $$TV_n = Z[(1 + r)^n] = Z[CF_n]$$

where $CF_n = (1 + r)^n$ and values for $CF_n$ can be found in 'compounding' or 'future value' tables (see Appendix Table A4.1). For example, for $n = 5$ years and $r = 0.10 (= 10\%$ p.a.),

$CF_5 = 1.6105$. Hence $1000 invested today at 10% p.a. is worth $1605 in 5 years time. This formula can be used, for example, in finding the terminal value after $n$ periods of a single coupon payment on a bond which is paid out today (and invested at $r$). Terminal or future values calculated using Excel are given in Appendix Table A4.1.

## TERMINAL VALUE (ORDINARY ANNUITY)

An annuity is a constant payment of $Z$ every year for $n$ years. Each $Z$ is reinvested when it is received and hence earns interest-on-interest. We assume that the first payment of $Z$ occurs *at the end of year 1* and all subsequent payments are made at the end of each year. If the reinvestment rate $r$ is assumed to be constant then the terminal value of the annuity is:

[4.2]
$$TV_a = Z(1 + r)^{n-1} + Z(1 + r)^{n-2} + \ldots + Z(1 + r) + Z$$

Using the formula for the sum of a geometric progression this reduces to (see Section 4.5):

[4.3]
$$TV_a = ZS_{n,r} \quad \text{where} \quad S_{n,r} = \frac{(1 + r)^n - 1}{r}$$

The term $S_{n,r}$ can be found in tables which give 'the sum of an annuity of $1 for $n$ periods at a rate $r$'. For example, if you are offered $Z = \$100$ at the end of *each year* for $n = 20$ years at a rate $r = 0.10$, then the terminal value is:

[4.4]
$$TV_n = \$100 \times S_{20,10} = \$100(57.275) = \$5727.50$$

The above formula is useful in calculating the terminal value of a *stream* of fixed coupon payments on a bond (assuming these coupons when paid out are each reinvested at $r$).

## TERMINAL VALUE (VARIABLE INTEREST RATES)

If the rate of interest varies in each year then we cannot use compounding tables but must simply undertake the following calculation:

[4.5]
$$TV_n = Z(1 + r_{0,1})(1 + r_{1,2})(1 + r_{2,3}) \ldots (1 + r_{n-1,n})$$

where $r_{0,1}$ is the interest rate between year 0 and year 1
$\quad r_{1,2}$ is the interest rate *expected* to prevail between year 1 and year 2, etc.

Note that at $t = 0$ you know the interest rate payable over the first year but for subsequent years you will have to forecast or form an expectation at $t = 0$ of what future 1-year rates $r_{1,2}, r_{2,3}, \ldots, r_{n-1,n}$ will be. Let us now turn to some general formulae for the calculation of DPV.

## DPV (CONSTANT DISCOUNT RATE)

If we have a *constant* discount rate $r$, then the DPV is:

[4.6]
$$DPV = \frac{V_1}{(1+r)} + \frac{V_2}{(1+r)^2} + \ldots + \frac{V_3}{(1+r)^3} + \ldots + \frac{V_n}{(1+r)^n}$$

$$= \delta V_1 + \delta^2 V_2 + \delta^3 V_3 + \ldots + \delta^n V_n$$

where $\delta = 1/(1+r)$ are the **discount factors** and can be obtained from discount tables—see Appendix Table A4.2. For example, if $r = 0.1$, then $\delta = (1/1.1) = 0.9091$, $\delta^2 = 1/(1.1)^2 = 0.8264$ and these figures are given in Table A4.2. Clearly, $\delta > \delta^2 > \delta^3$, etc. (with $0 < \delta < 1$) and therefore 'money' which accrues further in the future has a smaller 'present value' than 'money' which accrues in earlier years.

## DPV (ORDINARY ANNUITY)

If all future payments $V_i$ are constant in each year ($V_i = \$C$) and the first payment is at the end of the first year, then we have an **ordinary annuity**. The DPV of these payments is:

[4.7]
$$DPV_a = (\$C) \sum_{i=1}^{n} \frac{1}{(1+r)^i}$$

Using the formula for the sum of a geometric progression (see below), we can write the DPV of an ordinary annuity as:

[4.8]
$$DPV_a = C\,A_{n,r} \quad \text{where} \quad A_{n,r} = (1/r)[1 - 1/(1+r)^n]$$

The term $A_{n,r}$ is called the **annuity factor** and its numerical value is given in annuity tables, such as Appendix Table A4.3, for various values of $n$ and $r$. A variant on equation [4.8] is sometimes useful, where a project is *forecast* to earn a constant net cash flow per annum after a certain date. For example, suppose that after year 10 the cash flow is forecast to be a constant $C = \$100$ p.a. for a further $n$ years. The PV *in year 10* and *in year 0* of this annuity is:

$$PV_{10} = C\,A_{10,r} = 6.1446(\$100) = 614.46$$

$$DPV_0 = PV_{10}/(1+r)^{10} = 614.46(0.3855) = \$236.87$$

As we saw in Chapter 3 this is usually referred to as the **continuing value**. The overall DPV at $t = 0$, including the irregular cash flows $C_i$ in years 1 to 10 would therefore be:

$$DPV(project) = \sum_{i=1}^{10} \frac{C_i}{(1+r)^i} + DPV_0$$

In this way we can 'decompose' our forecast of net cash flows into a variable amount each year in the early years of a project and a constant cash flow in later years, when we presumably have less information about the precise fluctuations in revenues and costs.

A further special case of equation [4.8] arises when $n$ approaches infinity and the DPV of the fixed annuity payments is then given by the simple formula:

[4.9]     $DPV = C/r$

As we shall see in later chapters, equation [4.9] is used to price a bond called a perpetuity, which pays a fixed coupon of $\$C$ every year, for ever (but is never redeemed by the issuers). The annuity formula [4.8] can be used to find the DPV for many financial products involving constant payments, such as for mortgage payments, pension payments and also for pricing a coupon paying bond which is redeemable at some time in the future (see below).

There is a direct link between the terminal value of an annuity in equation [4.3], $TV_a = ZS_{n,r}$ and the DPV of an annuity in equation [4.8], $DPV_a = CA_{n,r}$. The value today (i.e. the DPV) of the terminal value of an annuity paying $Z = \$1$ is $[1/(1 + r)^n]S_{n,r}$ and this must equal $DPV_a$, hence:

[4.10]     $\dfrac{1}{(1 + r)^n} S_{n,r} = A_{n,r}$

Equation [4.10] links $S_{n,r}$ and $A_{n,r}$, however, as annuity tables give values for *both* $S_{n,r}$ and $A_{n,r}$ we do not need to use the above conversion formula.

## DPV (GROWING ANNUITY)

Suppose the income stream from an investment in a financial asset (e.g. a stock) or an investment project was $\$D_1$ at the *end of the first year*, $D_1(1 + g)$ at the end of the second year, etc. If the current payment at $t = 0$ is $D_0$, then note that $D_1 = (1 + g)D_0$, $D_2 = (1 + g)D_1 = (1 + g)^2 D_0$, etc. This sequence of receipts is called a growing annuity since the income stream grows at a rate $g$ (e.g. $g = 0.05$ represents 5% p.a. growth) *in all future periods*. A share pays out dividends and if these grew at a constant rate for ever, you would be prepared to pay today for the share, an amount equal to the DPV of these receipts. If we assume a constant discount rate $r$ then the DPV of the future dividends determines the 'fair price' of the share:

[4.11]     $P = \dfrac{D_0(1 + g)}{(1 + r)} + \dfrac{D_0(1 + g)^2}{(1 + r)^2} + \cdots$

Using the formula for the sum of a geometric series (see below) this expression simplifies to:

***Present value of growing annuity (as $t \to \infty$)***

[4.12]     $P = \dfrac{(1 + g)D_0}{r - g} = \dfrac{D_1}{(r - g)}$

The above is known as the **Gordon growth model** for evaluating the fair price of a share where dividends are expected to grow at a constant rate and is discussed in detail in Chapter 12. However, if an investment project had net revenues which were forecast to grow at a constant rate (from some point in time, which may be at $t > 0$) then equation [4.12] can be used to find the PV *at time* $t$. (This PV can then be discounted back to $t = 0$, as in our example, using the annuity formula above.)

What if the growing annuity starts with a (fixed) payment of $C$ at $t = 1$ and subsequent payments are $C(1 + g)$, $C(1 + g)^2$, ... as before, but the last payment is $C(1 + g)^n$ at $t = n$. The *present value* of the sum of these terms is:

***Present value of growing annuity (as t → n)***

$$DPV = C \, A_{n,r,g} \quad \text{where} \quad A_{n,r,g} = \left[ \frac{1}{(r - g)} - \frac{1}{r - g} \left( \frac{1 + g}{1 + r} \right)^n \right]$$

All of the above annuity formulae are therefore useful 'short-cuts' to calculating the DPV of a series of *constant* cash flows—although there are no new economic principles involved here.

## DPV (VARIABLE DISCOUNT RATE)

Note that in the above calculations of the DPV we assume that the interest rate used for discounting the future receipts was constant for all horizons. Suppose however that '1-year money' carries an interest rate of $r_1$, 2-year money costs $r_2$, etc. and we assume the future receipts are known with certainty (i.e. riskless). Then the DPV is given by:

[4.13]
$$DPV = \frac{V_1}{(1 + r_1)} + \frac{V_2}{(1 + r_2)^2} + \ldots + \frac{V_n}{(1 + r_n)^n} = \sum_{i=1}^{n} \delta_i V_i$$

where $\delta_i = 1/(1 + r_i)^i$ is the *discount factor*. The $r_i$ are known as ***spot rates*** of interest since they are rates that apply to borrowing (or lending money) for fixed periods. For example $r_1$ is the interest rate on money borrowed today with interest and principal paid back at the end of the year, $r_2$ is the rate charged on money borrowed today and paid back at the end of 2 years. (All interest rates are annual rates.) Most of the time, we find that longer term interest rates are higher than short-term interest rates (e.g. $r_1 = 3\%$, $r_2 = 3.5\%$, $r_3 = 4\%$). The relationship between 'time to maturity' and the corresponding spot rates $(r_i)$ on default free (riskless) assets (e.g. government bonds) is called the 'yield curve' (or term structure of interest rates) and is examined in Chapter 8.

In general, physical investment projects and investment in financial assets are not riskless, since the future receipts are uncertain. There are a number of alternative methods of dealing with uncertainty in the DPV calculation. One method is to assume the discount rate $\delta_i$ comprises a risk free spot rate $r_i$ plus a risk premium $rp_i$:

[4.14]
$$\delta_i = (1 + r_i + rp_i)^{-1}$$

Equation [4.14] is an identity and is not operational until we have a model of the risk premium (e.g. we could assume $rp_i$ is constant for all $i$). We examine some alternative models for $rp$ in later chapters, including the so-called capital asset pricing model (CAPM) and the arbitrage pricing theory (APT).

# 4.2 USING DPV IN FINANCIAL MARKETS

## PURE DISCOUNT BONDS: SPOT RATES

Instead of a physical investment project consider investing in a 'pure discount bond' (zero coupon bond). A **pure discount bond (or 'zero')** has a fixed redemption price $M$, a known maturity period $n$ and no default risk. A positive return $r_n$ on the zero arises because the market price is always below the maturity value $M$. Viewing the problem in terms of DPV we see that a 'zero' promises a known future payment of $M$ in $n$ years time in exchange for a capital cost paid out today of $P$. Hence the internal rate of return $r_n$ on the 'zero' is the solution of:

[4.15]
$$P = \frac{M}{(1 + r_n)^n}$$

The 'return' $r_n$ is the risk free rate applicable to a single payout at an $n$-year horizon and is therefore known as the 'spot rate' (for maturity $n$ years). There is an inverse relationship between the spot rate and the price.

## COUPON PAYING BONDS: YIELD TO MATURITY

A level coupon (non-callable) bond pays a fixed coupon $C$ at known fixed intervals (which we take to be every year) and has a fixed redemption price or maturity value $(M)$ payable when the bond matures. Suppose the bond has $n$ years left to maturity and a current market price $P_t$. The question is how do we measure the return on the bond if it is held to maturity? The bond is analogous to our physical investment project with the capital outlay today being $P_t$ and the future receipts being $C$ each year (plus the redemption price). The internal rate of return on the bond, which is called the 'yield to maturity' $y_t$ can be calculated from:

[4.16]
$$P_t = \frac{C}{(1 + y_t)} + \frac{C}{(1 + y_t)^2} + \ldots + \frac{C}{(1 + y_t)^n} + \frac{M}{(1 + y_t)^n}$$

Using the formula for the DPV of an ordinary annuity the above formula can be simplified to:

[4.17]
$$P_t = C\,A_{n,y} + M/(1 + y_t)^n \qquad \text{where} \quad A_{n,y} = [1 - 1/(1 + y)]/y$$

The yield to maturity is that *constant* rate of discount which, at a point in time, equates the DPV of future payments with the current market price. Since $P_t$, $M$ and $C$ are known values in the market, equation [4.16] can be solved to give the yield to maturity $y$. There is a subscript '$t$' on $y_t$ because as the market price falls, the yield to maturity rises (and vice versa) as a matter of actuarial arithmetic in equation [4.16]. Although widely used in the market and in the financial press there are some theoretical/conceptual problems in using the yield to maturity as an unambiguous measure of the return on a bond, even when it is held to maturity, and we deal with these issues in Chapter 7.

## PERPETUITY

A perpetuity is a (fixed) coupon bond that is never redeemed by the primary issuer (i.e. the number of payments $n \to \infty$). If the coupon is $\$C$ per annum and the current market price of the bond is $P_t$ then the yield to maturity (YTM) is given by equation [4.17], which as $n \to \infty$ reduces to the simple expression:

[4.18]   $$y = \frac{C}{P}$$

It is immediately obvious from equation [4.18] that the *percentage* change in the price of a *perpetuity* equals the percentage change in the yield to maturity (this is strictly true only for small changes).

## HOLDING PERIOD RETURN

Often bonds and stocks are held for a specific period of time and then sold. How can we measure the return, over a specific time horizon? Much empirical work on stocks deals with the one-period holding period return (HPR), where you buy the stock at (the end of) time period $t$ and sell it one period later at $t + 1$. The (discrete) holding period return $R_{t+1}$ is defined as:

[4.19]   $$R_{t+1} = \frac{(\text{sale price} + \text{dividends received}) - \text{purchase price}}{\text{purchase price}} = \frac{(P_{t+1} + D_{t+1}) - P_t}{P_t}$$

Rearranging equation [4.19] gives:

[4.20a]   $$R_{t+1} = \frac{(P_{t+1} - P_t)}{P_t} + \frac{D_{t+1}}{P_t}$$

or

[4.20b]   $$HPR = \text{capital gain} + \text{dividend yield}$$

The first term in equation [4.20] is the proportionate capital gain or loss (over one period) and the second term is the (proportionate) dividend yield. $R_{t+1}$ can be calculated ex-post but, of course, viewed from time $t$, $P_{t+1}$ and (perhaps) $D_{t+1}$ are uncertain and investors can only try and forecast them. Ex-post, if $\$A$ is invested in the stock (and all future dividend payments are reinvested in the stock) then the payout (terminal value) after $n$ periods is:

[4.21]   $$TV_n = \$A(1 + R_{t+1})(1 + R_{t+2}) \dots (1 + R_{t+n})$$

This is similar to equation [4.5] with the interest rate replaced by the HPR on the stock in each period. With slight modifications the one-period HPR can be defined for any asset. For a coupon paying bond with initial maturity of $n$ periods and coupon payment of $C$ we have:

$$[\textbf{4.22a}] \qquad R_{t+1} = \frac{(P_{t+1} - P_t)}{P_t} + \frac{C}{P_t}$$

$$[\textbf{4.22b}] \qquad \text{HPR (on bond)} = \text{capital gain} + \text{running yield}$$

and $R_{t+1}$ is often referred to as the (one-period) **holding period** *yield* **(HPY)**. The first term in equation [4.22] is the capital gain on the bond and the second is the coupon (or running) yield. Broadly speaking we can often apply the same type of economic ideas to explain movements in holding period returns for both stock and bonds (and other speculative assets) and we begin this analysis for bonds in Chapter 7 and for stocks (using the CAPM) in Chapter 10.

# 4.3 ALTERNATIVE MEASURES OF INTEREST

Much of the theoretical work in finance is conducted in terms of compound interest rates even though rates of interest quoted 'On the Street' often use 'simple interest'. For example, an interest rate of 2% payable every 3 months may be quoted as a **simple interest rate** of $R_s = 8\%$ per annum in the market. However, if an investor rolled over four 3-month investments *and the interest rate remained constant*, she could actually earn an annual 'compound rate' (often called the **'effective annual rate'**) of $(1.02)^4 = 1.0824$ or $R = 8.24\%$ p.a. The (annual, discrete) **compound rate** of return exceeds the simple rate because in the former case the investor earns 'interest-on-interest' over the last three 3-month periods.

We now examine the calculation of the terminal value of an investment when the *frequency* with which interest rates are compounded alters. Clearly, a quoted interest rate of 8% per annum when interest is calculated monthly will amount to more at the end of the year than if interest accrues only at the end of the year. Interest rates are usually presented as annual rates but it is important to know whether these annual figures are based on 'simple interest' $R_s$, 'discrete compounding' $R$, or so-called 'continuously compounded' $R_c$ rates.

So we can get used to 'day count conventions' which are actually used 'on the street'. We will let '$a$' be the number of days in the year and '$m$' the number of days to maturity (i.e. when you receive the payment on your investment). For simplicity we assume that there are 360 days in a year (i.e. $a = 360$). If the investment is for 3 months then we take $m = 90$ days and for an investment which lasts for 2 years we will usually take $m = 720$. It follows that the number of years or fraction of a year, $n$, to the maturity date is $n = (m/a) = m/360$. So from the above either $n = 90/360 = 0.25$ years (i.e. 3 months) or $n = 720/360 = 2$ years.

## SIMPLE INTEREST

Suppose you purchase an asset for $P_0 = \$100$ at $t = 0$ and sell it 3 months (1/4 of a year) later for $TV_{1/4} = \$102$. You have made 2% over 3 months which is a **simple annual return** $R_s$ of 8% over 1 year. The figure of 8% assumes that you do not earn any 'interest-on-interest' on the deal. It is as if you took the return of \$2 in the first 3 months and spent it and simply reinvested your initial $100 for the next 3 months, repeating this procedure at the end of 6 months, 9 months and 1 year. Hence you actually received a total of $8 over the whole year on an initial outlay of $100. The simple annual interest was calculated as:

[4.23]
$$R_s = \left(\frac{TV_{1/4}}{P_0} - 1\right)\frac{a}{m} = \left(\frac{TV_{1/4}}{P_0} - 1\right)\frac{1}{n}$$

$$= \left(\frac{102}{100} - 1\right)\frac{360}{90} = 0.08$$

A simple rearrangement of equation [4.23] gives:

[4.24]
$$P_0 = \frac{TV_{1/4}}{\left(1 + R_s\dfrac{m}{a}\right)} = \frac{TV_n}{(1 + R_s n)}$$

This equation says that the value today (i.e. the PV) of an amount $TV_{1/4} = \$102$, which accrues in 3 months time, when a simple interest rate of 8% p.a. is used, is $P_0 = \$100$. Let us change this problem around. Suppose we are told to invest $P_0 = \$100$ at simple annual rate of $R_s = 8\%$ p.a. over $n = 1/4$ of a year. Then what is the terminal value after $n$ years (or a fraction of a year)? Rearranging equation [4.24] gives:

[4.25]
$$TV_n = \$P_0(1 + R_s n)$$

Clearly, the above equations are all internally consistent. We can rearrange the same equation to determine either TV, $R_s$ or $P_0$. Note that when we quote $R_s$ as a percentage per annum, we also need to know the period over which the actual cash flow accrues (e.g. 1/4 of a year or every 3 months). Let us briefly consider the case of $n = 2$. Suppose now you again invested $P_0 = \$100$ but this time you receive $TV_n = \$108$ after $n = 2$ years ($= m/a$ $= 720/360$). The simple interest rate $R_s = 4\%$ p.a. It is easy to see that equations [4.24] and [4.25] hold for this case too.

## DISCRETE COMPOUNDING

Suppose you again purchase an asset for $P_0 = \$100$ at $t = 0$ and sell it 3 months ($n = 1/4$ of a year) later for $TV_{1/4} = \$102$. Your return over 3 months is 2% which implies a compound annual return of $R = (1.02)^4 - 1 = 0.0824$ or 8.24% p.a. This calculation assumes that the investment can be 'rolled over' so that all revenues earned can be reinvested in each successive 3-month period, at the same rate of return as in the first 3 months. Expressed algebraically, this can be stated as:

[4.26]
$$R = \left[\frac{TV_{1/4}}{P_0}\right]^{a/m} - 1 = \left[\frac{TV_{1/4}}{P_0}\right]^{1/n} - 1 = \left[\frac{102}{100}\right]^4 - 1 = 0.08243$$

Again a simple algebraic rearrangement gives the PV formula, to calculate the price of the asset given the TV and the compound annual rate:

[4.27]   $$P_0 = \frac{TV_{1/4}}{(1 + R)^n} = \frac{TV_{1/4}}{(1 + R)^{m/a}}$$

It also follows from the above that if you have $100 and invest it at a compound rate $R$ for a period of $n$ years (or a fraction of a year) it will eventually accrue to:

[4.28]   $$TV_n = P_0(1 + R)^n$$

For example, $100 invested at a compound rate of 8.243% p.a. will over 3 months (not surprisingly) accrue to:

[4.29]   $$TV_{1/4} = 100(1 + 0.08243)^{1/4} = \$102$$

Suppose you again invest $100, but this time you receive $108 after $n = 2$ years (i.e. equivalently, $a = 360$ days and $m = 720$ days). The annual compound return can be calculated from:

[4.30]   $$R = \left[\frac{108}{100}\right]^{1/2} - 1 = \left[\frac{TV_2}{P_0}\right]^{1/n} - 1 = 0.0392$$

This return is slightly less than 4% p.a. because the compound return assumes that the notional 'interest' earned at the end of year 1 is reinvested in the second year. Note that the above formulae work regardless of whether $n$ is in years or fractions of a year.

## CONTINUOUS COMPOUNDING

Let us now discuss a slight variant on the above example where interest is paid quarterly (i.e. $q = 4$ times per annum) and the simple annual rate is $R_s$. If the asset pays interest every $m = 90$ days and there are $a = 360$ days in a year then:

[4.31]   $$q = a/m = 4 \qquad \text{(valid only for } a \geqslant m \text{ and } q \text{ a whole number)}$$

The terminal value of $P_0$ at the end of $n$ years (where $n$ is a whole number of years, with $n \geqslant 1$) is:

[4.32]   $$TV_n = \$P_0(1 + R_s/q)^{qn}$$

$R_s/q$ is often referred to as the **periodic interest rate**. For example, suppose $R_s$ is 8% p.a. and interest is paid quarterly, $q = 4$ (times per year). Then the TV at the end of 2 years of a $1 investment is:

[4.33]   $$TV_2 = \$1(1 + 0.08/4)^{4(2)} = \$1.1716$$

Thus over 2 years the return is 17.16% which exceeds the simple annual rate of 16% ($= 2 \times 8\%$), the extra 1.16% being interest-on-interest.

Suppose we imagine the frequency of compounding increases so that $q$ increases from 1, 2, 3, ... to say 1000 times *per year*. What would be the terminal value at $t = 1$ of an investment of $P_0$? This is known as a continuously compounded rate and the investment accrues to:

[4.34]    $$TV_n = \lim_{q \to \infty} P_0(1 + R_s/q)^{qn}$$

This expression can be shown to be equal to:

[4.35]    $$TV_n = P_0\, e^{R_c n}$$

where $n$ is the number of years (or fraction of a year), e = 2.71828, and $R_c$ is the **continuously compounded annual rate**. Hence if we are given $R_c$ we can calculate TV. For example, if we assume $R_c$ is 0.10 (or 10%), then $P_0 = \$100$ accrues by the end of 1 year to $110.5171 ($TV_1 = \$100\, e^{0.10(1)}$).

For comparison suppose the simple interest rate $R_s$ is 10% p.a. then using equation [4.32] the terminal value *for different values of q* is given in Table 4.1. For practical purposes daily compounding, over say 1 year (i.e. $q = 365$) gives a result very close to continuous compounding (see last two entries in Table 4.1).

It follows from equation [4.35] that the price of an asset which has a continuously compounded return of $R_c$ and pays out $TV_n$ in $n$ years time is given by:

[4.36]    $$P_0 = (TV_n)e^{-R_c n}$$

For example, if you are offered a (zero coupon) bond which pays out $TV_1 = \$110.5171$ in 1 years time and the continuously compounded (annual) rate is $R_c = 0.10$, then its market price today should be $P_0 = \$110.5171\, e^{-0.10(1)} = \$100$. Similarly, if the bond pays out $100 in $n = 2$ years time and $R_c = 0.10$, then $P_0 = \$100\, e^{-0.10(2)} = \$81.87$. Tables of values for $e^{R_c n}$ and $e^{-R_c n}$ enable the TV and the PV to be easily calculated once you know $R_c$ and $n$. But this is also easy to do on a calculator).

## TABLE 4.1: Compounding frequency

| Compounding frequency | Value of $100 at end of year ($R_s = 10\%$ p.a.) |
| --- | --- |
| **Annually ($q = 1$)** | 110 |
| **Quarterly ($q = 4$)** | 110.38 |
| **Weekly ($q = 52$)** | 110.51 |
| **Daily ($q = 365$)** | 110.5155 |
| **Continuous, TV $= 100\, e^{0.10(1)}$ ($n = 1$)** | 110.5171 |

## 4.4 SWITCHING BETWEEN INTEREST RATES

### SIMPLE RATES AND COMPOUND RATES

It is often convenient in finance to use discrete or continuously compounded rates even though sometimes quoted rates 'On the Street' are simple rates. So far we have considered the situation where we are given either $R_s$, $R$ or $R_c$ and told to calculate either TV or PV. Here our task is rather different. It is to find values of $R_s$, $R$ or $R_c$ that *are equivalent to each other*. By this we mean that whichever of $R_s$, $R$ or $R_c$ we use (in the appropriate compounding formula) they will all give *the same value* for TV. (Hence they will also give the same value for PV as well.)

Suppose we are given a value for the ***annual* compound *rate* $R$**. Then $1 invested for $n$ years will have a $TV_n = [1 + R]^n$. The equivalent ***simple* interest *rate* $R_s$**, with payments $q$ times per year must yield the same terminal value, hence:

[4.37]     $\$1[1 + R]^n = \$1[1 + R_s/q]^{qn}$

The terms in the 'power of $n$' cancel so that equation [4.37] becomes:

---

**SWITCHING BETWEEN SIMPLE AND COMPOUND RATES**

[4.38]     $$[1 + R] = [1 + R_s/q]^q$$

---

We can use equation [4.38] to move from a simple annual rate to a compound rate and vice versa. For example, a simple interest rate $R_s$ (with quarterly payments $q = 4$) that would produce *the same terminal value* as a compound annual rate of $R = 12\%$ is the solution to:

[4.39a]     $1.12 = [1 + R_s/4]^4$

[4.39b]     $R_s = [(1.12)^{1/4} - 1]4 = 0.02874 \times 4 = \mathbf{11.49\%}$

Alternatively we can calculate $R_s$ by using the rules of logarithms (see Section 4.5 below):

[4.39c]     $4\ln(1 + R_s/4) = \ln(1.12)$

[4.39d]     $\ln(1 + R_s/4) = \ln(1.12)/4 = 0.02833$

Therefore:

[4.39e]     $1 + R_s/4 = e^{0.02833} = 1.02874$

[4.39f]     $R_s = 0.1149\ (\mathbf{11.49\%})$

Hence $R_s = 11.49\%$ is the simple annual rate for quarterly payments which *is equivalent to* an annual compound rate of $R = 12\%$. Again $R_s = 11.49\%$ is less than $R = 12\%$ because the former earns more interest-on-interest, yet both yield the same terminal value (by construction). Another way of expressing the equivalence of these two rates is to note that

$R_s/4 = 2.87\%$ payable each quarter would be quoted as a simple annual rate of $R_s = 11.48\%$ p.a. and this is equivalent to a 12% p.a. compound rate.

## DISCRETE AND CONTINUOUS COMPOUNDING

We can use a similar procedure to switch between the simple rate $R_s$ (per annum) and an equivalent continuously compounded rate $R_c$. One reason for doing this calculation is that much of the advanced theory of bond pricing and the pricing of futures and options uses continuously compounded rates.

Suppose we wish to calculate a value for $R_c$ which is equivalent to the $q$-period simple rate $R_s$. Since the terminal value after $n$ years of an investment of $\$A$ must be equal when using either interest rate we have:

[4.40]      $A\,e^{R_c n} = A[1 + R_s/q]^{qn}$

Using:

$$\ln e^{R_c n} = R_c n \quad \text{and} \quad \ln(1 + R_s/q)^{qn} = qn \ln(1 + R_s/q)$$

we have:

| SWITCHING: SIMPLE AND CONTINUOUSLY COMPOUNDED RATES |
|:---:|
| [4.41]      $R_c = q \ln(1 + R_s/q)$ |

So, if we are given the continuously compounded rate $R_c$ we can use the above equation to calculate the equivalent rate $R_s$ which applies when interest is calculated $q$ times per year:

[4.42]      $R_s = q[e^{R_c/q} - 1]$

We can perhaps best summarise the above array of alternative interest rates by using one final illustrative example. Suppose an investment pays a periodic interest rate of 5% every 6 months ($q = 2$, $R_s/2 = 0.05$). In the market, this would be quoted as a **simple annual rate** $R_s = 10\%$ p.a. An investment of $100, using discrete compounding, would yield $100(1 + (0.10/2))^2 = \$110.25$ after 1 year and therefore the **compound annual rate** $R = 10.25\%$ p.a. Suppose we now wish to convert this simple rate of $R_s = 0.10$ (with interest paid $q = 2$ times per year) to an *equivalent* continuously compounded rate. Using equation [4.42] with $q = 2$ we see that this is given by $R_c = 2 \ln(1 + 0.10/2) = 0.09758$ (i.e. 9.758% p.a.).

Of course, it must now be true that if interest is continuously compounded at a rate of $R_c = 9.758\%$ p.a., then $100 invested today would accrue to $e^{0.0975(1)} = \$110.25$ in $n = 1$ years time. The equivalent continuously compounded rate $R_c$ of 9.758% is less than the simple (discrete) rate $R_s$ of 10%, because in the former case interest is compounded continuously rather than only at the end of the first 6-month period. Yet the two interest rates are 'equivalent' because we have ensured that they give the same terminal value, by construction.

The formulae for switching between alternative measures of interest rates are given in Table 4.2.

## PV: USING ALTERNATIVE DISCOUNT RATES

In just the same way as we can calculate the terminal value using simple, discretely compounded and continuously compounded interest rates we can also apply these concepts to calculate the DPV of the future payment once we know what 'type' of interest or return is being quoted. It should be self-evident that for a payment of $TV_n$ in $n$ years time, we can calculate the PV according to the formulae given below:

[4.43]   **Simple rate**

$$PV_0 = \frac{TV_n}{(1 + R_s n)} \quad (n = \text{whole years or fraction of a year})$$

[4.44]   **Compound rate**

$$\text{(a) } PV_0 = \frac{TV_n}{(1 + R)^n} \quad (n = \text{whole years or fraction of a year})$$

$$\text{(b) } PV_0 = \frac{TV_n}{\left(1 + \dfrac{R_s}{q}\right)^{qn}} \quad (q = \text{frequency p.a.})$$

[4.45]   **Continuously compounded**

$$PV_0 = TV\,e^{-R_c n} \quad (n = \text{whole years or fraction of a year})$$

where $R_s$ is the simple annual rate

$R$ is the compound annual rate

$R_c$ is the continuously compounded annual rate

$q$ is the frequency of payments per year

$a$ is the number of days in a year

$m$ is the number of days to maturity

$n\,(= m/a)$ is the number of years (or fraction of a year) to maturity.

## TABLE 4.2: Switching between equivalent interest rates

| Simple rate $R_s$ with frequency $q$ per year and the equivalent compound rate, $R$ | Simple rate $R_s$ with frequency $q$ per year and the continuously compounded rate $R_c$ |
|---|---|
| $(1 + R)^n = [1 + R_s/q]^{qn}$ | $e^{R_c n} = [1 + R_s/q]^{qn}$ |

First note that equation [4.43] can be used to determine the price of some money market instruments (e.g. T-bills) where $R_s$ is the *'yield'* and $n < 1$. From equation [4.38] it can be seen that equations [4.44a] and [4.44b] are alternative ways of expressing the same relationship: equation [4.44a] uses the annual compound rate directly whereas equation [4.44b] uses the simple rate and then compounds it. Equations [4.44a] and [4.44b] are used for calculating the yield to maturity on bonds and equation [4.45] is used extensively in 'continuous time' bond pricing and in pricing derivatives—see Cuthbertson and Nitzsche (2001).

# 4.5 SIMPLE MATHEMATICAL RELATIONSHIPS

Not surprisingly, in finance it is impossible to avoid some mathematical and statistical terminology. We try to keep this to a minimum, although when dealing with options and statistical issues surrounding the measurement of 'risk', the level of maths and stats increases. Here, some very simple yet useful algebraic formulae are presented (with little or no formal proof). The reader can quickly go through these 'mathematical rules' and then return to them when they are referred to in later chapters.

## INVERSE

It is sometimes convenient to write $1/x$ or $1/x^2$, etc. as $x^{-1}$ or $x^{-2}$, respectively. In general:

[**4.46**]      $1/x^n = x^{-n}$

If we have two terms $x^n$ and $x^m$ then:

[**4.47a**]      $(x^n x^m) = x^{n+m}$

[**4.47b**]      $x^n x^{-m} = x^{n-m}$

For example, if $x = 2$, $n = 3$ and $m = 1$, it is easy to see that $(2^1)(2^3) = 2^4$ and $(2^3)(2^{-1}) = 2^2$.

## NATURAL LOGARITHMS

A calculator provides values of natural logarithms, for example for $r = 10$ or 1:

$\ln(10) = 2.3025$

$\ln(1) = 0$

If $r$ is 'small' (i.e. $-1 < r < 1$) then a useful *approximation* is:

[**4.48a**]      $\ln(1 + r) \approx r$

For example, if the interest $r = 0.01$ (1%) then:

[4.48b]    $\ln(1.01) = 0.00995$

which is very close to $r = 0.01$, so the approximation is a good one. Even for $r = 0.1$ (10%):

[4.48c]    $\ln(1.1) = 0.0953$

which is quite close to $r = 0.10$, so the approximation is not bad (and interest rates in developed industrial economies do not often exceed 10% p.a.). Clearly the closer $r$ is to zero the better the approximation. It is also the case that (for $1 > x > 0$):

[4.49]    $\ln(1 - x) \approx -x$

Now we consider how to calculate the logarithm of a ratio and the logarithm of a product. Take $x - 2$ and $y - 3$, so obviously $yx - 6$ and $y/x - 1.5$. Using a calculator $\ln(2) = 0.6934$, $\ln(3) = 1.0986$, while $\ln(6) = 1.7917$ and $\ln(1.5) = 0.4055$. Hence it is clear that the following relationships hold between logarithms:

[4.50a]    $\ln(y/x) = \ln(y) - \ln(x)$

[4.50b]    $\ln(yx) = \ln(y) + \ln(x)$

Another useful trick is the following. Note that for $y = 3$, $n = 2$: $y^n = 3^2 = 9$ and $\ln(9) = 2.1972$. However, $n \ln(y) = 2 \ln(3)$ also equals 2.1972. Hence:

[4.51]    $\ln(y^n) = n \ln(y)$

## PROPORTIONATE CHANGES AND LOGARITHMS

The first difference '$\Delta$' of the logarithm of a variable $x$ can be written in the following (broadly) equivalent ways:

[4.52]    $d[\ln(x)] = \Delta \ln(x) = \ln(x_1) - \ln(x_0) = \ln(x_1/x_0)$

Suppose $x$ is the price of a stock which moves from $x_0 = 100$ to $x_1 = 101$, then the proportionate change in $x$ is 0.01 $[= (x_1 - x_0)/x_0 = (101 - 100)/100]$ or 1%. We would say the return on the stock is 1%. Let us now examine the first difference of the logarithm of $x$:

[4.53]    $\Delta \ln(x) = \ln(x_1) - \ln(x_0) = \ln(x_1/x_0) = \ln(101/100) = 0.00995$

The number 0.00995 is extremely close to 0.01, the proportionate change in $x$, hence it appears that for small changes in $x$:

[4.54]    $d \ln(x) = \ln(x_1/x_0) \approx \Delta x_1/x_0 \equiv (x_1 - x_0)/x_0$

Taking $x$ to be the price of a stock, the term '$\ln(x_1/x_0)$' is referred to as the 'continuously compounded return'. If the change in price is 'small' then the continuously compounded return is very close to the usual proportionate (percentage) return, $\Delta x/x$. The continuously compounded return is widely used in finance, particularly when dealing with the pricing of derivatives. For those familiar with calculus, they will recognise that if $x$ is a function of time then:

[4.55] $$\frac{d(\ln x)}{dt} = \frac{1}{x}\frac{dx}{dt}$$

which is the proportionate change in $x$ (as $dt \to 0$).

## EXPONENTIAL FUNCTION

The exponential function is used extensively in futures and options pricing. The exponential function written $\exp(x)$ or $e^x$ is available on a calculator where 'e' $= 2.71828$ so that for example:

$$e^0 = 1$$

$$e^1 = 2.71828$$

$$e^2 = 7.3890$$

$$e^3 = 20.0855$$

Note that $e^3 = 20.08 = (e^2)(e^1) = (7.38)(2.71)$, hence the following two algebraic rules apply:

[4.56a] $$e^x e^y = e^{(x+y)}$$

[4.56b] $$e^x e^{-y} = e^{(x-y)}$$

If $x$ is small (i.e. close to zero) then an approximation to the value of $e^x$ (or $e^{-x}$) for $-1 < x < 1$ is:

[4.57a] $$e^x \approx 1 + x$$

[4.57b] $$e^{-x} \approx 1 - x$$

For example, for $x = 0.01$, $e^{0.01} = 1.01005$ which is very close to $(1 + x) = 1.01$. A better approximation to $e^x$ is to include more terms in $x$ and this is known as a Taylor series expansion:

[4.58] $$e^x = 1 + x + \frac{x^2}{2!} + \frac{x^3}{3!} + \dots$$

where $n! = n(n - 1)(n - 2) \dots 1$, so for example $3! = (3)(2)(1) = 6$. A Taylor series expansion can be used to approximate any non-linear (continuous) function and is widely used in finance. For example, the relationship between bond prices and yields (see above) is non-linear and we will approximate this relationship using 'duration' and 'convexity' (in Chapter 9), but these are nothing more than the first and second 'terms' in a Taylor series expansion. Another example is provided by the well-known Black–Scholes formula for the price of an option (see Chapter 21). This non-linear relationship can be simplified using a Taylor series expansion and this then gives rise to 'the Greeks' (i.e. the option's delta, gamma, vega, etc.) which have widespread use in hedging, portfolio insurance, financial engineering and risk management—see Cuthbertson and Nitzsche (2001).

## LOGARITHMS AND EXPONENTIAL

There are a couple of rather surprising algebraic relationships between logarithms and the exponential (function):

[4.59]    $\ln[e^x] = x$

[4.60]    $e^{(\ln x)} = x$

For example, to see that these are true use $x = 1$ on your calculator:

$$\ln(e^1) = \ln(2.718) = 1$$

$$e^{\ln(1)} = e^0 = 1$$

## GEOMETRIC PROGRESSION

If $x$ lies between $+1$ and $-1$ ($-1 < x < +1$) then it is often useful to know the *sum* of a series of $x$-values known as a geometric series (where here the sum is to infinity):

[4.61]    $S = 1 + x + x^2 + x^3 + \ldots$

For example for $x = 0.5$, we have $x^2 = 0.25$, $x^3 = 0.125$ so the sum $S$ looks as though it might be 2. The trick used to find the value of $S$ is to multiply equation [4.61] by $x$:

[4.62]    $xS = x + x^2 + x^3 + \ldots$

Subtracting equation [4.62] from equation [4.61] and ignoring the term in $x^n$ which approaches zero for large $n$ and $-1 < x < +1$:

[4.63a]    $S - xS = 1$

and hence

[4.63b]    $S_\infty = 1/(1 - x) = (1 - x)^{-1}$

For $x = 0.5$, we see that $S_\infty = 1/(1 - 0.5) = 2$, as expected. If the sum contains only values of $x$ up to $x^n$ then the same trick can be used. We need to find:

[4.64]    $S = [1 + x + x^2 + \ldots + x^{n-1} + x^n]$

Multiplying both sides of equation [4.64] by $x$ gives:

[4.65]     $xS = x + x^2 + x^3 + \ldots + x^n + x^{n+1}$

Hence subtracting equation [4.65] from equation [4.64] gives:

[4.66a]     $(1 - x)S = 1 - x^{n+1}$

or

[4.66b]     $S_n = \dfrac{1 - x^{n+1}}{1 - x}$

Using equation [4.66b] we can see how we obtained formula [4.8] for the DPV of an **ordinary annuity**, reproduced here:

[4.67]     $\text{DPV}_a = C\left[\dfrac{1}{(1+r)} + \dfrac{1}{(1+r)^2} + \ldots + \dfrac{1}{(1+r)^n}\right]$

Let $x = 1/(1+r)$ then:

[4.68]     $\text{DPV}_a = C[x + x^2 + x^3 + \ldots + x^n]$

$= Cx[1 + x + x^2 + \ldots + x^{n-1}]$

The term in square brackets is similar to that for $S_n$ in equation [4.64] except that one series ends at $n$ and the other at $n - 1$, hence:

[4.69]     $\text{DPV}_a = Cx\dfrac{(1 - x^n)}{(1 - x)}$

$= \dfrac{C}{(1+r)}\dfrac{\left[1 - \dfrac{1}{(1+r)^n}\right]}{\left[1 - \dfrac{1}{(1+r)}\right]} = \dfrac{C}{r}\left[1 - \dfrac{1}{(1+r)^n}\right]$

which is the formula in equation [4.8]. Notice that if $n \to \infty$, then $1/(1+r)^n \to 0$ and the DPV formula reduces to $\text{DPV} = C/r$ which is the formula for a perpetuity. For the DPV of a **growing annuity** we have from equation [4.11]:

[4.70]     $P = xD_0 + x^2 D_0 + x^3 D_0$

where $x = (1 + g)/(1 + r)$. Using equation [4.66b] this simplifies to:

[4.71]
$$P = D_0 x[1 + x + x^2 + \ldots]$$

$$= \frac{D_0 x}{1 - x} = \frac{D_0(1 + g)}{(r - g)}$$

where we have used $(1 - x) = (r - g)/(1 + r)$.

## 4.6 SUMMARY

In this chapter we have developed some basic tools for analysing behaviour in financial markets. There are many nuances on the topics discussed which we have not had time to elaborate in detail, and in future chapters these omissions will be rectified. The main conclusions to emerge are as follows.

- **Discounting and compounding** can be undertaken using simple rates, discretely compounded rates or continuously compounded interest rates. As long as the user knows the 'type' of interest rate being used, she can apply the appropriate compounding or discounting formulae.
- Discounting and compounding are useful in determining the **'fair price' of equities and bonds**.
- In some markets participants quote **'simple' interest rates** (e.g. money markets) but these can always be converted to **'effective'** or **compound rates** or to **continuously compounded rates**.
- Some **mathematical operations** involving logarithms, the exponential functions and summing a geometric series are useful in simplifying equations used in finance.

## END OF CHAPTER EXERCISES

Q1    What is an annuity? Give some practical examples.

Q2    How does the holding period return (yield) on equity differ from that on a coupon paying bond?

Q3    Interest on some assets is calculated using 'simple' interest. Wouldn't you earn more if compound interest was used?

Q4    What is the present value (PV) of monthly payments of $50 for the next 12 months, if the payments are made *at the end of the month*. The discount rate is 1% per month.

Q5    Compute how much you would have in a savings account 2 years from now if you invest $500 today, given an interest rate of 5.25% compounded:

(a) annually
(b) semi-annually
(c) quarterly
(d) continuously

**Q6** The (simple) annual rate quoted 'on the street' is 8% and interest is paid quarterly. What is the effective annual rate?

**Q7** The effective annual yield is $R_1 = 12\%$ p.a. What periodic rate $R_2$ paid quarterly would give the same terminal value at the end of the year?

# APPENDIX 4.1 TABLES

## TABLE A4.1: Future value $(1 + r)^n$

| Years | 0.01 | 0.02 | 0.03 | 0.04 | 0.05 | 0.06 | 0.07 | 0.08 | 0.09 | 0.1 | 0.11 | 0.12 | 0.13 | 0.14 | 0.15 |
|---|---|---|---|---|---|---|---|---|---|---|---|---|---|---|---|
| 1 | 1.0100 | 1.0200 | 1.0300 | 1.0400 | 1.0500 | 1.0600 | 1.0700 | 1.0800 | 1.0900 | 1.1000 | 1.1100 | 1.1200 | 1.1300 | 1.1400 | 1.150 |
| 2 | 1.0201 | 1.0404 | 1.0609 | 1.0816 | 1.1025 | 1.1236 | 1.1449 | 1.1664 | 1.1881 | 1.2100 | 1.2321 | 1.2544 | 1.2769 | 1.2996 | 1.3225 |
| 3 | 1.0303 | 1.0612 | 1.0927 | 1.1249 | 1.1576 | 1.1910 | 1.2250 | 1.2597 | 1.2950 | 1.3310 | 1.3676 | 1.4049 | 1.4429 | 1.4815 | 1.5209 |
| 4 | 1.0406 | 1.0824 | 1.1255 | 1.1699 | 1.2155 | 1.2625 | 1.3108 | 1.3605 | 1.4116 | 1.4641 | 1.5181 | 1.5735 | 1.6305 | 1.6890 | 1.7490 |
| 5 | 1.0510 | 1.1041 | 1.1593 | 1.2167 | 1.2763 | 1.3382 | 1.4026 | 1.4693 | 1.5386 | 1.6105 | 1.6851 | 1.7623 | 1.8424 | 1.9254 | 2.0114 |
| 6 | 1.0615 | 1.1262 | 1.1941 | 1.2653 | 1.3401 | 1.4185 | 1.5007 | 1.5869 | 1.6771 | 1.7716 | 1.8704 | 1.9738 | 2.0820 | 2.1950 | 2.3131 |
| 7 | 1.0721 | 1.1487 | 1.2299 | 1.3159 | 1.4071 | 1.5036 | 1.6058 | 1.7138 | 1.8280 | 1.9487 | 2.0762 | 2.2107 | 2.3526 | 2.5023 | 2.6600 |
| 8 | 1.0829 | 1.1717 | 1.2668 | 1.3686 | 1.4775 | 1.5938 | 1.7182 | 1.8509 | 1.9926 | 2.1436 | 2.3045 | 2.4760 | 2.6584 | 2.8526 | 3.0590 |
| 9 | 1.0937 | 1.1951 | 1.3048 | 1.4233 | 1.5513 | 1.6895 | 1.8385 | 1.9990 | 2.1719 | 2.3579 | 2.5580 | 2.7731 | 3.0040 | 3.2519 | 3.5179 |
| 10 | 1.1046 | 1.2190 | 1.3439 | 1.4802 | 1.6289 | 1.7908 | 1.9672 | 2.1589 | 2.3674 | 2.5937 | 2.8394 | 3.1058 | 3.3946 | 3.7072 | 4.0456 |
| 11 | 1.1157 | 1.2434 | 1.3842 | 1.5395 | 1.7103 | 1.8983 | 2.1049 | 2.3316 | 2.5804 | 2.8531 | 3.1518 | 3.4785 | 3.8359 | 4.2262 | 4.6524 |
| 12 | 1.1268 | 1.2682 | 1.4258 | 1.6010 | 1.7959 | 2.0122 | 2.2522 | 2.5182 | 2.8127 | 3.1384 | 3.4985 | 3.8960 | 4.3345 | 4.8179 | 5.3503 |

*continued overleaf*

## TABLE A4.1: (Continued)

| Years | 0.01 | 0.02 | 0.03 | 0.04 | 0.05 | 0.06 | 0.07 | 0.08 | 0.09 | 0.1 | 0.11 | 0.12 | 0.13 | 0.14 | 0.15 |
|---|---|---|---|---|---|---|---|---|---|---|---|---|---|---|---|
| 13 | 1.1381 | 1.2936 | 1.4685 | 1.6651 | 1.8856 | 2.1329 | 2.4098 | 2.7196 | 3.0658 | 3.4523 | 3.8833 | 4.3635 | 4.8980 | 5.4924 | 6.1528 |
| 14 | 1.1495 | 1.3195 | 1.5126 | 1.7317 | 1.9799 | 2.2609 | 2.5785 | 2.9372 | 3.3417 | 3.7975 | 4.3104 | 4.8871 | 5.5348 | 6.2613 | 7.0757 |
| 15 | 1.1610 | 1.3459 | 1.5580 | 1.8009 | 2.0789 | 2.3966 | 2.7590 | 3.1722 | 3.6425 | 4.1772 | 4.7846 | 5.4736 | 6.2543 | 7.1379 | 8.1371 |
| 16 | 1.1726 | 1.3728 | 1.6047 | 1.8730 | 2.1829 | 2.5404 | 2.9522 | 3.4259 | 3.9703 | 4.5950 | 5.3109 | 6.1304 | 7.0673 | 8.1372 | 9.3576 |
| 17 | 1.1843 | 1.4002 | 1.6528 | 1.9479 | 2.2920 | 2.6928 | 3.1588 | 3.7000 | 4.3276 | 5.0545 | 5.8951 | 6.8660 | 7.9861 | 9.2765 | 10.7613 |
| 18 | 1.1961 | 1.4282 | 1.7024 | 2.0258 | 2.4066 | 2.8543 | 3.3799 | 3.9960 | 4.7171 | 5.5599 | 6.5436 | 7.6900 | 9.0243 | 10.5752 | 12.3755 |
| 19 | 1.2081 | 1.4568 | 1.7535 | 2.1068 | 2.5270 | 3.0256 | 3.6165 | 4.3157 | 5.1417 | 6.1159 | 7.2633 | 8.6128 | 10.1974 | 12.0557 | 14.2318 |
| 20 | 1.2202 | 1.4859 | 1.8061 | 2.1911 | 2.6533 | 3.2071 | 3.8697 | 4.6610 | 5.6044 | 6.7275 | 8.0623 | 9.6463 | 11.5231 | 13.7435 | 16.3665 |
| 25 | 1.2824 | 1.6406 | 2.0938 | 2.6658 | 3.3864 | 4.2919 | 5.4274 | 6.8485 | 8.6231 | 10.8347 | 13.5855 | 17.0001 | 21.2305 | 26.4619 | 32.9190 |
| 30 | 1.3478 | 1.8114 | 2.4273 | 3.2434 | 4.3219 | 5.7435 | 7.6123 | 10.0627 | 13.2677 | 17.4494 | 22.8923 | 29.9599 | 39.1159 | 50.9502 | 66.2118 |

# TABLE A4.2: Present value $1/(1 + r)^n$

| Years | 0.01 | 0.02 | 0.03 | 0.04 | 0.05 | 0.06 | 0.07 | 0.08 | 0.09 | 0.1 | 0.11 | 0.12 | 0.13 | 0.14 | 0.15 |
|---|---|---|---|---|---|---|---|---|---|---|---|---|---|---|---|
| 1 | 0.9901 | 0.9804 | 0.9709 | 0.9615 | 0.9524 | 0.9434 | 0.9346 | 0.9259 | 0.9174 | 0.9091 | 0.9009 | 0.8929 | 0.8850 | 0.8772 | 0.8696 |
| 2 | 0.9803 | 0.9612 | 0.9426 | 0.9246 | 0.9070 | 0.8900 | 0.8734 | 0.8573 | 0.8417 | 0.8264 | 0.8116 | 0.7972 | 0.7831 | 0.7695 | 0.7561 |
| 3 | 0.9706 | 0.9423 | 0.9151 | 0.8890 | 0.8638 | 0.8396 | 0.8163 | 0.7938 | 0.7722 | 0.7513 | 0.7312 | 0.7118 | 0.6931 | 0.6750 | 0.6575 |
| 4 | 0.9610 | 0.9238 | 0.8885 | 0.8548 | 0.8227 | 0.7921 | 0.7629 | 0.7350 | 0.7084 | 0.6830 | 0.6587 | 0.6355 | 0.6133 | 0.5921 | 0.5718 |
| 5 | 0.9515 | 0.9057 | 0.8626 | 0.8219 | 0.7835 | 0.7473 | 0.7130 | 0.6806 | 0.6499 | 0.6209 | 0.5935 | 0.5674 | 0.5428 | 0.5194 | 0.4972 |
| 6 | 0.9420 | 0.8880 | 0.8375 | 0.7903 | 0.7462 | 0.7050 | 0.6663 | 0.6302 | 0.5963 | 0.5645 | 0.5346 | 0.5066 | 0.4803 | 0.4556 | 0.4323 |
| 7 | 0.9327 | 0.8706 | 0.8131 | 0.7599 | 0.7107 | 0.6651 | 0.6227 | 0.5835 | 0.5470 | 0.5132 | 0.4817 | 0.4523 | 0.4251 | 0.3996 | 0.3759 |
| 8 | 0.9235 | 0.8535 | 0.7894 | 0.7307 | 0.6768 | 0.6274 | 0.5820 | 0.5403 | 0.5019 | 0.4665 | 0.4339 | 0.4039 | 0.3762 | 0.3506 | 0.3269 |
| 9 | 0.9143 | 0.8368 | 0.7664 | 0.7026 | 0.6446 | 0.5919 | 0.5439 | 0.5002 | 0.4604 | 0.4241 | 0.3909 | 0.3605 | 0.3329 | 0.3075 | 0.2843 |
| 10 | 0.9053 | 0.8203 | 0.7441 | 0.6756 | 0.6139 | 0.5584 | 0.5083 | 0.4632 | 0.4224 | 0.3855 | 0.3522 | 0.3220 | 0.2946 | 0.2697 | 0.2472 |
| 11 | 0.8963 | 0.8043 | 0.7224 | 0.6496 | 0.5847 | 0.5268 | 0.4751 | 0.4289 | 0.3875 | 0.3505 | 0.3173 | 0.2875 | 0.2607 | 0.2366 | 0.2149 |
| 12 | 0.8874 | 0.7885 | 0.7014 | 0.6246 | 0.5568 | 0.4970 | 0.4440 | 0.3971 | 0.3555 | 0.3186 | 0.2858 | 0.2567 | 0.2307 | 0.2076 | 0.1869 |

*continued overleaf*

## TABLE A4.2: (*Continued*)

| Years | 0.01 | 0.02 | 0.03 | 0.04 | 0.05 | 0.06 | 0.07 | 0.08 | 0.09 | 0.1 | 0.11 | 0.12 | 0.13 | 0.14 | 0.15 |
|---|---|---|---|---|---|---|---|---|---|---|---|---|---|---|---|
| 13 | 0.8787 | 0.7730 | 0.6810 | 0.6006 | 0.5303 | 0.4688 | 0.4150 | 0.3677 | 0.3262 | 0.2897 | 0.2575 | 0.2292 | 0.2042 | 0.1821 | 0.1625 |
| 14 | 0.8700 | 0.7579 | 0.6611 | 0.5775 | 0.5051 | 0.4423 | 0.3878 | 0.3405 | 0.2992 | 0.2633 | 0.2320 | 0.2046 | 0.1807 | 0.1597 | 0.1413 |
| 15 | 0.8613 | 0.7430 | 0.6419 | 0.5553 | 0.4810 | 0.4173 | 0.3624 | 0.3152 | 0.2745 | 0.2394 | 0.2090 | 0.1827 | 0.1599 | 0.1401 | 0.1229 |
| 16 | 0.8528 | 0.7284 | 0.6232 | 0.5339 | 0.4581 | 0.3936 | 0.3387 | 0.2919 | 0.2519 | 0.2176 | 0.1883 | 0.1631 | 0.1415 | 0.1229 | 0.1069 |
| 17 | 0.8444 | 0.7142 | 0.6050 | 0.5134 | 0.4363 | 0.3714 | 0.3166 | 0.2703 | 0.2311 | 0.1978 | 0.1696 | 0.1456 | 0.1252 | 0.1078 | 0.0929 |
| 18 | 0.8360 | 0.7002 | 0.5874 | 0.4936 | 0.4155 | 0.3503 | 0.2959 | 0.2502 | 0.2120 | 0.1799 | 0.1528 | 0.1300 | 0.1108 | 0.0946 | 0.0808 |
| 19 | 0.8277 | 0.6864 | 0.5703 | 0.4746 | 0.3957 | 0.3305 | 0.2765 | 0.2317 | 0.1945 | 0.1635 | 0.1377 | 0.1161 | 0.0981 | 0.0829 | 0.0703 |
| 20 | 0.8195 | 0.6730 | 0.5537 | 0.4564 | 0.3769 | 0.3118 | 0.2584 | 0.2145 | 0.1784 | 0.1486 | 0.1240 | 0.1037 | 0.0868 | 0.0728 | 0.0611 |
| 25 | 0.7798 | 0.6095 | 0.4776 | 0.3751 | 0.2953 | 0.2330 | 0.1842 | 0.1460 | 0.1160 | 0.0923 | 0.0736 | 0.0588 | 0.0471 | 0.0378 | 0.0304 |
| 30 | 0.7419 | 0.5521 | 0.4120 | 0.3083 | 0.2314 | 0.1741 | 0.1314 | 0.0994 | 0.0754 | 0.0573 | 0.0437 | 0.0334 | 0.0256 | 0.0196 | 0.0151 |

## TABLE A4.3: Present Value Annuity $(1/r)[1 - 1/(1 + r)^n]$

| Years | 0.01 | 0.02 | 0.03 | 0.04 | 0.05 | 0.06 | 0.07 | 0.08 | 0.09 | 0.1 | 0.11 | 0.12 | 0.13 | 0.14 | 0.15 |
|---|---|---|---|---|---|---|---|---|---|---|---|---|---|---|---|
| 1 | 0.9901 | 0.9804 | 0.9709 | 0.9615 | 0.9524 | 0.9434 | 0.9346 | 0.9259 | 0.9174 | 0.9091 | 0.9009 | 0.8929 | 0.8850 | 0.8772 | 0.8696 |
| 2 | 1.9704 | 1.9416 | 1.9135 | 1.8861 | 1.8594 | 1.8334 | 1.8080 | 1.7833 | 1.7591 | 1.7355 | 1.7125 | 1.6901 | 1.6681 | 1.6467 | 1.6257 |
| 3 | 2.9410 | 2.8839 | 2.8286 | 2.7751 | 2.7232 | 2.6730 | 2.6243 | 2.5771 | 2.5313 | 2.4869 | 2.4437 | 2.4018 | 2.3612 | 2.3216 | 2.2832 |
| 4 | 3.9020 | 3.8077 | 3.7171 | 3.6299 | 3.5460 | 3.4651 | 3.3872 | 3.3121 | 3.2397 | 3.1699 | 3.1024 | 3.0373 | 2.9745 | 2.9137 | 2.8550 |
| 5 | 4.8534 | 4.7135 | 4.5797 | 4.4518 | 4.3295 | 4.2124 | 4.1002 | 3.9927 | 3.8897 | 3.7908 | 3.6959 | 3.6048 | 3.5172 | 3.4331 | 3.3522 |
| 6 | 5.7955 | 5.6014 | 5.4172 | 5.2421 | 5.0757 | 4.9173 | 4.7665 | 4.6229 | 4.4859 | 4.3553 | 4.2305 | 4.1114 | 3.9975 | 3.8887 | 3.7845 |
| 7 | 6.7282 | 6.4720 | 6.2303 | 6.0021 | 5.7864 | 5.5824 | 5.3893 | 5.2064 | 5.0330 | 4.8684 | 4.7122 | 4.5638 | 4.4226 | 4.2883 | 4.1604 |
| 8 | 7.6517 | 7.3255 | 7.0197 | 6.7327 | 6.4632 | 6.2098 | 5.9713 | 5.7466 | 5.5348 | 5.3349 | 5.1461 | 4.9676 | 4.7988 | 4.6389 | 4.4873 |
| 9 | 8.5660 | 8.1622 | 7.7861 | 7.4353 | 7.1078 | 6.8017 | 6.5152 | 6.2469 | 5.9952 | 5.7590 | 5.5370 | 5.3282 | 5.1317 | 4.9464 | 4.7716 |
| 10 | 9.4713 | 8.9826 | 8.5302 | 8.1109 | 7.7217 | 7.3601 | 7.0236 | 6.7101 | 6.4177 | 6.1446 | 5.8892 | 5.6502 | 5.4262 | 5.2161 | 5.0188 |
| 11 | 10.3676 | 9.7868 | 9.2526 | 8.7605 | 8.3064 | 7.8869 | 7.4987 | 7.1390 | 6.8052 | 6.4951 | 6.2065 | 5.9377 | 5.6869 | 5.4527 | 5.2337 |
| 12 | 11.2551 | 10.5753 | 9.9540 | 9.3851 | 8.8633 | 8.3838 | 7.9427 | 7.5361 | 7.1607 | 6.8137 | 6.4924 | 6.1944 | 5.9176 | 5.6603 | 5.4206 |

*continued overleaf*

## TABLE A4.3: (*Continued*)

| Years | 0.01 | 0.02 | 0.03 | 0.04 | 0.05 | 0.06 | 0.07 | 0.08 | 0.09 | 0.1 | 0.11 | 0.12 | 0.13 | 0.14 | 0.15 |
|---|---|---|---|---|---|---|---|---|---|---|---|---|---|---|---|
| 13 | 12.1337 | 11.3484 | 10.6350 | 9.9856 | 9.3936 | 8.8527 | 8.3577 | 7.9038 | 7.4869 | 7.1034 | 6.7499 | 6.4235 | 6.1218 | 5.8424 | 5.5831 |
| 14 | 13.0037 | 12.1062 | 11.2961 | 10.5631 | 9.8986 | 9.2950 | 8.7455 | 8.2442 | 7.7862 | 7.3667 | 6.9819 | 6.6282 | 6.3025 | 6.0021 | 5.7245 |
| 15 | 13.8651 | 12.8493 | 11.9379 | 11.1184 | 10.3797 | 9.7122 | 9.1079 | 8.5595 | 8.0607 | 7.6061 | 7.1909 | 6.8109 | 6.4624 | 6.1422 | 5.8474 |
| 16 | 14.7179 | 13.5777 | 12.5611 | 11.6523 | 10.8378 | 10.1059 | 9.4466 | 8.8514 | 8.3126 | 7.8237 | 7.3792 | 6.9740 | 6.6039 | 6.2651 | 5.9542 |
| 17 | 15.5623 | 14.2919 | 13.1661 | 12.1657 | 11.2741 | 10.4773 | 9.7632 | 9.1216 | 8.5436 | 8.0216 | 7.5488 | 7.1196 | 6.7291 | 6.3729 | 6.0472 |
| 18 | 16.3983 | 14.9920 | 13.7535 | 12.6593 | 11.6896 | 10.8276 | 10.0591 | 9.3719 | 8.7556 | 8.2014 | 7.7016 | 7.2497 | 6.8399 | 6.4674 | 6.1280 |
| 19 | 17.2260 | 15.6785 | 14.3238 | 13.1339 | 12.0853 | 11.1581 | 10.3356 | 9.6036 | 8.9501 | 8.3649 | 7.8393 | 7.3658 | 6.9380 | 6.5504 | 6.1982 |
| 20 | 18.0456 | 16.3514 | 14.8775 | 13.5903 | 12.4622 | 11.4699 | 10.5940 | 9.8181 | 9.1285 | 8.5136 | 7.9633 | 7.4694 | 7.0248 | 6.6231 | 6.2593 |
| 25 | 22.0232 | 19.5235 | 17.4131 | 15.6221 | 14.0939 | 12.7834 | 11.6536 | 10.6748 | 9.8226 | 9.0770 | 8.4217 | 7.8431 | 7.3300 | 6.8729 | 6.4641 |
| 30 | 25.8077 | 22.3965 | 19.6004 | 17.2920 | 15.3725 | 13.7648 | 12.4090 | 11.2578 | 10.2737 | 9.4269 | 8.6938 | 8.0552 | 7.4957 | 7.0027 | 6.5660 |

# Basic Statistics

In this section we introduce the basic ideas of random variables, probability distributions and some elementary statistical concepts used in finance for classifying data. Finance is the study of asset prices and asset values, which are often inherently stochastic or random, that is we cannot predict with certainty what their values will be tomorrow. We can only make probabilistic statements.

Broadly speaking, in statistics we try and establish some mathematical properties of theoretical models (e.g. for normally distributed variables) in terms of their 'true' or **population parameters**—that is, some constant values like the population mean and standard deviation. We cannot observe these population parameters since we do not have access to *all* possible data. Therefore we take a **sample** (subset) of the data (e.g. monthly stock returns between January 1994 and January 2000) and calculate sample statistics. We then see if these **sample statistics** are a 'good' estimate of the underlying 'true' population parameters and if not, 'how close' our sample statistics are to the 'true' population parameters. In this way we can assess our degree of ignorance or, equivalently, our degree of knowledge about 'important' financial concepts, such as the mean return and risk of a portfolio of assets, or the risk of bankruptcy of a firm or the impact on the equity price caused by the sale of a large block of shares. The link between the unobservable 'true' population parameters and their sample estimates requires formal statistical proofs and we merely present these results, rather than formally deriving them.

# 5.1 CALCULATING THE RATE OF RETURN

Very often 'raw' data consists of the *prices* of financial instruments (e.g. stock, bonds, spot FX prices) and price indices, such as the FTSE100 and the S&P500. However, investors and analysts usually use *rates of return* to analyse and compare financial assets. Figures 5.1 and 5.2 show the FTSE100 index and its monthly rate of return, respectively from February 1990 to August 2000. We can see that the FTSE price index rises over time while the *monthly returns* on the FTSE are very volatile, crossing the zero return 'line' frequently. The FTSE price index clearly has a mean value which increases through time and also its variance appears to alter through time, becoming more volatile after 1997. This property of having a time varying population mean or variance is known as **non-stationarity** (of course we are here inferring population parameters from a short sample of data, which can be dangerous!). In contrast the stock return (Figure 5.2) appears to have a constant mean and constant volatility and is said to be a **stationary series**. A stationary series because it frequently crosses its mean value (Figure 5.2) is said to be **mean reverting**, while a non-stationary series (Figure 5.1) rarely returns to its initial value.

Asset returns (e.g. for stocks, bonds, spot FX) are defined as the percentage change in the value of the asset price over a particular time horizon (i.e. day, week, month, year) plus any cash flows accruing to the asset (e.g. dividend payments). We can distinguish between the

**FIGURE 5.1: FTSE100 price index (January 1990–August 2000)**

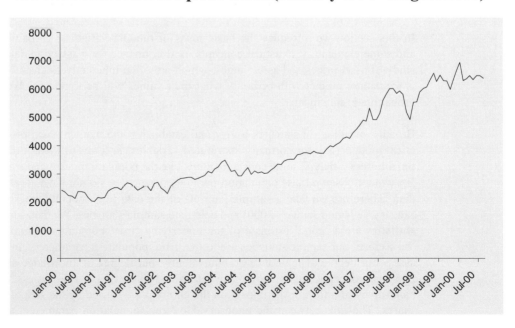

## FIGURE 5.2: Monthly returns on FTSE100 (February 1990–August 2000)

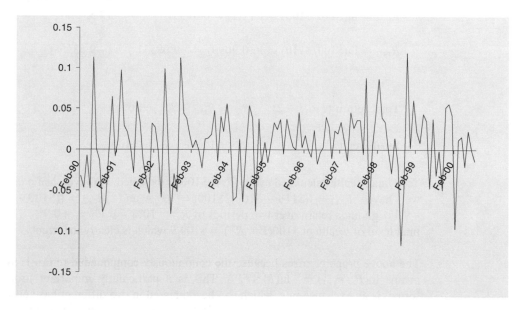

arithmetic rate of return and the continuously compounded rate of return. The **arithmetic rate of return** can be calculated as:

[5.1]
$$R_t = (P_t + D_{t-1} - P_{t-1})/P_{t-1} = (P_t - P_{t-1})/P_{t-1} + D_{t-1}/P_{t-1}$$

where $P_t$ = price at end of period $t$ and $D_{t-1}$ = dividends paid between $t-1$ and $t$. The 'return' therefore equals the capital gain plus the dividend–price ratio $(D_{t-1}/P_{t-1})$.

The **continuously compounded rate of return** is defined in terms of the logarithms of the price ratios:

[5.2]
$$R_t = \ln[(P_t + D_{t-1})/P_{t-1}] = \ln[P_t/P_{t-1} + D_{t-1}/P_{t-1}]$$

where, $P_t$ is the price of the asset at time $t$, $D_{t-1}$ is the dividend (or any other income) payments between $t-1$ and $t$.

There are several advantages in using the continuously compounded rate of return. Firstly, it does not allow negative *prices*. This is most easily seen by setting $D_t = 0$ and hence from equation [5.2], $P_t = P_{t-1}\exp(R_t)$. Now even if the return $R_t$ has a large negative value '$\exp(R_t)$' is always positive and therefore so is $P_t$. This property does not apply to equation [5.1] which can give negative prices for sufficiently large negative values of $R_t$.

Secondly, the continuous rate of return is 'additive' and gives the correct value for the final value of your wealth, after investing in the asset. Again for simplification set $D_t = 0$ and suppose the asset (e.g. equity) has prices $P_t = \$100$, $P_{t+1} = \$110$, $P_{t+2} = \$100$. If you hold one share at $t$ then clearly your wealth is unchanged at $t + 2$. The continuously compounded returns are:

$$R_{t+1} = \ln(\$110/\$100) = \ln(1.1) = 0.09531 \qquad (9.531\%)$$

$$R_{t+2} = \ln(\$100/\$110) = \ln(0.9090) = -0.09531 \qquad (-9.531\%)$$

Total return ($t$ to $t + 2$):    $R^* = R_{t+1} + R_{t+2} = 0\%$

Final wealth                      $= 100(1 + R^*) = 100$

Your final wealth calculated using $R^*$ is \$100 as expected. However, using arithmetic returns we have $R_{t+1} = [(\$110 - \$100)/\$100] = 10\%$ and $R_{t+2} = [(\$100 - \$110)/\$110] = -9.1\%$ giving a return over two periods of $R^* = 10\% - 9.1\% = +0.9\%$. This would give a final level of wealth of $\$100(1 + R^*) = \$100.9$ which is clearly incorrect.

The above property arises because the continuously compounded return is symmetric. That means $\ln(P_t/P_{t-1}) = -\ln(P_{t-1}/P_t)$. This is a particularly important property when the 'price' is an exchange rate, which can be expressed in two different base currencies (i.e. US dollars per Euro or Euros per US dollar). By having 'symmetric' returns our analysis of 'returns' is invariant to which currency we choose to measure the exchange rate.

If price changes are small (e.g. daily or monthly) then returns calculated using either the arithmetic or continuously compounded method give very similar values.

# 5.2 DESCRIBING DATA

Every day, analysts access a vast amount of financial data which are updated frequently. Most asset prices (e.g. for spot FX, bonds, stocks) change second-by-second. Other types of data, for example economic data (e.g. GDP, unemployment, inflation) are produced monthly or quarterly, while full company accounts are usually published annually.

To handle the flow of data effectively, it is important to summarise the data without losing too many of its individual characteristics. The simplest way to obtain an 'overview' of the data is to plot the data (e.g. time series graphs, scatter plots). Another way to summarise a large data series is to 'group' the individual observations (e.g. daily stock returns) into a frequency distribution. Another commonly used technique is the calculation of summary statistics (e.g. mean, standard deviation, correlation). Summary statistics can be calculated for grouped data as well as ungrouped data (i.e. using the individual observations). The definitions of these summary statistics are the same whether grouped or ungrouped data is used, but you would not expect to obtain exactly the same results, as some of the characteristics of the individual observations will have been lost when grouping the data. We discuss these concepts below.

## FREQUENCY DISTRIBUTION AND PERCENTILES

A useful way of analysing data sets is to construct an empirical frequency distribution. We can then 'see' whether this empirical distribution is similar to any of the standard distributions (e.g. normal, Poisson). In order to summarise a 'long' data series, we can group the observations into similar bands (e.g. number of company defaults per year between 0 and 10, 10 and 20, etc.). The **frequency distribution** is then a 'graph' of the frequency with which the data 'falls' into these bands. Table 5.1 shows the (absolute) frequency with which particular returns are observed for the 127 monthly returns of General Motors stocks from February 1990 to August 2000. From Table 5.1 we see that 32 monthly returns were between 0% and 5%, but only one of the monthly returns was less than −20%. The relative frequencies are simply:

$$\text{Relative frequency} = \frac{\text{absolute frequency}}{\text{total number of events}}$$

The total number of returns in all the 'bands' is 127. Hence for example the relative frequency for returns between 0% and 5% is 25.20% ($= 32/127$). The **cumulative frequency** as the name suggests gives the frequency with which returns lie over a particular

## TABLE 5.1: Frequency distributions of monthly returns: General Motors

| 'Bands' | Absolute frequency | Cumulative frequency | Relative frequency | Cumulative relative frequency |
|---|---|---|---|---|
| **More than 20%** | 4 | 127 | 0.0315 | 1 |
| **15% to under 20%** | 11 | 123 | 0.0866 | 0.9685 |
| **10% to under 15%** | 20 | 112 | 0.1575 | 0.8819 |
| **5% to under 10%** | 27 | 92 | 0.2126 | 0.7244 |
| **0% to under 5%** | 32 | 65 | 0.2520 | 0.5118 |
| **−5% to under 0%** | 23 | 33 | 0.1811 | 0.2598 |
| **−10% to under −5%** | 4 | 10 | 0.0315 | 0.0787 |
| **−15% to under −10%** | 4 | 6 | 0.0315 | 0.0472 |
| **−20% to under −15%** | 1 | 2 | 0.0079 | 0.0157 |
| **Less than −20%** | 1 | 1 | 0.0079 | 0.0079 |
| **Total frequency** | 127 | | 1 | |

Note: *Cumulative frequency* is the frequency up to the upper bound of the specific band. That is it includes the frequency of the current band and all previous bands. The *relative frequency* equals the 'absolute frequency/total frequency' *range* (starting from the smallest). For example (Table 5.1, column 4) the relative frequency with which returns fall between 'less than 20%' and '0% to 5%' is:

Cumulative frequency ('less than 20%' to '0% to 5%')

$$= 0.0079 + 0.0079 + 0.0315 + 0.0315 + 0.1811 + 0.2520 = \mathbf{0.5119}$$

Of course, the cumulative frequency for *all* the returns (i.e. from their most negative value) to their largest positive value, must be unity. An empirical frequency distribution is also usually referred to as a **histogram**. A histogram of the frequency distribution for the returns on General Motors shares is shown in Figure 5.3.

**Percentiles** determine the cut-off point of a data series for which, if all observations are arranged in ascending order, $q\%$ of the data points are below that cut-off point whereas $1 - q\%$ are above. The **median** is a special percentile—namely the 50th percentile. For example, from the final column of Table 5.1 we see that 0.0472 (i.e. 4.72%) of all returns fell 15% or more. Hence the 5th percentile for returns is (close to) *minus* 15%. Other percentiles for monthly stock returns on General Motors can be calculated from Table 5.1 and we report these in Table 5.2.

## SUMMARY STATISTICS

Summary statistics capture the general properties of the shape of a probability distribution. Generally they are called 'moments'. The mean or expected value is the 'first moment' and measures the central tendency of a data series. The variance (or standard deviation) is the

---

## FIGURE 5.3: Histogram of monthly General Motors returns

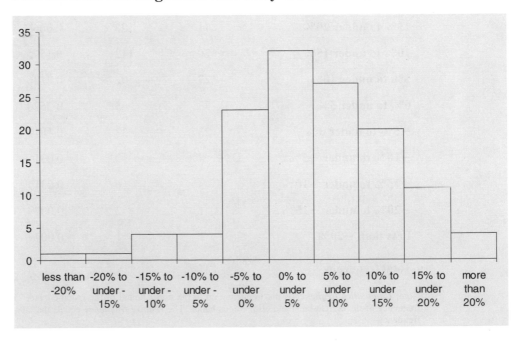

**TABLE 5.2: Percentiles on monthly returns of General Motors shares**

| Percentile | Value |
|---|---|
| 1 | −18.43% |
| 5 | −12.76% |
| 10 | −8.53% |
| 50 | −0.27% |
| 95 | 13.35% |
| 99 | 18.03% |

'second moment' and measures the dispersion of the data points around the mean. A measure of the symmetry (or non-symmetry) of the distribution is known as the skewness which is the 'third moment'. Finally, the degree of 'peakness' of the distribution is measured by the kurtosis (i.e. 'fourth moment'). In addition to these summary statistics for *individual* random variables, we are also interested in the relationship or co-movements of two (or more) variables. This can be measured by their covariance or correlation coefficient. A random variable is usually assumed to have population mean, variance, skewness measures, etc. that are all constant (over time). Sample statistics are then used to provide *estimates* of these 'population parameters'.

The arithmetic mean is the most widely used statistical measure of central tendency of a data series. (Other measures of central tendency include the geometric mean, the median and the mode.) Suppose we have a data series of $n$ monthly stock returns $X_i$ ($i = 1, 2, \ldots, n$) then the **sample (arithmetic) mean** is:

[5.3]
$$\bar{X} = \frac{\sum_{i=1}^{n} X_i}{n}$$

and the **sample (geometric) mean** is:

[5.4]
$$\bar{X} = \sqrt[n]{X_1 X_2 \cdots X_n}$$

The **median** is that return which lies in the 'middle' position when the returns are ordered by size from lowest to highest. For example, given returns {−3%, −3%, −2%, +2%, +1%} the median is −2%. The **mode** is the observation that occurs most often and given the above returns is −3%.

The **sample standard deviation** measures the spread around the mean and is calculated as:

[5.5]
$$\hat{\sigma} = \sqrt{\frac{\sum_{i=1}^{n}(X_i - \bar{X})^2}{n - 1}}$$

In equation [5.5] we divide by $(n - 1)$ rather than the sample size $n$, in order to get an unbiased estimate of the true population parameter $\sigma$. (In mathematical terms, unbiascdncss means that our values of $\hat{\sigma}$ are centered around the 'true' population value, $\sigma$.) The standard deviation has the same units as the $X_i$ (e.g. % or $) and is therefore a more useful measure than the sample variance, $\hat{\sigma}^2$. Because the 'units' are the same, the standard deviation can be directly compared to the mean. For example, a mean return of $\bar{X} = 10\%$ and a standard deviation of $\hat{\sigma} = 2\%$ implies we have a fairly accurate estimate of the 'true' population mean.

**Skewness** is a measure of the symmetry (or deviation from symmetry) of the distribution of the data. It is the 'third moment' of the (frequency) distribution and is calculated as:

[5.6]
$$\text{Skew} = \frac{n}{(n - 1)(n - 2)}\sum_{i=1}^{n}\left(\frac{X_i - \bar{X}}{\hat{\sigma}}\right)^3$$

If the distribution of returns were normal, then 'skew' would be zero. If 'skew' is positive then the frequency distribution of returns has a long 'right tail'. The 'fourth moment', **kurtosis**, measures the degree of 'peakness' and is given by:

[5.7]
$$\text{Kurt} = \left(\frac{n(n + 1)}{(n - 1)(n - 2)(n - 3)}\sum_{i=1}^{n}\left(\frac{X_i - \bar{X}}{\hat{\sigma}}\right)^4\right) - \frac{3(n - 1)^2}{(n - 2)(n - 3)}$$

The normal distribution has Kurt = 3. If the data are more peaked than in the normal distribution then Kurt > 3 (known as leptokurtic), whereas a 'lower peak' has Kurt < 3 and is known as platykurtic. As well as the above, there are other summary statistics which also measure the variability in the data set (i.e. range, modified range, absolute deviation, etc.), but these need not concern us.

## COVARIANCE AND CORRELATION COEFFICIENT

The degree of association between two variables $X$ and $Y$ can be measured using the **sample correlation coefficient**:

[5.8]
$$\hat{\rho} = \hat{\sigma}_{xy}/\hat{\sigma}_x\hat{\sigma}_y$$

where

$$\hat{\sigma}_{xy} = \frac{\sum_{i=1}^{n}(X_i - \overline{X})(Y_i - \overline{Y})}{n-1}$$

and $\hat{\sigma}_x$ is the sample standard deviation of $X$, $\hat{\sigma}_y$ is the sample standard deviation of $Y$. $\hat{\rho}$ is the sample estimate of the 'true' population correlation coefficient $\rho$ which has a similar formula to equation [5.8] (see equations [5.11] and [5.12]). $\hat{\sigma}_{xy}$ is known as the **covariance** between $X$ and $Y$ and can be positive, negative or zero. Unfortunately the value of $\hat{\sigma}_{xy}$ depends on the units used to measure $X$ and $Y$ and therefore the covariance for *different pairs* of variables cannot be meaningfully compared. This is why we use the correlation coefficient $\hat{\rho}$ which lies between $-1$ and $+1$, so that:

## TABLE 5.3: Summary statistics

| | Rate of return | | |
|---|---|---|---|
| | General Motors | Microsoft | S&P500 |
| **Mean** | 0.46 | 3.18 | 1.11 |
| **Standard deviation** | 8.60 | 9.82 | 3.67 |
| **Variance** | 73.94 | 96.46 | 13.47 |
| **Maximum value** | 26.61 | 28.17 | 11.95 |
| **Minimum value** | −28.35 | −21.31 | −11.23 |
| | **Correlation matrix** | | |
| **General Motors** | 1 | | |
| **Microsoft** | 0.1003 | 1 | |
| **S&P500** | 0.4350 | 0.4938 | 1 |
| | **Covariance matrix** | | |
| **General Motors** | 73.94 | | |
| **Microsoft** | 8.47 | 96.46 | |
| **S&P500** | 13.73 | 17.80 | 13.47 |

Note: Returns are monthly and measured as percentages over the sample period February 1990 to August 2000

$$\hat{\rho} = +1 \qquad X \text{ and } Y \text{ are perfectly positively related}$$

$$\hat{\rho} = -1 \qquad X \text{ and } Y \text{ are perfectly negatively related}$$

$$\hat{\rho} = 0 \qquad X \text{ and } Y \text{ are not (linearly) related}$$

Thus for instance, if $\hat{\rho} = +0.70$ between the returns on British Airways (BA) stock and the FTSE100 index, this implies that a positive return on BA is accompanied, about 70% of the time, by a positive return on the FTSE100 market index. Note that there is no causation implied by the correlation coefficient. Causation could be from $X$ to $Y$, or vice versa or in both directions. It might also be the case that a positive correlation between $X$ and $Y$ is due to both being influenced in the same direction by a third variable $Z$ (e.g. a fall in interest rates might cause both BA stock returns and the return on the FTSE100 to increase). To establish causality we require some kind of a 'model' or view of the world. Statistics can never establish causality, only associations between variables.

Table 5.3 shows summary statistics for the rate of return on Microsoft and General Motors shares, as well as the return on the S&P500 over the sample period of February 1990 to August 2000. General Motors has a lower mean return than Microsoft but the latter has a higher standard deviation. Microsoft's return and General Motors' returns have a very low correlation of 0.10 but both are moderately highly correlated with the S&P500.

These sample statistics provide the basic inputs when calculating the optimal holdings of each of these shares, as we shall see in Chapters 10 and 18.

# 5.3 PROBABILITY, RANDOM VARIABLES AND EXPECTATIONS

Many investment decisions have to be made under uncertainty. In order to quantify this uncertainty we can use probabilities and probability distributions. This enables us to say whether a particular event will or will not occur with a certain likelihood (probability).

The idea of random events and probabilities is fairly well understood for simple problems. For example, a single toss of a six-sided die has a probability of $1/6$ (0.1666) of yielding a single integer $X_i$ between 1 and 6. The probability distribution is uniform (see Figure 5.4) and has only six possible outcomes (also known as 'events'), and hence it is a discrete probability distribution and the variable $X_i$ is a **discrete random variable**. In contrast, we can also have a **continuous random variable**. Continuous random variables can take *any* value (over a specific range). Most financial time series are continuous random variables. The best known continuous probability distribution is the normal distribution which is symmetric and bell-shaped (see Section 5.5). Other continuous probability distributions are the Student's $t$-distribution, the lognormal distribution, the $F$-distribution and the 'chi-squared' $\chi^2$-distribution.

The **uniform distribution** gives an equal probability of drawing any number between zero and one and provides a 'building block' for other distributions and statistical procedures. Examples of discrete probability distributions are the binomial and Poisson distributions.

## FIGURE 5.4: Probabilities of throwing a die

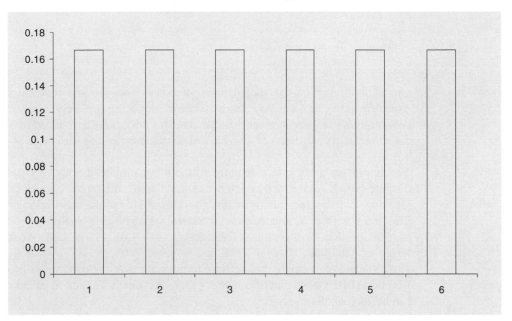

The binomial distribution is used in option pricing theory, whereas the Poisson distribution finds applications in the insurance industry (e.g. probability of car accidents or property damage by fire) as well as in determining the number of defaults (bankruptcies) in a group of firms. Below we discuss the binomial, Poisson and normal distributions in more detail, but first we need to look at the population parameters such as expected value, variance and covariance.

## EXPECTATIONS: MEAN AND DISPERSION

Useful summary statistics for theoretical probability distributions are the expected value and the variance (or standard deviation).

Suppose you threw a die a large number of times and received $X_i$ dollars depending on what number came up. The 'number' on the die is a **discrete random variable**, as is the amount of dollars you win on average, if you throw the die a number of times. This amount is given by the (theoretical) expected value $\mu$ (or $EX$):

[5.9] $$\mu \equiv EX = \sum_{i=1}^{6} p_i X_i$$

where $p_i$ denotes the probability for a particular outcome or 'event' (here $1/6$)
$X_i$ denotes the possible payoffs from these 'events' (here 1, 2, 3, 4, 5 or 6 dollars).

We can also measure the 'dispersion' of our winnings. Each throw gives a deviation from the mean of $(X_i - EX)$, with probability $p_i \, (= 1/6)$. A measure of the average dispersion is given by the (population) **standard deviation**:

[5.10]
$$\sigma = \sqrt{\sum_{i=1}^{6} p_i(X_i - EX)^2}$$

and $\sigma^2$ is known as the (population) **variance**. You can see that the formulae for the expected value and the population standard deviation are very similar to their sample counterparts (i.e. sample mean, sample standard deviation) introduced in Section 5.2. Table 5.4 shows some properties of discrete and continuous random variables.

The return on a stock is a random variable but, unlike the above outcomes, which are discrete (i.e. $X_i$ can only take integer values 1 to 6), the return on a stock can in principle take any value between minus infinity (but this would require short selling) and plus infinity. The stock return is a continuous random variable. The probability of observing any particular value for the return, for example $X = 1.0120\%$ is zero. We can only think in terms of the probability of obtaining a value between say $X_1 = 1.0119\%$ and $X_2 = 1.0121\%$ and to calculate this we have to integrate over the continuous **probability density function (PDF)**. Note that the range $X_1$ to $X_2$ for which we want to calculate the probability can be very small or very large.

## TWO OR MORE RANDOM VARIABLES

So far we have only looked at the population parameters for a single random variable. However, in the real world we have many random variables which may be related to each other. Therefore, it is useful to look at some additional population summary statistics which describe the relationship between two or more random variables. In the whole population of stock return data, if the return on one stock goes up does the return on the other stock go up as well, or does it go down or is it unaffected? The 'true' degree of association between the return on the two stocks (in the whole population) is known as the population **covariance** or

## TABLE 5.4: Properties of random variables

|  | Discrete | Continuous |
|---|---|---|
|  | $p_i \geqslant 0$ <br> $\sum p_i = 1$ | $\int_{-\infty}^{\infty} f(X)\mathrm{d}x = 1$ |
| **Mean (first moment)** | $\mu = EX = \sum p_i x_i$ | $\mu = EX = \int_{-\infty}^{\infty} Xf(X)\mathrm{d}x$ |
| **Variance (second moment)** | $\sigma \equiv \mathrm{Var}(X) = \sum p_i(X_i - EX)$ <br> $= \sum p_i X_i^2 - (EX)^2$ | $\sigma \equiv \mathrm{Var}(X) = \int_{-\infty}^{\infty} x^2 f(X)\mathrm{d}x$ |

**correlation coefficient**. If the 'true' correlation between two stock returns is positive, then each time the return on $X$ is positive, the return on $Y$ will also *tend to be* positive. The correlation coefficient ranges between $-1$ and $+1$. The formula for the **population covariance** is:

[5.11]  $$\mathrm{Cov}(X,\ Y) \equiv \sigma_{xy} = \sum_i \sum_j p_{ij}(X_i - EX)(Y_j - EY)$$

where $p_{ij}$ denotes the joint probability that outcomes $X_i$ and $Y_j$ occur simultaneously.

The **population correlation coefficient** is calculated as:

[5.12]  $$\rho_{xy} = \sigma_{xy}/\sigma_x \sigma_y$$

Clearly these definitions are similar to their sample counterparts, but they use the 'true' or population parameters $p_{ij}$, $EX$ and $EY$.

Another important concept in finance is the calculation of the expected value and variance of a *linear combination* of two or more random variables. For example this is used extensively in modern portfolio theory (see Chapter 10). The variance (or standard deviation) is often taken as a measure of the riskiness of a *portfolio* of assets since it measures the dispersion of outcomes from the mean. Suppose we form a *portfolio* consisting of $100, held in two stocks $X$ and $Y$. We allocate our funds as follows, $w_x = \frac{3}{4}$ (i.e. $75) in $X$ and $w_y = \frac{1}{4}$ (i.e. $25) in $Y$. Note that the weights $w_x$ and $w_y$ sum to 1. The actual return on our two-asset portfolio $R_p$ is a linear combination of the return on the individual assets:

[5.13a]  $$R_p = w_x R_x + w_y R_y$$

and the *expected* return is simply:

[5.13b]  $$ER_p = w_x ER_x + w_y ER_y$$

The variance and standard deviation of the portfolio can be shown to be:

[5.14a]  $$\sigma_{R_p}^2 = \mathrm{Var}(R_p) = w_x^2 \sigma_x^2 + w_y^2 \sigma_y^2 + 2 w_x w_y \rho \sigma_x \sigma_y$$

and

[5.14b]  $$\sigma_{R_p} = \mathrm{Std.\ dev}(R_p) = \sqrt{w_x^2 \sigma_x^2 + w_y^2 \sigma_y^2 + 2 w_x w_y \rho \sigma_x \sigma_y}$$

From equations [5.14a] and [5.14b] you can see that the variance or standard deviation is a (non-linear) weighted average of the individual variances $\sigma_i$ and the correlation coefficient $\rho$ between the two asset returns. As mentioned earlier, equations [5.13] and [5.14] form the basis for modern portfolio theory, which deals with optimal asset allocation, either across domestic assets or across all assets (i.e. including international assets). The above formulae are easily generalised to $n$ assets. It is probably useful here to state the general formulae using matrix notation. The formula for the expected portfolio return is:

[5.15]      $ER_p = \mathbf{w}'\mathbf{ER}_i$

where $\mathbf{ER}_i = [ER_1,\ ER_2,\ \ldots,\ ER_n]'$ and $\mathbf{w} = [w_1,\ w_2,\ \ldots,\ w_n]'$. The portfolio variance is:

[5.16]      $\mathrm{Var}(R_p) = \mathbf{w}'\mathbf{\Sigma}\mathbf{w}$

$$\text{where } \mathbf{\Sigma} = \begin{bmatrix} \sigma_{11} & \sigma_{12} & \cdots & \sigma_{1n} \\ \sigma_{21} & \sigma_{22} & \cdots & \sigma_{2n} \\ \vdots & \vdots & \ddots & \vdots \\ \sigma_{n1} & \sigma_{n2} & \cdots & \sigma_{nn} \end{bmatrix}$$

$ER_p$ is the expected *portfolio* return (scalar)
$\mathrm{Var}(R_p)$ is the *portfolio* variance (scalar)
w is an $(n \times 1)$ column vector of weights assigned to the individual assets
$\mathbf{ER}_i$ is an $(n \times 1)$ column vector of expected returns of the individual assets
$\mathbf{\Sigma}$ is the $(n \times n)$ variance–covariance matrix.

# 5.4  BINOMIAL AND POISSON DISTRIBUTIONS

## BINOMIAL PROBABILITY DISTRIBUTION

The binomial probability distribution is a discrete probability distribution. It can be used to model the path of stock prices (which provides a key input to the valuation of options). The binomial probability distribution can be used if:

- there are *only two mutually exclusive outcomes* (at any point in time), either a 'success' (e.g. a rise in the stock price) or a 'failure' (e.g. a fall in the stock price);
- the two events are *independent*—the latter implies that the probability of a 'rise' this period is independent of whether the stock price experienced a rise or a fall in previous periods;
- the probability of a 'success' is constant from 'trial to trial' (i.e. as we move through time).

If the probability of a success is $p$ this implies that the probability of a failure is $(1 - p)$ and these probabilities remain constant throughout the whole process. Suppose the initial stock price is $S = 100$ and hence after one 'up' move the stock price is $SU$ and after one 'down' move the stock price is $SD$, where for example we can take $U = 1.1$ and $D = 0.9091$ (note that $U = 1/D$). The stock price **lattice** or **tree** over $n = 2$ periods is given in Figure 5.5 for $p = 0.6$ and $1 - p = 0.4$.

The probability of $k$ 'up' moves after $n$ 'trials' (or time periods) is given by:

[5.17]      $\text{Probability}(k \text{ 'up' moves}) \equiv P_k = \begin{pmatrix} n \\ k \end{pmatrix} p^k (1 - p)^{n-k}$

## FIGURE 5.5: Two-period stock price lattice

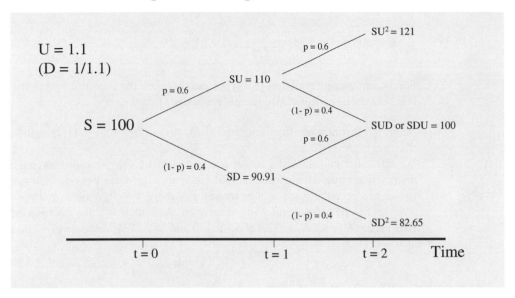

It is obvious that $k \leq n$. The first term in equation [5.17] is defined as:

[5.18]
$$\binom{n}{k} = \frac{n!}{(n-k)!\,k!}$$

where the symbol '!' indicates 'factorial' and $n! = n(n-1)(n-2)\ldots 1$ and $0! = 1$. The 'factorial term' in equation [5.18] is often given the symbol $C_{n,k}$ which stands for the number of combinations (or 'ways') you can get $k$ ups after $n$ trials (or time periods). Let's try it out for $n = 2$ (see Figure 5.5):

No. of possible paths with $k = 2$ 'ups' $= (2!)/(0!\,2!) = 1$   (i.e. UU)
No. of possible paths with $k = 1$ 'ups' $= (2!)/(1!\,1!) = 2$   (i.e. UD and DU)
No. of possible paths with $k = 0$ 'ups' $= (2!)/(2!\,0!) = 1$   (i.e. DD)

Hence, after $n = 2$ trials (i.e. time periods) there are two ways you can reach the point UD which has one 'up' move. There is only one way you can reach either the point UU (i.e. two 'up' moves) or DD (i.e. zero 'up' moves).

The probability of an 'up' move (over any single period) is $p$. Then given our independence assumption, the probability of two consecutive 'up' moves is $p^2$, or an 'up' followed by a 'down' is $p(1-p)$, while two consecutive 'down' moves has a probability of $(1-p)^2$. We now have the probabilities for the three 'nodes' at $n = 2$ (see Figure 5.5) and also the number of ways we can reach these nodes. For example, if $n = 2$ and $p = 0.6$, then equation [5.17] implies the probability of reaching node UU $= 0.36$, of node UD $= 0.48$ and of node DD $= 0.16$. Of course, the sum of these three possible outcomes is unity.

The cumulative probability distribution is simply the addition of the individual binomial probabilities from 0 to $k$, which can be stated as:

[5.19]    $$\text{Cum. prob.}(m|n, p) = \sum_{k=0}^{m} \binom{n}{k} p^k (1 - p)^{n-k}$$

For example using equation [5.19] we can calculate the probability that the stock price over the 2-day horizon would rise 'on not more than 1 day':

$$\Pr(\text{not more than one 'up' in 2 days}) = \Pr(0|2) + \Pr(1|2) = 0.84$$

We can also calculate the mean and variance of the possible outcomes of a binomial distribution (tree) at a particular trial (i.e. particular time period). Above we noted that at $n = 2$ the probability of $k$ 'up' moves $P_k$ where $k = 0$, 1 or 2 is $P_0 = (1 - p)^2 = 0.16$, $P_1 = p(1 - p) = 0.48$ and $P_2 = p^2 = 0.36$. Also at $n = 2$ the corresponding stock prices (see Figure 5.5) are $S_0 = 82.16$, $S_1 = 100$ and $S_2 = 121$, respectively. The mean stock price at $n = 2$ is:

$$ES = \sum_{k=0}^{2} P_k S_k$$

and

$$\text{Var}(S) = \sum_{k=0}^{2} P_k (S_k - ES)^2$$

The expected value of the stock price at $n = 2$ is therefore $ES = 0.36(121) + 0.48(100) + 0.26(82.65) = 104.78$ and the variance is $\text{Var}(S) = 0.36(121 - 104.78)^2 + 0.48(121 - 104.78)^2 + 0.16(82.65 - 104.78)^2 = 184.04$.

For the binomial model we can also calculate the expected value and variance of the *number of 'ups'*:

[5.20]    $$E(\text{'number of ups'}) = np$$

and

[5.21]    $$\text{Var}(\text{'number of ups'}) = np(1 - p)$$

In our example above the average number of 'ups' is $E(\text{'number of ups'}) = 1.2\ (= 2 \times 0.6)$, which means that in two trials we would expect to get on average 1.2 up moves. The variance of the 'ups' is $\text{Var}(\text{'number of ups'}) = 0.48\ (= 2 \times 0.6 \times 0.4)$.

In general equation [5.20] tells us the mean number of 'successes', which in our case is the average number of 'up' moves $EX = 1.2$, which is not a particularly interesting statistic. The binomial model is used more generally, for example in determining the mean number of defective items (e.g. batteries) in a subset of $n$ batteries. So, if the probability of a defective battery is $p = 0.3$ and you draw a sample of $n = 10$ batteries from the production line, you would expect $EX = 3$ defective batteries. Also, the standard deviation in the number of defective batteries would be 2.1 $(= 10(0.3)(0.7))^{1/2}$. Hence, if you found say eight defective batteries in your sample of 10, you would infer that there is something 'out of the ordinary' happening somewhere in the production process.

## POISSON PROBABILITY DISTRIBUTION

The Poisson distribution is widely used in insurance. For example, it can be used to calculate the probability of $k$ claims against fire or car insurance policies or the probability of default or bankruptcy of a firm. The Poisson distribution assumes:

- the events are independent of each other (i.e. that means if a policyholder makes a claim this claim does not affect other claims);
- the probability of an event occurring during a particular time interval is the same for all time periods;
- the number of possible events '$n$' is very large (i.e. $n \to \infty$);
- the probability of 'success' (e.g. a claim for fire insurance) is very small (i.e. tends to zero).

The latter two assumptions imply that the mean (number of claims) is constant (i.e. $\lambda = np$ is constant). The Poisson distribution is a limiting case of the binomial distribution when $n \to \infty$ and $p \to 0$. The Poisson distribution has only one parameter $\lambda$, the mean rate (of insurance claims). The Poisson distribution is defined as:

[5.22]
$$p(k) = e^{-\lambda} \frac{\lambda^k}{k!} \qquad \text{for } k = 0, 1, 2, 3, \ldots$$

where $k$ denotes the number of 'successes' (e.g. claims being made) which has infinitely many discrete possibilities (e.g. $0, 1, 2, 3, \ldots, \infty$) each with its own probability $p(k)$. For example, if on average there have been $\lambda = 3$ claims per year for fire insurance, then the probability of $k = 2$ claims in any 1 year is (see Figure 5.6, panel A):

## FIGURE 5.6: Poisson distribution

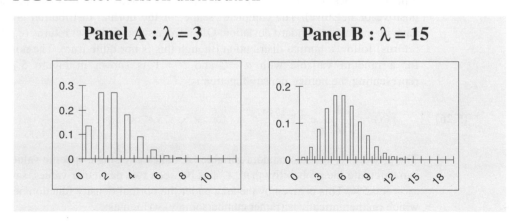

$$p(2) = \frac{e^{-3}3^2}{2!} = 0.224$$

The cumulative distribution is given by:

[5.23]      $\text{Cum. prob.}(m) = e^{-\lambda} \sum_{i=0}^{m} \frac{\lambda^i}{i!}$

Equation [5.23] gives the probability of *up to m* 'successes'. For example for $m = 3$ we require the probability of either 0, 1, 2 or 3 claims made. Similarly the probability that *not more than 4* claims are made in any 1 year is: $1 - \text{Cum. prob.}(3) = 1 - 0.6472 = 0.3528$. Note here, that in order to calculate the probability of more than 4 claims arising, we use the fact that this is equivalent to 1 minus the probability that either 3 or less than 3 claims are made.

The expected value and variance for the Poisson distribution can be shown to be:

[5.24]      $EX = \lambda$

and

[5.25]      $\text{Var}(X) = \lambda$

Quite coincidentally, the Poisson distribution has the property that the mean and variance are equal. It is also the case that the Poisson distribution is fairly symmetric if $\lambda$ is large and it may then be approximated by the normal distribution (see Figure 5.6, panel B, where $\lambda = 15$).

# 5.5 NORMAL DISTRIBUTION

The normal distribution is a theoretical (mathematical) distribution which is bell-shaped and symmetric around the mean. It assumes that 'events' are independent (e.g. the probability of a positive stock return this period is unrelated to whether the previous period's return was positive or negative). The complete 'shape' of the normal distribution is known once we have its mean and standard deviation. Often we assume that asset returns (e.g. monthly stock returns) follow a normal distribution (though this is not quite true). The normal distribution for a random variable with $\mu = 0$ and $\sigma = 1$ is shown in Figure 5.7. The equation representing the normal density function is:

[5.26]      $f(x) = \frac{1}{\sigma\sqrt{2\pi}} e^{-[(x-\mu/\sigma)^2/2]}$      for $-\infty < x < \infty$

The probability that the random variable '$X$' takes any single specific value is zero. But we can calculate the probability that '$X$' lies between two particular values, say $x_1 = -1\%$ and $x_2 = +0.5\%$. This is given by the area under the normal density function between $x_1$ and $x_2$, which mathematically is (rather cumbersomely) written as:

## FIGURE 5.7: Standard normal distribution N(0, 1)

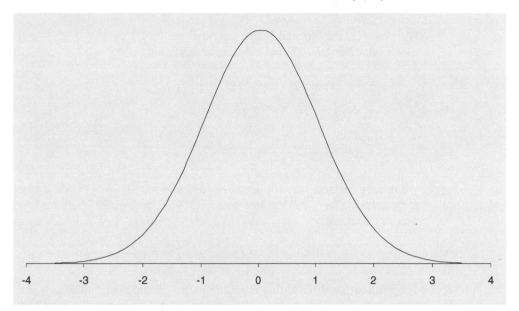

[5.27]    $$P(x_1 \leqslant X \leqslant x_2) = \int_{x_1}^{x_2} f(x)\mathrm{d}x = \Phi(x_1) - \Phi(x_2)$$

where $\Phi(x_1)$ is known as the cumulative density function for $x_1$. $\Phi(x_1)$ is the area of the 'normal curve' from $-\infty$ to $x_1$ and gives the probability that '$X$' lies between $-\infty$ and $x_1$. The standard normal distribution has $\mu = 0$ and $\sigma = 1$ and hence $\Phi(-1.96) = 2.5\%$ and $\Phi(0) = 50\%$ (see Appendix Table A5.1). The distribution is symmetric so the area between 0 and $+1.96$ of the standard normal distribution also 'contains' 47.5% of the area. The beauty of the normal distribution is that we can easily work out the probability that our stock return will lie in a particular range. For example we can be 95% confident that the stock return $X_i$ will lie in the range:

[5.28]    $$X_i = \mu \pm 1.96\sigma$$

since 95% of the 'area' of the standard normal distribution lies within $\pm 1.96$ standard deviations of zero. Using Appendix Table A5.1 allows us to read off probabilities when $\mu = 0$ and $\sigma = 1$ without having to solve equation [5.27]. However, for a normally distributed random variable $X_i$ with mean $\mu$ and standard deviation $\sigma$ we first need to transform $X_i$ into a *standard normal variable*:

[5.29]    $$z_i = \frac{(X_i - \mu)}{\sigma}$$

It is easy to show that $z_i \sim N(0, 1)$, that is $z_i$ is normally distributed with mean zero and standard deviation of unity. The equation for this probability density function is equation [5.27] above with $\sigma = 1$, that is:

[5.30] $$f(z) = \frac{1}{\sqrt{2\pi}} e^{-z^2/2}$$

For example, the probability that our stock return $X_i$ with $\overline{X} = 3.5\%$ and $\hat{\sigma} = 8.25\%$ will take a value between 0% and 10% can be easily obtained:

$X_1 = 0\%$ implies $z_1 = -0.4242$

and

$X_2 = 10\%$ implies $z_2 = 0.7879$

We require the area between $z_1 = -0.4242$ and $z_2 = 0.7879$. Since the normal distribution is symmetric this is also the area between 0.4242 and $-0.7879$. From Appendix Table A5.1 we can calculate:

$P(0\% < X < 10\%) = P(-0.4242 < z < 0.7879) = 0.448$ (or 44.8%)

The **Student's $t$-distribution** is similar to the normal distribution as it is symmetric around a mean of zero. However, the $t$-distribution has a flatter peak (i.e. platykurtic) and also fatter tails (see Figure 5.8 which compares the normal distribution and the $t$-distribution).

Asset *prices* (e.g. stock prices) tend to follow a **lognormal distribution**. The lognormal distribution only allows values of $X_i \geqslant 0$. The lognormal is like the normal distribution but with 'thinner' tails and with an elongated right tail. Hence the lognormal distribution is skewed. If a random variable $y_t$ is normally distributed with mean $\mu$ and standard deviation $\sigma$, then variable $X = e^y$ is lognormally distributed. The probability density function is given by:

---

## FIGURE 5.8: Student's $t$-distribution and the standard normal distribution

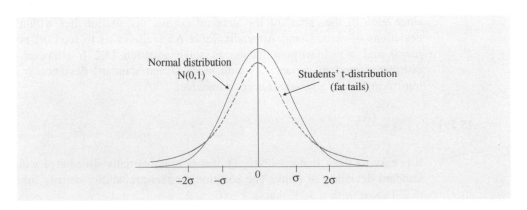

[5.31]
$$f(x) = \begin{cases} \dfrac{1}{\sigma^2 x\sqrt{2\pi}}\, e^{-0.5\left(\ln\left(\frac{x-\mu}{\sigma}\right)\right)^2} & \text{for } x \geqslant 0 \\ 0 & \text{otherwise} \end{cases}$$

The expected value and variance for the lognormal distribution are:

[5.32]
$$EX = e^{\mu + \sigma^2/2}$$

and

[5.33]
$$\text{Var}(X) = e^{2\mu + \sigma^2}(e^{\sigma^2} - 1)$$

The lognormal distribution is not 'tabulated' and therefore the 'area' (i.e. probability) between two points ($x_1$ and $x_2$) has to be calculated numerically (e.g. using Excel).

## 5.6  CENTRAL LIMIT THEOREM

An important statistical concept regarding the behaviour of the sample mean $\overline{X}$ is the Central Limit Theorem. The Central Limit Theorem states that the **sampling distribution of the mean** of a random variable approaches the normal distribution as the sample size increases. The latter result applies no matter what the 'shape' of the underlying distribution for $X$ (which is often not known). Hence, as long as the sample size '$n$' is large enough, any analysis of the sample mean of the variable can be conducted using the normal distribution: a very powerful result. A second property of the Central Limit Theorem is that the standard error (also known as the standard deviation) of the sample mean $\sigma_{\overline{X}}$ converges to zero as the sample size goes to infinity. Figure 5.9 demonstrates these properties for two variables $X_i (i = 1, 2)$ which have radically different population distributions. However, the means $\overline{X}_1$ and $\overline{X}_2$ both have distributions which approach the normal distribution as $n$ increases.

The standard error of the sample mean is given by:

[5.34]
$$\sigma_{\overline{X}} = \frac{\sigma}{\sqrt{n}}$$

where $\sigma$ is the population standard deviation of the individual observations $X_i$ and '$n$' is the sample size. To summarise, if we have a random variable $X_i$ with population mean $\mu_x$ and standard deviation $\sigma_x$ following *any* probability distribution (e.g. uniform, binomial or any other shape) then the sample mean $\overline{X}$ will have a probability distribution that approaches the normal distribution with mean $\mu_x$ and standard deviation $\sigma_{\overline{X}} = \sigma_x/\sqrt{n}$. We can therefore estimate the population mean $\mu_x$ with increasing accuracy as $n \to \infty$, by using the sample mean $\overline{X}$.

The theorem is extremely useful in Monte Carlo simulation (MCS) and can be used to value assets, companies or options. In MCS we 'simulate' say 100 values for $X_i$ (e.g. asset returns) and calculate the mean return $\overline{X} = \sum_1^{100} X_i/100$. We then repeat this simulation to obtain

## FIGURE 5.9: The Central Limit Theorem

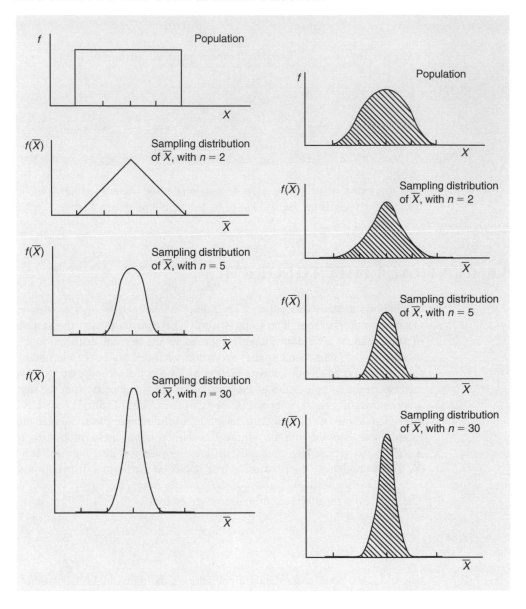

say $n = 10{,}000$ values of $\overline{X}$. We then know that the average of these 10,000 values of $\overline{X}$ will be a relatively precise estimate of the 'true' population mean, $\mu_x$ (which is unobservable).

# 5.7  REGRESSION ANALYSIS

The correlation coefficient (see Section 5.2) can be used to measure the association between two variables. Regression analysis is usually used when analysing more than two variables, but here we concentrate on a simple two-variable regression. The model used as an example here is known as the **single index model SIM** (or market model of stock returns). The SIM involves a regression of the (monthly) return of British Airways (BA) shares (variable $Y_t$) on the return of the FTSE100 stock market index (variable $X_t$). The resulting regression equation is:

[**5.35**]    $Y_t = \alpha + \beta X_t + \varepsilon_t$

where $\varepsilon_t$ is a random error term which 'picks up' anything that influences the return on BA shares, which is not explained by the return on the FTSE100. $\varepsilon_t$ is assumed to have a zero mean and constant variance. The more $X$ 'explains' movements in $Y$, the smaller will be the variance of $\varepsilon$. Using ordinary least squares (OLS) to obtain estimates of the parameters $\alpha$ and $\beta$, using monthly data for the sample period April 1990 to May 2000 (122 observations) we obtain:

[**5.36**]
$$Y_t = -\; 0.8711 \;+\; 1.6037 X^t$$
$$(0.6357) \quad (0.1445)$$
$$[-1.3704] \quad [11.10]$$

$$R^2 = 0.7116$$

where (.) = standard errors of the coefficient and [.] = $t$-statistic on the coefficient.

Note that equation [5.36] represents a straight line with an intercept $\hat{\alpha} = -0.8711$ and a slope coefficient (or gradient), $\hat{\beta} = +1.6037$. Using OLS gives values for $\hat{\alpha}$ and $\hat{\beta}$ which minimise the deviations of the actual observations from those on the regression line. Hence, the regression line which is described by equation [5.36] is also called the 'line of best fit'. The regression results can be interpreted as follows. When the return on the FTSE100 increases by 1% (one unit) then on average the return on BA shares increases by 1.6037% (units). The values in parentheses below the parameter estimates are the standard errors of the estimated coefficients and can be used to calculate confidence intervals or for hypothesis testing. The ratio $t_\beta = \hat{\beta}/\text{s.e.}(\hat{\beta})$ reported in equation [5.36] give us the likelihood that the 'true parameter' is equal to zero and therefore that no (linear) relationship between $Y_t$ and $X_t$ exists. The smaller is the value of s.e.$(\hat{\beta})$ relative to $\hat{\beta}$ itself, the higher is this $t$-ratio and the more confident we can be about the precision of our estimate of $\beta$. The ratio can be shown to have a Student's $t$-distribution, and if the absolute value of $t$ is greater than about 1.96 (this depends on the sample size) we can be 95% certain that $\beta$ is *statistically* significantly different from zero.

The '$R$-squared' ($R^2$) of the regression indicates how much of the actual variability in $Y_t$ is explained by the independent variable $X_t$. The *predicted values* of $Y_t$ are given by the following expression: $\hat{Y}_t = \hat{\alpha} + \hat{\beta}X_t = -0.8711 + 1.6037X_t$, which is our linear regression line. Figure 5.10 shows the scatter diagram of the returns of BA shares and the FTSE100 and the regression line (equation [5.36]). You can see from Figure 5.10 that as $X_t$ moves so does the predicted value $\hat{Y}_t$. However $\hat{Y}_t$ will not always coincide with the actual data series $Y_t$ at all points in time: there is a **prediction error** or **'residual'** which is calculated as:

## FIGURE 5.10: Regression analysis

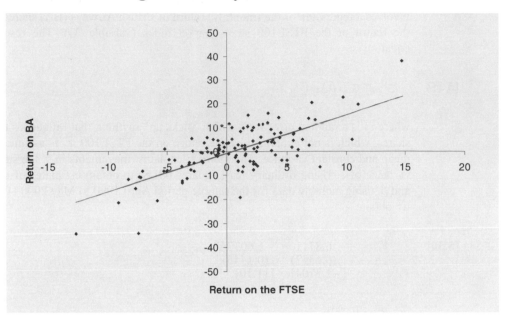

[5.37]    $e_t$ = actual value of $Y_t$ − predicted value of $Y_t$

$$= Y_t - \hat{Y}_t = Y_t - (\hat{a} + \hat{\beta} X_t)$$

$e_t$, the residual is actually an estimate of the 'true' error term $\varepsilon_t = Y_t - (\alpha + \beta X_t)$ where $(\alpha, \beta)$ are the 'true' unobservable parameters. If we have a 'good equation' then we expect that $Y_t \approx \hat{Y}_t$ most of the time and hence $e_t$ will be small. The OLS estimation technique actually 'chooses' $\hat{a}$ and $\hat{\beta}$ to make this prediction error as small as possible, but in practice it will not be zero for each data point in the sample. The $R^2$ of the regression measures the proportion of the variation in the actual $Y$ series accounted for by the variation in $\hat{Y}_t$. $R^2$ is calculated as:

[5.38]    $$R^2 = \frac{\sum_{t=1}^{n}(Y_t - \bar{Y})^2}{\sum_{t=1}^{n}(\hat{Y}_t - \bar{Y})^2}$$

An $R^2$ of say 0.3 implies that on average only 30% of the variation in $Y_t$ is accounted for by variation in the independent variable $X_t$ (and hence 70% is left unexplained). This implies that (since $\hat{\beta} > 0$) whenever $X_t$ increases, then only about 30% of the time will $Y_t$ also increase.

Using OLS it is easy to include many independent variables $X_1$, $X_2$, ..., $X_n$ on the right-hand side of the equation, to try and improve our 'explanation' of movements in $Y_t$. Possible $X$ variables, apart from the market return, which could influence stock returns include the dividend−price ratio, the book-to-market value of the firm, interest rates, exchange rates and inflation.

Here, we can only scratch the surface of the complexities involved in regression analysis, but there are a number of issues that need to be addressed if your equation is to be a success, including:

- Do the empirical results conform to your theoretical ideas (or model) or even just your gut instinct (e.g. do you expect stock returns to rise after an unexpected rise in dividends)?
- Are the key parameters ($\alpha$ and $\beta$) statistically significant and of the expected sign (i.e. positive or negative)?
- Are the residuals $e_t$ 'well behaved'? Usually we require the residuals to have a constant variance (i.e. homoscedastic), to be unrelated to each other (i.e. not autocorrelated) and not to 'explode' (i.e. to be stationary). One can test the residuals $e_t = Y_t - \hat{Y}_t$ for all of these desirable properties.
- If we estimate the equation using $n$ data points, are the parameters ($\alpha$ and $\beta$) stable and does the equation forecast well when we add additional data points at $n + 1$, $n + 2$, etc.? Again there are numerous procedures to test these propositions, one of the simplest being recursive least squares. Recursive OLS simply repeatedly re-estimates $\alpha$ and $\beta$ as we add extra data. We can then plot a graph of $\alpha$ (or $\beta$) as we 'move through' the sample and observe whether its estimated value remains reasonably stable, as we add more data points.

The above procedures are now standard features of many software regression packages (such as Microfit, TSP, PC Give, Eviews, RATS, etc.) and can also be found in Excel.

## 5.8 SUMMARY

- Asset returns are measured either by the **arithmetic return** or the **continuously compounded return**. The former is more familiar but the latter has some convenient properties (e.g. asset prices can never become negative).
- To summarise the vast amount of data on a single variable we can construct a **frequency distribution (or histogram)**. The sample mean, standard deviation, skewness and kurtosis (i.e. the four 'moments') as well as the correlation coefficient and covariances are **summary statistics** which are often used to describe the broad characteristics of data series.
- Asset prices (and returns) are **random variables** and hence follow **stochastic processes**. A **probability distribution** can be used to quantify the likelihood that a particular event occurs (or does not occur).
- The binomial, Poisson and normal (probability) distributions are widely used in finance. The **binomial distribution** can be used to model the evolution of stock prices. The **Poisson distribution** is used in insurance markets to predict such events as the number of claims against fire, car or life insurance or to calculate the probability of default (bankruptcy) of a particular firm in an industrial sector. The **normal distribution** is widely used to represent asset returns, particularly on stocks, bonds and spot FX.

> • **Regression analysis**, similar to correlation analysis, measures the association between different variables. A 'goodness of fit' measure is the $R^2$ which describes the amount of variability of the dependent variable which is explained by the variability in the explanatory variable(s).

## END OF CHAPTER EXERCISES

**Q1**   What does the normal distribution have that the Poisson distribution does not?

**Q2**   Intuitively, what does the $R$-squared of a regression represent? Does a high $R^2$ indicate that the equation would provide accurate forecasts?

**Q3**   What are the distinctive characteristics of a binomial process?

**Q4**   What does the Central Limit Theorem say about the (sample) estimate of the mean?

**Q5**   Use the Poisson distribution to calculate:

  (i)  The probability that more than 10 firms go bankrupt in any given month.
  (ii)  The probability that less than five dot.coms go bankrupt in any given month.

It has been calculated that on average nine 'dot.com' firms go bankrupt in any given month.

**Q6**   Assume that *monthly* returns on the dollar–pound sterling exchange rate are normally distributed with a mean of 1% and a standard deviation of 8%. What is the probability that monthly returns are (i) more than 1.5%, (ii) less than 3% and (iii) between −2% and 4%?

**Q7**   The probability that the market index rises on a particular day is 0.5. If we look at a 5-day horizon, what is the probability that the market index rises on 2 out of the 5 days? How many possible outcomes are there for the market index to rise on 2 of the 5 days?

## APPENDIX 5.1  NORMAL DISTRIBUTION

### TABLE A5.1: Probabilities for the Standard Normal Distribution

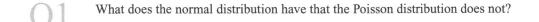

| $z$ | 0 | 0.01 | 0.02 | 0.03 | 0.04 | 0.05 | 0.06 | 0.07 | 0.08 | 0.09 |
|-----|------|------|------|------|------|------|------|------|------|------|
| **0** | 0.0000 | 0.0040 | 0.0080 | 0.0120 | 0.0160 | 0.0199 | 0.0239 | 0.0279 | 0.0319 | 0.0359 |
| **0.1** | 0.0398 | 0.0438 | 0.0478 | 0.0517 | 0.0557 | 0.0596 | 0.0636 | 0.0675 | 0.0714 | 0.0753 |
| **0.2** | 0.0793 | 0.0832 | 0.0871 | 0.0910 | 0.0948 | 0.0987 | 0.1026 | 0.1064 | 0.1103 | 0.1141 |

# TABLE A5.1: (*Continued*)

| z | 0 | 0.01 | 0.02 | 0.03 | 0.04 | 0.05 | 0.06 | 0.07 | 0.08 | 0.09 |
|---|---|------|------|------|------|------|------|------|------|------|
| **0.3** | 0.1179 | 0.1217 | 0.1255 | 0.1293 | 0.1331 | 0.1368 | 0.1406 | 0.1443 | 0.1480 | 0.1517 |
| **0.4** | 0.1554 | 0.1591 | 0.1628 | 0.1664 | 0.1700 | 0.1736 | 0.1772 | 0.1808 | 0.1844 | 0.1879 |
| **0.5** | 0.1915 | 0.1950 | 0.1985 | 0.2019 | 0.2054 | 0.2088 | 0.2123 | 0.2157 | 0.2190 | 0.2224 |
| **0.6** | 0.2257 | 0.2291 | 0.2324 | 0.2357 | 0.2389 | 0.2422 | 0.2454 | 0.2486 | 0.2517 | 0.2549 |
| **0.7** | 0.2580 | 0.2611 | 0.2642 | 0.2673 | 0.2704 | 0.2734 | 0.2764 | 0.2794 | 0.2823 | 0.2852 |
| **0.8** | 0.2881 | 0.2910 | 0.2939 | 0.2967 | 0.2995 | 0.3023 | 0.3051 | 0.3078 | 0.3106 | 0.3133 |
| **0.9** | 0.3159 | 0.3186 | 0.3212 | 0.3238 | 0.3264 | 0.3289 | 0.3315 | 0.3340 | 0.3365 | 0.3389 |
| **1** | 0.3413 | 0.3438 | 0.3461 | 0.3485 | 0.3508 | 0.3531 | 0.3554 | 0.3577 | 0.3599 | 0.3621 |
| **1.1** | 0.3643 | 0.3665 | 0.3686 | 0.3708 | 0.3729 | 0.3749 | 0.3770 | 0.3790 | 0.3810 | 0.3830 |
| **1.2** | 0.3849 | 0.3869 | 0.3888 | 0.3907 | 0.3925 | 0.3944 | 0.3962 | 0.3980 | 0.3997 | 0.4015 |
| **1.3** | 0.4032 | 0.4049 | 0.4066 | 0.4082 | 0.4099 | 0.4115 | 0.4131 | 0.4147 | 0.4162 | 0.4177 |
| **1.4** | 0.4192 | 0.4207 | 0.4222 | 0.4236 | 0.4251 | 0.4265 | 0.4279 | 0.4292 | 0.4306 | 0.4319 |
| **1.5** | 0.4332 | 0.4345 | 0.4357 | 0.4370 | 0.4382 | 0.4394 | 0.4406 | 0.4418 | 0.4429 | 0.4441 |
| **1.6** | 0.4452 | 0.4463 | 0.4474 | 0.4484 | 0.4495 | 0.4505 | 0.4515 | 0.4525 | 0.4535 | 0.4545 |
| **1.7** | 0.4554 | 0.4564 | 0.4573 | 0.4582 | 0.4591 | 0.4599 | 0.4608 | 0.4616 | 0.4625 | 0.4633 |
| **1.8** | 0.4641 | 0.4649 | 0.4656 | 0.4664 | 0.4671 | 0.4678 | 0.4686 | 0.4693 | 0.4699 | 0.4706 |
| **1.9** | 0.4713 | 0.4719 | 0.4726 | 0.4732 | 0.4738 | 0.4744 | 0.4750 | 0.4756 | 0.4761 | 0.4767 |
| **2** | 0.4772 | 0.4778 | 0.4783 | 0.4788 | 0.4793 | 0.4798 | 0.4803 | 0.4808 | 0.4812 | 0.4817 |
| **2.1** | 0.4821 | 0.4826 | 0.4830 | 0.4834 | 0.4838 | 0.4842 | 0.4846 | 0.4850 | 0.4854 | 0.4857 |
| **2.2** | 0.4861 | 0.4864 | 0.4868 | 0.4871 | 0.4875 | 0.4878 | 0.4881 | 0.4884 | 0.4887 | 0.4890 |
| **2.3** | 0.4893 | 0.4896 | 0.4898 | 0.4901 | 0.4904 | 0.4906 | 0.4909 | 0.4911 | 0.4913 | 0.4916 |
| **2.4** | 0.4918 | 0.4920 | 0.4922 | 0.4925 | 0.4927 | 0.4929 | 0.4931 | 0.4932 | 0.4934 | 0.4936 |
| **2.5** | 0.4938 | 0.4940 | 0.4941 | 0.4943 | 0.4945 | 0.4946 | 0.4948 | 0.4949 | 0.4951 | 0.4952 |
| **2.6** | 0.4953 | 0.4955 | 0.4956 | 0.4957 | 0.4959 | 0.4960 | 0.4961 | 0.4962 | 0.4963 | 0.4964 |
| **2.7** | 0.4965 | 0.4966 | 0.4967 | 0.4968 | 0.4969 | 0.4970 | 0.4971 | 0.4972 | 0.4973 | 0.4974 |

*continued overleaf*

## TABLE A5.1: (*Continued*)

| z | 0 | 0.01 | 0.02 | 0.03 | 0.04 | 0.05 | 0.06 | 0.07 | 0.08 | 0.09 |
|---|---|------|------|------|------|------|------|------|------|------|
| **2.8** | 0.4974 | 0.4975 | 0.4976 | 0.4977 | 0.4977 | 0.4978 | 0.4979 | 0.4979 | 0.4980 | 0.4981 |
| **2.9** | 0.4981 | 0.4982 | 0.4982 | 0.4983 | 0.4984 | 0.4984 | 0.4985 | 0.4985 | 0.4986 | 0.4986 |
| **3** | 0.4987 | 0.4987 | 0.4987 | 0.4988 | 0.4988 | 0.4989 | 0.4989 | 0.4989 | 0.4990 | 0.4990 |
| **3.1** | 0.4990 | 0.4991 | 0.4991 | 0.4991 | 0.4992 | 0.4992 | 0.4992 | 0.4992 | 0.4993 | 0.4993 |

Note: This table gives the area under the standard normal curve between zero and a point $z$ standard deviations above zero. For example the area between $z = 0$ and $z = 1.96$ is 47.5%, implying that the area to the right of $z = 1.96$ is 2.5% ($= 50\% - 47.5\%$)

# PART 3

# MONEY AND FIXED INCOME MARKETS

# 6

# Money Markets

---

**LEARNING OBJECTIVES**

- To demonstrate the relationships between **quoted rates of return and prices** in the money market, taking account of the various 'conventions' used in the different markets. These include **discount rates**, the **'dollar' discount** and **yield to maturity**.
- To discuss the main types of **money market instruments**, such as T-bills, banker's acceptances, bank deposits and loans (including the Euromarkets), commercial bills, certificates of deposit and repos.
- To provide an overview of the pratical **operation of these markets** particularly for the UK and the USA.

---

The money markets provide a means of borrowing and lending on a short-term basis, and the most liquid 'markets' comprise maturities of up to 6 months. The Central Bank uses the bill market to smooth out the daily and weekly cash payments or receipts, between the government sector and the private sector. For example, if government expenditure (payments) exceeds tax receipts on a particular day then the Central Bank may sell bills in the market to obtain additional 'cash'. The Central Bank also actively undertakes net purchases (or sales) in the bill market in order to inject or withdraw cash from the banking or private sector. These 'active' open market operations are usually an attempt to influence the 'monetary base', and hence ultimately the money supply. In doing so, the Bank can also have an impact on short-term yields when it enters the market as a net seller or net purchaser of bills.

The money market also facilitates borrowing and lending *within* the private sector. For example, a manufacturing firm that has surplus funds for 3 months may place them in a term deposit at a commercial bank or alternatively may purchase a 'bill' issued by another firm, which is short of cash. There is of course both a thriving new issues market for 'bills' and a highly liquid secondary market. Banks lend and borrow funds from each other in the interbank market while foreign residents are able to purchase 'domestic' money market assets. In large markets such as London, one can also purchase money market assets that are denominated in a foreign currency (e.g. US dollar certificates of deposit purchased in London).

Unfortunately, for the student (or embryonic market practitioner), there are a wide variety of 'conventions' used in money markets. One key distinction is whether 'returns' are calculated on a discount basis or a yield basis. For example, suppose I purchase a bill at $98 and its face value (i.e. maturity value) 3 months later is $100, then we could define the 'dollar discount' as $2 and describe the bill as a 'discount instrument'. It would seem sensible to calculate the percentage return (over 3 months) based on the $98 paid for the bill; the 'return' would be 0.02048 or 2.0408% [= ($100 − $98)/$98]. This method of calculation is referred to as being on a 'yield basis'. However, this convention does not apply to the Treasury bill market. The Treasury bill market quotes the percentage return based on the face value, that is 0.02 or 2% [− ($100 − $98)/$100] over 3 months, and this is known as the 'discount rate'. Hence T-bill rates are *quoted* on a 'discount basis' rather than a 'yield basis'.

Another issue which arises is the so-called day count convention, in grossing up the return from say 3 months to an annual return. Common sense suggests using the actual days to maturity. Hence if I purchase a bill on a Tuesday and sell it 33 days later the maturity period should be 33 (days). Also one might think that a (non-leap) year should amount to 365 days. However, day count conventions differ both between markets (e.g. US and UK Treasury bills) and between different instruments trading in the same market (e.g. US bills and bonds). Some markets assume there are 30 days in every month and (only) 360 days in a year! Clearly, these day count conventions need to be made explicit for the different instruments.

We have noted above that some money market instruments such as T-bills are sold on a 'discount basis'. Other instruments (e.g. certificates of deposit) earn interest in the conventional manner. That is, you lend $A$ now at a prearranged interest rate and collect the principal plus interest at the end of the investment period. In addition, some instruments have interest payments which vary with a particular reference rate (e.g. floating rate notes, FRNs). There is also the question of whether one uses simple interest or compound interest when converting from say a 3-month rate to an annual rate. In the money markets 'the street' uses simple interest, whereas textbooks tend to emphasise compound (or even continuously compounded) rates. For the practitioner all these calculations are usually done automatically using in-house software. However, it is still important to fully understand the basis of the conventions being used. There are a tremendous variety of money market assets and we will only consider a subset. Although we will say a little about the organisation of some of these markets, this is not the central theme of this section.

## 6.1 MONEY MARKET INSTRUMENTS

In this section we outline the main money market instruments including bank deposits and call money, interbank borrowing, Treasury bills, commercial bills and banker's acceptances, certificates of deposit (CDs) and repurchase agreements (repos). We begin with an account of these instruments for the UK and then note any major differences in the US market. As one might expect, similarly named instruments (e.g. Treasury bills, CDs) have similar functions in both the UK and US markets. Generally speaking, key differences are in such matters as day count conventions and market operations (e.g. differences in new issue procedures).

## PRICES, DISCOUNT RATES AND YIELDS

### DAY COUNT CONVENTIONS

The principal variables of interest in the purchase of financial assets are the price paid, the maturity value, any interest or coupon payments that may accrue and the dates on which money will change hands. For an instrument with a single payment at $t = 0$ and a single receipt at time $t \, (> 0)$, the important factors are what you pay out, what you receive and the time between the two events. The way you calculate 'the return' is then a matter of convenience (or custom and practice). In short, interest rates are of *secondary* importance, but it is these rates that are quoted when a transaction is agreed and only after this will the other details be sorted out. The quoted interest rates are related to the invoice price paid by simple formulae. There is an arbitrariness about the conventions used 'on the street'. For example, the use of 'simple' grossing up from quarterly rates to annual rates rather than using *compound* interest. However, since *all* participants use 'simple' grossing up, this does not create any problems. The markets do not all use the same day count conventions and possibilities include:

- Actual/actual      Actual days to maturity/actual days in the year
- Actual/360      Actual days to maturity/360 days in a year
- 30/360      Months are assumed to have 30 days and
a year is assumed to have 360 days.

### EUROMARKET INTEREST RATES

The Euromarket is a market in wholesale bank loans and deposits. A large volume of transactions consists of interbank lending and borrowing, although large corporates are also active in the market. Lending and borrowing can take place in all the major currencies. The origin of the term Euromarket is lending and borrowing the 'home currency' from a bank which is located offshore. So a UK company that borrows US dollars from a US bank in London is taking out a Eurodollar loan. The term 'Euro' does not imply that the loan has to originate from a bank situated in Europe.

Eurodollar deposits (and loans) are quoted on a simple yield basis (i.e. they are 'add on' rather than discount intruments). The conventions used in calculating interest in the Euromarkets can differ depending on the geographical location or currency in which one undertakes the borrowing and lending. The 'basis' can be either 360 or 365 days in a year. For example, a 365-day basis is used for sterling, the Irish pound, Kuwaiti dinar and Belgian franc. All other currencies use a 360-day basis. The day count convention is usually either **'actual/360'** or **'actual/365'**. However, by mutual agreement between the two parties, any basis can be used. For example, a quoted interest rate of 10% p.a. using alternative day count conventions results in:

- **10% over 90 days on US\$1m (360-day basis):**      $0.1 \left( \dfrac{90}{360} \right) \$1\text{m} = \$25,000$

- **10% over 90 days on US\$1m (365-day basis):**   $0.1\left(\dfrac{90}{365}\right)\$1m = \$24,657$

Hence 10% p.a. simple interest on a 365-day basis is equivalent to simple interest of 10.139% [$= 0.1(365/360)$] on a 360-day basis. There is a further method of calculating interest rates which is used in certain European countries for *domestic deposits* and we refer to this as the **continental** or **30/360 method**. Here each month is treated as if it had 30 days (and hence 360 days make 1 year), for example consider:

### A deal from 4th December to 12th May

| | |
|---|---|
| 4th December – 4th May | $= 5$ months $= 5 \times 30 = 150$ days |
| 4th May – 12th May | $= 8$ days |
| Total 'days' | $= 158$ days |
| Proportion of 1 year | $= 0.4388 \ (= 158/360)$ |

The actual number of days between 4th December and 12th May is 159, but this is of no consequence. What is important is the amount paid at the outset of the deal (at $t = 0$) and the amount received at the end (at $t = T$). We can then use whatever measure of 'return' is most convenient (e.g. simple interest, compound or continuously compounded rates).

Euromarket interest on deals less than 1 year (usually) pay the interest at maturity. For deals over 1 year interest is paid annually on the 'anniversary' of the deal with the final payment on say a $2\frac{1}{2}$-year deal being at maturity. So, a $2\frac{1}{2}$-year deal from 10th December will pay two interest payments in the following 2 years on 10th December, followed by a final interest payment (plus repayment of principal) on 10th June. If the anniversary is not a business day, then it will be rolled forward to the next business day, usually a Monday (providing this does not take you into the next month).

## LIBOR AND LIBID

LIBOR is the interest rate at which a first-class bank in London lends out (or offers) funds to another high credit rated bank in London. If a bank has funds deposited with it, then it pays out interest at the bid rate (LIBID). A 'round trip' for the bank would be to borrow funds at LIBID and on-lend them at LIBOR:

> **For the bank to make a 'round trip' profit:**
> **LIBOR > LIBID**

The 'usual' way to report bid–ask (offer) quotes differs in different geographical locations. For example:

| | | |
|---|---|---|
| **Quotes in USA:** | bid/offer | (e.g. $8\frac{1}{4} - \frac{1}{2}$) |
| **Quotes in London:** | offer/bid | (e.g. $8\frac{1}{2} - \frac{1}{4}$) |
| **Both quotes mean:** | I lend at $8\frac{1}{2}$% and borrow at $8\frac{1}{4}$% | |

In essence LIBID is the bank's funding cost (at the margin) for subsequent on-lending to say a commercial customer. In the language of economics it is the bank's 'marginal cost of funds' (ignoring reserve requirements and any taxation). The LIBOR rate you actually pay will differ depending on the size of the deal. The rate *quoted* will often be an average LIBOR rates taken from a sample of 'reference banks', usually at 11 a.m. London time, under the auspices of the British Bankers Association (BBA). LIBOR rates are applicable to any 'offshore' currency that banks borrow or lend in London. So, for example, there are Swiss franc, US dollar, yen, etc. LIBOR rates quoted in London. The equivalent rates elsewhere are NIBOR or NYBOR (New York), PIBOR (Paris), FIBOR (Frankfurt), MIBOR (Madrid), ADIBOR (Abu Dhabi), SIBOR (Saudi or Singapore) and HKIBOR (Hong Kong).

There is a complex little 'twist' that has arisen in Europe due to the adoption of a common currency (the euro) amongst 11 countries. You can now get a **euro-LIBOR** quote which is the (average) rate for borrowing the 'offshore' Euro (i.e. from beyond the euro zone's frontiers) by banks in London and is calculated by the BBA. It is also possible to borrow from bank's within the euro zone, based mainly on an average rate determined from a set of banks *within* the 11 'members' who are to use the euro. This is known as 'euro Euribor' or just **Euribor** for short. This is confusing to say the least, especially as payments on lots of other financial instruments are linked to one or other of these rival rates (e.g. FRNs, interest rate futures, options and swaps). It appears as if Euribor rates which are administered in Brussels will win this particular race. However, it is not of great importance *who* calculates the 'administered average' (i.e. Brussels or the BBA in London), what is important is where the assets are *traded,* since this determines the turnover in any financial centre—and London will probably take a large proportion of this business (e.g. issuing FRNs based on Euribor, trading Euribor futures and options).

## BANK DEPOSITS

A deposit placed in a bank from tomorrow and maturing the next business day is referred to as 'tomorrow/next' (or **tom/next**). A Euromarket deposit, unless stated otherwise, will begin on the **spot date**, which will be two business days from the day the trade took place (e.g. over the telephone). The **value date** is the maturity date of the deposit, when interest and any principal are normally repaid.

A **call deposit** is one which is repayable 'at call' which, although this sounds like immediate payment, usually involves payment two working days hence, to give time for the required paperwork to be completed.

An **overnight deposit** is a deposit which is repaid on (or rolled over) the next *business* day. Within a single time zone this poses no problems. Also, for example, Hong Kong can deal overnight in US dollar deposits since New York is about 13 hours behind, giving plenty of time for Hong Kong to complete the paperwork with New York. In contrast, London cannot easily deal overnight with Frankfurt in euros, since deals have to be completed by 8 a.m. in Frankfurt.

## PRICING OF PURE DISCOUNT INSTRUMENTS

The formulae outlined below are appropriate for pure discount instruments only. Bills of exchange, bank acceptances, commercial bills and Treasury bills have no coupon, they are traded at a discount: the market price is below the redemption (or face) value of the bill. For a bill with 1 year to maturity with a discount rate $d$% and face value FV = \$100 the price $P$ is (see Figure 6.1):

[6.1] $\qquad P = (1 - d/100)100$

Hence the discount rate ($d$) is:

[6.2] $\qquad d = \left(\dfrac{100 - P}{100}\right)100$

If the bill has less than 1 year to maturity the *discount rate*, which is the rate quoted 'On the Street', is an annualised percentage based on the *face value*:

[6.3] $\qquad d = \left(\dfrac{FV - P}{FV}\right)\left(\dfrac{a}{m}\right)100$

where $d$ is the discount rate (% per annum)
$\qquad$ $P$ is the purchase price (per \$100 nominal)
$\qquad$ $m$ is the number of days to maturity
$\qquad$ FV is the face value (\$100 nominal)
$\qquad$ $a$ is the number of days in a year.

If we know the discount rate we can rearrange equation [6.3] to determine the market price (see Figure 6.2).

[6.4] $\qquad P = FV\left[1 - \left(\dfrac{d}{100}\right)\left(\dfrac{m}{a}\right)\right]$

The difference between the face value and the market price paid is referred to as the (dollar or sterling) 'discount' $D$:

[6.5] $\qquad D = FV - P$

---

## FIGURE 6.1: Discount instruments: 1-year bills

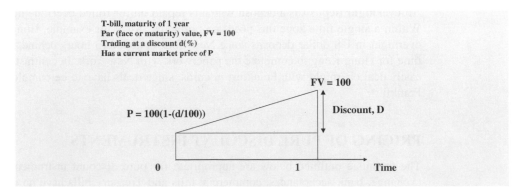

T-bill, maturity of 1 year
Par (face or maturity) value, FV = 100
Trading at a discount d(%)
Has a current market price of P

FV = 100

P = 100(1-(d/100))

Discount, D

0      1      Time

## FIGURE 6.2: Discount instruments: bills < 1 year

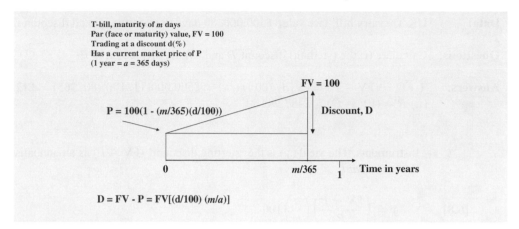

D = FV - P = FV[(d/100) (m/a)]

Using equations [6.4] and [6.5] we can also express the 'discount' as:

[6.6]
$$D = \text{FV}\left(\frac{d}{100}\right)\left(\frac{m}{a}\right)$$

If we are given the quoted price then it is straightforward to calculate the discount rate and the (sterling) discount (see Table 6.1).

'On the Street' market makers quote the discount rate on T-bills but using the above formulae one can calculate the current market price (see Table 6.2).

Finally note that if quotes are discount rates on a 30/360 day count basis, then on 1st April for a maturity date of 1st September, the discount rate ($d$) is given by:

[6.7]
$$d = [(\text{FV} - P)/\text{FV}](360/150)100$$

where 150 is the maturity period based on 30 days per month. The actual number of days to maturity is 153, but this is of no consequence since the participants all use the same convention in this market. Although for T-bills 'the street' quotes discount rates, it is possible to calculate the rate of return on a yield basis for comparison with other

## TABLE 6.1: Discount rate: UK T-bills

| Data: | UK Treasury bill, day count is actual/365<br>91-day bill, face value FV = £1m, market (purchase) price $P$ = £950,000 |
| --- | --- |
| Questions: | Calculate (i) the discount rate $d$ and (ii) the 'sterling discount' $D$ |
| Answers: | (i) $d = [(£1,000,000 - £950,000)/£1,000,000](365/91)100 = 20.05\%$<br>(ii) $D = \text{FV} - P = £1,000,000 - £950,000 = £50,000$ |

## TABLE 6.2: The 'discount' on UK T-bills

**Data:** UK Treasury bill, face value £500,000, 80 days to maturity, quoted discount rate 11% p.a.

**Questions:** Calculate (i) the (sterling) discount $D$ and (ii) the invoice price $P$

**Answers:** (i) $D = (FV - P) = FV(d/100)(m/a) = £500,000(11/100)(80/365) = £12,054.79$
(ii) $P = (FV - D) = £487,945.21$

instruments. The yield ($y$) is the 'sterling discount' ($FV - P$) as an annualised percentage of the *price paid*:

[6.8]
$$y = \left(\frac{FV - P}{P}\right)\left(\frac{a}{m}\right)100$$

So in Table 6.1 the yield on the T-bill is 21.11% whereas the discount rate is 20.02%. For any discount security the rate on a yield basis always exceeds the rate on a discount basis (because in the denominator in equation [6.8] the purchase price ($P$) is less than the face value (FV) which is in the denominator in equation [6.3]). Further, the magnitude of the difference between the two rates increases as rates increase. For example, for a price of 90 in the above example, the discount rate is 40.11% and the yield is 44.57%, a difference of 4.46% compared with a difference of 1.06% when the rates are around 20%.

It is easy to manipulate equations [6.8] and [6.4] to obtain the relationship between the quoted discount rate ($d$) and the return on a yield basis ($y$):

[6.9]
$$y = d\left(\frac{FV}{P}\right) = \frac{d}{\left[1 - \left(\dfrac{d}{100}\right)\left(\dfrac{m}{a}\right)\right]}$$

### YIELD INSTRUMENTS

For money market instruments such as a term deposit in a bank (e.g. a Eurodollar deposit or loan) or a certificate of deposit, 'the Street quote' is the return on a simple **yield basis**, which is the usual way we think of 'interest'. This is the same formula as equation [6.8], but we must interpret the final payment as a terminal value (TV). If the initial outlay or principal $P = \$100$ say is placed on deposit at a yield $y$ *for 1 year*, then the amount you receive after 1 year, the terminal value (see Figure 6.3) is:

[6.10]    $TV = P(1 + y/100)$

For yield instruments with less than 1 year to maturity 'the Street' uses simple interest to determine the terminal value (see Figure 6.4).

[6.11]    $TV = P[1 + (m/365)(y/100)]$

## FIGURE 6.3: Yield instruments: 1-year CDs

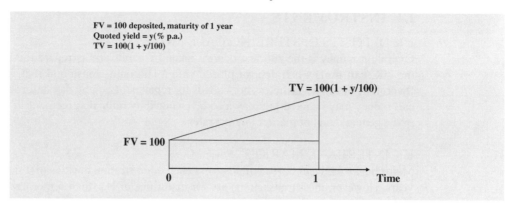

FV = 100 deposited, maturity of 1 year
Quoted yield = y(% p.a.)
TV = 100(1 + y/100)

TV = 100(1 + y/100)

FV = 100

0      1      Time

## FIGURE 6.4: Yield instruments: deposits < 1 year

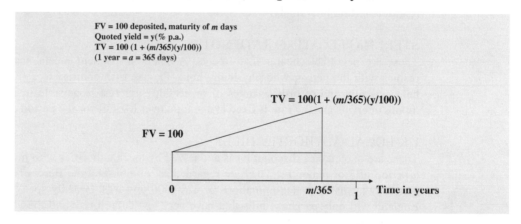

FV = 100 deposited, maturity of *m* days
Quoted yield = y(% p.a.)
TV = 100 (1 + (m/365)(y/100))
(1 year = *a* = 365 days)

TV = 100(1 + (m/365)(y/100))

FV = 100

0      m/365    1    Time in years

Alternatively, if you are promised a payment TV in *m* days time, the amount you would be prepared to pay today (i.e. the current price of the yield instrument) is:

[6.12]
$$P = \frac{TV}{1 + \left(\dfrac{m}{365}\right)\dfrac{y}{100}}$$

It follows that the yield ($y$) is given by:

[6.13]
$$y = \left(\frac{TV - P}{P}\right)\left(\frac{a}{m}\right)100$$

which is an equivalent form to equation [6.8]. Hence the 'calculated' yield on a T-bill and the *quoted yield* (equation [6.13]) on yield instruments (e.g. bank deposits) are on an equivalent basis.

## 6.2 UK AND US INSTRUMENTS

### UK INSTRUMENTS

#### UK DEPOSITS IN STERLING/CALL MONEY

Overnight money is the shortest deposit taken by banks and is repaid the next morning. In the UK, **call money** is a deposit placed with a Discount House and if it is for longer than 'overnight' it can nevertheless be 'called' for repayment on any day before noon. Interest on call money may be fixed but may also be changed by mutual agreement, if a trend develops in the general level of market interest rates.

#### UK INTERBANK MARKET

Major banks lend and borrow funds from each other from maturities of 1 day up to around 2 years. However, most transactions are for maturities of less than 6 months. Quotes are on a yield basis and the day count convention is actual/actual. Banks lend funds at the London Interbank Offer Rate (LIBOR) and pay the London Interbank Bid Rate (LIBID) on funds deposited with them. It follows that in order to make a profit LIBOR is greater than LIBID. These two interbank rates provide a reference rate for other (sterling) money market rates (e.g. for sterling FRNs).

#### STERLING FLOATING RATE NOTES

These are negotiable bearer instruments. A bearer instrument means that the ownership resides with the person who physically holds the asset (in contrast to a 'register' which is held centrally and records changes of ownership). Interest is payable in most cases at 3-month intervals and the rate is fixed at a margin over LIBOR for the period concerned.

#### UK LOCAL AUTHORITY BILLS

These are quoted on a discount basis and issued by local authorities with most maturities for a period of 3 or 6 months. They are regarded as 'eligible' by the Bank of England and are generally available in denominations of £250,000 upwards. Broadly speaking, the Bank of England will only purchase bills that have very low default risk and these are classified as 'eligible bills'.

#### UK TREASURY BILLS

T-bills are pure discount (i.e. non-coupon) *bearer* securities issued by the Treasury, under-taking to pay a fixed sum on a specified date. In the UK, offers of new T-bills are made on *Fridays* and may be taken up at any time during the following week. The date of take up is the *issue date* and most UK bills mature 91 days later. The most recently issued T-bills are referred to as 'hots' and these are issued in various denominations ranging from £5000 to £1m. The auction procedure for new issues is very similar to that for US T-bills, which is discussed below.

#### UK BILLS OF EXCHANGE: COMMERCIAL BILLS, BANKER'S ACCEPTANCES

These instruments are quoted on a discount basis. A bill of exchange enables a seller of goods (e.g. manufacturer) to extend credit to his customer. However, the manufacturer can obtain early payment of the extended credit by discounting the bill, with a bank or Discount House. The manufacturer will get his customer to sign the bill saying he owes the manufacturer £50,000, say. In the UK, bills that have been accepted are also known as 'two-name' paper since they bear the name of both the drawer (manufacturer) and the acceptor (customer). The manufacturer can then sell (discount) the bill to a bank or Discount House and obtain funds immediately and in this case the bill of exchange becomes a bank acceptance. (When a bill matures, it is normally presented for payment to the acceptor, i.e. the manufacturer's customer.) Calculation of the invoice (market) price of a bank acceptance, quoted 'On the Street' on a discount basis, is given in Table 6.3.

If the acceptor is not a bank the bill is a **trade bill**. Bills that are accepted by a bank are **bank bills** and within this group **eligible bills** are those accepted by 'eligible banks' (**ineligible bills** are those accepted by other banks). Until recent changes in the UK, the Bank of England would buy only eligible bills. In practice the Bank purchased these from the Discount Houses which endorsed the bills by adding their name to them, thus the Bank of England would buy only 'three-name' bills. Recent changes in the UK money market mean that the Bank of England will now deal with a large number of participants in the bill market and not just the Discount Houses (see the discussion of repos below).

## UK CERTIFICATES OF DEPOSIT

Certificates of deposit (CDs) are quoted on a yield basis. A CD is a bearer instrument which certifies that a sum of money has been deposited with the bank issuing the certificate, at a fixed yield, and that on the stated maturity date the deposit will be repaid by the issuing bank with interest. Interest may accrue on a 'periodic' basis or at maturity. If the CD is negotiable it can be sold in the secondary market, if immediate access to cash is required by the holder of the CD. (Cashing a non-negotiable CD usually involves a withdrawal penalty.) CDs in the UK are often referred to as wholesale deposits because the minimum deposit is large. Other market details for UK CDs are given in Box 6.1.

## TABLE 6.3: Example: UK bank acceptance

| | |
|---|---|
| **Data:** | Bank acceptance for £1m face value, with 87 days to maturity are sold at 12% discount |
| **Questions:** | Calculate (i) the 'discount' and (ii) the price of the security |
| **Answers:** | (i) $D = $ 'discount' $= £1m(12/100)(87/365) = £28,602.74$ <br> (ii) $P = (FV - D) = £971,397.26$ |

## Box 6.1    CDs: MARKET CONVENTIONS

The UK CD market is very liquid and the market conventions are broadly similar to those in other banking centres such as New York, the euro area and the Far East. Key features of the UK market are:

- Units of at least £500,000
- Minimum/maximum redemption period is 7 days/5 years
- Interest on 1 year (or less) CDs is paid on maturity
- Interest on CDs with maturity greater than 1 year is paid annually
- Settlement up to midday is by 'town clearing cheque' or banker's draft
- Afternoon dealings are settled the following business day
- Quotations ('On the Street') are on a yield basis
- Day count basis is actual/actual.

The CD is quoted on a 'simple' yield basis so Figure 6.4 applies when determining the (terminal) value at maturity. However, if the CD is selling in the secondary market, what is its invoice price? Its current invoice price $P$ is the DPV (using 'simple interest') of the known terminal receipts at maturity TV. Knowing the current quoted yield, say $y = 11\%$, the DPV can be calculated as in Table 6.4.

The algebraic formula for the current market price $P$ of a CD is found by first finding the maturity (terminal) value TV of the amount initially deposited (i.e. the face value) and then discounting this at the current yield $y_t$. The terminal value of a 90-day sterling CD with initial yield $y_0$ is:

$$[6.14] \qquad TV = FV\left[1 + y_0\left(\frac{90}{365}\right)\right]$$

If the CD was issued some time ago and it now has $m$ days to maturity then its current price in the secondary market is the DPV of the terminal value, discounted at the prevailing market yield $y_t$ (for $m$-day money):

## TABLE 6.4: Sterling CDs

| | |
|---|---|
| **Data:** | Quotes are on a (simple) yield basis<br>£1m CD issued at 12.5% for 120 days<br>Proposed purchase in secondary market at 11% current yield<br>Assume CD now has 62 days to maturity |
| **Question:** | Calculate the purchase price of the CD |
| **Answer:** | On maturity holder receives £1m $[1 + (12.5/100)\,(120/365)] = £1,041,095.89$<br>Hence price paid 62 days before maturity is the DPV at 11%<br>Price paid $= £1,041,095.89/[1 + (11/100)\,(62/365)] = £1,021,999.99$ |
| **Check:** | Purchase price paid $= £1,021,999.89$<br>Receipt at maturity $= £1,041,095.99$<br>Interest earned $= £19,096$<br>Yield $= (£19,096/£1,021,999.89)(365/62)100$<br>$= 11\%$ p.a. |

[6.15] $$P_t = \frac{\text{TV}}{\left[1 + y_t\left(\dfrac{m}{365}\right)\right]}$$

BID AND OFFER RATES

Market makers 'buy low' and 'sell high'. Hence their bid *price* for bills is below the offer *price*. However, in the interbank market banks 'bid' a rate for money (i.e. the *bid rate* is what they pay on money placed on *deposit* with them). Naturally, the banks wish to lend at a higher rate than that at which they borrow, so their offer *rate* (LIBOR) exceeds their bid *rate* (LIBID):

| | |
|---|---|
| **Interbank market:** | **offer rate (LIBOR) > bid rate (LIBID)** |
| **Bills and CDs:** | **bid price < offer price** |
| | ***therefore*** |
| | **bid rate > offer rate** |

UK money market rates are shown in Figure 6.5. The rates are presented as offer–bid, for example banks will lend overnight at 6% and will pay $5\frac{7}{8}$% on funds deposited with them. If

**FIGURE 6.5: Newspaper quotes (*Financial Times*). Reproduced with permission**

UK INTEREST RATES

LONDON MONEY RATES

| Oct 18 | Over-night | 7 days notice | One month | Three months | Six months | One year |
|---|---|---|---|---|---|---|
| Interbank Sterling | $5\frac{7}{8}$ - 5 | $5\frac{7}{8}$ - $5\frac{5}{8}$ | 6 - $5\frac{7}{8}$ | $6\frac{1}{8}$ - 6 | $6\frac{1}{4}$ - $6\frac{1}{8}$ | $6\frac{5}{16}$ - $6\frac{3}{16}$ |
| BBA Sterling LIBOR | - | $5\frac{15}{16}$ - | $6\frac{1}{16}$ - | $6\frac{3}{16}$ - | $6\frac{1}{4}$ - | $6\frac{3}{8}$ - |
| Sterling CDs | - | - | 6 - $5\frac{31}{32}$ | $6\frac{3}{32}$ - $6\frac{1}{16}$ | $6\frac{3}{16}$ - $6\frac{5}{32}$ | $6\frac{5}{16}$ - $6\frac{1}{4}$ |
| Treasury Bills | - | - | $5\frac{13}{16}$ - $5\frac{23}{32}$ | $5\frac{29}{32}$ - $5\frac{27}{32}$ | - | - |
| Bank Bills | - | - | $5\frac{29}{32}$ - $5\frac{27}{32}$ | $5\frac{31}{32}$ - $5\frac{29}{32}$ | - | - |
| Local authority deps. | - | $5\frac{7}{8}$ - $5\frac{13}{16}$ | 6 - $5\frac{7}{8}$ | $6\frac{1}{8}$ - 6 | $6\frac{1}{8}$ - 6 | $6\frac{1}{4}$ - 6 |
| Discount Market deps | 6 - $5\frac{7}{8}$ | $5\frac{7}{8}$ - $5\frac{11}{16}$ | - | - | - | - |

UK clearing bank base lending rate 6 per cent from Feb 10, 2000

| | Up to 1 month | 1-3 month | 3-6 months | 6-9 months | 9-12 months |
|---|---|---|---|---|---|
| Certs of Tax dep. (£100,000) | $2\frac{1}{4}$ | 5 | 5 | 5 | $5\frac{1}{4}$ |

Certs of Tax dep. under £100,000 is $2\frac{1}{4}$pc. Deposits withdrawn for cash $1\frac{1}{4}$pc.
Av. tndr rate of discount Sep 15, 5.8047pc. ECGD fixed rate Stlg. Export Finance. make up day Sep 27, 2000. Agreed rate for period Oct 25, 2000 to Nov 25, 2000, Scheme III 7.45pc. Reference rate for period Sep 1, 2000 to Sep 29, 2000, Scheme IV & V 6.209pc. Finance House Base Rate $6\frac{1}{2}$pc for October 2000. SONIA Oct 18 : 5.6645

we exclude the overnight interbank rates then the remaining rates increase with maturity. Taking interbank offer rates, these increase from $5\frac{7}{8}$% on 7-day money to $6\frac{5}{16}$% on 1-year loans. This is known as an upward sloping **yield curve** and is the subject of Chapter 8.

## US INSTRUMENTS

The quoted trading rates for **US Treasury bills**, **bank acceptances** and **commercial paper** are on a discount basis. The day count convention is actual/360, so the discount rate–price relationship is given by equation [6.4] and an example is provided in Table 6.5.

### US TREASURY BILLS

US 3 and 6-month bills are auctioned every Monday with the amounts to be auctioned usually announced on the previous Tuesday. 1-year bills are auctioned in the third week of every month (announced the preceding Friday). When it is temporarily short of cash the Treasury issues 'cash management bills' with maturities to match those of the projected shortfall. The US Treasury auction first involves deducting the total of non-competitive tenders (of up to $1m for each bid) and non-public purchasers (e.g. Federal Reserve). Non-competitive tenders are based on quantity (not 'price') and the price paid is the average price paid by the competitive bidders. The competitive bidders are allocated Treasury bills on the basis of the highest to the lowest bid prices. When the issue is exhausted, allocations are at the 'stop yield', and are in proportion to the quantities tendered. Those bidding at a higher yield (lower price) than the stop yield receive no allocation. The difference between the average yield of all the bids accepted and the stop is called the 'tail'. Note that although bids are submitted on a discount basis, the allocation is based on yields (which can be calculated from the discount rates).

An illustrative result from a Treasury auction is given in Table 6.6. After deducting non-competitive bids and the Feds, allocation, $7bn is available for competitive bidders. Those who bid at a yield of 6.01% or below (i.e. at a higher price) receive the entire amount for which they bid. This would leave $0.4bn [= $7bn – $6.6bn] to be allocated to those who bid at 6.02%. Each of these bidders will receive 26.67% [= $0.4bn/$1.5bn] of the amount they bid. The stop yield is therefore 6.02%. The average yield of full allocation bidders is 5.58% and completely unsuccessful bidders were 'shut out' at higher yields than 6.02%. The tail is therefore 0.04% (= 6.02% – 5.58%).

### US COMMERCIAL PAPER

Commercial paper (CP) is a means of short-term borrowing for large municipalities (i.e. local authorities in the UK) and corporates. It is an alternative to borrowing from banks. In

---

## TABLE 6.5: US Treasury bill (price and discount rate)

| | |
|---|---|
| **Data:** | Price = $97.912 per $100 of face value, days to maturity = 182<br>Day count convention: actual/360 |
| **Question:** | Calculate the quoted discount rate |
| **Answer:** | $d = [(100 - 97.912)/100]\,(360/182) = 4.13\%$ |

## TABLE 6.6: US Treasury auction: T-bills

| | |
|---|---|
| **Total issue** | $10.0bn |
| **Less non-competitive bids** | $0.5bn |
| **Less Federal Reserve** | $2.5bn |
| **Amount for competitive bidders** | $7.0bn |

*Competitive bids*

| Amount ($bn) | Cumulative bids | Bid (yield) |
|---|---|---|
| **0.5** | 0.5 | 5.55 |
| **0.7** | 1.2 | 5.56 |
| **0.8** | 2 | 5.57 |
| **1** | 3 | 5.58 |
| **1.1** | 4.1 | 5.59 |
| **1.2** | 5.3 | 6 |
| **1.3** | 6.6 | 6.01 |
| **1.5** | 8.1 | 6.02 |

the US commercial paper refers to an unsecured promissory note and differs from a bill of exchange in being a liability of the issuer directly, rather than indirectly via an acceptor. For this reason, US commercial paper is not quite equivalent to the UK commercial bill. CP may be issued on a pure discount basis or may bear interest at maturity (e.g. LIBOR + 1% on a floating rate basis). Paper of less than 270 days to maturity is a bearer instrument, for maturity periods of 270 days or more the paper must be registered (with the Securities and Exchange Commission SEC, which makes it more 'expensive' to issue). The most common maturity range is 30–50 days or less, since paper with less than 90 days to maturity is eligible collateral for a bank when dealing at the Fed discount window.

Backup lines of credit are needed to obtain a commercial paper rating. Issuers of commercial paper can increase their rating by using **credit enhancements**, that is finding a highly rated 'third party' who will guarantee repayment if the issuer defaults. This enables smaller, riskier firms to access the commercial paper market by using these enhancements. Firms can also raise their credit ratings by purchasing either **indemnity bonds** from insurance companies or **standby letters of credit** from banks. Both of these ensure that the third party will repay the 'paper' if the issuer defaults. The standby letter of credit is usually attached to the commercial paper and so the issuer 'rents' the credit rating of the bank. Studies have shown that equity prices respond positively to a commercial paper issue with a standby letter of credit attached, but there is no equity response when the letter of credit is omitted. Hence, the market sees the bank who issues the letter of credit as 'revealing' new information about the creditworthiness of the issuer. The markets therefore have less information than the banks on credit risk.

CP may be issued to a dealer ('dealer paper') or directly ('direct paper') to the lender. To pay off maturing CP the issuer usually sells a new tranche of CP to other investors. The issuer therefore faces **rollover risk** and because of this the CP is usually backed by unused lines of bank credit (for which a commitment fee is charged). CP is also rated by the credit rating agencies. The CP is usually held to maturity, so secondary market activity is smaller than the 'new issue' market.

## US CERTIFICATES OF DEPOSIT

As in the UK these are traded on a yield basis, however, US CDs use a day count of actual/360. CDs may be negotiable or non-negotiable. For the latter, the funds can only be withdrawn before the maturity date if a withdrawal penalty is paid. Negotiable CDs can be repeatedly sold in the open market. Negotiable CDs are usually issued in denominations of $1m or more and have maturities greater than 7 days and less than 1 year. However, some term CDs with maturities greater than 1 year are also issued. Normal CDs pay interest at maturity while term CDs pay interest semi-annually. The yield on CDs depends in part on the credit rating of the issuing bank, and their liquidity. CDs that are issued outside the US, but denominated in dollars, are known as Eurodollar CDs, while Yankee CDs are denominated in dollars but issued by a foreign bank with branches in the US. Table 6.7 shows the calculation of principal plus interest and Table 6.8 demonstrates how the purchase price of a CD in the secondary market is calculated.

## COMPARING RATES

Obviously, in comparing the return on two money market assets one cannot use a discount rate for one asset and the yield for another. Even when both assets are quoted on a yield basis one has to ascertain whether they use the same day count convention. In general, in comparing the rates on assets using different trading rates or day count basis, you should first convert to prices. The 'return' can then be recalculated on a consistent basis.

It is common usage to compare 'yields' based on *compound* annual yields since then the return on two assets can be compared over the same horizon and on the same basis. To demonstrate how we move from the rates quoted 'On the Street' to a measure of return, consider a US T-bill with 90 days to maturity with a quoted *discount rate* of 10% (actual/360) and a 90-day Eurodollar deposit (actual/360) with a quoted *yield* of 10%:

## TABLE 6.7: US certificates of deposit

| Data: | Notional $1m, 90-day CD with 7% yield |
|---|---|
| Question: | What are the payments at the end of 90 days? |
| Answer: | Payment = $1m[1 + (7/100)(90/360)] = $1,017,500 |

## TABLE 6.8: US marketable CDs (purchase price)

**Data:**     Day count basis: actual/360, quotation is yield basis
$5m CD originally issued at 7.25% for 60 days
Proposed purchase at 7% yield with 21 days to maturity

**Question:**     Calculate the purchase price $P$

**Answer:**     Except for the day count basis (and currency) the calculation is the same as for sterling CDs:

$$\text{Price paid} = \$5m\frac{[1 + (7.25/100)(60/360)]}{[1 + (7/100)(21/360)]}$$

$$= \$5,039,837.33$$

In the above calculation we first find the amount payable at the end of 60 days (i.e. principal + interest) and we then discount back to the present using the current yield of 7%

Price of T-bill = $100 − $10(90/360)     **= $97.50** (per $100 face value)
Dollar interest earned on the T-bill over 90 days     **= $2.50**

Simple annual return = $[(\$100/\$97.50)-1](365/90) = 0.1040$     **(10.40%)**
Compound return = $[(\$100/\$97.50)]^{(365/90)}-1 = 0.1081$     **(10.81%)**
Continuously compounded return = $(365/90)\ln(\$100/\$97.50) = 0.1027$     **(10.27%)**

Now $97.50 invested in a 90-day Eurodollar deposit gives:

Receipts after 90 days = $97.50[1 + 0.10(90/360)]$     **= $99.94**
Dollar interest earned on the CD over 90 days     **= $2.50**

Simple annual return = $[(\$99.94/\$97.50)-1](365/90) = 0.1015$     **(10.15%)**
Compound return = $[(\$99.94/\$97.50)]^{(365/90)}-1 = 0.1054$     **(10.54%)**
Continuously compounded return = $(365/90)\ln(\$99.94/\$97.50) = 0.1002$  **(10.02%)**

What is important in the comparison is what you pay, what you receive and the time between receipts and payments. The day count conventions are merely 'rules' for extracting these three elements. You can then use whatever method of calculating the 'annual return' you feel is most sensible. It should be immediately obvious that the T-bill has a higher 'return' than the Eurodollar deposit since the T-bill earns a dollar amount of $2.50 over 90 days, whereas the CD only earns $2.44 (both on an initial outlay of $97.50).

The *annual return* usually assumes that the initial 90-day investment can be reinvested (or rolled over) for the rest of the year, namely 4.055 (= 365/90) times. The method you use then depends on whether you assume the *dollar gains* (interest) made in the first (and only 'true' investment period) are subsequently reinvested or not.

Take for example the Eurodollar deposit. The **simple annual return** assumes the dollar gains of $2.44 are not reinvested in subsequent periods, but only the initial principal of $97.50 is reinvested each time (if you like the $2.44 earned each period is immediately spent). The **(discrete) compound rate** assumes any interest earned (i.e. $2.44 in the first period) as well as the principal of $97.50 is reinvested in the second and subsequent periods: that is we earn interest-on-interest. However, when *qualitatively* comparing the annual 'return' on the two assets you can use either simple annual interest or compound interest since they are on a comparable basis for both assets. They both give the same qualitative conclusion, namely that a T-bill with a *quoted discount rate* of 10% has a higher 'return' than a Eurodollar deposit with the same maturity and a *quoted yield* of 10%.

In fact both these returns (i.e. simple and compound) are not entirely a 'realistic measure' of what one could actually earn over the year, since when you come to roll over your initial investment, interest rates will have changed. However, they are both a 'reasonable' way of reporting returns on different instruments (on a comparable basis). Of course if a 90-day and a 365-day Eurodollar deposit both had a discrete annual compound return of 10.54% you would be wise to note that the 90-day deposit faces rollover (or reinvestment) risk, whereas the 365-day deposit does not.

The continuously compounded return may be less familiar, but again it gives the right qualitative answer (i.e. the T-bill has a higher 'return' than the Eurodollar deposit). In some respects the continuously compounded return is a little tricky. For example, for the Eurodollar deposit, why is *its* continuously compounded return of 10.02% less than *its* discrete compound return of 10.54%. This is because when using the continuously compounded return it is assumed that the interest-on-interest is earned continuously (e.g. daily) rather than just 4.055 times per year (as with the discrete compound return). Hence, you require a lower continuously compounded return to reach the same 'end point' than you do if interest is only compounded 4.055 times per year.

Due to the different assumptions regarding the length of a year, some care is required in comparing rates between the US money and bond markets. The US money market uses actual/360 while the US bond market uses actual/365. Hence when both are quoted on a yield basis (over the same time horizon) the yields are not comparable. To deal with this, money market yields are often quoted as a 'bond yield equivalent' ($BY$):

[**6.16**]    $BY = (365/360)y$

For reference, Table 6.9 shows the various rates calculated for the money and bond markets if the price in each one is 95 and the bond in question pays no interim coupon payments before it is to be sold. This example is intended only to illustrate the general difficulties in comparing rates. Discount rates use the face value of 100 as the denominator, whereas yield calculations use the market price. The day count conventions in the US money and bond markets are often different (i.e. actual/360 and actual/365, respectively).

The equality of the prices ($P = P_b = 95$) is reflected in the equality between the *bond*

## Table 6.9: US money and bond rates (a comparison)

| | | |
|---|---|---|
| Money market price | $P = 95, \text{FV} = 100, m = 91$ | |
| Bond market price | $P_b = 95, \text{FV} = 100, m = 91$ | |
| Money market discount rate | $d = \left(\dfrac{100 - P}{100}\right)\left(\dfrac{360}{91}\right)100$ | **19.78%** |
| Bond market discount rate (1) | $d^* = \left(\dfrac{100 - P_b}{100}\right)\left(\dfrac{365}{91}\right)100$ | **20.05%** |
| Money market yield | $y = \left(\dfrac{100 - P}{P}\right)\left(\dfrac{360}{91}\right)100$ | **20.82%** |
| Bond market yield | $Y = \left(\dfrac{100 - P_b}{P_b}\right)\left(\dfrac{365}{91}\right)100$ | **21.11%** |
| Money market 'bond yield equivalent' | $BY = \dfrac{365}{360}y$ | **21.11%** |

Note: 1. The bond market discount rate has no meaning in practice

*market yield* (*y*) and the *money market bond yield equivalent* (*BY*). Since *y* and *BY* are calculated on the same basis (i.e. yield basis and the same day count conventions), then if *y* = *BY* the two assets offer the same return. Note that the money market yield (*y*) and the two discount rates (*d*, *d\**) are all different, even though the two assets give the same 'return'.

## REPURCHASE AGREEMENT

A repo or more accurately a 'sale and repurchase agreement' is a form of collateralised borrowing. It is a bit like borrowing money to purchase a house. When you buy a house for say $300,000 the Savings and Loan Association (building society in the UK) or bank lends you about 90% of the cash but it takes the deeds of the house as collateral for the loan. The lender will repossess the house if you fail to make the interest payments. You only have to provide 10% of the value of the house (here $30,000) as an up front 'margin payment'. By doing so you obtain leverage, that is if the house increases in value by 20% you will have experienced an increase in value of $60,000 on an initial outlay of $30,000—this is a considerable 'bang per buck'.

Suppose a market maker wishes to borrow $10m overnight. He can agree to sell securities (e.g. T-bills or T-bonds) he holds, in exchange for cash and *simultaneously* agree to buy back the securities the next day. The implicit interest rate on this transaction is called the repo rate. The lender of the funds holds the securities as collateral. When viewed from the perspective of the supplier of the securities (i.e. the acquirer of funds) the transaction is a repo. From the point of view of the counterparty, the supplier of funds, it is called a *reverse repo*. Hence:

> **Repo = borrowing money by selling a security to a counterparty**
> **Reverse repo = lending money by purchasing a security from a counterparty**

The difference between the purchase price and the selling price is the 'dollar interest' on the loan. From Table 6.10 we see that an overnight repo with $r = 6.5\%$ on a loan of $10m will incur interest costs of $1806. Note that in principle any security can be used in a repo, such as a bill, bond or even equities.

Repos provide **leverage**. For example, suppose you wish to purchase $10m worth of T-notes (with 5 years to maturity). Instead of using your own funds or borrowing money from a bank, you could borrow the money from your broker, buy the 5-year T-notes and deposit these with your broker as collateral for the loan you used to buy the T-notes with in the first place. You then own $10m of T-bonds but you would have only had to pay say $1m cash to your broker as initial margin (i.e. we have assumed the initial margin is 10% of the total amount borrowed). You may even be lucky in that the T-bond may earn a coupon yield that exceeds the short-term repo cost of finance if the yield curve is upward sloping. (This is called positive 'cost of carry'.) If the market price of the bond should alter over the period of the repo this is immaterial since the buyback price in the repo is fixed. However, there is a danger here. If the price of the T-bond falls dramatically then you may be asked for additional margin payments (see below).

One can undertake a reverse repo to cover a short position. For example, if a dealer sold $20m of T-bills 3 weeks ago and now has to deliver the securities, he can agree to buy the

---

## TABLE 6.10: Overnight repo (USA)

| | |
|---|---|
| **Data:** | Overnight repo rate $r = 6.5\%$ <br> Face value of securities FV = $10m <br> Day count basis: actual/360 |
| **Question:** | Calculate the dollar interest ($D$) paid on an overnight repo. What is the equivalent repurchase price of the securities? |
| **Answer:** | $D = $ (face value)(repo rate)($m/360$) = ($10m)(6.5/100)(1/360) = $1806 |
| | The interest payment is equivalent to the borrower of the funds agreeing to repurchase the securities for ($10m + $1806) the next day |

securities now (from a third party) and sell them back at a future date (i.e. reverse repo). Eventually, of course, the dealer would need to buy the securities 'outright'.

There is credit risk in a repo agreement. Even though in the above example the lender of the cash retains the T-bills as collateral, the borrower could fail to repurchase the T-bills for ($10m + $1806). For example, if interest rates have risen overnight, the market value of the T-bills will be below $10m and the borrower might default. Clearly repos which have a maturity greater than 1 day have greater credit risk than overnight repos. The main characteristics of repo agreements in the USA are:

*Maturities*: Short-term, usually overnight to a few days. Some for 1, 2, 3 weeks and 1, 2, 3 months
*Principal*: For short-term maturities (< 1 week) usually about $25m or more. Minimum transactions with securities dealers is $1m
*Yields*: Typically, sale and repurchase price are equal with an agreed rate of interest to be paid. The alternative is a repurchase price above the sale price (i.e. an implicit interest rate and 'dollar discount')

To reduce credit risk exposure on a repo, the dealer (i.e. seller of T-bills) will receive less cash than the market value of the securities. This is called **'margin'** or colloquially 'a haircut' and the initial cash payment may be about 1–3% of market value for more creditworthy dealers (and up to 10% or more for less creditworthy dealers or less liquid securities). The initial margin provides the lender of the cash with a 'cushion' should T-bill prices fall over the term of the repo. Also, the cash to be paid will be periodically increased if the market value of the T-bills falls below some prearranged level (known as the 'maintenance margin'). This additional 'margin call' is sometimes referred to as the 'variation margin' (and is based on 'marking to market' the value of the T-bills or T-bonds). A classic case of a highly leveraged bond position using repos is that of Robert Citron, the Treasurer of Orange County (see Box 6.2) who on these and other instruments (known as reverse floating rate notes, FRNs) lost about $2bn in December 1994 on a notional bond portfolio of about $7bn.

## Box 6.2 ORANGE COUNTY (REPOS AND LEVERAGE)

Robert Citron, the Treasurer of Orange County (in California) managed a fund of around $7.7bn but he also borrowed $13bn via the repo market, posting T-bonds as collateral. This gave him considerable leverage and raised his overall exposure to about £20bn (after initial margin calls had been paid). Up to February 1994 all went well but then US interest rates began to rise and dealers asked for additional margin payments, as the bonds used as collateral in the repos fell in value.

Part of this cash came from a separate $600m bond issue by Orange County, but when its paper losses became known in December 1994 Credit Suisse First Boston refused to rollover $1.25bn of repos. Citron could not meet his margin requirements and

Orange County filed for bankruptcy, although many repo brokers had by then sold Citron's bonds held as collateral in the repos.

Although it was the **margin calls on the repos** which triggered Citron's collapse, the major losses occurred because of another type of leveraged transaction, known as 'reverse floaters' (i.e. reverse floating rate notes, FRNs). **Reverse (inverse) floaters** pay out to the holder if interest rates fall. But they also have 'embedded leverage' in that the payout formulae involve a multiplier whereby payments or receipts are a multiple of interest rate changes.

Citron held about $8bn of these leveraged inverse floaters, and with a multiplier of around three this implied an actual exposure of about $24bn. After February 1994 interest rates rose, so Orange County had to pay out on the inverse floaters and this was the major source of their $2bn losses. The purchase of some of these reverse floaters was financed from funds obtained in the repo market.

Ideally the securities should be delivered to the lender of the funds. However, this can be costly, particularly for short-term repos. Hence, often the borrower is allowed to place the securities (T-bills) in a segregated customer account or custodial account (for the lender) at the borrower's clearing bank. These methods provide some security for the lender, although not as much as actually holding the collateral (i.e. T-bills) himself.

Dealers use the repo market to finance their inventory and to cover short positions. Dealers will also attempt to earn profits by running a matched book, by taking on repos and reverse repos with the same maturity. For example, a dealer may enter into a term repo with a 'money market fund' for 5 days at a rate of 5.5% (i.e. borrows funds) and simultaneously enter into a reverse repo with a thrift (i.e. the equivalent of a building society in the UK) at a (lending) rate of 5.56%. If the collateral in the two deals is the same, then he has locked in a positive spread of 0.06%.

The Federal Reserve can influence interest rates by outright purchases or sales of T-bills. But, in general it uses the repo market instead to achieve the same aim. Note that, if the Fed sells securities it is not called a repo, but somewhat confusingly a *matched sale*. When it buys securities (i.e. lends funds) it is not referred to as a reverse repo but as a *system repo*.

## FEDERAL FUNDS RATE
The Federal Funds rate is not, as the name might suggest, the rate at which banks borrow from the Federal Reserve Board. It is in fact an interbank rate, namely the rate at which US banks borrow and lend from each other.

Depository institutions (i.e. commercial banks and thrifts) have to maintain reserves (which earn no interest) at the Federal Reserve, in proportion to their deposits or liabilities outstanding. If a commercial bank is short of reserves then it will bid for funds from surplus banks and pay the Fed Funds rate. Most transactions are for overnight funds, but longer term transactions of up to 6 months also occur. Commercial banks can also borrow in the repo market and, because the latter is a collateralised loan, whereas Federal Funds are not, the

Fed Funds rate is usually higher (by about 25 basis points) than the repo rate. Usually, as a last resort a bank will borrow from the 'discount window' of the Fed using short-term CP as collateral.

## 6.3 SUMMARY

- There are a wide **variety of 'conventions'** used in money markets. One key distinction is whether 'returns' are calculated on a **discount basis** (e.g. for T-bills and banker's acceptances) or on a **yield basis** (e.g. bank loans and deposits, commercial bills/paper and CDs).
- The **Euromarket** is a market in wholesale bank loans and deposits in 'offshore currencies'. A large volume of transactions consists of **interbank lending and borrowing**, although large corporates are also active in the market. Lending and borrowing can take place in all the **major currencies**.
- Major banks lend and borrow funds from each other from maturities of 1 day up to around 2 years, but most transactions are for maturities of less than 6 months. Banks in the UK lend funds at the **London Interbank Offer Rate (LIBOR)** and pay the **London Interbank Bid Rate (LIBID)** on funds deposited with them. Hence **LIBOR > LIBID**.
- **A repo** is a 'sale and repurchase agreement'. It is a form of collateralised borrowing. The lender of the funds usually holds the securities as collateral. A repo implies borrowing money by selling a security to a counterparty. A **reverse repo** applies when you are lending money by purchasing a security from a counterparty.
- The **Federal Funds** rate is *not* the rate at which banks borrow from the Federal Reserve Board but is the rate at which US banks borrow and lend *from each other*.

## END OF CHAPTER EXERCISES

**Q1** Which is higher, LIBOR or LIBID, and why? What is the higher, the bid *price* or the ask (offer) *price* on a T-bill?

**Q2** What is a 'repo'? Give a simple example of how you calculate the (simple annual) rate of interest (yield) on a 7-day T-bill repo. (Assume the day count convention is actual/365.)

**Q3** A UK T-bill with 60 days to maturity has a face value FV = £1m and a quoted discount rate $d = 10\%$. The day count convention is actual/365. Calculate:

(a) The (sterling) discount, $D$.
(b) The market price, $P$.
(c) The (simple annual) yield, $y$.

**Q4** A 6-month (US) T-bill was issued some time ago and now has a market price $P = \$98$ per $100 face value. The number of days left to maturity is now 90. The day count convention is 'actual/360'. Calculate:

(a) The quoted discount rate, $d$.

(b) The (simple) annual yield.

**Q5** A 1-year (UK) T-bill has a quoted discount rate of 8% and a face value FV = £100. The quoted yield on a 1-year (UK) CD is 8.5%.

(a) What is the (one year) holding period return HPR (yield) on the T-bill and the CD?

(b) Which gives the highest 'return' (if held to maturity)?

**Q6** A UK CD has a *'quoted'* current yield $y = 10\%$ p.a. and a face value of £1m. It now has 60 days to maturity but *when it was issued* it had an original maturity of 120 days and a quoted yield of $y = 12\%$ p.a. (Day count convention is actual/365.) Calculate:

(a) The current market price $P$ of the CD.

(b) Check that at this price you will earn 10% over the remaining life of the CD.

**Q7** The continuously compounded yield on a 180-day CD is 10.3% p.a. and on a 180-day T-bill the yield is 10.4% p.a. using discrete compounding every 90 days. Assuming both instruments use a day count convention of actual/360, which one provides the higher return?

# 7

# Bond Markets

---

**LEARNING OBJECTIVES**

- To explain the relationship between various measures of the return on a bond and the pricing of bonds. This includes the definition of **spot rates**, the **yield to maturity** and the **holding period yield**.
- To show that the fair price of a coupon paying bond is determined by spot rates of interest. Otherwise riskless arbitrage profits can be made by a strategy known as **coupon stripping**. The yield to maturity is then 'derived' from the price.
- To describe the key features of the government bond markets in the UK and the US, including price quotes, accrued interest and the **strips and repo markets**.
- To describe the corporate bond market including **floating rate notes (FRNs), deep discount bonds, callable and convertible bonds**. To show, in simple cases, how we might price a corporate bond.

---

As with money market instruments, there are a wide variety of different types of bond. A conventional government bond usually pays a fixed amount every 6 months to the holder (known as the coupon) plus the redemption value on a fixed maturity date. However, not all bonds have fixed coupons or fixed maturity dates. For example, some government and corporate bonds can be redeemed (or called) prior to their maturity date while some types of corporate bond (i.e. convertible bonds) can be exchanged for common stock (equity) of the issuer.

Bonds are usually issued to obtain long-term finance—their initial maturities are from 1 to 30 years (with some being non-redeemable and known as perpetuities or consols). They are issued by governments and their agencies (e.g. municipal securities in the US and local authority bonds in the UK) and by the corporate sector. They may be denominated in the home currency of the issuer or in a foreign currency (e.g. a UK corporate issuing dollar denominated bonds). A key difference between government issued bonds and those issued by corporates is default risk. Generally speaking, government bonds denominated in the home currency are described as 'risk free', meaning there is no default risk. This is because governments usually have the legal right to print their own currency to pay the interest and principal on the bonds (unless international agencies such as the IMF are able to prevent this). Of course, zero default risk would not necessarily be true for government bonds denominated in a foreign currency, as was the case for countries like Mexico in the 1980s and Russia in 1998, who effectively defaulted on dollar interest payments on their 'foreign bonds'.

In this chapter we first discuss 'risk free' government bonds, which provide the main analytic concepts for the reader to study the other types of bond mentioned above. We begin with an analysis of the various ways of measuring 'the return' on a bond and the relationship between 'yields' and prices. As with the money market, we shall see that there is a wide range of conventions and terminology. Next, the organisation of the UK and US government bond markets is discussed, including such topics as market makers, settlement procedures, new issues and the use of repos and the strips market. Finally, we present the main types of corporate bond and this is where we discuss convertible and callable bonds.

# 7.1 PRICES, YIELDS AND RETURN

This section deals with the various definitions of yields and the determination or calculation of bond prices. Unlike the money market, the bond market in the main uses compounding when calculating yields and the return on a bond. Bonds that have a single payout but have a maturity greater than 1 year are usually classified as **pure discount bonds or zero coupon bonds**.

After discussing 'zeros', we consider the three main ways 'the return' on a coupon paying bond may be measured: the running (or 'interest') yield, the yield to maturity and the 'total return'. Finally, we demonstrate how we can use riskless arbitrage to price a coupon paying bond by considering it as a series of zero coupon bonds. This allows a consistent methodology for the pricing of bonds and an analysis of the strips market, which concludes this section.

In the finance literature, interest rates and yields are often expressed as compound rates per annum—a convention not always adopted 'On the Street' (e.g. for T-bill rates). However, in the bond market most 'yield measures' involve some form of 'compounding'. We therefore deal with spot rates, yield to maturity and the relationship between yield and price for both zero coupon bonds and coupon paying bonds.

## PURE DISCOUNT/ZERO COUPON BONDS

A pure discount bond has a single payout $M$ in $n$ years time. If we know $M$ and the market price $P$, then we can calculate the current spot rate $r$ (Figure 7.1). Where we have this 'one off' single payment $M$, then $r$ is known as a spot rate of interest (or spot yield) for maturity date '$n$'. In the finance literature the spot rate is usually calculated as a compound rate of return expressed as an annual rate. Knowing $P$ and $M$, then $r$ is calculated from the discounted present value (DPV) formula (see Table 7.1):

[7.1]      $$P = \frac{M}{(1 + r)^n}$$

[7.2]      $$r = (M/P)^{1/n} - 1$$

## FIGURE 7.1: Spot rate zero coupon bond

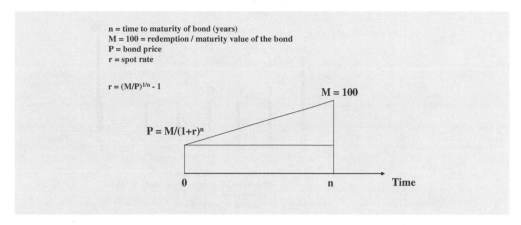

n = time to maturity of bond (years)
M = 100 = redemption / maturity value of the bond
P = bond price
r = spot rate

$r = (M/P)^{1/n} - 1$

$M = 100$

$P = M/(1+r)^n$

0    n    Time

## TABLE 7.1: Spot rate on a 'zero'

| Data: | $P$ = current price = \$62,321.30 |
|---|---|
| | $M$ = redemption value = \$100,000 |
| | $n - 6$ years |
| Question: | Calculate the spot rate $r$ |
| Answer: | $r = (\$100,000/\$62,321.30)^{1/6} - 1 = 0.082$ **(8.2% p.a.)** |

### COUPON PAYING BONDS

Coupon paying bonds provide a stream of income called coupon payments ($C$) which are known (in nominal terms) for all future periods, at the time the bond is purchased. On (conventional) government bonds the coupon payment is constant for all time periods. Most bonds are redeemable at a fixed date in the future for a known price, namely the **par value**, **redemption price** or **maturity value** ($M$) (see Figure 7.2). There are some bonds which, although they pay coupons, are never redeemed and these are known as **perpetuities** (e.g. '$2\frac{1}{2}$% consols' issued by the UK Government). The price quoted in the financial press and on electronic trading screens is known as the 'clean price'. The pricing formulae below all refer to the clean price. However, the actual price paid by an investor is known as the 'dirty price' or 'invoice price' and includes 'accrued' or 'rebate' interest. We deal with this additional complexity below.

### INTEREST YIELD, RUNNING YIELD, FLAT YIELD (CURRENT YIELD IN USA)

The interest yield on a bond is usually quoted in the financial press and is calculated as:

[7.3]    $$\text{Interest yield} = \frac{\text{annual coupon}}{\text{current clean price}} \times 100$$

## FIGURE 7.2: Coupon paying bond

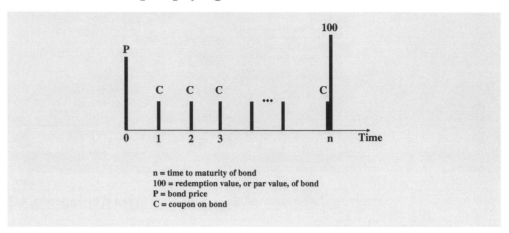

n = time to maturity of bond
100 = redemption value, or par value, of bond
P = bond price
C = coupon on bond

The interest yield is a very poor measure of the return on a bond since:

- it ignores any 'long-term' gains which occur if the bond is purchased at a discount and held to maturity;
- it ignores 'interest-on-interest' from coupon payments.

### YIELD TO MATURITY/REDEMPTION YIELD

The yield to maturity (YTM) is the internal rate of return of the bond. Knowing the market price $P$, the coupon $C$ and the maturity value $M$, the YTM ($= y$) is the solution to:

[7.4]
$$P = \frac{C_1}{(1+y)} + \frac{C_2}{(1+y)^2} + \ldots + \frac{(C_n + M)}{(1+y)^n}$$

Using the annuity formula this simplifies to:

[7.5a]
$$P = \frac{C}{y}\left[1 - \frac{1}{(1+y)^n}\right] + \frac{M}{(1+y)^n}$$

The YTM is that constant rate $y$ which equates the DPV of future cash flows $C_i$ (and the maturity value $M$) with the market price. Here $P$, $C_i$ and $M$ are known and we (or the *Financial Times*, calculate $y$, the YTM). An approximate formula to calculate $y$ is given by:

[7.5b]
$$y = \frac{C + (100 - P)/n}{(100 + 2P)/3}$$

Spreadsheets (such as Excel) can be used to calculate $y$. A simple example is given in Table 7.2. The YTM does not determine (in an economic sense) the price of the bond. It is merely a convenient single figure which summarises 'the average annual return' on the bond, given the market price. The YTM measures the (annual compound) rate of return on the bond if (i) it is held to maturity and (ii) all the coupon payments can be reinvested (on receipt) at a rate of interest equal to the (current) YTM. The YTM is made up of three elements:

## Table 7.2: Calculation of YTM

| Data: | Market price $= \$900$ |
|---|---|
| | 10% coupon bond, par value $= \$1000$ |
| | Semi-annual coupon payments, 3 years to maturity ($6 \times 6$ months) |
| **Question:** | Calculate the YTM |
| **Answer:** | $\$900 = \$50/(1 + y/2) + \$50/(1 + y/2)^2 + \ldots + \$50/(1 + y/2)^5 + \$1050/(1 + y/2)^6$ |

The solution to the above question can be found using simple computer spreadsheets (or by trial and error). **YTM = 14.2% p.a.** This can be verified by working out the DPV of the RHS using $y = 0.142$, which is found to be $900

> **YTM = coupon rate + interest on the coupons + capital gain (or loss) from the difference between the purchase price $P$ and the maturity value $M$**

If any of the above conditions does not hold, then the YTM will not correctly measure the 'return' on the bond even if it is held to maturity. However, it is still a widely used concept when discussing bond strategies amongst market participants. If the bond is not held to maturity then the correct measure of the return on the bond is the 'effective holding period return' (see below). If coupon payments are annual then $i = 1, 2, 3, \ldots$ refers to years and $y$ is at an annual (compound) rate. However, for government bonds the $C_i$ are usually fixed amounts paid semi-annually. For semi-annual coupons, we replace $y$ in the above formula by $y/2$ and $C_i$ is replaced by the semi-annual coupon payments $C/2$ and $i = 1, 2, 3, \ldots$ refers to 6, 12, 18, $\ldots$ months. It follows that $y/2$ is the semi-annual compound rate, with $y$ as the 'simple' grossed up annual rate (which in the US is known as 'the bond equivalent yield').

This 'simple' annual rate, $y$, is quoted 'On the Street'. The YTM can be calculated using the 'clean price' or the 'dirty price' but on dealers screens and in the financial press, it is usually the clean price that is used. Although the bond price is determined in an economic sense by the forces of supply and demand, nevertheless if we are given the YTM, then equation [7.4] can of course be used to calculate the current price (see Table 7.3). It is clear from equation [7.4] that the yield and price of a bond are negatively related and the relationship is non-linear (called 'convex'—see below).

### YTM AND COUPON RATE
The coupon *rate* is defined as $C/M$. There are some 'rules of thumb' used by traders when discussing the relationship between the YTM and the coupon rate of a bond. It is easy to show that if the coupon rate equals the YTM, then the bond is currently trading at a price equal to its par value. For example, consider a bond with a 10% coupon (annual), which also

---

## TABLE 7.3: Calculation of bond price (when YTM is given)

| | |
|---|---|
| **Data:** | 20-year, 10% coupon bond, par value of $1000 |
| | YTM is 11% p.a., semi-annual coupon payments |
| **Question:** | Calculate the price of the bond |
| **Answer:** | $C = 0.5(0.10(\$1000)) = \$50$, $n = 2(20) = 40$, $r = 0.11/2 = 0.055$ |
| | The DPV of the coupon payments is given by the ordinary annuity formula $Z = C[1 - 1/(1 + r)^n]/r = \$50[1 - 1/(1.055)^{40}]/0.055 = \$802.31$ PV (of $M$) $= \$1000/(1.055)^{40} = \$117.45$ |
| | Hence: **Price of bond** $= \$802.31 + \$117.45 = \mathbf{\$919.77}$ |

has a YTM of 10%, 2 years to maturity and a par value of £100. We can easily demonstrate that the market price of this bond equals its par value of £100, since using equation [7.4] we get:

[7.6] $$P = £10/(1.1) + £110/(1.1)^2 = £100$$

If the coupon rate $(C/M)$ is below the YTM, the market price will be below the par value (of £100) and the bond sells 'at a discount'. Conversely, if the coupon rate $C/M$ is above the YTM the bond is trading at a 'premium' (and will currently sell at a price above its par value). The qualitative relationship between market price, coupon rate, flat yield and YTM is given in Table 7.4 and can be deduced from the following rearrangement of the YTM equation [7.4]:

[7.7] $$\frac{P}{M} = \frac{C}{M}\left[\sum_{1}^{n}\frac{1}{(1+y)^i}\right] + \frac{1}{(1+y)^n}$$

[7.8] $$\frac{P}{M} = \frac{C}{M}\left[\frac{1 - (1+y)^n}{y}\right] + \frac{1}{(1+y)^n}$$

---

## TABLE 7.4: Yield and price relationship

| Bond sells at | Relationship |
|---|---|
| **Par** | Coupon rate = flat yield = YTM |
| **Discount** | Coupon rate < flat yield < YTM |
| **Premium** | Coupon rate > flat yield > YTM |

The coupon rate is $C/M$ and setting this to $y$ in equation [7.7] gives $P/M = 1$, that is the price of the bond equals its par value. Also, it follows that if $C/M$ is less than $y$ then $P/M < 1$ and the price is below the par value.

Consider two bonds with the same YTM, same maturity value and the same term to maturity, but bond A is selling above par and bond B below par. Since bond B will make a capital gain over its remaining life, while bond A will make a capital loss, the only way they could have the same yield is if bond A has higher coupon payments than bond B.

## TOTAL RETURN OR EFFECTIVE HOLDING PERIOD RETURN

The holding period return (HPR) is a measure of the (compound) rate of return, including coupon payments, interest-on-interest and any capital gain/loss. (Somewhat confusingly it is also referred to as the holding period *yield*.) Even if a bond is held to maturity, the HPR is uncertain because of uncertainty surrounding the future reinvestment rates for the coupon payments. If the bond is not held to maturity, but say for 1 year, then its future selling price is uncertain. For example, if the bond is purchased at a YTM of 10% but 1 year later the YTM falls to 9.5% then the market price of the bond will rise and the holder will make a capital gain, if he sells it. He will also have received two (6-monthly) coupon payments, the first of which will have been reinvested at whatever the prevailing yield on 6-month money happened to be at the end of the first 6-month period.

Some fund managers will actively trade bonds based on the expected HPR over a fixed horizon, sometimes called horizon analysis. The bond manager might purchase $1m of 10-year bonds and sell $1m of 5-year bonds because he feels the 10-year bonds will earn more, over the next 2 years. To calculate whether the return from this bond swap will be profitable he has to calculate the HPR for both bonds. To do so, the bond manager must assume a particular reinvestment rate for the coupon payments and a particular sale price at the end of the investment horizon (this would be the redemption price if the bond is held to maturity). Having calculated the terminal value (TV) of all payments (i.e. coupon and interest-on-interest + sale price) at the end of the chosen horizon (of $n$ years), the annual compound HPR ($r^*$) can be calculated from:

[7.9]     $$r^* = (TV/P)^{1/n} - 1$$

where TV is the value of all receipts at the end of the investment horizon, $P$ is the purchase price of the bond and $n$ is the number of years in the investment horizon.

An example of the calculation of the HPR is given in Table 7.5 and Figure 7.3. As coupon payments are often paid every 6 months and the annual YTM is measured as double the 6-month YTM, it is sometimes useful to measure the compound HPR assuming compounding over each 6-month period. In this case the formula becomes:

[7.10]     $$(1 + R^*/2)^h = TV/P$$

where $h = 2n$ (number of 6-month periods) and $R^*$ is the simple annual rate. Because of the uncertainty involved in calculating the effective HPR the bond manager will often undertake the calculations for a set of possible outcomes for future interest rates (i.e. scenario analysis).

## TABLE 7.5: Effective HPR

| | |
|---|---|
| **Data:** | 5-year, 10% coupon (annual) bond, par value $1000, trading at par (i.e. YTM = 10%) |

| | |
|---|---|
| **Question:** | Calculate the HPR assuming a horizon of 2 years, a reinvestment rate of 8% and a YTM in 2 years time of 9% |

**Answer:** Two coupons + interest on interest = $100 + $100(1.08)
$$= \$100\,(2.08) = \$208$$

Interest-on-interest is lower for an assumed reinvestment rate of either 10% or 9%

After 2 years the bond will have 3 years to maturity

$$\text{Expected price after 2 years} = \frac{\$100}{(1.09)} + \frac{\$100}{(1.09)^2} + \frac{\$100}{(1.09)^3} + \frac{\$1000}{(1.09)^3}$$

$$= \$100(2.5313) + \$1000(0.7722) = \$1025.33$$

A fall in the YTM produces a capital gain on the bond

Terminal value TV = $208 + $1025.33 = $1233.33

Approximate return = ($233.33/$1000)100 = 23.33% over 2 years (about 11.6% p.a.)

**HPR** (at compound annual rate) $= (1 + r^*)^2 = \$1233.33/\$1000 = \mathbf{1.23333}$

$r^* = \mathbf{0.1155\ (11.55\%)}$

## FIGURE 7.3: HPR over 2 years

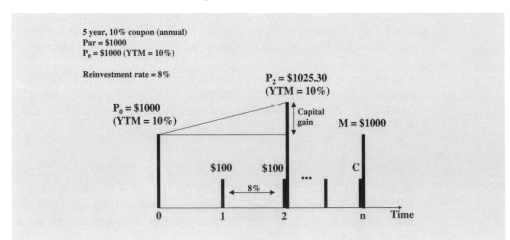

5 year, 10% coupon (annual)
Par = $1000
$P_0$ = $1000 (YTM = 10%)

Reinvestment rate = 8%

$P_2$ = $1025.30
(YTM = 10%)

$P_0$ = $1000
(YTM = 10%)

Capital gain

M = $1000

$100   $100

8%

0   1   2   n   Time

## PRICING COUPON PAYING BONDS USING SPOT RATES

This section discusses why bonds should be priced using spot rates. However, spot rates are not available at long maturities and therefore must be estimated from coupon paying bonds (see below). Bond prices that do not reflect prevailing spot rates can be subject to coupon stripping and riskless profit opportunities. The spot rate is the (annual compound) rate of return on an investment that has a 'one off' payout at time $n$. It is the return on a zero coupon bond:

[7.11]
$$P = \frac{M}{(1 + r_n)^n}$$

If there were zero coupon bonds for all maturities then we could observe their prices $P_1$, $P_2$, etc. and use equation [7.11] to calculate $r_1$, $r_2$, $r_3$, etc. These spot rates would be the outcome of the demand and supply for zero coupon bonds in the market. Any (non-callable) coupon bond can be viewed as a package/bundle of zero coupon securities and hence its price should equal the DPV of these coupon payments, where each coupon payment is discounted at the appropriate spot rate:

[7.12]
$$P = \frac{C_1}{(1 + r_1)} + \frac{C_2}{(1 + r_2)^2} + \ldots + \frac{C + M}{(1 + r_n)^n}$$

The $C_i$ may be viewed as the 'one off' payoffs at times 1, 2, 3, ... (and for most bonds $C_i = C$, a constant). The maturity value ($M$) is a one off payment at time $n$. Each separate coupon (and the redemption) payment may be considered as a zero coupon bond, discounted at the spot rate applicable to payments at $t = 1, 2, 3, \ldots$. Spot rates are the correct way to price government stock, since all coupons at time $t$ on different bonds are discounted at the same rate $r_t$. Once we have the spot rates, the price of a coupon paying bond is easy to calculate, as shown in Table 7.6.

---

## TABLE 7.6: Pricing coupon bonds using spot rates

| | |
|---|---|
| **Data:** | Bond A: Exchequer stock $8\frac{3}{4}\%$, annual coupon, 2 years maturity, par value = £100 |
| | Bond B: Exchequer stock 12%, annual coupon, 2 years maturity, par value = £100 |
| | Spot rates $r_1 = 0.05$ (5%), $r_2 = 0.06$ (6%) |
| **Question:** | Calculate the market price of the two bonds |
| **Answer:** | **Price (bond A)** $= £8.75/(1.05) + £108.75/(1.06)^2 = $ **£105.12** |
| | **Price (bond B)** $= £12/(1.05) + £112/(1.06)^2 = $ **£111.11** |

In contrast to using spot rates $r_1$, $r_2$, etc., the YTM discounts cash flows at $t = 1$ and $t = 2$ at the same rate $y$. Using a constant discount rate to price the bond can lead to profitable arbitrage opportunities via 'coupon stripping' (see below). Thus the YTM is best viewed as being arithmetically derived from the price of the bond (as illustrated above) and not as determining the 'correct' or 'theoretical' price of the bond.

## CALCULATION OF (THEORETICAL) SPOT RATES

We now turn to the problem of estimating spot rates when they are not directly observed in the market. In the US and the UK T-bills, which are risk free pure discount bonds, are only issued with maturities up to 1 year. In general, government bonds with maturities greater than 1 year are issued as coupon paying securities. However, spot yields can be calculated from coupon paying bonds in several ways and here we demonstrate the method known as **bootstrapping**. Table 7.7 considers the case where we observe spot rates $r_1$ and $r_2$ but not $r_3$. However, $r_3$ can be derived using the observed market price of a three-period coupon paying bond.

If we have coupon paying bonds for n = 2 years, 2.5 years, etc. then the bootstrapping procedure can be repeated to calculate $r_4$, $r_5$, etc. Where a coupon paying bond does not exist (e.g. for maturity of 3.5 years), then $r_7$ would be approximated using $r_6$ and $r_8$ (e.g. a simple method would be $r_7 = (r_6 + r_8)/2$).

## STRIPPED TREASURY SECURITIES AND COUPON STRIPPING

In the US (and recently in the UK) zero coupon securities are created by dealer firms, selling off the 'ownership' of the individual coupon payments from coupon paying bonds. These 'zeros' are therefore 'synthetic' securities. However, observed interest rates on 'stripped'

---

## TABLE 7.7: Calculation of spot rates by bootstrapping

| | |
|---|---|
| **Data:** | Two, zero coupon bonds (6 months and 1 year); $r_1 = 8\%$ p.a., $r_2 = 8.3\%$ p.a. |
| | Bond-B: coupon bond with maturity 1.5 years, coupon rate = 8.5%, coupons paid every 6 months, market price $P = 99.45$, par value = 100 |
| **Question:** | Calculate the 18-month spot rate $r_3$ |
| **Answer:** | The 'correct' price of bond-B is given by: |
| | $$99.45 = \frac{4.25}{(1 + r_1/2)} + \frac{4.25}{(1 + r_2/2)^2} + \frac{104.25}{(1 + r_3/2)^3}$$ |
| | Observed spot rates on 6m and 12m bills are $r_1 = 0.08$, $r_2 = 0.083$, hence $99.45 = 4.0865 + 3.9180 + 104.25/(1 + r_3/2)^3$ |
| | The only 'unknown' in the above equation is $r_3$; $r_3 = 0.0893$ **(8.93%)** p.a. on a bond equivalent yield basis |

Treasuries can give a misleading measure of risk free spot rates because (i) strips are less liquid/marketable, hence their yields reflect a liquidity premium, and (ii) there is preferential tax treatment for some holders of strips (e.g. some overseas purchasers) and this 'tax effect' is reflected in observed yields. Even though spot rates are observable in the strips market, it may still be necessary to use bootstrap procedures to obtain good estimates of the true risk free spot rates.

We now demonstrate why coupon paying bonds should be priced using spot rates. This is because if coupon bonds are *not* priced using spot rates, then there is a potential profit in 'coupon stripping' the bond. In Table 7.8 we see that the YTM on the coupon paying bond is 12.5% and its market price is $100. This implies that on setting the price, the first two coupons (and all the others) have implicitly been discounted at the YTM = 6.25% every 6 months. However, if the current spot rates are $r_1 = 4\%$ and $r_2 = 4.15\%$, then these first two coupons can be sold (as strips) to earn a riskless profit. It may be the case that the sums received from selling all 20 'coupons' as strips exceed the purchase price of $100. (This will depend on spot rates between years 2 and 10.) In this case the bond is mispriced, given prevailing spot rates.

---

## TABLE 7.8: Profits from coupon stripping

| | |
|---|---|
| **Data:** | Consider a $12\frac{1}{2}\%$ coupon bond, 10 years to maturity, selling at par ($100) with coupon payments every 6 months. The market price equals the par value and hence the YTM must equal 12.5% |
| | Hence: |
| | $$P = \$6.25/(1.0625) + \$6.25/(1.0625)^2 + \ldots + \$106.25/(1.0625)^{20}$$ $$= \$5.88 + \$5.53 + \$5.20 + \ldots + \$31.60 = \mathbf{\$100}$$ |
| | The actual spot rates for 6-month and 1-year money are 0.08 and 0.083, respectively |
| **Question:** | Show that in the first 2 years, coupon stripping is profitable |
| **Answer:** | We can expect to sell the first two coupons for: |
| | $$PV(C_1) = \$6.25/(1.04) = \$6.0096$$ |
| | $$PV(C_2) = \$6.25/(1.0415)^2 = \$5.7618$$ |
| | A market maker can therefore purchase the $12\frac{1}{2}\%$ coupon bond, 'unbundle' the coupons and sell each of the first two coupons as zero coupon bonds or Treasury strips. His profit today from selling the first two coupons is: |
| | $\$(6.0096 - 5.88) = \mathbf{\$0.1296}$ |
| | $\$(5.7618 - 5.53) = \mathbf{\$0.2318}$ |

In trying to realise his profit, in the above example, the dealer buys 12.5% coupon bonds causing an increase in their price (and hence a fall in the implicit YTM). By selling 1-year and 2-year strips, their prices fall (and their spot yields rise). Hence, arbitrage causes a narrowing in the profits to be made. Arbitrage will continue until the market price of the 12.5% coupon bond equals the sum of the receipts from coupon stripping (at current spot rates).

> **The market price of the coupon bond is determined by the current term structure of spot rates and the YTM is then derived by 'arithmetically inverting' the price–yield relationship**

The example in Table 7.9 shows that if a 2-year coupon paying bond is priced using spot rates then there will be no arbitrage profits from coupon stripping. This is because the present value (PV) of the coupons (and the maturity value) discounted at the appropriate spot rates gives a 'fair' price of $966.49 which equals the quoted market price.

## TABLE 7.9: Equilibrium price of coupon paying bonds

| | |
|---|---|
| **Data:** | Observed spot rate on 1-year bill $= 10\%$ |
| | Observed 2-year spot rate $= 11\%$ |
| | Coupon bond is Treasury, 2-year, 9% coupon (annual), par value $= \$1000$, with an observed market price of $P = \$966.4866$ |
| **Question:** | Calculate the 'fair' or 'equilibrum' price of the bond and hence show that there are no profits to be made from coupon stripping. Calculate the YTM of this bond |
| **Answer:** | PV from selling 1st coupon $= \$90/(1.10) = \$81.8182$ |
| | PV (2nd coupon + redemption value) $= \$1090/(1.11)^2 = \$884.6684$ |
| | Total receipts from coupon stripping $=$ 'fair' price $\hat{P} = \mathbf{\$966.4866}$ |
| | The actual market price of the bond equals the fair price, hence no arbitrage profits are possible. The YTM is the solution $y$ to: |
| | $$\frac{90}{(1+y)} + \frac{1090}{(1+y)^2} = 966.49 \text{ and hence } y = \mathbf{10.96\%}$$ |

# 7.2 MARKET STRUCTURE: UK AND US BOND MARKETS

In this section we look at the market structure of the UK and US bond markets, including the key market participants, settlement procedures, new issues and the index linked, repo and strips markets. The methods used for price quotes and the relationship between price quotes, accrued interest and the invoice price are also examined. We begin with the UK gilts market and then discuss the US Treasury bond market.

## BRITISH GOVERNMENT (GILT-EDGED) SECURITIES

In the UK, long-term government bonds (gilts) are issued to finance the government's budget deficit (or as it is often referred to in the UK, the public sector borrowing requirement, PSBR). The main holders of gilts include UK life assurance and pension funds, the personal sector and overseas residents. Conventional stocks (about 87% of the total) are issued with maturities up to about 30 years and index linked stocks (about 11% of the total), whose return is based on the rate of inflation, are also available (Figure 7.4). The outstanding stock is around £200bn. Until very recently about 20 gilt-edged market makers (GEMMs) acted as primary dealers and, although the system changed in 1996–97, it is instructive to look at these arrangements because many bond markets (particularly in emerging markets) operate broadly in this fashion. The GEMMs operate as follows:

- they must quote firm bid and offer prices at all times;
- quoted prices are good for at least £10m in conventional stocks;
- average value per bargain is about £1.5m;
- GEMMs have access to inter-dealer brokers (IDBs): this allows GEMMs to trade stocks on a 'no names basis' with other GEMMs;
- only GEMMs can borrow stock to cover short positions from approved stocklenders including stock exchange money brokers (SEMBs);
- information on all trades must be reported to the exchange (normally within 15 minutes, but within 5 minutes for trades over £100,000).

On conventional stocks a fixed rate of interest (the coupon) is paid every 6 months and there

## FIGURE 7.4: Nominal amount of gilts outstanding

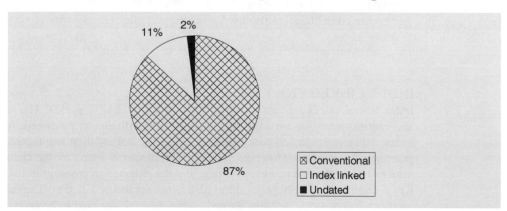

is usually a fixed repayment date and maturity value (usually the par value). For example, consider the Treasury 9%, 2008. The holder of this gilt will receive £9 interest each year (£4.5 every 6 months) on each £100 nominal of stock. The gilt will be redeemed at par on a specified date in 2008. Settlement procedures for the purchase and sale of gilts take place mainly through the Debt Management Office (DMO) and CrestCo which:

- record the ownership of stock in a central gilts register;
- moves stock electronically as ownership changes;
- arranges for a settlement bank to receive payments/receipts from purchases/sales of stock—these are aggregated daily.

*New issues* are by auction and tender, as described in Box 7.1. Small amounts (up to £500m) are also sold through the Bank's dealing room as tap stocks.

---

**Box 7.1    AUCTIONS AND TENDERS**

Suppose that £2000m of a new stock is to be sold by public offer. The following bids are received:

| | |
|---|---|
| At £99 | for £1000m |
| At £98–30/32 | for £500m |
| At £98–28/32 | for £1000m |

If the offer is taking place through an auction the Bank sells:

| | |
|---|---|
| £1000m | at £99 |
| £500m | at £98–30/32 |
| £500m | at £98–28/32, so that those bidding £98–28/32 receive 50% of the stock for which they bid |

If the offer is taking place through a tender, the Bank might sell £2000m at £98–28/32, with those who tendered above that price being allotted the full amount tendered and those who tendered £98–28/32 receiving 50% of the stock tendered for. The Bank might alternatively choose to allot stock at a higher price, and some of the stock would be retained in official portfolios for subsequent sale. The majority of new issues are by auction.

---

## INDEX LINKED STOCKS

Index linked stocks account for about 11% of the total gilts market. The coupon payments and redemption value are adjusted for changes in inflation as measured by the retail price index (RPI). Index linked gilts provide a hedge against inflation and therefore give a (near) guaranteed real return. However, inflation adjustment is based on the change in the RPI 8 months before the first coupon payment, and the redemption payment is also adjusted by the RPI 8 months previously (any capital gain is not subject to UK tax). The real rates of return on index linked stock are often quoted on the basis of assumed inflation rates of 3%, 5% or

10%. Because of the 'lag' in calculating the inflation adjustments, the higher is the assumed rate of inflation (e.g. 5% rather than 3%), the lower is the real rate. A stylised example of the adjustments to coupon and redemption payments is given in Table 7.10.

OPEN GILT REPO MARKET

Prior to the introduction of a gilt repo market in January 1996, only GEMMs (and the Discount Houses) could go short. In order to deliver the stock, the GEMMs could borrow from (and only from) SEMBs, who in turn borrowed from a lender approved by the Inland Revenue (i.e. the UK tax authorities). Also, the GEMMs could borrow cash against gilt collateral from the SEMBs, who in turn borrowed from the banking system. In a number of international securities markets, stock lending and borrowing takes place through sale and repurchase arrangements (repos), and this system also applies to the UK gilts market since 1996. The development of the gilt repo market involved two main changes:

- Any market participant can now borrow stock and such borrowing need not be for the sole purpose of filling a short position.
- The stock need not be lent/borrowed solely through a SEMB.

The repo allows participants to borrow cash against gilt collateral in order to finance long positions in other securities while a 'reverse repo' would enable participants to borrow gilts. Thus the special position of the GEMMs is eroded under the new repo arrangements. However, it should encourage wider participation in the market, particularly by international investors who are familiar with repo markets. Even after the introduction of the gilt repo market the GEMMs continue to retain their 'special arrangements', such as their direct dealing relationship with the Bank of England, access to IDB screens, secured borrowing from the Bank at 2.45 p.m. and the ability to participate in the Bank's twice-monthly money market repo facility.

## TABLE 7.10: Index linked stocks

| **Data:** | 4% index linked Treasury 2020 issued on 22nd July 1993 with interest payments due on 22nd January 1994 and every 6 months thereafter. Redemption date is 22nd July 2020 |
|---|---|
| | Base month for RPI is November 92 (i.e. 9 months prior to the issue date, July 93) and equals 135. Assume the RPI on 22nd July 2020 is 410.8. The RPI 8 months prior to 22nd January 94 is 140.1 |
| **Questions:** | What is the value of the first coupon payment? |
| | What is the value of the principal repayment on £100 nominal? |
| **Answers:** | First coupon payment $= (1/2)4(140.1/135) = £2.0755$ |
| | Redemption value $= £100(410.8/135) = £304.296$ |

## STRIPS IN THE UK GILTS MARKET

There is a proposal which has now been implemented that a STRIPS market in UK gilts be established (Bank of England, 1995). The term STRIP stands for 'Separate Trading of Registered Interest and Principal of Securities'. Originally 'stripping' referred to the practice of physically stripping coupons from a bearer bond certificate. In a strips market, an investor can exchange (all or part of) the coupons on a coupon paying bond for a set of individual coupons (which exactly match the cash flows of the parent bond). These separate coupons can then be sold in the market. Conversely, an investor can buy a set of strips and 'reconstitute' a coupon paying bond.

To develop liquidity in the market would require synchronisation of coupon dates on different bond issues. For example, a £5bn nominal issue of stock with an 8% coupon would produce semi-annual strips of only £200m. With aligned coupon dates, the registration of transactions via the DMO would not be too onerous. For example, if the longest strippable issue were on a 20-year gilt, then assuming one aligned coupon date, we would have 41 new zero coupon gilts plus the principal (redemption) payments on each strippable issue. The DMO would provide a 'stripping service' and charge a small fee for each reconstitution/ stripping transaction.

The advantage of a strips market from the investor's point of view is basically to avoid reinvestment risk, by purchasing strips to match a known future outflow of funds (e.g. pension payments by pension funds). Also, the strips market would increase the duration of existing gilts (see chapter 8). For example, the duration of the 'principal strip' of the longest conventional gilt would be more than twice that of the underlying coupon paying bond (at yield of around 6%). Hence pension funds which have long duration liabilities could more easily match the duration of their assets (and 'fine tune' the duration more precisely). Also, if index linked gilts were strippable then desired cash flow patterns in real terms could be achieved.

The strips market would allow synthetic gilt products to be manufactured. For example, 'deferred payment gilts' would result from the purchase of a coupon paying gilt and selling off the coupons for the early years, in the strips market. An 'annuity gilt' would involve selling the principal/redemption payment as a strip and retaining the coupon payments. To the extent that there is a demand by investors (both UK and international) for stripped gilts their introduction could reduce the government's cost of borrowing.

## US TREASURY BONDS

In broad terms the US system operates in a similar fashion in terms of dealing and settlement as the UK government bond market. In the US, Treasury securities with a maturity of 2 years or greater are issued as coupon paying securities. Maturities of 2, 3, 5, 7, 10 and 30 years are issued. Coupon securities with a maturity between 2 and 10 years are called 'notes' and those over 10 years are called 'bonds', but we will refer to both as bonds. The bonds are held in book entry form at the Federal Reserve so the investor only receives a receipt of ownership. As in the UK this allows low cost transfer of ownership. Although the Fed only deals with primary or recognised dealers, anyone can deal in government bonds. The auction procedure for new issues is on a yield basis—as described for UK T-bills. Trades in Treasury bonds are conducted through intermediaries known as government brokers who do not trade on their own account. They provide continuous 'highest bid', 'lowest offer' prices on their screens which can be 'hit' by a dealer, who then pays a commission to the government brokers. There is also a large active strips market in the US.

Dealer profits are made from (i) the bid–ask spread, (ii) any capital appreciation on their inventory (or depreciation on any securities held short) and (iii) the 'carry' earned on the difference between the interest earned on bonds and the cost of financing them. The primary dealers have near exclusive access to the prices on government dealer screens and the general public does not have access to these price quotes.

## STRIPPED TREASURY SECURITIES

Unlike the UK, the Treasury strips market has been active in the US since the early 1980s. The mechanism is that 'firms' (e.g. Merrill Lynch, Salomon Bros) purchase coupon bonds and place them in a custodial account at a bank. The firms then issue receipts representing ownership of each coupon and the principal (called the corpus). These 'receipts' are then sold to investors as 'Treasury strips'.

# PRICE QUOTES AND ACCRUED INTEREST

### Price quotes: US Treasury bonds

Price quotes on US bonds (and notes) are in units of $1/32$ of 1% of par (where par is $100). So 99-30 is a quote of $99$–$30/32$ (Figure 7.5). The minimum price movement (the tick size) is $1/32$ (of 1%) expressed in the *Wall Street Journal* as '+1' (Figure 7.5). An illustrative 'verbal' price quote is:

- '6% Feb 26 at $99: 07/99: 09$'. This signifies a 6% coupon bond redeemable in February 2026 and with a bid–ask price of $99$–$7/32$(bid) $= 99.21875$ and $99: 9/32$(ask) $= 99.28125$ per $100 nominal (see Figure 7.5 for similar newspaper quotes).

The 'Ask Yld' for US Treasuries is the yield to maturity (using the ask price) and 'n' after the date of the bond (e.g. 'Nov 02n') indicates a Treasury 'note'.

A useful rule of thumb is that on a par value of $100,000, a change in price of 1% equates to $1000 $(= (0.01)\$100,000)$. Also the 'tick value' on a par value of $100,000 is $(1/32)(0.01)\$100,000 = \$31.25$. The par value on different bonds can be different in the US (see Table 7.11). Hence when quoting bond prices, traders quote the price as a percentage of par value. A bond selling at par is quoted as 100. An illustrative example of quotes from five major government dealers (by telephone) is given in Table 7.11.

The largest ask price differential (dealer A – dealer E) is $4/32$. There is a variation in the bid–ask spread from $2/32$ (dealer B) to $4/32$ (dealer E), which is relatively large for such a liquid market.

### Price quotes: UK gilts

The quoted price is the clean price (i.e. excludes accrued or rebate interest). The price is quoted per £100 of nominal stock in decimals (see Figure 7.6). The following key features apply to quotes:

## FIGURE 7.5: T-bond quotes (*Wall Street Journal*). Reproduced with permission

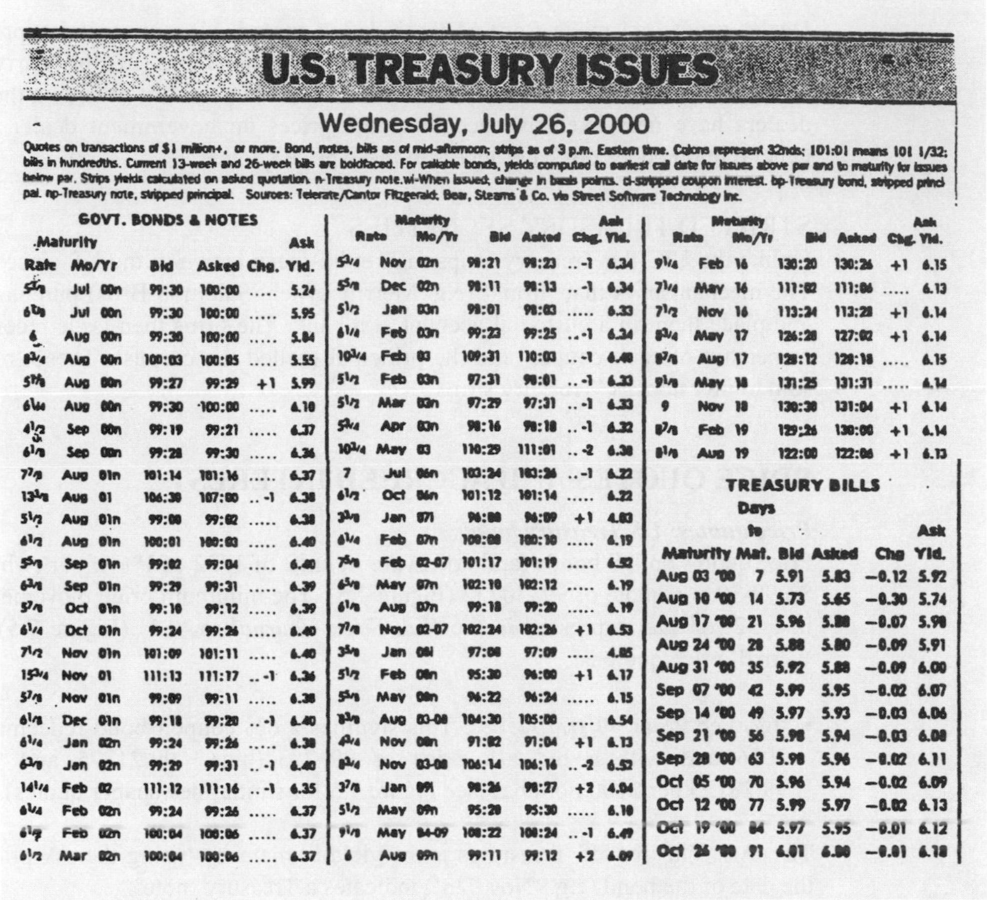

U.S. TREASURY ISSUES

Wednesday, July 26, 2000

Quotes on transactions of $1 million+, or more. Bond, notes, bills as of mid-afternoon; strips as of 3 p.m. Eastern time. Colons represent 32nds; 101:01 means 101 1/32; bills in hundredths. Current 13-week and 26-week bills are boldfaced. For callable bonds, yields computed to earliest call date for issues above par and to maturity for issues below par. Strips yields calculated on asked quotation. n-Treasury note. wi-When issued; change in basis points. ci-stripped coupon interest. bp-Treasury bond, stripped principal. np-Treasury note, stripped principal. Sources: Telerate/Cantor Fitzgerald; Bear, Stearns & Co. via Street Software Technology Inc.

GOVT. BONDS & NOTES

| Rate | Maturity Mo/Yr | Bid | Asked | Chg. | Ask Yld. |
|---|---|---|---|---|---|
| 5 7/8 | Jul 00n | 99:30 | 100:00 | ..... | 5.24 |
| 6 1/8 | Jul 00n | 99:30 | 100:00 | ..... | 5.95 |
| 6 | Aug 00n | 99:30 | 100:00 | ..... | 5.84 |
| 8 3/4 | Aug 00n | 100:03 | 100:05 | ..... | 5.55 |
| 5 7/8 | Aug 00n | 99:27 | 99:29 | +1 | 5.99 |
| 6 1/4 | Aug 00n | 99:30 | 100:00 | ..... | 6.10 |
| 4 1/2 | Sep 00n | 99:19 | 99:21 | ..... | 6.37 |
| 6 1/8 | Sep 00n | 99:28 | 99:30 | ..... | 6.36 |
| 7 7/8 | Aug 01n | 101:14 | 101:16 | ..... | 6.37 |
| 13 3/8 | Aug 01 | 106:30 | 107:00 | .. -1 | 6.38 |
| 5 1/2 | Aug 01n | 99:00 | 99:02 | ..... | 6.38 |
| 6 1/2 | Aug 01n | 100:01 | 100:03 | ..... | 6.40 |
| 5 5/8 | Sep 01n | 99:02 | 99:04 | ..... | 6.40 |
| 6 3/8 | Sep 01n | 99:29 | 99:31 | ..... | 6.39 |
| 5 7/8 | Oct 01n | 99:10 | 99:12 | ..... | 6.39 |
| 6 1/4 | Oct 01n | 99:24 | 99:26 | ..... | 6.40 |
| 7 1/2 | Nov 01n | 101:09 | 101:11 | ..... | 6.40 |
| 15 3/4 | Nov 01 | 111:13 | 111:17 | .. -1 | 6.36 |
| 5 7/8 | Nov 01n | 99:09 | 99:11 | ..... | 6.38 |
| 6 1/8 | Dec 01n | 99:18 | 99:20 | .. -1 | 6.40 |
| 6 1/4 | Jan 02n | 99:24 | 99:26 | ..... | 6.38 |
| 6 3/8 | Jan 02n | 99:29 | 99:31 | .. -1 | 6.40 |
| 14 1/4 | Feb 02 | 111:12 | 111:16 | .. -1 | 6.35 |
| 6 1/4 | Feb 02n | 99:24 | 99:26 | ..... | 6.37 |
| 6 1/8 | Feb 02n | 100:04 | 100:06 | ..... | 6.37 |
| 6 1/2 | Mar 02n | 100:04 | 100:06 | ..... | 6.37 |
| 5 3/4 | Nov 02n | 98:21 | 98:23 | .. -1 | 6.34 |
| 5 5/8 | Dec 02n | 98:11 | 98:13 | .. -1 | 6.34 |
| 5 1/2 | Jan 03n | 98:01 | 98:03 | ..... | 6.33 |
| 6 1/4 | Feb 03n | 99:23 | 99:25 | .. -1 | 6.34 |
| 10 3/4 | Feb 03 | 109:31 | 110:03 | .. -1 | 6.40 |
| 5 1/2 | Feb 03n | 97:31 | 98:01 | .. -1 | 6.33 |
| 5 1/2 | Mar 03n | 97:29 | 97:31 | .. -1 | 6.33 |
| 5 3/4 | Apr 03n | 98:16 | 98:18 | .. -1 | 6.32 |
| 10 3/4 | May 03 | 110:29 | 111:01 | .. -2 | 6.38 |
| 7 | Jul 06n | 103:24 | 103:26 | .. -1 | 6.22 |
| 6 1/2 | Oct 06n | 101:12 | 101:14 | ..... | 6.22 |
| 3 3/8 | Jan 07i | 96:08 | 96:09 | +1 | 4.03 |
| 6 1/4 | Feb 07n | 100:08 | 100:10 | ..... | 6.19 |
| 7 5/8 | Feb 02-07 | 101:17 | 101:19 | ..... | 6.52 |
| 6 5/8 | May 07n | 102:10 | 102:12 | ..... | 6.19 |
| 6 1/8 | Aug 07n | 99:18 | 99:20 | ..... | 6.19 |
| 7 7/8 | Nov 02-07 | 102:24 | 102:26 | +1 | 6.53 |
| 3 5/8 | Jan 08i | 97:08 | 97:09 | ..... | 4.05 |
| 5 1/2 | Feb 08n | 95:30 | 96:00 | +1 | 6.17 |
| 5 5/8 | May 08n | 96:22 | 96:24 | ..... | 6.15 |
| 8 3/8 | Aug 03-08 | 104:30 | 105:00 | ..... | 6.54 |
| 4 3/4 | Nov 08n | 91:02 | 91:04 | +1 | 6.13 |
| 8 3/4 | Nov 03-08 | 106:14 | 106:16 | .. -2 | 6.52 |
| 3 7/8 | Jan 09i | 98:26 | 98:27 | +2 | 4.04 |
| 5 1/2 | May 09n | 95:28 | 95:30 | ..... | 6.10 |
| 9 1/8 | May 04-09 | 108:22 | 108:24 | .. -1 | 6.49 |
| 6 | Aug 09n | 99:11 | 99:12 | +2 | 6.09 |
| 9 1/4 | Feb 16 | 130:20 | 130:26 | +1 | 6.15 |
| 7 1/4 | May 16 | 111:02 | 111:06 | ..... | 6.13 |
| 7 1/2 | Nov 16 | 113:24 | 113:28 | +1 | 6.14 |
| 8 3/4 | May 17 | 126:28 | 127:02 | +1 | 6.14 |
| 8 7/8 | Aug 17 | 128:12 | 128:18 | ..... | 6.15 |
| 9 1/8 | May 18 | 131:25 | 131:31 | ..... | 6.14 |
| 9 | Nov 18 | 130:30 | 131:04 | +1 | 6.14 |
| 8 7/8 | Feb 19 | 129:26 | 130:00 | +1 | 6.14 |
| 8 1/8 | Aug 19 | 122:00 | 122:06 | +1 | 6.13 |

TREASURY BILLS

| Maturity | Days to Mat. | Bid | Asked | Chg | Ask Yld. |
|---|---|---|---|---|---|
| Aug 03 '00 | 7 | 5.91 | 5.83 | −0.12 | 5.92 |
| Aug 10 '00 | 14 | 5.73 | 5.65 | −0.30 | 5.74 |
| Aug 17 '00 | 21 | 5.96 | 5.88 | −0.07 | 5.98 |
| Aug 24 '00 | 28 | 5.88 | 5.80 | −0.09 | 5.91 |
| Aug 31 '00 | 35 | 5.92 | 5.88 | −0.09 | 6.00 |
| Sep 07 '00 | 42 | 5.99 | 5.95 | −0.02 | 6.07 |
| Sep 14 '00 | 49 | 5.97 | 5.93 | −0.03 | 6.06 |
| Sep 21 '00 | 56 | 5.98 | 5.94 | −0.03 | 6.08 |
| Sep 28 '00 | 63 | 5.98 | 5.96 | −0.02 | 6.11 |
| Oct 05 '00 | 70 | 5.96 | 5.94 | −0.02 | 6.09 |
| Oct 12 '00 | 77 | 5.99 | 5.97 | −0.02 | 6.13 |
| Oct 19 '00 | 84 | 5.97 | 5.95 | −0.01 | 6.12 |
| Oct 26 '00 | 91 | 6.01 | 6.00 | −0.01 | 6.18 |

## TABLE 7.11: Alternative price quotes

| Dealer | Bid price(1) | Ask price(2) |
|---|---|---|
| A | 101:2 | 101:6 |
| B | 101:3 | 101:5 |
| C | 101:4 | 101:6 |
| D | 101:5 | 101:9 |
| E | 101:6 | 101:8 |

Notes: 1. Prices in 1/32 of 1%
2. Bid price = buying price 'bid' by market makers
3. Ask (offer) price = selling price offered by market maker

## FIGURE 7.6: Gilt Edged Stock: Quotes (*Financial Times*), reproduced with permission

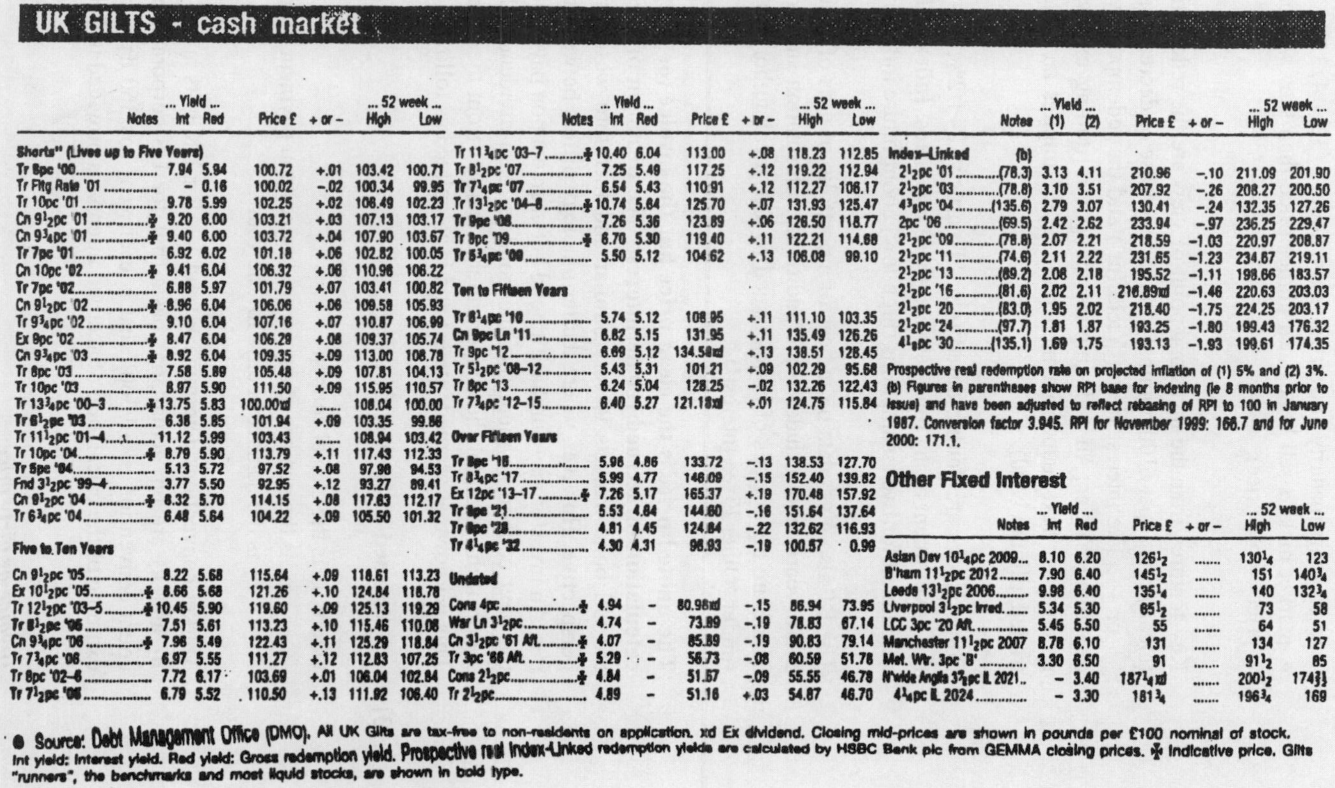

UK GILTS - cash market

| | Notes | Yield Int | Yield Red | Price £ | + or – | 52 week High | 52 week Low |
|---|---|---|---|---|---|---|---|
| **Shorts" (Lives up to Five Years)** | | | | | | | |
| Tr 8pc '00 | | 7.94 | 5.94 | 100.72 | +.01 | 103.42 | 100.71 |
| Tr Fltg Rate '01 | | – | 0.16 | 100.02 | –.02 | 100.34 | 99.95 |
| Tr 10pc '01 | | 9.78 | 5.99 | 102.25 | +.02 | 108.49 | 102.23 |
| Cn 9½pc '01 | ✤ | 9.20 | 6.00 | 103.21 | +.03 | 107.13 | 103.17 |
| Cn 9¾pc '01 | ✤ | 9.40 | 6.00 | 103.72 | +.04 | 107.90 | 103.67 |
| Tr 7pc '01 | | 6.92 | 6.02 | 101.18 | +.06 | 102.82 | 100.05 |
| Cn 10pc '02 | ✤ | 9.41 | 6.04 | 106.32 | +.06 | 110.98 | 106.22 |
| Tr 7pc '02 | | 6.88 | 5.97 | 101.79 | +.07 | 103.41 | 100.82 |
| Cn 9½pc '02 | ✤ | 8.96 | 6.04 | 106.06 | +.06 | 109.58 | 105.93 |
| Tr 9¾pc '02 | | 9.10 | 6.04 | 107.16 | +.07 | 110.87 | 106.99 |
| Ex 9pc '02 | ✤ | 8.47 | 6.04 | 106.28 | +.08 | 109.37 | 105.74 |
| Cn 9¾pc '03 | ✤ | 8.92 | 6.04 | 109.35 | +.09 | 113.00 | 108.78 |
| Tr 8pc '03 | | 7.58 | 5.89 | 105.48 | +.09 | 107.81 | 104.13 |
| Tr 10pc '03 | | 8.97 | 5.90 | 111.50 | +.09 | 115.95 | 110.57 |
| Tr 13¾pc '00–3 | ✤ | 13.75 | 5.83 | 100.00xd | ...... | 108.04 | 100.00 |
| Tr 6½pc '03 | | 6.38 | 5.85 | 101.94 | +.09 | 103.35 | 99.86 |
| Tr 11½pc '01–4 | | 11.12 | 5.99 | 103.43 | ...... | 108.94 | 103.42 |
| Tr 10pc '04 | ✤ | 8.79 | 5.90 | 113.79 | +.11 | 117.43 | 112.33 |
| Tr 5pc '04 | | 5.13 | 5.72 | 97.52 | +.08 | 97.98 | 94.53 |
| Fnd 3½pc '99–4 | | 3.77 | 5.50 | 92.95 | +.12 | 93.27 | 89.41 |
| Cn 9½pc '04 | ✤ | 8.32 | 5.70 | 114.15 | +.08 | 117.63 | 112.17 |
| Tr 6¾pc '04 | | 6.48 | 5.64 | 104.22 | +.09 | 105.50 | 101.32 |
| **Five to Ten Years** | | | | | | | |
| Cn 9½pc '05 | | 8.22 | 5.68 | 115.64 | +.09 | 118.61 | 113.23 |
| Ex 10½pc '05 | ✤ | 8.66 | 5.68 | 121.26 | +.10 | 124.84 | 118.78 |
| Tr 12½pc '03–5 | ✤ | 10.45 | 5.90 | 119.60 | +.09 | 125.13 | 119.29 |
| Tr 8½pc '05 | | 7.51 | 5.61 | 113.23 | +.10 | 115.46 | 110.08 |
| Cn 9¾pc '06 | ✤ | 7.96 | 5.49 | 122.43 | +.11 | 125.29 | 118.84 |
| Tr 7¾pc '06 | | 6.97 | 5.55 | 111.27 | +.12 | 112.83 | 107.25 |
| Tr 8pc '02–6 | | 7.72 | 6.17 | 103.69 | +.01 | 106.04 | 102.84 |
| Tr 7½pc '06 | | 6.79 | 5.52 | 110.50 | +.13 | 111.92 | 106.40 |
| Tr 11¾pc '03–7 | ✤ | 10.40 | 6.04 | 113.00 | +.08 | 118.23 | 112.85 |
| Tr 8½pc '07 | | 7.25 | 5.49 | 117.25 | +.12 | 119.22 | 112.94 |
| Tr 7¼pc '07 | | 6.54 | 5.43 | 110.91 | +.12 | 112.27 | 106.17 |
| Tr 13½pc '04–8 | ✤ | 10.74 | 5.64 | 125.70 | +.07 | 131.93 | 125.47 |
| Tr 9pc '08 | | 7.26 | 5.36 | 123.89 | +.06 | 126.50 | 118.77 |
| Tr 8pc '09 | ✤ | 6.70 | 5.30 | 119.40 | +.11 | 122.21 | 114.68 |
| Tr 5¾pc '09 | | 5.50 | 5.12 | 104.62 | +.13 | 106.08 | 99.10 |
| **Ten to Fifteen Years** | | | | | | | |
| Tr 6¼pc '10 | | 5.74 | 5.12 | 108.95 | +.11 | 111.10 | 103.35 |
| Cn 9pc Ln '11 | | 6.82 | 5.15 | 131.95 | +.11 | 135.49 | 126.26 |
| Tr 9pc '12 | | 6.69 | 5.12 | 134.58xd | +.13 | 138.51 | 128.45 |
| Tr 5½pc '08–12 | | 5.43 | 5.31 | 101.21 | +.09 | 102.29 | 95.68 |
| Tr 8pc '13 | | 6.24 | 5.04 | 128.25 | –.02 | 132.26 | 122.43 |
| Tr 7¾pc '12–15 | | 6.40 | 5.27 | 121.18xd | +.01 | 124.75 | 115.84 |
| **Over Fifteen Years** | | | | | | | |
| Tr 8pc '15 | | 5.98 | 4.86 | 133.72 | –.13 | 138.53 | 127.70 |
| Tr 8¾pc '17 | | 5.99 | 4.77 | 146.09 | –.15 | 152.40 | 139.82 |
| Ex 12pc '13–17 | ✤ | 7.26 | 5.17 | 165.37 | +.19 | 170.48 | 157.92 |
| Tr 8pc '21 | | 5.53 | 4.84 | 144.60 | –.16 | 151.64 | 137.64 |
| Tr 6pc '28 | | 4.81 | 4.45 | 124.84 | –.22 | 132.62 | 116.93 |
| Tr 4¼pc '32 | | 4.30 | 4.31 | 98.93 | –.19 | 100.57 | 0.99 |
| **Undated** | | | | | | | |
| Cons 4pc | ✤ | 4.94 | – | 80.98xd | –.15 | 86.94 | 73.95 |
| War Ln 3½pc | | 4.74 | – | 73.89 | –.19 | 78.83 | 67.14 |
| Cn 3½pc '61 Aft. | ✤ | 4.07 | – | 85.89 | –.19 | 90.83 | 79.14 |
| Tr 3pc '66 Aft. | ✤ | 5.29 | – | 56.73 | –.08 | 60.59 | 51.78 |
| Cons 2½pc | ✤ | 4.84 | – | 51.57 | –.09 | 55.55 | 46.78 |
| Tr 2½pc | | 4.89 | – | 51.16 | +.03 | 54.87 | 46.70 |

| | Notes | Yield (1) | Yield (2) | Price £ | + or – | 52 week High | 52 week Low |
|---|---|---|---|---|---|---|---|
| **Index-Linked** | (b) | | | | | | |
| 2½pc '01 | (78.3) | 3.13 | 4.11 | 210.96 | –.10 | 211.09 | 201.90 |
| 2½pc '03 | (78.8) | 3.10 | 3.51 | 207.92 | –.26 | 208.27 | 200.50 |
| 4⅜pc '04 | (135.6) | 2.79 | 3.07 | 130.41 | –.24 | 132.35 | 127.26 |
| 2pc '06 | (69.5) | 2.42 | 2.62 | 233.94 | –.97 | 236.25 | 229.47 |
| 2½pc '09 | (78.8) | 2.07 | 2.21 | 218.59 | –1.03 | 220.97 | 208.87 |
| 2½pc '11 | (74.6) | 2.11 | 2.22 | 231.65 | –1.23 | 234.67 | 219.11 |
| 2½pc '13 | (89.2) | 2.08 | 2.18 | 195.52 | –1.11 | 198.66 | 183.57 |
| 2½pc '16 | (81.6) | 2.02 | 2.11 | 216.89xd | –1.46 | 220.63 | 203.03 |
| 2½pc '20 | (83.0) | 1.95 | 2.02 | 218.40 | –1.75 | 224.25 | 203.17 |
| 2½pc '24 | (97.7) | 1.81 | 1.87 | 193.25 | –1.80 | 199.43 | 176.32 |
| 4⅛pc '30 | (135.1) | 1.69 | 1.75 | 193.13 | –1.93 | 199.61 | 174.35 |

Prospective real redemption rate on projected inflation of (1) 5% and (2) 3%. (b) Figures in parentheses show RPI base for indexing (ie 8 months prior to issue) and have been adjusted to reflect rebasing of RPI to 100 in January 1987. Conversion factor 3.945. RPI for November 1999: 166.7 and for June 2000: 171.1.

**Other Fixed Interest**

| | Notes | Yield Int | Yield Red | Price £ | + or – | 52 week High | 52 week Low |
|---|---|---|---|---|---|---|---|
| Asian Dev 10¼pc 2009 | | 8.10 | 6.20 | 126½ | ...... | 130¼ | 123 |
| B'ham 11½pc 2012 | | 7.90 | 6.40 | 145½ | ...... | 151 | 140¾ |
| Leeds 13½pc 2006 | | 9.98 | 6.40 | 135¼ | ...... | 140 | 132¾ |
| Liverpool 3½pc Irred. | | 5.34 | 5.30 | 65½ | ...... | 73 | 58 |
| LCC 3pc '20 Aft. | | 5.45 | 5.50 | 55 | ...... | 64 | 51 |
| Manchester 11½pc 2007 | | 8.78 | 6.10 | 131 | ...... | 134 | 127 |
| Met. Wtr. 3pc 'B' | | 3.30 | 6.50 | 91 | ...... | 91½ | 85 |
| N'wide Anglia 3⅞pc IL 2021 | | – | 3.40 | 187¼xd | ...... | 200½ | 174[illegible] |
| 4¼pc IL 2024 | | – | 3.30 | 181¾ | ...... | 196¾ | 169 |

● Source: Debt Management Office (DMO). All UK Gilts are tax-free to non-residents on application. xd Ex dividend. Closing mid-prices are shown in pounds per £100 nominal of stock. Int yield: Interest yield. Red yield: Gross redemption yield. Prospective real Index-Linked redemption yields are calculated by HSBC Bank plc from GEMMA closing prices. ✤ Indicative price. Gilts "runners", the benchmarks and most liquid stocks, are shown in bold type.

- an illustrative quote might be 107.16 implying a price of £107.16 per £100 nominal;
- tick size is 0.01(£1 per £100 nominal);
- bid–offer spreads for 'shorts' (i.e. less than 5 years) are about 1/32%, for 'longs' (i.e. 5 to 15 years maturity or over 15 years) about 2/32 – 4/32%;
- market makers sell bonds at a higher price than they will bid to buy the bond (i.e. offer price > bid price).

Key features from the investor's point of view are the redemption date, the coupon rate, the (clean) price (per £100 nominal) and the increase or decrease in price since the previous day '+ or −'. The interest yield ('Yield Int') and the redemption yield ('Yield Red') have been explained earlier. An 'xd' implies the gilt is trading ex-dividend (i.e. investor will not receive the next coupon payment) and a '⚬' implies an indicative price (i.e. for a thinly traded, illiquid bond).

Some stocks are **double dated** (e.g. 'Treasury 12–1/2%, 03–5') and can be redeemed by the government at any time between these two dates. **Index linked stocks** have their 'yields' calculated for two assumptions (high/low) about future inflation.

The FT also gives data on indices of a portfolio of gilts of different maturity 'bundles' (e.g. 5–10 years) and includes some additional information such as their duration (Figure 7.5). There are also details of bonds issued by UK local authorities and some large corporations (under 'Other Fixed Interest').

**The quoted price is the clean price but the invoice (or dirty) price to be paid requires calculation of accrued/rebate interest**. The treatment of **accrued interest** in the UK and the US bond markets is very similar and therefore we examine this mainly from a UK perspective. However, where the terminology differs between the two markets we point this out. An investor may purchase a bond between coupon payments. If the investor is to receive the next coupon payment (i.e. the bond is 'cum-dividend') then he must compensate the seller of the bond for the coupon interest earned from the time of the last coupon payment. This is known as accrued interest and is calculated as follows:

[7.13]     **Accrued interest** $= C(n_1/n_2)$

where   $C$ is the annual coupon
         $n_1$ is the number of days from last coupon payment to settlement date
         $n_2$ is the number of days in 'the year'.

Market conventions determine $n_1$ and $n_2$. For UK gilts and US Treasury coupon securities $n_1$ and $n_2$ are on 'actual/365' basis (but for US corporate and municipal bonds, the day count convention is '30/360', that is each year has 360 days and a month has 30 days). An example of the calculation of accrued interest is provided in Table 7.12.

### Invoice or dirty price
The quoted (clean) price assumes the owner of the bond will receive the next coupon payment. In the UK, gilts can be sold either cum-dividend or ex-dividend and this is reflected in the invoice or 'dirty price' paid per £100 nominal value.

## TABLE 7.12: UK gilts market (accrued interest)

| | |
|---|---|
| **Data:** | On 31st March 1993 (for settlement on 1st April) 9% Treasury 2012 was quoted at 106(3/16) |
| | Most recent coupon payment was 6th February 1993 |
| **Question:** | Calculate accrued interest |
| **Answer:** | 22 days from 6th February + 31 days in March + 1 day in April |
| | Hence $n_1 = 54$ days and the accrued interest AI is: |
| | **AI = £9 (54/365) = £1.3315 per £100 nominal of stock** |

**Cum-dividend**: The purchaser of the bond receives the next coupon payment and the seller does not, even though she has held the bond for part of this coupon period. The purchaser therefore compensates the seller and pays an invoice (dirty) price:

> **Dirty price = clean (quoted) price + accrued interest**

The invoice (dirty) price is the total proceeds (per £100 nominal) that the buyer pays the seller. The accrued interest compensates the seller of the bond for the fact that he will not receive the next coupon payment. In our example the dirty price is:

[7.14]     £106(3/16) + £1.3315 = £107.52 (per £100 nominal of stock)

**Ex-dividend**: The purchaser is excluded from receiving the next dividend but the clean price 'includes' the next dividend payment. Hence the seller (who will receive the next coupon payment) owes the purchaser **'rebate interest'** (see Table 7.13). The invoice (dirty) price paid by the purchaser (investor) is therefore lower than the clean price:

> **Dirty price = clean (quoted) price − rebate interest**

In the UK gilts market, the recipient of the coupon payment is determined about 37 days before actual payment, after which date the bond goes ex-dividend. In the US the invoice price (paid) by the purchaser, as in the UK, is the clean price with adjustment for accrued or rebate interest.

## TABLE 7.13: UK gilts (rebate interest)

| | |
|---|---|
| **Data:** | On 31st March 1993 (for settlement on 1st April 1993) 9% Treasury 2004 is quoted at £111(5/32) xd (i.e. clean price, xd = ex-dividend) |
| | Next coupon payment date is 25th April, 24 days hence (i.e. 25 − 1) |
| **Question:** | Calculate the rebate interest |
| **Answer:** | **Rebate interest** $= 9.0\,(24/365) =$ **£0.592 per £100 nominal** |
| | **Dirty price** $= £111\,(5/32) - £0.592 =$ **£110.56 (per £100 nominal)** |

# 7.3 CORPORATE BONDS

A corporate can raise long-term debt finance through bank loans or an issue of corporate bonds. We discussed the former in Chapter 1 and here we elaborate on raising finance through marketable debt, such as corporate bonds. A public issue of bonds follows a similar procedure to that for stocks. In general, the issue must be approved by the Board of Directors (and sometimes by a vote of the stockholders) and often a registration statement has to be issued to the regulatory authorities (e.g. the Securities and Exchange Commission, SEC in the US). The registration statement includes an **indenture** or **deed of trust** which is a written agreement between the bond issuer and a trust company. The trust company is appointed by the issuing company to represent the bondholders' interests and the **bond indenture** will cover the following issues:

- the 'cash' terms in the bond (e.g. amount of issue, par value of each bond, coupon rate, maturity date, etc.);
- collateral protecting the bondholder;
- sinking fund arrangements;
- protective covenants;
- convertible and call elements.

Let us consider each of these elements in turn. The bond issue might be for $100m total value, with each bond having a face value of $1000. A coupon of 10% p.a. payable every 6 months would imply dollar payments of $100 p.a. (10% of $1000) in two equal instalments of $50 every 6 months. The maturity date might be in 20 years time. The selling price of the bonds might be 99 which implics 99% of $1000 or $990 per bond. The bonds may be either registered or bearer bonds.

## COLLATERAL

The collateral protecting the bondholder can be of several types. For example, in the US a **collateral trust bond** has as collateral, shares owned by the company issuing the bonds. So if the bond issuer owns shares in another company, XYZ, then the latter can be sold and the proceeds used to pay the bondholders their coupon payments and repayment of the principal.

**Mortgage securities** are bonds which are secured on specific assets (e.g. railroad bonds are often secured on the company's rolling stock, which could be sold to other railroad companies, to pay off the bondholders).

The term **debenture** is a tricky concept since its meaning can vary in different countries. In the US a debenture is an unsecured bond. If the firm defaults, a debenture holder in the US will only receive payment, after payments have been made to mortgage and collateral trust bondholders. Most industrial and finance company bonds in the US are debentures, while the exceptions here are bonds issued by US utilities and railroads which are secured on specific assets. Another key factor in a bond issue is whether the bonds are senior debt or junior debt since this determines the 'order' in which debtors will be paid in the event of bankruptcy.

## SINKING FUND

Although the face value of *all* of the bonds issued could be paid at maturity, a sinking fund to pay off the bonds gradually over a period of time is more usual. Typically, the company makes equal annual payments to the trust company after a 'grace period' of several years (e.g. 7 years on a 20-year bond). These payments are sufficient to redeem at par say 80% of the outstanding bonds (with the remaining 20% *'balloon'* paid at maturity). The trust company uses these sinking fund payments to redeem the outstanding bonds either by purchasing them at market prices or by selecting bonds randomly (by lottery) and purchasing them at face (par) value.

The existence of a sinking fund allows bondholders an 'early warning' if the company is getting into financial distress, since it will then not be able to meet its sinking fund provision. But there are also advantages to the issuer. The company may have the option to either repurchase its bonds in the open market (when the market price is below par value) or repurchase at par (when the market price is above par value). Hence the company may 'gain' a valuable option from the sinking fund provisions.

## PROTECTIVE COVENANTS

These are either restrictions on things the company may want to do, that would harm the bondholders (i.e. **restrictive covenants**) or actions that the company must undertake to enhance the position of bondholders (i.e. **positive covenants**). Restrictive covenants might include:

- restrictions on the amount of dividends which can be paid to shareholders;
- restrictions on sales of company assets (e.g. of subsidiary companies);
- restrictions on issues of further long-term debt.

Positive covenants might include:

- forcing the company to hedge some of its interest rate risk;
- maintaining a minimum level of liquid assets to pay creditors.

The US corporate bond market is the largest in the world and Figure 7.7 (from the *Financial Times* of 4th October 2000) shows the (bid) yield price and credit ratings by S&P and Moody's. The yield and credit rating are (usually) inversely related, showing that the market views the relative credit risk, the same as the rating agencies. For example, in utilities 'Pac Bell' with an S&P rating of AA− has a yield of 6.98%, while 'CWE' with a BBB+ rating has a yield of 7.56%. In the last column of Figure 7.7 is the yield spread over government bonds (T-bonds) of the same maturity. Generally the yield spreads increase as the credit rating falls (e.g. see 'Industrials') as one would expect.

As we see below, these spreads are a measure of the 'risk premium' on the bond. Also, in the next chapter we see how the yields on corporate bonds can be used to calculate a market based measure of the probability of default of the corporate. These probabilities are used by banks in determining the probability of default of their *whole portfolio* of corporate bonds and corporate loans, and influences the amount of 'capital' they hold as a 'cushion' against these possible 'bad debts'. This whole area is known as credit risk assessment and is currently the subject of revised regulatory rules which are being prepared under the auspices of the Bank for International Settlements (BIS) in Basle—see Cuthbertson and Nitzsche (2001).

## FIGURE 7.7: Corporate bond quotes (*Financial Times*). Reproduced with permission

### US CORPORATE BONDS

| Oct 2 | Red date | Coupon | S&P* Rating | Moody's Rating | Bid price | Bid yield | Day's chge yield | Mth's chge yield | Spread vs Govts |
|---|---|---|---|---|---|---|---|---|---|
| **UTILITIES** | | | | | | | | | |
| Pac Bell | 07/02 | 7.25 | AA- | Aa3 | 100.5650 | 6.89 | -0.02 | -0.12 | +0.91 |
| NY Tel | 08/25 | 7.00 | A+ | A1 | 87.2194 | 8.21 | +0.06 | +0.24 | +2.28 |
| CWE | 05/08 | 8.00 | BBB+ | Baa1 | 102.4966 | 7.56 | +0.04 | +0.02 | +1.74 |
| **FINANCIALS** | | | | | | | | | |
| GECC | 05/07 | 8.75 | AAA | Aaa | 109.7673 | 6.88 | +0.01 | -0.09 | +1.06 |
| Banc One | 08/02 | 7.25 | A- | A1 | 100.6147 | 6.87 | -0.03 | -0.20 | +0.89 |
| CNA Fin | 01/18 | 6.95 | BBB | Baa1 | 80.9142 | 9.17 | +0.06 | +0.01 | +3.24 |
| **INDUSTRIALS** | | | | | | | | | |
| Lucent | 03/29 | 6.45 | A | A2 | 83.5154 | 7.91 | +0.05 | +0.28 | +1.98 |
| News Corp | 10/08 | 7.38 | BBB- | Baa3 | 97.1484 | 7.85 | +0.04 | +0.10 | +2.03 |
| TCI Comm | 05/03 | 6.38 | AA- | A2 | 98.5681 | 6.98 | -0.02 | -0.24 | +1.00 |
| **AGENCIES** | | | | | | | | | |
| FHLMC | 04/09 | 5.86 | N/A | Aaa | 93.4620 | 6.88 | +0.05 | +0.02 | +1.06 |
| SLMA | 05/04 | 7.01 | N/A | Aaa | 101.5041 | 6.53 | - | -0.16 | +0.69 |
| FNMA | 08/28 | 6.16 | N/A | Aaa | 90.1169 | 6.96 | +0.05 | +0.09 | +1.03 |
| FFCB | 05/02 | 5.25 | N/A | Aaa | 98.1827 | 6.47 | +0.01 | -0.12 | +0.49 |
| **HIGH YIELD** | | | | | | | | | |
| Charter Comm | 04/09 | 8.63 | B+ | B2 | 90.1250 | - | - | - | - |
| HMH Prop | 08/08 | 7.88 | BB | Ba2 | 92.2500 | - | - | - | - |
| AMC Ent | 02/11 | 9.50 | CCC+ | Caa3 | 46.0000 | - | - | - | - |

NY latest. *Standard & Poor's. Yields: semi-annual basis.  Source: Interactive Data/FT Information.

## CONVERTIBLE AND CALL PROVISIONS

### CALL PROVISIONS

In the US almost all debentures are callable. A **call provision** allows the company to *call* (i.e. repurchase) the bond at a known fixed value (the call price), at specific times in the future. Generally the call price is set above the face value. So, for example, a call price of $1050, with a par value of $1000, implies that the bond can be called for $1050, implying a **call premium** of $50. Often the call premium is initially set equal to the (dollar) coupon and then declines to zero over the life of the bond.

The call provision in a bond is an embedded option which benefits the company rather than the bondholders. Consider the following. If interest rates fall then the market price of the bond may rise to say $1100, above the call price of $1050. If so, the company may be able to call the bond at say $1050, whereas the market price is currently at $1100. After calling each bond and paying $1050, the company can reissue bonds *with the same coupon and maturity* at the higher market price of $1100 (or equivalently at a lower yield to maturity). The company therefore needs to issue fewer bonds **to refund** the existing bonds outstanding. (We ignore the transaction costs of refinancing here.)

> **A company aiming to maximise shareholder wealth should 'extract' any advantage it can get from bondholders. So, a firm should call its bonds (and refund its debt) as soon as the market price exceeds the call price (and any transaction costs).**

In practice, firms often do not call their bonds even when the market price is at a substantial premium to the call price, but the reasons for this are far from clear, perhaps the firm does not call the bond because it is trying to maximise *future* receipts from bond sales and therefore does not seek to expropriate all of its advantage from the current bondholders. Clearly a call provision is a disincentive to purchasing the bonds, since bondholders may be deprived of capital gains when interest rates fall sharply. Consequently, callable bonds offer higher coupons (and yields) compared to conventional (non-callable) bonds. Note also that the call provision is not usually operative in the first few years (e.g. for the first 7 years on a 20-year bond).

If the company has to pay a higher coupon (or yield) why would it issue callable bonds rather than conventional bonds? One reason might be for tax purposes. The higher coupons are tax deductible for the company but taxable for the bondholder. If the bondholder is in a lower tax bracket than the company, the company will gain more than the bondholder will lose in taxes. The company may use this tax saving to pass on in the form of higher coupons. Second, because the callable bond has a higher coupon, it has a lower duration and is therefore less sensitive to changes in interest rates and this *may* also benefit shareholders by reducing their risk. Perhaps the most cogent reason for issuing callable bonds is that the call provision gives the company the option to 'get rid of' any restrictive covenants in the bond indenture, prior to maturity of the bonds. For example, if the company sees a profitable acquisition target, but the bond covenants prohibit a takeover or merger, the company can go ahead with the acquisition by first calling the bonds.

## CONVERTIBLES

**Debt convertibles** (**convertible bonds** or **convertible loan stock**) are bonds which are 'convertible' into ordinary shares of the same firm, at the choice of the bondholder, after a period of time. The shares are 'paid for' by surrendering the bonds. The pro's and con's of convertibles are summarised in Box 7.2.

---

## Box 7.2 CONVERTIBLE BONDS

A convertible bond gives the holder the right (but not the obligation) to purchase a given number of shares at a fixed price at some time in the future. Convertible bonds will usually carry a yield below that on similar conventional bonds, because the convertible has a valuable 'embedded option'. They are usually unsecured and subordinated (i.e. junior debt). From the investor's point of view convertibles allow a periodic coupon payment, but if the firm is successful the investor can share in these higher profits by converting the bond into shares, at a later date. Hence, the investor does not have to be so worried about the firm issuing extra senior debt which would rank over the convertible. Also, if the company invests in high-risk projects then at least the holder of the convertible will share in the gains if these are successful (whereas an ordinary bondholder would only receive the fixed coupon payments). Convertibles are therefore useful to protect the bondholder against a wrong assessment of the risk of the firm and are often issued by smaller and more riskier firms.

Convertibles also usually have a provision whereby the issuer can **buy back (or 'call')** the convertible bond at a fixed price and the holder can usually choose to receive shares or receive the 'call price' in cash. This call provision is a way of forcing conversion and the issuer will undertake this option if the current market value of the bond is greater than the current value of the shares the issuer has to 'give up'.

Clearly, convertibles, if converted, alter the **debt-to-equity ratio** of the company. If they are converted then they also 'dilute' the holdings of the existing shareholders, since the profits of the company are now spread over a larger number of shareholders (of course the company also saves on the interest payments and the repayment of principal). Companies in their financial statements must show how their earnings per share would be affected by conversion.

It should be obvious that if the stock price rises sufficiently, then the convertibles will be exchanged by their holders, for stocks at a fixed price. This works as follows. Suppose the convertible is a 20-year bond with an 8% coupon and is issued at par (= $100) in 2000. The current share price is $2, the **conversion price** is $2.50 and the latter 'option' can be exercised at any time after 2003. The **conversion ratio** is:

$$\text{Conversion ratio} = \frac{\text{nominal value of bond}}{\text{conversion price}} = \frac{\$100}{\$2.50} = 40$$

So each bond can be converted into 40 shares. Convertibles are protected against stock splits and stock dividends. For example, if in the above case there was a 2 for 1 stock split the conversion ratio would be increased to 80 and the conversion price would drop to $1.25. Often the conversion price is stepped up over time to reflect the potential growth in the firm's profits.

The bondholder will only be tempted to exercise this option if the stock price after 2003 rises above the conversion price of $2.50 (the latter is equivalent to the strike price $K$ in a conventional option). The **conversion premium** is:

$$\text{Conversion premium} = \frac{K - S}{S} = \frac{\$2.50 - \$2}{\$2} = 25\%$$

If the stock price does not rise above $K = \$2.50$, then the bondholder will not exercise the 'embedded option' and will continue to receive the 8% coupon.

The **advantages to the issuer** of the convertible are:

- It can issue convertibles at lower yield than a conventional bond.
- If the firm believes its current stock price is artificially low, it can raise funds by issuing convertibles. If the stock price subsequently rises, the firm issues more shares when the bonds are 'converted' but it then does not have to use its cash flow to pay further coupons and principal (e.g. issuing convertibles can be useful for governments who wish to privatise state firms which have no track record in the market).
- The covenants on hybrid debt–equity such as a convertible are usually less than on conventional bonds (e.g. often unsecured and the holders do not impose restrictions on interest cover, etc.).
- Interest payments are tax deductible against profits.

The **advantages to the holder** of a convertible are:

- Periodic fixed coupon payments.
- Payment before any ordinary shareholders.
- They can share in higher profits if the firm does well since the bonds will then be converted to shares. Hence they are useful when the risk of a company is difficult to assess and when the scale of its future senior debt issues is uncertain.

Who issues convertible bonds? Well, in the main, relatively more convertibles are issued by:

- young high-growth firms, rather than established firms;
- firms with relatively low credit ratings rather than high credit ratings.

Convertibles are often unsecured and subordinated debt. In a sense, the payments profile for convertibles matches the expected revenues of firms that issue them. Young firms have low net cash flows in their early years and this is matched by the lower coupon payments of convertibles (relative to conventional bonds). However, later cash flows are expected to be high. While this makes conversion likely, it is at a time when the firm is strong enough to withstand 'dilution' and higher dividend payments. Issuing convertibles also partially solves the problem of accurately assessing the riskiness of young firms or the possibility that they may act in a risky or cavalier fashion, such as taking on high-risk strategies in the future without the consent of bondholders (i.e. an agency problem). Compared with a conventional bond, the holder of a convertible can share in the profits from these 'high-risk' projects if they are successful. Convertibles like warrants are 'equity kickers'.

There is one final aspect of convertibles you should be aware of. Most convertibles have a (deferred) call provision. When the convertible bond is called, the holder has the following choices:

- 'sell' the bond to the company and receive the call price in cash (of say $K = 105\%$ of $1000);
- convert the bond into shares at the known conversion value (i.e. conversion ratio $\times$ current share price).

Clearly the bondholder will convert to shares if the conversion value exceeds the call price of $K = \$1050$, otherwise she will take the cash of $1050. This choice clearly affects the cash flow of the firm and its debt-to-equity ratio.

Unfortunately, establishing the 'fair price' for warrants, convertibles and callable bonds is far from straightforward and we cannot deal with it in this book. However the interested reader should consult Cuthbertson and Nitzsche (2001).

## OTHER TYPES OF MARKETABLE DEBT

There are a number of permutations on the 'conventional' or 'plain vanilla' corporate bond, besides their convertible and callable properties. These are designed to appeal to particular investors and some of these are outlined below.

A **floating rate note (FRN)** is a bond on which the coupon payments $C are linked to a short-term interest rate such as 3 or 6-month LIBOR. FRNs are particularly popular in the Euromarkets. Future coupon payments on an FRN are uncertain, but, somewhat paradoxically, this implies that their market price does not fluctuate as much as that of a conventional 'fixed coupon' bond. Intuitively the price of the 'floater' does not alter much because as interest rates change both the numerator (i.e. the floating coupon payment) and the denominator (i.e. the interest rate) move in the same direction, partially cancelling each other out. In contrast, for a fixed coupon bond a change in interest rates only affects the denominator of the bond price formula and hence the price alters substantially. Since changes in inflation (expectations) are a major source of changes in interest rates, then 'floaters' can be seen as reducing inflation risk.

Floaters are often issued with 'floor' or 'floor and ceiling' provisions, which limit the range of coupon adjustments. These floors and ceilings are a form of embedded option. For example, if current interest rates are 10%, the FRN might have a floor of 8% and a ceiling of 12%, which limits the lowest and highest coupon rates payable in any period. So if, for example, current interest rates are 14%, the coupon payable will only be 12% (of the par value) in that period.

Some companies also raise finance by issuing **deep-discount bonds**. These are zero coupon bonds and they are attractive to institutions like pension funds which have a known *nominal* payment (e.g. a pension lump sum) at a specific date in the future. A 'zero' then provides a perfect hedge. Because coupon bonds can be 'stripped', there are relatively few deep-discount bonds issued. **Income bonds** (in the US) allow the issuer to defer coupon payments if the firm's income is insufficient, and this cannot lead to the company being in default. However, income bonds are not popular, partly because they 'have the smell of death' since they signal an increased probability of financial distress and partly because of the difficulties of measuring the firm's income and hence the coupons to be paid.

**Medium term notes (MTNs)** are very popular in the USA where they are issued by a corporate to an agent who then *offers them continuously* to investors in alternative amounts and maturities (e.g. 9 months to 1 year, 1 to 2 years and so on, up to 30 years). They fill the funding gap between commercial paper and long-term bonds. They can be fixed or floating rate debt, with coupons in domestic or foreign currency, or with coupons linked to an equity index. The more complex MTNs are known as **structured notes** since they are often tailored by the agent based on a specific request by an investor.

## PRICING CORPORATE BONDS

The pricing of corporate bonds, particularly those with convertible and callable properties, can be rather technical. The difficulty being trying to get a measure of the risk and cost of distress/bankruptcy, which should clearly affect the bond price. We can therefore only deal with highly simplified cases below (for futher details see Cuthbertson and Nitzsche, 2001). We deal with two rather different approaches. The 'conventional' appoach uses the familiar discounting technique, but we also briefly present a more 'modern' approach which uses options pricing theory.

Pricing a plain vanilla corporate bond can be tackled in a similar fashion to that for government bonds. However, each of the cash flows (and face value) $C$ on the corporate bond are *expected coupons $E[C]$*:

[7.15]
$$E[C] = (1 - p)C + p(\theta C)$$

where $p$ is the probability of default (in a particular year) and $\theta$ is the recovery rate if the corporate goes into default. (The default probability can be calculatcd from observed yields on corporates and this is illustrated in the next chapter.) If the probability of default is unrelated to other events in the economy then we could discount these cash flows at the risk free rate to obtain the bond price. However, in reality bonds do have some market risk (i.e. positive betas) and the probability of default depends on the state of the economy (e.g. recession or boom). Therefore one might (rather crudely) take the risk free spot rate $r$ and add a risk premium $rp$ to reflect uncertainty caused by the business cycle. The price of the corporate bond is given by:

[7.16]
$$P = \frac{E[C_1]}{(1 + r_1 + rp_1)} + \frac{E[C_2]}{(1 + r_2 + rp_2)^2} + \ldots + \frac{E[C_n + M]}{(1 + r_n + rp_n)^n}$$

Clearly one can speculate using corporate bonds either based on forecasts of changes in the risk free rate or changes in the credit (default) risk of the company. Since each corporate bond is affected in the same way by the changes in the risk free rate, speculators concentrate on predicting relative changes in the risk premium. For example, ideally you need to go long in a 10-year corporate bond whose credit standing (rating) you expect to improve and to short sell a 10-year corporate bond of a firm you expect to undergo a rating decline. Since you have equal (dollar) long and short positions (in matched duration bonds), the value of your speculative bond portfolio will remain unchanged if there are unexpected changes in risk free spot rates (i.e. shifts in the risk free yield curve). You are merely exposed to the relative credit risk of the two corporate bonds. If your guess about credit rating changes is correct then you will make a speculative profit, having used little of your own funds (since the proceeds from the short sale can be used to finance your long position).

## USING OPTIONS THEORY

Even with our limited knowledge of options theory we can gain some insights into the valuation of corporate debt. The key advantage of this approach is that it directly incorporates uncertainty and the volatility of the firm's assets directly affect the bond price.

Suppose for simplicity all bondholders held zero coupon bonds with a maturity of 10 years and maturity (face) value of $\$M$. If at the end of 10 years the value of the firm's assets $V_T$ is greater than $\$M$, then the bondholders will be repaid in full (and any excess $V_T - M$ accrues to the shareholders, not the bondholders). However, if $V_T < M$ then the shareholders, who have limited liability, can 'walk away' from the firm and the bondholders will not be repaid in full. The maturity value $M$ is like the strike price in an option contract. The bondholders receive the minimum of $M$ or $V_T$ and if $M > V_T$ their loss is $M - V_T$. The payoff to the bondholders is shown in Figure 7.8 and mathematically it can be expressed as:

[7.17]        Payoff to bondholders at $T = M - \max[0, M - V_T]$

---

## FIGURE 7.8: Shareholder and bondholder payoffs

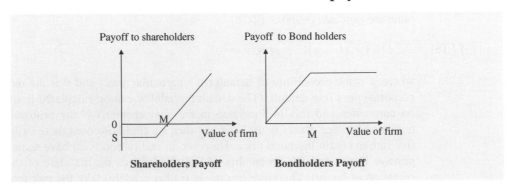

**Shareholders Payoff**          **Bondholders Payoff**

Figure 7.8 indicates that the bondholders' payoff is like a put option written on the firm's assets, with a strike price of $M$ (plus an amount of cash $M$).

So far, we have only given the possible payoffs at time $T$ (the maturity of the bond), but what we require is the market value of the corporate bond ($B_t$) today. However, once we know the payoff at $T$, options pricing theory can be used to determine $B_t$, which is given by a complicated formula (Merton, 1974) here expressed schematically as:

[7.18]     $$B_t = f[(M/V_T), \sigma, \tau, r]$$

where   $r$ is the risk free rate
$\sigma$ is the volatility (i.e. standard deviation of the value of the firm)
$\tau \ (= T - t)$ is the time to maturity of the bond
$f$ means 'function' of the variables in parentheses.

In particular, it is found that the current price of the bond is negatively related to the firm's leverage (i.e. proportion of debt outstanding $M/V_t$) and to the volatility of the firm's assets $\sigma$ (e.g. which would probably be higher for a firm selling electrical goods than for a firm selling groceries). The model also implies that the corporate–Treasury yield spread will widen, either with increased leverage or with higher volatility of the firm's assets. These are intuitively plausible results. In general, the value of a risky corporate bond can be calculated as:

> **Value of corporate bond $B_t$ = value of risk free bond – value of implied put option written by the bondholders**

There is another way we can tackle the valuation of a corporate bond using options. To do so, we somewhat paradoxically first look at the payoff to the equity holders. If $V_T < M$ then the equity holders get nothing, since even the bondholders cannot be paid in full. But if $V_T > M$ the shareholders receive all of the excess $V_T - M$, after paying the bondholders in full. Hence the payoff to the shareholders is like a call option (see Figure 7.8) with a strike price $M$. The shareholders have paid $S$, the initial equity investment in the firm, for this option. This (implied) call option is valuable to shareholders since they have limited downside risk but can benefit greatly if the firm is successful (remember that the bondholders only get the fixed amount $M$, no matter how successful the firm). To value this call option $P_t^c$ at time $t$, given the payoffs at time $T$, is again rather difficult. But once we have calculated $P_t^c$ we can calculate the value of the outstanding corporate bonds from:

> **Value of corporate bonds $B_t$ = value of the firm $V_t$ – value of the implied call $P_t^c$ held by the shareholders**

In practice, things are even more complicated since most bonds are coupon paying bonds, not zeros. Hence, for a 10-year annual coupon bond, the shareholders have 10 sequential call options with strike prices of $C, C, \ldots$ and $C + M$. In addition, if the shareholders do not exercise one of their call options (because $V_t < C$), the value of their 'later' call options is zero (since ownership of the firm's assets will pass to the bondholders, in liquidation). But these technical problems can be surmounted and options theory provides a useful approach to valuing risky debt.

## 7.4 SUMMARY

- **Bond prices** and the **yield to maturity (YTM)** are inversely related. **Spot rates** refer to the cost of lending and borrowing a given amount of money at a specific time. Spot rates can be observed at short horizons (e.g. up to 1 year) but have to be estimated from coupon paying bonds at longer horizons.
- **The YTM** is the return on a bond if it is held to maturity and all the future coupons can be reinvested at the current YTM. The **holding period yield (HPY)** is the return on a bond over a fixed horizon and includes the capital gain, any coupon payments and any interest-on-interest.
- The **'fair' or equilibrium price** of a coupon paying bond is determined by spot rates of interest, otherwise riskless arbitrage profits can be made by a strategy known as **coupon stripping**. Once we have calculated the 'fair' price we can then infer the YTM that is consistent with this price.
- The government bond markets in the UK and the US are very liquid and mainly include **conventional bonds** (and 'T-notes' in the US), although there are also some **index linked bonds** in the UK. There are active **strips** and **repo markets** in bonds too.
- Government bond markets in other developed countries operate in a similar manner to those in the US and UK. Some developing countries, particularly those prone to high inflation, do not have 'deep' liquid bond markets, often because of **fear of default** (e.g. Russian bond crisis of 1998).
- **Corporate bonds** are similar to government bonds and can be priced in the same way, except the discount rates used have to reflect the **default risk premium** as well as the risk free rate. Their price will alter if risk free rates change or if the risk of financial distress alters (e.g. as reflected in a change in S&P or Moody's bond rating).
- Corporate bonds come in the '**plain vanilla**' variety with either fixed or floating coupons but they are often callable and some are issued as convertibles. The latter two are equivalent to a plain vanilla bond plus an embedded option. The **callable bond** gives *the issuer* the option to buy back the bonds at a predetermined price over a certain time period. This gives the issuer added flexibility compared to a plain vanilla bond. The **convertible bond** can be exchanged for a certain number of stocks of the firm, at a predetermined price, at certain times in the future. It allows *the holder* the option of obtaining an 'equity stake' in the firm if it is subsequently successful.
- **Pricing plain vanilla corporate bonds** is similar to that for government bonds but

with the proviso that the coupon payments are subject to **default risk** and the discount rate may have to be adjusted to include a **risk premium**. Another approach to pricing plain vanilla corporate bonds is to use **options theory**, because the shareholders' limited liability is equivalent to holding an implied option. Also, when corporate bonds have embedded options to convert (to ordinary shares) or have call provisions, then clearly options theory is required for valuation (see Cuthbertson and Nitzsche, 2001).

# END OF CHAPTER EXERCISES

Q1 What is a Treasury (or gilt) 'strip'?

Q2 What are the key features of a bond which help determine its yield to maturity?

Q3 The quoted price for a UK gilt-edged stock is '£105.21875 xd' (xd = 'ex-dividend', that is excluding the next 'dividend'/coupon payment). What is the (clean) price of this gilt (per £100 nominal) and will this be the price paid by the investor?

Q4 Assume that you require a 10% (compound) return on a zero coupon bond with a par (face value) of £1000 and 5 years to maturity. What price would you pay for the bond?

Q5 Consider a 7% coupon, US government bond that has a par value of $1000 and matures 5 years from now. The coupon payments are made annually. The current yield to maturity YTM (redemption yield) for such bonds is 8%. Calculate the market price of the bond and state whether you expect this bond to sell at par, at a premium (over par) or at a discount.

Q6 Consider the following German government coupon bond (i.e. 'Bunds'):

Price = euros 769.42
Coupon = 7% p.a. (paid every 6 months)
Par value = euros 1000
Maturity = 15 years

Show that the semi-annual yield is $r = 5\%$, so that the yield to maturity on a 'bond equivalent basis' (i.e. simple annual yield) is 10%.

Q7 Why are coupon bonds priced using spot rates (yields)? What then is the significance of the yield to maturity YTM?

# CHAPTER 8

# Forward Rates, Yield Curves and the Term Structure

In this chapter we discuss the interrelated concepts of the forward rate (of interest), the yield curve and the term structure of interest rates. A forward–forward rate of interest (or 'forward rate' for short) applies over two specific periods in the future, but the rate is agreed today. Suppose you negotiate an agreement today to borrow $10m from a bank in 1 years time and to pay off the loan plus interest at the end of the second year. The interest rate payable is $f_{12} = 10\%$, *which is agreed today*. This is a type of **forward–forward agreement (FFA)** and $f_{12}$ is the quoted forward rate (of interest).

There are a number of other financial instruments which also allow you to negotiate a contract today, but where the interest payments/receipts occur in the future. Examples include a forward rate agreement (FRA), a floating rate note (FRN), interest rate swaps and interest rate futures and options contracts. A key issue is how to establish the 'fair' or 'correct' price for these contracts and the forward rate plays a pivotal role here. In this chapter we show how the cash flows from an FFA can be exactly replicated by borrowing and lending today in the cash (spot) market. Thus we can 'manufacture' a *synthetic FFA* and use the observed spot rates of interest to correctly calculate the 'fair' forward rate, which should be charged by the bank. Forward–forward agreements have now been superseded by forward rate agreements (FRAs), which are based on the same principle, but the institutional details of the contracts differ slightly.

Why are long rates of interest (e.g. on 10-year money) usually higher than short rates (e.g. on 1-year money)? The relationship between (spot) rates of interest of different maturities comes under the headings of the **term structure of interest rates** and the **yield curve**. Hence the latter part of this chapter outlines the main theories concerning the shape of the yield curve and how this may be used to infer the market's view of future inflation (in the price of goods and services).

Although *quoted* forward rates can be observed in the market, these rates usually only apply in highly liquid markets and over short horizons (of up to 1 year). But, to correctly price some instruments (e.g. swaps, FRNs and some FRAs) we require forward rates for long horizons. It turns out that these can be derived from spot rates of interest. However, as we discovered in the previous chapter, these long horizon spot rates have to be estimated from existing coupon paying bonds. We therefore have the problem of 'extracting' spot and forward rates from observed prices of coupon paying bonds. There are several methods available to 'fit' the yield curve and we discuss some of them in this chapter.

# 8.1 FORWARD RATES

We begin by showing how riskless arbitrage establishes the 'fair' or 'correct' or 'equilibrium' forward rate. This is done by 'engineering' a synthetic forward contract which has the same cash flows as the actual FFA, and hence the latter must have the same forward rate as our synthetic equivalent. A concrete example will make this clear.

Suppose you go to a bank *today* and negotiate to lend $100 *in 1 years time* and receive $110.50 at the end of year 2. This is a **forward–forward agreement** (FFA) with a **quoted** forward rate of $f_{12} = 10.5\%$ and the cash flows are shown in Figure 8.1. Note that you do not use any of your 'own funds' today.

The question is whether the 10.5% is a 'fair rate' for this loan. The answer to this question lies in 'manufacturing' a **synthetic forward contract**, which has the same cash flows as the actual FFA with the bank. Assume the *current* 1-year spot rate is $r_1 = 9\%$ and the 2-year spot rate is $r_2 = 10\%$. Consider the following two transactions undertaken today, in the spot market (for 'money'):

---

**SYNTHETIC FORWARD CONTRACT**
Borrow $91.74 for 1 year at $r_1 = 9\%$
Lend $91.74 for 2 years at $r_2 = 10\%$

---

## FIGURE 8.1: Actual forward–forward agreement

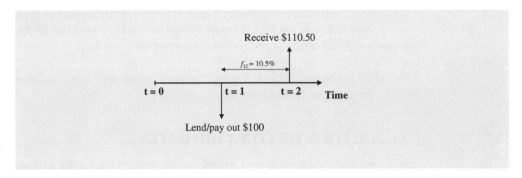

These give rise to the cash flows in Figure 8.2. Note that there are no 'own funds' used: the funds borrowed are immediately on-lent.

Borrowing $91.74 for 1 year implies a payment of $100 $[= \$91.74(1 + r_1)]$ at the end of year 1: this is the same cash outflow as in the actual FFA (see Figure 8.1). Lending $91.74 for 2 years leads to receipts of $111 $[= \$91.74(1 + r_2)^2]$ at the end of year 2. Our synthetic forward contract therefore leads to a cash outflow of $100 at $t = 1$ and an inflow of $111 at $t = 2$, which is equivalent to a **synthetic forward rate** applicable between $t = 1$ and $t = 2$ of $sf_{12} = 11\%$ $(= \$111/\$100)$. But the bank is quoting a rate of $f_{12} = 10.5\%$ on money lent between $t = 1$ and $t = 2$. You would not wish to lend your funds to the bank in 1 years time because you can 'manufacture' a better deal yourself by using the spot markets for 1-year and 2-year money. More importantly, faced with these interest rates you can make a riskless arbitrage profit as follows:

(i) agree today an FFA to borrow $100 from bank A in 1 years time at $f_{12} = 10.5\%$;
(ii) borrow $91.74 today, for 1 year at $r_1 = 9\%$ (from bank B);
(iii) lend $91.75 today, for 2 years at $r_2 = 10\%$ (from bank C);

## FIGURE 8.2: Synthetic forward ($sf_{12}$)

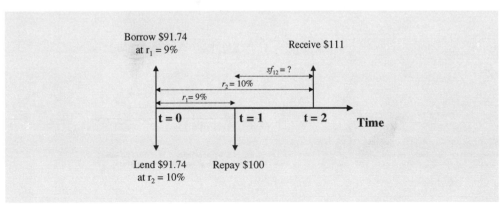

   (iv)  use the funds from the FFA in (i) at $t = 1$ to pay back the 1-year loan at $r_1 = 9\%$ from bank B, which now amounts to $100;

    (v)  at $t = 2$, receive $111 from the 2-year loan at $r_2 = 10\%$ made to bank C and pay bank A the $110.50 in the FFA. Overall this gives a riskless profit of $0.50, which is known at $t = 0$ (although the profit does not accrue until $t = 2$).

As we shall see below, if bank A doesn't wish to be 'duped' it should quote a forward rate equal to the synthetic forward rate $sf_{12} = 11\%$.

## CALCULATION OF FORWARD RATES

How do we directly calculate the forward rate (in the FFA) that bank A should quote in order that no riskless profits can be made? Figure 8.3 may help here, in terms of a heuristic argument. The 'fair' forward rate is based on the fact that investing $1 over 2 years at $r_2$ must give the same return (*over 2 years*) as investing at $r_1 = 9\%$ in the first year followed by an FFA at $f_{12}$ between years 1 and 2. This is because both strategies give a known return at $t = 0$ (since the rate $f_{12}$ is negotiated and known at $t = 0$, as is $r_1$).

In Figure 8.3 note that the 2-year investment earns 10% in *each* of the two years. Also, *in the first year*, the 2-year rate is 1% ($= 10\% - 9\%$) higher than the 1-year rate ($r_1 = 9\%$). Hence between $t = 1$ and $t = 2$ the forward contract must earn 10% plus the amount 'lost' in the first year. Hence the 'fair' forward rate is:

    **'Fair' forward rate $f_{12} = 10\% + (10\% - 9\%) = \mathbf{11\%}$**

$$= 2r_2 - r_1$$

This calculation ignores interest-on-interest which makes the correct forward rate a little higher at 11.009% (see below). More formally, let $f_{12}$ denote the 'fair' forward rate applicable between years 1 and 2. Then $A = \$91.74$ invested over 2 years gives

## FIGURE 8.3: Synthetic forward rate ($sf_{12}$)

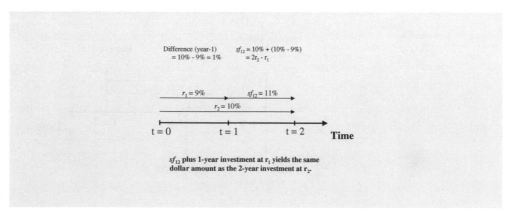

$sf_{12}$ plus 1-year investment at $r_1$ yields the same dollar amount as the 2-year investment at $r_2$.

$A(1 + r_2)^2 = \$111$ at $t = 2$ (see Figure 8.3). On the other hand, $A = \$91.74$ invested at $r_1$ gives $A(1 + r_1) = \$100$ which when reinvested in the FFA at $f_{12}$ gives $A(1 + r_1)(1 + f_{12})$ at $t = 2$. For these two amounts at $t = 2$ to be equal we must have:

[8.1]  $$(1 + r_2)^2 = (1 + r_1)(1 + f_{12})$$

Rearranging equation [8.1]:

[8.2]  $$(1 + f_{12}) = \frac{(1 + r_2)^2}{(1 + r_1)} = \frac{(1.10)^2}{(1.09)} = 1.11009$$

If we use the *approximation* $\ln(1 + z) = z$ (for $-1 < z < 1$) then equations [8.1] and [8.2] can be expressed as linear relationships:

[8.3a]  $$2r_2 \approx r_1 + f_{12}$$

or

[8.3b]  $$f_{12} \approx 2r_2 - r_1$$

If we use *continuously compounded* rates then the above linear relationships are exact, for example:

[8.4]  $$f_{c,12} = 2r_{c,2} - r_{c,1}$$

where $\ln(1 + r_i) = r_{c,i}$ ($i = 1,\ 2$) etc. We will for the moment assume the approximations in equation [8.3] are accurate and in our exposition we will mainly use discretely compounded rates. We can repeat the above argument for a three-period horizon to obtain:

[8.5]  $$(1 + r_3)^3 = (1 + r_1)(1 + f_{13})^2$$

[8.6]  $$3r_3 \approx r_1 + 2f_3$$

where $f_{13}$ is the implicit (annual) forward rate for the years $t + 1$ to $t + 3$ and hence applies to an investment horizon of $3 - 1 = 2$ years. Note also that we can compare our 3-year investment at $r_3$ with a known 2-year investment at $r_2$ and the forward rate $f_{23}$ between years 2 and 3:

[8.7]  $$(1 + r_3)^3 = (1 + r_2)^2(1 + f_{23})$$

[8.8]  $$3r_3 \approx 2r_2 + f_{23}$$

Equations [8.6] and [8.8] can be used to calculate the implicit forward rates $f_{13}$ and $f_{23}$ from the known spot rates. Implicit forward rates can be calculated for any horizon by using the appropriate recursive formula and data on spot rates. From the above, the following recursive equation is seen to hold for discrete and continuously compounded rates, respectively:

[8.9a]     Discrete     $f_{m,n} = \left[\dfrac{(1 + r_n)^n}{(1 + r_m)^m}\right]^{1/(n-m)} - 1$

[8.9b]     Continuous     $f_{m,n} = \left[\dfrac{n}{n - m}\right] r_n - \left[\dfrac{m}{n - m}\right] r_m = \left[\dfrac{nr_n - mr_m}{n - m}\right]$

where $n > m$. For example, for $n = 3$, $m = 2$ then equation [8.9b] gives $f_3 = 3r_3 - 2r_2$ which is of course the same as equation [8.8]. It is worth noting that the above equations use either discrete or continuously compounded rates whereas *quoted* market rates use simple interest (see below). In Table 8.1 we use data on 10 (continuously compounded) spot rates $r_1$ to $r_{10}$ to calculate the one-period forward rates $f_{t,t+j}$ ($j = 1, 2, \ldots$). In one case we have a rising spot yield curve and in the other we have a downward sloping yield curve. We then plot the spot rates and the corresponding forward rates against time to maturity: these are the spot and forward yield curves. It is a matter of arithmetic (and can be seen in Figure 8.4) that:

> **When spot rates increase with time to maturity (i.e.**
> $r_1 < r_2 < \ldots < r_{10}$) **then the forward rate curve**
> **lies *above* the spot rate curve (and vice versa)**

We now look at two key uses of forward rates, namely pricing a T-bill futures contract and a forward rate agreement (FRA). The latter is a key building block in the analysis of interest rate swaps.

## FUTURES CONTRACTS

Suppose you are offered at time $t = 0$ a contract which allowed you to purchase a 1-year T-bill at $t = 1$ for $100 and this T-bill had a face (maturity) value of $111, which of course would be paid 1-year later at $t = 2$. Note that at $t = 0$ no cash changes hands but at $t = 1$ you pay $100 and take delivery of the T-bill (for which you can receive $111 with certainty at $t = 2$). What we have described is in fact a forward or futures contract on a T-bill. The *price* agreed today (at $t = 0$) of $100 for delivery of the T-bill at maturity of the futures contract in 1 years time (i.e. at $T = 1$) is the forward (or futures) price denoted $F_0 = \$100$ (or more correctly $F_0^T$).

The above deal has the same cash flows as our FFA described above and hence the *price* agreed today of $F_0 = \$100$ must be the 'fair' or 'no arbitrage' price for the futures contract. Indirectly, we have therefore found a method of calculating the 'fair' T-bill *futures price*:

[8.10]     $F_0^T = \dfrac{M}{(1 + f_{1,2})}$

where $M$ is the face value (= $111). Now in practice, the T-bill delivered in a 'real world' futures contract has $M = \$100$, but this just means that the fair price will be $F_0 = \$90.09$.

## TABLE 8.1: Spot and forward yield curves

**Forward rates (continuously compounded)**

Upward sloping yield curve

| $m$ | 1 | 2 | 3 | 4 | 5 | 6 | 7 | 8 | 9 | 10 |
|---|---|---|---|---|---|---|---|---|---|---|
| 1 | | 0.07 | 0.077 | 0.082 | 0.0875 | 0.0908 | 0.094333 | 0.095714 | 0.09725 | 0.097778 |
| 2 | | | 0.084 | 0.088 | 0.093333 | 0.096 | 0.0992 | 0.1 | 0.101143 | 0.10125 |
| 3 | | | | 0.092 | 0.098 | 0.1 | 0.103 | 0.1032 | 0.104 | 0.103714 |
| 4 | | | | | 0.104 | 0.104 | 0.106667 | 0.106 | 0.1064 | 0.105667 |
| 5 | | | | | | 0.104 | 0.108 | 0.106667 | 0.107 | 0.106 |
| 6 | | | | | | | 0.112 | 0.108 | 0.108 | 0.1065 |
| 7 | | | | | | | | 0.104 | 0.106 | 0.104667 |
| 8 | | | | | | | | | 0.108 | 0.105 |
| 9 | | | | | | | | | | 0.102 |
| 10 | | | | | | | | | | |
| **Spot rates** | 0.05 | 0.06 | 0.068 | 0.074 | 0.08 | 0.084 | 0.088 | 0.09 | 0.092 | 0.093 |
| **Forward rates** | 0.07 | 0.077 | 0.082 | 0.0875 | 0.0908 | 0.094333 | 0.095714 | 0.09725 | 0.097778 | |

$n$

*continued overleaf*

223

## TABLE 8.1: (*Continued*)

**Forward rates (continuously compounded)**

Downward sloping yield curve

|  |  | | | | | | $n$ | | | |
|---|---|---|---|---|---|---|---|---|---|---|
|  | 1 | 2 | 3 | 4 | 5 | 6 | 7 | 8 | 9 | 10 |
| **1** | **0.02** | | **0.052** | **0.065333** | **0.075** | **0.0808** | **0.086** | **0.088571** | **0.091** | **0.092222** |
| 2 | | 0.024 | | 0.058 | 0.073333 | 0.081 | 0.0872 | 0.09 | 0.092571 | 0.09375 |
| 3 | | | 0.05 | | 0.077 | 0.086 | 0.0925 | 0.0948 | 0.097 | 0.097714 |
| 4 | | | | 0.104 | | 0.104 | 0.106667 | 0.106 | 0.1064 | 0.105667 |
| 5 | | | | | 0.164 | | 0.138 | 0.126667 | 0.122 | 0.118 |
| 6 | | | | | | 0.244 | | 0.174 | 0.152 | 0.1395 |
| 7 | | | | | | | 0.314 | | 0.211 | 0.174667 |
| 8 | | | | | | | | 0.38 | | 0.241 |
| 9 | | | | | | | | | 0.444 | |
| 10 | | | | | | | | | | |
| **Spot rates** | 0.1 | 0.09 | 0.082 | 0.074 | 0.068 | 0.062 | 0.058 | 0.056 | 0.054 | 0.053 |
| **Forward rates** | | 0.02 | 0.052 | 0.065333 | 0.075 | 0.0808 | 0.086 | 0.088571 | 0.091 | 0.092222 |

## FIGURE 8.4: Yield curves

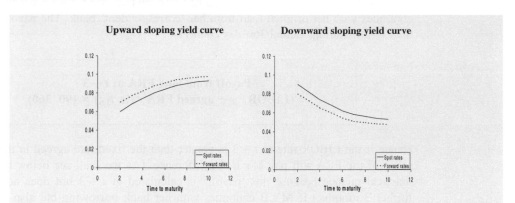

Hence the no arbitrage T-bill futures *price* is derived from the appropriate forward *rate* $f_{1,2}$ (which in turn is derived from observed spot rates at $t = 0$).

## FORWARD RATE AGREEMENTS

Forward–forward agreements (FFAs) as described above were provided by banks until the 1980s. The problem was that such agreements used up the banks' lines of credit with other banks and with their own customers (and hence the banks incurred capital charges). Also, the banks were subject to credit (default) risk on the whole of the principal in the forward– forward deal. Hence the banks developed an equivalent security known as a forward rate agreement (FRA), where the principal amount is not exchanged and the payments are based on the *difference* between two interest rates—this considerably reduced credit risk. The outcome from the FRA is (almost) equivalent to that from the FFA discussed above, although the institutional arrangements differ. We will now outline the practical issues surrounding the use of FRAs and will use the usual market convention, namely *simple* interest rates.

An FRA is a form of forward contract which allows one to 'lock in' or hedge interest rate risk for a specific period in the future. If you are borrowing money *in the future* (e.g. in 3 months time) you may fear a rise in interest rates since then, your future borrowing costs will be higher. Conversely if you are thinking of lending money in the future you will lose out if interest rates fall since your deposit will earn less interest. Hence:

> **To hedge a rise in future borrowing rates ⇒ buy ('go long') an FRA**
> **To hedge a fall in future lending rates ⇒ sell ('go short') an FRA**

An example will make this clear. Suppose M's B has borrowed $1m from a bank for 6 months with interest payments reset at the end of the first 3-month period, based on the prevailing 3-month LIBOR. For the first 3-month period the rate on the loan is fixed at the *current* 3-month LIBOR rate at $t = 0$ and she can do nothing about this. Assume, however, that M's B thinks LIBOR rates will rise in the future, hence increasing the cost of rolling over the loan 3 months from now. She can hedge this risk by buying an FRA today at an agreed FRA rate $f_{3,6}$ to begin in 3 months time and lasting for a further 90 days. She also continues with her original loan from her 'correspondent' bank. The payoff to M's B from the FRA (assuming 'actual/360' day count) is:

$$
\begin{aligned}
&\textbf{Payoff from long FRA at } t+3 \\
&= (\text{LIBOR}_{t+3} - \text{agreed FRA rate } f_{3,6}) \times (90/360)
\end{aligned}
$$

Hence if the LIBOR rate at $t+3$ is greater than the fixed rate agreed in the FRA then the seller of the FRA will pay M's B the difference. (As we shall see below there is a further practical nuance because this 'payoff' is calculated at $t+3$ but does not accrue until a further 3 months.) If M's B continues with her bank borrowing but also holds the (long) FRA then the effective cost of the loan repayments in 3 months time is:

$$
\begin{aligned}
\textbf{Effective cost of loan } &= (\text{LIBOR}_{t+3} - \text{pay off from FRA}) \times (90/360) \\
&= [\text{LIBOR}_{t+3} - (\text{LIBOR}_{t+3} - f_{3,6})] \times (90/360) \\
&= f_{3,6} \times (90/360)
\end{aligned}
$$

Hence by taking out the FRA, M's B has effectively swapped her floating rate payments on her original bank loan for fixed rate payments at the rate $f_{3,6}$ negotiated in the FRA. Of course, if LIBOR rates at $t+3$ turn out to be lower than the FRA rate $f_{3,6}$ (negotiated at $t=0$) then M's B will pay the seller of the FRA the difference. However, the payments on her original bank loan will be at the lower LIBOR rate so again she effectively ends up with net payments (i.e. the bank loan plus the FRA) equal to the fixed rate $f_{3,6}$ in the FRA.

Banks are the main participants in the FRA markets, which are over-the-counter (OTC) instruments, that is they are not traded continuously in a standardised format on an exchange but they can be tailored to suit individual requirements. By taking a long position in the FRA, M's B has effectively 'swapped' her payment on the bank borrowing at an unknown floating rate (i.e. LIBOR) for a known fixed rate payment at the FRA rate $f_{3,6}$. In fact, an **interest rate swap** is nothing more than a series of FRAs over a number of reset periods. For example, a 5-year swap with interest payments reset every 3 months is equivalent to 19 ($= 20 - 1$) separate FRAs. (Note that there are '19' FRAs because the first payment in the swap is at the current known LIBOR rate at $t=0$ — see Cuthbertson and Nitzschc, 2001 for further details on swaps.)

## CALCULATION OF THE FRA/FORWARD RATE

Having determined the payoff from an FRA we now turn to the calculation of the fair forward (FRA) rate. The quoted rate on an FRA is determined by the two relevant spot rates in the market and equals (ignoring the bid–ask spread) the 'implicit' or synthetic forward rate $sf_{3,6}$. If the quoted rate on the FRA did not equal the synthetic forward rate then riskless arbitrage profits could be made. Market participants use quotes based on *simple interest* to calculate the fair forward rate $f_{3,6}$. For the 3 month $\times$ 6 month FRA we assume:

(i) 30/360 day count basis (e.g. 3 months $= 90/360 = 1/4$);
(ii) $r_3 = 11.625$ (% p.a.), $r_6 = 11.8125$ (% p.a.)—*simple* interest rates.

The 'fair' forward rate $f_{3,6}$ is given by:

[8.11]        $(1 + r_6/2) = (1 + r_3/4)(1 + f_{3,6}/4)$

$(1.05906) = (1.02906)(1 + f_{3,6}/4)$

Hence:

$f_{3,6} = 0.116608$ (**11.6608% p.a.**)

Given the current 3 and 6-month spot rates a bank would provide a 3 month $\times$ 6 month FRA at an interest rate of 11.66% p.a. To see why the forward rate is set at this level consider a Corporate Treasurer who *will receive* $100m sales revenue in 3 months which he then wishes to place on deposit for 3 months. He can guarantee the interest rate he will receive by selling a 3 month $\times$ 6 month FRA (i.e. lending) to a bank at $f_{3,6} = 11.66\%$ p.a. Alternatively, the Corporate Treasurer can create a *synthetic FRA* by:

(i) borrowing the present value of $100m for 3 months; and
(ii) simultaneously lending the cash received for 6 months.

(The above cash flows are similar to those in Figure 8.2 but with $t = 1$ and $t = 2$, corresponding to 3 months and 6 months, respectively.) The cash flows today and in 3 months time are:

**Today:**            Borrow $97.1758m $= \$100m / [1 + 0.11625/4]$ for 3 months
                      Lend $97.1758m for 6 months
**After 3 months:**   Pay off borrowed funds ($97.1758m) plus interest of $2.83m with the
                      $100m sales revenue
**After 6 months:**   Receive $102.9152m $= \$97.1758m [1 + 0.118125/2]$ on the 6-month
                      bank deposit

From his *synthetic* FRA the Treasurer has earned $102.9152m at the end of 6 months for an outlay of $100m at the end of 3 months. The rate of interest he has earned is the 'synthetic forward rate' of $sf_{3,6} = [(102.9152/100) - 1] \times 4 = 2.09152\% \times 4 = 11.6608\%$ p.a. (simple annual rate). If the quoted rate for the 3 month $\times$ 6 month FRA is different from the synthetic rate then riskless arbitrage would ensue. For example, suppose the synthetic forward rate $sf_{3,6} = 11.6608\%$ and was greater than the quoted rate of $f_{3,6} = 11\%$ say offered by the bank. The Treasurer would not sell the FRA (i.e. would not lend directly to the bank) but could create his own synthetic forward contract by borrowing at the 3-month spot rate and lending at the 6-month spot rate. Hence $r_3$ would rise and $r_6$ would fall, until the equality in formula [8.11] is restored.

## SETTLEMENT PROCEDURES

Finally let us consider the actual settlement procedure for an FRA. An FRA is a contract on a notional principal amount $Q. However, there is no exchange of principal at the beginning and end of the contract, only the *difference* in interest payments on the notional principal amount is paid. The settlement (or benchmark) rate used in the contract is usually the LIBOR rate (or the equivalent interbank rate in any given currency).

We have already considered the 'payoff' from the FRA and noted that this can be calculated at $t + 3$, but the interest applies over the period $t + 3$ to $t + 6$ (for a 3 month $\times$ 6 month FRA). Hence the amount actually paid at $t + 3$ is the *present value* of the difference between LIBOR at the settlement date and the quoted forward rate agreed at the outset of the contract. For example, consider the payment at settlement on the following 3 month $\times$ 6 month FRA:

(i) $f_{3,6} = 8\%$ (set at $t = 0$) on a notional principal of $Q = \$1m$;
(ii) actual 3-month LIBOR rate *in 3 months time* (i.e. at $t + 3$) is $r_{t+3} = 10\%$.

Cash settlement is made at the end of 3 months. To calculate the cash settlement note that the amount owed at the end of 6 months is:

**Amount owed after 6 months $= Q(r_{t+3}-$FRA rate$)\ 90/360$**

Since payment takes place after 3 months (i.e. as soon as $r_{t+3}$ becomes known) the amount owing needs to be discounted, hence:

**Actual payment (after 3 months)** $= \dfrac{1}{(1 + 0.10/4)}[\$1m(10 - 8) \times (90/360)]$

$$= \$5000/1.025 = \textbf{\$4878.05}$$

Algebraically, the terminal value TV of the FRA *after 6 months* on a notional principal of $Q$ is:

[8.12]     $TV_6 = \dfrac{T - t}{360}(r_{t+3} - f_{3,6})Q$

where $T$ is the longer maturity leg (in days), $t$ is the shorter maturity leg (in days). Hence:

[8.13]     **Actual cash payment (at $t + 3$)** $= \dfrac{TV_6}{\left(1 + r_{t+3}\dfrac{(T - t)}{360}\right)}$

Only the 'difference in value' is paid because the Corporate Treasurer will already have long-term variable rate loan arrangements with his own bankers and uses the FRA to hedge these longer term loan commitments. In effect, as we noted earlier, he 'transforms' the floating rate payments on his bank borrowing into a known fixed payment at $f_{3,6}$.

Although it has not been the focus here, note that FRAs can also be used to speculate on the future course of interest rates. It should be obvious that since the payoff from our *long* FRA is $(r_{t+3} - f_{3,6})\ (90/360)$ then a speculator should:

---

**SPECULATING WITH FRAs**
Buy (go long) an FRA if you think interest rates will rise in the future
Sell (go short) an FRA if you think interest rates will fall in the future

---

Because FRAs are OTC instruments (with relatively high transactions costs) then in practice speculation on future changes in interest rates is usually undertaken with exchange traded derivative instruments such as interest rate futures and options contracts.

# 8.2 YIELD CURVES AND THE TERM STRUCTURE

Most governments at some time or another attempt to influence short-term interest rates as a lever on the real economy or in an attempt to influence the rate of inflation. This is usually accomplished by the monetary authority either engaging in open market operations using repos (i.e. buying or selling bills) or threatening to do so. Changes in short rates (with unchanged inflationary expectations) may influence real inventory holdings and consumers' expenditure, particularly on durable goods. Short-term interest rates may have an effect on *the level* of long-term interest rates on government bonds. This is the yield curve relationship.

Government bond rates will directly influence corporate bond rates, which in turn may affect real investment in plant and machinery. Hence, the government's interest rate policy can influence real economic activity via its effect on short rates and long rates. Also changes in domestic short rates may influence capital flows, the exchange rate and hence price competitiveness, the volume of net trade (exports minus imports) and the level of output and employment. We deal with the link between short rates and the exchange rate, the so-called uncovered interest parity relationship, in Chapter 16.

In this section we concentrate on the relationship between short rates and long rates on government debt, that is on the yield curve and the term structure of interest rates. There are various hypotheses as to why rates of interest on long maturity bonds are usually (but not always) higher than rates on short dated bonds. We begin by discussing these alternative theories before moving on to see how forward rates may be used to predict the future course of interest rates as well as the future rate of inflation. Finally we outline various methods of fitting a smooth curve to observed interest rates of different maturities. This provides the basis for calculating forward rates, which can then be used to price FRAs, FRNs, swaps and interest rate futures.

## THEORIES OF THE TERM STRUCTURE

The relationship between interest rates of different maturities on (default free) bonds is referred to as the term structure of interest rates. Graphically, this relationship is known as the yield curve, hence:

> **The yield curve is a graph showing the relationship
> between interest rates (yields) on bonds
> and their time to maturity**

Normally, the yield curve slopes upwards (A–A in Figure 8.5) and becomes flatter as the time to maturity lengthens.

A yield curve refers to a particular point in time (i.e. interest rates on a specific day) and the whole curve may shift up or down as the general level of all interest rates alters (B–B in Figure 8.5). The upward slope of the yield curve indicates, for example, that bonds with (say) 20 years to maturity will command a higher interest rate than those with 1 or 2 years to maturity. There are, however, circumstances in which the yield curve can slope downwards, a situation which occurs when future short rates are expected to be lower than the current short rate. Such a situation is unusual since long bonds carry additional risk relative to short-term bonds. This is because even if long bonds are held to maturity, the *real value* (i.e. in terms of purchasing power over goods and services) of the interest payments on long maturity bonds may be very uncertain, because of uncertainty over future inflation levels.

Theories which attempt to explain possible different shapes of the term structure include the expectations hypothesis, the liquidity preference hypothesis, market segmentation and the preferred habitat hypothesis. They differ only in their treatment of the term premium. We deal with each in turn and a summary is provided in Box 8.1.

---

## FIGURE 8.5: Yield curve

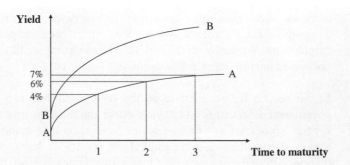

If short rates are expected to rise then $r_2 = 6\%$ and $r_3 = 7\%$.

## Box 8.1    THE TERM STRUCTURE: SUMMARY

**1. Pure expectations hypothesis (PEH)**
   (a) *Expected excess return is zero.*
   (b) *The term premium is zero for all maturities.*

$$r_{nt} - E_t(r_{t+j}\text{'s}) = 0$$

## 2. Expectations hypothesis (constant term premium)
(a) *Expected excess return equals a constant which is the same for all maturities.*
(b) *The term premium 'T' is a constant and the same for all maturities.*

$$r_{nt} - E_t(r_{t+j}\text{'s}) = T$$

## 3. Liquidity preference
(a) *Expected excess return on a bond of maturity n is a constant but the value of the constant is larger the longer the period to maturity.*
(b) *The term premium increases with n, the time period to maturity.*

$$r_{nt} - E_t(r_{t+j}\text{'s}) = T^{(n)}$$

*where $T^{(n)} > T^{(n-1)}$ ... etc.*

## 4. Time varying risk premium
(a) *Expected excess return on a bond of maturity n varies with n and over time.*
(b) *The term premium depends on the maturity n and varies over time.*

$$r_{nt} - E_t(r_{t+j}\text{'s}) = T(n, z_t)$$

*where $T(.)$ is some function of n and a set of variables $z_t$.*

## 5. Market segmentation
(a) *Excess returns are influenced at least in part by the outstanding stock of assets of different maturities.*
(b) *The term premium depends in part on the outstanding stock of assets of different maturities.*

$$r_{nt} - E_t(r_{t+j}\text{'s}) = T(z_t^{(n)})$$

*where $z_t^{(n)}$ is some measure of the proportionate holdings of assets of maturity 'n'.*

## 6. Preferred habitat theory
(a) *Bonds which mature at dates which are close together should be reasonably close substitutes and hence have similar term premia.*

The term structure of interest rates deals with the relationship between the yields on bonds of different maturities. Strictly speaking the yields in question are *spot yields* and therefore, conceptually, the analysis applies to pure discount bonds or zero coupon bonds. Pure discount government bonds for long maturities do not exist, nevertheless, spot yields can be derived from data on a set of coupon paying bonds (see below). A more familiar measure of the return on a bond is the *yield to maturity*, and it can be shown that theories of the term structure can also be applied with minor modification (and an element of approximation) using these yields to maturity (e.g. Shiller, 1989).

## PURE EXPECTATIONS HYPOTHESIS

The pure expectations hypothesis (PEH) applied to spot yields assumes investors are risk neutral, that is, they are indifferent to risk. The inherent variability or uncertainty concerning returns is of no consequence to their investment decisions. Consequently, they base their investment decisions only on *expected* returns. For example, consider investing $A$ in a 3-year (zero coupon) bond with yield $r_{3t}$. The terminal value of the investment is:

[8.14]       $TV = \$A(1 + r_{3t})^3$

where $r_{3t}$ is the rate on the three-period long bond (expressed at an annual rate). Next consider the alternative strategy of reinvesting $A$ and any interest earned in a series of 'rolled over' *one-period* investments, for 3 years. Ignoring transactions costs the *expected* terminal value $E_t(TV)$ of this series of *one-period investments* is:

[8.15]       $E_t(TV) = \$A(1 + r_t)(1 + E_t r_{t+1})(1 + E_t r_{t+2})$

where $E_t$ implies expectations are made at time $t$ and $r_{t+i}$ is the rate applicable between periods $t + i$ and $t + i + 1$. Hence $E_t r_{t+2}$ is the expectation at time $t$ of what the 1-year rate will be at the end of year 2. An investment in a zero coupon long bond gives a known terminal value since this bond is held to maturity. Investing in a series of 1-year bonds gives a terminal value which is subject to uncertainty, since the investor must guess the future values of the one-period spot yields, $r_{t+j}$. However, under the PEH, risk is ignored and hence the terminal values of the above two alternative investment strategies will be equalised:

[8.16]       $(1 + r_{3t})^3 = (1 + r_t)(1 + E_t r_{t+1})(1 + E_t r_{t+2})$

The equality holds because if the terminal value corresponding to investment in the long bond exceeds the *expected* terminal value of that on the sequence of 1-year investments, then investors would at time $t$ buy long bonds and sell the short bond. This would result in a rise in the current market price of the long bond and hence a fall in its yield, $r_{3t}$. Simultaneously, sales of the short bond would cause a fall in its current price and a rise in $r_t$. Hence the equality in equation [8.16] would be quickly (instantaneously) restored. We could *define* the expected 'excess' or 'abnormal profit' AP on a $1 investment in the long bond over the sequence of rolled over short investments as:

[8.17]       $E_t(AP_t) \equiv r_{nt} - E_t(r_{t+j}\text{'s})$

where $r_{nt}$ is the yield on the long maturity bond and the term '$E_t(r_{t+j}\text{'s})$' represents the RHS of equation [8.16]. The PEH applied to *spot yields* therefore implies that the *expected* excess or abnormal profit is zero. Taking logarithms of equation [8.16] and using the approximation $\ln(1 + z) \approx z$ for $|z| < 1$ we obtain the linear relationship:

[8.18]       $r_{3t} = (1/3)[r_t + E_t r_{t+1} + E_t r_{t+2}]$

One way of stating the PEH based on equation [8.18] is that it implies:

> **The long rate is a weighted average of current and expected future short rates**

In general when testing the PEH one should use *continuously compounded* spot rates since then there is no linearisation approximation involved in equation [8.18]. If we had considered a two-period investment horizon the PEH would have given:

[8.19] $$r_{2t} = (1/2)[r_t + E_t r_{t+1}]$$

## THE YIELD CURVE

The yield curve is a graph of the yield against the maturity of the bond. The PEH provides one way of analysing the shape of the (spot) yield curve. For example, viewed from time $t$, if short rates are expected to remain constant so that $r_t = r_{t+1} = r_{t+2} = 4\%$ (say), then using equations [8.18] and [8.19] the long rates $r_{2t}$ and $r_{3t}$ are also seen to equal 4%. Hence with constant expected short rates the yield curve is flat. However, if short rates are expected to rise (e.g. $r_t = 4\%$, $Er_{t+1} = 8\%$, $Er_{t+2} = 9\%$) then from equations [8.18] and [8.19] we have $r_{2t} = 6\%$, $r_{3t} = 7\%$ and the yield curve will be upward sloping (see Figure 8.5). Since expected future short rates are influenced by expectations of inflation (Fisher effect), the yield curve is likely to be upward sloping when inflation is expected to increase in future years. Hence the shape of yield curve gives an indication of the markets view of future inflation:

> **YIELD CURVE**      **INFLATION**
> **flat**              ⇒ **expected to remain unchanged**
> **upward sloping**    ⇒ **expected to rise in the future**
> **downward sloping**  ⇒ **expected to fall in the future**

In fact, as we shall see below, we can extract forward rates from the yield curve and use these to provide an explicit numerical forecast for future inflation.

The PEH ignores risk and hence the risk or **term premium** is zero for all maturities. Although the *nominal* return on a long bond is (reasonably) certain, the *real* return is likely to be more risky than on a series of rolled over 1-year investments. The rate paid on future 1-year investments is likely to be close to the rate of inflation in these future periods. But for the long bond the interest rate is fixed in nominal terms over the life of the bond and hence is uncertain in real terms (because of uncertainty about future inflation rates). Therefore, the return on long bonds ought to contain a 'reward for risk', that is a term premium $T_t^{(n)}$. So equation [8.17] now becomes:

[8.20] $$E_t(\text{AP}_t) \equiv r_{nt} - E_t(r_{t+j}\text{'s}) + T_t^{(n)}$$

Different theories of the term structure make different assumptions about the precise nature

233

of the term premium. Indeed if we assume the term premium is a (non-zero) constant in each year and doesn't depend on the maturity of the bond (i.e. $T_t^{(n)} = T$), this constitutes the **expectations hypothesis (EH)**. Obviously this yields similar predictions as the PEH.

## LIQUIDITY PREFERENCE

Here, the assumption is that the term premium does *not* vary over time but it does depend on the term to maturity of the bond (i.e. $T_t^{(n)} = T^{(n)}$). For example, bonds with longer periods to maturity may be viewed as being more 'risky' than those with a short period to maturity. If the liquidity (term) premium increases with the term to maturity then the basic qualitative shape of the yield curve will remain as described above, but it will be steeper (see Figure 8.6).

The increased risk on longer term bonds may be due to increased 'inflation risk' or because lenders like to lend at short horizons while borrowers prefer a longer horizon. Hence long rates contain a **liquidity premium** to induce lenders to lend at long horizons.

## MARKET SEGMENTATION

The market segmentation hypothesis states that the long–short interest rate spread on two bonds of different maturities depends on *all* the factors that influence the supply and demand for these assets (e.g. the proportion of wealth held in each of these assets, the variance of returns, price inflation, etc.). However, in practice the market segmentation hypothesis usually assumes that it is only when the proportion of debt held in bonds of maturity '$n$' increases that the yield $r_{nt}$ on these bonds also increases.

## PREFERRED HABITAT

The preferred habitat theory is, in effect, agnostic about the determinants of the term premium. It suggests that yields on bonds in widely differing maturity bands are largely unrelated. This is assumed to be because investors tend to operate only in specific maturity bands.

## FIGURE 8.6: Liquidity preference

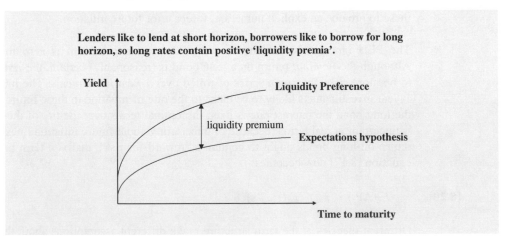

TIME VARYING RISK

If the risk or term premium varies over time and varies differently for bonds of different maturities then:

[8.21]     $r_{nt} = E_t(r_{t+j}\text{'s}) + T(n, z_t)$

where $z_t$ is a set of variables that influences investors' perceptions of risk. This is our most general model so far, but unless one specifies an explicit form of the function $T$, our model is not operational. Currently there is a lot of empirical work examining time varying risk under the assumption that once the market is perceived to be highly risky, it remains highly risky for some time. This is the concept of 'persistence' in ARCH and GARCH models (see Cuthbertson, 1996). Of course, if the term premium varies over time, then the direct link between the long rate and the sequence of expected future short rates is broken.

The empirical evidence suggests that the expectations hypothesis has a reasonable amount of support in most developed industrial economies (see Cuthbertson, 1996). While there is some evidence of small yet constant term premia between yields on different maturity bonds, it remains the case that long rates are primarily influenced by expected future short rates.

## 8.3  FORWARD RATES AND THE TERM STRUCTURE

Our theories of the term structure have been discussed in terms of spot rates. However, as forward rates can be calculated from spot rates, the term structure can be analysed using forward rates. To see this we return to the two-period case (with a slight change in notation) and examine variants of the expectations hypothesis (EH) in terms of forward rates. If the EH including a term premium $T_{02,t}$ holds, then arbitrage ensures:

[8.22]     $2r_{02,t} = r_{01,t} + E_t r_{12,t} + T_{02,t}$

But forward and spot rates are (arithmetically) related:

[8.23]     $2r_{02,t} = r_{01,t} + f_{12,t}$

Comparing equations [8.22] and [8.23] we see that:

[8.24]     $f_{12,t} = E_t r_{12,t} + T_{02,t}$

Hence the forward rate is equal to the market's expectation of the return on a one-period bond, starting one period from now, plus the term premium. If $T_{02,t} = 0$, then equation [8.24] is consistent with the pure expectations hypothesis.

---

**The PEH therefore implies that the forward rate is an
unbiased predictor of the expected future spot rate**
*and*
**Observable forward rates can be used to help predict
future values for nominal interest rates and hence inflation
rates (if real rates are constant)**

---

Subtracting $r_{01,t}$ from both sides of equation [8.24] we see that the EH also implies that the **forward premium** $(f_{12} - r_{01})$ is an unbiased predictor of the expected change in interest rates, $\Delta E_t r_{t+1} = E_t r_{12,t} - r_{01,t}$. More generally,

**Expected change in interest rates = forward premium − term premium**

[8.25]
$$\Delta E_t r_{t+1} = (f_{12,t} - r_{01,t}) - T_{02,t}$$

Tests of the expectations hypothesis are usually based on regressions of the form:

[8.26]
$$\Delta r_{t+1} = \alpha + \beta(f_{12,t} - r_{01,t}) + \varepsilon_t$$

(where we assume rational expectations—see Cuthbertson, 1996). Under the PEH we expect the forward premium to be an unbiased predictor of change in the future spot rate and hence $\beta = 1$. Mishkin (1988) examines equations like [8.26] over 2 to 6-month horizons, using data on US Treasury bills over the period 1959–82. He finds that for 1-month ahead forecasts $\hat{\beta} = 0.40$ (s.e. $= 0.11$) and $R^2 = 0.11$, but as the horizon is extended to changes in interest rates over 3, 4, 5 and 6 months, the forward premium generally has little or no predictive power (i.e. $\hat{\beta} \approx 0$ statistically). Fama and Bliss (1987) present results for much longer horizons using spot rates from 1 to 5-years maturity. They find that the forecast power of regressions like [8.26] improves as the horizon is lengthened. For example, for changes in spot rates over a 4-year horizon the forward premium explains 0.48% of the variability in future interest rates and we do not reject the hypothesis that $\hat{\beta} = 1$. So there does appear to be some predictive power in the forward premium, for future changes in interest rates. Hence if future changes in interest rates reflect future rates of inflation then current observed forward rates may help predict inflation.

## 8.4 YIELD CURVES AND INFLATION

The EH implies that long rates are a weighted average of current and future short rates and therefore the yield curve will be upward sloping if short rates *are expected to rise* in the future (e.g. because inflation is expected to be higher).

Suppose we have estimated the yield curve for a particular day and it shows short-term rates at about $r_{1,t} = 6.5\%$ with 4-year rates rising to $r_{4,t} = 9\%$ and becoming flat thereafter. The yield curve can be used to provide the market's expectation of future inflation. Consider our four-period spot rate $r_{4,t}$ for the period $t$ to $t + 4$. The Fisher hypothesis implies:

Nominal rate = real rate + expected inflation

[8.27]
$$r_{4,t} = rr_{4,t} + \pi^e_{4,t}$$

Hence the average annual expected inflation rate over the next 4 years can be calculated as:

Expected inflation = nominal rate − real rate

[8.28]
$$\pi^e_{4,t} = r_{4,t} - rr_{4,t}$$

If the real rate is assumed to be constant at $rr = 3.5\%$ p.a. then with $r_4 = 9\%$, **expected inflation** over the next 4 years would be 5.5% p.a. ($= 9\% - 3.5\%$) and with $r_1 = 6.5\%$, expected inflation over the next year would be 3% p.a. ($= 6.5\% - 3.5\%$). Hence, the *increase* in inflation between $t + 1$ and $t + 4$ is therefore predicted to be 2.5% ($= 5.5\% - 3\%$). If the real rate of interest is assumed to be constant (at 3.5%) then we can obtain this result directly:

---

**Change in expected inflation between $t + 1$ and $t + 4$**

$$= \text{(4-year rate } r_{4,t}) - \text{(1-year rate } r_{1,t}) = 9\% - 6.5\% = 2.5\%$$

---

If there is a market in index linked, default free government bonds, then the real rate (ignoring tax effects) is also observable and may change over time (reflecting productivity growth in the economy). Estimates of the real rate of interest (from index linked bonds) indicate that in the UK, variations in the real rate are usually quite small ($\pm 1\%$ p.a.) so the assumption of a constant real rate may be reasonable. Note that although the market's prediction of future inflation as calculated above may provide the best predictor available, nevertheless it may not be very accurate, because of large unforeseen events which occur between the time the forecast is made and the end of the forecast period.

Under the (pure) expectations hypothesis the forward rate is the best predictor of future interest rates (e.g. $E_t(r_{34,t}) = f_{34,t}$). So, for example, if we want to know what the market's current forecast of inflation is between years $t + 3$ and $t + 4$ then this is equal to ($f_{34,t}$ − real rate). Knowing the shape of the forward rate curve we can calculate the market's view of inflation over successive years. If the forward rate curve is upward (downward) sloping then market participants are expecting a rise (fall) in inflation in subsequent years.

In reality the relationship between nominal spot (and forward) rates and inflation expectations may be more complex than given by the basic Fisher hypothesis because of risk premia effects. A more complex Fisher equation is:

---

**Nominal rate of return = expected inflation + inflation risk premium + expected real rate + real rate risk premium**

---

Changes in the above risk premia may distort the information about future inflation contained in nominal rates. Even noting the above difficulties, Central Banks do use the above methodology to help forecast future inflation, although they will also examine many other factors (e.g. cost pressures from a falling currency, commodity price forecasts, the projected level of aggregate demand). Although forecasts obtained from market interest rates often get the direction of change in inflation right, nevertheless the quantitative forecast may not be very accurate (e.g. because of major unforeseen events such as the impact of a recession on actual inflation).

# 8.5 ESTIMATING YIELD CURVES

There are many different types of yield curve but all of them are a graph of some measure of 'yield' against maturity (e.g. spot yield curve, forward yield curve and the par yield curve). Because of the wide diversity of coupon paying bonds, with different coupon payment dates, different tax treatment, etc., some method of 'fitting' a smooth curve is required. Also, some maturities may not be traded or constitute a very thin market, so that observed prices may not be representative of actual traded prices. Hence not all bond yields will lie exactly on a single yield curve, and therefore we briefly consider techniques of fitting yield curves to observed market data. Having fitted a smooth continuous yield curve to the data, we can then 'read off' the estimated yield for any maturity.

## ESTIMATING SPOT RATES: REGRESSION

One method of estimating a yield curve for spot rates is based on a cross-section regression on a set of coupon paying bonds. Let us assume we have $n$ bonds ($i = 1, 2, 3, \ldots, n$) all of which have annual coupons which are paid exactly 1, 2, 3, $\ldots$, $n$ years in the future. Hence we have data on the coupons $C_i(1)$, $C_i(2)$, $\ldots$ where the $C_i$ differ for each bond. We can also observe the price $P_i$ of each bond. Consider the following equation:

[8.29] $$P_i = \delta_1 C_i(1) + \delta_2 C_i(2) + \delta_3 C_i(3) + \ldots + \varepsilon_i$$

where $\delta_t = 1/(1 + r_t)^t$ and $\varepsilon_t$ is a random error. The discount factors $\delta_t$ depend on the unobserved spot yields $r_t$. The random error arises because not all bonds (with exactly the same coupons) will have exactly the same price because of bid–ask spreads, non-synchronous trading, etc. At time $t$, if we have a set of bonds with different prices $P_i$ and coupons $C_i$, then equation [8.29] is a cross-section regression equation and we can estimate $\delta_i$ (often under the restriction that $\delta_1 < \delta_2 < \delta_3 \ldots$). Having obtained estimates for $\delta_i$ we can then solve our estimated spot rates $r_t$.

## DISCOUNT FUNCTION

The main problem with the above is that coupon payments on different bonds fall on different dates (i.e. the $C_i$'s for different bonds do not correspond to the same payment dates). We can mitigate this problem by assuming the discount rates (which are assumed to fall smoothly) are a polynomial function (of time), for example:

[8.30]     $\delta_t = a_0 + a_1 t + a_2 t^2$

Substituting equation [8.30] in equation [8.29]:

[8.31]     $$P_i = \sum_{t=1}^{m} \delta_t C_i(t)$$

[8.32]     $$P_i = a_0 \left[ \sum_t C_i(t) \right] + a_1 \left[ \sum_t t C_i(t) \right] + a_2 \left[ \sum_t t^2 C_i(t) \right]$$

For a cross-section of $n$ bonds ($i = 1, 2, 3, \ldots, n$) equation [8.32] is a linear regression with independent variables given by the terms in square brackets. Having estimated $a_0$, $a_1$ and $a_2$ then these can be substituted in equation [8.30] to obtain estimates of the discount rates $\delta_1, \delta_2, \delta_3, \ldots$ and hence the corresponding spot rates. There are a wide variety of sophisticated statistical methods now used to estimate yield curves (see Anderson *et al.*, 1996). Box 8.2 provides a fairly intuitive parametric method of fitting the (forward) yield curve based on Svensson (1994) and until recently the Bank of England used this approach. A slightly more complex approach but one that is quite widely used (currently by the Bank of England) is the so-called cubic spline method, and this is explained in Appendix 8.1.

## Box 8.2     YIELD CURVE ESTIMATION

We will illustrate with reference to the term structure of forward rates. For pedagogic purposes assume we have a set of implicit forward rates for various maturities and we wish to fit a (forward) yield curve. (In practice these forward rates are derived as part of the whole curve fitting exercise—see Appendix 8.1.) These forward rates will not cover all maturities and different bonds paying different coupons may give rise to different values for the forward rate at any particular maturity.

The yield curve can be (and usually is) a non-linear function of the term to maturity '$m$'. At any point in time we need a functional form that will allow either a horizontal or upward/downward sloping or even a humped yield curve, since the yield curve may change shape on different days. The estimated parameters determine the particular shape applicable on a particular day. The **Svensson (1994) approach** approximates the set of observed rates using a complex non-linear functional form:

$$f(m) = \beta_0 + \beta_1 \exp(-m/d_1) + \beta_2[(m/d_1) \exp(-m/d_1)]$$
$$+ \beta_3[(m/d_2) \exp(-m/d_2)]$$

where $f(m)$ is the forward rate at maturity $m$. Note that $\beta_i$ and $d_i$ are the parameters to be estimated. The different elements in the equation give rise to the possible shapes the yield curve might take:

$\beta_0$ = determines the long run level of rates

$\beta_1$ = determines a smooth upward ($\beta_1 < 0$) or downward ($\beta_1 > 0$) element of the fitted curve

$\beta_2, \beta_3$ = determines possible humps in the fitted curve.

These separate elements also result in a yield curve that is flat at long maturities. Broadly speaking, the cross-section data on $f(m)$ is derived from various coupon paying bonds (i.e. about 58 conventional nominal bonds) on a particular day. Conceptually (although not quite accurately) you can assume that the estimation procedure minimises the squared deviations of observed forward rates from the fitted rates from this cross-section regression. A new curve is fitted daily.

# 8.6 TERM STRUCTURE OF CREDIT RISK

In this section we give a simplified account of how we can 'extract' the probability of default in each future year, over the life of a corporate bond. This area is at the forefront of research, particularly models which use options theory, but the approach adopted here will only give us 'ball-park' estimates.

Given the yield curve for Treasury bonds (i.e. risk free government bonds), then the yield curves for AAA, AA, etc. rated bonds should all be above each other, with that for CCC rated being the 'highest'. This is because at any maturity (e.g. 10-year corporate) a CCC rated bond has a higher probability of default than a BBB, BB, etc. rated bond or the Treasury bond (which we assume has zero default risk).

To illustrate the issues involved suppose we have spot yields (and hence the implied forward yields) for Treasuries and BBB rated bonds (these spot yields might have to be estimated from coupon paying corporate and Treasury bonds).

**Treasuries** $\quad r_1 = 10\% \qquad r_2 = 11\% \qquad f_{12} = 12\%$

**Corporate BBB** $\quad r_{c1} = 12\% \qquad r_{c2} = 14\% \qquad f_{c,12} = 16\%$

Let $p_{01}$ = the probability of repayment for the corporate BBB bond in year-1 and hence $1 - p_{01}$ = the probability of default. Then *risk neutral* investors would be indifferent between investing \$1 in either the corporate or the Treasury bond if:

[8.33] $\qquad p_{01}(1 + r_{c1}) = (1 + r_1) \quad \text{and} \quad p_{01} = \dfrac{(1 + r_1)}{(1 + r_{c1})} = 0.982$

Hence:

Probability of default in year-1 = $(1 - p_{01}) = 0.018$ (1.8%)

A spread of 2% ($= 12\% - 10\%$) therefore implies a 1.8% probability of default in year 1.

The analysis can be made more realistic by assuming a recovery rate of $\theta$ ($>0$) if the corporate defaults. Then risk neutrality implies:

Expected return on the corporate = return on Treasury

$$(1 - p_{01})[\theta(1 + r_{c1})] + p_{01}(1 + r_{c1}) = 1 + r_1$$

We can easily solve the above equation for $p_{01}$ and for the credit spread:

**[8.34]**     Credit spread $= (r_{c1} - r_1) = \dfrac{1 + r_1}{(\theta + p_{01} - p_{01}\theta)} - (1 + r_1)$

The spread is therefore lower the higher is $\theta$ (the recovery rate), as one would expect. Also note that $p$ and $\theta$ have a symmetric effect on the spread. If you increase $p$ by 0.01 and reduce $\theta$ by 0.01, there is no change in the credit spread.

Let us continue with our simple example for year 2 where $p_{12}$ is the probability that the corporate does *not* default between years 1 and 2 (given that it has not defaulted in year 1). Hence $1 - p_{12}$ is the **marginal probability of default**, that is the probability of default in year 2, given that there has been no default in year 1. At $t = 0$, the expected return on \$1 invested *at the end of year 1* in the corporate is $p_{12}(1 + f_{c,12})$ hence, under risk neutrality:

$$p_{12}(1 + f_{c,12}) = (1 + f_{12}) \quad \text{and} \quad p_{12} = \frac{(1 + f_{12})}{(1 + f_{c,12})} = 0.965$$

Hence:

Marginal probability of default in year $2 = (1 - p_{12}) = 0.035$ (3.5%)

The **cumulative probability** of survival by the end of year 2 is:

$C_p(\text{survival, } 0\text{–}2) = p_{01}\,p_{02} = (0.982)(0.965) = 0.95$ (95%)

Hence, the cumulative probability of default by the end of year 2 is:

$C_p(\text{default, } 0\text{–}2) = 1 - p_{01}\,p_{02} = 0.05$ (5%)

Notice that the **cumulative** probability of default by the end of year 2 is 5%, which is *not* equal to the sum of the *marginal* probabilities of default $p_{01} = 1.8\%$ and $p_{12} = 3.5\%$. In our example the probability of default in year-1 is 1.8% and in year 2 (given 'survival' in year 1) is 3.5%. The yield curve of the corporate therefore reflects the market's view that there may be a recession in year-2, leading to a higher default rate. If (at $t = 0$) the market believed year-2 would be a boom year then this would be reflected in the yield curve, which would then imply a fall in default probability in year-2, compared with year-1. So, we have not only derived the default probabilities implicit in the observed term structure, but noted that these probabilities may have predictive power for future recessions or economic booms.

The nice feature of the above methodology is that it is forward looking. However, it has some severe drawbacks, including:

- The assumption of risk neutrality may be inappropriate.
- Spot yields on corporate bonds are assumed to reflect only the risk free rate and the default risk premium (i.e. there are no embedded options in the bond).
- Estimating corporate spot yields from the relatively illiquid corporate bond market is difficult because the majority of bonds are coupon paying and many have callable features.

The above drawbacks imply that a more thorough analysis requires the use of option pricing techniques.

## 8.7 SUMMARY

In this chapter our primary concerns have been the relationship between interest rates of different maturities and the relationship between spot rates and forward rates of interest. The key points are as follows.

- A **forward rate** quoted today is an interest rate which applies to an investment which occurs between two future time periods.
- It is possible to create a **synthetic forward** (interest rate) contract by borrowing and lending at the appropriate spot rates of interest. **Riskless arbitrage** then ensures that the *quoted* forward rate equals this synthetic forward rate.
- Forward rates are used to price **interest rate futures contracts** such as FFAs and FRAs (as well as FRNs, swaps and other interest rate derivatives), and they also provide an estimate of the market's view of inflation in future years.
- The **yield curve** is a relationship between interest rates for different maturities. An upward (downward) sloping yield curve implies inflation is expected to increase (decrease) in the future.
- The **expectations hypothesis** implies that the yield on a long maturity bond is a weighted average of current and future expected short rates. The **shape of the yield** curve therefore depends on the market's expectations about future short rates.
- Because all *observed* yields do not lie on a smooth curve, **the yield curve is usually estimated**. Two commonly used methods are the **(parametric) Svensson model** and some form of **cubic spline technique**.
- Yield curves for risk free government bonds and corporate bonds can be used to 'extract' an estimate of the implied (marginal) **probability of default** in each year for the corporate bond. This is a *forward looking* measure of default probability and can be used to set capital adequacy requirements for credit risk—see Cuthbertson and Nitzsche (2001).

## END OF CHAPTER EXERCISES

Q1    What is a forward–forward agreement and how does it differ from a forward rate agreement (FRA)?

**Q2**   What is the (spot) yield curve and why is it useful?

**Q3**   What are the two key features we require from a fitted yield curve?

**Q4**   The 1-year spot rate on US Treasury bonds (T-bonds) is 9%, the 2-year spot rate is 9.5% and the 3-year spot rate is 10%.

(a) Calculate the implied 1-year ahead, 1-year forward rate, $f_{12}$. Explain why a 1-year forward rate of 9.6% would not be expected to prevail in the market.
(b) Calculate the forward rates $f_{23}$ and $f_{13}$. Is there any link between $f_{12}$, $f_{23}$ and $f_{13}$?
(c) Very briefly, mention one practical use for spot rates and one practical use of the forward rate concept.

**Q5**   If the EH holds, why might the yield curve be:

(a) flat
(b) upward sloping
(c) downward sloping
(d) What might cause a parallel shift in the yield curve?
(e) The government implements a credible 'tight' monetary policy by raising short-term (e.g. 3-month) interest rates. Why might this result in a downward sloping yield curve?

**Q6**   (a) The bank offers to *borrow* $100 from *you* at an interest rate applicable between the end of year 1 and the end of year 2 at a rate of 13% (i.e. the forward rate). The spot rates for 1-year money and 2-year money are currently 10% p.a. and 12% p.a., respectively. Explain whether you would take the bank's offer.
(b) In principal, how can one calculate the forward rates $f_{13}$ (i.e. the rate of interest applicable between the end of year 1 and the end of year 3) and $f_{23}$?
(c) What are the practical uses of forward rates in finance?

**Q7**   Quoted spot (interest) rates are as follows:

| Year | Spot rate (%) |
|---|---|
| 1 | $r_1 = 5.00$ |
| 2 | $r_2 = 5.40$ |
| 3 | $r_3 = 5.70$ |
| 4 | $r_4 = 5.90$ |
| 5 | $r_5 = 6.00$ |

(a) What are the discount factors for each date (that is, the present value of $1 paid in year $t$)?

(b) Calculate the PV and hence the fair price of the following 'Treasury notes' (i.e. annual coupon paying bonds) all of which have a $1000 par value:

   (i)  5% coupon, 2-year note
   (ii)  5% coupon, 5-year note
   (iii)  10% coupon, 5-year note.

(c) What are the 1-year forward rates applicable between (i) year 1 and year 2, (ii) year 2 and year 3?

# APPENDIX 8.1 YIELD CURVE ESTIMATION

The **Svensson parametric method** described in Box 8.2 has several advantages:

- there are not many parameters to estimate;
- it gives a smooth forward rate curve;
- it is constrained to be flat at the long end. This implies that market participants, for example, believe that 1-year rates in 25 years time will be the same as 1-year rates in 30 years time.

However, being a fully parametric model, it does have one key drawback. When a data point is changed at the long end, the whole re-estimated curve will shift, particularly at the short end. This sensitivity (or parameter instability) may lead to a bad model, in the sense that when it is used to price bonds (which have not been used in the estimation) there may be large errors.

Because of the above problem, the Bank of England has changed its estimation method and now uses a **cubic spline technique** (i.e. a third order-polynomial function of maturity)—as do many other Central Banks. The spline technique splits the whole forward rate curve into separate segments and bond prices in each segment are approximated by separate 'cubic B-splines'. This overcomes the sensitivity/instability problem because a change in a data point at the long end has hardly any impact on the cubic spline 'segments' at the short end. The different segments can move largely independently of each other.

The cubic splines for each segment of the forward curve are joined at 'knot points' and the methodology ensures that the curve (and its first derivatives) are continuous at all points (including at the knot points). The objective function used in estimating the spline curve is to minimisc bond pricing errors, subject to a penalty for excessive curvature:

$$[A8.1] \qquad \sum_{L=1}^{N} \left( \frac{P_i - \Pi_i}{D_i} \right)^2 + \int_{0}^{M} \lambda(m)[f''(m)]^2 \mathrm{d}m$$

where  $N$ is the number of bonds in the sample
         $P_i$ is the price of bond $i$
         $\Pi_i$ is the fitted value of price using the cubic spline
         $D_i$ is the duration of bond $i$

$\lambda$ is the penalty for excessive curvature
$f''(m)$ is the second derivative of the forward rate curve
$M$ is the maximum maturity in the data set.

The first term is the usual price minimisation condition where division by $D_i$ makes it approximately equal to minimising squared *yield* errors. The second term ensures that the change in *curvature* of the forward rate curve is not too abrupt across different maturities (and $\lambda(m)$ depends on only three estimated parameters).

The cubic spline and the Svensson curve give very similar results (shapes) for maturities between 1 and 20 years, but the cubic spline fits better at the very short (i.e. 0–1 year) maturities and at the very long (i.e. 25–30 year) end of the curve (since the latter is not always flat as assumed in the Svensson model). Put another way, the cubic spline method tends to 'fit' bond prices (which were not used in the estimation) at the short and long ends better than the Svensson curve. (For an excellent overview, see Anderson and Sleath, 1999.)

# CHAPTER 9

# Bond Market Strategies

Bond market strategies are often classified as either 'passive' or 'active'. Naturally, they are indicative of the type of investor behaviour involved, but as we shall see, even a passive strategy involves rebalancing of the bond portfolio. The passive strategies we analyse are immunisation, cash flow matching and indexing. A pension fund manager is faced with a liability outflow in the future (i.e. pension payments) which is, in the main, known today. One problem she has is to ensure that these payments can be met. One method is to try to assemble a portfolio of bonds such that the coupon payments plus interest-on-interest plus any redemption value of the bonds come as close as possible to meeting these liabilities. However, what bonds should she choose and in what proportions should she hold each bond? The concept of 'duration' plays a key role here. Loosely speaking, if the duration of the bond portfolio equals the duration of the liabilities, then (to a first approximation) she will be hedged against changes in interest rates. This strategy is known as **duration matching** or **portfolio immunisation**.

The liabilities of a pension fund consist of a *series* of cash flows. To ensure these cash outflows can be met some form of **multiperiod immunisation** is required. Two practical solutions are available. First, one can match each individual cash outflow with a portfolio of bonds *dedicated* to that particular cash flow. Alternatively, one can try and ensure that the duration of the whole portfolio of bonds equals that of *all* the liabilities.

Some portfolio managers will speculate with part of the bond portfolio and will only immunise the portfolio if its value falls to some minimal level. This mixture of active and passive strategies is known as **contingent immunisation**.

An alternative passive strategy to immunisation is **cash flow matching**. Here projected cash outflows are met by purchasing a set of bonds whose coupon and maturity payouts exactly match those of the liabilities. **Bond indexing** provides our final passive strategy. Indexing requires bond portfolio managers to choose a relatively small number of bonds such that they 'track' the performance of a chosen bond index.

Finally, **active bond strategies** require bond managers to 'take a bet' on the future course of interest rate movements or shifts in the yield curve. The activities of the Central Bank are keenly monitored by bond dealers since the timing, size and direction of interest rate movements are crucial in switching between longs and shorts.

# 9.1 DURATION AND CONVEXITY

In this section we show how a coupon paying bond can be used to guarantee payment of a fixed sum at some future date, even if yields alter. The concepts of duration and convexity are then used to analyse changes in bond prices consequent on changes in yields.

## IMMUNISATION OF A SINGLE LIABILITY PAYMENT

Suppose an individual has a fixed liability of $A payable in 4 years time and she wishes to invest in a bond (or bonds) so that she can be assured of receiving this amount. Which bonds should she choose? Clearly, if pure discount bonds were available with a maturity of 4 years she could purchase these bonds today, so that they have a maturity value of $A in 4 years time.

If she purchased any coupon paying bond then she would face the uncertainty of reinvestment risk of the coupons and, if the bond had a maturity of greater that 4 years, she would also face an uncertain selling price in the fourth year. However, it is possible to choose a coupon bond which will meet a fixed 'one off' liability in 4 years time, *providing* we assume the reinvestment rate equals the YTM for all periods (i.e. the yield curve is flat). As we shall see later, the bond we choose has a 'duration' of 4 years.

If all interest rates should rise or fall by 1%, will the investor still receive his $A in 4 years time? The answer is 'yes' providing the duration of the bond is 4 years and spot rates at all maturities move by $\pm 1\%$ (i.e. a parallel shift in the yield curve). In Table 9.1 we assume a single liability of $165.95 which is payable in 4 years. We show that for a flat yield curve, a

---

## TABLE 9.1: Immunisation (single liability)

**Data:** Liability in 4 years time = $165.95

Purchase 5-year, 13.52% (annual) coupon bond, par value = $100, YTM = 11%

**Questions:** What are the total receipts in 4 years time assuming:

(1) a constant reinvestment rate equal to the YTM = 11%?

(2) a reinvestment rate of 12% or 10%?

Comment on your answer

**Answers:** _**Interest rates remain at 11%: receipts in 4 years**_

Expected price of bond in year 4 = $113.52/(1.11) = $102.270

Coupons + interest-on-interest = $13.52 $(1.11)^3$ + $13.52 $(1.11)^2$ + $13.52 $(1.11)^1$ + $13.52 = $63.68

Total receipts (year 4) = $165.95

_**Interest rates increase to 12%: receipts in 4 years**_

Expected price of bond in year 4 = $113.52/(1.12) = $101.36

Coupons + interest-on-interest = $13.52 $(1.12)^3$ + $13.52 $(1.12)^2$ + $13.52 $(1.12)^1$ + $13.52 = $64.62

Total receipts (year 4) = $165.97

_**Interest rates fall to 10%: receipts in 4 years**_

Expected price of bond in year 4 = $113.52 ie 113.52/(1.10)(1.10) = $103.20

Coupons + interest-on-interest = $13.52 $(1.10)^3$ + $13.52 $(1.10)^2$ + $13.52 $(1.10)^1$ + $13.52 = $62.75

Total receipts (year 4) = $165.95

**Analysis:** The bond must have a duration equal to that of the liability, that is 4 years

specific bond will exactly meet this liability even if there is a subsequent parallel shift in yields (to 12% or 10%).

In Table 9.1 it is clear that after a change in yield, any increase (decrease) in coupon payments and interest-on-interest is exactly offset by the decrease (increase) in the price of the bond in year 4. For example, if yields rise to 12% the price of the bond in year 4 falls from $102.27 to $101.35, but this is just offset by a rise in coupon interest payments from $63.67 to $64.61. This particular bond has 'immunised' the total receipts available in 4 years time, from any changes in interest rates.

> **The price response of a bond to a given change in interest rates depends on the characteristics of the bond, *namely its coupon and time to maturity***

These are summarised below (see Table 9.2).

- For a given change in yield (basis points) the actual price increase is greater than the price decrease (e.g. column 4, Table 9.2 for yields of 6% and 12%).

## TABLE 9.2: Price changes, coupons, maturity and yield

**Four bonds priced initially to yield 9%**

(1)  9% coupon, 5 years to maturity, initial price = 100

(2)  9% coupon, 20 years to maturity, initial price = 100

(3)  5% coupon, 5 years to maturity, initial price = 84.1746

(4)  5% coupon, 20 years to maturity, initial price = 63.1968

| Change in yield from 9% to: | Change (bp) | Percentage price change for bonds with different coupon and maturity | | | |
|---|---|---|---|---|---|
| | | (1) | (2) | (3) | (4) |
| | | 9%, 5 year | 9%, 20 year | 5%, 5 year | 5%, 20 year |
| 6.00 | (−300.00) | 12.80 | 34.67 | 13.73 | 39.95 |
| 8.00 | (−100.00) | 4.06 | 9.90 | 4.35 | 11.26 |
| 8.99 | (−1.00) | 0.04 | 0.09 | 0.04 | 0.10 |
| 9.01 | (1.00) | −0.04 | −0.09 | −0.04 | −0.10 |
| 10.00 | (100.00) | −3.86 | −8.58 | −4.13 | −9.64 |
| 12.00 | (−300.00) | −11.04 | −22.57 | −11.89 | −25.09 |

Note: The initial yield is 9% and the first two columns indicate the illustrative new yields (%) and the change in yield (bp). Columns (1)–(4) show the percentage change in bond price for different coupons and maturities

- Price change (volatility) is greater the lower the coupon rate (e.g. compare columns 1 and 3 or 2 and 4).
- Price change is greater the longer the term to maturity (e.g. compare columns 1 and 2 or 3 and 4).

The above properties are merely an 'arithmetic' consequence of the DPV formula for bond prices. It would be useful to summarise the response of bond prices to a change in yield in a single number, and this is known as the duration of the bond. However 'duration' only provides an approximation to the price change and an improved approximation is obtained by also considering the 'convexity' of the bond. Although duration only provides an approximation to price changes it is nevertheless extremely useful in choosing a bond portfolio that (to a first approximation) will ensure meeting a future liability. Hence duration plays a major role in immunising a liability stream of future cash payments.

> **The duration of a bond may be described as the time weighted average of the relative value of the coupon payments (with the weights being the present value of the coupon payments as a proportion of the bond price)**

Duration is calculated as:

[9.1]
$$D = \frac{[PV(C_1)1 + PV(C_2)2 + \ldots + PV(C_n + M)n]}{P}$$

where $P$ is the price of the bond
$n$ is the time to maturity
PV is the present value of the coupon payments (discounted by the YTM)
$PV(C_t) = C_t/(1 + y)^t$ is the present value of single coupon payment
$PV(C_n + M) = (C_n + M)/(1 + y)^n$.

Duration is useful because it allows us to summarise the price sensitivity of a bond in a single figure. It can be shown (see Appendix 9.1) that for small changes in yields, the proportionate price change of the bond is given by:

[9.2]
$$dP/P = -D \, dy/(1 + y)$$

$D$ is known as **Macaulay duration** (Macaulay, 1938). It follows that bonds with higher duration have larger price changes, for any given change in yields. The relationship between the bond price and the yield is actually non-linear (i.e. 'convex'), and duration provides a linear approxiation (see Figure 9.1).

The actual price rise will exceed that given by the duration equation [9.2] and the actual price fall will be less than that calculated using duration. For small changes in yield the actual price change and that given using equation [9.2] will be very close. We can rearrange equation [9.2] in a number of equivalent ways. For example:

## FIGURE 9.1: Duration and price change

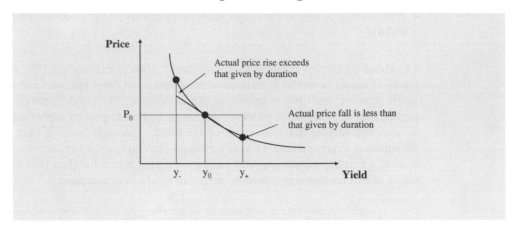

[**9.3**]     $dP/P = -(MD)\,dy$     where   $MD = D/(1 + y)$

The term MD is known as **modified duration**. A zero coupon bond of maturity $n$ has only one payment $M$ at time '$n$'. The present value of $\$M$, that is PV($M$) in the above notation, is also the price of the zero. Hence using equation [9.1]:

> **The duration of a zero coupon bond equals its maturity $n$**

We asserted that the bond in Table 9.1 has a duration of 4 years and in Table 9.3 we prove this to be the case. Sometimes it is a useful 'shorthand' to refer to the **dollar duration** DD of a bond which is defined as:

[**9.4**]     $dP = -(DD)\,dy$   where   $DD = (MD)P$

Knowing DD one can immediately calculate the (approximate) price change for a given change in yield. Going one step further, for a 1 bp change we have $dy = 0.0001$ $(= 1/10{,}000)$. Hence:

[**9.5**]     $dP(\text{for 1 bp}) = \dfrac{MD \times P}{10{,}000}$

The expression in equation [9.5] is known as '**price value of a basis point**' (**PVBP**). To illustrate the use of PVBP, consider a trader who has $P = \$1m$ in a bond with a modified duration $MD = 5$, hence PVBP is 500. This means that for every 1 bp (i.e. 0.01%) change in the yield, the value of the bond portfolio will change by $500.

Duration only provides a (first-order) approximation to the change in price of a bond and hence is only accurate for small changes in interest rates (e.g. up to 25 basis points). A more accurate approximation is found by also using the convexity of the bond:

---

## TABLE 9.3: Calculation of duration

**Data:** 5 years to maturity, 13.52% coupon (annual) par value = $100, YTM = 11%

**Question:** Calculate the duration and the change in price if the YTM increases to 12%

**Answer:** Current price $P = \$13.52/(1.11) + \$13.52/(1.11)^2 + \ldots + \$113.52/(1.11)^5$

$$= \$12.18 + \$10.97 + \ldots + \$67.37 = \textbf{\$109.31}$$

Hence PV$(C_1) = \$12.18$, PV$(C_2) = \$10.97$, etc.

$D = [\$12.18(1) + \$10.97(2) + \ldots + \$67.37(5)]/\$109.31 = 4$ years

***Change in price***

$\mathrm{d}P/P = -D\,\mathrm{d}y/(1+y)$

$$= -(3.991)0.01/(1.11) = -0.036\,(3.65\%)$$

New price (at YTM = 12%) = $\$109.31(1 - 0.036) = \$105.38$

---

> **Convexity measures the curvature of the price–yield relationship**

Convexity $V$ is defined as:

[9.6]
$$V = (1/2)\frac{\left[\sum_{t=1}^{N} t(t+1)C(t)/(1+y)^t\right]}{P}$$

Our improved approximation to the change in price is then given by:

[9.7]
$$\mathrm{d}P/P = -D\,\mathrm{d}y^* + V(\mathrm{d}y^*)^2 \quad \text{where} \quad \mathrm{d}y^* = \mathrm{d}y/(1+y)$$

The calculation of the price change using duration and 'duration plus convexity' is an approximation to the true price change. The actual (true) price change will differ from that given by the above formulae if either the change in yield is large or there is a non-parallel shift in the yield curve. Table 9.4 demonstrates these points.

---

## TABLE 9.4: Duration and convexity

| | |
|---|---|
| **Data:** | A 5-year pure discount bond, face value $1000, 5-year spot rate (=YTM) of 10% |
| **Questions:** | Calculate (1) duration, (2) convexity, (3) the approximate price change and (4) the actual price change for a 2% (200 bp) change in interest rates |
| **Answers:** | **1. Duration** |

$P = \$1000/(1.10)^5 = \$620.92$, PV($1000$) $= \$620.92$

$D = 5\text{PV}/P = 5$

The duration of a pure discount bond $=$ term to maturity

**2. Convexity**

$V = (1/2)[5(6)\$1000/(1.10)^5]/\$690.92 = 15$

**3a. Price change: using duration**

$dP/P = -5(0.02)/(1.10) = -0.0909 \ (-9.091\%)$

**3b. Price change: using D and V**

$dP/P = -0.0909 + 15(0.02/1.10)^2 = -0.0859 \ (-8.595\%)$

**4. Actual price change**

Initial price (at 10% interest) $= \$1000/(1.10)^5 = \$620.92$

Price (at 12% interest) $= \$1000/(1.12)^5 = \$567.43$

Actual price change $= -8.615\%$

Using duration *and* convexity provides a closer approximation to the actual change in price

## DURATION OF A PORTFOLIO OF BONDS

So far we have matched a single liability with a **single** bond of the same duration. However, more flexibility in the choice of bonds could be beneficial in terms of greater liquidity in the market. Here we choose the duration of our *portfolio* of bonds to equal that of the single liability. The 'portfolio duration' is simply a weighted average of the duration of the constituent bonds in the portfolio held in proportions $w_i$:

[9.8] $\qquad D_\text{p} = \sum w_i D_i$

where $0 < w_i < 1$ (assuming no short selling) and $\sum w_i = 1$. Hence, a single liability payable in 10 years may be duration matched by many different bond portfolios. A **bullet portfolio** would have bonds with durations close to 10 years, whereas a **barbell portfolio** has bonds with a wider span of durations. For example, if we have a single liability payable in 10 years then the duration of the liability is 10. We can duration match this liability with the following bond portfolios:

**Barbell portfolio:** 5 and 15-year duration bonds

$$D_p = (1/2)5 + (1/2)15 = 10$$

**Bullet portfolio:** 9 and 11-year duration bonds

$$D_p = (1/2)9 + (1/2)11 = 10$$

For non-parallel shifts in the yield curve, spot rates at different maturities alter by different amounts. Duration matching does not ensure immunisation for non-parallel shifts since it is spot rates that determine the reinvestment rate for coupon payments. For a bullet portfolio, the spot yields are 'closer to' each other than for a barbell portfolio. Hence, the bullet portfolio involves less immunisation risk than the barbell portfolio. However, the barbell allows a wider choice of bonds and hence may have lower dealing costs and greater liquidity. As well as reducing immunisation risk by choosing a bullet portfolio, one can try and incorporate non-parallel shifts of the yield curve by modifying the definition of duration (see below).

## IMMUNISATION RISK

Faced with multiple liability flows, matching the bond portfolio duration $D_p$ to the duration of the liabilities may not ensure:

(a) all multiple liability payments are met;
(b) the bond portfolio achieves a target rate of return over a particular horizon.

Alternatives to Macaulay duration are (i) maturity matching and (ii) multifactor immunisation. In practical terms, the evidence seems to suggest that Macaulay duration is more effective than maturity matching on the above criteria (Bierwag *et al.*, 1981; Leibowitz and Weinberger, 1983), and more complex multifactor models often do not radically outperform those based on the Macaulay duration (see Fong and Vasicek, 1984). Hence, duration matching provides a reasonably accurate yet fairly simple method of portfolio immunisation.

## 9.2 PORTFOLIO IMMUNISATION

The aim in this section is to examine some of the practical issues involved in immunisation strategies. *'Standard immunisation'* requires rebalancing of the bond portfolio, while a *'contingent immunisation'* allows an element of active portfolio management. Multiple liability payments cause additional complexities which may be tackled using either dedicated portfolios or by matching *portfolio* durations. Finally, problems caused by non-parallel shifts in the yield curve can be ameliorated by using more complex measures of duration.

The simplest form of immunisation strategy involves a single liability of $X$ payable at some future date $n$. A single liability payment has a duration equal to its maturity (i.e. its payout date). The criteria which ensure the single cash outflow will be met by the immunised bond portfolio are:

---

# IMMUNISATION

- Present value of the bond portfolio = present value of the liability.
- Duration of the bond portfolio equals the maturity (= duration) of the single liability.
- The yield curve is flat.
- Parallel shifts in the yield curve.

---

The duration of a bond portfolio $D$ alters merely because of the passage of time and also if the YTM changes (see equation [9.1]). The 'life of the liability' (= duration $D_L$) also changes over time. Hence the bond portfolio needs to be periodically rebalanced to ensure that $D_p = D_L$ at all times. The frequency of rebalancing depends on a trade off between the potential costs of a duration mismatch and the transactions costs of buying and selling bonds.

## CONTINGENT IMMUNISATION

This strategy allows the portfolio manager to pursue an active portfolio strategy until an adverse movement in rates reduces the future value of the portfolio down to a 'safety net' level. At this point the investment manager fully immunises the portfolio to lock in the 'safety net' level of return. Suppose the following data is available:

- $100m investment funds, desired 'safety net' return = 10% p.a. over 4 years. Immunised rate of return currently available = 12% p.a.
- Minimum target value in 4 years = $100m$(1.10)^4$ = $146.41m.
- At 12% current return, the value of an investment to achieve $146.41m in 4 years is $146.41m$/(1.12)^4$ = $93.05m.

Then:

(Dollar) safety cushion = $146.41m − $93.05m = **$53.36m**

The bond manager has a positive safety cushion and can therefore undertake an active bond strategy, purchasing bonds she believes will give a high holding period return (HPR). Let us take a rather extreme example to illustrate a contingent immunisation strategy. Suppose interest rates rise at the end of the first year to 14% so that to achieve her target of $146.41m in the remaining 3 years she requires funds of $98.82m ($= \$146.41m/(1.14)^3$). Also, assume that at the outset she had used the $100m to purchase bonds that paid $10m in coupons at the end of the first year, but the rise in interest rates caused these bonds to fall in price by $11m. The value of her bond portfolio at the end of the year is therefore $99m ($= \$100m + \$10m - \$11m$) and the safety cushion is virtually zero ($= \$99m - \$98.82m$). At this point the bond manager would use all the currently available funds to fully immunise the portfolio at current yields of 14%. In practice, bond managers use only a proportion of the available funds in active portfolio management and always use most of the funds to immunise the liabilities. This ensures that very large rises in interest rates do not push the losses on the active portfolio to extremely low levels, so that the target cannot be met.

## MULTIPERIOD IMMUNISATION

A pension fund, for example, has known pension payments over several successive years. One method of meeting these multiperiod cash outflows is to take *each* separate liability payment and duration match it with a *dedicated* portfolio of bonds. For example, in Table 9.5 a liability outflow of $1000 in 2 years time is matched with a portfolio of bonds whose weighted duration is 2 years (and whose current value is $1000). Similarly the cash outflow of $2000 at the end of year 4 is matched with a bond portfolio with $D = 4$ and current market value of $2000.

A second method is to match portfolio durations (see Appendix 9.2). Although the latter is not sufficient to ensure all cash flows will be met, even for parallel shifts in the yield curve, the method is quite effective and widely used in practice. An illustrative case is given in Table 9.6.

## NON-PARALLEL SHIFTS IN THE YIELD CURVE

There are no immunisation strategies that can be guaranteed to be successful for all possible shifts in the yield curve. However, we can analyse some alternatives to a parallel shift and examine the implications for the measurement of duration. If we take the short rate $r_1$ as our reference rate then a parallel shift for all maturities ($= n$) may be represented as:

[9.9a]    $\Delta r_n = \Delta r_1 \qquad (n = 2, 3, 4, \ldots)$

A non-parallel shift may be represented as:

[9.9b]    $\Delta r_n = g_n \Delta r_1$

## TABLE 9.5: Multiperiod immunisation: dedicated portfolio

|  | End year 2 | End year 4 |
|---|---|---|
| **Liabilities (cash flow)** | $1000 | $2000 |
| **Asset portfolio** | Portfolio of coupon paying bonds with $D = 2$ and PV = $1000 | Portfolio of coupon paying bonds with $D = 4$ and PV = $2000 |

## TABLE 9.6: Matching portfolio durations

**Data:**     Liabilities: $100 in each of next 5 years

Assets: (a) 1-year, 6% coupon bond (annual), par value = $100

(b) 4-year, 8% coupon bond (annual), par value = $100

Current YTM is 10% p.a.

**Question:**     Calculate the amounts invested in each bond in order to match portfolio durations

**Answers:**     ***Duration: liabilities***

$PV_L = \$100/(1.1) + \$100/(1.1)^2 + \ldots + \$100/(1.1)^5 = \$379.07$

$PV_1 = \$100/(1.1) = \$90.91$, $PV_2 = \$100/(1.1)^2 = \$82.64$, etc.

$D_L = (1PV_1 + 2PV_2 + \ldots + 5PV_5)/PV_L = 2.81$

***1-year bond: duration***

$Price = PV_a = \$106/(1.1) = \$93.36$     $D_1 = 1$ year

***4-year bond: duration***

$PV_b = price = \$8/(1.1) + \$8/(1.1)^2 + \$8/(1.1)^3 + \$108/(1.1)^4$

$= \$7.27 + \$6.61 + \$6.01 + \$73.77 = \$93.66$

$D_b = [\$7.27(1) + \$6.61(2) + \$6.01(3) + \$73.77(4)]/\$93.66 = 3.56$

***Proportions:*** $w_a + w_b = 1$

$1w_a + 3.56w_b = 2.81$ (bond portfolio duration = duration of liabilities)

Hence: $w_a = 0.293$ and $w_b = 0.707$

Amount in 1-year bond = $0.293(PV_L) = \$111.07$

Amount in 4-year bond = $0.707(PV_L) = \$267.86$

where, if long rates move less than short rates, we have $0 < g_i < 1$, and $g_2 > g_3 > \ldots > g_n$. A multifactor model allows rates to respond to more than one variable (factor). A two-factor model may be represented as:

[9.9e]     $\Delta r_n = g_n \Delta r_1 + b_n \Delta X$

where $\Delta X$ is any variable that affects the set of interest rates $r_n$ (e.g. $X$ might be the spread between long and short rates). Depending on the coefficients $g_n$ and $b_n$ this equation can allow for 'twists' in the yield curve. Equations [9.9b] and [9.9c] can be estimated from past data to obtain the coefficients $g_n$ and $b_n$ for each maturity. For example, for the 3-year rate we might obtain (for $X$ = long–short spread):

[9.10]     $\Delta r_3 = 0.95\Delta r_1 + 0.1\Delta X$

Thus, taking a view about the change in $\Delta r_1$ and $\Delta X$ we can work out $\Delta r_3$ and hence the change in the value of a coupon payment in year 3. It is also possible to amend our measure of duration to incorporate the influence of $g_n$ and $b_n$ (see Schaefer, 1984 and Reitano, 1992). If interest rates respond as in equation [9.9], then it is shown in Table 9.7 that the measure of duration on a 2-year bond is no longer $D = (PV_1 + 2PV_2)/P$ but becomes $D^* = (PV_1 + 2g_2PV_2)/P$. Appendix 9.3 shows how the calculation of duration can be modified when there are twists in the yield curve.

With the increase in computing power, non-parallel shifts can now be dealt with by simulating shifts in the yield curve and calculating price changes based on the *full* PV formula using spot rates (which avoids the approximations involved in using duration). This is a form of scenario analysis or stress testing (see Cuthbertson and Nitzsche, 2001). The impact on the value of the bond portfolio of alternative 'shapes' for the yield curve can be easily simulated and assessed.

---

## TABLE 9.7: Non-proportional shift in the yield curve

**Data:**     [1] $\dfrac{dr_n}{1 + r_n} = g_n \dfrac{dr_1}{(1 + r_1)}$

**Question:** For a two-period bond, calculate the algebraic expression for duration when the yield curve shifts according to the above formula

**Answer:**   ***Two-period bond***

$P = C/(1 + r_1) + (C + M)/(1 + r_2)^2$

$dP/P = \{[(-1)C/(1 + r_1)]dr_1/(1 + r_1) + [-2C/(1 + r_2)^2]dr_2/(1 + r_2)\}/P$

Substituting from [1] for $dr_2/(1 + r_2)$ we obtain:

$dP/P = -[1PV_1 + 2PV_2g_2)]dr_1/(1 + r_1)$

We may write the above as:

$dP/P = -D^*[dr_1/(1 + r_1)]$

where $D^* = [PV_1 + 2PV_2g_2]$

We have a new definition of duration $D^*$ which incorporates the non-parallel shift in the yield curve represented by the estimated parameter $g_2$

## 9.3  CASH FLOW (OR EXACT) MATCHING

Multiperiod liabilities can also be met by a strategy known as cash flow (or 'exact') matching. The aim is to find the lowest cost portfolio that generates a pattern of cash flows that exactly matches the stream of liability payments. In this process we begin with the last liability payment $L_T$ and work back to the present as follows (see Figure 9.2).

- Choose a bond A with maturity date $T$ and final year payout $C_A + M_A$ equal to $L_T$.
- Coupon payments from bond A at $T - 1$ are used to meet part of the liabilities $L_{T-1}$ so that we require additional funds $(L_{T-1} - C_A)$ at $T - 1$. We purchase bond B with maturity $T - 1$ and final payment $(C_B + M_B) = (L_{T-1} - C_A)$.
- Repeat the above until the first liability payment is covered, each time purchasing the lowest cost bond (in terms of transactions costs).

This is a passive strategy, requiring no bond sales or rebalancing, and the only risk is credit risk. So far, we have ignored interest-on-interest from coupons. A variant on the above would be to assume a low expected reinvestment rate and to use these *prospective* funds to meet future liability payments. Clearly, there is some market risk in this strategy since actual reinvestment rates might fall below those expected. Appendix 9.4 shows how this more complex procedure can be set up as a linear programming problem.

### COMBINATION MATCHING (HORIZON MATCHING)

With multiperiod liabilities, matching the duration of the *portfolio* of assets to that of the liabilities does not guarantee meeting cash flow liabilities in all periods. Also, non-parallel shifts in the yield curve, which tend to occur at shorter maturities, would undermine an immunisation strategy. In combination matching these risks are minimised by (i) cash flow matching for the first few years (say 5 years) and then (ii) duration matching the portfolio in later years.

## FIGURE 9.2: Cash flow matching

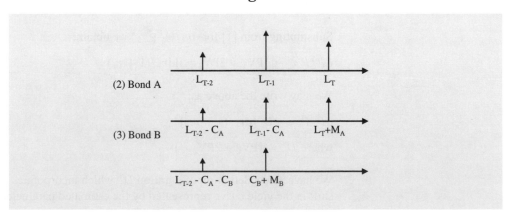

# 9.4 BOND INDEXING

Portfolio theory implies that the best investors can do is to hold the market portfolio. A broad based bond index is not necessarily *the* market portfolio (i.e. it excludes many assets, for example equities and commodities), but such a bond index will represent a well-diversified bond portfolio. There are three main types of bond market index:

- broad based (e.g. Lehman Bros, Salomon Bros, Merrill Lynch);
- specialised market (e.g. high-grade corporate index);
- customised (e.g. Salomon Pension Fund Index).

A *broad market index*, as its name suggests, will include government bonds, agency and corporates. A *customised index* such as a Pension Fund Index will, for example, contain bonds of long duration and hence will closely match the duration of the pension liabilities of the customer.

Bond indexing requires the bond portfolio manager to choose a *sample* of bonds that constitute his 'replication index'. This replication index will be chosen to closely 'track' a particular bond index quoted in the market. Obviously the bond manager will not hold all the bonds in the market index as this would involve prohibitive transactions costs. The performance of a bond index over *a fixed horizon* is often measured by the (effective) HPR, denoted $R$, where:

[9.11]
$$(1 + R) = \frac{\text{coupons} + \text{reinvestment income} + \text{change in value}}{\text{initial portfolio value}}$$

Also of interest to bond managers is the variability in $R$ over the investment horizon. For example, if $R$ is measured every month, the variance (or standard deviation) of monthly returns over a year will give some indication of the variability in returns. Tracking error is the difference between the performance of the bond manager's 'replication index' portfolio and the market index itself. Sources of **tracking error** include:

- transactions costs in constructing the replication portfolio;
- difference in composition of the replication portfolio and the index itself;
- discrepancies between transactions prices (e.g. bid–ask) of the replication index and the prices used in constructing the market index.

## REPLICATING THE INDEX

There are two broad methods (which are not necessarily mutually exclusive) of trying to replicate the chosen index: (i) stratified sampling and (ii) optimisation approach. In **stratified sampling** the bonds *in the market bond index* are classified according to chosen characteristics, as in Table 9.8. Hence, the number of stratified cells = $2 \times 3 \times 3 = 18$. The fund manager will then choose a subset of the bonds from the market index to replicate the above characteristics. For example, if the market index has 10% which are corporate AAA bonds, then in the replication index the fund manager will also hold 10% chosen from a subset of AAAs in the market index.

## TABLE 9.8: Stratified sampling

| 1. **Duration** | (a) less than 5 years | (b) greater than 5 years | |
| 2. **Sectors** | (a) Treasury | (b) agency | (c) corporates |
| 3. **Rating** | (a) triple-A | (b) AA and A | (c) BBB |

## TABLE 9.9: Tracking error monthly returns (bp)[1]

| Index | Mean return[2] | Standard deviation[3] | Cumulative total return[4] |
| --- | --- | --- | --- |
| **Broad market** | 2 | 54 | 34 |
| **Government** | 2 | 2 | 31 |
| **Corporate** | 9 | 17 | 156 |

Notes: 1. 2-year period, January 1985 – November 1986
2. Difference between monthly return on replication index and actual index—averaged over 2 years, expressed in basis points
3. Standard deviation of monthly tracking error (bp)
4. Sum of tracking error of monthly returns over 2-year period—at an annual rate in basis points

In the **optimisation approach** the fund manager will have an explicit quantitative target. For example, she might try and maximise total return $R$ over a specific horizon while still matching the cell breakdown described above. Alternatively, based on historic data she may choose those bonds that minimise the variance of the past tracking errors (see Seix and Akoury, 1986). So far we have described what is usually referred to as 'plain vanilla' indexing. In **enhanced indexing** the aim is to exceed the performance of the benchmark index, pursuing an active strategy with part of the available funds (e.g. undertaking substitution swaps, namely buying bonds that are underpriced and selling an equal amount of those that are overpriced).

The tracking error of monthly HPRs over a 2-year period for a number of replication indices is given in Table 9.9. The mean (monthly) return tracking errors for the broad market and government replication indexes are low at 2 bp (i.e. 0.02%), with that for corporates being higher at 9 bp. These figures are also reflected in the cumulative tracking error over a 2-year period. The standard deviation of the tracking error is large for corporates, and this high figure is also reflected in the figure of 54 bp for the standard deviation of the broad market replication index, which includes corporates.

# 9.5 ACTIVE BOND STRATEGIES

The variety of active strategies in the bond market is not as numerous as those in the equity market. In part this is because government bonds are relatively homogeneous, compared to equities, differing only in their maturity and coupon payments. A large proportion of government bond portfolios are managed using passive strategies described in the previous section. At the margin, the decision concerning the proportion of funds to be held in stocks relative to bonds is a crucial one, and this is often determined by such factors as the state of the business cycle and inflation.

For example, near the peak of the business cycle, inflationary pressures are likely to build up and one might expect interest rates to rise in the near future. Hence the portfolio manager might switch out of bonds into stocks. Stock returns may remain high for some time as company profits continue to rise. If the peak of the business cycle is imminent this may indicate the onset of a recession and hence a fall in future profits. The latter, coupled with interest rate rises (i.e. the discount factor in the PV formula), will lead to a fall in stock prices. A good **'market timer'** will now also move out of stocks (and bonds) and into cash. Some of the cash may then be invested in bonds and stocks of another country, which is just emerging from a recession. This is **tactical asset allocation**. However, the portfolio choices we are concerned with here are more limited and concern either:

- moving between bonds and cash;
- a 'switch' between two different bonds one of which is overpriced and the other underpriced.

Both strategies require the investor to either forecast future changes in interest rates or shifts in the yield curve. Both of these types of forecast are subject to wide margins of uncertainty and therefore active strategies can be highly risky.

## SHIFTS IN THE YIELD CURVE

An obvious strategy is for a bond manager to switch to longer duration bonds if she expects a fall in all rates (i.e. rise in price)—and vice versa. Longer duration bonds have larger price changes. Some analysts try and predict twists in the yield curve. For example, if the analyst expects an easing of monetary tightness then she would expect short rates to fall. However, if monetary laxity implied higher rates of inflation in the future she might expect long rates to rise to reflect the inflation premium. To take advantage of this twist in the yield curve she would move out of long duration bonds and into short duration bonds.

## REGRESSION TECHNIQUES

Regression techniques can be used to try and predict current interest rate changes from previous changes in interest rates and from the long–short spread. According to the expectations hypothesis the spread should have predictive power for future interest rate changes. Consider changes in the 3-year rate, which depend on the 3 year–1 year spread:

[9.12] $$\Delta r_{3t} = a_1 \Delta r_{3t-1} - b_1 (r_3 - r_1)_{t-1} + c_1$$

Estimates of $a_1$, $b_1$ and $c_1$ ($b_1$, $c_1 > 0$) can be obtained. Equation [9.12] is a form of error correction model (ECM). In static equilibrium, when all interest rates are assumed to be constant (i.e. $\Delta r = 0$) then the equation gives $r_3 = r_1 + c_1/b_1$, where the term $(c_1/b_1)$

represents the liquidity premium. In addition, the dynamic equation implies that if $r_3 > r_1$ at time $t - 1$ then $r_3$ will fall next period (i.e. $\Delta r_{3t} < 0$)—ceteris paribus. Knowing values of the RHS variables at $t - 1$ we can predict the change in the 3-year rate next period and hence the capital gain on the bond. The above equation is merely illustrative and in practice it might also contain other lagged values of the change in interest rates as well as other spreads, for example the 6 month–1 month spread (see Cuthbertson, 1996).

Similar equations for the change in interest rates for other maturities $r_i$ ($i = 2, 4, 5$, etc.) can also be estimated. If we have a set of equations explaining $\Delta r_1$, $\Delta r_2$, etc. then we can predict interest rate movements along the whole of the yield curve and hence predict bond price changes for bonds of different maturities. The analyst can then decide on a reallocation of his portfolio across the maturity spectrum to maximise his expected holding period return from a switching strategy.

Instead of forecasting interest rates and then calculating what will happen to bond prices, we can forecast the latter directly. One simple forecasting rule can be derived by assuming the expected one-period holding period yield $H_{t+1}$ is equal to the risk free rate (i.e. the short rate) plus a risk (term) premium $T_t$:

[9.13]     $E_t H_{t+1} = r_t + T_t$

where $H_{t+1}$ *is defined* as the capital gain plus running yield $ry_t$:

[9.14]     $H_{t+1} = \Delta P_{t+1}/P_t + ry_t$

and $ry_t = C/P_t$. Rearranging the above we obtain an expression for the capital gain:

Capital gain $= -(\text{yield gap/spread}) + \text{term premium}$

[9.15]     $E_t \Delta P_{t+1}/P_t = -(ry_t - r_t) + T_t$

Under the expectations hypothesis, it can be shown that when the spread is positive we expect bond prices to fall. In practice, however, the opposite is usually the case. A regression of $\Delta P_{t+1}/P_t$ on the spread often gives a positive coefficient. Wright (1995) provides an example of this for the USA. (Note, Wright uses $\Delta P_{t+1}$ as the dependent variable.)

[9.16]     $\Delta P_{t+1}/P_t = 1.246\,(ry - r)_t + (8, \text{lagged bond price changes})$

OLS, 1960(1)–1972(4), $R^2 = 0.097$

Wright also estimates two other (largely ad hoc) equations with independent variables which include (i) the lagged bond price *level* and (ii) the lagged real interest rate. He estimates these equations recursively and uses them to forecast bond prices one quarter ahead. 'Active' and 'passive' trading strategies are then as follows.

**Active strategy:**     Hold bonds if the prediction from the regression equation [9.16] exceeds the 'market prediction' based on equation [9.15] (with $T = 0$), which is given by $-(ry_t - r_t)$. Otherwise hold cash.

**Passive strategy:**     'Buy and hold' the bond portfolio.

He finds weak evidence for positive excess returns (over a risk free rate) from the active strategy. The active strategy does not always produce a return that exceeds the average return from a 'buy and hold' strategy, but the *variability* in returns for the active strategy is lower. Wright therefore provides some evidence that regression equations can be used to formulate active bond strategies that give a positive excess return (on average), with relatively low ex-post variability.

## SUBSTITUTION SWAP

If the yield curve correctly represents behaviour in the bond market (e.g. as represented by the expectations hypothesis) then all bond yields should lie close to the curve. Any mispriced bonds will have yields that lie some distance from the fitted yield curve (Figure 9.3). If the current yield curve is Q–Q, then the investor looks for two bonds like A and B. Bond A has an abnormally high yield which will be *expected* to fall in the future (towards the yield curve) and hence its price will rise. The converse applies to bond B.

A **substitution swap** involves buying A and selling B. This affords some protection against an unforeseen upward or downward parallel shift in the yield curve, while one waits for the mispricing to be corrected. For example, if after switching the yield curve immediately moved up to Z–Z then the investor would lose a little on A as its yield would rise towards the new yield curve Z–Z (i.e. price would fall). However, she gains substantially on B since she can buy it back at a much lower price in the future after the large fall in yield towards the curve Z–Z. Buying only A would have resulted in an overall loss. Sometimes in a substitution swap a portfolio manager will buy A and sell B in proportions that do not involve a change in portfolio duration from its desired value. There are two obvious uncertainties in basing active bond strategies on the yield curve:

## FIGURE 9.3: Substitution swap

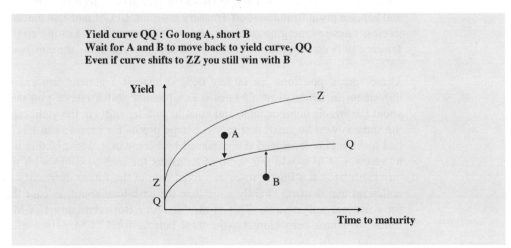

265

- The yield curve is estimated—it is therefore subject to approximation error.
- The yield curve might shift substantially before any mispricing is corrected.

A variant on the substitution swap is to take bets on the spread between two yields on assets with different credit risks. Clearly the differential between the yield on a corporate bond and on US T-bonds will depend on perceived changes in the risk of default (or of a ratings downgrade): the greater the risk of default the wider the spread against Treasuries. The hedge fund *Long Term Capital Management* lost over \$4bn in 1998, when executing spread strategies (see Box 9.1).

## Box 9.1     LONG TERM CAPITAL MANAGEMENT

In September 1998 LTCM, a hedge fund, was rescued by a consortium of New York banks (under the direction of the Federal Reserve Board). Ordinary commercial banks had lent money long term to LTCM, which had a debt-to-equity ratio of around 50 to 1. The fund was founded in 1994 by John Meriwether, a former head of Salomon Bros bond arbitrage division who left after the 1991 Salomon bond scandal. In the latter, Paul Mozer, a bond trader reporting to Meriwether, had tried to 'corner' the primary Treasury auction market by submitting bids in excess of the firm's approved limits. Meriwether was alleged to have failed to supervise traders properly and was subsequently fined \$50,000 by the SEC. Two Nobel prize winners in Economics, Robert Merton and Myron Scholes (of Black–Scholes–Merton option pricing fame) also joined the firm.

Although LTCM's positions were **highly leveraged** (sometimes by using options), a good idea of what occurred can be seen by considering a bet on a narrowing of the yield *differential* between US corporate bonds and US Treasuries, $(r_c - r)$—so-called 'relative value' or '**convergence trades**'. If you are long corporates and short Treasuries, then if the yield spread narrows, you will make profits. The fall in $r_c$ implies a rise in corporate bond prices and hence a gain on the long corporate position. A rise in yields on Treasuries (which also narrows the spread) will lead to a fall in T-bond prices and hence a profit from the short Treasury position. LTCM had also placed such bets on interest rates in emerging markets, and on interest rates in Europe converging as the January 1999 date for the introduction of a common currency (the euro) grew closer.

These spread positions are largely hedged against a general upward or downward movement in the level of all rates (i.e. a parallel shift). Hence you need not worry about the largely unpredictable and volatile parallel shifts in the yield curve. However, the spreads were so small that to make large profits for investors in LTCM, the trades had to be highly leveraged (i.e. financed by borrowing). Most of this borrowing was by repos. LTCM would sell some of its assets for cash to banks with the promise to buy them back at a higher price at a fixed date in the future. Normally banks require collateral that is worth slightly more than the cash loaned out, in case the assets used for collateral fall in value. This is the 'haircut'. But seemingly LTCM were loaned funds with near zero haircuts (the total haircut for LTCM £10bn of borrowing is reported by Jorion, 2000 to be as little as $500) and they also had a $900m credit line from major US banks.

By the end of 1997, LTCM total fees were of the order of $1.5bn and the 16 partners in LTCM had invested about $1.9bn of their own money in the fund. The balance sheet had assets of $125bn, supported by equity of $5bn—a leverage ratio of 25 to 1. To control risk LTCM stated that their target maximum risk level was set equal to the volatility of an unleveraged position in US equities. The firm also charged relatively large annual fees of about 2% of capital plus 25% of profits (whereas other hedge funds have about a 1% fixed fee and charge 20% of profits).

Unfortunately for LTCM, after Russia defaulted on its debt in August 1998 ('the thousand year storm'), spreads against Treasuries rose. Also, LTCM was long rouble denominated debt and short Russian foreign denominated debt, believing that this gave them a natural hedge, since if Russia defaulted on its rouble denominated debt it would also default on its foreign currency debt. In fact Russia only defaulted on its rouble denominated debt, so the hedge failed. Contagion spread to other emerging markets and, faced with falling corporate and emerging market bond prices, LTCM sought to unwind its long positions. But the market in some of these emerging market bonds was very illiquid, so it was difficult to sell without causing prices to plummet. This is known as liquidity risk. LTCM also faced margin calls on its T-bond futures positions. By the end of September 1998 LTCM had lost $4.4bn (compared with end-97), of which $1.9bn was the partners' money, about $700m from the Union Bank of Switzerland and $1.8bn losses by other investors in LTCM.

If LTCM's counterparties had to liquidate LTCM's collateral in the repos (with near zero haircuts) then this would have meant losses for these banks and possible bankruptcy for some banks. Had LTCM gone bust, then many banks would have suffered severe losses on their loans to LTCM in a 'fire sale'. Therefore the Fed stepped in to organise a rescue operation. The whole episode has led to calls for hedge funds to come under some regulatory control.

However, those banks who, under the direction of the Fed, pumped money into the rescue (i.e. of about $3.6bn to give them a 90% equity stake in LTCM) have since made profits as spreads returned to their normal pattern and narrowed in 1999. But the original lenders to LTCM have lost substantial amounts (see above). Some of the above spread strategies were actually conducted with options on interest rates (rather than in the underlying bonds themselves) and with equity options. This allowed large positions to be taken with only relatively small payments for the option premia—that is LTCM used options to leverage their positions.

Finally, scenario analysis (or stress testing) is often used to assess the impact of various non-parallel shifts in the yield curve on the value of a bond portfolio. The scenarios are based on the types of yield curve shifts observed in the past. Also, Monte Carlo simulation can be used to assess the riskiness of a particular 'open' or 'speculative' position in bonds (Cuthbertson and Nitzsche, 2001).

## 9.6 SUMMARY

- **Duration and convexity** can be used to provide an approximation to the change in price of a bond for a given change in the yield to maturity.
- **Matching the duration** of a bond with the duration of a single future cash outflow (e.g. a 'one off' lump sum pension payment), ensures that the reinvested coupons and the receipts from the sale of the bond will be sufficient to meet the cash outflow. This is an **immunisation strategy**.
- In practice, immunisation is not perfect when there are **multiperiod liabilities** (i.e. cash payouts over many periods) and **non-parallel shifts** in the yield curve.
- **Cash flow matching** to meet multiperiod liabilities, requires the fund manager to find a set of bonds where the timing of coupon payments and maturity value of the bonds exactly coincide with the timing of the liability payouts.
- **Bond indexing** is not designed to meet a future known set of cash payouts but merely to hold a bond portfolio that accurately **tracks the rate of return** on a (bond) market index.
- **Active bond strategies** involve speculation with part (or all) of the bond portfolio. Given a forecast of a general fall in yields, speculators might switch towards bonds with longer durations. **Regression techniques** can be used to try and predict bond yield and bond price changes. Bonds whose yields are a long way from an estimated yield curve are mispriced and may provide a profitable speculative opportunity using a **substitution swap** or convergence trades.

## END OF CHAPTER EXERCISES

**Q1** Give two reasons why the concept of duration is useful.

**Q2** What is meant by the convexity of a bond? Why might you be willing to pay more for bond-A which has a greater convexity than bond-B?

**Q3** Why might a pension fund use cash flow matching? Will it use this technique for the whole of its bond portfolio?

**Q4** Consider a 10% coupon bond (annual coupons) with par value $100, yield to maturity $y = 10\%$ and 5 years to maturity. Calculate:

(a) The current market price $P$.
(b) The Macaulay duration $D$.
(c) The (approximate) price change if the yield to maturity rises to 10.5% or falls to 9.5%.
(d) The 'true' price change for $y = 10.5\%$ and $y = 9.5\%$.

**Q5** What conditions are necessary to ensure a successful immunisation strategy? Are these conditions met in practice?

**Q6**    What are the difficulties in implementing a bond indexing strategy?

**Q7**    ***Portfolio A***: 1-year discount bond, face value = $2000
                         10-year discount bond, face value = $6000
    ***Portfolio B***: 5.95-year discount bond, face value = $5000

Current flat yield curve is $y = 10\%$ p.a. (continuously compounded).

(a) Show that the duration of portfolio-A equals that of portfolio-B.
(b) What is the **Actual** percentage change in value of portfolio-A for a 10 bp increase in yield?
    Does the duration formula give approximately the same answer?
(c) Repeat (b) for portfolios A and B for an increase in yield of 5% p.a.
    Which portfolio has the higher convexity?

# APPENDIX 9.1   DURATION AND CONVEXITY

The price of a coupon paying bond is a non-linear (convex) function of the yield to maturity, $y$:

[A9.1]    $$P = \frac{C}{(1+y)} + \frac{C}{(1+y)^2} + \ldots + \frac{(C+M)}{(1+y)^n}$$

Any non-linear function can be approximated by a Taylor series expansion of which the first two terms are:

[A9.2]    $$\frac{dP}{P} = \frac{1}{P}\left[\frac{dP}{dy}dy + \frac{1}{2}\frac{d^2P}{dy^2}(dy)^2\right]$$

Differentiating equation [A9.1] with respect to $y$ gives:

[A9.3]    $$\frac{dP}{dy} = \frac{-C}{(1+y)^2} - \frac{2C}{(1+y)^3} - \ldots - n\frac{(n+M)}{(1+y)^{n+1}}$$

$$= \frac{-1}{(1+y)}\left[\frac{C}{(1+y)} + \frac{2C}{(1+y)^2} + \ldots + n\frac{(n+M)}{(1+y)^n}\right]$$

It follows that:

[A9.4]    $$\frac{1}{P}\frac{dP}{dy} = \frac{-D}{(1+y)}$$

where

[A9.5]    $$D = \frac{1}{P}\left[\frac{1C}{(1+y)} + \frac{2C}{(1+y)^2} + \ldots + \frac{C+M}{(1+y)^n}\right]$$

Equation [A9.4] provides the formula for the price change in terms of duration given the definition of $D$ in equation [A9.5]. To calculate an expression for convexity we note from equation [A9.2] that we need to differentiate equation [A9.3] a second time:

[A9.6]
$$\frac{d^2 P}{dy^2} = \left[\frac{(1)(2)C}{(1+y)} + \frac{(2)(3)C}{(1+y)^2} + \dots + \frac{n(n+1)(C+M)}{(1+y)^n}\right] \frac{1}{(1+y)^2}$$

If we now define convexity $V$ as:

[A9.7]
$$V = \frac{1}{2}\left[\sum_{i=1}^{n} \frac{i(i+1)}{(1+y)^i}\right]\frac{1}{P}$$

Then equation [A9.2] becomes:

[A9.8]
$$\frac{dP}{P} = \frac{-D}{(1+y)}dy + V\left[\frac{dy}{(1+y)}\right]^2$$

## ZERO COUPON BOND

It is straightforward to show that the duration of a zero coupon bond equals its maturity. We have:

[A9.9]
$$P = \frac{M}{(1+y)^n}$$

and

[A9.10]
$$\frac{dP}{P} = -n\left[\frac{M}{(1+y)^{n+1}}\right]\frac{dy}{P}$$

Substituting for $P$ from equation [A9.9] into equation [A9.10]:

[A9.11]
$$\frac{dP}{P} = \frac{-n}{(1+y)}dy$$

Duration is defined by:

[A9.12]
$$\frac{dP}{P} = \frac{-D}{(1+y)}dy$$

Comparing equations [A9.11] and [A9.12] we see that the duration of a zero equals its maturity, $n$.

# APPENDIX 9.2  CONDITIONS FOR SUCCESSFUL IMMUNISATION

Assume all the cash flows of the liabilities have a present value $PV_L$ where the discount rate used is the yield to maturity YTM, $y$. The present value of the liabilities is therefore a function of the cash flows and $y$, hence $PV_L = f(\text{cash flows}, y)$.

For ease of exposition assume we have a portfolio containing only two bonds with current prices $P_1$ and $P_2$. The current value of the bond portfolio is:

[A9.13]     $V_B = N_1 P_1 + N_2 P_2$

where $N_1$, $N_2$ are the number of bonds held (of each type). Differentiating equation [A9.13] with respect to $y$:

[A9.14]     $$dV_B = N_1 \left(\frac{dP_1}{P_1}\right) P_1 + N_2 \left(\frac{dP_2}{P_2}\right) P_2$$

$$= V_1 \left(\frac{dP_1}{P_1}\right) + V_2 \left(\frac{dP_2}{P_2}\right) = -(V_1 D_1 + V_2 D_2)\, dy$$

where $V_i = N_i P_i$ is the dollar amount held in each bond and we have substituted $dP_i / P_i = -D_i\, dy$, assuming continuously compounded yields. The change in the (present) value of the liabilities is:

[A9.15]     $d(PV_L) = -(D_L\, dy)PV_L$

Equating [A9.14] and [A9.15] and imposing the initial condition that:

[A9.16]     $PV_B = PV_L$

we obtain:

[A9.17]     $$\frac{(V_1 D_1 + V_2 D_2)}{PV_B} = D_L$$

But the left-hand side of equation [A9.17] is simply the duration of the bond *portfolio* $D_p$, since:

[A9.18]     $D_p = w_1 D_1 + w_2 D_2$   where   $w_i = V_i / PV_B$

Hence equation [A9.17] demonstrates that successful immunisation requires the duration of the bond portfolio to equal the duration of the interest sensitive liabilities.

# APPENDIX 9.3  MULTIFACTOR MODEL AND DURATION

We demonstrate how a multifactor model produces measures of duration that incorporate non-parallel shifts in the yield curve. The number of factors in the interest rate model provides an equal number of measures of duration. So for a two-factor model we require two distinct measures of duration.

**Problem:** Calculate the bond price change for non-parallel shifts in the yield curve.

**Two factor model:** Factor 1 = long (spot) rate $r_L$

Factor 2 = variable $X$ (e.g. long–short spread).

[A9.19]     $$\Delta r_i = a_i \Delta r_L + b_i \Delta X \qquad i = 1, 2, 3, \ldots$$

Equation [A9.19] is a regression equation which allows for non-parallel shifts in the yield curve. For a 1-year horizon we regress $\Delta r_1$ on $\Delta r_L$ and $\Delta X$ to obtain estimates of $a_1$ and $b_1$. Similarly for $r_2$, $r_3$, etc. The variable $\Delta X$ is often taken to be the change in the long–short spread (i.e. $\Delta X = \Delta r_L - \Delta r_1$), but can be any variable that is thought to influence the shape or position of the yield curve.

## COUPON BOND AND DURATION

We take a three-period bond as an example where the third coupon $C_3$ includes the maturity value and we use continuously compounded rates:

[A9.20]     $$P = C_1 \exp(-r_1) + C_2 \exp(-2r_2) + C_3 \exp(-3r_3) = \sum_{t=1}^{3} C_t \exp(-r_t t)$$

[A9.21]     $$dP/P = P^{-1} \sum_{t=1}^{3} (-t) C_t \exp(-r_t t)\, dr_t = -\sum_{t=1}^{3} t(PV_t/P)\, dr_t$$

where

[A9.22]     $$PV_t = C_t \exp(-r_t t)$$

From equation [A9.21]:

[A9.23]     $$dP/P = -\frac{[(PV_1)\, dr_1 + 2(PV_2)\, dr_2 + 3(PV_3)\, dr_3]}{P}$$

Substituting for $dr_2$, $dr_3$, etc. from the yield curve relationship [A9.19] (we use '$\Delta$' and 'd' interchangeably):

$$dP/P = -(PV_1/P)[a_1\, dr_L + b_1\, dX] - 2(PV_2/P)[a_2\, dr_L + b_2\, dX]$$

[A9.24a]     $$- 3(PV_3/P)[a_3\, dr_L + b_3\, dX]$$

Rearranging equation [A9.24a]:

$$dP/P = -[a_1(\text{PV}_1/P) + 2a_2(\text{PV}_2/P) + 3a_3(\text{PV}_3/P)]\,dr_\text{L} - [b_1(\text{PV}_1/P)$$

[A9.24b]
$$+ 2b_2(\text{PV}_2/P) + 3b_3(\text{PV}_3/P)]\,dX$$

If we define the terms in square brackets as the 'long rate duration' $D_\text{L}$ and the 'spread duration' $D_\text{X}$ then:

[A9.25]
$$dP/P = -D_\text{L}\,dr_\text{L} - D_\text{X}\,dX$$

$D_\text{L}$ and $D_\text{X}$ take into account non-parallel shifts in the yield curve represented by the parameters $a_i$ on reference rate $r_\text{L}$ and the parameters $b_i$ on the variable $dX$. Given estimates of $(a_i, b_i)$ we can calculate $D_\text{L}$ and $D_\text{X}$ in the usual way. If we had used non-continuously compounded rates then all terms $dr$ and $dX$ would be replaced by $dr/(1+r)$, $dX/(1+X)$.

An illustration of the use of the multifactor interest rate model for non-parallel shifts in the yield curve is given in Table A9.1. It can be seen that the interest rate equation [A9.19] gives a non-parallel shift in the yield curve since $dr_1 = 78$ bp, $dr_2 = 67$ bp and $dr_3 = 51$ bp. We then use the estimates of $(a_i, b_i)$ to calculate $D_\text{L} = 3.71$ and $D_\text{X} = 0.4$. Finally equation [A9.25] gives the price change of the bond for the non-parallel shift in the yield curve:

$$dP/P = 2.843(0.005) - 0.308(0.001) = -0.0145\,(1.45\%)$$

---

## TABLE A9.1: Multifactor model and duration

**Data:**  3-year, 10% (annual) coupon bond, par value £100. The yield curve is initially flat with $r_1 = r_2 = r_3 = 10\%\ (0.1)$. Interest rate regressions (using continuously compounded rates) are:

$$dr_i = a_i\,dr_\text{L} + b_i\,dX$$

where $dr_\text{L}$ = change in the long spot rate

$dX$ = change in long–short spread

$\{a_1, a_2, a_3\} = \{1.5, 1.3, 1.0\}$

$\{b_1, b_2, b_3\} = \{0.3, 0.2, 0.1\}$

**Questions:**  1. Calculate the change in the 1, 2 and 3-year spot rates for a 50 bp change in the long (15-year) rate and a 10 bp change in the spread. Does the yield curve twist?

2. Calculate the 'long rate' and 'spread' durations.

3. Use duration to calculate the new bond price and check to see if this provides a reasonable approximation.

*continued overleaf*

## TABLE A9.1: (*Continued*)

**Answers:**   1. $dr_1 = 1.5(50) + 0.3(10) = 78$ bp (0.78%)

$dr_2 = 1.3(50) + 0.2(10) = 67$ bp (0.67%)

$dr_3 = 1.0(50) + 0.1(10) = 51$ bp (0.51%)

Hence the yield curve 'twists' and moves up more at the short end (0.78 bp) than the long end (0.51 bp). The 3-year maturity moves 51 bp, almost the same as the 15-year maturity ($dr_L = 50$ bp).

2. $PV_1 = 10 \exp(-0.1) = £9.048$

$PV_2 = 10 \exp(-0.2) = £8.187$

$PV_3 = 110 \exp(-0.3) = £81.49$

$P = PV_1 + PV_2 + PV_3 = £98.72$

$D_L = 1.5(£9.048/£98.72) + 2(1.3)(£8.187/£98.72) + 3(1.0)(£81.49/£98.72) = 2.843$

$D_X = 0.3(£9.048/£98.72) + 2(0.2)(£8.187/£98.72) + 3(0.1)(£81.49/£98.72) = 0.308$

3. Using duration, the change in the bond price is:

$dP/P = -D_L \, dr_L - D_X \, dX$

$= -2.843(0.005) - 0.308(0.001) = -0.0145 \,(1.45\%)$

The (approximate) new price is $P = £98.72 - 0.0145(£98.72) = $ **£97.29**

The *actual* new price is $P = 10 \exp(-0.1078) + 10 \exp(-0.1067 \times 2)$ $+110 \exp(-0.1051 \times 3) = $ **£97.31**, so the duration approximation is quite accurate.

# APPENDIX 9.4   CASH FLOW MATCHING (LINEAR PROGRAMMING PROBLEM)

In cash flow matching one objective is to choose a set of bonds to minimise the cost of the chosen portfolio:

$$\text{Min} \sum_i N(i)P(i, \, t)$$

where $N(i) =$ number of bonds of type $i$
   $P(i) =$ price of bond of type $i$.

The constraints might include:

1. Cash flows $C(i, t)$ are sufficient to meet liability flows $L(t)$

$$\sum_i N(i)C(i, t) \geqslant L(t) \text{ for all } t$$

2. The investor cannot issue bonds

$$N(i) \geqslant 0 \text{ for all } i$$

In the above there is no allowance either for interest-on-interest from the coupon flows or for reinvestment of any excess funds after meeting a particular liability. If we let the reinvestment rate $= r_t$ and $S_{t-1} =$ the excess funds available at $t - 1$ then we can include additional constraints.

3. Replace the constraints in (2) with

$$\sum N(i)C(i, t) + S_{t-1}[1 + r(t)] = L(t) + S_t$$

Bond cash flows + reinvestment income = liabilities + new investment in bonds

4. Reinvestment funds are positive (or zero)

$$S_0 = 0 \qquad \text{and} \qquad S_{t-1} \geqslant 0$$

# PART 4

# PORTFOLIO THEORY AND CAPITAL STRUCTURE

# CHAPTER 10

# Portfolio Theory and Asset Returns

## LEARNING OBJECTIVES

- To explain why it is beneficial for investors to hold a **diversified portfolio** consisting of a number of risky assets rather than say one single risky asset or a small subset of all the available risky assets. This involves trading off risk against expected return and gives rise to the **efficient frontier**.

- To determine how much an individual investor will borrow (or lend) at the safe rate in order to increase (decrease) her exposure to the 'bundle' of risky assets. This is in part determined by the **capital market line (CML)** which, together with the efficient frontier, allows us to calculate the *optimal* proportions in which to hold the risky assets. This is the **mean–variance model** of portfolio choice.

- To analyse the determinants of the **equilibrium expected return** on an individual security, so that all the risky assets are willingly held by investors.

- To show how we can measure the risk premium on an asset and hence determine its 'correct' or equilibrium rate of return. Two key competing theories are the **capital asset pricing model (CAPM)** and the **arbitrage pricing theory (APT)**. In the CAPM the riskiness of an individual asset (held as part of a diversified portfolio) is given by the **asset's 'beta'**. The latter plays a key role in finance.

In this chapter we analyse the **mean–variance model** of portfolio choice and derive the (basic one-period) capital asset pricing model, CAPM. The CAPM, interpreted as a model of equilibrium asset returns, is widely used in the finance literature and the concepts which underlie its derivation, such as portfolio diversification, measures of risk and return and the concept of the market portfolio, are also fundamental to the analysis of all asset prices. At the end of this chapter we also present a brief account of the arbitrage pricing theory, APT. This relates the expected return on a security to a set of variables called 'factors' which could include marketwide effects due to interest rates, exchange rates, etc. Throughout this chapter we will consider that the only risky securities are equities (stocks), although strictly the model applies to choices amongst *all* risky assets (i.e. stocks, bonds, real estate, etc.).

The concepts behind portfolio theory can be used to determine asset allocation strategies.

For example, a fund manager has to decide how to distribute her funds across different equities in different countries. A set of optimal proportions (e.g. 25% in UK stocks, 75% in US stocks) can be determined using portfolio theory. A fund manager might also wish to put some of her own funds in a 'safe asset' (e.g. bank deposit), with the remainder placed in risky equities. Alternatively, if she is not too worried about risk but likes a high return she may be willing to borrow money at the safe rate (e.g. bank loan) and add this to her own funds and put 'the lot' in the stock market. Portfolio theory can also help in this borrowing–lending decision. Finally, when deciding whether to invest in new plant and machinery, the discount rate in the PV calculation should reflect the riskiness of the project, and the CAPM provides a way of calculating the correct adjustment for risk (for an all equity financed firm). The concepts used, before we finally 'make it' to the results of mean–variance portfolio theory and the CAPM are quite numerous and somewhat complex. Hence it is useful at the outset to sketch the main concepts and ideas we will meet and draw out some basic implications of the approach.

# 10.1  AN OVERVIEW

We restrict our world to one in which investors can choose a set of risky assets (stocks) plus an asset which is risk free over the fixed holding period (e.g. fixed term bank deposit or a Treasury bill). Investors can borrow and lend as much as they like at the risk free rate. We assume investors like higher expected returns but dislike risk (i.e. they are risk averse). The expected return on an *individual* security we denote as $ER_i$, and we assume that the risk on an *individual* security can be measured by the variance $\sigma_i^2$ or standard deviation $\sigma_i$ of its return. We assume all individuals form the same (i.e. homogeneous) expectations about expected returns and the variances and covariances (correlation) between the various returns. Transactions costs and taxes are assumed to be zero.

## PORTFOLIO DIVERSIFICATION

$\sigma_{12}$ is the covariance between two returns and is related to the correlation coefficient $\rho$ by the formula:

[10.1]     $$\rho = \sigma_{12}/\sigma_1 \sigma_2$$

The covariance and correlation coefficient will both have the same sign but the covariance has the annoying property that it is dependent on the units used to measure returns (e.g. proportions or percentages), whereas the correlation coefficient is 'dimensionless' and must always lie between $+1$ and $-1$. If $\rho = +1$ the two asset returns are perfectly positively (linearly) related and the asset returns *always* move in the same *direction* (but not necessarily by the same percentage amount). For $\rho = -1$ the converse applies and for $\rho = 0$ the asset returns are not (linearly) related. As we see below, the 'riskiness' of the portfolio consisting of both assets, 1 and 2, depends crucially on the sign and size of the correlation coefficient, $\rho$. If $\rho = -1$, risk may be completely eliminated by holding a specific proportion of initial wealth in both assets. Even if $\rho$ is positive (but less than $+1$) the riskiness of the overall portfolio is reduced (although not to zero).

Consider the reason for holding a **diversified portfolio** consisting of a **set** of risky assets. Assume for the moment that the funds allocated to the safe asset have already been fixed. Putting all your wealth in asset 1, you incur an expected return $ER_1$ and a risk element $\sigma_1^2$. Similarly holding just asset 2 you expect to earn $ER_2$ and incur risk $\sigma_2^2$. Let us assume a two-asset world where there is a negative covariance of returns $\sigma_{12} < 0$. Hence when the return on asset 1 rises that on asset 2 tends to fall. (This also implies a negative correlation coefficient $\rho_{12} = \sigma_{12}/\sigma_1\sigma_2$.) Hence if you diversify and hold both assets, this would seem to reduce the variance of the *overall* portfolio (i.e. of asset 1 plus asset 2). To simplify even further suppose that $ER_1 = ER_2 = 10\%$ and $\sigma_1^2 = \sigma_2^2$. In addition assume that when the return on asset 1 increases by 1%, that on asset 2 falls by 1% (i.e. returns are perfectly negatively correlated, $\rho = -1$). Under these conditions when you hold half your initial wealth in each of the risky assets, the expected return on the overall portfolio is $ER_p = 0.5ER_1 + 0.5ER_2 = 10\%$. However, diversification has reduced the risk on this portfolio to zero: an above average return on asset 1 is always matched by an equal below average return on asset 2 (since $\rho = -1$). Our example is a special case. But in general, even if the covariance of returns is zero or positive (but not perfectly positively correlated) it still pays to diversify and hold a combination of both assets.

The key inputs in mean–variance portfolio theory which determine asset allocation decisions are the expected return, variances and correlation between returns. We can derive a 'theoretical' optimum that depends on these 'inputs', but we then have to estimate them. Table 10.1 gives historic sample averages for these statistics based on monthly stock returns for different US industrial sectors (over the period January 1990 to September 2000). The average monthly return on the Entertainment sector at 1.31% exceeds that for the Financial sector at 1.25%, and what is more the Entertainment sector has a lower standard deviation at

## TABLE 10.1: Monthly stock market returns S&P industrial sectors (January 1990 to September 2000)

| | Chemical | Entertainment | Financial | Automobiles | Oil |
|---|---|---|---|---|---|
| **Mean return** | 0.56 | 1.31 | 1.26 | 0.83 | 0.73 |
| **Standard deviation** | 6.20 | 5.71 | 6.24 | 7.20 | 4.41 |
| | | **Correlation matrix** | | | |
| **Chemical** | 1 | | | | |
| **Entertainment** | 0.3476 | 1 | | | |
| **Financial** | 0.6245 | 0.5623 | 1 | | |
| **Automobiles** | 0.5138 | 0.4258 | 0.5062 | 1 | |
| **Oil** | 0.5578 | 0.1020 | 0.4604 | 0.2039 | 1 |

5.71% than the Financial sector at 6.24%. If these historical figures are good estimates of the (constant) population parameters then why would anyone hold shares in the Financial sector, rather than putting all their money in the Entertainment sector? The reason given above for having some of *both* assets as part of your portfolio is that if the correlation between returns is less that +1, then there may be some diversification benefit to be had from including Financials along with Entertainment shares. Indeed the historic correlation coefficient between the returns in these two sectors is 0.5623 (Table 10.1). It is also clear from Table 10.1 that you might also include the Oil sector in your portfolio because, although it has a rather low average return of 0.73% p.m., it has relatively low correlations with all other sectors.

So, the benefits of diversification in reducing risk depend on returns having less than perfect (positive) correlation. In fact even a little diversification quickly reduces risk. If we *randomly* choose a one-stock portfolio, a two-stock portfolio, etc. (from stocks in the S&P500 index) and calculate the *portfolio* standard deviation $\sigma_p$, then 'risk' drops to a level $C$ (Figure 10.1) with only about 25 stocks. Hence, less than perfect (positive) correlation eliminates **diversifiable** or **idiosyncratic** risk. Hence, in general, portfolio diversification effects arise from:

> **Portfolio diversification arises from $\rho < +1$, and the law of large numbers $n \rightarrow \infty$**

For example, consider $n = 2$ for illustrative purposes, then:

[10.2]
$$\sigma_p^2 = w_1^2 \sigma_1^2 + w_2^2 \sigma_2^2 + 2w_1 w_2 \rho \sigma_1 \sigma_2$$

- if $\rho = 1$: $\sigma_p = (w_1\sigma_1 + w_2\sigma_2)$ and $\sigma_p$ is a (linear) weighted average of $\sigma_1$ and $\sigma_2$
- if $\rho < 1$: $\sigma_p < (w_1\sigma_1 + w_2\sigma_2)$ and $\sigma_p$ *must be less than* the weighted average of $\sigma_1$ and $\sigma_2$

This is the portfolio diversification effect. If $\rho = 0$, equation [10.2] becomes:

[10.3]
$$\sigma_p^2 = w_1^2 \sigma_2^2 + w_2^2 \sigma_2^2$$

For example, suppose $\sigma_1 = \sigma_2 = \sigma$ and $w_1 = 1/2$, then $\sigma_p = \sigma/\sqrt{2}$ and in general, as we see below: $\sigma_p = \sigma/\sqrt{n}$. This is the 'law of large numbers' or 'insurance effect'. A large number of uncorrelated ($\rho = 0$) events have a low variance (i.e. $\sigma_p \rightarrow 0$ as $n \rightarrow \infty$). This is why your car insurance premium is low relative to the replacement value of the car. If the car insurer has a large number of customers who have accidents which are largely independent of each other then the risk of the whole 'portfolio' of customers is relatively small. (The reason, in practice, that the risk does not approach zero as the number of customers increases is that there is some small positive correlation between accidents from claimants within the same company. It usually 'takes two to make an accident' and they may be with the same insurance company.)

The **systematic risk** of a portfolio is defined as risk which cannot be diversified away by adding extra securities to the portfolio. (It is also referred to as '**non-diversifiable**', '**portfolio**' or '**market risk**'.) There is always some non-zero risk even in a well-diversified portfolio, and this is because of the covariance or correlation effect. To see this note that the variance of a portfolio of $n$ assets held in proportions $w_i$ $(0 < w_i < 1)$ is:

[**10.4**] $$\sigma^2_{\mathrm{p}} = \sum_i^n w_i^2 \sigma_i^2 + \sum_i^n \sum_j^n w_i w_j \sigma_{ij}$$

With $n$ assets there are $n$ variance terms $\sigma_i^2$ and $n(n-1)/2$ covariance terms $\sigma_{ij}$ that contribute to the variance of the portfolio. The number of covariance terms rises much faster than the number of assets in the portfolio, and hence the number of variance terms (both the latter increase at the same rate, $n$). To illustrate this dependence on the covariance term consider a simplified portfolio where all assets are held in the same proportion $(w_i = 1/n)$ and where all variances and covariances are constant (i.e. $\sigma_i^2 = V$ and $\sigma_{ij} = C$, where '$V$' and '$C$' are constants). Then equation [10.4] becomes:

[**10.5**] $$\sigma^2_{\mathrm{p}} = n[n^{-2}V] + n(n-1)[n^{-2}C] = (1/n)V + (1 - 1/n)C$$

It follows that as $n \to \infty$ the influence of the variance term approaches zero and $\sigma^2_{\mathrm{p}}$ is the (constant) covariance, $C$. (Figure 10.1) Thus the variance of *individual* securities, which represents (idiosyncratic) risk particular to that firm or industry, can be diversified away. However, covariance risk cannot, and it is the covariance terms that (in a loose sense) give rise to market/non-diversifiable or systematic risk, which as we shall see, is represented by the beta of the security.

## LIMITED INVESTMENT AND PORTFOLIO VARIANCE

In general the agent may reduce $\sigma_{\mathrm{p}}$ by including additional stocks in her portfolio. (Particularly those that have negative covariances with the existing stocks already held.) In fact the portfolio variance $\sigma^2_{\mathrm{p}}$ falls very quickly as one increases the number of stocks held from 1 to 25 and thereafter the reduction in portfolio variance is quite small (Figure 10.1). This, coupled with the brokerage fees and information costs of monitoring a large number

## FIGURE 10.1: Increasing size of portfolio

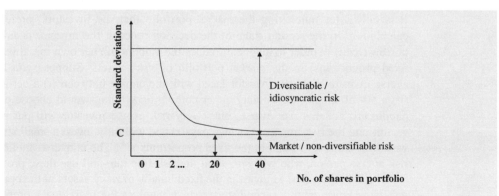

of stocks, may explain why individuals tend to invest in only a relatively small number of stocks. Individuals may also obtain the benefits of diversification by investing in mutual funds (unit trusts), closed-end mutual funds (investment trusts) and pension funds, since these use funds from a large number of individuals to invest in a very wide range of financial assets and each individual then owns a proportion of this 'large portfolio'.

The above discussion also points to the reason why investors as a whole are willing to hold *all* available stocks in the market. To demonstrate this point we set up a counter-example. If *one* stock were initially not desired by any of the investors then its current price would fall as investors sold it. However, a fall in the current price implies that the *expected return* over the coming period is higher, ceteris paribus (assuming one expected it to pay some dividends in the future). One might therefore see the current price fall until the expected return increases so that the stock is sufficiently attractive to hold.

## TASTES AND PREFERENCES FOR RISK VERSUS RETURN

The reader may by now, be surmising that the individual investor's tastes or preferences must come into the analysis at some point. Indeed, there is a quite remarkable result, known as the ***separation principle***. The investment decision can be broken down into two separate decisions. The first decision concerns the choice of the *optimal proportions* $w_i^*$ of risky assets held and this is *independent of the individual's preferences* concerning her subjective trade off between risk and return. This choice only depends on the individual's views about the objective market variables, namely expected returns, variances and covariances. Hence we can use portfolio theory to assist the fund manager in her asset allocation decision. Now if we are willing to assume (and it's a big 'if') that expectations about variances, etc. are the same for all investors, then we find that all investors hold the same proportions of the risky assets (e.g. all investors hold 1/20 of 'A shares', 1/80 of 'B shares', etc.) irrespective of their preferences. Hence, aggregating, all individuals will hold these risky assets in the same proportion as in the (aggregate) market portfolio (e.g. if the share of ICI in the total stock market index is 1/20 by value, then all investors hold 1/20 of their *own* risky asset portfolio in ICI shares). Note that even if all investors do not have the same view about variances, expected return, etc. then portfolio theory can still be used to calculate a *particular investor's* optimal asset allocation strategy. So all is not lost! However, we cannot call the resulting portfolio 'the market portfolio'.

It is only after mimicking the market portfolio that the investors' preferences enter the calculation. In the second stage of the decision process, the investor decides how much to borrow (lend) in order to augment (reduce the amount of) her own initial wealth invested (in fixed proportions) in the market portfolio of risky assets. Suppose you have a *very* risk averse investor. Such an investor faced with the choice between (i) a certain gain of $5 or (ii) a 50–50 chance of winning either nothing or $100bn, would choose option '(i)'. Most people are not this risk averse, but a very risk averse investor will put most of her own wealth into the risk free asset (which pays $r$) and will only invest a small amount of her own wealth in the risky assets, in the fixed proportions $w_i^*$. The converse applies to a much less risk averse person, who will *borrow* at the risk free rate and use these proceeds (as well as her own initial wealth) to invest in the fixed bundle of risky assets in the optimal proportions $w_i^*$. Note however, this second stage, which involves the individual's preferences, does not impinge on the *relative demands* for the risky assets (i.e. the proportions $w_i^*$ which are fixed). Hence if all investors agree about variances and covariances then the *equilibrium expected return* on any risky asset is independent of individuals' preferences (and level of initial wealth).

Throughout this chapter we shall use the following equivalent ways of expressing expected returns, variances and covariances:

- **Expected return** $\equiv \mu_i \equiv ER_i$
- **Variance of returns** $\equiv \sigma_i^2 \equiv \text{Var}(R_i)$
- **Covariance of returns** $\equiv \sigma_{ij} \equiv \text{Cov}(R_i, R_j)$

## CAPM AND BETA

Let us turn now to some specific results about equilibrium returns which arise from the CAPM. The CAPM provides an elegant model of the determinants of the equilibrium expected return $ER_i$ on any *individual* risky asset in the market. It predicts that the expected return on an individual risky asset $ER_i$ consists of the risk free rate $r$, plus a risk premium $rp_i$. However, it provides an explicit expression for the risk premium:

[10.6]     $ER_i = r + rp_i$

where $rp_i = \beta_i(ER_m - r)$ and $\beta_i = \text{Cov}(R_i, R_m)/\text{Var}(R_m)$. The risk premium is proportional to the excess market return $(ER_m - r)$ with the constant of proportionality given by the **beta** of the individual risky asset. The CAPM can be rewritten:

[10.7]     $(ER_i - r) = \beta_i(ER_m - r)$

$ER_m$ is the expected return on the market portfolio, that is the 'average' expected return from holding *all* assets in the optimal proportions $w_i^*$. Since actual returns on the market portfolio differ from expected returns, the variance $\text{Var}(R_m)$ on the market portfolio is non-zero. The definition of firm $i$'s **beta** $\beta_i$ indicates that:

- it depends on the covariance between the return on security $i$ and the market portfolio, $\text{Cov}(R_i, R_m)$;
- it is inversely related to the variance of the market portfolio, $\text{Var}(R_m)$.

Loosely speaking, if ex-post (or actual) returns when averaged, approximate the ex-ante expected return $ER_i$, then we can think of the CAPM as explaining the average monthly return (over say a 12-month period) on security $i$. What does the CAPM tell us about equilibrium returns on individual securities in the stock market? First note that $(ER_m - r) > 0$, otherwise no risk averse agent would hold the market portfolio of risky assets when he could earn more, *for certain,* by investing all his wealth in the risk free asset.

Returns on individual stocks tend to move in the same direction and hence, in general, $\text{Cov}(R_i, R_m) \geqslant 0$ and $\beta_i \geqslant 0$. The CAPM predicts that for those stocks which have a zero covariance with the market portfolio, they will be willingly held as long as they have an expected return equal to the risk free rate—put $\beta_i = 0$ in equation [10.7]. Securities that have a large positive covariance with the market return ($\beta_i > 0$) will have to earn a relatively high expected return: this is because the addition of such a security to the portfolio does little to reduce *overall portfolio* variance.

The CAPM also allows one to assess the relative volatility of the expected returns on individual stocks on the basis of their $\beta_i$ values (which we assume are accurately measured). Stocks for which $\beta_i = 1$ have a return that is expected to move one-for-one with the market portfolio (i.e. $ER_i = ER_m$) and are termed **'neutral stocks'**. If $\beta_i > 1$ the stock is said to be an **aggressive stock** since it moves *more* than changes in the expected market return (either up or down) and conversely **defensive stocks** have $\beta_i < 1$. Therefore investors can use betas to rank the relative safety of various securities and can combine different shares to give a desired beta for the portfolio. However, the latter should not detract from one of the theory's key predictions, namely that *all* investors should hold stocks in the same optimal proportions $w_i^*$. Hence the 'market portfolio' held by all investors will include neutral, aggressive and defensive stocks held in the *optimal proportions* $w_i^*$. Of course, a portfolio manager who wishes to 'take a position' in particular stocks may use betas to rank the stocks to include in her portfolio (i.e. she doesn't obey the assumptions of the CAPM and therefore doesn't attempt to mimic the market portfolio). Also if our portfolio manager has different views about variances and covariances to other portfolio managers, she can still use portfolio theory to calculate her optimal asset allocation proportions ($w_i$), but these will then differ from other portfolio manager's optimal proportions.

# 10.2 PORTFOLIO THEORY

Our main aim in this section is to introduce the key concepts in portfolio theory and show how these are used in determining the optimal asset allocation. The material is presented in the following order:

- Mean–variance criterion
- Efficient set of portfolios
    two risky assets
    $n$ risky assets
- Transformation line
    = one safe asset + one risky asset (or 'bundle')
- Capital market line (CML) and the market portfolio
    = one safe asset + $n$ risky assets.

## MEAN–VARIANCE CRITERION

We assume that the investor would prefer a higher expected return $ER_p$ rather than a lower expected return, but she dislikes risk (i.e. is risk averse). We choose to measure risk by the variance (or standard deviation) of the returns on the portfolio of risky assets. More risk implies less 'satisfaction'. In the jargon of economics, the investor's utility ($U$) is assumed to depend only on expected return and the variance (or standard deviation) of the return:

[10.8]  $$U = U(ER_p, \sigma_p)$$

Thus, if the agent is presented with a portfolio A (of $n$ securities) and a portfolio B (of a different set of $n$ securities), then according to the mean–variance criterion MVC, portfolio A is preferred to portfolio B if:

**[10.9a]**     $E_A(R_p) \geqslant E_B(R_p)$

and

**[10.9b]**     $\sigma_A^2(R_p) \leqslant \sigma_B^2(R_p)$   or   $\sigma_A(R_p) \leqslant \sigma_B(R_p)$

where $\sigma$ is the standard deviation of the return of the portfolio.

Of course if, for example, $E_A(R_p) > E_B(R_p)$ but $\sigma_A(R_p) > \sigma_B(R_p)$ then we cannot say what portfolio the investor prefers using the MVC. Portfolios that satisfy the MVC are known as the set of **efficient portfolios**. A portfolio A that has a lower expected return *and* a higher variance than another portfolio B is said to be 'inefficient' and an individual would (in principle) never hold a portfolio such as A if portfolio B is available (i.e. portfolio A is 'dominated' by portfolio B).

## PREFERENCES

For any individual we can represent her preferences in a $(ER_p, \sigma_p)$ graph (Figure 10.2). At all points on the indifference curve $I_1$, the individual is equally 'happy' (i.e. has constant utility). If you increase risk from Y to Z, then in order to compensate for this loss of satisfaction, the individual must be given a higher expected return (Z to B) to return to the same level of 'happiness'. Indifference curve $I_2$ represents higher levels of satisfaction than $I_1$. The individual would prefer to be at A rather than B since both points have the same expected return but at A the individual bears less risk.

## EFFICIENT FRONTIER: TWO RISKY ASSETS

To simplify matters we assume there are only four possible scenarios (see Table 10.2). A 'high' level of interest rates is detrimental to equity returns but high (real) growth in the

## FIGURE 10.2: Individual preferences

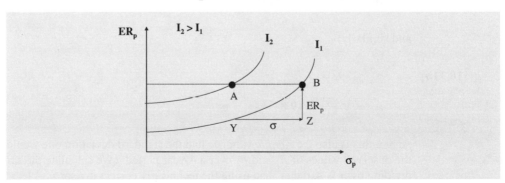

## TABLE 10.2: Two risky assets

| State | Interest | Growth | Probability | Return | |
|---|---|---|---|---|---|
| | | | | Equity 1 | Equity 2 |
| 1 | high | low | 0.25 | −5 | 45 |
| 2 | high | high | 0.25 | 5 | 35 |
| 3 | low | low | 0.25 | 10 | 10 |
| 4 | low | high | 0.25 | 25 | −5 |

economy leads to high expected returns. This is because high interest rates (tight monetary policy) generally imply lower profits, while high growth implies high profits. Some of these profits will then be distributed as dividends and may lead to capital gains on the stock. The four combinations of possible scenarios have an equal probability of occurrence (of 1/4 each). Given the returns $(R_1, R_2)$ on the two assets *under each scenario,* we can calculate the expected return:

[10.10a] $$ER_1 = \tfrac{1}{4}(-5) + \tfrac{1}{4}(5) + \tfrac{1}{4}(10) + \tfrac{1}{4}(25) = 8.75$$

and similarly:

[10.10b] $$ER_2 = 21.25$$

Note that the expected return, using probabilities, is the same as the *sample average* of the return, if we had observed $R_1 = (-5, 5, 10, 25)$ over a 4-year period. The variance and standard deviation are given by:

[10.11a] $$\sigma_1^2 = \tfrac{1}{4}(-5 - 8.75)^2 + \tfrac{1}{4}(5 - 8.75)^2 + \tfrac{1}{4}(10 - 8.75)^2 + \tfrac{1}{4}(25 - 8.75)^2 = 117.28$$

$$\sigma_1 = \sqrt{117.28} = 10.83$$

and similarly:

[10.11b] $$\sigma_2^2 = 392$$

$$\sigma_2 = \sqrt{392} = 19.8$$

Again, this is also the *sample* variance and the standard deviation one would calculate, given the observed values of $R_1$ and $R_2$ over a 4-year period. (We calculate the sample variance by dividing by $n = 4$, rather than using the technically correct divisor $n - 1 = 3$.)

> **The standard deviation $\sigma_i$ (or variance) of an asset's return is a measure of its 'own riskiness', (*i.e. it is the only asset held by the investor*)**

We can also work out the covariance and correlation coefficient between the returns on these two assets. The returns on the two assets are negatively correlated. When the return on '1' is high, then that on '2' tends to be low. The covariance and correlation coefficient are:

[10.12]
$$\sigma_{12} = \tfrac{1}{4}(-5 - 8.75)(45 - 21.25) + \tfrac{1}{4}(5 - 8.75)(35 - 21.25) + \tfrac{1}{4}(10 - 8.75)(10 - 21.25)$$
$$+ \tfrac{1}{4}(25 - 8.75)(-5 - 21.25) = -204.68$$

[10.13]
$$\rho = \frac{\sigma_{12}}{\sigma_1 \sigma_2} = \frac{-204.68}{(10.83)(19.8)} = -0.9549$$

Suppose the investor at this stage is not allowed to borrow or lend the safe asset. What opportunities are open to her when faced with assets '1' and '2' with variances $\sigma_1$ and $\sigma_2$ and covariance $\sigma_{12}$ or correlation $\rho$ between the two returns (see Table 10.3).

We can calculate the combinations of expected return and standard deviation of return available to her as she varies the proportion of her *own* wealth (remember there is no borrowing or lending at this stage) held in either equity 1 or equity 2. We begin with an algebraic exposition but then demonstrate the points made using a simple numerical example. Suppose the investor chooses to hold a proportion of her wealth $w_1$ in asset 1 and a proportion $w_2 = (1 - w_1)$ in asset 2. The **actual return** on this diversified portfolio (which will not be revealed until one period later) is:

[10.14a]
$$R_p = w_1 R_1 + w_2 R_2$$

## TABLE 10.3: Summary statistics (two risky assets)

|  | Risky assets | |
| --- | --- | --- |
|  | Equity 1 | Equity 2 |
| **Mean, $ER_i$** | 8.75% | 21.25% |
| **Std. dev., $\sigma_i$** | 10.83% | 19.80% |
| **Correlation (equity 1, equity 2)** |  | −0.9549 |
| **Covariance (equity 1, equity 2)** |  | −204.688 |

289

The *expected* return on the portfolio is:

[**10.14b**]     $ER_p = w_1 ER_1 + w_2 ER_2$

The *variance of the portfolio* is given by:

[**10.15**]     $\sigma_p^2 = E(R_p - ER_p)^2 = E[w_1(R_1 - ER_1) + w_2(R_2 - ER_2)]^2$

$= \sigma_p^2 = w_1^2 \sigma_1^2 + w_2^2 \sigma_2^2 + 2w_1 w_2 (\rho \sigma_1 \sigma_2)$

where we have used $\sigma_{12} = \rho \sigma_1 \sigma_2$. The question we now ask is:

> **How do $ER_p$ and $\sigma_p$ vary, relative to each other, as the investor *alters the proportion of her own wealth held in each of the risky assets*? This is the opportunity set**

Remember that $ER_1$, $ER_2$, $\sigma_1$, $\sigma_2$ and $\sigma_{12}$ (or $\rho$) are fixed and known and we simply alter the proportions of wealth: $w_1$ in asset 1 and $w_2$ ($= 1 - w_1$) in asset 2. (Note that there is no maximisation/minimisation problem here. It is a purely *arithmetic* calculation given the definitions of $ER_p$ and $\sigma_p$.) A numerical example is given in Table 10.4.

For example, for $w_1 = 0.75$, $w_2 = 0.25$ we get:

[**10.16**]     $ER_p = 0.75(8.75) + 0.25(21.25) = 11.88$

## TABLE 10.4: Portfolio risk and return

| | Share of | | Portfolio | |
| --- | --- | --- | --- | --- |
| | Equity 1 | Equity 2 | $ER_p$ | $\sigma_p$ |
| **State** | $w_1$ | $w_2$ | | |
| 1 | 1 | 0 | 8.75% | 10.83% |
| 2 | 0.75 | 0.25 | 11.88% | 3.70% |
| 3 | 0.5 | 0.5 | 15% | 5% |
| 4 | 0 | 1 | 21.25% | 19.80% |

and

[**10.17**]    $\sigma_p^2 = (0.75)^2(10.83)^2 + (0.25)^2(19.80)^2$

$+ 2(0.75)(0.25)[-0.95(10.83)(19.80)] = 13.7\ (\sigma_p = 3.7)$

This is marked in Figure 10.3. The risk–return combinations in Figure 10.3 represent a **feasible set** or **opportunity set** for every investor. However, the investor would never choose points along the lower portion of the curve because points along the upper portion have a higher expected return but no more risk, hence:

> **The locus of points above and to the right of (0.75, 0.25) is known as the efficient frontier**

For two risky assets, the efficient set is a **non-linear** locus of points in $(ER_p, \sigma_p)$ space, each point representing different proportions ($w_1$ and $w_2$) of the two risky assets. It is clear that combining the two assets into a portfolio gives the investor a wider set of risk–return combinations than holding either of the two assets. This is the principle of diversification.

## DIFFERENT VALUES OF THE CORRELATION COEFFICIENT

At any point in time there will only be one value for the correlation coefficient $\rho$ given by the (past) behaviour of the two returns. However, it is interesting to see what happens to the efficient frontier when $\rho$ moves from $+1$ to $-1$. (Over time, in the real world $\rho$ may change, and therefore so will the efficient frontier.) This is done in Table 10.5 where we construct the mean–variance combinations for different values of $\rho$. In general, as $\rho$ approaches $-1$ the $(\mu_p, \sigma_p)$ locus moves closer to the vertical axis indicating that a greater reduction in portfolio risk is possible for any given expected return (Figure 10.4). For $\rho = -1$ the curve

## FIGURE 10.3: Efficient frontier

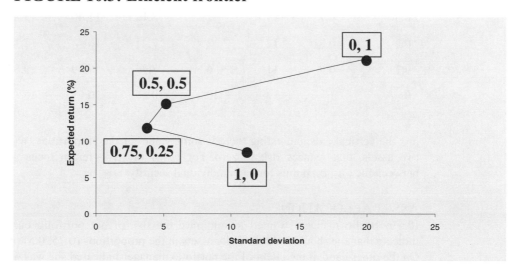

## TABLE 10.5: Risk–return locus for different correlation coefficients

| | | | Summary statistics of individual assets | |
|---|---|---|---|---|
| | | | Asset 1 | Asset 2 |
| **Mean** | | | 10 | 20 |
| **Std. dev.** | | | 10 | 30 |

| | | | Portfolio (of two assets) | | | | |
|---|---|---|---|---|---|---|---|
| $w_1$ | $w_2$ | Return | Std. dev. | Std. dev. | Std. dev. | Std. dev. | Std. dev. |
| | | | $\rho = -1$ | $\rho = -0.5$ | $\rho = 0$ | $\rho = 0.5$ | $\rho = 1$ |
| 1 | 0 | 20 | 30 | 30 | 30 | 30 | 30 |
| 0.9 | 0.1 | 19 | 26 | 26.51 | 27.02 | 27.51 | 28 |
| 0.8 | 0.2 | 18 | 22 | 23.07 | 24.08 | 25.06 | 26 |
| 0.7 | 0.3 | 17 | 18 | 19.67 | 21.21 | 22.65 | 24 |
| 0.6 | 0.4 | 16 | 14 | 16.37 | 18.44 | 20.30 | 22 |
| 0.5 | 0.5 | 15 | 10 | 13.23 | 15.81 | 18.03 | 20 |
| 0.4 | 0.6 | 14 | 6 | 10.39 | 13.42 | 15.87 | 18 |
| 0.3 | 0.7 | 13 | 2 | 8.19 | 11.40 | 13.89 | 16 |
| 0.2 | 0.8 | 12 | 2 | 7.21 | 10 | 12.17 | 14 |
| 0.1 | 0.9 | 11 | 6 | 7.94 | 9.49 | 10.82 | 12 |
| 0 | 1 | 10 | 10 | 10 | 10 | 10 | 10 |

hits the vertical axis, indicating there is some value for the proportions ($w_1$, $w_2$) held in the two assets, that reduces risk to zero. For $\rho = 1$ the risk–return locus is a straight line between the ($\mu_i$, $\sigma_i$) points for each individual security.

## ASSET ALLOCATION

If a portfolio manager wanted to minimise the risk of her portfolio our analysis would indicate that she should hold the risky assets in the proportions (0.75, 0.5) (see Figure 10.3). On the other hand, if the client of the portfolio manager indicated she was willing to tolerate

# FIGURE 10.4: Risk reduction through diversification

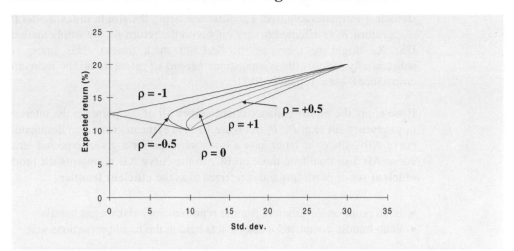

risk of only $\sigma = 5\%$, then the portfolio manager would suggest that the highest return she could **expect** to obtain was 15%, and this would require an asset allocation of (0.5, 0.5). The converse of this argument is that if the client asks the portfolio manager how much risk she would have to bear to achieve an expected return of say 20%, the answer would be $\sigma = 19.8\%$ with asset allocation (0, 1). All of the above assumes no borrowing or lending, but only investing the client's own wealth.

## EFFICIENT FRONTIER: *n*-RISKY ASSETS

We now consider the case of $n$ assets. When we vary the proportions $w_i$ ($i = 1, 2, \ldots, n$) to form portfolios it is obvious that there is potentially a large number of such portfolios. We can form asset portfolios consisting of two or three or $n$ assets. We can also form portfolios consisting of a fixed number of assets but in different proportions. All of these possible portfolios are represented by the points on and inside a convex 'egg' (Figure 10.5). These points represent the opportunity set of asset proportions (the $w_i$) of the risky assets. Note that when the number of assets is large then to calculate the variance of the portfolio

# FIGURE 10.5: Efficient frontier (= AB)

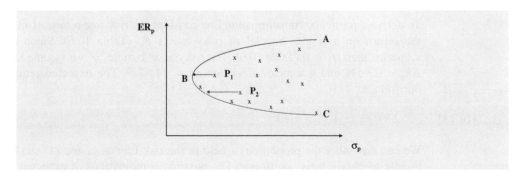

requires statistical estimates of $n$ variances and $n(n-1)/2$ covariances. So for $n = 25$ this amounts to 325 separate estimates. There are 'short cuts' available to reduce the number of statistical estimates required, a popular one being the **single index model (SIM)**. Here each asset return $R_i$ is assumed to vary only with the return on the whole market $R_m$ (e.g. for the US, $R_m$ might be taken as the S&P500 stock index). This linear regression model substantially reduces the computations needed to calculate all the individual variances and covariances—see Appendix 10.1.

If we apply the mean–variance criterion then all of the points in the interior of the **portfolio opportunity set** (e.g. $P_1$, $P_2$ in Figure 10.5) are (mean–variance) dominated by those on the curve ABC since the latter have a lower variance for a given expected return. Points on the curve AB also dominate those on BC, so the curve AB represents the proportions $w_i$ in the **efficient set** of portfolios and is referred to as the **efficient frontier**.

- Each point on the efficient frontier represents one risky asset bundle.
- Each bundle comprises $n$ risky assets held in the fixed proportions $w_i$.

## THE TRANSFORMATION LINE

Let us now take *one* risky bundle (of $n$ assets held in *fixed* proportions $w_i$). For $n = 3$ we might have $w_1 = 20\%$, $w_2 = 25\%$ and $w_3 = 55\%$, which makes up our one risky bundle. Now allow the investor to borrow or lend unlimited amounts at the safe rate of interest $r$. Because $r$ is fixed over the holding period, the variance of the risk free asset is zero, as is its covariance with our own risky bundle. Thus, the investor can:

- invest all of her wealth in the one risky bundle and undertake no lending or borrowing;
- invest less than her total wealth in the single risky bundle and use the remainder to lend at the risk free rate;
- invest more than her total wealth in the risky bundle by borrowing additional funds at the risk free rate. In this case she is said to hold a *levered portfolio*.

The above choices are represented by the *transformation line* which is a relationship between expected return and risk for a portfolio consisting of: one safe asset plus one risky bundle. The transformation line holds for *any* portfolio consisting of these two assets and it turns out that the relationship between expected return and risk (measured by the standard deviation of the 'new' portfolio) is a straight line.

To derive a particular transformation line consider the risk free return $r$ (on say a T-bill) and the return on a single 'bundle' of risky assets $R_q$ (Table 10.6). Since $r = 10\%$ for all scenarios then $\sigma_r = 0$ (Table 10.6). The risky asset bundle '$q$' we assume has a mean return $ER_q = 22.5\%$ and a standard deviation $\sigma_q = 24.87\%$. The expected return on this 'new' portfolio is:

[**10.18**]    $ER_N = xr + (1-x)ER_q$

We can now alter the proportions $x$ held in the risk free asset and $(1-x)$ held in the risky bundle to obtain 'new' portfolios. The possible combinations of expected return $ER_N$ and

## TABLE 10.6: Transformation line

| | Return | |
|---|---|---|
| | T-bill (safe) | Equity (risky) |
| **Mean** | $r = 10\%$ | $r_q = 22.5\%$ |
| **Std. dev.** | $\sigma_r = 0$ | $\sigma_q = 24.87\%$ |

risk $\sigma_N$ on these 'new' portfolios are shown in the last two columns of Table 10.7. This **linear opportunity set** is shown in Figure 10.6 as the transformation line.

The transformation line has an intercept equal to the risk free rate ($r = 10\%$). Here the investor puts *all* her wealth in the safe asset ($x = 1$). When *all* of the investor's own wealth is held in the risky bundle ($x = 0$) then the 'new' portfolio has $ER_N = 22.5\%$ and $\sigma_N = 24.9\%$, these are of course the expected return and standard deviation of the risky bundle ($ER_q$ and $\sigma_q$). This is the 'no borrow/no lend' portfolio.

When $x = 1$ all wealth is invested in the risk free asset and $ER_N = r$ and $\sigma_N = 0$. For $0 < x < 1$ some wealth is lent out at the risk free rate and the remainder is put in the risky asset bundle. When $x = 0$ all her wealth is invested in stocks and $ER_N = ER_q$. For $x < 0$ the agent borrows money at the risk free rate $r$ to invest in the risky assets. For example, when $x = -0.5$ and initial wealth $= \$100$, the individual borrows $50 (at an interest rate $r$) and invests $150 in stocks (i.e. a levered position). From Table 10.7 we see that this gives $ER_N = 28.75\%$ and $\sigma_N = 37.3\%$ and is also shown in Figure 10.6.

## TABLE 10.7: 'New' portfolio: risk free + risky asset

| | Share of wealth in | | 'New' portfolio | |
|---|---|---|---|---|
| **State** | T-bill | Equity | $ER_N$ | $\sigma_N$ |
| | $w_1$ | $w_2$ | | |
| **1** | 1 | 0 | 10% | 0% |
| **2** | 0.5 | 0.5 | 16.25% | 12.44% |
| **3** | 0 | 1 | 22.5% | 24.87% |
| **4** | −0.5 | 1.5 | 28.75% | 37.31% |

## FIGURE 10.6: Transformation line: (1 riskless + 1 risky asset)

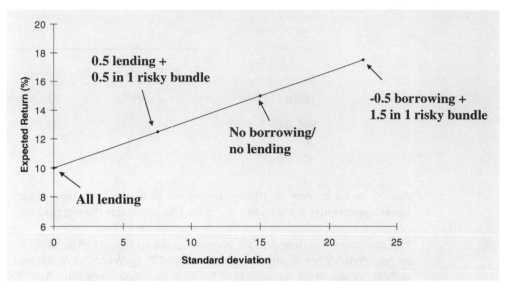

The transformation line gives us the *linear* risk–return relationship for *any* portfolio consisting of a combination of investment in one safe asset *and* one 'bundle' of risky assets. At *every* point on a given transformation line the investor holds the risky assets in the *same fixed proportions* $w_i$

All the points (except the intercept) on the transformation line represent a combination of $w_i = 20\%$, 25% and 55% in our one risky bundle (of $n = 3$ risky assets, 'alpha', 'beta' and 'gamma'). The only 'quantity' that varies along the transformation line is the proportion held in the *one* risky bundle of assets relative to that held in the *one* safe asset. The investor can borrow or lend and be anywhere along the transformation line. For example, the (0.5, 0.5) point represents 50% in the safe asset and 50% in the single bundle of risky securities. Hence an investor with $100 would hold $50 in the risk free asset and $50 in the one risky bundle made up of (0.2)$50 = $10 in alpha and (0.25)$50 = $12.5 in beta and (0.55)$50 = $27.5 in the gamma securities.

Since $r$ is known and fixed over the holding period then the standard deviation of the 'new' portfolio depends only on the standard deviation of the one risky bundle, and this is why the opportunity set in this case is a straight line. For *any* portfolio consisting of two assets, one of which is a single risky bundle and the other is a safe asset, the relationship between the expected return on this new portfolio $ER_N$ and its standard deviation $\sigma_N$ *is linear* with intercept $= r$. When a portfolio consists only of $n$ *risky* assets then, as we have seen, the efficient frontier in $(ER_p, \sigma_p)$ space is curved. This should not be unduly confusing since the portfolios considered in the two cases are very different.

If we choose a single risky bundle '$k$' with $\sigma_k = 30\%$ and $ER_k = 15\%$ then we can draw the corresponding transformation line $rL$ (Figure 10.7). Similarly for our original single risky bundle $\sigma_q = 25\%$ ($ER_q = 22.5\%$) we have a higher transformation line $rL$. Hence each single risky bundle (each with different fixed weights $w_i$) has its *own* transformation line.

## FIGURE 10.7: Transformation lines: (1 safe + risky 'bundles')

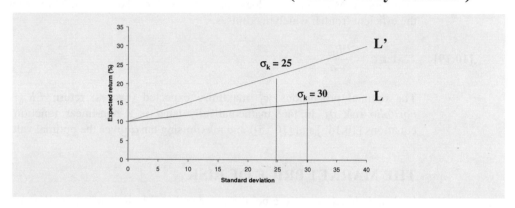

## THE MARKET PORTFOLIO AND THE CML

Although an investor can attain any point along $rL$ in Figure 10.7, *any* investor (regardless of her preferences) would prefer to be on the transformation line $rL'$. This is because at any point on $rL'$ the investor has a greater expected return for any given level of risk compared with points on $rL$. The 'highest' transformation line that is tangent to the efficient frontier provides the investor with the highest possible return per unit of risk. Point M in Figure 10.8 represents a 'bundle' of $n$ risky assets held in certain *fixed* proportions ($w_i$). In our simple model with only two risky assets these optimal proportions at M are seen to be $w_1 = 0.5$ and $w_2 = 0.5$ (Figure 10.8). M is always a single bundle of stocks held in fixed proportions, by *all* investors. Hence point M is known as the **market portfolio** and $rL'$ is known as the **capital market line, CML**.

## FIGURE 10.8: Efficient frontier and CML

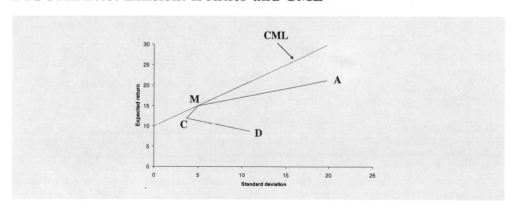

> **The CML is therefore the transformation line which is tangential to the efficient frontier**

When we have many risky assets the efficient frontier is a smooth curve (Figure 10.9) and the market portfolio M represents the optimal proportions $w_i^*$ of the risky assets held by all investors. At M the investor does not borrow or lend. Notice that M represents that point on the efficient frontier which maximises:

[10.19]     $$\tan \alpha = \frac{ER_m - r}{\sigma_m}$$

The optimal proportions $w_i^*$ maximise expected (excess) return $ER_m - r$ per unit of *portfolio* risk $\sigma_p$. In fact mathematically $\tan \alpha$ is a non-linear function of the $w_i$ (see equations [10.14b] and [10.15]) and maximising $\tan \alpha$ gives the optimal values for the $w_i$.

## THE MARKET PRICE OF RISK

If all individuals are at the point represented by M, then they can all earn the **same** excess return per unit of risk. The *market price of risk* (derived in Appendix 10.2) is given by:

[10.20]     $$\lambda_m = \frac{ER_m - r}{\sigma_m}$$

If every investor had homogeneous expectations then $\lambda_m$ would be the same for all investors. However, if investors have heterogeneous expectations then this ratio can be different for each investor. This would break one of the assumptions underlying the CAPM, but allows us to use the ***Sharpe ratio*** as a measure of the relative performance of different investors. If an investor holds *any portfolio 'p'* of stocks composed of a *subset* of the assets of the market portfolio then the Sharpe ratio is:

---

## FIGURE 10.9: CML and market portfolio (M)

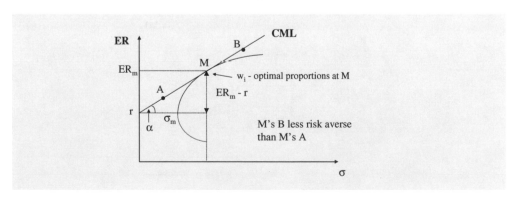

**[10.21]**     $S = (ER_p - r)/\sigma_p$

The higher is $S$, the higher is the expected (excess) return $ER_p - r$ per unit risk (i.e. the portfolio standard deviation $\sigma_p$). Thus for two investment managers, the one whose portfolio has a higher Sharpe ratio, may be deemed the more successful in trading off return against risk. The Sharpe ratio is therefore a type of **performance index** which can be used to rank the relative success of different investment managers or investment strategies.

## ONE SAFE ASSET PLUS ONE RISKY ASSET BUNDLE

If we now allow investors to borrow or lend then they will 'mix' the risk free asset with the risky bundle represented by M, to get to their preferred position along the CML. Hence investors' preferences determine at which point along the CML each *individual* investor ends up. For example an investor with little or no aversion to risk would end up at a point like B (Figure 10.9). She borrows money (at $r$) to augment her own wealth and then invests the borrowed money and all her own wealth in the risky bundle represented by M (but she still holds *all* her $n$ risky assets in the fixed proportions $w_i^*$).

## SEPARATION PRINCIPLE

The investor makes two separate decisions.

(i) Knowledge of expected returns, variances and covariances determines the efficient frontier. The investor then determines point M as the *point of tangency* of the line from $r$ to the efficient frontier. All this is accomplished without any recourse to the individual's preferences. *All* investors, regardless of preferences (but with the same view about expected returns, etc.) will 'home in' on the portfolio proportions $w_i^*$ of the risky securities represented by M. All investors hold the *market portfolio*, or more correctly all investors hold their $n$ risky assets in the same proportions as their relative value in the market. Thus if the value of ICI shares constitutes 10% of the total stock market valuation then each investor holds 10% of her own risky portfolio in ICI shares.

(ii) The investor now determines how she will combine the market portfolio (consisting of a bundle of $n$ risky assets) with the safe asset. This decision does depend on her subjective risk–return preferences. At a point such as A (Figure 10.10) the *individual* investor is reasonably risk averse and holds most of her wealth in the safe asset, putting only a little into the market portfolio (in the fixed optimal proportions $w_i^*$). In contrast, M's B is less risk averse than M's A and ends up at B (to the right of M), with a levered portfolio (i.e. she borrows to increase her holding in the market portfolio, in excess of her own initial wealth). An investor who ends up at M is moderately risk averse, and puts all of her wealth into the market portfolio and neither borrows nor lends at the risk free rate.

## ASSET ALLOCATION

It should now be clear how portfolio theory can be used to determine the optimal asset allocation strategy for *any* investor. The portfolio manager first agrees with the client on the likely future outcomes for expected returns $ER_i$, variances $\sigma_i$ and covariances $\sigma_{ij}$ (or $\rho_{ij}$).

## FIGURE 10.10: Preferences of M's A and M's B

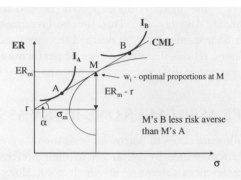

These are likely to be based on historic values plus 'hunches' about particular markets. The analysis might initially be applied only to the **industry asset allocation** problem, namely the optimal proportions to 'place' in the major domestic industries (e.g. chemicals, engineering, services, electrical). The efficient frontier is constructed and if the client doesn't wish to borrow or lend, the analyst can suggest alternative risk–return combinations available. The client will choose one of these (e.g. minimum variance point) based on her risk–return preferences. However, if the client is willing to borrow or lend then she can increase her 'opportunity set' by moving up and down the CML. The optimal asset allocation is then given by her market portfolio M (and proportions $w_i^*$) and the lending–borrowing decision then depends on her degree of risk aversion.

Although mean–variance portfolio theory is one of the cornerstones of modern finance, it is debatable how important it is in practical asset allocation in large investment houses. There are a whole host of issues to consider when moving from theory to practice, and some of these are discussed in Chapter 18. However, at this point it is worth looking at the asset allocation decisions actually made by large investment houses. These are outlined in Box 10.1.

## Box 10.1    ASSET ALLOCATION IN PRACTICE

*The Economist's* **quarterly portfolio poll** of large investment houses for third quarter 1999 shows an average equity holding of 54%, bond holdings of 42% and only 4% held in cash (Table B10.1). Although most of the major stock markets around the world had experienced a very long bull market in equities, the low proportion of cash held (at 4%) indicates that investors were not expecting the 'global equity bubble' to burst in the near future. There was no 'flight to cash'.

All of the banks, except Daiwa, held broadly similar proportions of **equities** lying between 45% and 55% of their total portfolios. Compared to the previous quarter, Daiwa increased its share in equities by over 5% points and held 70% in equities at the end of 1999. Although Daiwa increased its overall share in equities, it did redistribute its equity portfolio away from the US (reducing its US share by over 5% points to 45%) and towards Britain and the euro area. Several other investment houses (i.e. Robeco Group, Commerz Int. and Standard Life) also reduced their equity holdings in the US. Clearly, there appears to have been a fairly widespread view that the US stock market might have been subject to 'irrational over-exuberance' in the past and that a 'correction' was imminent. Hence the move into European equities.

Turning now to **bond holdings**. The average holding in the US (at 48%) is much higher than the 'neutral position' (as represented by the proportions held in the Salomon Bros World Government Bond Index). In contrast, the average bond holdings in yen at 11% are 'underweight' (i.e. less than the 24% held in yen in the Salomon Bros Index). Several houses increased the share held in bonds in the euro zone by more than 5% points (compared with the previous quarter) and all but Credit Suisse were overweight in bonds in the euro zone.

These figures show that market participants do not have **homogeneous views** about risk and return (as assumed by the theory) since their asset proportions differ. Considerations other than historic measures of expected return, variances and covariances undoubtedly influence asset allocation decisions. Investment houses 'look forward' and their estimates of these inputs depend on future government policies and the uncertainties surrounding the implementation of these policies. They may also be more worried by possible downside outcomes than an equal upside potential, as witnessed in 'flights to quality' when the outlook is very uncertain (e.g. after the Asia crisis of 1997/8 there was a move to investments in 'quality' G7 countries).

In fact, portfolio theory is still applicable no matter how investors form their forecasts of expected returns, variances and covariances, as long as only the latter influence the investment decision. Portfolio theory can also accommodate many other 'real world' issues, such as not being allowed to change asset proportions by more than (say) 2% in any one month, or not being allowed to short sell, or undertaking a sensitivity analysis of the portfolio allocation decision. These and other issues are discussed further in Chapter 18.

## 10.3 CAPITAL ASSET PRICING MODEL

The capital asset pricing model CAPM is a logical consequence of mean−variance portfolio theory. It provides an equation to determine the return required by investors to willingly hold any particular risky asset:

[10.22]

**Required return on asset-$i$ = risk free rate + risk premium**

$$ER_i = r + \beta_i(ER_m - r)$$

where $\beta_i$ is the asset's beta (see below). Let us see how the CAPM arises from portfolio theory. In order that the efficient frontier be the same for *all* investors they must have

## TABLE B10.1: International asset allocation

| | Holding by instruments (%) | | |
| --- | --- | --- | --- |
| | Equities | Bonds | Cash |
| **Robeco Group** | 45 | 55 | 0 |
| **Julius Baer** | 50(−) | 45(+) | 5 |
| **Commerz Int.** | 53(−) | 47(+) | 0 |
| **Credit Suisse** | 50 | 47 | 3 |
| **Lehman Bros** | 55 | 45 | 0 |
| **Standard Life** | 55 | 37(−−) | 8(++) |
| **Daiwa** | 70(++) | 20 | 10(−−) |
| **Average** | **54** | **42** | **4** |

*continued overleaf*

**TABLE B10.1: (Continued)**

| | United States | Other Americas | Britain | Germany | France | Other Europe | Japan | Other Asia |
|---|---|---|---|---|---|---|---|---|
| | | | | | Equity holding by area (%) | | | |
| Robeco Group | 48(−) | 1 | 12(+) | 5 | 4 | 12 | 13 | 5(−) |
| Julius Baer | 50 | 0 | 6 | 6 | 5 | 16 | 14 | 3 |
| Commerz Int. | 45(−) | 0 | 7(+) | 7 | 6(−) | 16(−−) | 16(++) | 3(+) |
| Credit Suisse | 44 | 0 | 8 | 8 | 4 | 14 | 18 | 4 |
| Lehman Bros | 45 | 2 | 14 | 8 | 7(+) | 16(−) | 6(+) | 2 |
| Standard Life | 50(−) | 2(−) | 14 | 4(−) | 4 | 12(+) | 13(+) | 1 |
| Daiwa | 45(−−) | 0(−) | 10(+) | 7(+) | 6(+) | 12(+) | 15 | 5(−) |
| Average | 47 | 1 | 10 | 7 | 6 | 12 | 14 | 3 |
| Neutral* | 50 | 2 | 10 | 5 | 5 | 13 | 14 | 1 |

*continued overleaf*

303

**TABLE B10.1:** (*Continued*)

| | Bond holding by currency (%) | | | | |
|---|---|---|---|---|---|
| | Dollar | Yen | Sterling | Euro zone | Other |
| **Robeco Group** | 42(++) | 3(--) | 4(--) | 28(++) | 23(+) |
| **Julius Baer** | 79(--) | 0 | 0 | 14(++) | 7 |
| **Commerz Int.** | 34(-) | 18(+) | 4(-) | 42(++) | 2(-) |
| **Credit Suisse** | 96 | 0 | 4 | 0 | 0 |
| **Lehman Bros** | 33 | 12 | 5 | 46 | 4 |
| **Standard Life** | 28(-) | 20(+) | 9(+) | 37(-) | 6(+) |
| **Daiwa** | 23(--) | 24(-) | 5(+) | 42(++) | 6(-) |
| **Average** | **48** | **11** | **4** | **30** | **7** |
| **Neutral\*** | **28** | **24** | **6** | **37** | **5** |

Notes: Figures are for third quarter 1999
(++) indicates a change of more than +5% points on last quarter
(+) indicates a change of less than +5% points on last quarter
(--) indicates a change of more than −5% points on last quarter
(−) indicates a change on less than −5% points on last quarter
\* Neutral position equities = proportions as held in Morgan Stanley Capital International, World Equity Index
\* Neutral position bonds = proportions as held in Salomon Bros, World Government Bond Index
Source: *The Economist*, 9th October 1999, p. 132. © The Economist Newspaper Limited, London. Reproduced with permission.

homogeneous expectations about the underlying market variables $ER_i$, $\sigma_i^2$ and $\sigma_{ij}$. Hence with homogeneous expectations *all* investors hold *all* the risky assets in the proportions given by point M, the market portfolio. The assumption of homogeneous expectations is crucial in producing a **market equilibrium** where all risky assets are willingly held in the optimal proportions $w_i^*$ given by M or, in other words, in producing *market clearing*.

Because all $n$ assets are held at M, there is also a set of equilibrium expected returns $ER_i$ (for the $n$ assets) corresponding to point M. The equation representing the equilibrium returns for asset-*i* takes account of the fact that, when held as part of a portfolio, asset-*i* might reduce the risk of the overall portfolio (i.e. low or negative covariances again), hence:

> **The riskiness of asset-*i*, when *considered as part of a diversified portfolio*, is not its own variance $\sigma_i^2$ but the covariance between $R_i$ and the market return $R_m$**

More formally, the CAPM (embodied in point M in Figure 10.10) gives the risk adjusted equilibrium return on asset-*i* as:

[10.23]
$$ER_i - r = \beta_i(ER_m - r) \quad \text{where} \quad \beta_i = \text{Cov}(R_i, R_m)/\sigma_m^2$$

It therefore provides an explicit form for the risk premium, namely $rp_i = \beta_i(ER_m - r)$. An estimate of an asset's beta can be obtained using a time series regression. For example the monthly return on asset-*i*, over say the last 5 years (in excess of the risk free rate) is regressed on the monthly excess return on the market $(ER_m - r)$ and the slope gives a measure of $\beta_i$. In practice some aggregate stock index such as the S&P500 or the FT Actuaries Index is used as a measure of the return on the market portfolio, $ER_m$. As we see in the next chapter, the risk adjusted discount rate for firm-*i* used in capital budgeting is often taken to be $ER_i$ (for an all equity financed firm). It can be calculated once we have estimated $\beta_i$ and formed a view about the likely values of $ER_m$ and $r$.

The CAPM must not be confused with the single index model SIM, $R_{it} = \theta_i + \delta_1 I_t + \varepsilon_{it}$ (see Appendix 10.1) which is merely a *statistical relationship* between $R_{it}$ and an 'index' $I_t$, which could be the market return or some other variable (e.g. the dividend–price ratio). Hence, $I_t$ could be any variable which is found to be *correlated* with $R_{it}$. The SIM embodies no specific theoretical model to explain this observed correlation. Clearly, the equation for the SIM and the CAPM equation [10.23] do differ, because the former incorporates the risk free rate $r$ and has a zero intercept term. However, in some of the literature the CAPM and SIM are often treated as equivalent (which they are not), and the reader should be aware of this.

## BETA AND SYSTEMATIC RISK

The CAPM predicts that only the covariance of returns between asset-*i* and the market portfolio influences the excess return on asset-*i*. No additional variables such as the dividend-price ratio, or the size of the firm or the price–earnings ratio should influence expected excess returns. All changes in the portfolio risk of asset-$i$ are summed up in its beta. The beta of a security represents that part of the risk that cannot be diversified away, hence:

> **Beta represents an asset's systematic (market or non-diversifiable) risk**

An individual investor may choose not to use the full mean–variance optimisation procedure. However, 'beta' may still be a useful practical metric. For example, if an investor requires a portfolio with a specific beta (e.g. 'aggressive portfolio' with $\beta_p > 1$) then this can be easily constructed by combining securities with different betas in different proportions (with $\sum w_i = 1$):

[10.24] $\qquad \beta_p = \sum w_i \beta_i$

Of course, the weights $w_i$ would then be arbitrary and would not represent the optimal weights given by our mean–variance theory.

## SECURITY MARKET LINE

The CAPM can be 'rearranged' and expressed in terms of the security market line SML. Suppose that the average historic value of $(ER_m - r)$ is 8% p.a. and the risk free rate is 5%, then the CAPM becomes:

[10.25] $\qquad ER_i = 5 + 8\beta_i$

This is a linear relationship between $ER_i$ and $\beta_i$ (Figure 10.11) and is known as the **security market line, SML**.

## FIGURE 10.11: Security market line (SML)

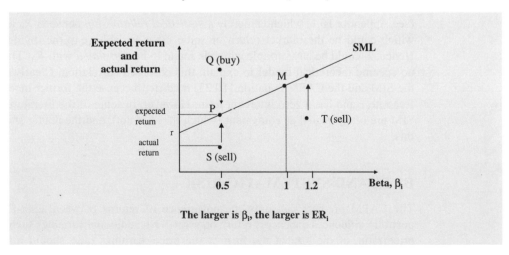

The larger is $\beta_i$, the larger is $ER_i$

> **The SML relates the average return $ER_i$ on security $i$ with its beta-$\beta_i$.**
> **If the CAPM is correct then all securities should lie on the SML**

According to the CAPM/SML the average monthly return (say over the last year) on each asset $ER_i$ should be proportional to that asset's beta, $\beta_i$. Given the definition of $\beta_i$ in equation [10.23] we see that the market portfolio M has a beta of 1, since $\text{Cov}(R_i, R_m) = 1$ if asset-$i$ is the market portfolio. If a security has $\beta_i = 0$ then it will earn a return equal to the risk free rate. The SML indicates that a security with a high beta has a high risk and therefore should earn a high average return, or mathematically:

[10.26]
$$\frac{\text{Excess return on security } i}{\text{Excess return on security } j} = \frac{(ER_i - r)}{(ER_j - r)} = \frac{\beta_i}{\beta_j}$$

The SML can be used to try to pick underpriced and overpriced stocks. To see this consider a security S (Figure 10.11) with a beta of 0.5. You could duplicate the beta of security S by buying a portfolio with 50% in the safe asset and 50% in a security with a beta of unity. But this synthetic portfolio would lie on the SML (e.g. at P), have a higher expected return and hence would dominate S. Hence S would be sold, since its actual return is less than its equilibrium return given by the SML. If S were sold its current price would fall and this would raise its expected return, so that S moved towards P. (Similarly, a security T with $\beta_i = 1.2$ could be duplicated by borrowing 20% of your wealth at the safe rate and using your own funds plus borrowed funds to invest in a security with $\beta_i = 1$.)

Alternatively, a security like Q currently has a higher average return given its $\beta$ of 0.5, than is indicated by the SML. An investor should purchase Q. Securities like Q and S are currently mispriced (i.e. they are not on the SML). A speculator might purchase Q and short sell S in order to make an expected capital gain on Q and S. (i.e. purchase S at a lower price in the future). To implement an active switching strategy one has to graph the average historic return on a set of securities $\bar{R}_i$ (say monthly returns averaged over the past year) against their estimates of $\beta_i$ and look for 'outlier securities' like Q and S. This investment strategy is risky since it assumes the CAPM is true and that any mispricing will be corrected over a reasonably short time horizon.

# 10.4 PERFORMANCE MEASURES

The CAPM predicts that the excess return on any stock adjusted for the risk on that stock $\beta_i$ should be the same for all stocks (and all portfolios). Algebraically this may be expressed as:

[10.27]
$$(ER_i - r)/\beta_i = (ER_j - r)/\beta_j = \ldots$$

Equation [10.27] applies of course, under the somewhat restrictive assumptions of the standard CAPM which include:

- all agents have homogeneous expectations;
- agents minimise the standard deviation of the portfolio subject to a given expected return;
- agents can borrow or lend unlimited amounts at the riskless rate;
- the market is in equilibrium at all times.

In the real world however, it is possible that over short periods the market is not in equilibrium and profitable opportunities arise. This is more likely to be the case either if agents have divergent expectations, or if they take time to learn about a new environment which affects the returns on stocks of a particular company, or if there are some agents who base their investment decisions on what they perceive are 'trends' in the market. As we shall see in future chapters, if there is a large enough group of agents who 'follow trends' then the rational agents (smart money) will have to take account of the movements in stock prices produced by these 'trend followers' or noise traders (as they are often called in the academic literature).

It would be useful if we could assess actual investment performance against some overall index of performance. Such an index would have to measure the actual returns of traders relative to some equilibrium risk–return relationship. A trader who consistently turns in a higher *return* than all other traders is not necessarily 'the best' trader, since his portfolio might carry a higher level of risk than that borne by other traders. Hence, any performance index has to consider the return *relative to* the risk of the portfolio and then rank alternative portfolios accordingly.

One area where a performance index would be useful is in ranking the performance of specific mutual funds. A mutual fund allows the managers of that fund to invest in a wide portfolio of securities. Put to one side for the moment, the difference in transactions costs of the individual versus the mutual fund manager (who buys and sells in large quantities and may reap economies of scale). What one might wish to know is whether the mutual fund manager provides a 'better return' than is provided by a random selection of stocks by the individual. It may also be the case that whatever performance index we choose, it may itself be useful in predicting the **future performance** of a particular mutual fund. Any chief executive or group manager of a mutual fund will wish to know whether his subordinates are investing wisely. Again, a performance index ought to be able to tell us whether some investment fund managers are either doing better than other managers or better than a policy of mere random selection of stocks. The indices we will look at are known as the Sharpe, Treynor and Jensen performance indices.

## SHARPE'S PERFORMANCE INDEX

The index suggested by Sharpe is a *reward to variability ratio* and is defined for portfolio-$i$ as:

[10.28] $$S_i = \frac{ER_i - r}{\sigma_i}$$

where $ER_i$ is the expected return on portfolio $i$, $\sigma_i$ is the standard deviation of portfolio $i$, $r$ is the risk free rate. Sharpe's index measures the slope of the transformation line and can be calculated for any portfolio using historic data. Over a run of (say) monthly periods we can work out the average ex-post return and the standard deviation on the portfolio, held by the mutual fund manager. We can also do the same for a portfolio of stocks which has been randomly selected. The mutual fund manager will be outperforming the random selection strategy providing his value of $S_i$ is greater than that given by the randomly selected portfolio. The reason for this is that the mutual fund portfolio will then have a transformation line with a higher slope than that given by the randomly selected portfolio. It follows that any investor could end up with a higher level of expected utility if he mixed the portfolio of the mutual fund manager with the riskless asset. Underlying the use of Sharpe's performance index are the following assumptions:

- Investors hold only one risky portfolio (either the mutual fund or a randomly selected portfolio) together with the risk free asset.
- Investors are risk averse and returns are normally distributed (the latter assumption is required if we are to use the mean–variance framework).

## TREYNOR'S PERFORMANCE INDEX

When discussing Sharpe's performance index we assumed that individual investors hold only the riskless asset and a single portfolio of risky assets. Treynor's performance index assumes that the individual investor has a choice between the mutual fund or another portfolio of risky assets. Treynor's index is given by:

[10.29]
$$T_i = \frac{ER_i - r}{\beta_i}$$

It is therefore a measure of excess return per unit of risk, but this time the risk is measured by the beta of the portfolio. The Treynor index comes directly from the CAPM which may be written as:

[10.30]
$$\frac{ER_i - r}{\beta_i} = ER_m - r$$

Under the CAPM the value of $T_i$ should be the same for all portfolios of securities when the market is in equilibrium. It follows that if the mutual fund manager invests in a portfolio where the value of $T_i$ exceeds the excess return on the market portfolio he will be earning an abnormal return relative to that given by the CAPM. We can calculate the sample value of the excess return on the *market* portfolio given by the right-hand side of equation [10.30]. We can also estimate $\beta_i$ for any given portfolio using a time series regression of $(R_i - r)_t$ on $(R_m - r)_t$. Then given the fund manager's historic average excess return $(ER_i - r)$ we can compute all the elements of equation [10.30]. The fund manager outperforms the market if his particular portfolio (denoted $i$) has a value of $T_i$ which exceeds the average return on the market portfolio. Values of $T_i$ can be used to rank individual investment manager's portfolios. There are difficulties in interpreting the Treynor index if $\beta_i < 0$, but this is uncommon in practice.

## JENSEN'S PERFORMANCE INDEX

Jensen's performance index also assumes that investors can hold either the mutual fund denoted $i$ or a well-diversified portfolio such as the market portfolio. Jensen's index is given by the intercept $J_i$ in the following regression:

[10.31]    $E_t R_{it+1} - r_t = J_i + \beta_i (E_t R_{\mathrm{m}t+1} - r_t)$

To run regression we need time series data on the expected excess return on the market portfolio and the expected excess return on portfolio-$i$ chosen by the mutual fund manager. We then obtain estimates for $J_i$ and $\beta_i$. In practice, one replaces the expected return variables by the actual return (by invoking the rational expectations assumption—see Chapter 5). It is immediately apparent from equation [10.31] that if $J_i = 0$ then we have the standard CAPM. Hence, mutual fund-$i$ earns a return in excess of that given by the CAPM if $J_i$ is greater than zero. For $J_i$ less than zero, the mutual fund manager has underperformed relative to the risk adjusted rate of return given by the CAPM. Hence Jensen's index actually measures the *abnormal return* on the portfolio of the mutual fund manager (i.e. a return different from that given by the CAPM).

## COMPARING TREYNOR AND JENSEN PERFORMANCE MEASURES

We can rearrange equation [10.31] as follows:

[10.32]    $\dfrac{ER_i - r}{\beta_i} = \dfrac{J_i}{\beta_i} + (E_t R_{\mathrm{m}t+1} - r_t)$

The left-hand side of equation [10.32] is simply Treynor's index $T_i$. If beta is positive (which it is for most portfolios) then it is easy to see that when $T_i > 0$ then $J_i$ is greater than zero. Hence 'success' using the Treynor index also implies 'success' on Jensen's index. However, it may be shown that when ranking two mutual funds say X and Y, by these indices, then they can give different inferences. That is to say a higher value of $T_i$ for fund Y over fund X may be consistent with a value of $J_i$ for fund Y which is less than that for fund X. Hence, the relative performance of two mutual funds depends on the index chosen. In Chapter 13 we use the above indices to rank alternative portfolios based on a particular 'passive' and a particular 'active' investment strategy. This allows us to ascertain whether the active strategy outperforms a 'buy-and-hold' strategy.

## PERFORMANCE OF MUTUAL FUNDS

There have been a large number of studies of mutual fund performance using the above three indices. Most studies have found that fund managers are unable to systematically beat the market and hence they do not outperform an unmanaged (yet diversified) portfolio, such as the S&P index. Shawky (1982) examines the performance of 255 mutual funds covering the period 1973–77. First he finds that the same ranking is obtained for all three indices. This is because there is a very strong correlation between the $\sigma_i$ and $\beta_i$ for each portfolio.

On calculating Jensen's performance index, Shawky found that it was significantly different from zero in only 25 out of the 255 mutual funds studied, and of these, 16 had negative values of $J_i$ and only nine had positive values. Thus, out of more than 250 mutual funds only nine outperformed an unmanaged diversified portfolio such as the S&P index. Using Sharpe's index, between 15 and 20% of mutual funds outperformed an unmanaged portfolio, while for Treynor's index the figure was slightly higher, with around 33% outperforming the unmanaged portfolio. Hence, although there are *some* mutual funds which outperform an unmanaged portfolio, there are not many.

Given the above evidence, there seems to be something of a paradox in that 'managed funds' are highly popular, and their growth in Western developed nations throughout the 1970 to 2000 period has been substantial. While it is true that 'managed' funds on average do not outperform the 'unmanaged' S&P index, nevertheless, they do outperform almost any unmanaged portfolio consisting of only a small number of shares. Relatively high transactions costs for small investors often imply that investing in the S&P index is not a viable alternative, and hence they purchase mutual funds. The key results to emerge from this section are:

- Sharpe's reward-to-variability index is an appropriate performance measure when the investor holds mutual fund shares plus a riskless asset.
- Treynor's and Jensen's performance indices are appropriate when the investor is assumed to diversify his portfolio and holds both mutual fund shares, together with many other risky assets and the riskless asset.

# 10.5 THE ARBITRAGE PRICING THEORY

For most people, the arbitrage pricing theory APT is a little difficult to grasp as its derivation is not as intuitively appealing as the CAPM. The APT is a multifactor model since, unlike the CAPM, it allows a number of potential variables (factors) to influence the expected return on asset-$i$, whereas the CAPM has only one factor, namely the asset's beta. Broadly speaking the APT allows the *actual return* $R_{it}$ on asset-$i$ to be influenced by a number of marketwide variables or 'factors', such as interest rates, the exchange rate, etc. The sensitivity of the return on asset-$i$ to each of these factors is known as the 'factor betas' $b_{ij}$ so we have:

[**10.33**] $$R_{it} = a_i + \sum_{i=1}^{k} b_{ij} F_{jt} + \varepsilon_{it}$$

where $F_j$ is the $j$th factor (variable), $b_{ij}$ is the factor's beta, $\varepsilon_{it}$ is a random error. These factor betas are of course conceptually different from 'the beta' in the CAPM. Using a relatively sophisticated proof based on risk free arbitrage, it is possible to show (see Appendix 10.3) that equation [10.33] gives an explicit expression for the *equilibrium return* $ER_{it}$ on an asset:

[**10.34**] $$ER_i = \lambda_0 + \lambda_1 b_{i1} + \lambda_2 b_{i2} + \ldots + \lambda_k b_{ik}$$

Equation [10.33] is similar to the CAPM equation if we assume there is only a single factor which is the excess return on the market portfolio. Similarly, equation [10.34] is the APT equivalent of the SML of the CAPM, since it shows that the equilibrium return depends on a set of (factor) betas.

Note that in the APT a particular factor can influence *actual* returns but that does not necessarily imply it has an effect on *equilibrium* returns (i.e. its $\lambda$ value may be zero—see below). If a factor does not influence equilibrium returns, the factor is said to be 'not priced'. Assume we have three factors, inflation, interest rates and output, with only two factors influencing equilibrium returns (i.e. only inflation and interest rates are priced):

[10.35] $\qquad R_{it} = a_1 + b_{i1}F_{1t} + b_{i2}F_{2t} + b_{i3}F_{3t} + \varepsilon_{it}$

[10.36] $\qquad ER_i = \lambda_0 + \lambda_1 b_{i1} + \lambda_2 b_{i2}$

where $\quad R_{it}$ is the actual return on stock-$i$ $\qquad ER_i$ is the equilibrium return on stock-$i$
$\qquad\qquad b_{ij}$ are the 'risk' factor weights $\qquad\quad F_{1t}$ is the change in inflation
$\qquad\qquad F_{2t}$ is the change in interest rates $\qquad F_{3t}$ is the change in output

Strictly, the factors $F_{it}$ are unexpected events or 'surprises'. In practice, the change in a variable is often deemed to be unforecastable and is taken as a measure of an unexpected event. Notice that the APT implies that the $\lambda$'s are the same for all stocks (but the $b_{ij}$ differ). The theory therefore assumes that stocks with the same sensitivity to economic factors (i.e. same $b_{ij}$'s) will offer the same equilibrium return. This is because the factors that are 'priced' give rise to 'risk' that cannot be diversified away and therefore must influence the risk adjusted (required) return on the stock.

## HEURISTIC DERIVATION OF THE APT

Broadly speaking, the APT implies that the return on a security can be broken down into an expected return and an unexpected or surprise component. For any individual stock this surprise or news component can be further broken down into 'general news' that affects all stocks and 'specific news' that affects only this particular stock. For example, news which affects all stocks might be an unexpected announcement of an increase in interest rates by the Central Bank. News that affects the stocks of a specific industrial sector, for example, might be the invention of a new radar system which might be thought to influence the aerospace industry but not other industries like chemical and service industries. The APT predicts that 'general news' will affect the rate of return on *all* stocks but by different amounts. For example, a 1% unexpected rise in interest rates might affect the return on stocks of a company that was highly leveraged, more than that for a company that was not levered. The APT may be represented as:

[10.37] $\qquad R_{it} = ER_{it} + u_{it}$

where $R_{it}$ is the actual rate of return on the $i$th stock, $ER_{it}$ is the expected return on the $i$th stock and $u_{it}$ is the unexpected, surprise or news element. We can further subdivide the surprise or news element $u_{it}$ into **systematic** or **market risk** ($m_t$), that is risk that affects a large number of stocks each to a greater or lesser degree and **unsystematic** or **idiosyncratic** or **specific risk** ($\varepsilon_{it}$) which specifically affects a single firm or small group of firms:

[10.38] $\qquad u_{it} = m_t + \varepsilon_{it}$

As in the case of the CAPM, we shall find that systematic risk cannot be diversified away because this element of news or new information affects *all* companies. However, as we see below unsystematic or specific risk may be diversified away. In order to make the APT operational we need some idea of what causes systematic risk. News about economy-wide variables is, for example, a government announcement that GDP is higher than expected or a sudden increase in interest rates by the Central Bank. These economy-wide **factors** $F$ (indexed by $j$) may have different effects on different securities and this is reflected in the different values for the coefficients $b_{ij}$ or 'betas' given below:

[10.39]     $$m_t = b_{i1}(F_{1t} - EF_{1t}) + b_{i2}(F_{2t} - EF_{2t}) + \ldots$$

where the expectations operator $E$ applies to information at time $t - 1$ or earlier. For example, if for a particular firm the beta attached to the surprise in interest rates is equal to 0.5, then for every 1% that the interest rate rises above its expected level this would increase the return on security-$i$ by 0.5% (above its expected value). Note that the 'betas' here are *not* the same as the CAPM betas and hence are denoted $b$ rather than $\beta$. A crucial assumption of the APT is that the idiosyncratic or specific risk $\varepsilon_i$ is uncorrelated across different securities, $\text{Cov}(\varepsilon_i, \varepsilon_j) = 0$.

## PORTFOLIO RETURNS

Specific risk can be diversified away by holding a large number of securities. For simplicity, suppose there is only one systematic risk factor, $F_t$, and $n$ securities in the portfolio (held in proportions $x_i$), hence:

[10.40]     $$R_{pt} = \sum_{i=1}^{n} x_i R_{it} = \sum_{i=1}^{n} x_i (ER_{it} + b_i F_t + \varepsilon_{it}) = \sum_{i=1}^{n} x_i ER_{it} + \left( \sum_{i=1}^{n} x_i b_i \right) F_t + \sum_{i=1}^{n} x_i \varepsilon_{it}$$

Thus the return on the portfolio is a weighted average of the expected return *plus* the weighted average of the beta for each security (multiplied by the factor $F$) *plus* a weighted average of the specific risk terms $\varepsilon_i$. If the specific risk is uncorrelated across securities then some of the $\varepsilon_i$ will be positive and some negative, but their weighted sum is likely to be close to zero. In fact, as the number of securities increases the last term on the right-hand side of equation [10.40] will approach zero and the specific risk will have been diversified away. Hence in general the APT predicts that:

> **The 'APT' return on the *portfolio is* made up of the expected returns on the individual securities and the systematic risk as represented by the economy-wide news 'factor' $F$**

It is the possibility of diversifying away the systematic risk that allows one to construct a 'zero risk arbitrage portfolio' (see Appendix 10.3) which then results in the two key equations [10.33] and [10.34] of the APT, one to determine *actual returns* and the other to determine *equilibrium returns*.

## 10.6 SUMMARY

- **Mean–variance (M–V) portfolio theory** gives the **optimal proportions** in which risky assets are held. It assumes all investors have the same view about the 'market determined variables', expected returns, variances and covariances. Since the risky assets are all willingly held, this also gives rise to a model of equilibrium returns for all of the individual assets in the portfolio, and this is known as the CAPM.

- MV portfolio theory predicts that:
  (i) **All investors** hold their risky assets in the same proportions regardless of their preferences for risk versus return. These optimal proportions constitute the market portfolio.
  (ii) **Investors' preferences** enter in the second stage of the decision process, namely the choice between the 'fixed bundle' of risky securities and the risk free asset. The more **risk averse** the individual is, the smaller the proportion of her wealth will be placed in the bundle of risky assets.

- **The CAPM** implies that in equilibrium, the expected excess return on any *single* risky asset $ER_i - r$ is proportional to the excess return on the market portfolio $(ER_m - r)$. The constant of proportionality is the asset's beta, where $\beta_i = \text{Cov}(R_i, R_m)/\sigma_m^2$.

- **Beta** provides a measure of the **risk premium** on an individual security when it is held as part of a diversified portfolio. If **different investors have different views** about market determined variables, then MV portfolio theory can still be used to:
  (i) predict the **'individual's' efficient frontier** and her optimal asset allocation (over risky assets);
  (ii) once the investor's preferences are known, to then determine the **individual's** optimal amount of **borrowing or lending**.

- Strictly speaking the CAPM model of equilibrium returns does not hold, if investors do not have the same expectations about market variables. However, if the agents who are highly active in the market (i.e. are 'on the margin', in the economics jargon) have reasonably homogeneous expectations, then the CAPM may provide a good approximation to the determination of equilibrium returns.
- An alternative model to the CAPM for determining equilibrium returns is the APT. The **key features of the APT** are:

  (i) *actual* returns may depend on a number of marketwide variables or **'factors'** (e.g. interest rates), each of which has its own 'beta';
  (ii) *equilibrium* returns on asset $i$ depend on a weighted average of its **'factor betas'**. These weights $\lambda$ are the same for all assets and are known as **'the price of risk'**.

# END OF CHAPTER EXERCISES

Q1  If you have one risky asset and one riskless (safe) asset, what is meant by the opportunity set? (This particular opportunity set is often referred to as 'the transformation line'.)

Q2  If you have $n$ risky assets, what is meant by the efficient frontier?

Q3  What is the Sharpe ratio and intuitively why would an investor choose asset proportions in such a way as to maximise the Sharpe ratio?

Q4  The returns on a Treasury bill (i.e. safe asset) and on equity (i.e. risky asset) are given below (for four 'states' of the economy):

| | | Return (% p.a.) | |
| --- | --- | --- | --- |
| State of the economy | Prob. (state of economy occurring) | T-bill | Equity |
| 1 | 0.25 | 4 | −10 |
| 2 | 0.25 | 4 | 0 |
| 3 | 0.25 | 4 | 15 |
| 4 | 0.25 | 4 | 50 |

The maturity of the T-bill equals the holding period of 1 year and hence is the risk free asset.

(a) Calculate the expected return $ER$ and the standard deviation $SD$ of the returns on (i) the Treasury bill and (ii) the equity share. (Use $n = 4$ rather than $n - 1 = 3$ when calculating $SD$.)

(b) Calculate the expected return $ER$ and the standard deviation $SD$ of a **portfolio** consisting of the risk free asset and the risky asset (equity), corresponding to the following proportions '$x$' held in each asset:

| Share of | |
| --- | --- |
| T-bill ($x$) | Equity ($1 - x$) |
| 1 | 0 |
| 0.5 | 0.5 |
| 0 | 1 |
| −0.5 | 1.5 |

(c) Plot a graph of the expected return against the standard deviation for each value of '$x$' and indicate on the graph the proportions of each asset held.

(d) What is meant by 'leverage' in the context of this graph? Why do you obtain leverage when $x = -0.5$ and $(1 - x) = 1.5$, if you have 'own funds' of $100?

## Q5

The return from equity-1 (risky asset) and equity-2 (risky asset) depends on the state of the economy:

| | | Rate of return (%) | |
| --- | --- | --- | --- |
| **State of the economy** | **Probability** $p_i$ | **Equity 1** | **Equity 2** |
| 1 | 0.25 | 0 | 35 |
| 2 | 0.25 | 0 | 15 |
| 3 | 0.25 | 7.5 | 10 |
| 4 | 0.25 | 15 | 10 |

(a) Calculate the expected return $ER$ and the standard deviation $\sigma_i$ of the returns on equity-1 and equity-2, and the correlation coefficient between the two returns.

(Note: $ER = \sum_{j=1}^{4} p_j R_j$, for each asset and $\sigma_1 = \sum_{j=1}^{4} p_j (R_j - ER_1)^2$,

$\sigma_{12} = \sum_{j=1}^{4} p_j (R_{1j} - ER_1)(R_{2j} - ER_2)$ and $\rho = \sigma_{12}/\sigma_1\sigma_2$.

(b) Calculate the expected return $ER_p$ and the standard deviation $\sigma_p$ **on a portfolio** of equity-1 and equity-2 (i.e. two risky assets) corresponding to the following proportions $w_i$ held in each asset:

| Share of | |
| --- | --- |
| **Equity-1** $w_1$ | **Equity-2:** $w_2 = (1 - w_1)$ |
| 1 | 0 |
| 0.75 | 0.25 |
| 0.5 | 0.5 |
| 0 | 1 |

(Note: $ER_p = w_1 ER_1 + w_2 ER_2$, and $\sigma_p^2 = w_1^2 \sigma_1^2 + w_2^2 \sigma_2^2 + 2w_1 w_2 \rho \sigma_1 \sigma_2$)

(c) For each portfolio (i.e. combination of $w_1$, $w_2$) plot a graph of the expected return ($ER_p$) against the standard deviation ($SD = \sigma_p$) and indicate on the graph the proportions of each asset held. What is the opportunity set and the efficient frontier?

(d) What is the proportion of each risky asset held in the minimum variance ($SD$) portfolio?

(e) Suppose there is a safe asset (e.g. T-bill) which has a (safe) return of 4%. What are the optimal proportions of the two risky assets (equity-1 and equity-2) any investor would hold? What is meant by 'optimal' here?

(f) How would your answer to (e) change if the rate of return on the risk free asset is 10% rather than 4%?

Assume investors like high (expected) returns but do not like high levels of risk (where we measure risk by the standard deviation of the portfolio of risky assets held). Mathematically, this can be expressed as:

$$U = U(ER_p, \sigma_p)$$

where $U$ = level of satisfaction (or 'utility') and when $ER$ increases so does $U$, but when $\sigma_p$ increases there is a fall in $U$.

(a) Briefly explain what we mean by this investor's 'indifference curve' and what general shape does it have (in an $ER_p$ against $\sigma_p$ graph)?

(b) Draw two indifference curves, one for a very risk averse investor and the other for a person for whom risk is not a major concern.

(c) According to mean–variance portfolio theory how would the portfolio held by the extremely risk averse investor and the not so risk averse investor differ? For example, would one of them hold 70% of a 'high risk' share and 30% of a 'low risk' share, while the other held exactly the opposite *proportions* of these two risky assets?

The CAPM predicts that the equilibrium rate of return on any risky asset-$i$ is given by:

$$ER_i = r + \beta_i (ER_m - r)$$

where $ER_m$ = expected market return, $r$ = risk free rate.

(a) Explain the intuitive logic behind the CAPM relationship. How would you measure beta?

(b) Intuitively, when a risky asset earns less than the risk free return $r$, why would you continue to hold this risky asset?

# APPENDIX 10.1 THE SINGLE INDEX MODEL

This is not really a 'model' in the sense that it embodies any behavioural hypotheses, it is merely a *statistical assumption* that the return on *any* security $R_{it}$ may be adequately represented as a linear function of a single (economic) variable $I_t$ (e.g. inflation):

[A10.1]     $R_{it} = \theta_i + \delta_i I_t + \varepsilon_{it}$

where $\varepsilon_{it}$ is white noise and equation [A10.1] holds for $i = 1, 2, \ldots, m$ securities and for all time periods. If the unexplained element of the return $\varepsilon_{it}$ for any security-$i$ is independent of that for any other security-$j$, we have:

[A10.2]     $\text{Cov}(\varepsilon_{it}, \varepsilon_{jt}) = E(\varepsilon_{it}, \varepsilon_{jt}) = 0 \qquad i \neq j$

and if $I_t$ is independent of $\varepsilon_{it}$:

[A10.3]     $\text{Cov}(I_t, \varepsilon_{it}) = 0 \qquad$ for all $i$ and $t$

Under the above assumptions, unbiased estimates of $(\theta_i, \delta_i)$ for each security (or a portfolio of securities) can be obtained by an OLS regression using equation [A10.1] on time series data for $R_{it}$ and $I_t$. The popularity of the single index model SIM arises from the fact that it considerably reduces the number of parameters (or inputs) used to calculate the mean and variance of a portfolio of $n$ securities and hence to calculate the efficient portfolio. Given our assumptions, it is easy to show that:

[A10.4]     $ER_i = \theta_i + \delta_i EI_t$

[A10.5]     $\sigma_i^2 = \delta_i^2 \sigma_I^2 + \sigma_{\varepsilon_i}^2$

[A10.6]     $\sigma_{ij} = \delta_i \delta_j \sigma_i^2$

For a portfolio of $n$ securities we have:

[A10.7]     $ER_p = \sum_{i=1}^{n} x_i ER_i$

[A10.8]     $\sigma_p^2 = \sum_{i=1}^{n} x_i \sigma_i^2 + \sum_{i=1}^{n} \sum_{j=1}^{n} x_i x_j \sigma_{ij}$

To calculate the optimal proportions, *in general* we require: $n$ expected returns $ER_i$, $n$ variances and $n(n-1)/2$ covariances as 'inputs'. However, if the SIM is a good statistical description of asset returns all we require to calculate $ER_p$ and $\sigma_p$ are the $n$ values of $(\theta_i, \delta_i)$ and one value for each of $EI_t$ and $\sigma_I^2$. (It can be shown that in a well-diversified portfolio terms involving $\sigma_{\varepsilon_i}^2 \to 0$ and hence can be ignored.) Note that to calculate *all* the covariance terms $\sigma_{ij}$ we do not require any *additional* information (see equation [A10.6]) and compared with the general case equation [A10.8] we 'save' on $n(n-1)/2$ calculations: if $n$ is large this is a considerable advantage of the SIM.

> **The SIM considerably reduces the number of inputs required to calculate the expected return and standard deviation of a portfolio of assets**

When the SIM is used in this way the 'single index' $I_t$ is often taken to be the actual (ex-post) return on the *market* portfolio with variance $\sigma_m^2$ (replacing $\sigma_I^2$ above). The *expected value* of the market return $ER_m$ and $\sigma_m$ might then be based on (historic) sample averages over a recent data period. The SIM is not a particularly good representation of expected returns within one country, and in particular the independence assumption $E(\varepsilon_i \varepsilon_j) = 0$ rarely holds in practice. The reason for this is that if $R_i$ for two (or more) securities depends on more than one index then $\varepsilon_i$ and $\varepsilon_j$ will not be uncorrelated. (This is a case of omitted variables bias with a common omitted variable in each equation.) Put another way, it is unlikely that shocks or news which influence returns on firm A do not also influence the returns on firm B. When comparing returns in different countries the SIM has somewhat greater applicability, since macroeconomic shocks (e.g. changes in interest rates) may not be synchronised across countries. Despite its defects, the SIM is quite widely used in practice (see Chapter 12 and Cuthbertson and Nitzsche, 2001).

# APPENDIX 10.2  BETA AND THE MARKET PRICE OF RISK

## BETA AND THE RISK OF THE MARKET PORTFOLIO

The $\beta_i$ of a security can be shown to measure the *relative* impact of security-$i$ on the risk of the *overall* portfolio of stocks $\sigma_m$. We can rearrange the definition of the variance of a portfolio as follows:

[A10.9]
$$\sigma_m^2 = w_1(w_1\sigma_{11} + w_2\sigma_{12} + w_3\sigma_{13} + \ldots + w_n\sigma_{1n})$$
$$+ w_2(w_1\sigma_{21} + w_2\sigma_{22} + w_3\sigma_{23} + \ldots + w_n\sigma_{2n}) + \ldots$$
$$+ w_n(w_1\sigma_{n1} + w_2\sigma_{n2} + \ldots + w_n\sigma_{nn})$$

where we have rewritten $\sigma_i^2$ as $\sigma_{ii}$. If the $w_i$ correspond to those for the market portfolio then we can denote the portfolio variance as $\sigma_m^2$. The contribution of security-2 to the portfolio variance may be interpreted as the bracketed term in the second line of equation [A10.9] which is then 'weighted' by the proportion of security-2 ($w_2$) held in the portfolio. The bracketed term contains the covariance between security-2 with all other securities including itself (i.e. the term $w_2\sigma_{22}$) and each covariance is weighted by the proportion of each asset in the market portfolio. It is easy to show that the term in brackets in the second line of equation [A10.9] is the covariance of security-2 with the return on the market portfolio $R_m$:

[A10.10]
$$\text{Cov}(R_2, R_m) = E\sum_{i=1}^{n} w_i(R_i - ER_i)(R_m - ER_m)$$
$$= w_1\sigma_{21} + w_2\sigma_{22} + w_3\sigma_{32} + \ldots + w_n\sigma_{n2}$$

It is also easy to show that the contribution of security-2 to the risk of the portfolio is given by the above expression since $\partial\sigma_m^2/\partial w_2 = 2\,\text{Cov}(R_2, R_m)$. Hence, in general the variance of the market portfolio may be written:

[A10.11]     $\sigma_{\mathrm{m}}^2 = w_1 \, \mathrm{Cov}(R_1, R_m) + w_2 \, \mathrm{Cov}(R_2, R_m) + \ldots + w_n \, \mathrm{Cov}(R_n, R_m)$

Now, rearranging the expression for the definition of $\beta_i$:

[A10.12]     $\mathrm{Cov}(R_i, R_{\mathrm{m}}) = \beta_i \sigma_{\mathrm{m}}^2$

and substituting equation [A10.12] in equation [A10.11] we have:

[A10.13]     $\displaystyle\sum_{i=1}^{n} w_i \beta_i = 1$

> **The beta of a security therefore measures the *relative*
> impact of security-*i* on the risk of the portfolio of stocks,
> as a proportion of the total variance of the portfolio**

A security with $\beta_i = 0$ when added to the portfolio has zero *additional* proportionate influence on total variance, whereas $\beta_i < 0$ reduces the relative variance of the portfolio. Of course, the greater the amount of security-*i* held (i.e. the larger is the absolute value of $w_i$) the greater is the impact of $\beta_i$ on the total portfolio variance, ceteris paribus. Since an asset with a small value of $\beta_i$ considerably reduces the overall variance of a risky portfolio, it will be willingly held even though the security has a relatively low expected return. All investors are trading off risk, which they dislike, against expected return, which they do like. Assets which reduce overall portfolio risk therefore command relatively low returns but are nevertheless willingly held in equilibrium.

## THE CAPITAL MARKET LINE AND THE MARKET PRICE OF RISK

The capital market line CML, which is tangential at M (see Figure 10.10), has intercept $r$ and slope $(ER_{\mathrm{m}} - r)/\sigma_{\mathrm{m}}$ and hence has the form:

[A10.14]     $ER_{\mathrm{N}} = r + \left[\dfrac{\mu_{\mathrm{m}} - r}{\sigma_{\mathrm{m}}}\right]\sigma_{\mathrm{N}} \equiv r + \left(\dfrac{ER_{\mathrm{m}} - r}{\sigma_{\mathrm{m}}}\right)\sigma_{\mathrm{N}}$

where the slope of CML $= (ER_{\mathrm{m}} - r)/\sigma_{\mathrm{m}}$.

The slope of the CML is often referred to as the **'market price of risk'**. All investors' portfolios lie on the CML and therefore they all face the same market price of risk. The slope of an indifference curve is known as the marginal rate of substitution (MRS). The individual's MRS is the rate at which the individual is willing to take on more risk while being compensated by a higher expected return (so that she just remains equally 'happy')—see Figure 10.2. From Figure 10.10 it is clear that for *both* investors at A and K the MRS (i.e. the *slope* of the indifference curve for either A or K) equals the market price of risk (i.e. slope of the CML), hence:

> **In the CAPM, *all* investors have the same trade off between risk and return**

The derivation of the efficient frontier and the market portfolio uses the standard deviation as a measure of risk. When risk is measured in terms of the variance of the portfolio we have:

[A10.15]  $\lambda_m = (\mu_m - r)/\sigma_m^2$

which is also frequently referred to as **the market price of risk**. Since $\sigma_m$ and $\sigma_m^2$ are conceptually very similar, this need not cause undue confusion (see Roll, 1977 for a discussion of the differences in the representation of the CAPM when risk is measured in these two different ways).

# APPENDIX 10.3  FORMAL DERIVATION OF THE ARBITRAGE PRICING THEORY

The 'beauty' of the APT is that it does not require any assumptions about utility theory or that the mean and variance of a portfolio are the only two elements in the investor's objective function. The model is really a mechanism (an algorithm almost) that allows one to derive an expression for the expected return on a security (or a portfolio of securities) based on the idea that *riskless* arbitrage opportunities will be instantaneously eliminated. Not surprisingly the APT does, however, require *some* (arbitrary) assumptions. We assume that agents have homogeneous expectations and that the return $R_{it}$ on *any* stock is *linearly* related to a set of $k$ factors $F_{jt}$:

[A10.16]  $R_{it} = a_i + b_{ij}F_{jt} + \varepsilon_{it}$

where the $b_{ij}$ are known as *factor weights*. Taking expectations of equation [A10.16], assuming $E\varepsilon_{it} = 0$ and subtracting it from itself gives:

[A10.17]  $R_{it} = ER_{it} + b_{ij}(F_{jt} - EF_{jt}) + \varepsilon_{it}$

Equation [A10.17] shows that although each security is affected by all the factors, the impact of any particular $F_k$ depends on the value of $b_{ik}$, and this is different for each security. This is the source of the covariance between return $R_{it}$ on different securities. We assume that we can continue adding factors to equation [A10.17] until the unexplained part of the return $\varepsilon_i$ is such that:

[A10.18]  $E(\varepsilon_i\varepsilon_j) = 0$ for all $i$ and $j$ and all time periods

[A10.19]     $E[\varepsilon_i(F_j - EF_j)] = 0$ for all stocks and factors and all time periods

Respectively, equation [A10.18] and equation [A10.19] state that the **unsystematic** (or specific) risk is uncorrelated across securities and is independent of the factors $F$, that is of *systematic risk*. Note that the factors $F$ are common across *all* securities. Now we perform an 'experiment' where investors form a **zero-beta portfolio** with *zero net investment*. The zero-beta portfolio must satisfy:

[A10.20]     $\displaystyle\sum_{i=1}^{n} x_i b_{ij} = 0$     for all $j = 1, 2, \ldots, k$

and the assumption of zero investment implies:

[A10.21]     $\displaystyle\sum_{i=1}^{n} x_i = 0$

It follows from equation [A10.21] that some $x_i$ are less than zero, that is some stocks are held short and the proceeds invested in other securities. The next part of the argument introduces the arbitrage element. If investors use no 'own funds' and the zero-beta portfolio earns a non-zero expected return, then a risk free profit can be earned by arbitrage. This arbitrage condition places a restriction on the expected return of the portfolio, so using equation [A10.17]:

[A10.22]     $\displaystyle R_{pt} = \sum_{i=1}^{n} x_i R_{it} = \sum_{i=1}^{n} x_i ER_{it} + b_{1p}(F_{1t} - EF_{1t})$

$\displaystyle \qquad\qquad + b_{2p}(F_{2t} - EF_{2t}) + \ldots + \sum_{i=1}^{n} x_i \varepsilon_{it}$

where $b_{1p} = \sum x_i b_{i1}$ etc. is the portfolio beta for the first factor.

Using equation [A10.20] and the assumption that for a large well-diversified portfolio the last term on the RHS of equation [A10.22] approaches zero we have:

[A10.23]     $\displaystyle R_{pt} = \sum_{i=1}^{n} x_i ER_{it} \equiv ER_{pt}$

where the second equality holds *by definition*. Since this artificially constructed portfolio has an *actual* rate of return equal to the expected return, there is zero *variability* in its return and it is therefore riskless. Arbitrage arguments then suggest that this riskless return must be zero:

[A10.24]     $\displaystyle\sum_{i=1}^{n} x_i ER_{it} = 0$

We now have to invoke a proof based on linear algebra. Given the conditions [A10.19],

[A10.20], [A10.21] and [A10.24], which are known as orthogonality conditions, then it may be shown that the expected return on any security-$i$ may be written as a linear combination of the factor weightings $b_{ij}$. For example, for a **two-factor model** we have:

[A10.25]     $$ER_i = \lambda_0 + \lambda_1 b_{i1} + \lambda_2 \beta_{i2}$$

We noted above that $b_{i1}$ and $b_{i2}$ in equation [A10.17] are specific to security-$i$. The expected return on security-$i$ weights these security specific betas by a weight $\lambda_j$ that is *the same for all securities*. Hence $\lambda_j$ may be interpreted as the extra expected return required because of a security's sensitivity to the $j$th factor (e.g. GNP or interest rates).

## IMPLEMENTATION OF THE APT

The APT may be summed up in two equations:

[A10.26]     $$R_{it} = a_i + \sum_{j=1}^{k} b_{ij} F_{jt} + \varepsilon_{it}$$

[A10.27]     $$ER_{it} = \lambda_0 + \sum_{j=1}^{k} b_{ij} \lambda_j$$

The APT may be implemented in the following (stylised) way. A 'first-pass' time series regression of $R_{it}$ on a set of factors $F_{jt}$ (e.g. inflation, GDP growth, interest rates) will yield estimates of $a_i$ and the $b_{i1}$, $b_{i2}$, etc. This can be repeated for $i = 1, 2, \ldots, m$ securities so that we have $m$ values for *each* of the betas, one for each of the different securities. In the 'second-pass' regression the $b_i$ vary over the $m$ securities and are therefore the RHS *variables* in equation [A10.27]. Hence in equation [A10.27] the $b_{ij}$ are the variables which are different across the $m$ securities. The $\lambda_j$ are the same for *all* securities and hence these can be estimated from the cross-section regression [A10.27] of $R_i$ on the $b_{ij}$ (for $i = 1, 2, \ldots, m$).

The above estimation is a two-step procedure. There exists a superior procedure (in principle at least) whereby both equations [A10.26] and [A10.27] are estimated simultaneously. This is known as *factor analysis*. Factor analysis chooses a subset of all the factors $F_j$ so that the covariance between each equation's residuals is (close to) zero (i.e. $E(\varepsilon_i \varepsilon_j) = 0$), which is consistent with the theoretical assumption that the portfolio is fully diversified. One stops adding factors $F_j$ when the next factor adds 'little' additional explanation. Thus we simultaneously estimate the appropriate number of $F_j$'s and their corresponding $b_{ij}$'s. The $\lambda_j$'s are then estimated from the cross section regression equation [A10.27].

There are, however, problems in interpreting the results from factor analysis. First, the signs on the $b_{ij}$'s and $\lambda_j$'s are arbitrary and could be reversed (e.g. a positive $b_{ij}$ and a negative $\lambda_j$ is statistically indistinguishable from a negative $b_{ij}$ and a positive $\lambda_j$). Second, there is a scaling problem in that the results still hold if the $\beta_{ij}$ are doubled and the $\lambda_j$ halved. Finally, if the regressions are repeated on different samples of data there is no guarantee that the same factors will appear in the same order of importance. Thus, the only a priori constraints in the APT model are that some $\lambda_j$ and $b_{ij}$ are (statistically) non-zero: there is not a great deal of economic intuition one can impart to this result.

The reason we have spent a little time, at this point, in discussing the testing of the APT is that although the structure of the model is very general (based on arbitrage arguments plus a few other minimal restrictive assumptions) nevertheless, it is difficult to implement and make operational. As well as the problems of interpretation of the $b_{ij}$ and $\lambda_j$ which we cannot 'sign' a priori (i.e. either could be positive or negative), we might also have problems in that the $b_{ij}$ or $\lambda_j$ may not be constant over time. In general terms, applied work has concentrated on regressions of equation [A10.26] in an effort to isolate a few factors that explain actual returns.

## SUMMARY

The APT model involves some rather subtle arguments and is not easily interpreted at an intuitive level. The main elements are:

- It provides a structure for determining equilibrium returns based on constructing a portfolio that has zero risk (i.e. zero-beta portfolio) and requires no cash investment. Arbitrage arguments imply that such a riskless portfolio has an actual and expected return of zero.
- The above conditions, plus the assumptions of linear factor weightings and a large enough number of securities to give an infinitely small (zero) specific risk, allow orthogonality restrictions to be placed on the parameters of the expected returns equation. These restrictions give rise to an expected returns equation that depends on the factor loadings ($b_{ij}$) and the indices of risk ($\lambda_j$).
- The APT does not rely on any assumptions about utility functions or that agents consider only the mean and variance of prospective portfolios. The APT does, however, require homogeneous expectations.
- The APT contains arbitrary elements when we consider its empirical implementation (e.g. what are the appropriate factors $F_j$? Are the $b_{ij}$ constant over time?) and may be difficult to interpret (e.g. there are no a priori restrictions on the signs of the $b_{ij}$ and $\lambda_j$).
- The CAPM is more restrictive than the APT but it has a more immediate intuitive appeal and is somewhat easier to test in that the 'factor' is more easily 'pinned down' (e.g. in the standard CAPM it is the excess return on the market portfolio).

# CHAPTER 11

# Valuing Firms: Capital Structure and the Cost of Capital

(EVA), but is closely related to an earlier methodology known as residual income and also to the more recently introduced concepts of **economic profit**, the **return on capital (ROC)** and the **risk adjusted return on capital (RAROC)** used by financial intermediaries. The EVA approach can also be used to rank different companies as well as divisions within the same company.

- We show that under certain restrictive conditions a 'high' or 'low' dividend payout has no effect on the value of the firm. This is the **Modigliani–Miller dividend irrelevance proposition**. We examine what determines dividend payout, in practice, and find that firms alter dividends depending on a variety of factors, including personal and corporate tax rates, and they also tend to 'smooth' dividend payments.

Project appraisal implies that a financial manager who wishes to maximise the value of the firm should undertake all those physical investment projects for which the NPV is positive. The overall value of the firm is nothing more than the sum of all the positive NPV investment projects which the firm is currently undertaking (or has firm plans to undertake).

By and large we have sidestepped the issues of how capital projects are financed and the appropriate discount rate to use in the NPV calculation. We can now bring together the individual investor decisions about what stocks to hold and the firm's appropriate choice of discount rate. In the previous chapter, we found that mean–variance portfolio theory provides investors with a method of calculating the optimal amount to place in each risky asset, which so far we have taken to consist of equity (shares). The CAPM provides a measure of the risk adjusted return on equity $ER_i$ required by investors, to willingly hold the equity of a particular firm. If the firm is financing its capital project solely by the issue of new equity, then it seems fairly obvious that the discount rate to use should be the CAPM (or APT) equilibrium required return, $ER_i$. After all, this is the risk adjusted rate of return required by investors. But suppose the financial manager can finance the capital investment project with a mixture of debt (e.g. corporate bonds and bank loans) and equity. Is there an optimal mix of debt and equity which will increase the value of the firm by reducing the overall 'debt plus equity' cost of finance?

This is the so-called **capital structure question**. Modigliani–Miller in a famous paper show that, under certain conditions, the proportion of debt-to-equity finance makes absolutely no difference to the value of the firm. The implication is that a financial manager can finance a project with NPV $> 0$ with any *arbitrary* mix of debt and equity, without affecting the overall value of the firm. However, we still have *to calculate* this overall cost of capital when we have a mix of debt and equity finance: this is known as the **weighted average cost of capital, WACC.** It is the WACC that should be used as the discount factor for a physical investment project, when the project is financed by a mixture of debt and equity.

By the end of this chapter the reader will become aware that there are no easy *practical* solutions to the capital structure question. It is as if we had employed the proverbial two-handed lawyer to adjudicate on the practical results to be drawn from the various theoretical models, namely 'on the one hand ... whilst on the other hand ...'. However, the models do bring out the key elements in the debate.

# 11.1 CAPITAL STRUCTURE

In this section we first look at the relationship between the WACC and the value of the firm, before moving on to examine why shareholders require a higher return on equity the greater is the debt-to-equity ratio. Next we examine the so-called 'traditional view' which suggests that there is a particular level for the debt-to-equity ratio which will maximise the value of the firm. We contrast the 'traditional view' with the Modigliani–Miller model (in the absence of corporate taxes) which, under certain restrictive assumptions, implies that a firm can have any debt-to-equity ratio it likes and this will not affect the value of the firm. In this MM world there is therefore no optimal debt-to-equity ratio. Finally, we introduce corporate taxes into the MM model and find that we obtain a very different conclusion, namely that the optimal level of debt finance is 100%. That is to say, the value of the firm (with taxable profits) reaches a maximum value when the firm has no equity finance but is instead 100% debt financed. Later in the chapter we try and understand whether these diverse results apply in the real world.

The key question we want to analyse in this section is whether it is possible to increase the value of the firm (i.e. shareholder wealth) by increasing leverage (i.e. gearing)—that is, by increasing the proportion of debt relative to equity finance. First, we need to know how we measure the value of the firm. This is determined by the present value PV of the earnings of the firm. A reasonable assumption to make is that a firm's net cash flows or earnings (before interest payments and depreciation) are independent of capital structure. This is because these net cash flows are determined primarily by management effort in generating sales revenues and lowering running costs of the firm. To simplify the exposition, we assume these are a *constant* $\$Y$ p.a. (i.e. an annuity flow).

In practice, a company may be financed mainly via equity $S$, or it may be highly leveraged and be financed mainly from issuing debt $B$ (e.g. leveraged buyouts using junk bonds). The overall cost of funds (capital) to the firm, $R_w$, is a weighted average of the cost of equity (shares) $R_s$, and debt (bonds) $R_b$, so that:

[11.1] $$\text{WACC} \equiv R_w = (1 - z)R_s + zR_b$$

where $z = B/(S + B)$ is the proportion of debt finance and $(1 - z) = S/(S + B)$ is the proportion of equity finance. $R_w$ is known as the weighted average cost of capital, WACC.

> **The WACC is a weighted average of the cost of equity/
> share finance and the cost of debt/bond finance**

The value of the firm is:

[11.2] $$V = \frac{\$Y}{\text{WACC}}$$

If $Y$ is independent of leverage then the value of the firm can only change if the debt-to-equity mix alters the WACC, hence:

**Minimising the WACC will also maximise the value of the firm**

The capital structure question merely asks whether it makes any difference to the **market value** of the firm $V$ if the firm is financed by all equity ($z = 0$), all debt ($z = 1$) or a mixture of equity and debt ($0 < z < 1$). The 'traditional view' suggests that a firm's leverage (i.e. debt-to-equity ratio $B/S$) is significant in determining the overall cost of capital, while Modigliani–Miller (MM) argue that, under certain conditions, the value of the firm is independent of the debt-to-equity ratio. An analogy may help in understanding the MM proposition. Consider the firm as equivalent to one pizza. No matter how you divide the pizza (i.e. debt and equity), the total value of the pizza is unchanged. The value of the pizza depends solely on the ingredients and the skill of the chef in making it, and not how you divide it up.

From equation [11.2] the crucial question is whether an increase in leverage $z$ leads to a fall in $R_w$ and hence an increase in the value of the firm. The so-called **traditional view** assumes that because debt finance costs less than equity finance (i.e. $R_b < R_s$), then increasing the *proportion* of debt finance (i.e. increasing $z$) from say 0% to 10–25% would initially lower $R_w$ and hence increase $V$ (Figure 11.1). The latter point assumes $R_s$ initially remains constant as $z$ increases. However, as debt levels are increased to say over 80% leverage, then shareholders would require a higher return $R_s$. This is because a small downturn in earnings might imply that after paying out 'high' interest payments to bondholders, there would be no funds left to distribute to shareholders. (In the extreme case, earnings would also be insufficient to even pay all the interest owed to bondholders.) Hence, rising debt levels eventually imply an increased risk of distress and possible bankruptcy. This would make shareholders require a higher return $R_s$ in order to willingly hold the shares of a very highly leveraged, highly risky company. As $R_s$ rises then so does $R_w$ (ceteris paribus), and hence the value of the firm begins to fall at high debt levels. Hence, increased leverage first causes $R_w$ to fall and $V$ to rise but eventually increased leverage causes $R_w$ to rise and hence $V$ to fall. There is therefore an optimal level of leverage (i.e. debt-to-equity ratio) which

# FIGURE 11.1: Traditional view: cost of capital

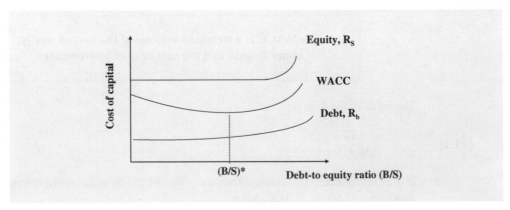

maximises the value of the firm. This is the traditional view, which sounds very plausible and realistic.

Franco Modigliani and Merton Miller, in a landmark 1958 paper, argued against the traditional view. They stated that (under certain conditions) the value of the firm is independent of the mix of debt-to-equity finance. Two firms with the same expected earnings stream would have the same value, whether the firm was 10% or 90% debt financed. This is an astounding and somewhat counter-intuitive result. Surely the 90% debt financed firm has greater risk of non-payment to shareholders and therefore the latter would require an enormous return $R_s$ to keep even their 10% stake in the firm. This would raise $R_w$ and hence lower the market value $V$ of the firm's future earnings. It turns out that the Modigliani–Miller result does not deny that as you substitute more and more of the cheaper debt finance (i.e. '$z$' increases) then $R_s$ does rise. However (put somewhat crudely) the increase in '$z$' in equation [11.1] and hence fall in $(1 - z)$ is *exactly offset* by the rise in $R_s$, such that the overall cost of capital $R_w$ remains constant. If $R_w$ remains constant as leverage rises, then the value of the firm $V$ remains unchanged.

## WACC AND LEVERAGE

Let us see how the WACC varies as we alter the level of leverage $z$. Suppose $R_b = 10\%$ p.a. The required return to shareholders $R_s$ will exceed $R_b$ because shareholders receive earnings only *after* the bondholders have received their interest payments. (This is also true if the firm goes into liquidation.) Hence shares are more risky than bonds. To start the ball rolling, if leverage $z = 20\%$, let us assume shareholders require $R_s = 15\%$ p.a. Hence:

$$R_w = (1 - z)R_s + zR_b = 0.8(15\%) + 0.2(10\%) = 14\%$$

If we increase leverage to $z = 50\%$ and $R_s$ *remains unchanged* at 15% then:

$$\text{WACC} \equiv R_w = 0.5(15\%) + 0.5(10\%) = 12.5\%$$

Hence $R_w$ has fallen. This is the assumption used in the 'traditional view', when leverage is increased from an initial low level. It follows that since the WACC has fallen, then the value of the firm $V = Y/\text{WACC}$ will increase as the debt level initially increases. However, as $z$ reaches some threshold, further increases in $z$ will lead to a substantial rise in $R_s$, so that $V$ eventually does fall. Hence, according to the traditional view, there is a particular debt-to-equity mix which maximises $V$.

The Modigliani–Miller assumption is that as leverage $z$ increases from $z_0 = 0.2$ to $z_1 = 0.5$ then $R_s$ will rise, but it rises just enough so that $R_w$ remains constant. For example, in a Modigliani–Miller world the required return by shareholders $R_s$ would rise to 18% p.a. as leverage increased to 50%, so that $R_w$ remains unchanged at 14%:

$$R_w = 0.5(18\%) + 0.5(10\%) = 14\%$$

The reason we get this rather special outcome in Modigliani–Miller is rather subtle, but it is to do with that ever-pervasive concept in finance, (riskless) arbitrage. It is shown below that an investor can create the same cash flows that are generated by a levered firm by investing in an unlevered firm (i.e. 100% equity financed) and borrowing from the bank. The latter we call 'home-made leverage'. The 'home-made' levered firm must have the same *market value* as the real levered firm, as both have the same cash flows. Arbitrage then ensures that the value of the actual levered firm equals that of an unlevered firm, and hence the market value of a firm is independent of the different proportions of debt-to-finance.

## WHY DO SHAREHOLDERS REQUIRE HIGHER RETURNS?

The reason shareholders require higher average returns $R_s$ as leverage increases is because increased leverage increases the *variability* of shareholder returns. For a given variability in earnings, the fact that interest payments are paid first to bondholders magnifies the variability in returns to shareholders. This can be seen in Table 11.1.

Consider a firm that has raised $10m in capital and its realised earnings $Y_i$ then turn out to be either $0.5m, $2m or $4m, depending on the future state of the economy. We assume these three possible outcomes are equally likely (i.e. probability of each outcome equals 1/3). This possible variability in earnings is known as **business risk** and arises from unexpected changes in sales, costs and prices. Such potential variability in earnings has nothing to do with how the firm is financed.

For an all equity (zero leverage) firm, all of the earnings $Y_i$ accrue to shareholders who have possible returns $R_i = 5\%$, 20% or 40%. The expected return is therefore $ER_{0\%} = 21.7$ with standard deviation $\sigma_{0\%} = 14.3$. If the firm has 20% gearing then it must have issued $2m in debt and raised $8m in equity. Interest payments on the debt are fixed at $rB = 0.1(2m) = \$0.2m$, regardless of the outcome for earnings $Y_i$. If earnings are high (e.g. $Y_3 = \$4m$) then the shareholders will receive all of the excess over the $0.2m interest payments. Shareholders receive $Y_3 - rB = 3.8m$ which gives a return of $R_3 = 3.8/8 = 47.5\%$. However, if earnings are low, $Y_1 = \$0.2m$, then $R_1 = 3.75\%$ (which is less than that for the unlevered firm of $R_1 = 5\%$). The expected return for the shareholders in the 20% levered firm is $ER_{20\%} = 24.6$ with $\sigma_{20\%} = 17.9$. The increased leverage has led to a higher average return but an *increased variability* in returns, compared with the all equity (unlevered) firm.

Finally, with 50% leverage and $Y_1 = \$0.5m$, there are no distributed earnings and the shareholder's return is 0%. When earnings are higher (e.g. $Y_2 = \$2m$ or $Y_3 = \$4m$) the shareholders of the 50% levered firm do really well because they receive *all* of these earnings after the *fixed* debt interest of $rB = \$0.5m$ has been paid. Not only that, the earnings distributed to shareholders of $1.5m and $3.5m have a small equity base of only $5m. Hence, shareholder returns in 'average' and 'good' times are high at 30% and 70%, respectively.

The key feature of the 50% levered firm relative to the 20% or 0% levered firm is the wider variability in returns to equityholders (which range from 0% to 70% for the 50% levered firm). This increase in risk, due simply to higher leverage, could be termed **leverage risk**. Leverage risk for the 20% levered firm is $(\sigma_{20\%}^2 - \sigma_{0\%}^2)^{1/2} = 10.8$ and leverage risk for the 50% levered firm is $(\sigma_{50\%}^2 - \sigma_{0\%}^2)^{1/2} = 15.6$. This increase in leverage risk is compensated for by the higher average return (i.e. $ER_{50} > ER_{30}$).

# TABLE 11.1: Leverage and the return on equity

**Capital raised = $10m = S + B = shares + debt (bonds)**

**Cost of debt = 10%**

| | 1. Poor | 2. Average | 3. Good |
|---|---|---|---|
| **Earnings before interest $Y_i$ (equal probability)** | $Y_1 = \$0.5$ | $Y_2 = \$2$ | $Y_3 = \$4$ |

**A. 100% equity (0% leverage)**

**($S = $10m equity)**

| | | | |
|---|---|---|---|
| Debt interest $rB$ | 0 | 0 | 0 |
| Earnings/dividends for shareholders | $0.5 | $200 | $4 |
| Return on shares $R_i = \text{Div}/S$ | $0.5/10 = 5\%$ | $2/10 = 20\%$ | $4/10 = 40\%$ |
| Expected return (standard deviation) | **21.7% (14.3)** | | |

**B. 20% levered ($z = B/V = 2/10$)**

**($B = $2m debt, $S = $8m equity)**

| | | | |
|---|---|---|---|
| Debt interest $rB$ | $0.2 | $0.2 | $0.2 |
| Earnings/dividends for shareholders | $0.3 | $1.8 | $3.8 |
| Return on shares $R_i = \text{Div}/S$ | $0.3/8 = 3.75\%$, | $1.8/8 = 22.5\%$, | $3.8/8 = 47.5\%$ |
| Expected return (standard deviation) | **24.6% (17.9)** | | |

**C. 50% levered ($z = 5/10$)**

**($B = $5m debt, $S = $5m equity)**

| | | | |
|---|---|---|---|
| Debt interest $rB$ | $0.5 | $0.5 | $0.5 |
| Earnings/dividends for shareholders | $0.0 | $1.5 | $3.5 |
| Return on shares $R_i = \text{Div}/S$ | $0/5 = 0\%$ | $1.5/5 = 30\%$ | $3.5/5 = 70\%$ |
| Expected return (standard deviation) | **33.3% (21.2)** | | |

Note: Standard deviations are calculated as $\sigma = [\sum_{i=1}^{3} p_i(R_i - ER)^2]^{1/2}$ where $p_i$ = probability of 'poor', 'average' or 'good' and here $p_i = 1/3$ (i.e. equal probabilities)

Thus for a given variability in earnings, the variability in equity returns increases with the degree of leverage, as does the average return on equity. That is, $R_s$ increases as leverage increases. The latter relationship is shown in Figure 11.2 for an unlevered (i.e. all equity financed) firm and a 50% levered firm. One can see that as earnings $Y$ vary between $1m

# FIGURE 11.2: How leverage affects equity returns

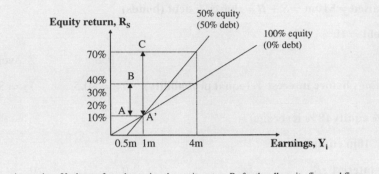

As earnings $Y_i$ change from 1m to 4m, the equity return $R_s$ for the all equity financed firm moves from 10% to 40% (A to B) but for the 50% levered firm the equity return changes much more, from 10% to 70% (A' to C).

and \$4m the variability of $R_s$ is much higher for the levered firm (i.e. distance A'C) than for the unlevered firm (i.e. distance AB). The positive relationship between $R_s$ and the degree of leverage is formally derived in Appendix 11.1.

Having set out the basic concepts in both the traditional and Modigliani–Miller approach let us examine these ideas in a little more depth.

## TRADITIONAL VIEW

Consider an *initial* all equity financed company. The traditional view is that as the firm acquires increasing amounts of debt, then the WACC first falls but eventually rises, thus leading to an optimal debt-to-equity ratio at $(B/S)^*$ (Figure 11.1). The reason for the initial fall in the overall cost of capital is:

- the cost of debt $R_b$ is less than the cost of equity $R_s$
- the cost of equity initially remains constant.

Hence, as you increase the proportion of debt, $R_w$ falls. However, as more debt is added the cost of *equity capital* $R_s$ begins to rise because:

- the *variability* of future earnings (after deduction of interest payments) increases with leverage (as interest must be paid to bondholders regardless of the gross earnings of the company);
- the risk of bankruptcy increases (and bondholders are 'paid' before equity holders).

The increase in risk as perceived by shareholders will mean they require a higher return in order to hold (existing and any new issues of) equity. In addition, even debtholders may require a higher yield as leverage increases because of the increased risk of bankruptcy. Although not based on a sophisticated economic model, the traditional view is probably widely held in company boardrooms.

---

**TRADITIONAL VIEW**
There is a debt-to-equity mix which minimises the WACC
and hence maximises the firm's market value

---

## MODIGLIANI–MILLER—NO CORPORATE TAXES

The increase in management buyouts and takeovers financed using debt, particularly in the 1980s (e.g. using junk bonds), has given some practical impetus to the view that the value of a company is independent of the degree of leverage: an issue to which we now turn.

Merton Miller put forward the following analogy to explain the MM Proposition I. Suppose the firm is a giant tub of whole milk. You could sell the 'whole milk'. Alternatively you could separate out the cream and the remainder would be skimmed milk. The cream would sell at a high price but the skimmed milk would sell at a low price. The MM Proposition I effectively says that the 'whole milk' and the 'cream plus skimmed milk' would sell for the same total amount of money. Arbitrage would ensure that this is the case. If, for example, the whole milk sold for $90, which was less than the 'cream plus skimmed milk' of $70 + $30, then you could buy the whole milk at a cost of $90, separate it into cream and skimmed milk (at zero transactions cost) and sell them for $100, thus making an arbitrage profit of $10. As everyone bought whole milk this would bid up its price, while the price of cream and skimmed milk would fall as supply increased. Hence, prices of the 'whole milk' and 'cream plus skimmed milk' would be brought into equality. The ability to divide up the firm's output or value (i.e. into home-made 'cream plus skimmed milk') and the ability to undertake arbitrage means that the *constituents* of the whole milk just sell for the same price as the whole milk itself. Similarly, the way you finance the firm's activities does not affect the value of the firm, which is ultimately determined by the future earnings from its products.

More formally, the MM view is also based on the idea that the value of a company is ultimately determined by the capitalised value (i.e. PV) of the future income stream from its activities in production, sales, marketing and investment in 'plant and machinery'. In an MM world this future income stream is assumed to be independent of the way in which the firm's activities are financed. If the PV of future income streams of two otherwise identical companies (i.e. with equal business risk) are equal, then the value of the firm should be independent of the proportions of equity and debt used for its finance (Figure 11.3). Suppose firm A and firm B both have a PV of future (net) income of $100m. Firm A has 80% debt finance and 20% equity finance, while for firm B the proportions are 20% debt and 80% equity. The MM view implies that the market value should be the same for both firms (and equal to $100m). Basically the idea is this. If two firms X and Y are identical except for their capital structure, yet you can purchase the securities of X for less than the securities of Y, then an arbitrageur should short sell the securities of Y and buy the securities of X, thus making an *immediate* cash profit. Since the future cash flows from the identical firms X and Y are the same (in PV terms) then there are zero *net* cash flows in *future* periods, from the long and short positions in X and Y.

## FIGURE 11.3: The value of the firm. MM Proposition I (no taxes)

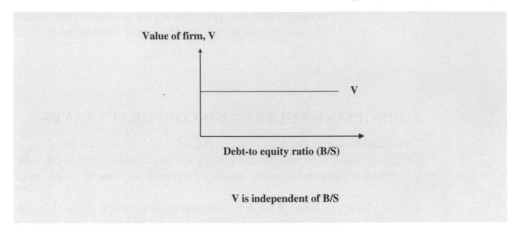

MODIGLIANI–MILLER 'PROPOSITION I'
The WACC and the value of the firm are both independent
of the debt-to-equity mix used in financing the
firm's activities

As we see below, the MM analysis relies on the fact that an investor can create a 'home-made' or synthetic levered firm by borrowing and then investing in an all equity (unlevered) company. This synthetic levered portfolio should cost the same as a direct investment in the levered company. Arbitrage then ensures that the values of the levered and unlevered companies are equal. The MM analysis is based on the following simplifying assumptions:

### ASSUMPTIONS: MODIGLIANI–MILLER APPROACH

- Perfect capital markets with borrowing and lending rates equal and the same for companies and persons.
- No corporate or personal taxes or transactions costs.
- Other firms exist with the same business (systematic) risk but different leverage.
- Net cash flows from physical investment projects can be regarded as perpetuities and are independent of the debt-to-equity mix

Broadly speaking a firm can obtain funds for physical investment from retained earnings, issuing equity (i.e. ordinary shares) or from issuing debt (i.e. corporate bonds, bank loans). To simplify matters we will consider 'equity' as comprising only ordinary shares and 'debt' as comprising only corporate bonds. Retained earnings will be ignored for the moment and we assume all earnings are distributed. In an efficient market the $-market value $V$ of the firm is reflected in the market value of its outstanding $-equity (shares) $S$ and the $-value of its debt $B$, since these are the ultimate recipients of the future cash flows, hence:

**[11.3]**    $V = S + B$

We develop the MM argument by considering investment in two otherwise identical firms, except one is unlevered U (i.e. all equity financed) and the other levered L (i.e. mix of equity and debt finance). Then we will create a synthetic levered firm by borrowing, and using the funds to invest in the all equity (unlevered) firm. The net profits from the **synthetic levered firm SL** and the actual levered firm L are equal. Hence we can deduce that arbitrage will ensure that the *costs* of the two strategies are equal and this results in the Modigliani–Miller Proposition I:

**Value of levered firm $V_L$ = value of unlevered firm $V_U$**

The capital structure of the two companies is shown in Table 11.2. We will use arbitrage to determine the value of $S_L$ and hence $V_L$, but note that it is crucial that both firms earn the same revenue $Y = \$800$ (i.e. they are identical except for their capital structure). Investing 10% in the unlevered and the levered companies gives the results shown in Table 11.3a and b.

## TABLE 11.2: Capital structure

| Unlevered | Levered |
|---|---|
| $V_U - \$1000$ | $V_L = ?$ |
| $B_U = \$0$ | $B_L = \$200$ |
| | $S_L = ?$ |
| | $R_b = 0.05$ |

Note: Future cash flow from both firms is $Y = \$800$

Cases U and L are not directly comparable because they involve different amounts of invested capital and different returns. When investing in 10% of the shares of the levered company L the initial investment is lower because the bondholders have also provided some funds. However, the $-return from the levered company is also lower because the firm deducts interest payments on the debt before distributing the funds to shareholders.

## TABLE 11.3: Levered and unlevered company

| Transaction | $ Investment | $ Return |
|---|---|---|
| **(a) Case U: buy 10% of unlevered company** | | |
| **Buy 0.10 of $V_U$** | $\$100 = 0.10 V_U$ | $0.10 Y$ |
| **(b) Case L: buy 10% of levered company** | | |
| **Buy 0.10 of $V_L$** | $0.10 S_L = 0.10(V_L - B_L)$ | $0.10[Y - 0.05 \times 200]$ |
| | | $= 0.10(Y - R_b B_L)$ |

Looking at the last column of case L (Table 11.3b) we can see that the return is $0.10(Y - R_b B_L)$. However, the investor can 'manufacture' this return by creating home-made leverage. To see this consider an investor who *borrows* $\$B_L$ at an interest rate $R_b$ and also purchases (using her own funds) 10% of the *unlevered* company.

Comparing case SL (Table 11.4) and case L (Table 11.3b), the dollar returns are equal. For case L the return is $0.10(Y - R_b B_L)$ in direct payment of dividends, while for case SL the return comprises dividends of $0.10Y$ from the unlevered firm less personal interest payments of $(0.10)R_b B_L$. Since the $-returns are equal, arbitrage will ensure that the *cost* of these two strategies must be equal:

Cost of L $=$ Cost of SL

$$0.10(V_L - B_L) = 0.10(V_U - B_L)$$

Hence:

$$V_L = V_U$$

We can now fill in the gaps in Table 11.2:

$$V_L = V_U = \$1000 \text{ and } S_L = V_L - B_L = \$1000 - \$200 = \$800$$

## PROFITABLE ARBITRAGE

To show that home-made leverage and arbitrage ensures that $V_L = V_U$, consider starting with $S_L^* = \$1300$ so that we are in disequillibrium:

[11.4]     $V_L^* = S_L^* + B_L = \$1500 > V_U = \$1000$

The levered company $V_L^*$ is overvalued and directly purchasing 10% of the levered company gives case L$^*$. Given the above figures direct investment in the levered firm (case L$^*$) yields a dollar return of $79 for an investment of $130 (Table 11.5). However, an investor would not purchase L$^*$ directly because it is overvalued. Instead case SL$^*$ (Table 11.6) shows that the investor can obtain the same *return* as in the levered firm, by using home-made leverage.

---

## TABLE 11.4: Synthetic leveraged company

| Transaction | $ Investment | $ Return |
|---|---|---|
| **Case SL: synthetic leverage = borrow and invest in levered company** | | |
| **Borrow 0.10 of $B_L$** | $-0.10B_L$ | $-0.10R_b B_L + 0.10\ Y$ |
| **Buy 0.10 of $V_U$** | $+0.10V_U$ | |
| | Net inv. $= 0.10(V_U - B_L)$ | Return $= 0.10(Y - R_b B_L)$ |

## TABLE 11.5: Direct investment in levered company

| Transaction | $ Investment | $ Return |
|---|---|---|
| **Case L\*: buy 10% of levered company** | | |
| **Buy 0.10 of $S_L^*$** | $(0.10)S_L^* = (0.10)\$1300$ | $0.10(Y - R_b B_L)$ |
| | $= \$130$ | $= 0.10(\$800 - 0.05(\$200))$ |
| | | $= \$79$ |

## TABLE 11.6: Cost of home-made leverage

| Transaction | $ Investment | $ Return |
|---|---|---|
| **Case SL\*: borrow and invest in unlevered company** | | |
| **Borrow 0.10 of $B_L$** | $-0.10 B_L = 0.10(\$200) = 20$ | $-0.10 R_b B_L = -1$ |
| **Buy 0.10 of $V_U$** | $+0.10 V_U = 0.10(\$1000) = 100$ | $+0.10Y = 80$ |
| | **Net inv. = \$80** | **Net return = \$79** |
| | $= 0.10(V_U - B_L)$ | $= 0.10(Y - R_b B_L)$ |

That is, she borrows $(0.10)B_L$ and simultaneously purchases 10% of the *unlevered* firm. However, the cost of investing in the unlevered firm will be less because $S_U = V_U < V_L^*$.

Synthetic leverage (Table 11.6) involves borrowing $20 (= 0.10B_L)$ and simultaneously purchasing 10% of the unlevered firm at a cost of $100 (= 0.10V_U = 0.10 \times \$1000)$. Here the *net* investment is $80 [= 0.10(V_U - B_L) = \$100 - \$20]$.

The *dollar return* from home-made leverage is $79, the same as direct investment in the levered firm. But the cost of the home-made leverage is lower, at $80, than direct investment in the levered firm of $130. Hence rational agents have an arbitrage opportunity, which involves borrowing and purchasing shares in the unlevered company while also selling shares in the levered company. This causes $S_U$ and hence $V_U (= S_U)$ to rise, and selling the equity of the levered firm causes $S_L$ (and hence $V_L$) to fall. Arbitrage will continue until $V_L = V_U$. Hence the capital structure of the company does not affect the company's overall value. Put differently, a 10% debt–90% equity financed firm should have the same market value as a firm financed by 90% equity and 10% debt.

## LEVERAGE AND THE REQUIRED RATE OF RETURN ON EQUITY

We have noted that the MM proposition implies that the *overall cost of capital $R_w$* is independent of the degree of leverage. One implication of this is that the WACC formula (equation [11.1]) can be rearranged to show that the equilibrium expected return *on equity* (shares) $R_s$ is positively related to leverage. In equation [11.1], substitute $z = B/V = B/(S + B)$ and rearrange to give:

[11.5]
$$R_s = R_w + (R_w - R_b)\frac{B}{S}$$

The WACC does not change with the amount of leverage—MM Proposition I. Note also that $R_w - R_b$ is positive because, even for an unlevered firm, shares are risky and their return should exceed the return on riskless debt. Hence equation [11.5] implies:

---

**MODIGLIANI–MILLER 'PROPOSITION II'**
**Since the WACC is independent of the debt-to-equity**
**ratio, this implies that the cost of equity capital $R_s$**
**rises with the debt-to-equity ratio $B/S$**

---

Figure 11.3 shows that the value of the firm does not depend on the debt-to-equity mix. Figure 11.4 shows that an increase in the debt-to-equity ratio $B/S$ requires an increase in the required return on equity, $R_s$ and if $R_b$ stays constant then this relationship is linear. In practice it is possible that if debt holders bear some of the firm's *business risk* and demand a higher return $R_b$ as debt increases, then the slope of the $R_s$ line might taper off at high debt levels (from equation [11.5] a higher value for $R_b$ tends to reduce the required return of equity holders since they no longer carry all the firm's business risk). Note that here we are considering the division of business risk between the debt and equity holders and we are *not* claiming that $R_b$ rises because of an increased risk of bankruptcy.

## MODIGLIANI–MILLER WITH CORPORATE TAXES

If we keep all the original assumptions of Modigliani–Miller but allow the firm to deduct interest income against earnings, before paying tax, then we get a remarkable turnaround. In this 'new' Modigliani–Miller world, there *is* an optimal debt ratio:

---

# FIGURE 11.4: The cost of equity finance. MM Proposition II (no taxes)

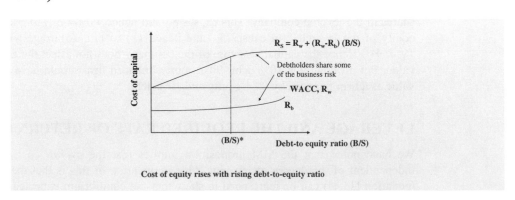

Cost of equity rises with rising debt-to-equity ratio

> **For two firms with the same business risk, then with corporate taxes the optimal debt ratio that maximises the value of the firm involves 100% leverage (i.e. all debt financed)!**

First let's look at a heuristic argument for this proposition. Note that for MM *without taxes*, the value of the firm is independent of leverage because the WACC remains constant as leverage $z$ increases. The latter arises because, although $R_s$ rises with leverage, the lower cost of debt $zR_b$ is just offset by the rising $(1 - z)R_s$. However, *with taxes*, the cost of debt finance is lower and equal to $R_b(1 - t)$ (where $t$ = corporation tax rate). Hence although $R_s$ still rises with increased leverage, it does not completely offset this lower *after-tax* borrowing cost. Hence, the WACC falls continuously as leverage increases and the value of the firm $V = Y/\text{WACC}$ rises. As long as the firm has taxable profits an increase in leverage to 100% raises firm value! Clearly this 'tax shield' is very important in the model.

To develop this argument a little further note that, with corporate taxes, the value of an unlevered firm $V_U$ (i.e. 100% equity financed) equals the constant after-tax earnings $Y(1 - t)$ discounted at the risk adjusted discount rate *for an unlevered (i.e. all equity) firm $\rho_s^u$*:

$$V_U = \frac{Y(1 - t)}{\rho_s^u}$$

Using a more sophisticated argument than above, it is shown in Appendix 11.2A that (with taxes) the values of the levered firm $V_L$ and the unlevered firm $V_U$ are related, namely:

> **MM PROPOSITION I (WITH CORPORATE TAXES)**
>
> **Value of a levered firm $V_L$ = value of an unlevered firm $V_U$ + value of the 'tax shield', $tB$**
>
> $$V_L = V_U + tB$$

The 'tax shield' is the additional value imparted to the levered firm because the tax system allows the levered firm to deduct interest income on its debt before it is subject to corporation tax. In contrast, for an unlevered firm which has no debt interest, all of its earnings are subject to tax before any distribution to shareholders. The unlevered firm therefore has a lower value than the levered firm. It follows from the above equation that as the amount of debt $B$ increases then the value of the levered firm increases and is maximised at 100% debt finance.

At this point it is worth making a small change in notation. Because we have introduced the rate of return on equity *in an unlevered* (i.e. 100% equity financed) firm $\rho_s^u$, we will now denote the rate of return on equity in a *levered* firm as $R_s^L$ (rather than simply $R_s$). Also we will use $B_L$ and $S_L$ for the debt and equity of the *levered* firm. These changes we hope will make the following (rather tricky) analysis a little easier.

What about MM Proposition II in the presence of corporate taxes? Is it still the case that the cost of equity capital $R_s^L$ in the levered firm rises with the debt-to-equity ratio (i.e. with leverage)? The answer is yes. This result still holds because, if you remember, it was based on the increased volatility in the returns to equity holders in the levered firm and corporate taxes do not qualitatively alter this result. It is shown in Appendix 11.2B that the return on equity $R_s^L$ in the levered firm is:

$$R_s^L = \rho_s^u + (1 - t)(\rho_s^u - R_b)\frac{B_L}{S_L}$$

where $\rho_s^u$ is the risk adjusted return on equity in an unlevered (i.e. 100% equity) firm, hence from the above equation:

> **MM PROPOSITION II (WITH CORPORATE TAXES)**
> **There is a positive relationship between the required**
> **return on equity in a levered firm $R_s^L$**
> **and the debt-to-equity ratio $B_L/S_L$**

# 11.2 NPV AND THE COST OF CAPITAL

This section is concerned with the calculation of the NPV of an investment project, undertaken by a levered firm. There are two main approaches. The first approach discounts the after-tax cash flows from the investment project using the WACC. The second approach is known as adjusted present value (APV). This method discounts the after-tax cash flows using the return on equity of an *unlevered* firm $\rho_s^u$ and then makes an adjustment for the present value of the tax shield(s) which accrue to the levered firm. This method requires us to calculate $\rho_s^u$ which is (usually) not directly observable. The latter somewhat esoteric problem is formally taken up in Appendix 11.3.

When a firm is trying to calculate the net present value (NPV) of a new investment project (e.g. the purchase of plant and machinery) it must use a discount rate that reflects the cost of funds required to finance the project. Three main sources of funds are equity, debt and retained earnings. Essentially, the cost of capital can be viewed as the weighted average of the cost of each of these sources of funds. Ideally, the appropriate measure of the cost of funds incorporates all the risk elements of the new investment project, since potential investors (i.e. shareholders or bondholders) will only hold these 'assets' if their expected return compensates them for the risks involved. In practice, calculations of the cost of capital often require some simplifying assumptions.

## COST OF EQUITY

The cost of *new* equity is the return that has to be paid to the new stockholders. There are numerous models of what determines equilibrium returns on equity, and we have already discussed the CAPM/SML approach and the APT. For example, we can use the SML:

[11.6] $$ER_s = r + \beta_s(ER_m - r) = 3 + 8\beta_s$$

where $r$ is the risk free rate ($= 3\%$ say), ($ER_m - r$) is the excess return on the market portfolio ($= 8\%$ say), and $\beta_s$ is the firm's estimated beta. Suppose a cross-section regression of the average return (over the last year) on a set of stocks and on their betas gives the estimates of the intercept ($= 3$) and the slope ($= 8$). Taking a single (levered) firm with beta equal to $\beta_s = 1.5$ say, then this implies a cost of equity of $ER_s = 15\%$. The APT requires estimates of the factor loadings $b_{ij}$ and the price of risk $\lambda_i$ for each of these factors. It is then straightforward to calculate the cost of equity for firm $i$:

$$ER_s = \lambda_1 b_{s1} + \lambda_2 b_{s2} + \dots$$

Either of these measures can be used as a measure of the cost of equity finance.

## COST OF DEBT

The cost of *new* debt is the return that must be paid (in the future) to the new debtholders. The cost of *existing* debt we take to be the interest rate (yield to maturity) on that debt, $R_b$ and this will reflect the existing credit rating of the firm (e.g. using Standard & Poor's or Moody's rating service). Since corporations can deduct interest payments from their debt payments, their after-tax cost of debt is:

[11.7] $$R_b^* = (1 - t)R_b$$

where $t$ is the marginal corporate tax rate. The yield $R_b$ is the *promised* rate on the new debt assuming the firm does not go into liquidation. However, as the firm issues new debt there may be an increased *risk* of bankruptcy (with consequent loss of sales) as well as the additional costs of actual bankruptcy (e.g. fire sale of assets, etc.). Hence the true *expected* cost of debt may be higher than that in equation [11.7]. However, default probabilities and the expected value of debt after an actual default are difficult to measure (e.g. after bankruptcy proceedings—'Chapter 11' in the USA and compulsory liquidation in the UK). Hence the quoted yield is usually used in practice. (We could also measure $R_b$ using the SML and the firm's beta on existing bonds, but because of a paucity of readily available estimates of 'bond betas', this method is usually not used.)

## RETAINED EARNINGS

Retained earnings are frequently used to finance new investment projects. However, the cost of such funds is not zero. All of the retained earnings could be distributed to shareholders and the firm could then issue more shares to obtain more funds. Hence, broadly speaking the opportunity cost of retained earnings is equal to the cost of raising equity capital. The only true cost advantage of retained earnings over external finance is the saving in issue and floatation costs and in administrative costs of keeping shareholders informed about the progress of the company. It follows that if we can work out the overall cost of equity finance, this figure can also be applied to retained earnings.

## WEIGHTED AVERAGE COST OF CAPITAL

Having calculated the cost of equity and the cost of debt we can now determine the weighted average cost of capital, WACC. Assume equity and bonds are the only sources of finance. The total annual expected cost of issuing $\$B$ of debt and $\$S$ of equity (stocks) finance is:

[11.8]    $$C = R_s S + R_b (1 - t) B$$

The total value of the firm's capital is:

[11.9]    $$V = S + B$$

and hence the WACC, namely the dollar amount the firm expects to pay out to the bond and stockholders per unit of capital raised, is:

[11.10]    $$R_w (\text{WACC}) = \frac{\text{total cost}}{\text{total value}} = \left( \frac{S}{S + B} \right) R_s + \left( \frac{B}{S + B} \right) R_b (1 - t)$$

$$= (1 - z) R_s + z R_b (1 - t)$$

where $z = B/(B + S)$ is the degree of leverage. With no corporate taxes we simply set $t = 0$ in the above equation. An example of the calculation of the WACC is given in Table 11.7. The WACC should be used as the discount rate in the NPV formula to discount after-tax earnings $Y(1 - t)$ for the marginal capital investment project as long as the following conditions hold.

---

### USING THE WACC IN PROJECT APPRAISAL

WACC can be used:

(i) If the new project gives rise to cash flows that have the same degree of business risk as the existing general cash flows of the firm, that is, the project is 'scale enhancing' (e.g. when expanding your chain of hamburger outlets).

(ii) If the project does not lead to a (large) change in the firm's **debt ratio**.

In fact, the WACC calculation assumes that the amount of debt outstanding is rebalanced every period to maintain a **constant ratio** $B_L/V_L$ for the firm as a whole (see Appendix 11.4 for a formal proof).

---

## TABLE 11.7: Calculating the weighted average cost of capital

| Data: | Market value of debt $B = \$40m$ | Number of outstanding shares $= 4m$ |
|---|---|---|
| | Share price $= \$15$ | Yield on existing debt $= 10\%$ |
| | Corporate tax rate $t = 30\%$ | Excess market return $R_m - r = 8.5\%$ |
| | Risk free rate $r = 5\%$ | Firm's beta $= 1.2$ |
| **Question:** | Calculate the WACC | |
| **Answer:** | *Cost of equity* | |
| | $R_s = 5\% + 1.2(8.5\%) = \mathbf{15.2\%}$ | |
| | *Cost of debt (after tax)* | |
| | $R_b^* = (1 - 0.3)10\% = \mathbf{7\%}$ | |
| | *Cost of capital* | |
| | Value of equity $S = \$60m \ (= 4m \times \$15)$ | Value of debt $B = \$40m$ |
| | $R_w(\text{WACC}) = 0.6(15.2\%) + 0.4(7\%) = \mathbf{11.92\%}$ | |

Note: This calculation of the WACC assumes that the debt-to-equity ratio remains constant so that we can use the firm's current cost of equity capital of 15.2% (if the debt-to-equity ratio increases substantially then according to MM-I the cost of equity would increase with increasing leverage)

In other words the WACC works for the 'average' project. The earnings $Y(1 - t)$ are not adjusted for interest payments on the debt because the value added by the tax shield is picked up in the lower WACC in equation [11.10] when $t > 0$. When the project radically alters the degree of leverage then the above WACC formula should not be used in calculating the NPV of the project. So if the above two assumptions do not hold, then use of the WACC becomes problematic and rather complex ad hoc adjustments to $R_w$ may be required. For example, if a manufacturing firm is investing in office building then the equity beta of firms that operate purely in the real estate sector might be used (rather than the beta of manufacturing firms).

## ADJUSTED PRESENT VALUE

The 'standard' WACC approach discounts all future after-tax earnings $Y(1 - t)$ at the same discount rate and hence assumes the project is scale enhancing and that leverage does not change dramatically with the new project. When these conditions do not hold an alternative PV technique known as **adjusted present value** (APV) has been advocated (although it does not appear to be very widely used in practice). The APV approach does not make adjustments to the discount rate, but instead adjusts the cash flows for the costs or benefits from the type of financing undertaken (e.g. debt finance, depreciation of capital assets and subsidised loans from government). It is implemented as follows.

(i) Value the after-tax earnings of the project $Y(1 - t)$ using the discount rate for an *all equity financed* firm, $\rho_s^u$ to give:

$$\text{NPV(all equity)} = -\text{KC} + Y(1 - t)/\rho_s^u$$

where KC = capital cost of the project. We do not usually observe $\rho_s^u$ since in practice all firms are levered, however Appendix 11.3 shows how $\rho_s^u$ can be measured.

(ii) Add the PV of any tax shields due to financing, to obtain the APV:

$$\text{APV} = \text{NPV(all equity)} + \text{PV(tax shields from financing decisions)}$$

The idea of APV is rooted in MM Proposition I with corporate taxes, namely that the value of the levered firm $V_L = V_U + \text{PV (tax shield)}$. The flexibility of the APV approach arises from the fact that tax shields from other tax deductible expenses such as floatation costs and subsidised finance can be relatively easily calculated, whereas one cannot adjust the WACC discount rate to accommodate these factors. For example, if the capital investment were $1m and the firm used 'straight-line depreciation' then the tax saving each year for 5 years would be ($t \times \$200{,}000$) p.a., so the present value of the tax shield would be:

$$\text{PV(tax shield from depreciation)} = t(200{,}000) \times \frac{1}{R_b}\left[1 - \frac{1}{(1 + R_b)^5}\right]$$

where we have used the 5-year annuity value to obtain the present value. Suppose the total tax savings in each year from the 'debt' tax shield plus the value of the depreciation tax shield are $Z = (tR_b B) + t(200{,}000)$. If these tax savings are certain, then the tax shield can be discounted at the risk free rate $R_b$. On the other hand if the tax savings *depend on the cash flows from the project itself*, which may be highly uncertain (i.e. rather than from the general business of the firm), then the tax shield in each year should be discounted at the discount rate for the all equity firm $\rho_s^u$ to reflect their general business risk.

It should now be obvious to the reader that we have been searching around deep in the entrails of academia to try and 'solve' this general problem of an appropriate way of calculating the NPV of a project. We do not have a definitive answer, although we have some useful approaches. Given the uncertainties over cash flow forecasts themselves and estimation of a firm's beta, the above rather esoteric issues do not seem worth pursuing further at this point. On a practical note our conclusions might be:

---

**WACC versus APV**

- Discounting using the 'standard' WACC is useful for projects that are broadly scale enhancing and that do not drastically alter the degree of leverage.
- The APV approach is feasible for projects where the value of tax shields is likely to be of importance.

---

It is worth repeating that although NPV calculations seem fairly straightforward in textbooks, nevertheless in practice they are an art rather than an exact science.

## INCENTIVES AND ECONOMIC VALUE ADDED

Managers are supposed to act in the interests of shareholders and undertake investment projects with positive NPV, which then maximises the value of the firm. The costs of monitoring managers' efforts and actions are known as agency costs, and in practice the shareholders delegate this responsibility to the board of directors. Because it is difficult to monitor the managers' 'efforts', rewards for top management often include a basic salary (for effort or 'input') plus performance bonuses and stock options, which are rewards based on 'output'. However, the stock price can be a poor measure of the managers' contributions to 'output' because it depends on so many other outside factors (e.g. general state of the economy). A better measure might be the firm's stock price performance relative to a set of 'benchmark' competitors rather than the absolute change in the firm's stock price. Even then the firm could just 'get lucky' and the managers would then receive payment even though their managerial skills played no part in the success of the firm. Note that payouts to managers are invariably asymmetric: they do not have to pay out to the shareholders if the firm subsequently does badly, because of their bad decisions. Indeed their contracts are likely to involve a massive golden parachute payment if they are dismissed or resign.

**Economic value added (EVA)** as promoted by the firm Stern–Stewart & Co. has been suggested as a method of measuring and monitoring the performance of divisions within a firm and also for comparing economic performance across different firms. (An earlier approach known as the **residual income theory** is similar to EVA.) EVA is connected with what has become known as the **value based management** approach. Clearly, managers should not be told to maximise (accounting) earnings since this may involve huge capital costs and hence imply undertaking projects with negative NPVs. EVA recognises that (dollar) earnings must be compared with the capital used to finance the project. In its simplest form EVA is defined as:

$$\text{EVA (or residual income)} = \text{earnings after tax, EAT} - \text{capital used}$$

$$= \text{EAT} - (\text{WACC} \times \text{KC})$$

For example, if EAT from the project equals \$100m, KC = \$1000m and the WACC = 9%, then EVA = \$10m and the manager would invest in the project, since EVA > 0. The project is therefore deemed to be worthwhile and the managers are 'adding value' for the shareholders. Note that there are some rather difficult issues surrounding the definition of 'earnings' (e.g. whether to deduct economic depreciation) and the capital stock figures used (e.g. net or gross capital stock) – see Copeland et al. 2000.

Another commonly used 'statistic' in project appraisal is the **return on capital (employed), ROC** (sometimes called the return on investment), defined as:

**Return on capital** ROC = EAT/KC = \$100m/\$1000m = 10%

The investment decision is then:

Invest in project if $ROC > WACC$

But it is easy to see that EVA and ROC are the same decision rule. Finally, note that McKinsey & Co. use a concept called economic profit EP defined as:

**Economic profit** $EP = (ROC - WACC) \times KC = (0.10 - 0.09) \times \$1000m = \$10m$

and the criterion is that managers invest in the project if $EP > 0$. Again this decision rule is easily seen to be the same as our earlier EVA and ROC rules. These three methods all have the virtue that they look at the 'return' on the investment, relative to the amount of capital tied up in the project. This makes managers focus on reducing capital employed (e.g. reducing inventories/office space/unused machinery) as well as focus on projects which increase earnings. However, in its 'raw form' presented here it only considers earnings over the next year (or a short horizon of a few years) so it is not the same as the NPV (or the APV) criterion.

Is there any connection between EVA, NPV and APV? Yes there is. They can be shown to be equivalent under certain restrictive assumptions (see Copeland *et al.*, 2000). To see the relationship between NPV and EVA in a simple case, suppose the estimate of EAT in the EVA calculation was an 'average value' that was expected to persist in all future years of the project (i.e. $n \to \infty$). Economists will recognise this 'average value' as being the annuity value of the PV of the future earnings, sometimes called 'permanent earnings/income'. The PV of the annuity flow EAT is, $PV = EAT/WACC$ and the NPV criterion is:

Invest in the project if   $PV(earnings) > KC$       where $PV = EAT/WACC$

or                $EAT - WACC \times KC > 0$

Hence, the NPV criterion and the EVA criterion are now equivalent. So the key difference between the two criteria is whether the 'earnings' figures used in EVA represent the 'average earnings' over future years. If earnings projections in EVA are only for the next few years then the EVA criterion might give misleading signals about the performance of divisions or the whole company (e.g. for a biotechnology company where earnings only accrue after many years of R&D costs). In more advanced texts it is shown that NPV, EVA and APV give identical results as long as the discount rates used in the different methods are consistent, but this need not concern us here (see Copeland *et al.*, 2000, chapter 8 for more details).

*Fortune* magazine (of 10th November 1997) provided figures for the EVA ($m) of companies, from which the following have been extracted:

|  | EVA | Capital | ROC | WACC |
|---|---|---|---|---|
| **General Electric** | 2515 | 51,017 | 17.7 | 12.7 |
| **General Motors** | −3527 | 94,268 | 5.9 | 9.7 |
| **Johnson & Johnson** | 1327 | 15,603 | 21.8 | 13.3 |

Clearly, you can have a positive return on capital of 5.9% (General Motors) but if this requires a large amount of capital then your EVA may be negative. Also Johnson & Johnson has a higher ROC than General Electric but the latter has a higher EVA partly because it has a lower WACC.

Above we have been (implicitly) discussing non-financial firms. A form of 'return on capital' is also used in the banking sector and other financial intermediaries, but here it is known as the **'risk adjusted return on capital' RAROC** (initially introduced by Bankers Trust in the 1970s). Broadly speaking the bank is interested in whether its various divisions' earnings, after allowance for the 'capital' they use, achieve the return required by shareholders. A bank's earnings arise from:

- the 'spread' it earns on its loans over the interest it has to pay on its deposits;
- any fees it earns (e.g. loan arranging fees, fees on FX transactions);
- less expected losses on its loan portfolio;
- less its operating costs (e.g. salaries).

The denominator 'capital' is measured in a rather sophisticated way and refers to *unexpected* losses on (say) a bank loan, known as the 'capital at risk', which is (see Cuthbertson and Nitzsche, 2001 for further details):

$$\text{Capital at risk} = \text{loan exposure} \times \text{LGD} \times (\sigma_L \times \text{percentile level})$$

where LGD = loss given default and $\sigma_L$ = standard deviation of losses (for this 'risk class' of customer). Assuming normality, the 1st 'percentile level' would be 2.33. Hence for a face value $100m bank loan, LGD = 20% and $\sigma_L = 30\%$ (for this 'risk class' of customer):

$$\text{Capital at risk} = \$100m \times 0.20 \times 0.30 \times 2.33 = 13.98m$$

The RAROC is defined similarly to the ROC above, namely:

---

**RISK ADJUSTED RETURN ON CAPITAL: RAROC**
**RAROC = 'earnings'/'capital at risk'**

---

Only those activities (e.g. bank loans to a company) where the RAROC exceeds the required return on equity (or WACC) would be accepted. Clearly, if RAROC > WACC then:

$$\text{EVA} = \text{'earnings'} - \text{capital at risk} \times \text{WACC} > 0$$

and RAROC can be seen to be a type of EVA criterion. In practice EVA (and allied approaches) can be seen as a simplified form of NPV which gives managers an incentive to act in the interest of shareholders and also allows the board of directors to monitor both (divisional) managers' performance and that of the whole firm relative to its competitors (see Box 11.1).

## Box 11.1     IS EVA POPULAR?

EVA and its near equivalents economic profit (EP) and return on capital (ROC) have recently been adopted by major US firms such as AT&T, Quaker Oats, Walt Disney and Coca-Cola and in the UK by Lucas Varity, BAT Industries and Carlton Communications. As we have already noted, key issues concern the measurement of earnings/ profits and what exactly constitutes 'capital'. Different assumptions can give rise to very different figures for EVA. Stern–Stewart & Co. suggest around 160 adjustments need to be made to accounting data to obtain correct figures for 'earnings' and economic capital employed.

Consider the difficulties in calculating the EVA for Glaxo–Wellcome for 1995. (The figures used are based on the *Investor's Chronicle* of 17th January 1997, p. 19.) Take 'capital' first. Relatively easily measured are shareholders' equity (£91m), total debt (£4347m) plus 'minority interests' (£130m). But what do we do about 'goodwill' and R&D expenditure?

Clearly, **R&D** helps add value and is an 'investment' but in accounting terms it is written off against profits. Hence, we should add say the last *4 years* of R&D expenditure (£3322m) to our 'capital' figures and also add back to 1995 profits that year's R&D expenditure (£130m).

When Glaxo acquired Wellcome it wrote off 'goodwill' estimated at £5197m and, as this can be viewed as part of the assets of Glaxo–Wellcome, it is added back to 'capital'. So we have:

**Capital (£m)**

| | |
|---|---|
| Shareholders' equity | 91 |
| Debt | 4347 |
| Minority interests | 130 |
| R&D (4 years) | 3322 |
| Goodwill | 5197 |
| Capital used | **13,087** |

On the earnings side, we have operating profit of £2126m (plus the R&D costs for 1995 which, as noted above, have to be added back to get the 'true' operating profit). The profit figures for 1995 for Glaxo contained a deduction of about $1.2bn to fund the costs of integration with Wellcome. However, most of this was not actually spent in 1995 but merely added to provisions. Hence a figure of £1169m, representing 'unspent' provisions, is added back to profits. Finally, on the revenue side, we need to deduct 1995 tax payments of £564m.

**Profit/income statement**

| | |
|---|---|
| Operating profit | 2126 |
| *Plus* R&D costs | 1130 |
| *Plus* provisions | 1169 |

*Minus* tax                              <u>564</u>
Earnings/profit (after tax)              **3861**

Glaxo–Wellcome has about 70% equity and 30% debt finance. Using the CAPM gives a required return on equity of 13.4% and the average cost of debt is 7%, giving **WACC = 11.5%**. We can now calculate the ROC and EVA for Glaxo–Wellcome:

$$ROC = (EADT/KC)100\% = (386/13087)100 = \textbf{29.5\%}$$

$$EVA = EADT - (WACC \times KC) = 3861 - 0.115(13,087) = \textbf{£2356m}$$

The ROC exceeds the WACC, so the managers of Glaxo–Wellcome are 'adding value' and this is confirmed by the positive figure of £2356m for EVA. Note however the implicit assumptions used, such as including 4 years R&D expenditure in 'capital' (why not 5 years?) as well as 'goodwill'. The earnings figures are only for 1 year and therefore are unlikely to reflect Glaxo–Wellcome's 'average' (or permanent) earnings over future years. Changes in some of these assumptions could radically alter the calculated value of EVA.

Source: *Investor's Chronicle*, 17th January 1997, p. 19

# 11.3 EVIDENCE

If MM Proposition I is correct then $V$ is independent of the debt-to-equity ratio and hence we should expect to observe a random distribution of debt-to-equity ratios across 'similar' companies. This simple version of the theory cannot be correct since we actually observe that *most* companies in a particular industrial sector have low debt-to-equity ratios (e.g. chemicals). In other sectors such as banking, debt-to-equity ratios are uniformly high. With the advent of junk bonds in the 1980s there was an increase in management buyouts and in small firms taking over large firms. This was accomplished by raising finance by issuing low credit rated debt which offered high coupons. Thus for some firms in an industry, debt-to-equity ratios rose and became more random, bringing us closer to MM. In general, however, there is not a random distribution of debt-to-equity ratios across firms in the same industries (i.e. those that can broadly be expected to have similar future profits). The assumptions of the theory can be relaxed to try and accommodate these stylised facts. We therefore need to consider the following factors:

- that borrowing rates are not the same for companies and individuals;
- that the roles of corporate taxes and investment allowances are complex and may favour debt over equity (as explicitly incorporated in the APV approach);
- that perceived bankruptcy and other agency costs may be substantial;
- that the volatility of cash flows influences the firm's ability to service debt interest payments and this may lead to a rise in the cost of debt $R_b$ and hence a fall in the firm's value, as the debt-to-equity ratio rises.

All of the above factors could invalidate the MM propositions and this would imply that the financial manager might be able to reduce the overall cost of finance (and hence increase the value of the firm) by altering the mix of debt and equity finance. Sometimes, however, the firm's debt-to-equity mix has to be altered just to ensure survival, as can be seen from Box 11.2 on the Eurotunnel refinancing package.

## Box 11.2    EUROTUNNEL RESTRUCTURING

Eurotunnel initially raised around **£1bn from equity shareholders** and **£5bn in debt** (i.e. bank loans from a consortium of 225 banks) to build (part of) the Channel Tunnel rail link between England and France. Its initial debt-to-equity ratio was therefore high. Delays in building the tunnel, overshoot on costs and a shortfall on revenue projections meant that towards the end of 1996 it had debts of around £9bn. Interest costs were around £2m *per day* which could not be met from its net revenues. It had already, by 1995, suspended payments in its junior debt (for up to 18 months).

Eurotunnel's debtors (the 225 banks) could have forced it into liquidation, but this would have resulted in protracted legal wrangling to sort out the position of each creditor in the 'pecking order'. Instead, a **debt-for-equity swap** was agreed between Eurotunnel's chairman Sir Alastair Morton and the 225 banks.

A debt-for-equity swap dilutes the original shareholders' capital, but it would allow Eurotunnel to pay less interest on the reduced level of debt.

The deal involved the banks owning about 45% of the company through a **£1bn debt-for-equity swap**, with the shares valued at 130p (£1.30). In total, the restructuring involves about £4.5bn of Eurotunnel's £9bn debt. Additional measures were also implemented to reduce the interest burden from around £650m p.a. to £400m p.a. (over the period until the end of December 2003). As is usual in such cases, the restructuring involves quite complex arrangements, which include:

(i) £1.5bn of **fixed rate debt swapped for resettable bonds** (i.e. on which the interest rate can be periodically adjusted).

(ii) £1bn of **debt to be swapped for 'equity notes'** (i.e. bonds convertible into Eurotunnel shares at 155p (£1.55) per share after December 2003).

(iii) £1.2bn of debt exchanged for **'loan notes'** which pay (only) 1% fixed interest plus 30% of Eurotunnel's net profits. Clearly, these 'loan notes' are a hybrid debt–equity security.

(iv) Eurotunnel could not pay even the lower interest payments of £400m p.a. after the above restructuring (since its free cash flow was then only £125m p.a.). Hence, it also agreed to issue £1.85bn of **'stabilisation notes'** which 'roll-up' interest free until 2006 but can be converted to shares before then at 130p. Again, a hybrid debt–equity security.

If Eurotunnel's net revenues increase sufficiently, then the restructuring may pay off. There is a mild 'sweetener' for the original shareholders in the form of an issue of free **warrants**, with an exercise price of 150p (£1.50) and exercisable until December

2003. If Eurotunnel's net profits improve by this time, then shareholders will exercise the warrants and the funds obtained can be used to redeem the equity notes held by the banks. If Eurotonnel's fortunes do not improve, then the banks will end up owning about 75% of Eurotunnel and the problem of what to do with it.

The overall conclusion is that in the 'real world', the debt-to-equity mix of the firm may well affect its perceived future survival prospects, simply because its net revenues may turn out not to be sufficient to cover the interest payments on its debt. The risk and costs of bankruptcy (or restructuring) are sufficiently important to firms and suppliers of funds that the simple Modigliani–Miller model may not be an adequate description of the real world. However, the Modigliani–Miller thesis provides a valuable starting point from which to build more realistic models of the firm's financing decisions.

Source: *Financial Times*—various issues, *Investor's Chronicle*—various issues

The Modigliani–Miller approach (either with or without taxes) provides a clear and intellectually rigorous model. It is a useful starting point but it does not 'fit' the real world. So what other factors might be important when altering debt levels and how in practice might these affect the WACC and the value of the firm? It is unlikely that our assumption of no difference in borrowing rates between companies and individuals is a major source of worry, since many individuals who want to buy shares and borrow money can do so by using a margin account with their broker and this implies they face a borrowing rate which is very close to that for companies.

Textbooks at this point generally introduce the **costs of bankruptcy** into the calculation of optimal capital structure. Clearly as you add more debt, the probability of 'financial distress' or outright bankruptcy will increase. The expected loss in value from bankruptcy is equal to the probability of bankruptcy times the financial cost of bankruptcy. Hence the value of the levered firm with bankruptcy costs (and taxes) is:

$$V_L = V_U + \text{PV(tax shields)} - \text{PV(costs of financial distress)}$$

The relationships between firm value and leverage for the three cases are depicted in Figure 11.5. With zero bankruptcy costs, $V_L = V_U + tB_L$ and the leveraged firm's value increases linearly with the level of debt. When we add bankruptcy costs there is now an optimal debt ratio, since at some point the losses from bankruptcy will outweigh the value of the tax shield. However, the *expected* bankruptcy cost (as debt varies) is very difficult to measure and hence the optimal level of leverage is virtually impossible to calculate. So, although valid in general terms, this analysis does not really help to establish the optimal debt-to-equity ratio in practice. In any case there is a long 'list' of potential factors which could invalidate other key MM assumptions, and these are equally difficult to evaluate. We discuss some of these below.

The first set of factors comes under the general heading of **agency costs**. Agency costs are

## FIGURE 11.5: Value of the firm.
## MM Proposition I (with taxes and bankruptcy)

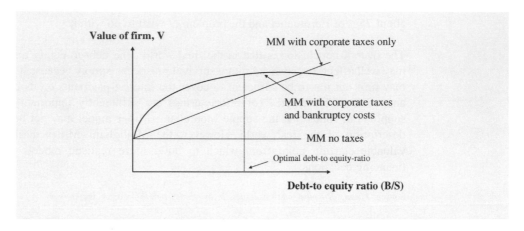

the costs of ensuring that managers (the agents) act in the best interests of the shareholders (i.e. the owners or principals) and meet the terms in any debt agreements (i.e. covenants).

Debt agreements (e.g. for bonds, bank loans) usually contain **restrictive covenants** and other conditions. Such conditions might preclude the managers from investing in particular sectors or in highly risky ventures. In principle, this limits managerial flexibility and may lead managers to try and hide crucial facts from bondholders (e.g. on the true riskiness of a project). Hence, bondholders suffer from *information asymmetry*. To investigate the behaviour of managers requires expenditure on monitoring by the debtholders and hence they may insist on a higher interest rate as leverage increases. This breaks one of the MM assumptions and will tend to increase the WACC and lower the firm's market value.

In the extreme case where the firm is already in financial distress, the shareholders have an incentive to persuade managers to undertake highly risky projects. If the gamble pays off, the high returns will all accrue to the shareholders (and all the bondholders get is their fixed interest payments). If the projects fail, the shareholders are hardly any worse off (but the bondholders will probably experience defaults). However, this 'go-for-broke' strategy by managers will be tempered by the fact that the managers themselves may lose their jobs, if the investment projects are unsuccessful.

In the real world, lenders prefer secured lending, so if the firm defaults on its interest payments, the debtholders can receive a payout from the sale of the firm's assets (e.g. plant, machinery, buildings). But there is a limit to a firm's ownership of highly marketable assets. For example, an advertising agency or 'high-tech' biotechnology firm might have very few tangible assets it can easily sell, whereas a mainstream engineering firm may have a large amount of tangible assets. This may mean that as leverage increases, the interest cost of (unsecured) borrowing rises more for the advertising firm than for the engineering firm. The latter has a higher 'debt capacity' than the former.

Managers might eschew high levels of debt because, if profitable projects arise in the future, it may be very difficult to persuade the market to provide even more debt finance (at reasonable cost) for new projects. Therefore, if managers keep debt levels low they get the benefit of an 'option to expand' into profitable projects, which might arise unexpectedly in the future.

If leverage increases the probability of bankruptcy then customers (e.g. for consumer durable goods like cars) might be less willing to purchase and suppliers (e.g. raw materials, etc.) might require higher prices, just in case the firm defaults. Thus leverage and the firm's cash flows $Y$ might not be independent (as assumed in MM). Also, if debtholders perceive this as a potential problem area, they too might raise debt interest costs as leverage increases. The perceived probability and costs of distress will of course depend on such factors as:

(i)  The greater the variability in earnings the higher the risk of liquidation or 'distress' (e.g. compare the earnings volatility of a 'high-fashion' retailer with those of a large department store or of a 'dot.com' retailer selling holidays with those of an established company such as Thomas Cook).
(ii) The costs of distress will be lower the greater the liquidity and marketability of the firm's assets (e.g. it is often easier to sell a building in a city centre rather than a specific piece of machinery or a factory on an out-of-town greenfield site). Also, since bondage is illegal, one cannot sell off the expertise of the employees of a failed 'dot.com' firm!)
(iii) The probability and costs of distress are lower the higher the proportion of variable to fixed costs (e.g. if you can quickly reduce staffing costs, you may lower the probability and costs of default).

So, firms with less volatile earnings, with highly marketable assets and 'flexible labour' (e.g. workers on short-term contracts) might be able to have higher leverage without the interest cost on their marginal debt increasing. Another way in which debt levels might influence future cash flows is if they affect managerial incentives. Firms with high leverage have to meet high interest payments every year or the firm fails and managers lose their jobs. This may provide strong incentives for managers (and other workers) to increase productivity, cut costs and concentrate on their 'core competencies'. Also, highly leveraged firms may not have a high level of earnings after paying debt interest. This means they cannot 'empire build' since there are little or no 'free cash flows'. They can only 'empire build' by subjecting themselves to outside scrutiny by 'going to market' for additional funds, and this they may be reluctant to do. Hence, high leverage might increase profits by discouraging 'empire building'.

It is also the case that highly concentrated shareholdings (e.g. family held shares) rather than a highly diffuse shareholder base (i.e. thousands of shareholders) might improve efficiency. Therefore moving to a smaller shareholder base by buying back equity with funds obtained from additional debt finance might improve efficiency and the cash flow of the firm. The counter-argument is that 'diffuse shareholders' are not really diffuse since, effectively, voting at the AGM is dominated by a few large institutional shareholders (e.g. insurance and pension funds).

## SIGNALLING AND PECKING ORDER

Given the investment plans and dividend payouts of the firm (which tend to be 'sticky') then any fluctuations in earnings may require changes in the degree of external finance. In terms of 'hassle' for managers, it is clearly easiest to finance projects from retained earnings, followed by debt issues and finally by issuing equity. This is called the **'pecking order'** and arises because the justification and information managers have to provide increases as one moves from internal finance, to debt, to equity.

With a 'pecking order' each firm's observed debt ratio could simply reflect its past cumulative requirements for external finance. Indeed, if it is generally accepted that highly profitable firms use mostly internal finance, then a firm issuing a large amount of debt (or a fortiori equity finance) is giving a 'signal' to the market that its current and future profitability is in doubt. This is likely to raise the cost of such finance. Also, if the firm does issue equity (e.g. a rights issue) investors might see this as a signal that the firm thinks its shares are overvalued and it is trying to obtain funds now, since 'rough times' are ahead. They will therefore only supply new finance at a much lower market price (i.e. they require a higher future return on equity). The pecking order theory appears to explain *intra*-industry debt patterns amongst mature firms quite well, since within an established industry (e.g. chemicals) those firms with lower profits also have higher debt ratios. However, the theory does not do so well at an *inter*-industy level and for 'young' companies. Here we see some rapidly growing firms (e.g. in biotechnology) with relatively low earnings, yet with very low debt ratios and much of their external finance coming from equity (e.g. via venture capitalists and new issues).

## WHERE DOES THIS LEAVE US?

Well, it leaves us without a well-defined theory of the optimal debt-to-equity mix that actually 'fits the facts'. This is why we regularly read in the financial press that some firms in an industry are either issuing more debt and using the funds to buy back equity or are using retained earnings to buy back equity—both of which increase leverage. Meanwhile, other firms in the same sector might have unchanged leverage. Buybacks such as the *Virgin Group* (Richard Branson) and the *Really Useful Group* (Andrew Lloyd Webber) increase leverage. Also, junk bonds were used extensively in the 1980s in management buyouts (MBO) and takeovers, again increasing leverage in these firms (sometimes to extremely high levels). Meanwhile, other firms (e.g. *Carphone Warehouse,* the *JCB* group that produce mechanical diggers of that name and *Barbour* who produce waxed jackets) have near zero debt.

Certainly therefore, some executives do believe that there is an optimal debt-to-equity ratio for their firms and therefore the WACC may be U-shaped. However, precisely what is the optimal leveraged position (e.g. is it 50% or 60%?) requires a careful assessment of many factors and we do not have one single overarching 'theory' that can provide the answer.

# 11.4  DIVIDEND POLICY

One of the key decisions to be made is how much of the profits (earnings) of the firm should be distributed in dividends and how much should be retained by the firm. If the firm has surplus funds then what should it do? Some possibilities include:

- Undertake new investment projects.
- Repurchase its own shares or reduce its debt.
- Acquire additional companies by merger or takeover.
- Purchase financial assets.
- Distribute more in dividends.

In this section we want to explore some of these issues but, be warned, financial economists have not come up with well-developed theoretical models which give unambiguous answers to these questions. The 'state of the art' here is much like the capital structure question discussed above. Different models provide useful insights into the main factors influencing these decisions but we cannot say precisely what determines the *optimal* policy in real world situations.

We first briefly discuss the effect of dividend announcements and actual dividend payouts on the share price. Next we examine yet a further proposition put forward by Modigliani–Miller, namely that 'dividend policy' does not affect the market value of the firm. This is the famous 'dividend irrelevance proposition' and applies in a 'no tax' world. We then find that when we include corporate and personal taxes in our model, the 'irrelevance proposition' breaks down and the tax regime can have a powerful effect on dividend policy. Finally, we discuss further 'real world' factors that appear to influence the dividend policy of the firm.

## SHARE PRICES AND DIVIDENDS

It is a well-established empirical fact that an *announcement* of a higher dividend payout in the near future (e.g. in 1 months time) leads to an immediate rise in the stock price. This appears to be because shareholders *perceive* that managers like to keep dividend payments fairly smooth over time and not to cut dividends in any year. Hence, the announcement of a higher current dividend is taken as a *signal* that earnings of the firm will also be higher in the future. (Hence the announcement of a higher *current* dividend is *not* taken as a signal that *future* dividends will be lower.) These higher dividends signal higher productivity, lower costs or increased sales prospects. Given this signalling mechanism it is perfectly rational that in an efficient market this should result in an immediate rise in stock prices (this is extensively discussed in Part 5 of the book).

Now consider a very different scenario. What happens to the stock price on the day of the actual dividend payment? Suppose a dividend payment is announced on 15th January and is to be paid on 15th February. In the US, on the **'date of record'**, say 1st February, a list of who currently owns the shares is made. All shareholders who hold shares five business days before the 'date of record' will receive the next dividend payment (i.e. the share is selling **cum-dividend**). But if the share is purchased four working days or less from the 'date of record' (i.e. from 28th January), then that person will not receive the next dividend payment (i.e. the share trades **ex-dividend**). Suppose that on the ex-dividend day 28th January, the share price is $P$. What price would you have paid for the share 1-day before? If the known dividend payment was $D$, then you would be willing to pay $P + D(1 - t_p)$ where $t_p$ = personal income tax rate (e.g. $t_p = 0.3$). Hence, on the ex-dividend day, in the first few minutes of trading, the stock price will fall by $D(1 - t_p)$. We have ignored the minor discounting problem that $D$ is not actually paid until 15th February and issues of future capital gain taxes, but these do not materially affect our conclusion.

## TIMING OF DIVIDENDS

We now want to show under what conditions the *timing* of dividend payouts does *not* affect the value of the firm. (This section follows the approach in Ross *et al.*, 1996 and Brealey and Myers, 2000.) The assumptions required for Modigliani–Miller's dividend irrelevance proposition are:

- No taxes or transaction costs.
- The investment expenditures of the firm are already set and are not altered by the dividend decision. All positive NPV projects have already been financed and future earnings of the firm are known.
- All investors have the same (i.e. homogeneous) expectations about future earnings.

Let's keep things as simple as possible. Assume the earnings of the firm are currently $1000 and will also be $1000 in 1 years time. Initially we assume all earnings are paid as dividends and the discount rate for this all equity firm is $r = 0.1$ (10%). The value of the firm is:

$$V = 1000 + \frac{1000}{1.1} = \$1909$$

If there are 100 shares outstanding, the dividends per share are $10 each period and the current share price is $19.09. After the immediate dividend of $10 is paid, the stock price will fall to $9.09.

In this Modigliani–Miller world 'dividend policy' is very specific. It is a choice *to reallocate dividends over time* (while the investment expenditure and hence earnings/cash flows of the firm are held fixed). For example, would an increased payment of $100 in dividends in year 1 lead to a change in the value of the firm and in the stock price (with the earnings profile unchanged)? The answer is 'no'.

To see this note that, as earnings in year 1 are $1000, the additional $100 must be financed externally. If the firm issues $100 worth of shares to *new* investors, they will only purchase them if they have a promised return of 10% (i.e. the return on equity) and hence the new shareholders receive $110 in dividends at the end of year 1. This only leaves $890 ($1000−$110) to pay dividends to the *old* shareholders. Hence for the old shareholders we have:

|                                      | $t = 0$ | $t = 1$ |
|--------------------------------------|---------|---------|
| Total dividends (old shareholders)   | $1100   | $890    |
| Dividends per share (old shareholders) | $11   | $8.90   |

The 'new' value of the firm is therefore:

$$V_{new} = 1100 + \frac{890}{1.1} = \$1909$$

which is unchanged from our previous calculation. Hence, in a world with no taxes and fixed expectations about future earnings and investment expenditures:

---

**MODIGLIANI–MILLER DIVIDEND IRRELEVANCE PROPOSITION**
**The value of the firm is independent of the time profile of**
**dividend payments**

---

In passing, note that the *new* shareholders do not receive the immediate dividend. They would therefore pay \$8.09 (= 8.90/1.1) per share and hence 123.6 (= 1000/8.09) new shares would be issued.

Why is $V$ unchanged by this change in the time profile of dividend payments? One intuitive way to think about this is to note that it is the earnings of the firm from its investment projects that determine the value of the firm. Therefore, the retention–distribution decision over time is immaterial. This is rather like the 'cutting up the pizza' argument in the capital structure debate.

Another approach is to consider the dividend irrelevance proposition arising from **'home-made' dividends**. Suppose investors would prefer dividend payments of \$10 in each period but the firm decides to increase payments to \$11 immediately and \$8.90 in 1 years time. Faced with this situation the investor can take \$1 of her cash dividends and reinvest it at $r = 10\%$ giving \$1.1 at $t = 1$. She then has \$10 cash at $t = 0$ and at $t = 1$, \$8.09 in dividends plus \$1.1, also giving \$10 at $t = 1$. The investor has created 'home-made dividends' of \$1.1 at $t = 1$ by selling \$1 of the company's shares at $t = 0$.

How about the converse case? Assume the investor prefers dividends of \$11 and \$8.90 but the company issues dividends of \$10 in each period. The investor immediately sells \$1 of the company's shares and hence at $t = 0$ has \$11 (= \$10 in dividends + \$1 from the sale of shares). Because she has sold \$1 of shares at $t = 0$, she will receive \$1.1 [= \$1(1 + r)] lower dividend payments from the company at $t = 1$. Hence at $t = 1$ she receives \$8.90 (= \$10 −\$1.1).

The dividend irrelevance proposition arises because the investor can create home-made dividends either by reinvesting her 'surplus' dividends or selling off shares. So, she is able to achieve any cash flow she likes, regardless of the payoff profile of *actual* dividend payments by the firm.

## DIVIDEND POLICY AND TAXES

The Modigliani–Miller dividend irrelevancy proposition does not necessarily hold in the presence of corporate and personal taxes (or with tax allowances/breaks). In fact, the dividend payout policy depends crucially on these tax rates. Suppose the personal tax rate $t_p = 0.30$ and the corporate tax rate is higher at $t_c = 0.40$, but the corporate receives tax breaks on certain investments. For example, suppose that if the firm invests in the shares of another firm, then the first 70% say of dividend income is not taxable, leaving only $z = 0.3$ (30%) which is taxable. The firm now has a choice of:

- Issuing $1 in additional dividends to shareholders today, who can then invest the funds themselves in financial assets. This is a 'high' dividend policy.
- Retaining the dividends, with the firm investing them in financial assets (earning income at a rate $r$) and then paying the funds to shareholders at a later date. This is a 'low' dividend policy.

Which policy, 'high' dividend payout or 'low' dividend payout today, will provide the greatest benefit to shareholders in say $n = 2$ years time? The after-tax return to the shareholders investing their own cash is $r(1 - t_p)$, but for the firm investing the cash, it is $r(1 - t_c z)$, the latter being an effective tax rate of $t_c z = 0.12$ [ $= 0.4 \times 0.3$]. If the firm takes $1 of additional cash and does not immediately distribute it in dividends but invests it for $n$ years, this will accrue to $1[1 + r(1 - t_c z)]^n$. If this is paid to the shareholders in year $n$, they will receive:

Shareholder receipts from delayed dividend payment

[11.11]     $= \$1[1 + r(1 - t_c z)]^n (1 - t_p) = \$0.8286$

On the other hand, if the firm distributes the $1 in dividends at $t = 0$, the investors receive only $1(1 - t_p)$ after tax. This can then be reinvested for $n = 2$ years at a rate $r(1 - t_p)$ to give an after-tax final payment of:

Shareholder receipts from immediate dividend payment

$= [\$1(1 - t_p)][1 + r(1 - t_p)]^n (1 - t_p)$

[11.12]     $= \$0.7865$

Comparing equations [11.11] and [11.12] we see that, with our figures, it is more favourable to the shareholders if the company has lower current dividends and reinvests the excess cash itself. In general:

Receipts from immediate dividends $<$ receipts from delayed dividends when $t_p > t_c z$

In our example $t_p = 0.30$ and $t_c z = (0.4)(0.3) = 0.12$ and hence this is consistent with the company delaying the payment of dividends. However, different tax rates and tax breaks could produce the opposite result (e.g. some pension funds might pay zero effective tax on dividends), hence:

> **High personal income tax rates and low (effective)**
> **corporate tax rates favour low current dividends**

Note that in terms of the above analysis the 'extra cash' retained is not spent on investment projects since we assume that all positive NPV projects have already been financed from a mixture of debt and equity.

## REAL WORLD CONSIDERATIONS

In the real world, firms smooth dividends and try to avoid any fall in dividends. A reasonable representation of this 'smoothness' property is provided by the **partial adjustment model**. Firms have a desired long run level of dividends (per share) $D^*$ which is set by the desired payout ratio $p$ $(= 0.4$ for example) and the level of current earnings:

$$D^* = pE_t$$

However, if current earnings increase and hence $D^*$ increases, they do not immediately pay out all of this cash flow in additional current dividends. Instead they pay out a fraction $\theta$ (e.g. $\theta = 0.9$) in extra dividends:

$$D_{t+1} - D_t = \theta(D^* - D_{t-1}) \qquad \text{or} \qquad D_{t+1} = \theta pE_t + (1 - \theta)D_{t-1}$$

Hence, if current earnings $E_t$ increase by $1, the increase in dividends next period is only $0.36 $(= 0.9 \times 0.4)$. The observed pattern of dividends paid out is therefore 'smooth', even though earnings might be quite variable from year to year. There might also be an asymmetric effect, in that when $E_t$ falls slightly, this does not lead to any fall in dividends (except in extreme cases). As we have already seen, in practice retained earnings (of $0.64) may be used to finance additional investment projects (the 'pecking order' hypothesis) or to repay debt if the firm is highly geared. There is some evidence to suggest that firms also increase retained earnings to help finance mergers and takeovers (even though these often turn out to harm the existing shareholders). Hence, because of the complexity of a firm's goals and objectives, the tax laws, as well as the signalling function of dividends, we find that our theories only suggest possible reasons for different dividend policies of firms. There is not a particular formula one can apply to determine the optimal dividend policy. One thing is clear however, firms do not behave as if dividend policy is irrelevant.

# 11.5  SUMMARY

In this chapter we have analysed some of the key propositions in corporate finance, namely the relationship between alternative methods of financing the firm's activities, the overall cost of capital and the market value of the firm. The key results are as follows.

> • **Modigliani–Miller (MM) 'Proposition I' (no corporate taxes)** demonstrates that under certain restrictive assumptions, **the WACC and hence the value of the firm are independent of the debt-to-equity mix**. Under Proposition I a firm should undertake all those projects with positive NPV and not worry whether they are financed from debt or equity. Business decisions and finance decisions are independent.

- Given that the overall WACC, $R_w$ is independent of the debt-to-equity mix (i.e. MM Proposition I) then we can deduce that the required return on equity in a levered firm, $R_s^L$, is *not* independent of the debt-to-equity mix. In fact **the required return on equity $R_s^L$ depends *positively* on the debt-to-equity ratio $B_L/S_L$. This is MM 'Proposition II' (no corporate taxes)** and arises because with greater leverage shareholders experience greater variability in earnings and hence greater business risk, for which they demand additional return.

- For two firms with the same business risk, then **including corporate taxes overturns the original MM Proposition** I. The value of the levered firm $V_L$ equals the value of the unlevered firm $V_U$ plus the value of the 'tax shield' $tB$: $V_L = V_U + tB_L$. Hence **the optimal capital structure is to have 100% debt finance**. MM Proposition II in the presence of corporate taxes implies a positive relationship between the required return on equity in a levered firm $R_s^L$ and the debt-to-equity ratio $B_L/S_L$. (This result is qualitatively similar to the 'no tax' case.)

- **It is unlikely that the above MM propositions hold in practice** because the assumptions on which they are based are overly restrictive. Because the **probability and costs of 'distress' and bankruptcy** increase with the debt-to-equity ratio, then the WACC is likely to rise after some debt level has been reached. Also, a firm's debt levels might affect managerial incentives and hence company earnings. Both of these factors would tend to lead to a fall in the value of the firm as the debt-to-equity ratio increases past some critical point. Hence in practice there is some optimal debt-to-equity ratio for the firm.

- **There may be an optimal debt-to-equity ratio in practice**, nevertheless it is very difficult to precisely determine exactly what level is optimal. This leaves plenty of scope for companies to justify (in the financial press) why their proposed changes in capital structure will add to shareholder value.

- When calculating the NPV of a project for a levered firm two broad approaches are available. The first **discounts after-tax earnings using the after-tax WACC** as the discount rate. This is valid for projects that are (i) carbon copies of the existing projects of the firm and hence are scale enhancing and (ii) do not alter the firm-wide leverage ratio. Adjustments are possible to overcome the latter restrictive assumption but are difficult to implement in practice.

- A second approach is **adjusted present value (APV)**, whereby the **after-tax cash flows are discounted at the 'all equity' discount rate** and the PV of any **tax shields** are added to give the APV. This method is more appealing when the value of the tax shields is likely to be substantial.

- Whatever method is chosen to calculate the NPV it is worthwhile remembering that they all involve considerable uncertainties and therefore there comes a point when 'sophisticated' adjustments based on *alternative financing arrangements* may not be worthwhile. Remember the key element of value added for the firm is in **choosing projects where net cash flows are high in relation to their *business risk***, and where strategic business objectives can be met. (The latter has been aided by the use of **real options**—see Cuthbertson and Nitzsche, 2001.) Prospective gains from 'tax shields' may therefore often be of secondary importance.

- Some **'simpler' alternatives to NPV** have been advocated, which seek to provide incentives for managers to act in the interests of shareholders when deciding on specific investment projects. These methodologies are rather similar and come under the heading of **Economic Value Added (EVA)**, **Economic Profit (EP)**, the **return on capital (ROC)** and the **risk adjusted return on capital (RAROC)** the latter is used by financial intermediaries. The EVA approach can be used to rank different companies, as well as divisions within the same company.

- Under certain restrictive assumptions, **the rescheduling of dividend payments over time is irrelevant**. Put another way, neither a 'high' nor 'low' dividend payout has any effect on the value of the firm. This is the **Modigliani–Miller dividend irrelevance proposition**. In practice firms 'smooth' dividend payments and do not cut them except when the firm is in financial distress.

# END OF CHAPTER EXERCISES

**Q1** Broadly speaking what determines the 'value of a firm'?

**Q2** Under what conditions does the WACC fall continuously as the debt-to-equity ratio (i.e. leverage) increases?

**Q3** Why can we consider the value of the firm to be equal to (i) the PV of future earnings and (ii) the market value of equity $S$ plus the value of debt $B$? Isn't this contradictory?

**Q4** Two firms have identical possible earning flows $Y$ in the future. Firm-A is all equity financed while firm-B is financed with 90% debt and 10% equity. Why would the equityholders of firm-B demand a higher expected (required) return than the equityholders of firm-A?

**Q5** Why do the 'traditionalists' believe that there is a debt-to-equity ratio that will maximise the value of the firm?

**Q6** Show that:

(a) $R_w = (1 - z)R_s + zR_b$ where $z = B/(B + S)$ can be rearranged to give:
(b) $R_s = R_w + (R_w - R_b)B/S$

Hence, demonstrate under what conditions the cost of equity capital rises with the debt-to-equity ratio.

**Q7** In a Modigliani–Miller world without corporate taxes, the value of the firm is independent of the debt-to-equity ratio, but if we include corporate taxes in the model then the value of the firm is maximised with 100% debt. Intuitively, what is the cause of this dramatic change in outcomes?

# APPENDIX 11.1  LEVERAGE AND THE RETURN ON EQUITY (NO CORPORATE TAXES)

We want to derive the algebra that underlies the numerical calculations in Table 11.1 and Figure 11.2, that is the relationship between the return on equity $R_s^L$ and income $Y$, as the degree of leverage $z$ changes. We assume (i) no taxes and (ii) all earnings (after interest payments) are distributed in dividends.

$Y=$ earnings (cash flow, profits) before interest, tax and depreciation for either a levered
    L or unlevered U firm
$S_L=$ \$-value of equity in a levered firm
$B_L=$ \$-value of debt (bonds) in a levered firm
$V_i=$ \$-value of the firm ($i =$ U or L)
$R_b=$ interest cost of debt
$R_s^L=$ return on equity in levered firm
$z \equiv B_L/V_L =$ degree of leverage (and $1 - z \equiv S_L/V_L$)
Div$=$ total dividends paid to all shareholders

The return on equity is defined as:

[A11.1]     $R_s^L = (\text{Div})/S_L$

Using $S_L \equiv (1 - z)V_L$ and Div $= Y - R_b B_L = Y - R_b(zV_L)$ then:

[A11.2]     $R_s^L = \dfrac{Y - R_b(zV_L)}{(1 - z)V_L} = \dfrac{Y}{V_L(1 - z)} - R_b\dfrac{z}{(1 - z)}$

Clearly, $R_s^L$ depends on $Y$ and leverage $z$. In Table 11.1 a crucial assumption is that the mix of debt and equity is decided before the income of the firm $Y$ is realised. Remember that $Y$ is 'uncertain', but we can work out the impact on $R_s^L$ of different possible values for $Y$, for 'identical' firms (except for their degree of leverage $z$). From equation [A11.2] a graph of $R_s^L$ against $Y$ has a slope $1/V_L(1 - z)$ and an intercept $-(R_b z)/(1 - z)$. Hence as $z$ increases the slope of this graph increases (and the intercept becomes more negative)—see Figure 11.2. If $Y$ increases or decreases by 1 unit then $R_s^L$ changes by $\Delta R_s^L = (\Delta Y)/V(1 - z)$. For example, for $V = \$10m$ and $z = 0.2$, or $z = 0.5$ we have $\Delta R_s^L = 1.25\Delta Y$, $\Delta R_s^L = 2\Delta Y$, respectively. Hence for higher values of leverage $z$, the variability in $\Delta R_s^L$ increases for different realisations of $Y$. For an all equity firm $z = 0$, hence:

[A11.3]     $R_s = Y/V_L$

where we have dropped the 'L' in the notation. So, a graph of $R_s$ against $Y$ goes through the origin (see Figure 11.2). The value of $Y$ for which the all equity and a levered firm give an *equal* value for $R_s$ is given by equating [A11.2] and [A11.3], from which we obtain:

$Y^* = R_b V$

In the text $Y^* = 0.1(\$10m) = \$1m$ which can be seen as the 'cross-over point' in Figure 11.2. You might also note that equation [A11.2] can also be obtained by rearranging

$V_L = Y/\text{WACC}$ to solve for $R_s^L$, where $\text{WACC} = (1-z)R_s^L + zR_b$. This is perfectly consistent as long as we realise that in Table 11.1, $V_L$ is held constant and only the *proportions* of $S$ and $B$ are being altered (i.e. leverage), which then has a direct effect on $R_s^L$. The overall result from Table 11.1, and equation [A11.2] is that the *expected return on equity* and the *volatility* of equity returns, are both higher the greater the degree of leverage $z$.

# APPENDIX 11.2  MODIGLIANI–MILLER WITH CORPORATE TAXES

In this appendix we derive the following relationships for a levered firm which is subject to corporate taxes:

(A) We show how ***Modigliani–Miller Proposition I*** is altered in the presence of corporate taxes. The relationship between the value of a levered firm and an unlevered firm is:

[A11.4]     $V_L = V_U + tB_L$

> **The value of the levered firm increases with the amount of debt $B_L$**
> **Therefore our original 'no tax' MM Proposition I that $V_L$ is independent of debt $B_L$ does *not* hold in the presence of corporate taxes**

(B) We demonstrate that the cost of equity capital $R_s^L$ in a levered firm is given by:

[A11.5]     $R_s^L = \rho_s^u + (1-t)(\rho_s^u - R_b)\dfrac{B_L}{S_L}$

where $\rho_s^u$ is the cost of equity capital in an unlevered firm (i.e. 100% equity financed), hence:

> **Our original *MM Proposition II* that $R_s^L$ rises with the degree of leverage $(B_L/S_L)$ still holds in the presence of corporate taxes**

Throughout we assume the levered and unlevered firms have the same degree of business risk and hence the same *expected* earnings $Y$, before interest and taxes. We also assume (expected) earnings $Y$ are a constant amount per annum forever (i.e. $Y$ is a perpetuity). All earnings are distributed to shareholders.

## (A) THE VALUE OF AN UNLEVERED AND LEVERED FIRM

For an unlevered (i.e. 100% equity financed) firm, after-tax earnings are $Y(1-t)$ and the value of the firm is:

[A11.6] $$V_U = \frac{Y(1-t)}{\rho_s^u}$$

where $\rho_s^u$ = risk adjusted discount rate for an *all equity financed firm*. For the levered firm, corporate taxes are calculated after deduction of interest payments. Hence, interest income paid to bondholders and the earnings available to shareholders are:

Interest income of bondholders $= R_b B_L$

Shareholder earnings $= (Y - R_b B_L)(1 - t)$

Therefore, the total income accruing to both stakeholders in a levered firm is:

[A11.7] $$\text{Total income of levered firm} = (Y - R_b B_L)(1 - t) + R_b B_L = Y(1 - t) + t(R_b B_L)$$

$$= \text{income of unlevered firm} + \text{'tax shield'}$$

Note that $Y(1-t)$ equals the income accruing to an equivalent unlevered firm (see equation [A11.6]) and hence should be discounted at $\rho_s^u$ the risk adjusted discount rate for an all equity firm. The income from the tax shield arises because the firm holds debt of $B_L$. If the tax shield is riskless it should be discounted at the rate $R_b$. Therefore, from equation [A11.7] the value of the levered firm $V_L$ is:

[A11.8] $$V_L = \frac{Y(1-t)}{\rho_s^u} + \frac{R_b t B_L}{R_b} = V_U + t B_L$$

> **MM PROPOSITION I (WITH CORPORATE TAXES)**
> **Value of levered firm = value of unlevered firm + value of tax shield**

In fact, it can be shown that equation [A11.8] only holds when the *level* of debt $B_L$ is constant over time. An alternative assumption is that the debt-to-equity *ratio* $B_L/S_L$ is constant over time and here a slightly different formula applies (see Miles and Ezzel, 1980). Also, the Miles–Ezzell approach allows us to continue using an amended WACC formula as the discount rate when the debt ratio $B_L/V_L$ changes because of the specific project:

$$\text{WACC}^* = \rho_s^u - (B_L/V_L)T(1 + \rho_s^u)/(1 + R_b)$$

where $T$ is the net tax saving per dollar of interest paid. The latter is difficult to estimate in practice so the marginal corporate tax rate $t$ is usually used instead. The validity of the above formula for the WACC still depends on the restrictive assumption that the firm as a whole adjusts its debt as the value of the firm alters, to maintain a constant overall ratio of debt-to-market value. This more complex approach seems unlikely to be applied in practice.

## (B) RETURN ON EQUITY OF A LEVERED FIRM, $R_s^L$ AND THE DEBT-TO-EQUITY RATIO, $B_L/S_L$

The relationship between the cost of equity in a levered firm $R_s^L$ and the debt-to-equity ratio $B_L/S_L$ is a little involved. First, consider the balance sheet of the levered firm (paying corporate taxes):

**LEVERED FIRM'S BALANCE SHEET**

| Assets | | Liabilities | |
|---|---|---|---|
| **Value unlevered firm** | $V_U$ | **Debt (bonds)** | $B_L$ |
| **Value tax shield** | $tB_L$ | **Equity** | $S_L$ |
| **Total** | $V_U + tB_L$ | | $B_L + S_L$ |

The expected cash flow (perpetuity) *per annum* from $V_U$ and the tax shield $tB_L$ is:

[A11.9]     Expected cash flow from assets $= \rho_s^u V_U + R_b(tB_L)$

The expected cash flow to equity and bondholders is:

[A11.10]     $R_s^L S_L + R_b B_L$

Since there are no retained earnings, the two cash flows in equations [A11.9] and [A11.10] must be equal, which gives after rearrangement:

[A11.11]     $R_s^L = V_U \dfrac{\rho_s^u}{S_L} - (1-t)\dfrac{B_L}{S_L} R_b$

But from equation [A11.8] and the fact that in an efficient market the value of the firm $V_L$ is equal to the market value of equity plus debt:

[A11.12]     $V_L = V_U + tB_L = S_L + B_L$

Hence:

[A11.13]     $V_U = S_L - (1-t)B_L$

Substituting equation [A11.13] in equation [A11.11] for $V_U$:

$$R_s^L = \frac{\rho_s^u}{S_L}[S_L - (1-t)B_L] - (1-t)\left(\frac{B_L}{S_L}\right) R_b$$

[A11.14] $\qquad R_s^L = \rho_s^u + (1-t)(\rho_s^u - R_b)\dfrac{B_L}{S_L}$ where $\rho_s^u > R_b$

---

**MM PROPOSITION II (WITH CORPORATE TAXES)**
The required return on equity *in a levered firm* $R_s^L$
increases with the debt-to-equity ratio $B_L/S_L$

---

Note that for each unit increase in $B_L/S_L$ the required return on equity $R_s^L$ increases by $(1-t)(\rho_s^u - R_b)$, which is less than under the no tax case (i.e. $t = 0$). This concludes our proof of MM Proposition II.

# APPENDIX 11.3  THE RETURN ON EQUITY IN AN UNLEVERED FIRM AND ADJUSTED PRESENT VALUE

In this appendix we derive an expression for the return on equity in an unlevered firm $\rho_s^u$ in terms of the return on equity in a levered firm $R_s^L$ and the bond return $R_b$. This enables us to calculate $\rho_s^u$ in terms of the observables $R_s^L$ and $R_b$.

---

**We can then use our 'calculated' $\rho_s^u$ as the discount rate in the adjusted NPV technique**

---

To apply the APV technique of project appraisal, we need a measure of the discount rate on an unlevered firm $\rho_s^u$. This can be obtained from the CAPM/SML:

[A11.15] $\qquad \rho_s^u = r + \beta^u(ER_m - r)$

However, we now require $\beta^u$, the beta of an unlevered firm. Unfortunately, (nearly) all firms are levered, so what we observe in the data is the beta of a levered firm $\beta^L$. Can we link $\beta^u$ to $\beta^L$? The answer is yes. But the method is rather involved. We therefore consider the no tax case, before moving on to the case where we have corporate taxes.

## CASE A: NO CORPORATE TAXES

We begin with the fact that the beta of a levered firm is a weighted average of the debt $\beta_b^L$ and equity $\beta_s^L$ betas (and the 'weights' sum to unity):

[A11.16] $\qquad \beta^L = \left(\dfrac{B_L}{V_L}\right)\beta_b^L + \left(\dfrac{S_L}{V_L}\right)\beta_s^L$

$\beta_b^L$ and $\beta_s^L$ are observable/measurable from the SML, using data on returns on debt and equity for levered firms. **MM Proposition I** implies that the beta of an unlevered firm $\beta^u$ (with equal business risk) equals that of a levered firm, hence:

[A11.17] $\qquad \beta^u = \left(\dfrac{B_L}{V_L}\right)\beta_b^L + \left(\dfrac{S_L}{V_L}\right)\beta_s^L \equiv z\beta_b^L + (1-z)\beta_s^L$

where $z = B_L/V_L$. Equation [A11.17] allows us to calculate $\beta^u$ from the observed $\beta_b^L$ and $\beta_s^L$. Now, $\beta_b^L < \beta_s^L$ because debt is less risky than equity, so equation [A11.17] implies:

[A11.18] $\qquad \beta^u < \beta_s^L$

Hence, the beta of an all equity firm is less than the equity beta of a levered firm. This also fits with MM-II where we found that the equity of a levered firm has higher risk than an 'equivalent' unlevered (100% equity) firm. If $\beta_b^L \approx 0$ then equation [A11.17] becomes:

[A11.19] $\qquad \beta^u = \left(\dfrac{S_L}{V_L}\right)\beta_s^L$

and it is easy in this case to see that $\beta^u < \beta_s^L$.

## CASE B: WITH CORPORATE TAXES

Again we want to obtain an expression for the unobservable $\beta^u$ in terms of the observable/measurable values $\beta_b^L$ and $\beta_s^L$. The derivation is a little involved so we immediately present the equation we are looking for, which is:

[A11.20] $\qquad \beta^u = \left[\dfrac{B_L(1-t)}{B_L(1-t)+S_L}\right]\beta_b^L + \left[\dfrac{S_L}{(1-t)B_L+S_L}\right]\beta_s^L$

This is very similar to equation [A11.17] since in both equation [A11.17] and equation [A11.20], $\beta^u$ is a weighted average of $\beta_b^L$ and $\beta_s^L$ with the weights summing to unity. In equation [A11.20] the 'weights' contain the tax rate $t$, as we might expect. Of course, if you set $t = 0$ in equation [A11.20] it 'collapses' to equation [A11.17], the 'no tax' form of the equation. To prove equation [A11.20] we begin with the value of a levered firm, given by MM-I (with taxes):

[A11.21] $\qquad V_L = V_U + tB_L$

By definition, the value of the levered firm is equal to the market value of its debt and equity:

[A11.22] $\qquad V_L = B_L + S_L$

From equations [A11.21] and [A11.22]:

[A11.23] $\qquad V_U = (1-t)B_L + S_L$

The *definition* of the beta of a levered firm is:

[A11.24] $\qquad \beta^L = \left(\dfrac{B_L}{V_L}\right)\beta_b^L + \left(\dfrac{S_L}{V_L}\right)\beta_s^L$

The next point holds the key to the derivation. From MM-I with taxes we have $V_L = V_U + tB_L$. Hence, the beta of a levered firm can also be viewed as a weighted average of the beta of an unlevered (100% equity financed) firm and the beta of the tax shield ($tB$). Hence:

[A11.25]
$$\beta_L = \left(\frac{V_U}{V_L}\right)\beta^u + \left(\frac{tB_L}{V_L}\right)\beta_b^L$$

The beta of the cash flow from the tax shield is the 'debt beta', since here *we assume* the tax shield is riskless. We are now nearly there. Equating [A11.24] and [A11.25] and rearranging:

[A11.26]
$$\beta^u = \left[\frac{B_L(1-t)}{V_U}\right]\beta_b^L + \left[\frac{S_L}{V_U}\right]\beta_s^L$$

Substituting for $V_U$ from equation [A11.23] gives the expression required:

[A11.27]
$$\beta^u = \left[\frac{B_L(1-t)}{(1-t)B_L + S_L}\right]\beta_b^L + \left[\frac{S_L}{(1-t)B_L + S_L}\right]\beta_s^L$$

> The 'unobservable' beta of an *unlevered* firm is equal
> to a weighted average of the 'observable' betas on debt
> and equity of the *levered* firm

The 'weights' on $\beta_b^L$ and $\beta_s^L$ in equation [A11.27] sum to unity. Again, note that since $\beta_b^L < \beta_s^L$ then from equation [A11.27] the beta of the equity of an unlevered (100% equity financed) firm is less than the beta of the equity of a levered firm:

[A11.28]
$$\beta^u < \beta_s^L$$

This again fits with our MM-II (with taxes), which implies that levered equity is more risky than unlevered equity. If we set $\beta_b^L = 0$ in equation [A11.27] then it is easy to see that in this case $\beta^u < \beta_s^L$.

# APPENDIX 11.4  ASSUMPTIONS WHEN USING WACC

For a levered firm, the after-tax WACC is used in discounting the future cash flows from an investment project. For this to be a valid procedure, we can show that the following restrictive assumptions are required:

(i) the new project must produce constant annual earnings $Y$ *in perpetuity*;
(ii) the firm must maintain its *initial* debt ratio ($B_L/V_L$) when financing the project.

The latter assumption is usually expressed as the WACC being valid for the 'average project'. To demonstrate the above, let the firm's capital cost (at $t = 0$) be KC dollars. Hence given (ii):

$$\text{Dollar amount of debt} = \left(\frac{B_\text{L}}{V_\text{L}}\right)\text{KC} \quad \text{and} \quad \text{Dollar amount of equity} = \left(\frac{S_\text{L}}{V_\text{L}}\right)\text{KC}$$

The total dollar cost *per annum* of the debt and equity is:

$$\text{Total dollar cost of finance p.a.} = (1 - t)R_\text{b}\left(\frac{B_\text{L}}{V_\text{L}}\right)\text{KC} + R_\text{s}^\text{L}\left(\frac{S_\text{L}}{V_\text{L}}\right)\text{KC}$$

A viable investment project requires perpetual earnings $Y$ p.a. from the project to exceed the dollar cost p.a., that is:

$$Y \geqslant (1 - t)R_\text{b}\left(\frac{B_\text{L}}{V_\text{L}}\right)\text{KC} + R_\text{s}^\text{L}\left(\frac{S_\text{L}}{V_\text{L}}\right)\text{KC}$$

or

$$\frac{Y}{\text{KC}} \geqslant (1 - t)R_\text{b}\left(\frac{B_\text{L}}{V_\text{L}}\right) + R_\text{s}^\text{L}\left(\frac{S_\text{L}}{V_\text{L}}\right) = \text{WACC}$$

Note that $Y/\text{KC}$ is the project's annual rate of return. Hence, a viable project is one where the return on the project exceeds the WACC, where the latter assumes the debt ratio $B_\text{L}/V_\text{L}$ for the project, is the same as for the firm as a whole.

# PART 5

# EQUITY MARKETS

# Equity Finance and Stock Valuation

In Chapter 1 we presented a brief overview of how the firm raises finance by issuing equity and debt while in Chapter 7 we went into more detail about the various forms of marketable debt finance, provided by corporate bonds, floating rate notes, convertible and callable bonds. Here, in the first section of this chapter we return to the issue of alternative sources of equity finance. In particular we elaborate on the factors involved in new equity issues as well as additional sales of shares by a mature corporation. The rest of this chapter then deals with the pricing of ordinary shares.

Portfolio theory suggests that if all investors have the same expectations about returns and their (co)variances and they wish to 'trade off' risk against return, then they will all hold the market portfolio. They passively alter their portfolio of assets to maintain the 'optimal balance' between risk and expected return. However, in the real world some investors might feel they have superior information about some stocks and will speculate with part of their portfolio of assets. Broadly speaking, if they think a stock is undervalued, that is its 'true' or 'fair value' $V$ is above the current market price $P$, then they will purchase it, hoping its price will rise and they will earn a positive return which outweighs any risk in the strategy. To undertake such a speculative strategy the investor has to be able to calculate the 'fair value' of the stock, and the various methods to do this are outlined in this chapter.

In earlier chapters we noted that the fair value of an asset is determined by the PV of future cash flows. For equity (stocks) there are two major problems. First, future cash flows (dividends) are uncertain and we need some forecasting method to predict them. Second, the discount rate should reflect the riskiness of these cash flows. Broadly speaking, the greater the risk the greater the discount factor. We have already noted the 'mirror image' relationship between DPV and the internal rate of return (IRR). This also applies to 'stock-picking', where we can classify under (over)valued shares using either the DPV or IRR approach.

# 12.1 FINANCING THE FIRM: SHARE CAPITAL

Firms can raise debt finance from bank loans and this does not affect the ownership of the firm, which may initially be in the hands of a small number of 'initial investors' whose shares are not traded. (These may be 'family firms' or firms with a minority shareholder interest from business angels or venture capitalists.) However, at some point the firm may wish to raise additional equity finance by an initial public offering (IPO) of shares. The ownership of the firm will then pass to the 'new' shareholders (as a group), and in this section we begin by discussing the difference between ordinary and preference shares. In addition, a 'mature' publicly quoted firm may wish to raise additional equity finance; one method for doing so is a 'rights issue' and this is discussed below. We also discuss the use of scrip issues and stock splits.

## ORDINARY SHARES

In general, there are two types of shares issued: ordinary and preference shares. Essentially, ordinary shareholders are the owners of the firm, with a residual claim on profits (after tax and payment of interest on debt). Such 'earnings' are either retained or distributed as dividends to shareholders. **Ordinary shares** (of UK companies) have the following characteristics:

- Voting rights (usually one vote per share) as set down in the Memorandum of Association, which include the right to appoint the Board of Directors and the auditors.
- Shares are normally non-redeemable with a par value (i.e. fully paid up value), but they can be issued 'partly paid' and then paid for in instalments.
- Shareholders are the residual claimants on the firm's profits and therefore may not receive dividends if current (or previous retained) earnings are low.

'Preferred ordinary' and 'deferred ordinary' shares rank behind 'ordinary shares' for receipt of payment. 'Deferred' are second in the 'pecking order' for payment. Some firms also have non-voting shares.

## PREFERENCE SHARES

Preference shares have some characteristics of ordinary shares and some characteristics of debt instruments. The characteristics of **preference shares** are:

- Holders have a claim on dividends which takes 'preference' over ordinary shareholders. Dividends are often paid at a predefined rate (either fixed or floating) and are often 'cumulative' rather than 'non-cumulative' (i.e. if 'cumulative' then any shortfall in dividend payments is made up in future years, before any further payments to ordinary shareholders).
- They are usually non-voting, but they are often granted voting rights if preferred dividends have not been paid for some time. Preferred stock holders cannot put the firm into liquidation.
- If the firm goes into liquidation, payments to preference shareholders are paid after those to debt holders but before any payments to ordinary shareholders.
- In the US preferred stock dividends cannot be deducted as an 'interest expense' when calculating the issuer's corporate tax payments. (So US companies with losses have an incentive to issue preferred stock.) For most US investors preferred dividends are taxed as income, but for US corporates who hold preferred stock of other companies 80% of the dividends are tax deductible. Hence if the corporate tax rate were say 35% on bond income received, the effective tax rate on preferred dividends received would only be 7% ($= 0.2 \times 0.35$). Not surprisingly, most preferred stock in the US is held by corporates and because of the low effective tax rate, its pre-tax yield can often be below that on T-bonds.

Some preference shares are convertible into ordinary shares at a predetermined rate on specific dates, at the option of the holder. These **convertible preference shares** are often issued as 'mezzanine finance' to venture capitalists. Hence investors get a fixed return and they can convert to ordinary shares if the firm is ultimately successful.

## RIGHTS ISSUE

When a company initially 'goes public' (i.e. becomes a corporation) it usually obtains finance by issuing **ordinary shares** in an IPO or private placement, after which it can raise additional finance from debt (e.g. additional bank loans or corporate bond issues) or from preference shares. However, after some years, the Board of Directors may decide that additional ordinary share capital is required to finance fixed investment or to repay existing debt.

Suppose a public company has been in existence for some time and it initially obtained finance via an IPO (i.e. unseasoned new issue). It now wants to raise additional equity finance. It could simply sell additional shares on the open market, which would constitute a **seasoned new issue**. However since the *new* shareholders will receive dividends, the funds available for *existing* shareholders are likely to be reduced: their holding has become **diluted**. Because of the latter adverse effect, it is customary (or a legal requirement) to offer the new shares to *existing* shareholders in proportion to their existing holdings: this is a ***pre-emptive rights issue***. (Another reason for a rights issue is to fund a takeover by issuing the new shares to the shareholders of the company to be taken over, but here no cash is raised.)

The cost of a rights issue (for cash) usually amounts to about 2 to 5% of total receipts from the issue.

However, countries differ over pre-emptive rights. In the USA and Germany some companies can issue additional shares by auction (i.e. a seasoned new issue) and do not have to first offer them to existing shareholders. If the Directors sell some of 'the rights' to financial institutions by prior arrangement, this is known as a *private placement*.

An example of a 'one for three' rights issue is given in Table 12.1. Existing equity for *Longevity.com* is 1m shares, at a current price of $100 per share, and hence the market value is $100m. To ensure that the rights are taken up, the offer price in the rights issue must be less than $100. Suppose *Longevity.com* chooses a share offer price of $80 (allowing for a contingency of a 20% fall in price, below which the rights issue would not be taken up). It wants to raise $26,666m to expand its range of funeral parlours, hence (ignoring rounding errors):

$$\text{Number of new shares} = \frac{\text{funds required}}{\text{subscription price}} = \frac{\$26.666m}{\$80} = 333{,}333$$

---

## TABLE 12.1: Rights issue: *Longevity.com*

| | |
|---|---|
| **Data:** | Existing equity = 1m shares (at $25 par value) |
| | Current share price = $100 |
| | Current market cap = $100m (= 1m × $100) |
| | Extra funds required = $26.666m |
| | Offer price for new shares = $80 |
| **Questions:** | What is the value of the shares after the rights issue (i.e. the 'ex-rights' price)? |
| | What could you sell your 'rights' for? |
| **Answers:** | Number of new shares issued = $26.666m/$80 = 333,333 shares |
| | Hence, we have to issue one new share for every three existing shares |
| | This is a 'one for three' rights issue: |
| | 3 old shares @ $100 = $300 |
| | 1 new share @ $80 = $80 |
| | Hence, 4 shares are worth = $380 |
| | Value of 1 share (ex-rights) = $95 |
| | Hence, value of 1 right = $15 (= $95 − $80) |

Shareholders ('by convention') always get one right for each share they own, and hence 1m rights are issued. However, the crucial point is how many 'rights' must be exercised to receive one new share:

$$\text{Number of rights needed to buy one new share} = \frac{\text{number of old shares}}{\text{number of new shares}}$$

$$= \frac{1m}{333,333} = \text{three rights}$$

This is a 'one for three' rights issue (Table 12.1). The rights clearly have value to existing shareholders since they have the option to purchase 'new' shares at $80, when the existing shares are currently worth $100. However, it is not quite as simple as this. If we assume future earnings per share are unchanged by the rights issue, then these earnings are now 'spread over' more shares, so the price of the shares should fall after the rights issue. What will the ex-rights share price be? Suppose the investor initially held three shares then:

**After the offer**

```
3 old shares @ $100        = $300
1 new share @ $80          = $80
Hence, 4 shares are worth  = $380
Value of 1 share (ex-rights) =  $95
```

Hence:

Value of 1 right = new price − subscription price

$$= \$95 - \$80 = \mathbf{\$15}$$

The ex-rights price will be $95 if the market price of the old shares remains at $100. The shareholder is no better off after taking up the rights since she now holds four shares worth $95 per share (= $380), whereas before she owned three shares worth $100 per share, but she has also paid an extra $80 for the one share in the rights issue.

If a shareholder did *not* take up her rights issue then the value of her shareholding would fall by $15, since she now has three shares at $95 (= $285), whereas she started off with three shares at $100 (= $300). However, the shareholder receives an allotment letter for the new shares and if she doesn't wish to take up the rights, she can sell the allotment letter, for a premium. Given the one for three rights issue she could sell the rights for $15 per share since she holds the allotment letter. The 'old' shareholder then ends up with three shares at $95 plus $15 in cash, a total of $300, which equals the pre-rights value of her initial three shares. The person who purchases the rights for $15 per share pays the subscription price of $80 and hence a total payment of $95 per share. The latter of course equals the ex-rights price she would pay by buying the share in the open market at $95.

It is always possible that the share price falls below $80, say to $70 before the rights are taken up. In this case none of the existing shareholders would take up the rights at a price of

$80. Hence the rights issue has to be underwritten, for which the underwriter gets a small 'standby fee'. However, in practice the subscription price is set relatively low so that it is rare for rights issues not to be fully taken up.

The Directors decide the ratio of 'new to old' shares depending on whether they think the current price is too high. If they wish to lower the ex-rights price substantially (for a given amount of funds to raise) they will issue many more new shares (e.g. one for two rights issue). For example, if the subscription price for *Longevity.com* is set at $53.33 (i.e. 2/3 of $80) then:

$$\text{Number of new shares} = \frac{\$26.666m}{\$53.33} = 500,000$$

Given that the initial number of shares is 1m this implies that $26.666m can be raised with a subscription price of $53.33 and a one for two rights issue.

## SCRIPT ISSUES AND SPLITS

Script issues and stock splits are rather peculiar 'animals' since they do not raise additional finance and merely result in a 'cosmetic' change to the share price, but no overall change in share value. Their main *raison d'etre* is that investors psychologically seem to like 'low' quoted prices—although what constitutes 'low' varies from country to country.

In a **script issue**, new shares are *given* to existing shareholders. A script issue may ensue if the Directors feel the quoted share price is too high. In a one for one script issue, one new share is given free for each existing share held by an investor. In a one for two **stock split**, each share held by an investor with par value $1 is replaced by two shares with par value $0.5. In both of these cases the market price of each share held falls by one-half (but of course the total value of the shares held is the same). To give another example, if the share price was currently $100 then a four for one script issue would result in a market price of $20.

A **script dividend** (or **stock dividend**) is an issue of shares in lieu of a cash dividend and is usually an option given to shareholders. The firm does not have to pay out any cash, there is some share dilution and the shareholder gains additional shares (which may be taxed at a lower effective rate than the cash dividend).

In the UK the 'acceptable' range of market prices is from £1 to £10, whereas in the US prices up to $100 seem 'acceptable' and in Switzerland quoted prices equivalent to over $1000 are not uncommon. Of course, one possible advantage of a low quoted price is that 'small' investors can purchase at least one stock! But given the transactions cost of buying one share this is hardly a compelling reason for stock splits and script issues to lower the quoted price. Note that a **reverse split** or **conversion** sometimes takes place when the stock price is at a very low level. So replacing four old shares with one new share will quadruple the quoted price.

Having outlined how a firm raises finance via equity issues we now turn to the problem of establishing a 'fair price' for the shares. A subsidiary factor here is whether there is an optimal time for the firm to issue new shares. If the firm knows that its current share price $P$ is above its 'true' or 'fair value' $V$, then it should issue shares today since it will have to issue less shares for any *given amount of finance it wishes to raise*. However, in an 'efficient market' we shall see that the firm does not have such a 'timing advantage' since the market price will always equal the 'fair value'. Also, if speculators can accurately calculate the fair value and this differs from the market price then they could earn profits by buying underpriced shares (i.e. where $P < V$) and short selling overpriced shares (i.e. where $P > V$).

## 12.2 FAIR VALUE AND EFFICIENT MARKETS

The fair value $V$ of a stock is the DPV of future expected dividends. Because future dividends are uncertain (Figure 12.1), the discount rates $R_t$ should reflect the riskiness of these dividend payments:

[12.1]
$$V = E\left[\frac{D_1}{(1 + R_1)} + \frac{D_2}{(1 + R_2)^2} \cdots\right]$$

where $D_t$ are the dividend payments ($t = 1, 2, 3 \ldots$ years)
$\quad R_t$ is the risk adjusted discount rate for year $t$ ($t = 1, 2, 3 \ldots$ years)
$\quad E$ is the 'expected value', with expectations formed at time $t = 0$.

It can be shown (see Appendix 12.1) that the DPV formula does not require investors to consider holding the stock forever. All we require is that investors calculate their expected selling price at time $t + m$, based on dividends which they expect to accrue from $t + m$ onwards. Suppose investors use all available information to forecast future dividends and discount rates and they use equation [12.1] to calculate the fair value of the stock, which we assume is $V = \$10$. If the actual price is $P = \$8$ then investors would buy the stock, since they would expect the actual price to move towards the fair value, hence making a capital gain of $2. As all 'informed' investors execute this strategy, then the actual price will quickly rise to equal the fair value of $10.

## FIGURE 12.1: Equities—cash flow

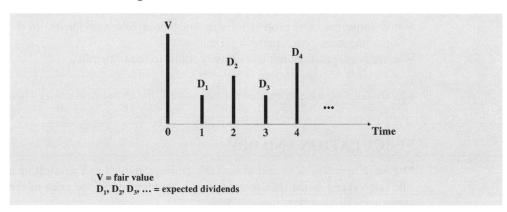

V = fair value
$D_1, D_2, D_3, \ldots$ = expected dividends

In addition, as new information becomes available this will be reflected in the market price. For example, the announcement of a successful new drug would result in higher profits and dividends. Hence one might expect this to lead to a reappraisal of the fair value to say $V = \$12$ and for the actual price to immediately rise to $12. The ideas discussed above are the basis for what financial economists call the **efficient markets hypothesis EMH**:

---

### EFFICIENT MARKETS HYPOTHESIS

- Investors use all available (relevant) information to calculate the fair value of the stock. This is sometimes referred to as *informational efficiency* or *rational expectations*.
- Stock prices immediately move to reflect fair value, so that $P = V$ at all times.
- Prices are 'marked up' so quickly (instantaneously), that it is impossible to make a profit which is greater than the risk involved in the investment strategy. That is, it is impossible to make 'abnormal' or 'supernormal' profits (i.e. profits corrected for risk) by trying to 'pick winners'.

---

It is important to adjust profits for the risks undertaken, and it is this which makes the EMH difficult to test. In the above example, the potential capital gain of $2 as the price moves up from $P = \$8$ to $V = \$10$ might involve substantial risk, and hence although a profit on the trade might be made, this may not warrant the risks involved. We discuss the EMH in greater detail in the next chapter as it forms a 'baseline' for assessing investment strategies.

If the EMH always held, then $P$ would always be equal to $V$ and there would be no profits to be made. This is similar to the apocryphal story of the student who joyfully explained to his finance professor that when walking down the street he spotted a $100 bill on the pavement (sidewalk) in the town's covered market. The professor replies, 'I don't believe you, the market is efficient so someone would have already picked it up'. Well, not quite correct perhaps, but you don't see many $100 bills (or even $1 bills) on the sidewalk do you? Hence it follows that, faced with the EMH, a successful speculative strategy at a minimum requires:

- that some investors process information (about future dividends) in different ways and some investors have superior information;
- some stock prices do not immediately adjust to their fair value.

Clearly once we have calculated the fair value $V$, the investment strategy is straightforward.

## SPECULATION AND DPV

The basic idea here is similar to the DPV concept applied to a physical investment decision. The fair value $V$ is the DPV of receipts (i.e. dividends) and the price of the stock ($P$) is the capital cost of your 'investment'. Hence:

> **If $P < V$**      **then purchase the stock**
> **If $P > V$**      **then (short) sell the stock**

If investors are rational, then if you purchase a stock with $P < V$, the market price should rise towards the fair value, giving you a capital gain. The key areas of uncertainty in this strategy are:

- $V$ may be calculated incorrectly.
- After purchasing a stock for which $P < V$, bad news about dividends arrives so that the market reappraises its view about $V$. Hence $V$ falls below $P$, before the initial mispricing is corrected. Hence you now hold a stock which is overvalued ($P > V$).

The above investment rule is nothing more than our usual DPV rule for investment projects applied to stocks. We could equally have stated our investment rule as 'invest in the stock if the NPV is positive'. Refinements on the above basic strategy use sophisticated quantitative techniques to forecast dividends in all future years (see below), and sometimes a forecast of future discount rates is also used (see Cuthbertson, 1996). These are inputs to the DPV formula to calculate an estimate of the fair value $V$.

It is possible to use past data to obtain a time series of fair values $V_t$ (for $t = 1$ to $n$ years). To see this in a simple way, suppose that the fair value depends only on next period dividend $D_{t+1}$ and the discount rate is the safe rate $r_t$. In addition assume that the best forecast of next period dividend is this period dividend (i.e. $E_t(D_{t+1}) = D_t$, this is the random walk assumption for dividend behaviour). Then:

[12.2]      $$V_t = \frac{D_t}{(1 + r_t)}$$

Using past data on $D_t$ and $r_t$ we can obtain a time series for $V_t$. So far we have no empirical evidence on how quickly $P$ might move towards $V$, and how accurate this relationship might be. But this is vital for an equity trader. This information can be obtained by looking at the relationship between the 'gap' or disequilibrium $(V - P)_t$ in the historic data and *subsequent* capital gains (or returns) over the next month, using regression analysis. Using time series data an estimate of this equation might be:

[12.3]      Capital gain over 1 month $= 0.5 \times$ ('mispricing')

$$\frac{\Delta P_{t+1}}{P_t} = 0.5 \times (V - P)_t$$

where we have assumed the estimated adjustment coefficient is 0.5. Hence, broadly speaking, when $V$ exceeds $P$ by say 10% we expect a capital gain of 5% over the next month. Usually such equations do not forecast accurately over 'short' horizons of 1 month, but they are quite good over longer horizons of 1–5 years. Also if the $R^2$ for this regression is say 0.75, it tells us that on average any positive gap $(V - P) > 0$ subsequently leads to a capital gain 75% of the time. The above statistical relationship is known as an **error**

**correction model ECM**, since the mispricing error $(V - P) > 0$ leads to a rise in price in the future. But if $P$ rises then $V - P$ gets smaller and hence the mispricing is (partially) 'corrected' or reduced (see Cuthbertson, 1996 for further details). It also follows that $(V - P) < 0$ leads to a subsequent fall in $P$, which also tends to 'correct' the mispricing error.

## CALCULATING THE FAIR VALUE

Having outlined the broad principles we now turn to some alternative methods for calculating the fair value. A major difficulty is in deciding the risk adjustment to use for the discount factors. In general the required rate of return on a stock-$i$ at time $t$ $(R_{it})$ may be written as:

[12.4]    $R_{it}$ = risk free nominal rate $r_t$ + risk premium $rp_{it}$

The safe rate $(r)$ does not differ between different stocks but it will be different for different time horizons, if the yield curve is not flat. The risk premium $rp$ is different for different stocks and we can use the CAPM/SML to provide an estimate. (Later we also use the APT.)

### CASE A: USING THE YIELD CURVE

If the yield curve is not flat then the risk free rate is different for each maturity and can be obtained from the (spot) yield curve. For example the current yield curve might give $r_1 = 10\%$, $r_2 = 11\%$ and $r_t = 10\%$ $(t > 2)$ as in Table 12.2.

In this approach the risk premium is generally assumed to be constant over time. One way of obtaining a ball-park estimate for the risk premium for a particular firm is to use the average return over the last few years on comparable stocks in that industry (and then deduct the average value of the risk free rate). For example, the risk premium for Marks and Spencer might be calculated using the (annual) average return on the stocks of other food retailers such as Sainsburys, Tesco, etc. over the last 5 years. If the average return for all food retailers over the last 5 years is 8% and the average risk free rate is 5%, then the *average* risk premium $rp = ER - r = 3\%$. The discount rate for each period $R_t = r_i + 3\%$ then varies because of the yield curve and the fair value is calculated in Table 12.2.

### CASE B: USING THE CAPM

According to the CAPM the risk adjusted required rate of return is:

[12.5]    $ER_i = r + \beta_i(ER_m - r)$

As before, we could assume that the safe rate varies over different maturities. However, to simplify matters and because the risk premium is thought to be relatively more important, $r$ is usually taken to be constant and equal to its recent historic average value. An estimate of the firm's beta is usually obtained from a time series regression using about the last 5 years of (monthly returns) data or obtained directly from a risk measurement service (see below). The excess return on the market $(ER_m - r)$ is also usually an historic average. Hence in using the CAPM to calculate the discount rate, it is assumed that the market return $R_m$ and the risk free rate $r$ will remain fairly constant in the future and that we have an accurate measure of $\beta_i$. Given this basic information it is straightforward to calculate the fair value and the stock selection decision, as shown in Table 12.3.

## TABLE 12.2: Yield curve and stock valuation

| | |
|---|---|
| **Data:** | Spot rates from the yield curve are $r_1 = 10\%$, $r_2 = 11\%$, $r_i = 10\%$ (for $i > 2$) |
| | The market risk premium $rp$ on stock XYZ is 3% over the risk free rate |
| | Current dividends $= 10p$ (pence) |
| | Expected dividends at end of years 1, 2 and 3 are 12p, 14p and 14p, respectively |
| | After year 3, expected dividend growth $= 7\%$ p.a. |
| **Questions:** | Calculate the fair price of XYZ |
| | If the current market price is 180p should you purchase XYZ? |
| **Answers:** | The risk adjusted rates of return in each year are given by $R_i = r_i + rp$. Hence: |
| | $R_1 = 10\% + 3\% = 13\%$ |
| | $R_2 = 11\% + 3\% = 14\%$ |
| | $R_i = 10\% + 3\% = 13\%$ (for $i > 2$) |
| | The fair value using these required rates of return is: |
| | $V_0 = 12p/(1.13) + 14p/(1.14)^2 + V_3/(1.13)^3$ |
| | $V_3 = D_3(1 + g)/(R - g) = 14(1.07)/(0.13 - 0.07) = 249.7p$ |
| | Hence: |
| | $V_0 = 12p/(1.13) + 14p/(1.14)^2 + 249.7p/(1.13)^3 = 194.45p$ |
| | Purchase XYZ since the fair value $V$ exceeds the current market price of 180p |

### CASE C: USING THE SML

The problem with using the CAPM to calculate $ER_i$ is that it is rather sensitive to the average values chosen for the excess market return ($ER_m - r$). The SML 'averages out' the relationship between expected return $ER_i$ and the firm's beta $\beta_i$ by using regression analysis. In effect the *slope* of the SML provides an average value for $ER_m - r$ and provides a better estimate of $ER_i$. Remember that to estimate the SML we require data on the *average* monthly return $R_i$ (over say the previous year) on a set of say 500 stocks ($i = 1$, 2, 3, ..., 500) along with their estimated betas $\beta_i$ (Figure 12.2). Suppose this cross-section regression on these 500 stocks gives the SML:

[12.6]     $R_i = 5 + 8\beta_i$

so that the average value of $ER_m - r$ in the historic data is 8% and the average risk free rate is 5%. For firm Q with $\beta_i = 0.5$, its risk adjusted discount rate would be $ER_i = 9\%$ and this would be used in the DPV formula (if the project was all equity financed).

## TABLE 12.3: CAPM and stock valuation

| | |
|---|---|
| **Data:** | Risk free rate = 3% p.a. |
| | Stock XYZ has $\beta = 1.5$ |
| | Dividend expected end-year on XYZ = 10p |
| | Average market return $R_m = 10\%$ p.a. |
| | Expected dividend growth = 5% p.a. |
| **Questions:** | 1. What is the risk adjusted rate of return $ER_i$ on XYZ assuming the CAPM holds? |
| | 2. What is the fair price $V$ of XYZ? |
| | 3. If the current market price of XYZ is 120p should you purchase the stock? |
| | 4. What are the risks attached to your investment strategy? |
| **Answers:** | 1. $ER_i = r + \beta_i(ER_m - r) = 3\% + 1.5(10\% - 3\%) = 13.5\%$ |
| | 2. $V = D/(ER_i - g) = 10p/(0.135 - 0.05) = 117.65p$ |
| | 3. Do not purchase the stock. Sell or short sell the stock since $P > V$ |
| | 4. After (short) selling the stock, the price may not fall within the 'assessment period' for the portfolio manager. Unexpected high profits or 'good' company news may be released. Hence expected dividends would now be higher and $V$ might increase beyond $P$ (i.e. the stock is now undervalued). The CAPM measure $ER_i$ may not hold for all future periods in the DPV formula. If there is a 'bubble' present then the actual price may diverge from $V$ for substantial periods of time. Any irrational or 'noise traders' can move $P$ independently of $V$ (see chapter 14) |

## FIGURE 12.2: Security market line

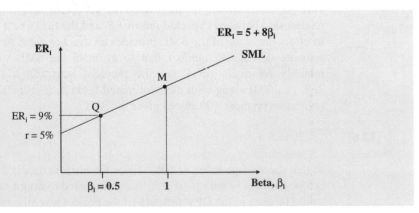

## GORDON GROWTH MODEL

There are further 'rules of thumb' that are used to simplify the DPV formula and the inputs required to calculate the fair value. Suppose dividend growth ($g$) and the required rate of return ($R$) are assumed constant over time (but differ across different firms). The time path of dividends is given in Figure 12.3 and the fair value is:

[12.7]
$$V_0 = \frac{D_0(1 + g)}{(1 + R)} + \frac{D_0(1 + g)^2}{(1 + R)^2} + \dots$$

Using the DPV formula for a growing annuity:

[12.8a]
$$V_0 = \frac{D_1}{(R - g)}$$

where $D_1$ = dividends at the end of the first year (i.e. $D_1 = D_0(1 + g)$). For a constant level of dividends (i.e. $g = 0$) this reduces to:

[12.8b]
$$V_0 = D/R$$

(Note that the above formula is equivalent to that which we derived for the price of a bond with a fixed coupon, payable forever, with a yield to maturity of $R$—see Chapter 7.)

Sometimes analysts think they can produce good estimates of dividends over say the next 3 years, but then their best guess is that dividends will grow at a constant rate from then on. This gives rise to the *two-period model*:

[12.9]
$$V = \frac{D_1}{(1 + R_1)} + \frac{D_2}{(1 + R_2)^2} + \frac{D_3}{(1 + R_3)^3} + \frac{V_4}{(1 + R_4)^4}$$

where $V_4$ is the DPV (calculated for time $t = 4$) of all future dividends in years 5, 6, ... If $R$ is the (constant) discount rate applicable to years 5, 6, ... etc., then:

## FIGURE 12.3: Gordon growth model

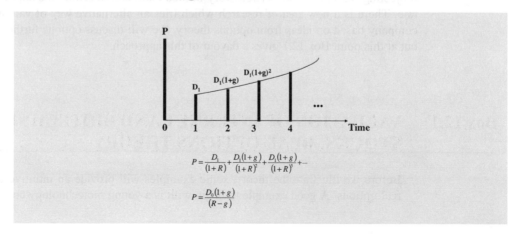

[12.10] $$V_4 = \frac{D_5}{R - g}$$

Since $V_4$ is measured at $t = 4$, then its contribution to the *current* price (at $t = 0$) implies we have to discount $V_4$ back to time $t = 0$ (i.e. hence the term $1/(1 + R_4)^4$ in 12.9).

## STOCK PRICE VOLATILITY

The Gordon growth model can be used to illustrate why stock prices may be highly volatile even though investors act in a perfectly rational way and the market always prices stocks efficiently (i.e. $P = V$). Suppose that in January investors think that dividends next year will be $D_1 = \$10$ and they will then grow at 3% p.a. (i.e. $g = 0.03$) and the risk adjusted rate of return is $R = 0.10$. The price of the stock in an efficient market will be $P = D_1/(R - g)$ $= \$142.86$. Now suppose that 1 month later investors revise the growth rate of dividends down to $g = 0.02$, then the new price will be set at $P = \$125$. This is a capital loss of over 12% in 1 month, for anyone who holds the stock. Hence, it is not surprising that the stock market is highly volatile since new information (or 'news' for short) about future dividend growth or the appropriate discount rate to use in the DPV formula can lead to large changes in price, even when traders are acting in a rational way. However, it has been argued (e.g. see Cuthbertson, 1996) that the stock market is *excessively* volatile and the observed volatility in actual prices is greater than would occur if investors were always rational and the market were truly efficient (see next chapter).

## INTERNET AND BIOTECHNOLOGY STOCKS

The stock market valuation of internet and biotechnology companies can sometimes appear excessively high, given that many of these companies have relatively low revenues and often negative operating profit (i.e. earnings before interest, taxes, depreciation and amortisation, EBITDA). Certainly, their stock valuation is also highly volatile. Are these stock prices justified or are these stocks excessively overvalued, and if so, by how much might we expect the price to fall if underlying market conditions changed? A stock analyst using conventional DPV techniques to value these types of companies has a major problem both in projecting future cash flows (from very limited data) and in setting the appropriate discount rate. There is a new area of research which tries an alternative way of valuing this type of company based on ideas from options theory. We will discuss options further in Chapter 21 but at this point Box 12.1 gives a flavour of this approach.

## Box 12.1    VALUATION OF INTERNET AND BIOTECHNOLOGY STOCKS: REAL OPTIONS THEORY

Before we illustrate the theory, some examples will provide an intuitive overview of real options. A good example to begin with is a young biotechnology company which is considering 'stage I' of a research project to discover 'blockbuster' drugs, such as a cure for certain types of cancer or AIDS. The share price $P$ for an all equity firm is:

$P$ = PV of firm's investment projects/number of shares outstanding

So we need to value the firm in order to determine the 'fair price' for its shares. Suppose the research projects will proceed in stages, the early stages providing possible breakthroughs for later developments and 'spin-off' drugs. Suppose there are only two stages. When using a conventional NPV calculation the stock analyst will assess the *expected* present value of the net revenues over the life (of say 5 years) for 'stage I' using probabilities of a 'low', medium' or 'major' breakthrough. This can then be compared with the (present value) of the capital costs of the research equipment for 'stage I'. The cash flows will be discounted using the company's risk adjusted discount rate. Suppose the 'conventional' NPV for 'stage I' equals *minus* $10m. Should the analyst advise clients not to invest in stage I or has she missed some vital advantages of the project?

Suppose the research being considered in stage I will allow an assessment of the prospects for a further 'breakthrough drug' being discovered at a later date. If so, the biotechnology company would exploit this new knowledge in 'stage II', given the 'know-how' acquired in stage I. Hence, the 'stage I' project has an embedded option, namely the possible expansion into stage II, in say 5 years time. The value of the stage I investment is not only its own cash flows but also the option to exploit stage II. This **embedded option to expand** has value, which should be added to the NPV calculation for 'stage I'. Of course, one cannot know at $t = 0$ whether this option to exploit 'stage II' will be undertaken in 5 years time. This depends on future research progress which we cannot know today. However, the option to expand still has a value at $t = 0$. Indeed, if the value of the option to expand is greater than $10m, then we should go ahead with 'stage I' even though it has a 'conventional' negative NPV.

Surely there is a 'downside' to the above 'fiddling of the figures'. Well there is a 'downside', since if there is no breakthrough in 5 years time, the option to expand will be worth zero (i.e. we will not exploit 'stage II'). But note that the downside is limited to zero. In fact the embedded option to expand is a **call option** with a strike price equal to the additional investment required (at $t = 5$) to exploit 'stage II' of the research project.

The potential upside is very large, while the downside is truncated at zero (profit) if we do not go ahead—the typical **asymmetric payoff** from an option. The larger is the variance $\sigma$ of possible outcomes in stage II the larger the possible upside, while the downside payoff remains at zero. Hence it should not be surprising that this call option (like all options) is worth more the greater the degree of uncertainty $\sigma$ in future revenues. (This is taken up in Chapter 21.) So, other things equal, we have the somewhat paradoxical result that stage I, including its embedded option, is worth more today the *greater is the uncertainty* about future revenues in stage II. Because 'conventional' NPV calculation concentrates on *expected outcomes*, it does not correctly value these embedded options.

One can easily see that the above analysis could apply to internet or 'dot.com' companies, in general. Most of these companies have a very high share price, even though they have relatively low revenues and very often negative profits and hence negative 'conventional' NPVs. But their share price reflects the possibility of expansion into other similar internet business areas, given the knowledge gained in the current business. This embedded *option to expand* is reflected in their *current* share price.

To value an internet or biotechnology company using options theory we need to model the stochastic behaviour of the key economic variables faced by these internet firms such as revenues and costs. Schwartz and Moon (2000) did this for the **internet company *Amazon.com***, at the end of 1999. Their model has two sources of uncertainty; one is the actual change in revenues, $R$ and the other is the *expected* (or mean) growth in revenues, $\mu$.

The *actual growth* in revenues is assumed to equal a 'trend value' plus a random element, which initially has a very large volatility ($\sigma_0 = 20\%$ p.a.) that slowly falls to a long run level ($\overline{\sigma} = 10\%$ p.a.), as the whole internet sector becomes established. Also the *expected growth* rate $\mu_t$ changes over time, beginning at its end-1999 high value ($\mu_0 = 44\%$ p.a.) and slowly falling to a lower long run value ($\overline{\mu} = 6\%$ p.a.), as more competitors enter the internet business. Not only this, but the expected growth rate is itself uncertain, beginning with an initial standard deviation of $\eta_0 = 60\%$ p.a which then slowly falls to zero. Costs are assumed to be equal to 94% of revenues (on average) and hence there is a 6% profit margin over sales. The cash flow of the firm is:

$$Y_t = R_t - C_t$$

In practice the cash flow $Y$ is 'earnings before interest, tax, depreciation and amortisation', EBITDA—but we ignore these complications here. We assume all cash is 'retained' and earns the risk free rate $r$. If cash balances fall to zero, the firm is assumed to go bankrupt (i.e. we ignore the possibility of raising additional financing or of a merger in future years).

Although the above model is highly simplified we do have the 'basic ingredients' to value the firm. Schwartz and Moon assume the value of Amazon is equal to 10 times EBITDA ($= Y_T$) at $T = 25$ years (they use Monte Carlo simulation MCS to obtain a 'representative' or 'average' value for the firm). Schwartz and Moon (2000) used a more complex model than the above, and they show that as of December 1999, the model gave a value for *Amazon.com* of \$5.5bn, in their 'baseline' case. Hence, it is possible for internet companies to have a high valuation if the 'embedded options' for future expansion are factored into the calculation.

But we cannot expect such a simplified model (with imprecisely estimated parameters) to accurately price an internet stock, rather the analysis allows one to assess whether such prices are 'beyond belief' and also to assess how sensitive the price is to changing circumstances. For example, the model also shows that one can expect internet stocks to be highly volatile as investors' views about key parameter estimates change by relatively small amounts, particularly the variances $\eta_0$ and $\sigma_0$ and the profit margin. These issues are discussed in greater depth in Cuthbertson and Nitzsche (2001).

## INTERNAL RATE OF RETURN OF A STOCK

In just the same way as we examine the feasibility of a physical investment project either by using NPV or IRR, we can also do this for investment in stocks. The internal rate of return (IRR) $y$ on a stock is that (constant) rate of return that equates the *observed market price P* with the DPV of (expected) dividends:

[12.11a]
$$P = E\left[\frac{D_1}{(1 + y)} + \frac{D_2}{(1 + y)^2} + \frac{D_3}{(1 + y)^3} + \cdots\right]$$

Once we have a forecast of dividends and the known market price we can solve equation [12.11a] for $y$. However, if dividend growth is constant (i.e. Gordon growth model) then:

[12.11b]
$$P = D_1/(y - g)$$

Hence the solution for the IRR is simplified, namely:

**IRR = dividend yield + growth rate of dividends**

[12.12]
$$y = D_1/P + g$$

Our earlier investment strategy was invest if $P > V$ where $V$ is calculated using the risk adjusted rate of return $ER_i$. An equivalent strategy, based on the IRR is:

> **Buy stocks if**      **IRR > required risk adjusted rate of return $ER_i$**
> **Sell stocks if**      **IRR < required rate of return $ER_i$**

Thus one purchases the stock if the IRR, based on the current market price, exceeds the required (or risk adjusted) rate of return. An example showing the equivalence of the IRR and DPV criterion is given in Table 12.4.

## STOCK SELECTION: THE ARBITRAGE PRICING THEORY

As we have seen, the arbitrage pricing theory APT provides an alternative model of equilibrium returns on a stock $ER_i$ to the CAPM. Hence the APT can also be used to 'stock-pick', either by using the value of $ER_i$ from the APT in the DPV formula to provide an

## TABLE 12.4: IRR and DPV

| | |
|---|---|
| **Data:** | Stock XYZ |
| | CAPM required rate of return $ER_i = 13.5\%$ p.a. |
| | Dividends at end-year $= 10p$ (pence) |
| | Expected dividend growth $= 5\%$ p.a. |
| | Current price $= 110p$ |
| **Questions:** | 1. Calculate the fair price and your investment decision |
| | 2. Calculate the IRR on the stock and your investment decision |
| **Answers:** | 1. $V = 10p/(0.135 - 0.05) = 117.65p$ |
| | $P = 110p < 117.65p$      **Hence purchase the stock** |
| | 2. $y = D/P + g = (10p/110p) + 0.05 = 0.1409$ (14.09%) |
| | $y = 14.09\% > ER_i = 13.5\%$      **Hence purchase the stock** |
| | For the Gordon growth model either of the two investment rules gives the same |
| | investment decision |

estimate of 'fair value' or $ER_i$ can be directly compared with the IRR of the stock. Let us review the APT and examine the practical aspects of using the APT in stock selection. Remember that the APT is a multifactor model of equilibrium returns and the key elements are:

- The unexpected return on a stock responds to unexpected events (factors) in the economy (e.g. unexpected increases or decreases in inflation).
- Each factor can have a different impact on actual returns (i.e. the factor sensitivities or $b_{ij}$'s differ across securities).
- Some (but not all) of the factors will influence the *equilibrium* return on the stock.

Hence, a factor can influence *unexpected* returns but may not impact on *equilibrium* returns (i.e. its $\lambda$ value may be zero—see below). If a factor does not influence equilibrium returns, the factor is said to be 'not priced'. We assume three factors, inflation, interest rates and output, with only two factors influencing equilibrium returns (i.e. only inflation and interest rates are priced). Two equations summarise the above:

[12.13]      $R_{it} = a_1 + b_{i1}F_{1t} + b_{i2}F_{2t} + b_{i3}F_{3t} + \varepsilon_i$

[12.14]      $ER_i = \lambda_0 + \lambda_1 b_{i1} + \lambda_2 b_{i2}$

where $R_{it}$ is the actual return on stock $i$

$ER_i$ is the equilibrium return on stock $i$

$b_{ij}$ are the 'risk' factor weights

$F_{1t}$ is the change in inflation, $F_{2t}$ is the change in interest rates, $F_{3t}$ is the change in output.

Strictly, the factors $F_{it}$ are unexpected events or 'surprises'. In practice, the change in a variable is often deemed to be unforecastable and is taken as a measure of an unexpected event. The $b_{ij}$ can be estimated from a *time series* regression of returns $R_{it}$ on the factors $F_{it}$. Given the $b_{ij}$ then $\lambda_0$, $\lambda_1$ and $\lambda_2$ can be obtained from a cross-section regression on a group of stocks (where $ER_i$ for each stock is measured as the average monthly return (say) over 1 year). Suppose the $\lambda$'s from the cross-section regression on $b_{i1}$, $b_{i2}$ and $b_{i3}$ take on the following values:

[12.15]    $ER_i = 6 + 2b_{i1} + 0.8b_{i2}$

with $b_{i3} = 0$. Notice that the APT implies that the $\lambda$'s are the same for all stocks (but the $b_{ij}$ differ). The theory therefore assumes that stocks with the same sensitivity to economic factors (i.e. same $b_{ij}$'s) will offer the same equilibrium return. This is because the factors that are 'priced' give rise to 'risk' that cannot be diversified away and therefore must influence the risk adjusted (required) return on the stock. Although three factors influence actual returns (equation [12.13]), only two of these factors (i.e. inflation and interest rates) are 'priced' in the market. For asset-1 suppose the estimates of the risk factor weightings are $b_{11} = 4$ and $b_{12} = 2$. Then equilibrium returns on asset-1 should be:

[12.16]    $ER_1 = 6 + 2(4) + 0.8(2) = 15.6$

Hence the APT allows one to calculate an equilibrium risk adjusted return $ER_i$ (see equation [12.14] or [12.15]) and this can be used to calculate the 'fair value' or it can be directly compared with the IRR of the stock, to identify mispriced stocks. Note that the CAPM is an equation similar to [12.13] but with only one factor, namely the market return $R_m$, so $F_{1t} = R_m$ and all other factors are ignored. Similarly, equation [12.14] is the multivariate equivalent of the SML of the CAPM. The SML is a relationship between $R_i$ and $b_i$ (the stock's beta with the market) whereas equation [12.14] allows several 'factor betas' to influence the equilibrium return $ER_i$.

## EXPLICIT FORECASTS

If an investor believes he can forecast say a rise in inflation (factor 1) then he should move into stocks that have a high (positive) risk exposure to inflation (i.e. a large positive value of $b_{i1}$). These are not mispriced securities, it is merely that the investor thinks he has superior forecasting performance about inflation and wishes to hold those stocks whose returns are very sensitive to positive inflation shocks. The analogy with the CAPM is holding stocks with high positive beta values if you believe the market return is going to rise.

## SPECIFIC EXPOSURE

Key issues that any practical application of the APT depend on are:

• Isolating the factors $F$ that have constant beta coefficients over different time periods.

- Noting that factors that influence returns might differ in different time periods (e.g. oil prices in the 1970s but not in the 1990s).
- Ascertaining which factors are priced (the $\lambda$'s) and assessing whether the $\lambda$'s remain constant over different time periods.

All of the above considerations imply that it may be difficult to precisely calculate the equilibrium risk adjusted return $ER_i$. There is a voluminous literature in this area (see Cuthbertson, 1996 for a summary) and the ideas behind the APT have been used by some practitioners (see Lofthouse, 1994 for a summary).

# 12.3 INDUSTRY STUDIES: FORECASTING EARNINGS

Analysts who are trying to pick mispriced securities will use a variety of methods to forecast future earnings and hence fair value. We will use the term 'earnings' here but this is simply the 'free cash flow' for the whole firm discussed in Chapter 3. Often they will concentrate on prospects for specific sectors in terms of sales and (after-tax) earnings (profits), particularly over the next few years. In the very short term they will be concerned with any announcements about earnings made by the company. Analysts take a view of future earnings and this is then reflected in the current market price of the share. However, if the company announces higher earnings *than the market had expected*, this will imply higher dividends and an increase in fair value. Analysts then rush to inform their traders and clients, to purchase this stock before the price rises. If the analyst and her traders act quickly they may be able to purchase the stock before the price rises substantially in the market. If they are correct then they will earn a capital gain. In other words 'the quick get rich' (and if the financial incentives are right, maybe 'the rich stay quick'). This is why analysts continually watch the 'news services' on their Reuters and Bloomberg screens: they are looking for price sensitive information which signals a change in fair value.

Over the longer term, analysts will have more sophisticated models of predicting earnings. Detailed scrutiny of company statements about new markets, wage claims, commodity (input) prices, etc. helps in forecasting future earnings in the industry as a whole. Firm specific factors (e.g. higher than average expenditure on marketing or R&D) will then be used to adjust these forecasts of industry earnings, up or down. Also analysts might use a time series equation to forecast future industry earnings $E_t$, for example an **autoregressive model**:

[12.17]     $$E_t = 0.8E_{t-1} + 0.15E_{t-2}$$

where the weights (0.8, 0.15) might be imposed (e.g. EWMA) or estimated from past data. If today is $t = 1$, then future values of $E$ will be given by:

$$E_2 = 0.8E_1 + 0.15E_0 \quad \text{and} \quad E_3 = 0.8E_2 + 0.15E_1$$

This is a recursive forecast. Additional variables (e.g. output growth) might also be included in equation [12.17].

A quoted **price–earnings ratio** (or '$P–E$ ratio') of say 20 simply represents the fact that the market currently values the share at 'twenty times earnings'. The $P-E$ ratio of a particular firm can vary substantially from year to year and $P-E$ ratios vary across firms in a particular sector. For example (on 7th September 2000) some $P-E$ ratios of banks were:

|                | $P-E$ ratio |
|----------------|-------------|
| ABN Amro       | 16.3        |
| Abbey National | 9.7         |
| Barclays       | 11.4        |
| HSBC           | 19.8        |
| Lloyds TSB     | 13.1        |

The $P-E$ ratio is often used as a crude method of finding the fair value of the shares of a firm in a particular industrial sector. For example, if the whole banking sector has an average $P-E$ ratio of 18 and you find that the shares of 'bank-X' have a $P-E$ ratio of 14, then you might be tempted to purchase these 'undervalued' shares. You hope that the market has temporarily mispriced bank-X and that when the market corrects this mispricing, the price of bank-X will rise until its $P-E$ ratio equals that for the sector as a whole. Of course this is a risky strategy since the observed lower $P-E$ ratio of 14 may be simply due to the fact that the market has correctly noted that 'bank-X' is relatively 'inefficient' and its earnings only justify a price equal to 14 times earnings. To put this issue more bluntly, note that a firm with abnormally low current earnings will nevertheless have a high $P-E$ ratio, but this does not imply that *in the future* its shares will perform well. It is therefore a risky strategy to buy shares with low $P-E$ ratios (and short sell those with high $P-E$ ratios), and only detailed statistical analysis can determine whether in the past this would have been a successful speculative strategy—see Chapter 13 on anomalies for further details.

$P-E$ analysis is used in corporate finance to provide a crude 'first shot' at valuing potential merger and takeover targets. Suppose 'Little Bank' has a fairly stable historic $P-E$ ratio of $PE = 20$. It has earnings of $10 per share under the current management and there are $N = 1m$ shares outstanding, so that the current value of the bank is $V = \$200m$ ($= 20 \times \$10 \times 1m$). 'Shark Bank' is looking for prospective takeover targets and thinks that if it swallows up Little Bank it will be able to cut its branch network, consolidate its retail products and increase earnings of Little Bank by 10% to $11 per share. It therefore values Little Bank at $V_{new} = PE \times E_{new} \times N = \$220m$ and this is the maximum it is willing to offer for Little Bank. (We assume the acquisition of Little Bank does not affect the rest of Shark Bank's earnings.) As it bids for Little Bank it will push up the market value of Little Bank's shares and it will cease bidding if the cost of acquiring Little Bank exceeds $220m. A more sophisticated analysis of the takeover decision would involve PV techniques (as outlined in Chapter 3), but $P-E$ analysis provides a 'ball-park' first estimate.

The PV formula can be adapted to incorporate earnings forecasts. Suppose earnings (per share) next year are forecast to be $E_1 = \$100$. Analysts will often assume a particular *constant* value for the proportion of funds paid out in dividends, where $p = $ payout ratio (e.g. if $p = 40\%$ then $D = \$40$). It follows that the retention ratio is $(1 - p) = 60\%$ and the retained earnings (RE) are $60 per share. (The latter are usually assumed to be primarily used to finance new physical investment projects.) Hence:

> **Total earnings (per share) = retained earnings + dividend payments**
>
> $$E = RE + D$$

with $D = pE$ and $RE = (1 - p)E$

A forecast of earnings can then be translated into a forecast for dividends and the usual PV formula used to establish 'fair value'. Note that if $D = pE$ then the growth in dividends equals the growth in earnings. For the special case of the Gordon growth model, the fair value $V$ and hence in equilibrium, the market price is given by:

[**12.18a**]     $$P = V = \frac{pE_1}{(R - g)}$$

The equilibrium price–earnings ratio is therefore:

[**12.18b**]     $$\frac{P}{E_1} = \frac{p}{(R - g)}$$

The above formula indicates (in a constant growth scenario) the 'drivers' of the $P-E$ ratio (to use corporate strategy jargon).

> **A firm will have a higher $P-E$ ratio:**
> **The higher is the payout ratio $p$**
> **The lower is the cost of capital $R$**
> **The higher is the growth rate of earnings $g$**

However, the above bald statement although 'arithmetically correct' can be very misleading since it ignores the economics that lie behind equation [12.18b]. For example, if we increase the payout ratio, then this implies lower retained earnings and this in turn may lead to lower fixed investment and hence lower growth of earnings, $g$. These issues were discussed in Chapter 3 when valuing companies. The perfectionists might wish to note that the above analysis can be reconciled with the valuation procedures in Chapter 3, if you make the assumption that all retained earnings are spent on fixed investment $I$. Then $RE = (1 - p)E = I$ so $I/E = 1 - p$ = retentions ratio. Hence, where in Chapter 3 we defined the 'investment ratio' $IR \equiv I/E$ it is here equivalent to $(1 - p)$ = retentions ratio, since all retentions are spent on fixed investment.

## RISK MEASUREMENT (BETA) SERVICES

Newspaper quotes provide very basic summary statistics on companies as shown in Figure 12.4, which is an extract from the *Financial Times*. The stock price (closing mid price) for each firm in pence is given together with the increase or decrease ('+ or −') from the previous day and the 'high' and 'low' prices over the previous '52 weeks'. The column marked 'Volume' is the number of shares traded the previous day (thousands). The gross dividend yield ('Yield') is

## FIGURE 12.4: Newspaper quotes: (a) *Wall Street Journal* reproduced with permission

# LONDON SHARE SERVICE

| | | | | | |
|---|---|---|---|---|---|
| ♣ BrndywnRlty | 1908 | 21 | 20 15/16 | 21 | + 1/16 |
| BrazilFd | 682 | 18 1/16 | 18 | 18 1/16 | ... |
| BrazilTelecom | 1424 | 75 1/8 | 71 13/16 | 74 13/16 | + 9/16 |
| ♣ BrazilEqty | 239 | 6 1/8 | 6 1/8 | 6 1/8 | − 1/8 |
| BriggsStrat | 567 | 34 13/16 | 34 5/16 | 34 3/8 | − 1/8 |
| BrilAuto ADS | 5074 | 34 3/4 | 32 1/16 | 33 7/8 | + 8 5/16 |
| Brinkerint | 1798 | 31 | 29 11/16 | 30 11/16 | + 5/16 |
| BrisMyrsSqb | 99498 | 49 | 47 3/8 | 47 3/4 | − 1 1/16 |
| BritAir | 276 | 58 1/8 | 56 3/4 | 57 1/4 | + 2 1/2 |
| BritEngy ADS | 135 | 15 1/8 | 14 13/16 | 15 1/8 | + 3/16 |
| BritTele | 525 | 133 7/8 | 131 3/8 | 132 5/16 | − 1 15/16 |
| Broadwing | 6388 | 28 11/16 | 27 13/16 | 28 3/8 | + 1/8 |
| BrokenHill | 635 | 23 1/8 | 22 5/16 | 23 | + 3/8 |
| BritldProp | 656 | 16 3/8 | 14 3/4 | 14 7/8 | ... |
| BrownShrp A | 90 | 2 3/16 | 2 1/2 | 2 9/16 | + 1/16 |
| Brown&Brown | 181 | 49 13/16 | 48 1/8 | 49 7/8 | + 1 1/8 |
| ♣ BrownFormn A | 25 | 49 1/2 | 49 1/8 | 49 1/8 | − 5/8 |
| BrownShoe | 1539 | 14 7/8 | 14 3/4 | 14 13/16 | − 1/16 |
| ♣ BrownFormn B | 883 | 50 7/8 | 50 | 50 1/8 | − 3/4 |
| Brunswick | 2189 | 19 5/16 | 18 7/8 | 18 7/8 | − 1/8 |
| ♣ BrushEngr | 301 | 17 1/8 | 16 15/16 | 17 | + 1/8 |
| ♣ BuckeyePtr | 174 | 27 1/2 | 27 3/16 | 27 3/8 | + 1/8 |
| BuckTech | 2419 | 24 1/8 | 23 3/4 | 24 1/4 | + 7/16 |
| ♣ BuckleInc | 88 | 13 3/4 | 13 5/8 | 13 5/8 | − 1/16 |
| ♣ BudgetGrp | 2182 | 4 11/16 | 4 3/8 | 4 1/2 | − 1/16 |
| Buenavnt ADR | 624 | 16 11/16 | 16 1/2 | 16 5/16 | + 1/16 |
| Bufete ADR | 814 | 13/32 | 5/16 | 3/8 | + 1/16 |
| BurlgtnCoal | 39 | 11 11/16 | 11 1/2 | 11 1/2 | − 1/8 |
| BurlgtnInd | 5840 | 2 1/8 | 1 7/8 | 2 | − 1/8 |
| BurlNthSF | 23477 | 24 3/8 | 22 | 22 1/2 | − 2 |
| BurlgtnRes | 18711 | 34 1/16 | 32 1/2 | 34 | + 1 1/4 |
| ♣ BurnhmPacP | 538 | 7 | 6 15/16 | 7 | + 1/16 |
| ♣ BurnsIntSvc | 69 | 13 5/16 | 12 15/16 | 13 1/16 | + 1/16 |
| BushBoake | 4300 | 41 7/8 | 41 7/16 | 41 7/8 | + 5/16 |
| ButlrMfg | 197 | 20 3/4 | 20 1/16 | 20 3/4 | + 1/16 |

**-C-C-C-**

| | | | | | |
|---|---|---|---|---|---|
| CANTV ADR | 3160 | 26 | 24 7/8 | 25 1/4 | − 13/16 |
| C&D Tch | 5311 | 48 1/2 | 38 15/16 | 40 1/8 | + 3 1/16 |
| CBD Pao ADR | 761 | 35 5/16 | 34 | 34 5/16 | − 1/16 |
| ♣ CBL Assoc | 1071 | 24 13/16 | 24 5/16 | 24 7/8 | + 1/4 |
| ♣ CBL Assoc pfA | 38 | 20 7/8 | 20 3/4 | 20 7/8 | ... |
| CB RichEllSvc | 153 | 11 9/16 | 11 3/8 | 11 1/2 | + 1/16 |
| CDI | 215 | 20 1/16 | 18 1/2 | 19 3/8 | − 5/8 |
| CEC Entn | 811 | 29 7/16 | 29 | 29 5/16 | − 1/16 |
| CGG | 55 | 14 3/4 | 14 11/16 | 14 11/16 | − 1/8 |
| CGI Gp A | 302 | 7 1/16 | 6 3/4 | 7 | + 1/4 |
| ♣ CH Engy | 547 | 32 1/4 | 31 7/8 | 32 5/16 | + 1/4 |
| CIGNA | 9814 | 98 | 96 3/4 | 98 | + 1 1/16 |
| CIGNA High | 731 | 5 7/8 | 5 3/4 | 5 3/4 | − 1/8 |
| CIT Gp A | 7982 | 18 7/8 | 18 5/16 | 18 5/16 | − 1/16 |
| CKE Restr | 877 | 3 | 2 15/16 | 3 | ... |
| CMI Cp | 267 | 2 15/16 | 2 7/8 | 2 15/16 | + 1/16 |
| CMP Gp | 192 | 29 1/4 | 29 1/4 | 29 5/16 | − 1/16 |
| CMS Engy | 6773 | 25 | 24 5/16 | 24 9/16 | ... |
| CMS EngyTr | 512 | 31 3/8 | 30 7/8 | 31 | + 1/16 |
| CNA Fnl | 2071 | 38 7/16 | 38 3/4 | 38 1/16 | + 1 1/16 |
| CNA IncoShr | 68 | 8 5/8 | 8 11/16 | 8 11/16 | − 1/16 |
| CNA Surety | 824 | 11 5/16 | 10 15/16 | 10 15/16 | − 3/16 |
| CNB CapTr SpuRS | 42 | 30 3/4 | 30 3/4 | 30 3/4 | − 1/16 |
| CNF Trnsp | 2302 | 26 | 25 3/4 | 25 15/16 | − 1/2 |
| ♣ CNH Global | 7003 | 8 1/16 | 7 5/16 | 7 1/2 | − 1/4 |

| | | | | | |
|---|---|---|---|---|---|
| ♣ ChoicePoint | 1250 | 41 5/8 | 40 1/8 | 40 1/2 | − 1 3/8 |
| ChrisCrft | 589 | 70 3/16 | 68 3/4 | 68 15/16 | − 3/4 |
| Chromcrft | 25 | 11 5/16 | 11 5/16 | 11 1/4 | + 1/8 |
| Chubb | 33782 | 75 | 71 | 74 1/2 | + 2 5/8 |
| Church&Dwt | 521 | 18 15/16 | 18 1/4 | 18 15/16 | + 5/16 |
| Chyron | 544 | 2 9/16 | 2 7/16 | 2 1/2 | − 1/16 |
| CIBER | 3060 | 11 11/16 | 10 13/16 | 11 7/16 | + 1/2 |
| ♣ CINergyCp | 3054 | 28 5/16 | 28 1/8 | 28 5/16 | − 1/8 |
| Circorint | 93 | 7 1/16 | 7 | 7 | ... |
| CircCity | 116330 | 25 15/16 | 23 5/8 | 23 7/8 | − 2 1/8 |
| CircCtyCrmx | 1797 | 3 3/4 | 3 5/16 | 3 5/16 | ... |
| CiticpCap pfA | 49 | 22 1/4 | 21 15/16 | 21 15/16 | − 1/16 |
| CitigpCap pfX | 120 | 21 15/16 | 21 5/8 | 21 15/16 | + 3/16 |
| Citigroup | 70376 | 70 7/8 | 69 5/16 | 69 5/8 | − 7/8 |
| Citigroup pfG | 761 | 45 3/4 | 44 15/16 | 45 3/4 | − 1/2 |
| Citigroup pfK | 24 | 25 11/16 | 25 1/2 | 25 1/2 | + 1/16 |
| CitigpCap pfN | 52 | 21 5/16 | 21 3/4 | 21 5/8 | − 1/16 |
| CitigpCap pfE | 94 | 24 3/4 | 24 1/2 | 24 1/2 | − 1/4 |
| Citigroup pfW | 120 | 21 15/16 | 21 3/4 | 21 15/16 | + 1/16 |
| CtznComm | 3953 | 17 7/8 | 17 1/16 | 17 7/8 | + 1/2 |
| CtznUtil EPPICS | 20 | 68 3/4 | 68 3/4 | 68 3/4 | ... |
| CityNtl | 2078 | 37 | 36 3/4 | 36 15/16 | + 1/16 |
| ♣ ClairStrs | 3819 | 18 5/16 | 17 5/8 | 18 1/16 | ... |
| ♣ CLARCOR | 267 | 20 5/8 | 20 | 20 5/8 | + 7/16 |
| ClaytnHms | 2769 | 8 7/16 | 8 1/8 | 8 3/8 | + 1/16 |
| ClearChanl | 23739 | 77 7/16 | 73 1/8 | 73 1/16 | − 2 1/2 |
| ♣ CLECO | 201 | 36 11/16 | 36 1/4 | 36 7/16 | − 1/16 |
| ClemteStral | 28 | 13 1/4 | 13 3/16 | 13 1/4 | + 1/4 |
| ClvlndClfs | 274 | 25 | 24 1/8 | 24 7/8 | + 5/16 |
| Clorox | 3082 | 42 3/8 | 41 5/8 | 41 3/4 | − 5/8 |
| ♣ Coachmen | 130 | 10 3/8 | 10 5/16 | 10 5/16 | − 1/16 |
| Coastal | 12988 | 58 15/16 | 57 1/4 | 58 | − 1 7/16 |
| CstlCpGwth | 25 | 31 1/8 | 30 | 30 | − 1 1/8 |
| CalFnl TOPrS | 1114 | 23 1/4 | 23 | 23 1/4 | + 1/16 |
| Coastcast | 1215 | 14 | 13 3/4 | 13 7/8 | + 3/8 |
| CocaCola | 33990 | 60 | 58 1/8 | 59 1/8 | − 1/8 |
| CCFemsa ADR | 2283 | 19 13/16 | 19 5/16 | 19 5/16 | − 5/8 |
| CocaColaEnt | 4275 | 19 1/8 | 18 11/16 | 18 3/4 | − 3/8 |
| Coeur dAlén | 2294 | 2 | 1 15/16 | 2 | + 1/16 |
| ♣ CohenStrsTR | 100 | 11 13/16 | 11 13/16 | 11 15/16 | + 1/8 |
| ColeNtl A | 30 | 6 11/16 | 6 5/16 | 6 5/16 | + 1/16 |
| ColgatePalm | 13749 | 58 3/4 | 55 1/8 | 55 5/16 | − 3/4 |
| CollinsAikman | 191 | 5 1/2 | 5 1/4 | 5 1/2 | + 1/8 |
| ColonlBcgp | 983 | 10 1/8 | 10 | 10 1/2 | + 1/16 |
| ♣ ColonlHiInco | 485 | 6 3/4 | 6 1/2 | 6 5/16 | ... |
| ♣ ColonlIntmk | 20 | 8 13/16 | 8 3/4 | 8 3/4 | − 1/16 |
| ♣ ColonlnsHi | 604 | 5 13/16 | 5 11/16 | 5 13/16 | + 1/8 |
| ♣ ColonlInvMun | 25 | 9 5/16 | 9 5/16 | 9 5/16 | + 1/16 |
| ♣ ColonlMuni | 198 | 6 1/16 | 5 7/8 | 5 15/16 | + 1/16 |
| ♣ ColonlProp | 318 | 27 5/16 | 27 3/16 | 27 5/16 | + 3/16 |
| ♣ ColonlProp pfA | 66 | 21 7/8 | 21 3/4 | 21 3/4 | − 1/8 |
| ColumEngy | 7848 | 68 11/16 | 68 1/16 | 68 7/16 | + 1/4 |
| CmbsSe A | 175 | 23 13/16 | 23 5/8 | 23 103/128 | − 27/128 |
| Comdisco | 18258 | 30 7/8 | 27 7/8 | 29 5/8 | − 1 1/4 |
| Comerica | 6227 | 53 | 51 5/16 | 51 15/16 | − 15/16 |
| CmfrtSysUSA | 175 | 4 13/16 | 4 5/16 | 4 5/16 | − 1/8 |
| ComrcBcpNJ | 2013 | 50 7/16 | 48 13/16 | 50 | − 1/2 |
| CommrcGpInc | 369 | 28 | 25 1/16 | 28 | + 1 1/16 |
| ComrclFed | 1320 | 17 1/4 | 17 | 17 1/4 | − 5/16 |
| ComrclMtls | 428 | 28 3/16 | 27 3/4 | 28 3/16 | + 5/16 |
| CmrclNetRlty | 2089 | 10 13/16 | 10 11/16 | 10 3/4 | ... |
| Commscope | 6278 | 35 1/8 | 33 13/16 | 34 11/16 | + 1 1/16 |
| CmntyBkSys | 177 | 22 | 21 15/16 | 22 | + 1/16 |

| | | | | | |
|---|---|---|---|---|---|
| Doncasters | 119 | 15 1/8 | 15 | 15 | ... |
| DonnaKrn | 225 | 6 5/16 | 6 | 6 1/8 | ... |
| DonlleyRR | 2371 | 22 11/16 | 21 7/8 | 22 1/8 | − 1 1/16 |
| DotHillSys | 1209 | 10 5/16 | 9 5/16 | 9 11/16 | − 1/2 |
| DoverCp | 4350 | 47 3/4 | 46 3/4 | 46 1/2 | − 1 |
| ♣ DoverDowns | 139 | 11 13/16 | 11 5/16 | 11 13/16 | + 3/8 |
| DowChem | 32350 | 29 5/16 | 28 | 28 5/16 | − 1 1/16 |
| ♣ DowJones | 3423 | 67 11/16 | 66 3/4 | 66 9/16 | − 1 |
| DowneyFnl | 502 | 34 1/16 | 33 5/16 | 33 13/16 | − 3/4 |
| ♣ Drsdnr RCM | 458 | 6 7/16 | 6 3/8 | 6 3/8 | ... |
| DryfsHiYldFd | 1221 | 9 1/4 | 9 1/8 | 9 1/8 | + 1/16 |
| DreyfStrGv | 235 | 9 1/4 | 9 3/16 | 9 1/4 | ... |
| DreyfStMnBd | 863 | 8 5/16 | 8 3/16 | 8 5/16 | − 1/8 |
| DreyfStrMuni | 1008 | 8 3/8 | 8 5/16 | 8 5/16 | + 1/8 |
| DrilQuip | 70 | 41 1/8 | 40 1/2 | 41 | ... |
| DuPont | 49627 | 45 3/4 | 43 1/2 | 44 15/16 | + 1 3/16 |
| DuPont pfB | 41 | 64 51/64 | 64 45/64 | 64 51/64 | + 13/64 |
| DuaneReade | 936 | 25 1/8 | 24 1/2 | 24 9/16 | − 9/16 |
| DucatiMtr | 158 | 26 1/16 | 24 7/8 | 25 3/8 | + 1/2 |
| Ducommun | 291 | 14 3/8 | 13 3/4 | 14 1/8 | ... |
| DufPhlpsUtl | 1758 | 9 3/8 | 9 1/2 | 9 3/8 | ... |
| DufPhlpsTF | 152 | 12 3/4 | 12 11/16 | 12 3/4 | − 1/16 |
| DufPhlpsBnd | 448 | 11 5/8 | 11 7/16 | 11 5/8 | + 1/16 |
| DukeCap QUIPS | 114 | 22 1/2 | 22 1/4 | 22 1/8 | − 1/8 |
| DukeCap TOPrS | 77 | 22 3/8 | 22 1/4 | 22 1/8 | − 1/8 |
| DukeCap TruPs | 32 | 25 1/8 | 25 | 25 1/8 | + 1/16 |
| DukeCap pfO | 143 | 22 1/8 | 21 3/4 | 22 | ... |
| DukeCap pfV | 104 | 22 5/16 | 22 1/16 | 22 1/4 | ... |
| DukeEngy | 7430 | 63 3/8 | 62 7/16 | 62 1/2 | − 1 |
| DukeEngy C | 54 | 22 1/8 | 22 | 22 1/16 | + 1/16 |
| ♣ DukeWks | 3737 | 24 1/2 | 23 13/16 | 24 7/16 | + 3/8 |
| ♣ DukeWks pfA | 97 | 24 5/16 | 24 | 24 5/16 | + 5/16 |
| ♣ DukeWks pfD | 19 | 23 1/2 | 23 1/4 | 23 1/2 | − 1/16 |
| ♣ DukeWks pfE | 48 | 22 3/8 | 21 3/4 | 21 7/8 | − 15/16 |
| ♣ DukeWks pfF | 25 | 21 5/16 | 21 1/8 | 21 5/16 | + 1/4 |
| DunBradst | 3646 | 28 15/16 | 28 5/16 | 28 11/16 | − 7/16 |
| Dycomind | 1878 | 48 | 44 | 45 5/16 | − 1/2 |
| Dynegy A | 10898 | 72 15/16 | 68 3/4 | 69 1/2 | − 3 7/16 |
| DynexCap | 104 | 1 7/16 | 1 3/8 | 1 3/8 | ... |

**-E-E-E-**

| | | | | | |
|---|---|---|---|---|---|
| ECC Intl | 29 | 3 1/8 | 3 1/8 | 3 1/8 | ... |
| EDF London pfA | 279 | 24 | 23 15/16 | 24 | ... |
| EDO | 78 | 6 | 5 3/4 | 5 3/4 | − 1/8 |
| EEX Cp | 1035 | 5 1/16 | 4 3/4 | 4 7/8 | ... |
| E4L | 2719 | 1 | 7/8 | 15/16 | − 1/16 |
| EK ChemChina | 52 | 2 7/16 | 2 7/16 | 2 7/16 | ... |
| ♣ EMC Cp | 66408 | 88 1/2 | 85 1/16 | 86 3/4 | − 1/2 |
| ENI Spa | 328 | 56 3/4 | 56 1/8 | 56 1/8 | − 1/8 |
| E O G Res | 13013 | 28 5/16 | 27 | 27 15/16 | + 13/16 |
| EOTT Engy | 275 | 13 15/16 | 13 13/16 | 13 3/4 | + 5/16 |
| E.ON | 164 | 54 1/2 | 53 1/8 | 53 1/8 | + 13/16 |
| Earthgrains | 518 | 18 3/4 | 18 3/4 | 18 3/4 | + 1/8 |
| EstAm SPERS | 21 | 14 5/16 | 14 1/8 | 14 3/8 | + 1/16 |
| EasternEnt | 1671 | 62 3/4 | 62 3/4 | 62 11/16 | − 1/16 |
| Eastgroup | 354 | 23 1/8 | 22 1/2 | 23 1/8 | + 5/16 |
| EastmanChm | 3699 | 48 3/4 | 45 3/4 | 48 3/4 | − 1/2 |
| EKodak | 18246 | 55 11/16 | 54 1/2 | 55 | − 5/8 |
| Eaton | 4049 | 68 3/4 | 66 15/16 | 67 11/16 | − 11/16 |
| EatonVance | 320 | 50 1/2 | 49 15/16 | 50 1/2 | ... |
| EtnVnc MIT | 307 | 11 1/16 | 11 1/8 | 11 3/8 | + 1/16 |
| EtnVncInco | 481 | 9 7/16 | 9 5/16 | 9 7/16 | + 1/16 |
| Ecolab | 3189 | 38 | 34 3/4 | 34 7/8 | − 1 5/16 |

last year's dividend payments as a proportion of the current price. The final column contains the price–earnings ratio ('*P–E*')—where earnings are based on the latest annual reports plus any interim figures. When 'xd' appears after the price quote it implies the share has gone 'ex-dividend' and if you purchase the share, you will not receive the next dividend—this 'loss' to

## FIGURE 12.4: (*Continued*)
## (b) *Financial Times* reproduced with permission

# LONDON SHARE SERVICE

### SOFTWARE & COMPUTER SERVICES - Continued

| | Notes | Price | + or − | 52 week high | 52 week low | Volume '000s | Yield | P/E |
|---|---|---|---|---|---|---|---|---|
| Geo Interactive Med | | 1170 | +7½ | 3525 | 93½ | 848 | – | Φ |
| Gladstone | | 135½ | −1 | 690 | 80 | 88 | – | – |
| Gresham Comp | | 33½ | −1 | 101½ | 25½ | 83 | – | – |
| Guardian IT | ♣ | 1357½ | −2½ | *1621¾ | 570½ | 70 | 0.1 | – |
| Horizon Technology | | 470 | −7½ | 852½ | 217½ | 1 | – | – |
| ICM Computer | ♣ | 320 | ....... | 1215 | 235½ | 5 | 0.9 | 21.1 |
| I S Solutions | ♣h | 225 | −3½ | *275½ | 47 | 261 | 0.4 | 64.0 |
| ITG | | 597½ | −30 | 1575 | 375 | 29 | – | Φ |
| ITNET | | 680 | −7½ | 1152½ | 398 | 125 | 0.5 | 61.3 |
| Infobank Intl | ♣ | 837½ | −57½ | 4375 | 101½ | 743 | – | – |
| Innovation | | 366 | +1 | 385 | 265 | 12 | – | – |
| Intec Telecom | | 401 | +12½ | 414 | 205 | 230 | – | – |
| Interactive Investor Intl | | 51 | ....... | 466½ | 36½ | 136 | – | – |
| JSB Software | ♣ | 1862½ | −20 | 3900 | 305 | 483 | – | – |
| Jasmin | ♣ | 137½ | ....... | 218½ | 90 | 6 | 1.5 | – |
| Kalamazoo Cmptr | ♣ | 33½ | −1 | 129½ | 29½ | 42 | – | – |
| Kewill Syst | ♣ | 1015 | +50 | 3332½ | 387½ | 1,080 | – | – |
| Knowledge Mngmt Sftw | | 170 | +2½ | 267½ | 105 | 463 | – | – |
| Knowledge Support | | 403½ | +1 | 410 | 195 | 180 | – | – |
| Logica | ♣† | 1743 | −18 | 2940 | 659 | 1,549 | 0.2 | – |
| London Bridge Software | ♣P | 827½ | −22½ | 1570 | 405 | 59 | 0.1 | – |
| Lynx Group | ♣ | 140xd | +1½ | 376 | 86½ | 48 | 1.8 | 30.6 |
| MERANT | | 150 | −1½ | 495 | 124½ | 1,052 | – | 21.9 |
| MMT Comp | † | 630 | ....... | 1045 | 475 | 1 | 3.0 | 19.4 |
| MSW Technology | ♣‡ | 41½ | −1 | 140 | 26½ | 18 | – | – |
| Macro 4 | | 875 | ....... | 1445 | 597½ | 0 | 3.0 | 25.1 |
| Microgen | ♣ | 392½ | −5 | 917½ | 144 | 10 | 0.5 | 74.7 |
| Misys | † | 605 | +12 | 1292 | 454 | 1,137 | 0.6 | 37.4 |
| Morse | ♣ | 482½ | +2½ | 810 | 205½ | 222 | – | 28.7 |
| NSB Retail Sys | ♣h | 300 | +5 | *365 | 63 | 307 | – | – |
| NetBenefit | | 485 | −45 | 2400 | 202 | 10 | – | – |
| Netstore | | 124 | ....... | 158 | 124 | 1,507 | – | – |
| Nettec | ♣ | 152½ | ....... | 275 | 135 | 245 | – | – |
| Northgate Info Solutions | g | 47 | −¾ | 109½ | 17 | 2,187 | 0.8 | – |
| Orchestream | | 447 | +17 | 485 | 200 | 182 | – | – |
| Parity | | 143¾ | −3¼ | 710 | 130 | 371 | 1.7 | 17.7 |
| Patsystems | | 165 | −1½ | 174 | 109 | 24 | – | – |
| Planit | | 121½xd | −2 | 209½ | 42 | 30 | 0.2 | Φ |
| Primar–E | ♣ | 15¼# | ....... | 22½ | 1¾ | – | – | – |
| QSP | ♣ | 123½ | ....... | 297½ | 89½ | 11 | – | 4.4 |
| RM | ♣† | 770 | +2½ | 1047½ | 519½ | 14 | 0.4 | – |
| Recognition Sys | | 347½ | +5½ | 662½ | 15 | 695 | – | – |
| Redbus Interhouse | q | 203½ | −6 | 312½ | 22 | 79 | – | – |
| Reflex Grp I£ | | 10 | ....... | 17 | 3¼ | – | – | 24.8 |
| Retail Decisions | ♣ | 149½ | +17 | 389 | 63½ | 1,904 | – | – |
| Rolfe & Nolan | ♣ | 355 | +2½ | 762½ | 172½ | 64 | 1.2 | 32.9 |
| Royalblue | s | 1492½ | ....... | 2787½ | 482½ | 4 | 0.3 | – |
| SDL | | 290 | −2½ | 850 | 280 | 18 | – | – |
| Sage | ✣† | 544 | +9 | 975 | 250 | 3,924 | – | – |
| Sema | ♣ | 1068½ | +31½ | 1848 | 554 | 6,055 | 0.3 | 75.2 |
| Service Power Techs | | 90 | −1½ | 126 | 78 | 5 | – | – |
| Sherwood Intl | ♣ | 717 | +42 | 1750 | 410 | 968 | 0.3 | 32.4 |
| Skillsgroup | ♣† | 137 | ....... | 377 | 124 | 386 | 4.3 | 13.2 |
| Staffware | ♣ | 2837½ | +137½ | 4650 | 235 | 60 | – | – |
| Statpro | | 88½ | −1 | 98 | 63½ | 2 | – | – |
| Superscape | ♣ | 287 | −1½ | 622½ | 76½ | 205 | – | – |
| Synstar | ♣ | 68 | −1 | 248½ | 65½ | 111 | – | 13.9 |
| TeleCity | | 1212½ | +20 | 1227½ | 800 | 133 | – | – |
| Telme.Com | | 42½ | ....... | 262½ | 27½ | 65 | – | – |
| Terence Chapman | ♣† | 209 | −1 | 676½ | 127½ | 0 | 0.7 | 78.2 |
| Torex | ♣ | 565 | ....... | 672½ | 256½ | 9 | 0.5 | 38.3 |
| Total Systems | ♣ | 107 | +9 | 164½ | 34½ | 142 | 1.9 | – |
| Trace Comps | ♣ | 73½ | ....... | 175 | 62 | 0 | – | 7.1 |

### SUPPORT SERVICES - Continued

| | Notes | Price | + or − | 52 week high | 52 week low | Volume '000s | Yield | P/E |
|---|---|---|---|---|---|---|---|---|
| Ricardo | ♣† | 505 | ....... | 536 | 326½ | 89 | 1.4 | 29.5 |
| Robert Walters | | 195 | ....... | 195½ | 175 | 100 | – | – |
| SHL | † | 285½xd | −½ | 325 | 180 | 1 | 2.1 | 18.3 |
| Securicor | † | 123¼ | −¼ | 198 | 110 | 203 | 1.0 | – |
| Semple Cochrane | ‡ | 71 | ....... | 408½ | 62½ | 2 | 4.6 | – |
| Serco | ♣h | 577½ | −2½ | 610 | 222½ | 689 | 0.2 | – |
| Shanks | ♣ | 203½xd | +1 | 259½ | 152½ | 619 | 2.6 | 18.3 |
| Simon Group | | 49 | ....... | 82 | 47½ | 158 | 2.2 | 8.4 |
| Spring Group | ♣ | 114½xd | −3 | 357½ | 99½ | 32 | 0.2 | – |
| Stat–Plus | | 70½ | ....... | 154 | 54½ | – | 9.9 | 8.2 |
| Staveley Inds | | 54 | ....... | 78½ | 47½ | 964 | – | – |
| Tilbury Douglas | ♣ | 363½ | ....... | 365 | 252 | 18 | 3.0 | 16.5 |
| TNT Post NLG | ✣ | £16 17/32 | +¼ | £18 9/16 | £13 11/32 | – | 1.4 | Φ |
| Tyco Intl $ | ✣♣P | £34xd | ....... | £34 | £0 7/32 | 1 | – | – |
| Universal Salvage | ♣ | 324½xd | +1 | 334 | 98 | 0 | 1.1 | Φ |
| WSP | ♣ | 318½ | −3½ | 375½ | 195½ | 21 | 1.2 | 24.0 |
| Waste Recycling | | 420 | +13 | 470 | 342 | 107 | 0.8 | 24.2 |
| Waterman Part | ♣† | 96½ | +2 | 116½ | 75½ | 3 | 4.4 | 11.2 |
| White Young Green | ♣† | 170 | +2½ | 184½ | 117½ | 2 | 2.4 | 17.0 |
| Whitehead Mann | | 300xd | ....... | 337½ | 230 | 1 | 3.5 | 13.4 |
| Williams | ♣ | 356 | −½ | 400 | 213 | 3,037 | 4.6 | 16.9 |
| 8p Cnv Pref | | 124½ | ....... | 137½ | 108½ | – | 6.4 | – |

### TELECOMMUNICATION SERVICES

| | Notes | Price | + or − | 52 week high | 52 week low | Volume '000s | Yield | P/E |
|---|---|---|---|---|---|---|---|---|
| Atlantic Telecom | | 430 | −10 | 1290 | 289½ | 188 | – | – |
| BT | ✣♣ | 868 | −10 | 1520¾ | 803 | 14,020 | 2.6 | 25.1 |
| Cable & Wireless | ✣ | 1220xd | −32 | 1578½ | 637½ | 7,505 | 1.2 | 69.4 |
| 7pc Cv Ln '08 | | £595 | −6 | £752 | £314 | – | 1.2 | – |
| COLT Telecom | | 2430 | +50 | 4172 | 1185 | 1,282 | – | – |
| Deutsche Telekom | | £31 13/32 | +1 3/16 | £62 13/16 | £30 13/32 | – | – | – |
| eircom | | 175¾xd | +1 | 357 | 157¼ | 424 | 1.6 | Φ |
| Energis | ✣ | 590 | −5 | *812 | 267¼ | 2,280 | – | – |
| Estonian Telecom | ♣ | 446½ | +¾ | 598¼ | 427¾ | – | – | – |
| European Telecom | ♣ | 483½ | −1½ | 611½ | 95½ | 27 | 0.7 | Φ |
| Fibernet Group | ♣ | 1780 | +2½ | 3055 | 423½ | 7 | – | – |
| FLAG Telecom $ | | 1118¼ | +75 | 2229¼ | 803½ | – | – | – |
| GN Gt Nordic DKr | | £82 3/32 | −1 1/32 | £92⅛ | £19 1/16 | – | 0.2 | – |
| IMS | ♣† | 135 | −11 | *503½ | 101¾ | 388 | 3.1 | 16.8 |
| JWE Telecom | ♣ | 112½ | −1 | 232 | 42½ | 6 | – | 54.5 |
| KPN Fl | ✣P | £25 31/32 | −⅛ | *£45 3/16 | £12 11/32 | – | 1.3 | 42.6 |
| Kingston Comms | ♣ | 593 | +2 | 1609¾ | 297 | 1,200 | 0.1 | – |
| Nippon T & T Y | s | £7780 7/32 | −236 13/32 | £11592⅝ | £6679 13/32 | – | 0.4 | 34.2 |
| PNC Tele.com | ♣ | 233½ | −1½ | 435 | 56½ | 19 | – | – |
| Redstone Telecom | ♣ | 274 | −3½ | *954 | 164½ | 46 | – | – |
| TeleWest | ✣♣ | 193 | −17 | 569¾ | 185 | 60,749 | – | – |
| Thus | | 245 | −2 | 645 | 240 | 1,568 | – | – |
| Vodafone AirTouch | ✣ | 304xd | +4½ | 401 | 202½ | 99,049 | 0.4 | 66.4 |

### TOBACCO

| | Notes | Price | + or − | 52 week high | 52 week low | Volume '000s | Yield | P/E |
|---|---|---|---|---|---|---|---|---|
| British American Tobacco | ✣♣s | 390 | −9 | 545 | 224 | 13,504 | 5.7 | 17.5 |
| Gallaher | | 360 | ....... | 460 | 203 | 446 | 6.2 | 9.7 |
| Imperial Tobacco | † | 656xd | +3 | 770 | 364 | 8,730 | 4.4 | 11.0 |

the purchaser is reflected in a lower price quote. The symbol ✣ indicates the share is included in the 'FT Global 500' index. (The other symbols need not concern us.)

In order to analyse past and future company performance, more information is needed.

Detailed statistical data on company and industry equity performance, at the heart of which is the estimation of betas for different companies, is provided by so-called risk measurement services (RMS). Box 12.2 explains the various uses for beta.

---

## Box 12.2    USES FOR 'BETAS'

- **Market timing**—for example, move into high beta shares if you expect the market to rise.
- **Performance measures**—if a stock (or portfolio of stocks) earns a higher return than given by the CAPM/SML equilibrium return then it has performed 'abnormally well'.
- **Betas** are used in the calculation of (i) the weighted average cost of capital, (ii) the risk adjusted discount rate, used in DPV calculations of *physical* capital projects and (iii) in calculating the fair value of a stock using the risk adjusted discount rate.
- **Betas** can be used to construct **customised portfolios** with a specific value of beta chosen by the client. The portfolio beta is simply a weighted average of the firm's betas, $\beta_p = \sum w_i \beta_i$. For example, a client who is relatively highly risk averse may 'stock pick' only those shares which either have betas less than 1 (i.e. defensive stocks) or if she includes stocks with $\beta > 1$, these will be offset by short selling positive beta stocks, so that the overall portfolio beta is small.
- **Betas** can be used to simplify the calculation of the market risk (e.g. J.P. Morgan's 'Value at Risk') of a stock portfolio and hence the overall **'position risk'** of equity traders and investment managers (see Cuthbertson and Nitzsche, 2001).

---

RMS often provide lists of 'high' and 'low' beta companies so that portfolio managers can easily form portfolios with a given beta value. Note that although a 'high' beta portfolio (e.g. $\beta = 1.5$) will have returns that on average move more than the market return, such a portfolio is not (necessarily) earning an abnormal return. The high average return simply compensates for the higher market (non-diversifiable or systematic) risk.

An illustrative set of data provided by these RMS is given in Table 12.5. The definitions used are as follows:

**Market cap**
> This is the market value of a company's ordinary shares outstanding (£m).

**Trading frequency**
> Average number of days from the previous recorded trade to the month end (e.g. '0' = very frequent, '99' = 99 or more days).

**Trading velocity**
> Value of shares recently traded as a percentage of market capitalisation.

**R-squared ($R^2$)**
> The proportion of the variability in the company return explained by the market return. This is a measure of how accurately the CAPM explains the movements in the return on a stock, $R_i$. An $R$-squared of 0.3 indicates 30% of past movements in $R_i$ are explained by movements in $R_m$.

## TABLE 12.5: Risk measurement services

| Company (sector) | (1) Market cap (£m) | (2) Trading frequency | (3) Velocity (% p.a.) | (4) Beta | (5) Beta s.e. | (6) $R^2$ (%) | (7) Variability (% p.a.) | (8) Specific risk (% p.a.) | (9) Annual abnormal return (%) | (10) Annual actual return (%) |
|---|---|---|---|---|---|---|---|---|---|---|
| 1. Trafalgar House (conglomerate) | 913 | 0 | 83 | 1.64 | 0.26 | 26 | 53 | 46 | 8 | 40 |
| 2. Forte (hotel & catering) | 1924 | 0 | 72 | 1.45 | 0.16 | 54 | 33 | 22 | −9 | 21 |
| 3. Liberty (store) | 73 | 2 | 2.4 | 0.29 | 0.19 | 3 | 28 | 28 | −8 | 6 |
| 4. Ingham (wool) | 22 | 3 | 112 | 0.11 | 0.28 | 0.1 | 47 | 47 | 18 | 141 |

Reproduced from E. Dimson and P. R. Marsh (Eds) *Risk Management Service* London Business School

398

### Standard error of beta

Broadly speaking we can be 95% certain that the true value of beta lies in the range $\hat{\beta} + 2\text{s.e.}(\hat{\beta})$ where $\text{s.e.}(\hat{\beta}) = $ estimated standard error of the $\hat{\beta}$.

### Variability

Standard deviation of the annual percentage return on the share. Broadly speaking the return on the share will exceed its 'mean return plus its variability' (i.e. $ER + \sigma$) about one year in six. The return will also fall short by an amount $\sigma$ about one year in six. The 'one in six' rule arises because for a normal distribution about 65% of returns are *within* '$\pm\sigma$', hence about 17.5% ($= 35/2$) will *exceed* and 17.5% will *fall short* of the mean. The figure of 17.5% is approximately 'one in six'.

### Specific risk

This is the risk of non-market related fluctuations in the share price. Even given an unchanged market return, the annual percentage return on stock $i$ will fall short of expectations by at least its specific risk, in about one year in six. Most of this specific risk is eliminated in a diversified portfolio.

### Annual abnormal return (AAR)

This is the performance of the share relative to its equilibrium return. The equilibrium return is measured by $\beta_i R_m$ and is a simplified version of the CAPM relationship. (In fact, it is the single index model SIM with a zero intercept):

[12.19] $$\text{AAR}_i = R_i - \beta_i(R_m)$$

where $R_i$ is the actual return on the share, $\beta_i$ is the beta of the shares and $R_m$ is the market return (% p.a.). The ARR is similar to Jensen's performance index (see Chapter 10).

### Annual actual return (holding period return)

This is the percentage price change plus the dividend yield over the past year. (Gross dividends are assumed to be reinvested in the share at the end of the month in which they are paid.)

The usefulness of most of the above statistics is fairly self-explanatory. Trading frequency and velocity (columns 2 and 3, Table 12.5) are broad indicators of the liquidity or thinness of the market in these shares. Relatively small capitalisation stocks (e.g. Liberty, Table 12.5, row 3) often have low trading frequency and velocity. However, some small-cap stocks (e.g. Ingham, Table 12.5, row 4) in specific periods might be purchased in large volume by fund managers and others (e.g. during a takeover bid). The variability (column 7) or market risk of individual stocks can be quite high. However, diversification can reduce the 'variability' of a portfolio of stocks (relative to that for any single stock) and, of course, specific risk (column 8) in a well-diversified portfolio can be reduced to near zero.

In assessing stock performance we usually require a measure which applies to a portfolio of stocks. The **annual abnormal return** for *a portfolio* (AAR$_p$) can be determined using either the beta of the portfolio $\beta_p$:

[12.20] $$\text{AAR}_p = R_p - \beta_p R_m$$

or by the weighted average of the AAR$_i$ for each security:

[12.21] $$\text{AAR}_p = \sum_{i=1}^{n} w_i \text{AAR}_i$$

Equations [12.20] and [12.21] are equivalent since:

[**12.22**]
$$\text{AAR}_\text{p} = \sum_{i=1}^{n} w_i(R_i - \beta_i R_\text{m}) = \sum_{i=1}^{n} \left( w_i R_i - \sum_{i=1}^{n} w_i \beta_i \right) R_\text{m} = R_\text{p} - \beta_\text{p} R_\text{m}$$

where $R_\text{p} = \sum_{i=1}^{n} w_i R_i$ and $\beta_\text{p} = \sum_{i=1}^{n} w_i \beta_i$. The $\text{AAR}_\text{p}$ is one measure of the performance of the portfolio, which has been adjusted for the riskiness of the portfolio. An analyst with an $\text{AAR}_\text{p}$ which is positive could be said to have 'beaten the market', and the $\text{AAR}_\text{p}$ of different analysts can be used to rank their (risk adjusted) investment performance. The $\text{AAR}_\text{p}$ is an alternative performance measure to those discussed in Chapter 10 and is quite similar to Jensen's index.

Thus the above type of information provided commercially can be useful for stock analysts in assessing company shares.

## 12.4 SUMMARY

- Firms can **raise new equity finance by issuing ordinary or preference shares**. The former have voting rights and they are the owners of the firm, the latter do not have voting rights but are entitled to receive dividend payments before the ordinary shareholders, who are 'last in the queue'. No shareholders receive any dividends before debt holders have been paid.
- A publicly quoted company can raise capital by issuing additional shares. Often (but not always) these **shares have to be offered to existing shareholders** rather than sold directly in the market. This is then called a **rights issue**.
- An **efficient market** is one in which prices (returns) reflect all available relevant information and in which **it is impossible to earn abnormal profits** (corrected for risk). In short, the EMH implies that it is impossible to do better than the passive investment strategy of holding the market portfolio.
- In an efficient market **the fair value of a stock** is given by the PV of expected future dividends, discounted using a risk adjusted discount rate.
- **Speculators** who believe they can 'beat the market' should purchase (sell) stocks when the market price is below (above) fair value or equivalently when the internal rate of return exceeds (is less than) the risk adjusted required rate of return $ER_i$.
- The **equilibrium risk adjusted rate of return $ER_i$** used in **calculating fair value** (for an all equity financed firm) can be estimated from either the **CAPM/SML or the APT**.
- Certain private firms provide the latest **estimates of company betas** and other stock market information, to aid investment analysts and to enable them to assess portfolio performance.

## END OF CHAPTER EXERCISES

Q1    Does the dividend discount model ignore the mass of investors who have bought their shares with the intention of selling them in say 3 years time?

**Q2**    What practical use is there in knowing the beta of your stock portfolio?

**Q3**    Why might stock prices be highly volatile even though all investors act in a perfectly rational way?

**Q4**    Why is it better to short sell an overvalued stock and to simultaneously buy a different undervalued stock, rather than simply just buying the undervalued stock?

**Q5**    The dividends of company X are expected to grow at the constant rate of 5% p.a. The last dividend payout was $1.80 per share. The risk adjusted (required) rate of return is $ER = 11\%$ p.a. The current market price of the share is $35. Should you purchase the share?

**Q6**    'Internet' plc is expected to produce earnings per share in 2001 of 20 cents and in 2002 of 26 cents. Earnings growth thereafter is expected to be 10%. Past performance is indicated below:

|  | 1988 | 1989 | 1990 |
|---|---|---|---|
| **Earnings per share (cents)** | 10 | 12 | 15 |
| **Dividends per share (cents)** | 4 | 4.8 | 6 |

(a) If the rate of return on Internet required by investors is 14% then what is the fair price for the share at the end of 2000?

(b) In the past 5 years Internet shares have provided a 10%, 12%, 3%, 6% and 8% return. Estimate the expected return and standard deviation of Internet plc.

(c) The expected return on the market is 7%, the standard deviation of market risk is 6%, correlation of Internet with the market is 0.7 and the risk free rate is 5%. If the current market price of Internet is $P = 235$, is Internet a 'good buy'?

**Q7**    A firm is expected to pay dividends of 20p at the end of the year $t = 1$. Dividends are then expected to grow at 5%. The (risk adjusted) required rate of return for this firm is 11%. What would you expect its current market price to be? If the dividend payout ratio is 60% what would you expect the price earnings ratio to be?

# APPENDIX 12.1   RELATIONSHIP BETWEEN RETURNS AND FAIR VALUE

There is a direct link between the *return* on a stock and the *price* of the stock. We can show that a particular assumption about the one-period holding period return (HPR) on a stock implies that the DPV formula for stock prices must hold (and vice versa). We simplify the algebra by omitting expectations signs (e.g. $ED_t$ will be written simply as $D_t$). Next, we assume that investors will willingly hold the stock if its expected return equals the risk free rate $r$ (which we take to be constant, $r = 0.1$):

Expected HPR $\equiv$ (capital gain + dividend yield) = $r$

[A12.1]     $(P_1 - P_0)/P_0 + D_1/P_0 = r$

Rearranging:

[A12.2]     $P_0 = \delta P_1 + \delta D_1$

where $\delta = 1/(1 + r) = $ discount factor (e.g. $\delta = 0.909$).

Equation [A12.2] implies that the price today $P_0$ depends on expected dividends tomorrow plus the price you expect to sell the stock for tomorrow. If investors are rational, then the price tomorrow $P_1$ is given by a similar equation to [A12.2]:

[A12.3]     $P_1 = \delta P_2 + \delta D_2$

Substituting equation [A12.3] in equation [A12.2]:

[A12.4]     $P_0 = \delta^2 P_2 + \delta D_1 + \delta^2 D_2$

Repeating the above for $P_2$, $P_3$, etc. and assuming that $\delta^t P_t \to 0$ as $t \to \infty$ then:

[A12.5]     $P_0 = \delta D_1 + \delta^2 D_2 + \delta^3 D_3 + \ldots$

Even if some investors only wish to hold the stock for one period, they have to calculate the selling price $P_1$. The only way they can do this is to calculate all future prices $P_2$, $P_3$, ... etc. Hence, although they have a 'short horizon', as long as they are 'rational' and base $P_2$ on expected future dividends, then the 'infinite sum' DPV formula for stock prices will hold. Hence the DPV formula does not imply that all investors want to hold the stock for ever, merely that they calculate the future selling price, based on future expected dividends.

Note that the above 'link' between the determinants of stock returns and the DPV for stock prices is perfectly general. For example, if the equilibrium return depends on $r$ which is expected to vary in the future then we still obtain an equation like [A12.5], but the discount factors vary every period, namely:

[A12.6]     $P_0 = \delta_1 D_1 + \delta_1 \delta_2 D_2 + \delta_1 \delta_2 \delta_3 D_3 + \ldots$

where $\delta_1 = 1/(1 + r_{01})$, $\delta_2 = 1/(1 + r_{12})$ etc.
$r_{ij}$ is the one-period spot rate between time period $i$ and period $j$.

## SPECULATIVE BUBBLES

It is also worth noting that the rather innocuous assumption $\delta^t P_t \to 0$ as $t \to \infty$ rules out the possibility of (rational) 'bubbles'. If this condition does not hold then the solution for $P_0$ in equation [A12.5] has an additional 'bubble term' which arises because people *believe* that the stock price will rise even though future dividends are expected to remain constant. If there is a 'bubble' then the market price does not equal its 'fair value' but (for a positive bubble) is higher than its fair value. Investors are prepared to pay a higher market price than the 'fair value' because they think the next person will be willing to pay an even higher price. Such speculative bubbles could be the cause of large rapid price movements, as for example tulip mania in the 16th century, the South Sea Bubble and even the stock market crashes of 1929, 1974 and 1987. For further analysis of speculative bubbles see Cuthbertson (1996).

# CHAPTER 13

# Efficient Markets and Predictability

### LEARNING OBJECTIVES

- To explain the practical implications of the **efficient markets hypothesis (EMH)** for investment strategy, aspects of corporate finance and the regulation of financial markets and institutions.
- To assess the **empirical validity of the EMH** applied to the stock market by looking at various tests of the predictability of asset returns. To examine the related issue of **'excess volatility'** in stock markets.
- To examine whether it is possible to earn **abnormal profits** (i.e. corrected for risk and transactions costs) by undertaking 'active' investment strategies.

The efficient markets hypothesis (EMH) may be expressed in a number of alternative ways, and the differences between these alternative representations can easily become rather esoteric, technical and subtle (see LeRoy, 1989). We try and avoid such technical issues and present the ideas in intuitive terms. The concepts behind the EMH can be applied to all speculative asset returns (e.g. stocks, bonds, derivatives), but we restrict our discussion to the equity market.

When economists speak of capital markets as being *efficient* they usually mean that they view asset prices and returns as being determined as the outcome trading between rational agents in a competitive market. The first key aspect of the EMH is that traders rapidly assimilate any information that is relevant to the determination of asset prices or returns (e.g. future dividend prospects). This is the **rational expectations** element of the EMH. Hence, individuals do not have different comparative advantages in the acquisition of information.

The second key element is that these rational traders instantaneously 'move' market prices to equal fair value, as determined by the PV of future dividends. It follows that in such a world there should be no opportunities for making a return on a stock that is in excess of a fair payment for the riskiness of that stock (and any transactions costs in buying and selling). In short, abnormal profits from trading should be zero. Thus, agents process information efficiently and immediately incorporate this information into stock prices. If current and past information is immediately incorporated into current prices, then only new information or 'news' should cause changes in prices. Since news is by definition unforecastable, then price changes (or returns) should be unforecastable: no information at time $t$ or earlier should help to improve the forecast of returns (or equivalently to reduce the forecast error made by the individual). In the finance literature the concepts behind the EMH provide a 'benchmark' against which we can judge the actual behaviour of asset returns (and prices).

# 13.1 IMPLICATIONS OF THE EMH

The view that the return on shares is determined by the actions of rational agents in a competitive market, and that equilibrium returns reflect all available public information, is probably quite widely held amongst financial economists. The slightly stronger assertion, namely that stock prices also reflect their fair (or fundamental) value (i.e. the PV of future dividends) is also widely held. What then are the implications of the EMH applied to the stock market?

As far as a risk averse investor is concerned the EMH means that he should adopt a 'buy and hold' policy. He should spread his risks and hold the 'market portfolio' (or the 25 or so shares that mimic the market portfolio). Such advice as 'put all your eggs in one basket and watch the basket' should be avoided. The role for investment analysis, if the EMH is correct, is very limited and would for example include:

- Advising on the choice of the 20 or so shares that mimic the market portfolio.
- Altering the proportion of wealth held in each asset to reflect the market share portfolio weights (the $w_i^*$ of the portfolio theory) which will alter over time. The optimal weights change as estimates of expected returns, variances and covariances change, when new data becomes available.
- Altering the portfolio as taxes change (e.g. if dividends are more highly taxed than capital gains, then for high rate income tax payers, it is optimal at the margin to move to shares which have low dividends and high expected capital gains).
- 'Shopping-around' in order to minimise transactions costs of buying and selling.

Under the EMH the current share price incorporates all relevant publicly available information. One somewhat technical way of expressing the EMH, under the mean–variance optimisation assumption, is that all securities lie on the SML. Hence, the investment analyst cannot pick winners by reanalysing publicly available information or by using trading rules (e.g. buy 'low', wait for a price rise and sell 'high'). Thus the EMH implies that a major part of the current activities of investment managers is wasteful.

It is worth noting that most individuals and institutions do not hold anything like the 'market portfolio' of all marketable assets. Except for residents of the USA this would require most investors to hold predominantly *foreign securities* (i.e. most corporations would be owned by foreigners). This is the **home bias puzzle**. Also, most mutual funds and unit trusts *specialise* and sell funds in particular sectors (e.g. chemicals or services) or specific geographical areas (e.g. Japanese stocks). There is a marketing reason for this. If finance houses operate a number of such funds, then *they* effectively hold the market portfolio, whilst the individual can speculate on individual 'packages' of mutual funds. Also with this strategy, the finance house will usually have at least one fund it can boast has 'beaten the market'.

## 13.2  PUBLIC POLICY ISSUES

Let us turn now to some public policy issues. The stock market is supposed to provide the 'correct' signals for the allocation of real resources (i.e. fixed investment). Only a small proportion of corporate investment is financed from new issues (e.g. about 4% on a gross basis in the UK). Nevertheless, the rate of return of a quoted company on the stock market provides a measure of cost of equity finance. The latter can be used as the discount rate in the DPV formula for physical investment projects (for an all equity financed project). Other things equal, if profits from a firm's new investment project are expected to be high, the existing share price will be 'high' and the firm can obtain its required funds by issuing fewer shares. However, if the share price does not reflect *fundamentals* (e.g. expected future dividends) but is influenced by whims or fads of 'irrational' investors, then this link is broken. An abnormally low share price which reflects ill-informed extraneous factors (e.g. irrational market prejudice) will then inhibit a firm from embarking on what (on a rational calculation) is a viable investment project.

The above analysis also applies to takeovers. If the stock market is myopic, that is only considers profits and dividends that accrue in the *near* future, then managers fearful of a takeover may distribute more in current dividends rather than using the retained profits to undertake profitable real investment say on R&D expenditure. This strategy will boost the share price and this is generally known as **'short-termism'**. A possible response by government to such short-termism might be to forbid hostile takeovers (e.g. as in Japan). The impact of short-termism on share prices might also be exacerbated by an incentive system whereby part of a manager's remuneration is in the form of share options.

The opposite view to the above, namely that hostile takeovers are welfare enhancing (i.e. in terms of the output and profits of the firm) requires the assumption that markets are efficient and that takeovers enable 'bad' incumbent managers to be replaced. In this scenario, the hostile bidder recognises that the incumbent 'bad' management has led shareholders to mark down the firm's share price. The hostile bidder then pays a price in excess of the existing share price. After replacing the 'bad' managers and reorganising the firm, the ensuing higher future profits are just sufficient to compensate for the higher price the bidder paid for the shares.

In the 1960s and 1970s there was a wave of conglomerate formation, followed in the 1980s by leveraged buyouts and conglomerate breakups (i.e. 'asset stripping'). Conglomerate mergers were sometimes justified on the grounds that the acquisition of unrelated firms by 'firm A' reduced risk to the shareholder who held A's shares, since the 'conglomerate' constituted a diversified portfolio of 'firms'. However, as diversification is easily accomplished by individuals altering *their own* portfolio of stocks, then the above reason for the formation of conglomerates is invalid. (Of course it carries slightly more weight if, for some reason, risk averse individuals do not diversify their shareholdings.)

Note that if share prices do reflect fundamentals (i.e. future dividends) but **'news'** occurs frequently and is expected to make a substantial impact on a firm's future performance, then one would still expect to observe *highly volatile* share prices, even if the market is efficient. However, if on occasions such volatility had adverse implications for parts of the real economy (i.e. an 'externality')—for example that a stock market crash led to insolvencies in financial institutions, a 'credit crunch' and less physical investment—this would at least provide a prima facie argument for governments to try and limit share price movements (for example, by closing markets for a 'cooling off period'). Also, where **systemic risk** is involved (e.g. the failure of one financial institution could lead to a collapse of many others) one might be prepared to prohibit certain institutions from holding 'highly volatile' assets such as shares (e.g. S&Ls and until recently banks in the USA—the Glass–Steagall Act).

By definition, 'news' is random around zero. Hence 'news' will not influence the level of share prices over a long horizon. Therefore, except in exceptional circumstances 'news' would be unlikely to cause panics leading to a 'run' on banks or financial institutions by their depositors. However, if the market is inefficient and prices are subject to longer term 'irrational swings' then stock price volatility may be greater than that predicted from the efficient markets hypothesis. Here, there is a prima facie case to insist that financial institutions have enough resources (reserves) to weather such storms. This is one argument for general **capital adequacy rules** applied to financial institutions such as the Basle Accord (BIS, 1988) on credit risk and their later proposals on capital adequacy for market risk. If there are systemic risks (i.e. a form of externality) then, in principle, government action is required to ensure that the level of capital reflects the marginal social costs of the systematic risk, rather than the marginal private costs (for any individual financial institution).

What are the implications of market efficiency in stock and bond markets for issues in corporate finance? If the market is efficient then there is no point in delaying a physical investment project in the hope that 'financing conditions will improve' (i.e. that the share price will be higher): under the EMH the current price is the correct price and reflects expected future earnings from the project. Also, in an efficient market, the Modigliani–Miller theorem (in the absence of taxes and bankruptcy) suggests that the cost of capital is independent of the capital mix (i.e. debt-to-equity ratio). So you cannot increase the value of the firm by altering the mix of finance. The issue of capital mix can also be applied to the maturity (term) structure of debt. Since rates on long and short corporate bonds fully reflect available information, the proportion of long debt to short debt will also not alter the cost of capital to the firm.

It follows from the above arguments that the role of the Corporate Treasurer as an 'active manager', either as regards the choice over the appropriate 'mix' of finance or in analysing the optimum time to float new stock or bond issues, is futile under the EMH. Of course, if the market is not efficient, the Corporate Treasurer may attempt to 'beat the market' and he can also alter the stock market valuation of the firm by his chosen dividend policy or by share repurchase schemes, etc.

As one might imagine, the issue economists find hard to evaluate is what are the precise implications for public policy and the behaviour of firms if markets are *not fully* efficient at all times (i.e. a so-called 'second best' policy). If markets are efficient there is a presumption that government intervention is not required. If markets are inefficient there is a prima facie case for government intervention. However, given uncertainty about the impact of any government policies on the behaviour of economic agents, the government should only intervene if, on balance, it feels the expected return from its policies outweighs the risks attached to such policies. Any model of market *in*efficiency needs to ascertain how far from efficiency the market is on average and what implications this has for public policy decisions and economic welfare in general. This is a rather difficult task given present knowledge.

## 13.3 PREDICTABILITY OF STOCK RETURNS AND PRICES

The EMH consists of three interrelated elements:

---

### EFFICIENT MARKETS HYPOTHESIS

- **Rational expectations (RE)**—Investors use all available relevant information to forecast asset returns (or prices) and they do not make systematic forecast errors (i.e. their forecast *errors* are random, with a mean of zero).
- **Informational efficiency**—Equilibrium excess returns (i.e. returns adjusted for risk and transactions costs) are independent of currently available information.
- **Abnormal profits**—It is impossible to consistently make abnormal profits (i.e. profits adjusted for risk and transactions costs) using a 'stock picking' strategy.

---

To test the EMH we need some model of what determines *equilibrium expected* returns. The simplest assumption is that **equilibrium returns are constant** $= \mu$—and this is not an unreasonable hypothesis over short horizons. What would stock returns and prices look like if we use this model? Over a small interval of time $\Delta t = 0.01$ years (i.e. approximately 3.5 days):

[13.1]     Expected stock return $ER_t \equiv (S_t/S_{t-1}) - 1 = \mu \Delta t$

where $\mu$ is the mean (expected) annual growth rate (e.g. $15\% = 0.15$). What about the variability of stock returns? If $\sigma$ is the annual standard deviation of stock returns (e.g. $20\% = 0.20$) then in a small interval of time the standard deviation is $\sigma\sqrt{\Delta t}$. Assume each period the stock price is 'hit' by a random shock $\varepsilon_t$ which is normally distributed N(0, 1) with unit variance. It is now relatively easy to simulate a random path for the stock price (known as a **Brownian motion**) using:

[13.2]     $S_t = [1 + \mu \Delta t + \sigma \varepsilon_t \sqrt{\Delta t}]S_{t-1}$

In Table 13.1 we generate a random series for $S$ over 1 year (i.e. $\Delta t = 0.01$ years and the number of data intervals $= 100$) using $\sigma = 20\%$ p.a., $\mu = 15\%$ p.a., setting $S_0 = 100$ and

## TABLE 13.1: Random series for stock prices

**Calculation of a series for stock prices assuming constant expected returns**

***Step 1***: Set the parameters (e.g. starting value, expected return/drift parameter $\mu$, volatility for $S$, time step)

***Step 2***: Generate 100 observations of a normally distributed random variable, $\varepsilon \sim N(0, 1)$

***Step 3***: Calculate values for $S$, the level of stock prices, using the formula for Brownian motion (you can then also calculate the % return on the stock)

***Step 4***: Plot graph

| | |
|---|---|
| Stock price $S$ ($t = 0$) | **100** |
| Expected return $\mu$ | **0.15** |
| Volatility $\sigma$ | **0.25** |
| Time step $\Delta t$ | **0.01** |

Formula: $S(t + 1) = S(t)(1 + \mu \Delta t + \sigma \varepsilon \Delta t^{1/2})$

| Time | Asset | Random number $\varepsilon \sim N(0, 1)$ | Percent return |
|---|---|---|---|
| **0** | 100 | | |
| **0.01** | 101.3779 | 0.491165 | 1.377912 |
| **0.02** | 103.469 | 0.765074 | 2.062684 |
| **0.03** | 99.84991 | −1.45911 | −3.49777 |
| **0.04** | 96.15962 | −1.53834 | −3.69584 |
| **0.05** | 94.95969 | −0.55914 | −1.24785 |
| **0.06** | 91.80535 | −1.38871 | −3.32177 |
| **0.07** | 92.56665 | 0.271701 | 0.829253 |
| **0.08** | 94.93839 | 0.964881 | 2.562202 |
| **0.09** | 96.24902 | 0.4922 | 1.380501 |
| **0.1** | 94.6048 | −0.74332 | −1.70829 |
| ... | ... | ... | ... |
| **0.9** | 127.032 | 0.770931 | 2.077327 |
| **0.91** | 128.7983 | 0.496177 | 1.390443 |

*continued overleaf*

## TABLE 13.1: (*Continued*)

| Time | Asset | Random number $\varepsilon \sim N(0, 1)$ | Percent return |
|------|-------|------------------------------------------|----------------|
| **0.92** | 131.5721 | 0.80146 | 2.153651 |
| **0.93** | 125.0483 | −2.04336 | −4.9584 |
| **0.94** | 122.5072 | −0.87282 | −2.03204 |
| **0.95** | 120.4523 | −0.73097 | −1.67742 |
| **0.96** | 120.5356 | −0.03233 | 0.069186 |
| **0.97** | 126.5748 | 1.944118 | 5.010294 |
| **0.98** | 122.8392 | −1.24051 | −2.95126 |
| **0.99** | 122.1106 | −0.29727 | −0.59318 |
| **1** | 123.4938 | 0.393114 | 1.132786 |

drawing successive values for $\varepsilon_1$, $\varepsilon_2$, $\varepsilon_3$ … from an $\varepsilon \sim N(0, 1)$ distribution. This gives the series shown in Figure 13.1 which over the year does rise by around 15% but with substantial variation around this mean value within the year. Wc also include the generated returns series $R$ in Table 13.1, which is a random, normally distributed variable with mean $\mu$ and standard deviation $\sigma$.

## FIGURE 13.1: Stock price (Brownian motion)

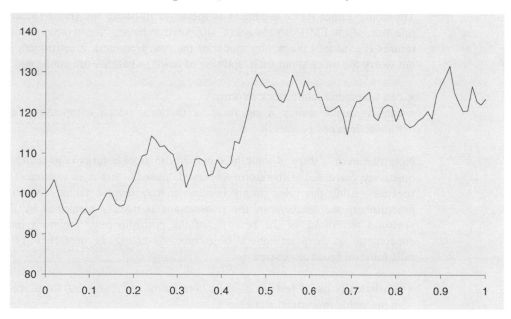

The above is about the simplest model of stock prices and it is a reasonable approximation for returns over say 1 day to 1 week which are found to be largely (but not quite) normal, identically and independently distributed, *niid*. But, as we see below, for longer horizons the above model is inadequate.

To elaborate slightly let us now assume the equilibrium expected return on a stock, between 'today' ($= t$) and 'tomorrow' ($= t+1$), denoted $E_t R_{t+1}$ depends on the risk free rate $r_t$ and a constant risk premium $rp = 8\%$ p.a. Our 'theory' is:

[13.3] $$E_t R_{t+1} = r_t + 8\%$$

We can think of $E_t R_{t+1}$ as the monthly return on the stock. Since investors are rational, the expected return $E_t R_{t+1}$ and the actual return $R_{t+1}$ will differ only by a random error (which has a mean of zero). Hence *on average* expected return and actual return will move together. Note that since $r_t$ is known today (at time $t$) then the expected and actual return $R_{t+1}$ are in part predictable *even under the EMH*. It is easy to see why. If the interest rate $r_t$ is high (low) for a number of months then we expect to observe the stock return $R_{t+1}$ also to be high (on average) in subsequent months. Hence, the EMH does not necessarily imply that actual stock returns are not predictable. From past data, what it does imply (in our example) is that the stock return in *excess* of the risk free rate and adjusted for the risk premium is not predictable (from other past information), that is:

> **Under the EMH:**
> **The expected stock return *less* the risk free rate and the risk premium is independent of any current (or past) information**

The above rather subtle argument is meant to illustrate the (rather academic) point that rejection of the EMH can always be attributed to having the 'wrong' model of equilibrium returns (i.e. usually the wrong model of the risk premium). Practitioners in the market do not worry too much about such 'splitting of hairs', what they are concerned about is:

- can we predict future stock returns;
- can we make money using these predictions, which compensate for the risks and transactions costs involved.

Note that even if there is some predictability in stock returns (e.g. returns 'tomorrow' are positively correlated with returns observed 'today'), this does not mean that you should speculate using this rule, simply because it may involve taking on too much risk. For practitioners the riskiness of the transactions is usually measured by the variability in portfolio returns $\sigma_p$ or the beta $\beta_p$ of the portfolio (e.g. Treynor's index). Below, we concentrate on the practitioners' objectives. Assessing the predictability of stock returns falls into two broad categories:

- **Statistically based tests** (e.g. using correlation and regression to forecast returns, to use in profitable investment strategies).

- Trading strategies based on 'rules of thumb' (e.g. buy low price–earnings ratio stocks) which are often referred to as **stock market anomalies**.

Clearly the distinction between these two approaches is not absolutely clear-cut since an 'anomaly' usually involves some form of statistical analysis. In this chapter we deal with statistically based tests, leaving anomalies to the next chapter. There are a wide variety of alternative statistical tests of asset return predictability including correlation, regression and various types of variance ratio statistics. The most frequently used approach is to regress stock returns (or returns in excess of the risk free rate) on a set of variables known today, which we designate as $\Omega_t$:

[13.4] $\qquad R_{t+1} = \alpha + \beta'\Omega_t + \varepsilon_t$

where $R_{t+1}$ is the stock return between time $t$ and $t+1$, $\varepsilon_t$ is a random error. These regression tests vary, depending on the information assumed which is usually of the following type:

- data on past returns $R_{t-j}$ ($j = 0, 1, 2, \ldots, m$);
- data on variables such as the dividend–price ratio, the earnings–price ratio, book-to-market value and 'size';
- data on past forecast errors, $\varepsilon_{t-j}$ (= actual return at $t - j$ minus the predicted return for $t - j$).

Using past returns as independent variables in equation [13.4] is similar to examining the correlation coefficient between current returns and lagged returns. (The latter are the autocorrelation and partial autocorrelation coefficients and are summarised in the correlogram.) The above tests can be done for alternative holding periods of a day, a week, a month or even over many years. We may find predictability and possible violations of the EMH at some horizons but not at others.

## LONG HORIZON RETURNS

Are stock returns **mean reverting**, that is higher than average returns are followed by lower returns in the future? Fama and French (1992) and Poterba and Summers (1988) find evidence of mean reversion in stock returns over long horizons (i.e. in excess of 18 months). For example, Fama and French estimate an autoregression where the return over the interval $t - N$ to $t$, call this $R_{t-N|t}$, determines future returns $R_{t|t+N}$:

[13.5] $\qquad R_{t|t+N} = \alpha + \beta R_{t-N|t} + \varepsilon_t$

Fama and French consider return horizons $N$ from 1 to 10 years. They found little or no autocorrelation, except for holding periods of between $N = 2$ and $N = 7$ years, for which $\beta$ is less than zero (i.e. mean reversion). There was a peak at $N = 5$ years when $\beta = -0.5$, indicating that a 10% negative return over 5 years is, on average, followed by a 5% positive return over the next 5 years. The $R$-squared in the regressions for the 3–5 year horizons are about 35%. Such mean reversion ($\beta < 0$) is consistent with that from the 'anomalies literature' on contrarian investment strategies—see the next chapter. Note however that the Fama–French results appear to be mainly due to the inclusion of the 1930s sample period (Fama and French, 1992, p. 4).

Poterba and Summers (1988) investigate mean reversion by looking at the variance of returns over different horizons. If (continuously compounded) stock returns are random then it can be shown that the standard deviation of returns over $T$ periods is given by the '$\sqrt{T}$-rule':

[13.6] $$\sigma_T = \sqrt{T}\sigma \quad \text{and} \quad \sigma_T^2 = T\sigma^2$$

where $\sigma_T$ is the standard deviation over $T$ periods
   $\sigma$ is the standard deviation over one period.

For example, if $\sigma = 20\%$ is the standard deviation over 1 year, then if stock returns are random, the standard deviation over 4 years should be $\sigma_T = 40\%$ ($= \sqrt{4} \times 20\%$). Poterba and Summers (1988) find that the variance of returns increases at a rate which is less than in proportion to $T$, and hence returns are mean reverting for horizons of $T$ between 3 and 8 years. This conclusion is generally upheld when using a number of alternative stock price indexes.

## MULTIVARIATE TESTS

The Fama–French and Poterba–Summers results are univariate tests. However, a number of variables other than past returns have also been found to help predict current returns. For example, Keim and Stambaugh (1986) using monthly excess returns on US common stocks (over the T-bill rate) for the period from about 1930 to 1978 find that for a number of portfolios (based on size) the following (somewhat arbitrary) variables are usually statistically significant:

- the difference in the yield between low grade corporate bonds and the yield on 1-month T-bills (i.e. a risk premium);
- the deviation of last period's (real) S&P index from its average over the past 5 years;
- the level of the stock price index based only on 'small stocks'.

However, it should be noted that for monthly return data on stocks, the regressions only explain about 0.6–2.0% of the actual excess return. Fama and French (1992) extend their earlier univariate study on the predictability of expected returns over different horizons and examine the relationship between (nominal and real) returns and the dividend yield, $D/P$:

[13.7] $$R_{t|t+N} = \alpha + \beta(D/P)_t + \varepsilon_t$$

The equation is run for monthly and quarterly returns and for annual returns of 1 to 4 years on the NYSE index. They also test the robustness of the equation by running it over various subperiods. For monthly and quarterly data the dividend yield is often statistically significant (and $\beta > 0$), but only explains about 5% of the variability in actual returns. For longer horizons the explanatory power increases. For example, for nominal returns over the 1941–86 period the explanatory power for 1, 2, 3 and 4-year return horizons is 12, 17, 29 and 49%. The longer return horizon regressions are also useful in forecasting 'out-of-sample'.

When looking at regression equations that attempt to explain returns, an econometrician would be interested in general diagnostic tests (e.g. are the residuals normally distributed, serially uncorrelated and homoscedastic?), as well as the outside sample forecasting performance of the equations and the temporal stability of the parameters. In many of the above studies this useful statistical information is not always fully presented, so it becomes difficult to ascertain whether the results are as 'robust' as they seem. However, Pesaran and Timmermann (1994) provide a study of stock returns which attempts to meet the above criticisms of earlier work.

Pesaran and Timmermann looked at excess returns on the S&P500 index and the Dow Jones Index measured over 1 year, 1 quarter and 1 month for the period 1954–71 and subperiods. For annual excess returns a small set of independent variables including the dividend yield, annual inflation, the change in the 3-month interest rate and the term premium, explain about 60% of the variability in the excess return. For quarterly and monthly data broadly similar variables explain about 18% and 10% of excess returns, respectively. Interestingly, for monthly and quarterly regressions they find a non-linear effect of previous excess returns on current returns. For example, squared previous excess returns are often statistically significant while past positive returns have a different impact than past negative returns on future returns. (The authors also provide diagnostic tests for serial correlation, heteroscedasticity, normality and 'correct' functional form, and these test statistics indicate no misspecification in the equations.)

To test the predictive power of these equations they use recursive estimation (OLS) and predict the *sign* of 'next period' excess return (i.e. at $t + 1$) based on estimated coefficients which only use data up to period $t$. For annual returns, 70–80% of the predicted returns have the correct sign, while for quarterly excess returns the regressions still yield a (healthy) 65% correct prediction of the sign of returns. Thus Pesaran and Timmermann (1994) reinforce the earlier results that excess returns are predictable and can be explained quite well by a relatively small number of independent variables.

## PROFITABLE TRADING STRATEGIES

The key question, however, is whether 'predictability' can be used to make profits adjusted for risk and transactions costs. Transactions costs in stock and bond trades arise from the bid–ask spread (i.e. dealers buy stock at a low price and sell to the investor at a high price) and the commission charged on a particular 'buy' or 'sell' order given to the broker. Pesaran and Timmermann use 'closing prices' which may be either 'bid' or 'ask' prices. They therefore assume that all trading costs are adequately represented by a fixed transactions cost per dollar of sales. They assume costs are higher for stocks $c_s$ than for bonds $c_b$. They consider a simple trading rule, namely:

> **SWITCHING STRATEGY**
> **If the predicted excess return (from the recursive regression) is positive then hold the market portfolio of stocks**
> **otherwise**
> **hold government bonds with a maturity equal to the length of the trading horizon (i.e. annual, quarterly, monthly)**

The above 'switching strategy' has no problems of potential bankruptcy since assets are not sold short and there is no gearing (borrowing). The alternative benchmark strategy is a 'passive one', namely holding the market portfolio at all times. They assess the profitability of the switching strategy over the passive strategy for transactions costs that are 'low', 'medium' or 'high'. (The values of $c_s$ are 0, 0.5 and 1.0% for stocks and for bonds $c_b$ equals 0 and 0.1%.)

In general terms they find that the returns from the switching strategy are higher than those for the passive strategy for annual returns (i.e. switching once per year in January), even when transactions costs are 'high' (see Table 13.2). However, it pays to trade at quarterly or monthly intervals only if transactions costs are less than 0.5% for stocks. In addition they find that the standard deviation of returns for the switching portfolio using annual returns (see Table 13.2) and quarterly (but not monthly) returns is below that for the passive portfolio (even under a high transactions cost scenario). Hence, the switching portfolio dominates the passive portfolio on the mean–variance criterion (over the whole data period 1960–90).

The above results are found to be robust with respect to different sets of regressors in the excess return equations and over subperiods 1960–70, 1970–80, 1980–90. In Table 13.2 are reported the Sharpe, Treynor and Jensen indices of mean–variance efficiency for the switching and passive portfolios for the 1-year horizon. For any portfolio 'p' these are given by:

[13.8a] $\qquad S = (ER_p - r)/\sigma_p$ $\qquad$ **(Sharpe ratio)**

[13.8b] $\qquad T = (ER_p - r)/\beta_p$ $\qquad$ **(Treynor ratio)**

[13.8c] $\qquad (R_p - r)_t = J + S(R_m - r)_t$ $\qquad$ **(Jensen index)**

One can calculate Sharpe and Treynor ratios for the switching and market portfolios. The Jensen index is the intercept $J$ in the above regression. In general, except for the monthly trading strategy under the 'high transactions cost' scenario, they find that the performance indices imply that the switching portfolio has the higher risk adjusted return.

## VOLATILITY TESTS

Do movements in stock prices $P_t$ reflect changes in the fair value $V_t$ of a stock? If so then the market is efficient. In an efficient market we would still expect stock prices to be quite volatile since any 'news' (e.g. 'interest rates unexpectedly reduced by the Central Bank', or

## TABLE 13.2: Performance measures of the S&P500 switching portfolio relative to the market portfolio annual returns, 1960–90

| | Portfolios | | | | | |
| --- | --- | --- | --- | --- | --- | --- |
| | (1) Passive strategy | | | (2) Switching strategy | | |
| Transaction cost (%) | Low | Med. | High | Low | Med. | High |
| Stocks | 0.000 | 0.500 | 1.000 | 0.000 | 0.500 | 1.000 |
| T-bills | – | – | – | 0.000 | 0.100 | 0.100 |
| Arithmetic mean return (%) | 10.780 | 10.720 | 10.670 | 12.700 | 13.430 | 12.210 |
| Standard deviation of return (%) | 13.090 | 13.090 | 13.090 | 7.240 | 7.200 | 7.160 |
| Sharpe's index | 0.310 | 0.300 | 0.300 | 0.820 | 0.790 | 0.760 |
| Treynor's index | 0.040 | 0.040 | 0.039 | 0.089 | 0.085 | 0.081 |
| Jensen's index | – | – | – | 0.045 | 0.043 | 0.041 |
| | – | – | – | (4.63) | (4.42) | (4.25) |
| Wealth at end of period (starting from $100 in January 1960) | 1913.000 | 1884.0 | 1855.0 | 3833.0 | 3559.0 | 3346.0 |

Notes: The switching portfolio is based on recursive regressions of excess returns on the change in the 3-month interest rate, the term premium, the inflation rate and the dividend yield. The switching rule assumes that portfolio selection takes place once per year on the last trading day of January. The 'passive strategy' involves a 'buy and hold' strategy where the investor purchases the market index (i.e. the S&P500 index). The results are presented for three different levels of transactions costs, namely 'low', 'medium' and 'high'
Source: Pesaran and Timmermann (1994). © John Wiley & Sons, Limited. Reproduced with permission

'profit growth figures revised upwards') that is expected to alter current or future dividends or the discount rate can lead to a substantial revision of the fair value and hence of the market price. On the other hand, stock prices might be heavily influenced by irrational 'fads and fashion' so that stock prices are *excessively* volatile and there may be long periods when stock prices are below (or above) their fair value. When stock prices are below their fair value this can cause problems for the managers of the firm since their strategy for the firm (which may be perfectly rational and sensible) begins to be criticised by (institutional) shareholders. Their time is then spent in PR exercises in the City (or Wall Street) to soothe the fears of shareholders. This is also connected with the problem of 'short-termism' since the share price might be artificially low because the market does not correctly evaluate the long-term earning power of the firm. These types of issue have certainly affected some entrepreneurs who floated their companies on the stock market only to want (and sometimes succeed) to buy them back at a later date, in part because they felt an 'irrational' market continually undervalued their shares (see Box 13.1).

---

**Box 13.1    FLOAT AND SINK?**

Several well-known firms have floated on the stock market only to become disillusioned by the behaviour of stockholders, who they believe undervalue the company's shares. These firms initially floated to gain access to finance for expansion. Richard Branson floated his *Virgin* group in 1986 and bought it back in 1988. Andrew Lloyd-Webber, the theatrical (musical) entrepreneur who wrote the music for shows such as *Cats* and *Phantom of the Opera*, floated his company, known as *The Really Useful Theatre Group*, in 1986, and bought it back in 1990. In fact, both Branson and Lloyd-Webber did rather well in the buyback. Branson bought back in 1988 at the same share price as at floatation and then sold off the music division (to EMI for £510m) for more than the buyback cost for the *whole* group. Lloyd-Webber floated for £36m, bought back in 1990 for £77.5m but then sold 30% of the group to Polygram (the record company) for around £78m a year later.

Another 'high-profile' company that became disillusioned with the City is Anita and Gordon Roddicks' *Body Shop*, the 'green' cosmetics group floated for £4.6m in 1984. The Roddicks have criticised the 'pinstripe dinosaurs' and 'short-termist' attitudes in the City. In 1992, the share price fell 40% in a day after a profit warning. The Roddicks have complained that institutional investors do not understand the culture and long-term goals of the firm. This involves expanding into foreign markets (e.g. USA, Asia) where large profits will only accrue after substantial investment in marketing and retail outlets.

The Roddicks, in 1995, tried to convert their 'plc' into a charitable trust so they could rid themselves of the 'short-termism' of the City institutional investors. This would have involved buying out the institutional shareholders and an original founder, Mr Ian McGlinn, who owned 28% of the shares (the Roddicks own 24% of the shares).

In November 1995 Body Shop shares traded at around 156p and the City view was that a buyback would require an offer of around 175p per share, valuing the company at £330m. However, the buyback would have required substantial mezzanine finance (i.e. mainly bank loans), with the concomitant risk of high gearing and interference from creditors, had interest payments not been met. For these reasons, in March 1996 the Roddicks abandoned their buyback plans.

The above shows that some entrepreneurs, perhaps in somewhat unconventional industries and with 'unconventional' management styles, do believe that shareholders persistently underprice their shares and are 'short-termist'. Clearly, if you 'go public', you incur an obligation that a private company does not, namely to effectively communicate your business strategy to the shareholders and to maximise shareholder value. These entrepreneurs became disillusioned because, despite their efforts at communication, they believed the City undervalued their companies.

> The question is whether this anecdotal evidence holds true for a large number of companies. Is it the case that some shares are persistently undervalued while others may also be overvalued? (The latter, presumably, do not complain.) Put another way, is the stock market excessively volatile? For this we require the more formal tests as set out in this and subsequent chapters.

The 'evidence' in Box 13.1 is interesting but it is anecdotal rather than scientific. Now 'scientific tests' in the finance area do not always yield unambiguous conclusions. However, there are a set of techniques which have been used to formally assess whether stock prices are excessively volatile and persistently deviate from their fair value. How can we test the proposition that stock prices alter from day to day or week to week by large amounts, which does not reflect changes in fundamentals (i.e. expected future dividends)? If the EMH holds then $P_t = V_t$ at all times. The difficulty in testing this proposition is obtaining a time series of fair values $V_t$ since this depends on *expected* future dividends which are not directly observable. The 'trick' in these tests has been either to forecast future dividends in some way or to assume that 'on average' *actual* dividends are a good representation of expected dividends (i.e. the rational expectations hypothesis again).

Barsky and DeLong (1993) provide an informal test that $P_t$ moves with $V_t$ by using the Gordon growth model and a forecast of the growth rate of dividends $g_t$ which varies over time. The Gordon (1962) growth model is $V_t = D_t/(R - g_t)$ where $R$ is the average (real) rate of return and $g_t$ is the expected growth rate of (real) dividends (based on information up to time $t$). Barsky and DeLong assume investors continually update their estimate of the future growth in dividends. They then compare $V_t$ with the actual S&P index $P_t$ in the US over the period 1880–1988. Even for the simple case of a constant value of $(R - g)^{-1} = 20$ and hence $V_t = 20D_t$, the broad movements of dividends (which directly determine $V_t$) over a long horizon of 10 years explain 67% of the variability in $P_t$ (Barsky and DeLong, 1993, table III, p. 302) with the pre-World War II movements in the two data series being even closer. They then propose that agents estimate $g_t$ at any point in time as a long distributed lag of past dividend growth rates. When $g_t$ is updated in this manner then the volatility of 1-year changes in $V_t$ is as high as 76% of the volatility in $P_t$ (Barsky and DeLong, 1993, table III, p. 302). However, it should be noted that although long swings in $P_t$ are in part explained by this model, changes over shorter horizons such as 1 year or even 5 years are not well explained. The above evidence is broadly consistent with the view that real dividends and real prices move together in the long run, but price and fair value can diverge quite substantially for a number of years.

Shiller (1989) pioneered the use of **volatility tests** to measure the degree of association between $P_t$ and $V_t$ and whether prices are excessively volatile. Fair value is determined by the DPV of expected future dividends and in an efficient market $P_t$ should equal $V_t$:

[13.9]
$$P_t = V_t = \sum_{i=1}^{n-1} \delta^i E_t D_{t+i} + \delta^n E_t P_{t+n}$$

where $P_{t+n}$ is the expected 'terminal price' at time $t + n$. To simplify matters assume all investors form the same expectation of future dividends and that the discount factor $\delta$ $(0 < \delta < 1)$ is a constant in all future periods. Note that $\delta = 1/(1 + r)$ where $r$ is the average safe rate of return. For example, if $r = 10\%$, $\delta = 0.909$.

To set the ball rolling, it is instructive to note that if, for each time period $t$, we had data on *expected* future dividends, the expected terminal price and the constant $\delta$, then we could work out the right-hand side of equation [13.9] and compare it with the actual stock price $P_t$. Of course, at time $t$, we do not know what investors' forecasts of expected future dividends would have been. However, Shiller (1981) proposed a simple yet very ingenious way of getting around this problem. We have data on actual dividends in the past, say from 1900 onwards, and we have the actual price $P_{t+n}$ today, say in 1996. We assume $\delta$ is a known value, say 0.909 for annual data. Then, using the DPV formula we can calculate what the stock price in 1900 would have been, if investors had forecast dividends exactly, in all years from 1900 onwards. We call this the **perfect foresight stock price**, $P_t^*$ in 1900. By moving 1 year forward and repeating the above, we can obtain a data series for $P_t^*$ for all years from 1900 onwards. As described above, the data series $P_t^*$ has been computed using the following formula:

[13.10]
$$P_t^* = \sum_{i=1}^{n-1} \delta^i D_{t+i} + \delta^n P_{t+n}$$

When calculating $P_t^*$ for 1900 the influence of the terminal price $P_{t+n}$ is fairly minimal since $n$ is large and $\delta^n$ is relatively small. As we approach the end-point of 1996, the term $\delta^n P_{t+n}$ carries more weight in our calculation of $P^*$. One option is therefore to truncate our sample say 10 years prior to the present in order to apply the DPV formula. Alternatively, we can assume that the *actual* price at the *terminal date* is 'close to' its expected value $E_t P_{t+n}^*$ and the latter is usually done in empirical work.

Comparing $P_t$ and $P_t^*$ in equations [13.9] and [13.10] we see that they differ by the sum of the forecast errors of dividends $\omega_{t+i}$ (weighted by the discount factors $\delta^i$) where $\omega_{t+i}$ is the forecast error ($= D_{t+i} - E_t D_{t+i}$). If investors do not make *systematic* forecast errors then we expect these errors in a long sample of data to be positive, about as many times as they are negative (and on average for them to be close to zero). This is the rational expectations assumption. Hence we might expect the (weighted) sum of $\omega_{t+i}$ to be relatively small and the broad movements in $P_t^*$ should be much like those for actual prices, $P_t$. However, the volatility of $P_t^*$ will exceed the volatility of the *actual* price $P_t$ because the former 'contains' (the squared) errors $\omega_{t+i}^2$ when forecasting dividends (whereas $P_t$ does not—see equation [13.9]).

Shiller (1981) provides a graph of (detrended) $P_t$ and $P_t^*$ (in real terms) for the period 1871–1979 and the correlation between $P_t$ and $P_t^*$ is found to be low, implying a rejection of the view that stock prices are wholly determined by the DPV of future dividends, in an efficient market. However, we can do better than just 'eyeball' the two series, and Shiller examines the relationship between the variances of $P_t$ and $P_t^*$. It can be shown (see Cuthbertson, 1996) that if $P_t = V_t$ then the *volatility (variance)* of the perfect foresight price should *exceed* the volatility of the actual price series:

**[13.11]**   $\mathrm{Var}(P_t^*) > \mathrm{Var}(P_t)$

However, the *opposite* of equation [13.11] is found to apply using actual data, and hence the EMH applied to stock prices is rejected. Not all investors appear to make rational forecasts of future dividends, and there are long periods when $P_t$ does not equal $V_t$. However, the reader should note that there are many nuances and statistical problems surrounding these variance bounds tests. Subsequent work in the 1980s pointed out deficiencies in Shiller's original approach (e.g. Kleidon, 1986; Flavin, 1983), but Shiller's (1989) later work rather successfully answered his critics. However, very recent work (e.g. Mankiw *et al.*, 1991; Gilles and LeRoy, 1991) has certainly demonstrated that violations of the EMH are statistically not absolutely clear-cut, and considerable judgement is required in reaching a balanced view on this matter.

Many of the above tests have also been applied to bond markets where the underlying theoretical models are usually taken as the expectations hypothesis of the term structure. In general, these tests favour the EMH, in contrast to those based on stocks (see Cuthbertson, 1996).


## PESO PROBLEMS

It should now be obvious that there are some complex statistical issues involved in assessing the EMH. One of these is known as the 'Peso problem', which arises in the following way. Suppose we have a sample of data during which investors attach a small probability to the possibility of a very 'high' level in dividends in the future. Investors' *expectations* of dividends at the beginning of the sample (i.e. at time $t$, say) $E_t D_{t+j}$ is a weighted average of the 'high' dividends and the 'normal' level of dividends. Hence, the dividend discount model will imply a relatively 'high' fair value for stock prices and, if agents are rational, actual stock prices $P_t$ will therefore also be high. However, suppose that during this period these 'high' *forecasts* for dividends do not occur and *actual* dividends remain at their 'normal' level. Investors have therefore made a systematic forecast error within this sample period.

If we assume rational expectations, our *ex-post* measure of fair value $V_{\text{ex-p}}$ using the dividend discount model will (erroneously) use *actual* dividends as an unbiased measure of expected dividends. Therefore we will find that $V_t < P_t$ for this particular sample of data and it looks as if the market is not efficient. But in fact the EMH holds, it is just that we have mismeasured dividend expectations.

If the sample period is extended then we would also observe other periods ('regimes') when investors *forecast* lower dividends, but these never occur, so that here $D_{t+j} > E_t D_{t+j}$ and hence over the extended 'full' sample, forecast errors average zero. The Peso problem arises because we only 'observe' the first sample of data.

The Peso problem arises because of one-off 'special events', which could take place within the sample period, but in actual fact do not. It considerably complicates tests of hypotheses based on rational expectations such as the EMH, that assume out-turn data differ from expectations by a (zero mean) random error. So, the Peso problem can affect tests of any asset pricing model which depends on expectations of future events (e.g. stocks, bonds, FX).

Clearly, the more the economy is subject to **regime changes** (e.g. periods of high growth followed by low growth, etc.) the more pervasive the Peso problem will be.

## 13.4 SUMMARY

We have considered the basic ideas that underlie the EMH, tests of the predictability of stock returns, excess volatility and whether active trading strategies earn profits (after correcting for risk and transactions costs). Our main conclusions are the following.

- The outcome of **tests of the EMH are important in assessing public policy** issues such as the desirability of mergers and takeovers, short-termism and regulation of financial institutions.
- **The EMH assumes investors process information efficiently so that persistent abnormal profits cannot be made by trading in financial assets**. The equilibrium return on stocks comprises a 'payment' to compensate for (systematic) risk, and information available in the market cannot be used to increase this risk adjusted return.
- Tests indicate that **stock returns and excess returns are predictable**. There is also considerable evidence that actual trading strategies based on the predictions from regression equations can result in profits, net of dealing costs.
- **The key question** for the validity or otherwise of the EMH and the degree of 'success' from a market analyst's point of view is whether these **profits fully compensate for the risk exposure undertaken**. There is certainly evidence that this might well be the case, although it can always be argued that methods used to correct for the risk of the portfolio (e.g. use of sample variance of returns) are inadequate.
- There appears to be *excess* volatility in stock markets.
- Where the balance of the **evidence for the EMH** lies is very difficult to ascertain given the plethora of somewhat conflicting results and the acute problems of statistical inference involved. To the authors it appears that on balance the evidence is against the EMH, in equity markets. To use Shiller's colourful phrase, the equity market is probably subject to bouts of **'irrational over-exuberance'**.

## END OF CHAPTER EXERCISES

Q1   What is Brownian motion?

Q2   Does the EMH imply that you should never change the proportions in which you hold stocks in your portfolio?

Q3   If the EMH were true would there ever be any takeovers?

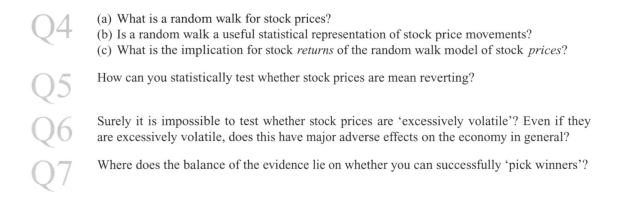

**Q4** (a) What is a random walk for stock prices?
(b) Is a random walk a useful statistical representation of stock price movements?
(c) What is the implication for stock *returns* of the random walk model of stock *prices*?

**Q5** How can you statistically test whether stock prices are mean reverting?

**Q6** Surely it is impossible to test whether stock prices are 'excessively volatile'? Even if they are excessively volatile, does this have major adverse effects on the economy in general?

**Q7** Where does the balance of the evidence lie on whether you can successfully 'pick winners'?

# Anomalies, Noise Traders and Chaos

In an 'efficient market' all investors have access to the same information, they process the information in the same 'rational way', and all have equal opportunities for borrowing and lending. In the real world these conditions are unlikely to be met. For example, different investors may form different probability assessments about future outcomes or use different economic models in determining expected returns. They may also face differences in transactions costs (e.g. mutual funds versus individuals when purchasing shares), or face different tax rates, and of course they will each devote a different amount of resources (i.e. time and money) to collecting and processing information. Of course, if these heterogeneous elements play a rather minor role then asset prices and rates of return will be determined solely by economic fundamentals and rational behaviour. But if not, prices may deviate substantially and persistently from their fair values. As we see below it is often the assumption of *heterogeneity* in behaviour which allows us to analyse why markets may not be efficient.

In this chapter we examine the EMH from a slightly different angle from the technical statistical research outlined in the previous chapter and concentrate on stock market anomalies, models of noise traders and chaos models.

# 14.1 STOCK MARKET ANOMALIES

## WEEKEND AND JANUARY EFFECTS

> **The weekend effect refers to the fact that there appears to be a systematic fall in the price of (some) stocks between Friday closing and Monday opening**

One explanation of the weekend effect is that firms and governments release 'good news' between Monday and Friday but wait until the weekend to release bad news. The bad news is then reflected in 'low' stock prices on Monday. However, in an efficient market this implies some agents should recognise this and should (short) sell on Friday (price is 'high') and buy on Monday (price is 'low') assuming that is, that the expected profit more than covers transactions costs and a payment for risk. This should then lead to a 'removal' of the anomaly since these rational traders will tend to depress prices on Fridays and raise prices on Mondays.

The so-called January effect is a similar phenomenon to the weekend effect. The daily rate of return on common stocks appears to be unusually high during the early days of the month of January. For the USA, one explanation is due to year-end selling of stock in order to generate some capital losses which can be set against capital gains in order to reduce tax liability. (This is known as 'bed and breakfasting' in the UK.) In January, investors wish to return to their equilibrium portfolios and therefore move into the market to purchase stock. Again if the EMH holds, this pattern of price changes should lead to purchases by non-tax payers (e.g. pension funds) in December when the price is low and selling in January when the price is high, thus eliminating the profitable arbitrage opportunity. The January effect seems to take place in the first five trading days of January (Keen, 1983) and also appears to be concentrated in the stocks of small firms (Reinganum, 1983).

## SMALL FIRM EFFECT

Between 1960 and the middle of the 1980s all small-capitalised companies earned on average a higher rate of return than the overall stock market index. This is the 'small cap' effect. Of course, according to the CAPM this could be due to the higher risks attached to these small firms which should be reflected in their higher beta values. However, Reinganum (1983) suggests that the rate of return, even after adjustment for risk, is higher on stocks of small-capitalised firms. Hence Reinganum has found that stocks of small firms *do not* lie on the security market line. In the last 15 years, this anomaly 'disappeared', after being prevalent for many decades. So the market may *ultimately* be efficient but clearly it can be 'inefficient' for very long periods before enough arbitrageurs learn about the anomaly.

## CLOSED-END FUNDS

Closed-end funds issue a fixed number of shares at the outset and trading in those shares then takes place between investors. Shares which comprise the 'basket' in the closed-end fund are generally also traded openly on the stock market. The value of the fund ought therefore to equal the *market value* of the individual shares in the fund. But it is often the case that closed-end funds trade at a discount on their market value (and very occasionally at a premium), and the discounts on different funds tend to move together over time. This violates the EMH, for investors could buy the closed-end fund's shares at the discount price and at the same time sell short a portfolio of stocks identical to that held by the fund. The investor thereby ensures she earns a riskless profit equal to the discount. Also, if movements in the discount are predictable over time, then investors could also make money. They would buy the funds when the discount is expected to fall (i.e. fund value rise) and finance this strategy by shorting the shares which comprise the fund.

Several reasons have been offered for such closed-end fund discounts. First, closed-end fund members face a tax liability (in the form of capital gains tax) if the fund should sell securities after they have appreciated. This potential tax liability justifies paying a lower price than the market value of the underlying securities. Second, some of the assets in the closed-end fund are less marketable (i.e. have 'thin' markets). Third, agency costs in the form of management fees might also explain the discounts. However Malkiel (1977) found that the discounts were substantially in excess of what could be explained by the above reasons, while Lee *et al.* (1990) find that the discounts on closed-end funds are primarily determined by the behaviour of stocks of small firms.

There is a further anomaly. This occurs because at the initial public offering of the closed-end fund shares, they incur underwriting costs and the shares in the fund are therefore priced at a premium over their true market value. The value of the closed-end fund then generally moves to a discount within 6 months. The anomaly is then why any investors purchase the initial public offering and thereby pay the underwriting costs via the future capital loss. Why don't investors just wait 6 months before purchasing the mutual fund at the lower price?

Some noise trader models that are discussed below incorporate herding behaviour by investors, and clearly this would explain why the discounts on closed-end funds move together over time.

## VALUE LINE ENIGMA

The Value Line Investment Survey (VLIS) produces reports on public traded firms and ranks these stocks in terms of their 'timeliness', by which it means the desirability of purchasing them. 'Rank-3' stocks are designated as those that are expected to increase in line with the market, while 'rank-1' stocks are a *'good buy'* and 'rank-5' stocks a *'bad buy'*, in terms of their expected future returns. It is found that 'rank-1' stocks earn a higher return than 'rank-3' stocks. This could be due to the fact that 'rank-1' stocks have higher risk (reflected in higher betas) than do 'rank-3' stocks. Also, in order for a trading strategy to be profitable we must take account of transactions costs. Holloway (1981) found that even after adjustments for risk and transactions costs, a strategy of purchasing 'rank-1' stocks at the beginning of the year and selling them at the end of the year outperformed that of buying the 'average' 'rank-3' stocks. The Value Line Ranking System therefore does provide profitable information for a successful speculative strategy, and this is inconsistent with the EMH.

## LOW PRICE–EARNINGS RATIOS

There is a longstanding view held by some 'stock pickers' that:

> **Stocks with low $P-E$ ratios give positive abnormal returns, although under the EMH this should not be possible**

This result is equivalent to that reported above for regressions where high 'earnings (or dividend) to price ratio stocks' are positively correlated with higher future stock returns. Abnormal returns are usually measured as:

- a return in excess of the market return $\quad AR_1 = R_i - R_m$
- a return in excess of that given by the CAPM $\quad AR_2 = R_i - [\alpha_i + \beta_i(R_m - r)]$

Empirical results are fairly invariant to either measure of abnormal return. The problem in assessing the validity of the low $P-E$ view of stock returns is to separate out the performance of low $P-E$ shares from other attributes such as small stocks (i.e. size effect), high book-to-market value stocks, etc. For example low $P-E$ stocks might on average also be 'small' stocks and it would be useful to separate out the true source of the abnormal profit.

Consider trying to separate the effects of low $P-E$ ratios from size effects. To get around the dual causality problem we first choose a random sample comprising small, medium and large firms. We then undertake the following stages (with say a sample of 1000 shares):

1. Form five quintiles from the largest 'size' stocks (i.e. market value) to the smallest.
2. Take the smallest 'size' quintile and 'arrange' these stocks in order of $P-E$ ratios. Split these into five quintiles based on $P-E$ ratios.
3. Repeat steps 1 and 2 for all the remaining size quintiles.
4. Now we regroup the data. That is:
   From every size quintile take the lowest $P-E$ ratio stocks and form a single composite 'low $P-E$ ratio group'. This composite group is random with respect to size.
5. Repeat step 4 with the second lowest $P-E$ ratio group and so on.
6. We end up with five quintiles based on high to low $P-E$ ratios, but randomised with respect to size.

One can also obtain five quintiles ordered according to size but with random $P-E$ ratios. Indeed we can use the randomisation procedure for any two attributes (e.g. size and book-to-market value) and 'order' stocks with respect to one attribute while randomising on another. Clearly a weakness of the method is that we can only choose bivariate combinations of attributes (multiple regression can overcome this problem, see below).

Having ordered the stocks by say $P-E$ ratios at the beginning of the year we can then calculate the abnormal monthly returns over the next 12 months. We can then 'reorder' the stocks at the end of the year and repeat the returns analysis, ending up with a monthly abnormal return averaged over several years. Levis (1993) for the UK and Jaffe *et al.* (1989) for the US find evidence in favour of an independent effect from low $P-E$ ratio stocks. Jaffe *et al.* use a regression to work out the impact on returns of $P-E$ ratios and 'size'. In moving from quintile-1 (high) to quintile-5 (low) for $P-E$ ratios, they find a 3.2% p.a. increase in returns. Levis (1993) also finds an independent $P-E$ ratio effect, after correcting for either size, yield or price, of about 3.5% p.a. However, not all the evidence favours low $P-E$ ratio stocks. Fama and French (1992) suggest that if regression analysis is used to control for size and market-to-book value, then low $P-E$ ratio stocks offer no extra return (see also Miles and Timmermann, 1996).

## WINNER'S CURSE/CONTRARIAN STRATEGIES

There exists a strong negative serial correlation for stock *returns* for those stocks that have experienced extreme price movements (particularly those which experience a price fall *followed by* a price rise). Thus for some stocks (or portfolios of stocks) there is *mean reversion* in stock price behaviour. Put another way there is some predictability in stock returns. Hence:

---

**CONTRARIAN STRATEGY**
A risk adjusted profit might be made by buying (selling)
those stocks that have recently fallen (risen) sharply
(relative to all other stocks)

---

DeBondt and Thaler (1985) take 35 of the most extreme 'winners' and 35 of the extreme 'losers' over the 5 years from January 1928 to December 1932 (based on monthly return data from the NYSE) and form two distinct portfolios of these companies' shares. They follow these companies for the next 5 years (= 'test period'). They repeat the exercise 46 times by advancing the start date by 1 year each time. Finally, they calculate the average 'test period' performance (in excess of the return on the *whole* NYSE index) giving equal weight (rather than value weights) to each of the 35 companies. They find:

- The 5-year price reversal for the 'loser portfolio' (at about +30%) is more pronounced than for the 'winner portfolio' (at −10%).
- The excess returns on the 'loser portfolio' occur in January (i.e. 'January effect').
- The returns on the portfolios are mean reverting over the 5-year horizon (i.e. a price fall is followed by a price rise and vice versa).

It is worth emphasising that the so-called 'loser portfolio' (i.e. one where prices have fallen dramatically *in the past*) is in fact the one that makes high returns *in the future*: a somewhat paradoxical definition of 'loser'. An arbitrage strategy of selling the 'winner portfolio' short and buying the 'loser portfolio' earns profits at an annual rate of around 5–8% (see DeBondt and Thaler, 1989). Bremer and Sweeney (1991) find that the above results also hold for very short time periods. For example, for a 'loser portfolio' comprising stocks where the *1-day* price fall has been greater than 10%, the subsequent returns are 3.95% *after 5 days*. They use stocks of *large firms only*. Therefore they have no problem that the bid–ask spread is a large percentage of the price (which could distort the results). Also they avoid problems with 'the small firm effect' (i.e. smaller firms are more 'risky' and hence require a greater than average equilibrium excess return). Hence Bremer and Sweeney (1991) also seem to find evidence of supernormal profits and a violation of the EMH.

One explanation of the above results is that 'perceived risk' and actual risk may diverge. That is the perceived risk of the 'loser portfolio' is judged to be 'high', hence requiring a high excess return in the future, if one is to hold it. Evidence from psychological studies suggests that misperceptions of risk do occur. For example, people rank the probability of dying from homicide greater than the risk of death from diabetes, but probabilistically they are wrong.

The above evidence certainly casts doubt on the EMH in that it may be possible to make supernormal profits because of some predictability in stock prices. However, it must be noted that many of the above anomalies are most prominent among small firms (e.g. January effect and winner's curse of DeBondt and Thaler, 1985) and discounts on closed-end funds (Lee *et al.*, 1990). If the 'big players' (e.g. pension funds) do not trade in small-firm stocks then it is possible that the markets are too thin and information gathering is costly, so the EMH doesn't apply. The EMH may therefore be a better paradigm for the stocks of large firms. These will be actively traded by the 'big players' who can be expected to have the resources to quickly process all relevant information and have access to cash and credit to execute trades so that prices (of such stocks) always equal fundamental value. Of course, without independent confirmation this is mere conjecture.

# 14.2  NOISE TRADERS AND SMART MONEY

The EMH does not require that *all* participants in the market are 'efficient' and well informed. There can be a set of irrational or 'noise traders' in the market who do not quote prices equal to fair value. All the EMH requires is that there is sufficient 'smart money' around who recognise that $P$ will eventually equal fair value $V$. So, if some irrational traders quote $P < V$, the 'smart money' will quickly move in and purchase stocks from the irrational traders, thus pushing $P$ quickly towards $V$. However, if irrational traders, who are perhaps new to the game, are continually entering the market, it may be possible for prices to diverge from fundamental value for some considerable time. Also it has recently been shown that irrational investors are able to survive in the market (DeLong *et al.*, 1990).

Investors who have finite horizons will be concerned about the price at some future time $N$. If they base their expectations of the value of $E_t P_{t+N}$ on expected future dividends from $t + N$ onwards, then we are back to the infinite horizon assumption of the rational investor (see previous chapter). However, if we allow heterogeneous agents in our model, then if agents believe the world is not dominated by rational investors, the price at $t + N$ will depend in part on what the rational investor feels the irrational investor's view of $P_{t+N}$ will be (i.e. Keynes' beauty contest). This general argument also applies if rational investors know that other rational investors use different models of equilibrium asset returns. Here we are rejecting the EMH assumption that all investors instantaneously know the true model or, equivalently, that learning by market participants about the changing structure of the economy (e.g. 'shipbuilding in decline, chemicals to grow') is instantaneous. In these cases, rational investors may take the view that the actual price is a weighted average of the rational valuation (or alternative rational valuations) and effect on price of the irrational traders (e.g. chartists). Hence the price does not always equal the fundamental value at $t + N$. Rational traders might be prevented from buying or selling, until the market price equals what perhaps *only they* believe is the fundamental value, because of the risks involved. Bonus payments to market traders based on profits over a fixed time period (e.g. monthly) might reinforce such behaviour. The challenge is to devise testable models that mimic noise trader behaviour.

A great deal of the analysis of financial markets relies on the principle of arbitrage (e.g. Shleifer and Summers, 1990). **Arbitrageurs** or **smart money** or rational speculators continually watch the market and quickly eliminate any divergence between the actual price and the fundamental value, and hence immediately eliminate any profitable opportunities. If a security has a perfect substitute then arbitrage is riskless. For example, a (very simple) mutual fund where 1 unit of the fund consists of '1 alpha + 2 beta' shares should sell at the same price for which one can purchase this bundle of *individual* shares in the open market. If the mutual fund is 'underpriced' then a rational trader should purchase the fund and simultaneously sell (or short sell) the securities which constitute the fund, on the stock market, thus ensuring a riskless profit (i.e. buy 'low', sell 'high'). If the smart money has unlimited funds and recognises and acts on this profit opportunity then this should quickly lead to a rise in price of the mutual fund (as demand increases) and a fall in price of the individual securities on the stock exchange (due to increased sales). Riskless arbitrage ensures that *relative* prices are equalised. However, if there are no close substitutes, so that arbitrage is risky, then arbitrage may not pin down the *absolute* price levels of stocks as a whole.

The smart money may consider short selling a share that appears to be overpriced relative to its fair value. They do so in the expectation that they can purchase it later when the actual price falls to the price dictated by fundamentals. If enough of the smart money acts on this premise then their actions will ensure that the price does fall as they all start short selling. The risks faced by the smart money are twofold. First, dividends may turn out to be 'better than expected' and hence the actual price of the share rises even further: this we can call **fundamentals risk**. Second, if arbitrageurs know that there are non-rational traders or **noise traders** in the market, who can, by their collective herding instincts or 'fads' push prices even higher than they are at present, then the arbitrageurs can again lose money: this is *noise trader risk*.

The risk in taking an arbitrage position only occurs if the smart money has a finite horizon. The smart money, who hold stocks short, may believe that prices will *ultimately* fall to their fundamental value and hence, in the long term, profits will be made. However, if arbitrageurs have to either borrow cash or securities (for short sales) to implement their trades and hence pay *per period fees* or report their profit position on their 'book' to their superiors at frequent intervals (e.g. monthly, quarterly), then an infinite horizon certainly cannot apply to all or even most trades undertaken by the smart money.

It may be that there are enough arbitrageurs with sufficient funds in the aggregate, so that even over a finite horizon, risky profitable opportunities are arbitraged away. The force of the latter argument is weakened, however, if we recognise that any single arbitrageur is unlikely to accurately know either the fundamental value of a security or to realise when observed price changes are due to deviations from the fundamental price. Arbitrageurs as a group are also likely to disagree amongst themselves about fundamental value (i.e. they have heterogeneous expectations), and this will increase the general uncertainty they perceive about profitable opportunities, even in the long term. Therefore, the smart money has difficulty in *identifying* any mispricing in the market and, if funds are limited (i.e. a less than perfectly elastic demand for the underpriced securities by arbitrageurs) or horizons are finite, it is possible that profitable *risky* arbitrage opportunities can persist in the market for some time.

If one recognises that 'information costs' (e.g. man-hours, machines, buildings) may be substantial and that marginal costs rise with the number of different shares to monitor and assess, then this also provides some limit on arbitrage activity in some areas of the market. For example, to take an extreme case, if information costs are so high that dealers either concentrate solely on bonds or solely on stocks (i.e. complete market segmentation), then differences in expected returns between bonds and stocks (corrected for risk) will not be arbitraged away.

## HERDING

Above, we have explained why risky arbitrage may be limited and insufficient to keep actual prices of stocks in line with their fundamental value. We now turn to discuss why a market might contain *a substantial number* of noise traders who follow simple 'rules of thumb' or 'trends' or waves of investor sentiment (herding behaviour) rather than act on the basis of fundamentals.

> **In order that noise traders as a group are capable of influencing market prices their demand shifts must broadly move in unison (i.e. be correlated across noise traders)**

We can obtain some general information on these issues from psychological experiments (see Shleifer and Summers, 1990 and Shiller, 1989 for a summary) which tend to show that *individuals* make systematic (i.e. non-random) mistakes. Subjects are found to overreact to new information (news) and they tend to extrapolate past price trends. They are over-confident, which makes them take on excessive risk.

As the stock market involves groups of traders it is useful to consider some experiments on *group behaviour* (see Shiller, 1989). In Sherif's (1937) 'autokinetic experiment' individuals in total darkness were asked to predict the movement of a pencil of light. In the experiment with individuals there was no consensus about the degree of movement (which in fact was zero). When a group of individuals performed the same experiment but this time each individual could hear the views of the others, then a consensus emerged (which differed across groups) about the degree of movement. In an experiment by Asch (1952) individuals acting alone compared lengths of line segments. The experiment was then repeated with a group where all other members of the group were primed to give the *same wrong answers*. The individual when alone usually gave correct answers, but when faced with group pressure the 'individual' frequently gave wrong answers. After the experiment it was ascertained that the individual usually knew the correct answer but was afraid to contradict the group. If there is no generally accepted view of what is the correct or fundamental price of a given stock then investors may face uncertainty rather than risk. This is likely to make them more susceptible to investor sentiment.

Models of the *diffusion of opinions* are often rather imprecise. There is evidence that ideas can remain dormant for long periods and then be triggered by some seemingly trivial event. The news media obviously play a role here, but research on persuasion often finds that informal face-to-face communication among family, friends and co-workers is of greater importance in the diffusion of views than is the media. With the internet, opinions can be quickly communicated. In fact the Securities and Exchange Commission in the USA is worried about some internet traders purchasing shares and then posting unsubstantiated views about particular companies on the internet (e.g. 'takover bid imminent') in order that 'uninformed' traders will also purchase the shares, pushing prices up, so the initial buyer sells at a profit.

There are mathematical theories of the diffusion of information based on models of epidemics. In such models there are 'carriers' who meet 'susceptibles' and create 'new carriers'. Carriers die off at a 'removal rate'. The epidemic can give rise to a humped shape pattern if the infection 'takes off'. If the infection doesn't take off (i.e. because of either a low infection rate or a low number of susceptibles or a high removal rate) then the number of new carriers declines monotonically. The difficulty in applying such a model to investor sentiment is that one cannot accurately quantify the behavioural determinants of the various variables (e.g. the infection rate) in the model, which are likely to differ from case to case.

Shiller (1989) uses the above ideas to suggest that the bull market of the 1950s and 1960s may have had something to do with the speed at which general information about how to invest in stocks and shares (e.g. investment clubs) spread amongst individuals. He also notes the growth in institutional demand (e.g. pension funds) for stocks over this period, which could not be offset by individuals selling their own holdings to keep their *total* savings constant. This was because individuals' holdings of stocks were not large or evenly distributed (most being held by wealthy individuals): some people in occupational pension funds simply had no shares to sell. Herding behaviour or 'following the trend' has frequently been observed in the housing market, in the stock market crash of 1987 (see Shiller, 1990) and in the foreign exchange market (Frankel and Froot, 1990; Allen and Taylor, 1989b).

## SURVIVAL OF NOISE TRADERS

If we envisage a market in which there are smart speculators who tend to set prices equal to fair value and noise traders who operate on rules of thumb, then a question arises as to how the noise traders can survive in this market. If noise traders hold stocks when the price is above the fundamental value, then the smart money should sell these assets to the noise traders, thus pushing down the price. As the price falls towards its fundamental value the noise traders lose money and tend towards bankruptcy, while the smart money can, if they wish, buy back the stocks at the lower price. On the other hand, if the noise traders hold assets whose price is below fundamental value, then the smart money should purchase such assets from the noise traders and they will then make a profit as the price rises towards the fundamental value. Hence the net effect is that the noise traders lose money and therefore should disappear from the market, leaving only the smart money. When this happens prices should then reflect fundamentals.

Of course, if there were an army of noise traders who *continually entered* the market (and continually went bankrupt) it would be possible for prices to diverge from fundamental value for some significant time. One might argue that it is hardly likely that noise traders would enter a market where previous noise traders had gone bankrupt in large numbers. However, entrepreneurs often believe they can succeed where others have failed. To put the reverse argument, some noise traders will be successful over a finite horizon and this may encourage others to attempt to imitate them and enter the market, ignoring the fact that the successful noise traders had in fact taken on more risk and just happened to get lucky. The advent of new technology in the form of cheap internet connections which lower the costs of share dealing may increase the demand for share trading by 'new' noise traders who are subject to common 'fads and fashions' (see Box 14.1).

| Box 14.1 | ELECTRONIC DAY TRADING |
|---|---|

By the end of 1999, there had been a tremendous growth in on-line share dealing. It is estimated that in the US in 1999, there were about 8m 'casual amateurs' who trade on average about twice a month, 250,000 'active amateurs' who trade about twice a day, and about 5000 on-site professionals who trade about 50 times per day. Their daily trading volume accounts for about 15% of the volume in NASDAQ. Professional day traders often trade from electronic trading firms such as *Tradescape, Mount Pleasant* and *Momentum Securities*, in order to simulate some of the excitement of being on the floor of an exchange.

Professional day traders are usually young (25–35) and are self-employed. They pay the electronic trading firms a commission of around $1.50 per 100 shares traded and they are linked directly to a market maker (rather than a broker).

Hence, the technological revolution of the internet is **democratising share trading**. As dealing costs fall, these on-line traders will be able to obtain 'news' items, real time prices and deal as quickly as the big market professionals. Some have argued that this 'internet dealing' helped to keep the market buoyant at the end of 1999.

The **national regulators** (e.g. the Securities and Exchange Commission, SEC in the US and the Financial Services Authority, FSA in the UK) are becoming worried about issues of fair competition and fraud in internet trading. The SEC is increasing its number of 'cyberforce attorneys' to detect fraud and to ensure that orders placed through brokers are executed efficiently and at the best available prices.

Although there are (unverifiable) stories of electronic day traders making 5–10% *per day* (albeit in a rising market), it is obvious that this is a highly risky occupation (or hobby). In fact, after being prevented from day trading via his electronic trading centre in Atlanta (because he had lost all his collateral), Mark Barton returned and shot and killed nine people. This was an additional risk day traders had not foreseen. However, it seems that when the downturn in the market arrives and day traders possibly lose large amounts of money, there may be yet more harrowing stories to emerge. The efficient markets hypothesis, if valid, could ruin the lives of a lot of day traders. When that happens, they and others may not end up 'Having a nice day'.

Can we explain why an *existing cohort* of noise traders can still make profits in a market which contains smart money? The answer really has to do with the potential for herding behaviour. No individual smart money trader can know that all other smart money traders will force the market price towards its fundamental value in the period of time for which he is contemplating holding the stock. Thus any strategy that the sophisticated traders adopt given the presence of noise traders in the market is certainly not riskless. There is always the possibility that the noise traders will push the price even further away from the fundamental value, and this may result in a loss for the smart money. Thus risk averse smart money may not fully arbitrage away the influence of the noise traders. If there are enough noise traders who follow *common* fads then noise trader risk will be pervasive (systematic). It cannot be diversified away and must therefore earn a reward or risk premium in equilibrium. Noise trading is therefore consistent with an average return which is greater than that given by equilibrium asset pricing models such as the CAPM. If noise traders hold a large share of assets subject to noise trader risk, they *may* earn above average returns and survive in the market. If there are some variables at time $t$ which influence the 'mechanical' behaviour of noise traders and noise trader behaviour is persistent, then such variables may influence expected returns in the market. This may explain why additional variables, when added to the CAPM, prove to be statistically significant.

The impact of noise traders on prices may well be greater when most investors follow the advice given in finance textbooks and *passively* hold the market portfolio. If noise traders move into a particular group of shares based on 'hunch', the holders of the market portfolio will do nothing (unless the movement is so great as to require a change in the 'market value' proportions held in each asset). The actions of the noise traders need to be countered by a set of genuine arbitrageurs who are active in the market. In the extreme, if *all* investors hold the market portfolio but *one* noise trader enters the market wishing to purchase shares of a particular firm then its price will be driven to infinity.

The smart money may not only predict fundamentals (e.g. future dividends) but may also divert their energies to anticipating changes in demand by the noise traders. If noise traders are optimistic about particular securities it will pay smart money to create more of them (e.g. junk bonds, Asian mutual funds, oil stocks) via, for example, the expansion of the activities of the securities business of investment banks. Suppose a conglomerate has interests in the oil market and noise traders are temporarily attracted by 'oil', then it may pay 'asset strippers' to take over the conglomerate, split off the oil division and sell off the separate parts of the business. The arbitrageurs (e.g. an investment bank) can then earn a share of profits from the 'abnormally high priced' issues of new oil shares which are currently in vogue with noise traders.

Arbitrageurs will also behave like noise traders in that they attempt to *pick stocks* that noise trader sentiment is likely to favour: the arbitrageurs do not necessarily counter shifts in demand by noise traders. Just as entrepreneurs invest in casinos to exploit gamblers, it pays the smart money to spend considerable resources in gathering information on possible future noise trader demand shifts (e.g. by studying chartists' forecasts). Hence arbitrageurs have an incentive to behave like noise traders—'if you can't beat 'em join 'em'. For example, if noise traders are perceived by arbitrageurs to be positive feedback traders then as prices are pushed above fundamental value, arbitrageurs get in on the bandwagon themselves in the hope that they can sell out 'near the top'. They therefore 'amplify the fad'. Arbitrageurs may expect prices in the longer term to return to fundamentals (perhaps aided by arbitrage sales), but in the short term arbitrageurs will 'follow the trend'. This evidence is consistent with findings of positive autocorrelation in returns at short horizons (e.g. weeks or months) as arbitrageurs follow the short-term trend and negative correlation at longer horizons (e.g. over two or more years) as some arbitrageurs take a long horizon view and sell overpriced shares. Also, if 'news' triggers noise trader demand, then this is consistent with prices overreacting to 'news'.

We noted the **equity premium puzzle** in Chapter 1, that is the fact that the high long run average return on say US stocks (e.g. the S&P500) in excess of the risk free rate cannot be explained by conventional asset pricing models (e.g. CAPM and APT). Put another way, the degree of risk aversion required to explain the excess return on stocks is just too high to be believable. Of course, it may be that the US stock market is a-typical and that taking world stock markets as a whole, the equity premium puzzle may not be so severe. Recently, formal approaches to solving the equity premium puzzle have been mainly centred on the US literature and often focus on the following: (i) using 'better' ways of mathematically representing people's aversion to risk using different utility functions (e.g. habit persistence, hyperbolic discount functions, disappointment aversion and loss aversion utility, whereby gains and losses are not treated equally—see Ang *et al.*, 2000); (ii) assuming some investors are credit constrained (Constantinides *et al.*, 1988); (iii) investigating alternative expectations mechanisms (e.g. assuming individuals misperceive how persistent 'shocks' to economic variables, like inflation, can be and their degree of mean reversion—Gatev and Ross, 2000); (iv) alternative learning models whereby agents have to estimate the relevant parameters such as the mean returns and variances and are therefore subject to estimation error, which introduces additional risk into the market (e.g. Lewellen and Shanken, 2000); (v) using optimisation rules that are robust under uncertainty, rather than optimal (e.g. the robust-$H_\infty$ approach—see Tornell, 2000). These are all reasonable (and difficult) research areas, but none have yet solved the puzzle. In this book we can only outline a small subset of behavioural finance models and we concentrate on ones which tend to consider either misperceptions or herding behaviour, as an explanation of why average returns on stocks are relatively high and also excessively volatile.

As one might imagine, it is by no means easy to introduce noise trader behaviour in any fully optimising framework since almost by definition noise traders are irrational—they misperceive the true state of the world. Noise trader models therefore contain somewhat arbitrary (non-maximising) assumptions about behaviour. Nevertheless, the outcome of the *interaction* between smart money traders (who do maximise a well-defined objective function) and the (ad hoc) noise traders is of interest since we can then ascertain whether such models confirm the general conjectures made above. Generally speaking, as we shall see, these more formal models do not contradict our 'armchair speculations' as outlined above.

## FORMAL MODELS OF NOISE TRADERS

In the model of DeLong *et al.* (1990), both smart money and noise traders are risk averse. Because there is a finite investment horizon, arbitrage is risky. Noise traders create risk for themselves and the smart money, by generating fads in demand for the risky asset. The smart money forms optimal forecasts of the future price based on the correct distribution of price changes, but noise traders develop biased forecasts. The degree of *price misperception* of noise traders $\rho_t$ represents the *difference* between the noise trader forecasts and optimal forecasts. In the DeLong *et al.* model $\rho_t$ is a random variable, normally distributed with mean $\rho^*$ and variance $\sigma^2$:

[14.1] $$\rho_t \sim N(\rho^*, \sigma^2)$$

If $\rho^* = 0$, noise traders agree on their forecasts with the smart money (on average). If noise traders are on average pessimistic (e.g. in a bear market) then $\rho^* < 0$, and the stock price will be below fundamental value. If noise traders are optimistic, $\rho^* > 0$, the converse applies. As well as having this long run view ($= \rho^*$) of the divergence of their forecasts from the optimal forecasts, 'news' also arises, so there can be *abnormal but temporary* variations in optimism and pessimism (given by a term $\rho - \rho^*$). The specification of $\rho_t$ is ad hoc but does have an intuitive appeal based on introspection and evidence from behavioural/group experiments.

In the DeLong *et al.* model the *fundamental value V* of the stock is a constant and is arbitrarily set at unity. The market clears to give an expression for the equilibrium price $P$ which looks rather complicated. However, we can give some intuitive feel for what is going on. The DeLong *et al.* equation for $P$ is:

[14.2] $$P_t = V_t + (\mu/r)\rho^* + [\mu/(1+r)][\rho_t - \rho^*] - 2\gamma\mu^2\sigma^2/r(1+r)^2$$

where $V_t$ is the fair value of the stock at time $t$
  $\mu$ is the proportion of investors who are noise traders
  $r$ is the riskless real rate of interest
  $\gamma$ is the degree of (absolute) risk aversion
  $\sigma^2$ is the variance of noise trader misperceptions.

If there are no noise traders $\mu = 0$ and equation [14.2] predicts that the market price equals its fundamental value (of unity) as set by the smart money. Now let us suppose that at a particular point in time, noise traders have the same long run view of the stock price as does the smart money (i.e. $\rho^* = 0$), and that there are no 'surprises' (i.e. no abnormal bullishness or bearishness), so that $(\rho_t - \rho^*) = 0$. We now have a position where the noise traders have the same view about future prices as does the smart money. However, the equilibrium market price still *does not solely reflect fundamentals*, and in fact the market price will be less than the fundamental price by the amount given by the last term on the RHS of equation [14.2]. The price is below fundamental value, so that the smart money (and noise traders) may obtain a positive expected return (i.e. capital gain) as a payment for 'noise trader risk'. Here, risk is generated entirely by fads and not by uncertainty about fundamentals. This mispricing is probably the key result of the model and involves a *permanent* deviation of price from fundamentals.

## 'INEFFICIENCY' AND SHORT-TERMISM

In a world of only smart money, the fact that some of these investors take a 'short-term' view of returns should not lead to a deviation of price from fundamentals. The argument is based on the implicit forward recursion of the present value formula. If you buy today at time $t$ in order to sell tomorrow, your return depends (in part) on the expected capital gain and hence on the price you can get tomorrow. But the latter depends on what the person you sell to at $t + 1$ thinks the price will be at $t + 2$, etc. Hence a linked chain of short-term 'rational fundamental' investors performs the same calculation as an investor with an infinite horizon.

With a finite investment horizon and the presence of noise traders the above argument doesn't hold. True, the longer the horizon of the smart money the more willing he may be to undertake risky arbitrage based on divergences between price and fundamental value. The reason being that in the meantime he receives the insurance of dividend payments each period and he has a number of periods over which he can wait for the price to rise to fundamental value. However, even with a 'long' but finite horizon there is some price resale risk. The share in the total return from dividend payments over a 'long' holding period is large, but there is still some risk present from uncertainty about the price in the 'final period'.

In the noise trader model of DeLong *et al.* (1990), if a firm can make its equity appear less subject to noise trader sentiment (i.e. reduce $\sigma$) then its underpricing will become less severe and its price will rise. This reduction in uncertainty might be accomplished by:

(i) raising current dividends (rather than investing profits in an uncertain long-term investment project, for example R&D expenditures);
(ii) swapping debt for equity;
(iii) share buybacks.

Empirical work by Jensen (1968) has shown that items (i)–(iii) do tend to lead to an increase in the firm's share price, and this is consistent with our interpretation of the influence of noise traders described above. It also follows that in the presence of noise traders one might expect changes in capital structure to affect the value of the firm (contrary to the Modigliani–Miller hypothesis). Firms will look for different 'clienteles' of investors who are willing to pay high prices for the patterns of cash flows they desire. For example, they will issue shares to investors who are very optimistic about the firm's prospects and debt to those who think the firm is just performing at an 'average' level. Firms will also issue shares (e.g. IPO, seasoned offerings) in 'hot markets', that is when they think investor sentiment favours their sector (e.g. telecoms, IT, banking sectors), and hence they can raise finance at lower cost. They might also see these 'hot periods' as a good time for acquisitions, since they can use their (temporarily) overvalued shares to pay the shareholders of the acquired company.

If stock market collapses (or exchange rate crises) cause severe bankruptcies and subsequent lower levels of fixed investment (e.g. SE Asia in 1997/8) then the social costs of 'inefficiency' can be high. If it is individual investors who lose out on average, relative to institutional investors (due to mispricing), then perhaps allowing individuals to manage their own Social Security saving might not be a good idea. Of course positive sentiment in an 'inefficient' market for some shares (e.g. internet shares) may not be totally bad since it does provide incentives (i.e. potential 'dot.com' multimillionaires) for creative entrepreneurs to exploit risky yet innovative business opportunities. If the market is subject to fads and fashions then clearly there is a case for financial regulation in the form of legal rules, disclosure requirements and bankruptcy proceedings. The latter allow creditors to prevent 'insiders' (e.g. managers and directors) from expropriating the remaining assets of the firm (e.g. by paying excessive severance payments, or selling off assets to related companies controlled by the directors)—see Shleifer (2000).

## NOISE TRADERS AND CONTAGION

We now discuss a noise trader model based on Kirman (1993). Kirman's model is very different to that of DeLong *et al.* (1990) in that it explicitly deals with the interaction between individuals, the rate at which individuals' opinions are altered by recruitment, and hence the phenomenon of 'herding' and 'epidemics'. The basic phenomenon of 'herding' was noted by entomologists. It was noted that ants, when 'placed' equidistant from two identical food sources which were constantly replenished, distributed themselves between each source in an asymmetric fashion. After a time, 80% of the ants ate from one source and 20% from the other. Sometimes a 'flip' occurred which resulted in the opposite concentrations at the two food sources. The experiment was repeated with one food source and two symmetric bridges leading to the food. Again, initially 80% of the ants used one bridge and only 20% used the other, whereas intuitively one might have expected that the ants would be split 50–50 between the bridges. One type of recruitment process in an ant colony is 'tandem recruiting' whereby the ant that finds the food returns to the nest and recruits by contact or chemical secretion. Kirman (1993) notes that Becker (1991) documents similar herding behaviour when people are faced with very similar restaurants in terms of price, food, service, etc. on either side of the road. A large majority choose one restaurant rather than the other even though they have to 'wait in line' (queue). Note that there may be externalities in being 'part of the crowd' at work here which we assume do not apply to ants. However, one still needs to explain any 'flip' from one restaurant to another.

We have already noted that stock prices may deviate for long periods from fundamental value, and in a later chapter we will also see that the spot exchange rate appears to be only loosely tied to 'economic fundamentals'. The parallel with the behaviour of the ants is obvious. A model that explains 'recruitment', and results in a concentration at one source for a considerable time period and then a possibility of a 'flip', clearly has relevance to the observed behaviour of speculative asset prices. Kirman (1993) makes the point that although economists (unlike entomologists) tend to prefer models based on optimising behaviour, optimisation is not necessary for survival (e.g. plants survive because they have evolved a system whereby their leaves follow the sun but they might have done much better to develop feet which would have enabled them to walk into the sunlight).

Kirman (1991) uses this type of model to examine the possible behaviour of a speculative asset price (e.g. stock prices or the exchange rate) determined by a *weighted average* of smart money and noise traders' views. The proportion of each type of trader *w* depends on the process of conversion (via a Markov chain process). The weights are endogenous and incorporate Keynes' beauty queen idea. Individuals meet each other and are either converted or not. They then try and assess which opinion is in the majority and base their forecasts on who they think is in the majority, smart money or noise traders. Thus the investor does not base his forecast on his own beliefs but on what he perceives is the majority view. The model is then simulated and exhibits a pattern that resembles the actual observed broad movements in stock prices.

There is very little evidence on the behaviour of noise traders and the diffusion of opinions in financial markets. Allen and Taylor (1989a) use survey techniques to investigate the behaviour of chartists in the FX market. These 'players' base their views about the future course of the spot exchange rate as extrapolations from graphs of the past behaviour of the exchange rate and believe they can exploit recurring patterns in the graphs (e.g. 'head and shoulders'—see Chapter 17). Allen and Taylor find that chart analysis is mainly used for short horizons (intra-day to 1–3 months) and then 'fundamentals' become more important. Also there is a tendency for chartists to underpredict the spot rate in a rising market and vice versa. Hence the elasticity of expectations is less than one (i.e. a rise in the actual rate does not lead to expectations of a bigger rise next period). They argue that the heterogeneity in chartists' forecasts (i.e. some forecast 'up' when others are forecasting 'down') means that they probably do not as a group influence the market overstrongly and hence are not destabilising.

# 14.3  CHAOS THEORY

Chaos theory attempts to explain the random patterns we see in asset prices and returns by using deterministic non-linear models. Before commencing our analysis of chaotic systems it is useful to briefly review the nature of the solutions to a dynamic linear *deterministic* system such as:

[**14.3**]     $y_t = a + by_{t-1} + cy_{t-2}$

Equation [14.3] is a second-order difference equation. Given starting values $y_0$ and $y_1$ and the parameters (*a*, *b* and *c*) we can determine all future values of $y_t$ to any degree of accuracy by repeated substitution in equation [14.3]. The time path of $y_t$ can converge on a stable equilibrium value $\bar{y} = a/(1 - b - c)$ and for certain parameter values may either have an oscillatory path or a monotonic path. For some parameter values the path may either be oscillatory and explosive (i.e. cycles of everincreasing amplitude) or monotonic and explosive. The problem in basing models on deterministic equations like [14.3] is that in the 'real world' we do not appear to observe deterministic paths for economic variables.

So far, our models to explain the random nature of stock price (returns) data have involved introducing explicit 'stochastic processes' somewhere into the model. For example, stock prices only move in response to news about dividends, that is the *random* forecast errors in the stochastic dividend process. In contrast to the above:

> **In *chaotic models*, apparent random patterns that we observe in real world data can be generated by a *non-linear* system that is purely *deterministic***

There is no commonly agreed definition of chaos, but loosely speaking chaotic systems are deterministic, yet they exhibit seemingly random and irregular time series patterns. The time series produced by chaotic systems are highly sensitive to the initial conditions (i.e. the starting point $y_0$ of the system) and to slight changes in the parameter values. However, this sensitivity to initial conditions and parameter values does not rule out the possibility of producing reasonably accurate forecasts *over short* horizons. This is because the time series from a chaotic system will be broadly repetitive in the early part of the time series, even if the initial conditions differ slightly.

The 'sensitivity' of chaotic systems is such that if the same chaotic system is simulated on two 'identical' computers (which estimate each data point to a precision of $10^{-8}$ say) then after a certain time, the path of the two series will differ substantially because of the minute rounding errors reacting with the highly non-linear system. This kind of result is the source of the observation that if the weather can be represented as a chaotic system then, 'A butterfly flapping its wings in China may result in a hurricane in the Caribbean'.

Although chaotic systems produce apparent random patterns in the time domain they nevertheless have a discernible structure (e.g. a specific frequency distribution) which can be used to provide statistical tests for the presence of chaos. Space constraints mean we shall not analyse these tests (but see DeGrauwe *et al.*, 1993). As one might imagine it can be very difficult to ascertain whether a particular 'random looking' time series has been generated from a deterministic chaotic system or from a genuinely stochastic system. The latter becomes even more difficult if the chaotic system is *occasionally* hit by 'small' random shocks: this is known as 'noisy chaos'. Tests for chaotic systems require a large amount of data, if inferences are to be reliable (e.g. in excess of 20,000 data points), and hence with the 'length' of most economic data this becomes an acute problem.

Most people would agree that human behaviour is not wholly deterministic and therefore the analysis of chaotic models only provides a starting point in explaining movements in asset prices. In essence, chaos theory suggests that financial economists take greater note of the possibility of non-linearities in relationships. Having obtained a model that is non-linear in the variables one can always 'add on' stochastic elements to represent the randomness in human behaviour. Hence as a first step we need to examine the dynamics produced by non-linear systems. If asset prices appear random and returns are largely unpredictable we must at least entertain the possibility that these results might be generated in chaotic systems. We have, so far, spoken in rather general terms about chaos. We now briefly discuss an explicit chaotic system and outline how economic models based on noise traders and smart money may generate chaotic behaviour.

## THE LOGISTIC EQUATION

About the simplest representation of a system capable of chaotic behaviour is the (non-linear) logistic equation:

[14.4] $$P_{t+1} = \lambda P_t (1 - P_t)$$

The steady state $P^*$ is given when $P_{t+1} = P_t = P^*$:

[14.5] $$P^* = \lambda P^* (1 - P^*)$$

and the two solutions are:

[14.6a] $$P^* = 0$$

and

[14.6b] $$P^* = 1 - (1/\lambda)$$

Not all non-linear systems give rise to chaotic behaviour: it depends on the parameter values and initial conditions. For some values of $\lambda$ the system is globally stable and given *any* starting value $P_0$, the system will converge to one of the steady state solutions $P^*$. For other values of $\lambda$ the solution is a *limit cycle* whereby the time series eventually oscillates (for ever) between *two* values $P_1^*$ and $P_2^*$ (where $P_i^* \neq P^*$ for $i = 1, 2$). This is known as a two-cycle. The 'solution' to the system is therefore a differential equation and is known as a *bifurcation*. Again for different values of $\lambda$ the series can alter from a two-cycle to a 4, 8, 16-cyclic pattern. Finally, for a range of values of $\lambda$ the time series of $P$ appears random and chaotic behaviour occurs. In this case, if the starting value is altered from $P_0 = 0.3$ to 0.30001, the 'random' time path differs after about 20 time periods, demonstrating the sensitivity to very slight parameter changes.

The dynamics of the non-linear logistic system in the single variable $P_t$ have to be solved by simulation rather than analytically. The latter usually applies a fortiori to more complex single variable non-linear equations and to a system of non-linear equations where variables $X$, $Y$, $Z$ say interact with each other. A wide variety of very diverse patterns which are seemingly random or irregular can arise in such models.

A simple model that yields a logistic equation is to assume a long run equilibrium level for prices $P^*$, determined by future dividends which we assume are constant (so that

$P^* = D/R$ where $R =$ constant discount rate—see Chapter 12). Now assume that the change in price is proportional to the gap between $P^*$ and last period's actual value $P_{t-1}$:

[14.7]     $\Delta P_t = \theta(P^* - P_{t-1})$     $\theta > 0$

This is a form of **error correction model**, ECM. If $P_{t-1}$ is below its long run equilibrium $P^*$ then $P$ increases next period: this then reduces the gap or 'error' $P^* - P_t$ next period. The model in equation [14.7] also **represents mean reversion**, since if $P_{t-1}$ is below $P^*$ it moves back towards $P^*$ next period. Let us now assume (rather arbitrarily, it must be admitted) that:

[14.8]     $\theta = \lambda P_{t-1}$     $\lambda > 0$

Hence, if the stock price is high, then the adjustment speed (i.e. the value of $\theta$) will be quicker. (This is a **non-linear error correction model**.) Substituting equation [14.8] into equation [14.7]:

[14.9]     $\Delta P_t = \lambda P_{t-1}(P^* - P_{t-1})$

$P_t = (1 + \lambda P^*)P_{t-1} - \lambda P_{t-1}^2$

Since $P^*$ is a constant (by assumption) we can arbitrarily set:

[14.10]     $P^* = -(1 - \lambda)/\lambda$

and equation [14.9] then becomes the logistic equation:

[14.11]     $P_t = \lambda P_{t-1}(1 - P_{t-1})$

which is capable of generating chaotic behaviour. The above 'model' is very simple (and a little contrived). However, if we can introduce non-linearities into a more realistic deterministic model, it may also yield chaotic behaviour.

In recent years, there has been much empirical work on non-linear (ECM) models in many areas of economics, and indeed the non-linearities are often also assumed to be asymmetric (see Cuthbertson, 1996 and Granger and Terasvirta, 1993 for an overview). The basic idea is similar to that set out above, but in equation [14.7] the adjustment parameter $\theta$ is assumed to be a non-linear function (often a logistic function) of the 'distance' from equilibrium (i.e. $\theta$ is a function of $(P^*_{t-1} - P_{t-1})$). Hence the speed of adjustment $\theta$ is faster the further you are from equilibrium (i.e. the larger is $(P^*_{t-1} - P_{t-1})$). The danger with such models is that the *estimated* non-linearity is due to some single large 'one off' rise or fall in $P$ (e.g. currency crisis) and the non-linear effect is therefore a rather sophisticated way of taking account of an 'outlier' in the data. However, careful tests of the stability of the key non-linear parameters to changes in the data set, can usually distinguish between these competing explanations.

## NOISE TRADERS AND SMART MONEY

It is not difficult to set up ad hoc models of the interaction of noise traders and smart money that are non-linear in the variables and hence that may exhibit chaos. When we say ad hoc we imply that the noise traders and smart money need not necessarily maximise some well-defined function (e.g. the mean–variance approach in portfolio theory). DeGrauwe *et al.* (1993) provide an interesting model of this interaction where noise traders exhibit extrapolative behaviour (positive feedback) and the smart money have negative feedback since they sell when the price is above fundamentals. The model generates a time series that approximates that found in actual high-frequency (e.g. daily) data for speculative prices such as stock prices and the exchange rate. The apparent randomness in the price series is of course not the result of random events or 'news', but is due to a purely deterministic non-linear system. Hence the rational expectations assumption is not required in order to yield apparent random behaviour in asset prices and asset returns.

Clearly, the above analysis is a long way from providing a coherent theory of asset price movements, but it does alert one to alternative possibilities to the rational expectations paradigm where all agents have homogeneous expectations, know the true model of the economy (instantly) and use all available useful information when forecasting. The key conclusions from chaotic models are:

- A purely non-linear yet deterministic process can produce 'random patterns' which do not repeat themselves. These random patterns need not necessarily be highly variable (although they might be) and they have a finite variance.
- The time series produced by chaotic systems are highly sensitive to the initial conditions and to slight changes in the parameter values. In chaotic systems even a small difference in the starting value can make a substantial difference to the forecast path. In conventional (linear) models the fact that the model parameters are estimated (but unbiased) does not unduly influence our forecasts, but with chaotic models even the slightest difference in a parameter can lead to very different forecasts.
- However, the sensitivity to initial conditions and parameter values does not rule out the possibility of producing reasonably accurate forecasts *over short* horizons. This is because the time series from a chaotic system will be broadly repetitive in the early part of the time series, even if the initial conditions differ slightly (e.g. weather forecasts 1 to 5 days ahead are pretty accurate but they are not particularly accurate over longer horizons).

# 14.4 SUMMARY

The key points in this chapter are as follows.

- Some stock market anomalies are simply manifestations of the **'small firm effect'**. Thus the **January effect** appears to be concentrated primarily amongst small firms, as are the profits to be made from **closed-end mutual funds**, where the discount available is highly correlated with the presence of small firms in the portfolio.
- There may be some market segmentation taking place whereby the **smart money** only deals in large tranches of frequently traded stocks of large companies. The market for small firms' stocks may be rather 'thin' and dominated by **noise traders**, hence allowing anomalies to persist.

- The idea of noise traders co-existing with smart money is a recent and important theoretical innovation. Here the price can diverge from fundamentals simply because of the extra uncertainty introduced by the noise traders. Also the noise traders co-exist alongside the smart money and do not necessarily go bankrupt.
- The presence of noise traders can in principle explain sharp movements in stock prices (i.e. bull and bear markets) and indeed the **excess volatility** experienced in the stock market. Nevertheless, these models embrace some ad hoc assumptions about behaviour (e.g. that 'opinions' or 'fads' are persistent).
- **Chaos theory** demonstrates how a *non-linear* deterministic system can generate apparently random behaviour. What is perhaps most important about this strand of the literature is that it alerts us to the possibility of non-linearities in economic behavioural equations. However, at present, 'chaos' is very much a 'technique in search of a good economic theory'.
- A major difficulty in trying to analyse chaotic models is the very large amount of data required to detect a chaotic (as opposed to a stochastic) process. A reasonable conjecture might be that chaotic dynamics (and the allied non-linear technique, neural networks) could become important statistical tools in forecasting of asset prices over very short horizons (e.g. tick-by-tick data). However, unless they are allied to economic theory models, their usefulness in general policy analysis will be very limited.

## END OF CHAPTER EXERCISES

**Q1** How would you define a 'noise trader' and a 'smart money' trader?

**Q2** Can noise traders outperform rational traders and hence stay in the market?

**Q3** How do the interactions of noise traders and 'smart money' lead to mispriced shares?

**Q4** What is the essence of chaos theory and why are the results counterintuitive?

**Q5** Name one stock market anomaly that you believe provides a profitable trading strategy.

**Q6** At the end of 1999 and in the first 3 months of 2000, certain 'dot.com' companies were being floated for hundreds of millions of dollars, even though they had only been trading for a few years, had very small turnover (e.g. $1m p.a.) and had not yet shown a profit. Is this irrational or a classic example of 'noise traders' and a (non-rational) bubble?

**Q7** Can noise trader behaviour explain the discounts found in closed-end funds (i.e. investment trusts in the UK)?

# PART 6

# THE FOREX MARKET

# CHAPTER 15

# The Foreign Exchange Market

## LEARNING OBJECTIVES

- To provide a brief overview of the evolution of the **international monetary system** and the move between alternative exchange rate regimes (e.g. fixed but adjustable rates, freely floating rates, currency bands and common currency areas).
- To explain the mechanics of **spot FX deals**, bid–ask spreads and cross-rates.
- To show how the **forward rate** is determined by riskless arbitrage (i.e. **covered interest parity**) and how a forward position can be hedged using either the money markets or an **FX swap**.
- To demonstrate how **speculation** in the spot FX market is influenced by domestic and foreign interest rates and expectations of future spot rates—this is **uncovered interest parity**.
- To explain the concept of price competitiveness and **purchasing power parity PPP** and their role in analysing trade flows.
- To show the relationship between the forward FX rate and the *future* spot rate—the so-called **forward rate unbiasedness proposition FRU**.
- To discuss the convergence (or otherwise) of real interest rates in different countries. This is the so-called **international Fisher effect**.
- To analyse how PPP, UIP and the international Fisher effect have implications for the success of the **Maastricht conditions** and entry into a **currency union**, such as EMU.

The FX market is the largest and most active financial market with trillions of dollars changing hands daily. The spot FX rate is also a 'price' which attracts much media and government attention because changes in the exchange rate can have far reaching implications for the rest of the economy. In this chapter we cover all the main issues concerning spot and forward FX markets and their impact on trade. The terminology used in this area can become rather complex, particularly that for the forward market. However, the basic ideas are not too difficult and these provide the concepts required to understand models of the exchange rate discussed in the next chapter.

We set the scene with a brief history of the international monetary system, emphasising the importance to 'small open economies' (i.e. those with a large export/import sector) of the exchange rate system adopted. We then move on to the more detailed working of the spot market, including bid, offer and cross-rates and how these are used by market participants. The next section deals with the forward market, including price quotes and the use of swap points by market makers. We then deal with hedging in the forward market and the evidence in favour of covered interest parity. The next section covers speculation in the spot market (i.e. uncovered interest parity), and this is followed by a discussion of price competitiveness and purchasing power parity. In the final sections we show how these basic concepts are interlinked and how they can be used to assess the prospects for entry into a currency union, such as EMU.

# 15.1 OVERVIEW OF THE INTERNATIONAL MONETARY SYSTEM

The behaviour of the exchange rate, particularly for small open economies that undertake a substantial amount of international trade, has been at the centre of macroeconomic policy debates for many years. There is no doubt that economists' views about the best exchange rate system to adopt have changed over the years, partly because new evidence has accumulated as the system has moved through various exchange rate regimes. It is worthwhile briefly outlining the main issues.

After World War II the **Bretton Woods arrangement** of 'fixed but adjustable exchange rates' applied to most major currencies. As capital flows were small and often subject to government restrictions, the emphasis was on price competitiveness. Countries that had faster rates of inflation than their trading partners were initially allowed to borrow from the **International Monetary Fund IMF** to finance their trade deficit. If a 'fundamental disequilibrium' in the trade account developed, then after consultation the deficit country was allowed to fix its exchange rate at a new lower parity (against the US dollar). After a devaluation, the IMF would also usually insist on a set of austerity measures, such as cuts in public expenditure, to ensure that real resources (i.e. labour and capital) were available to switch into export growth and import substitution. The system worked relatively well for a number of years and succeeded in avoiding the re-emergence of the use of tariffs and quotas that had been a feature of 1930s protectionism.

The US dollar was the **anchor currency** of the Bretton Woods system and the dollar was linked to gold at a fixed price of $35 per ounce. The system began to come under strain in the middle of the 1960s. Deficit countries could not persuade surplus countries to mitigate the competitiveness problem, by a revaluation of the surplus country's currency. There was an **asymmetric adjustment process** which invariably meant the deficit country had to devalue. The possibility of a large step devaluation allowed speculators a 'one way bet' and encouraged speculative attacks on those countries that were perceived to have poor current account imbalances, even if it could be reasonably argued that these imbalances were temporary.

The US ran large current account deficits which increased the amount of dollars held by foreigners (either as private sector foreign assets or as official foreign exchange reserves).

Hence, the US Government was able to exchange US dollars (which could be produced at near zero cost in terms of real resources) in return for valuable 'real resources' (e.g. oil, rubber, coal). This is known as **seniorage**, and is a benefit obtained if your currency becomes a **vehicle currency** (i.e. used to settle foreign trade between third countries) or is used as part of another country's foreign exchange reserves. Eventually, the amount of these externally held dollars exceeded the value of gold in Fort Knox, when valued at the 'official price' of $35 an ounce. At the official price, free convertibility of dollars into gold became impossible. A two-tier gold market developed (with the free market price of gold very much higher than the official price) and eventually convertibility of the dollar into gold was suspended by the US authorities. By the early 1970s, pressures on the system were increasing. International capital became more mobile and differential inflation rates between countries widened and caused large deficits or surpluses on the current accounts of different countries. By 1972/3 most major industrial countries had de facto left the Bretton Woods system, and floated their currencies.

In part, the switch to a **floating exchange rate regime** had been influenced by monetary economists. They argued that control of the domestic money supply would ensure a desired inflation and exchange rate path. In addition, stabilising speculation by rational agents would ensure that large persistent swings in the *real* exchange rate (i.e. price competitiveness) could be avoided by an announced credible monetary policy (often in the form of money supply targets). We will evaluate some of these monetary models of exchange rate determination in the next chapter.

Towards the end of the 1970s a seminal paper by Dornbusch (1976) showed that if FOREX dealers are rational, yet goods prices are 'sticky', then **exchange rate overshooting** could occur. Hence, a contractionary monetary policy (e.g. a cut in the money supply or a rise in domestic interest rates) could result in a major loss in price competitiveness over a substantial period, with obvious deflationary consequences for real trade, output and employment. Although in long run equilibrium the economy would move towards full employment and lower inflation, the loss of output in the transition period could be more substantial in the Dornbusch model than in earlier (non-rational) monetary models, which assume that prices are 'flexible'.

The volatile movement in nominal and real exchange rates in the 1970s led Europeans to consider a move back towards more managed exchange rates, which was eventually reflected in the workings of the **Exchange Rate Mechanism, ERM** from the early 1980s. European countries that joined the ERM agreed to try and keep their bilateral exchange rates within announced bands around a central parity. The bands could be either wide ($\pm6\%$) or narrow ($\pm2.25\%$). The Deutsche Mark (DM) became the anchor currency. In part the ERM was a device to replace national monetary targets with German monetary policy, as a means to combat inflation. Faced with a fixed exchange rate against the DM, a high inflation country has a clear signal that it must quickly reduce its rate of inflation to that pertaining in Germany. Otherwise, unemployment would ensue in the high inflation country, which would then provide a 'painful mechanism' for reducing inflation. The ERM had a facility for countries to realign their (central) exchange rates in the case of a fundamental misalignment. However, when a currency hits the bottom of its band because of a speculative attack, all the European Central Banks in the ERM system could agree to support the weak currency by co-ordinated intervention in the FX market.

The perceived success of the ERM in reducing inflation and exchange rate volatility in the 1980s led the G10 countries to consider a policy of co-ordinated intervention (e.g. the Plaza and Louvre accords) to mitigate persistent and large, under and overvaluations of their own currencies. The latter was epitomised by the 'inexorable' rise of the US dollar in 1983–85 and its subsequent fall, which seemed to be totally unrelated to changes in economic fundamentals (e.g. changes in interest rates, or the current account deficit). Recently, some economists have suggested a more formal arrangement for **currency zones and currency bands** for the major world currencies (e.g. US dollar, yen, euro) along the lines of rules used for the ERM.

In the early 1990s the ERM came under considerable strain. Increasing capital mobility and the removal of all exchange controls in the ERM countries facilitated a speculative attack on the Italian lira, sterling and the French franc around 16th September 1992 (known as Black Wednesday). Sterling and the lira left the ERM and allowed their currencies to float. About 1 year later, faced with further currency turmoil, most ERM bands were widened to ±15%. The move to a single European currency and a currency union (i.e. **Economic and Monetary Union, EMU**) was thrown into some confusion by the events of Black Wednesday. The economic reasons for a move to monetary union in Europe are complex, but one is undoubtedly the desire to 'remove' the problem of floating or quasi-managed exchange rates. (The latter issues are dealt with further in the next chapter.) The move to monetary union was formally started at a meeting of EU leaders on 10th December 1991 at Maastricht in the Netherlands where 'convergence criteria' were set out for entry into the common currency and culminated in 11 countries entering 'Euroland'—see Box 15.1.

## Box 15.1    MAASTRICHT CRITERIA AND EMU

The Maastricht Treaty is an amendment to the Treaty of Rome. The **Maastricht 'convergence criteria'** of December 1991 set out the conditions for entry into the common currency zone, which we refer to as 'Euroland'. The criteria are:

(1) The inflation rate should be within 1.5 percentage points of the average rate of inflation in the three EU countries with the lowest inflation rates.
(2) Long-term interest rates must be within 2% points of the average rate of the three EU states with the lowest interest rates.
(3) The national budget deficit must be below 3% of GNP.
(4) The national debt must not exceed 60% of GNP.
(5) The national currency must have remained within the 2.25% fluctuation margin in the currency band of the European Monetary System (EMS) and must not have been devalued for 2 years.

The Maastricht Treaty also proposed limited harmonisation of social policy (e.g. consumer protection, safety at work and immigration) and moves towards a common defence and foreign policy, but these do not concern us here.

As we shall see in this part of the book, some of these criteria are well founded in economic theory. The inflation and exchange rate criteria are there to ensure that on entry a particular country is not wildly price uncompetitive, thus avoiding a sharp fall in that country's output after entry. This concept is known as **purchasing power parity, PPP**. Similarly, the interest rate and exchange rate criteria taken together imply that investors will have no strong incentive to switch between financial assets of a particular country and the rest of the potential Euroland countries, which could result in pressure on exchange rates. This is known as the **uncovered interest parity, UIP** condition. Both PPP and UIP are discussed in this chapter.

The **budget deficit criterion** is somewhat arbitrary at 3% of GDP. But it is there so that countries after entering a common currency area will not have to undertake large bond issues to finance the budget deficit. (Remember a country within Euroland cannot issue 'money'.) The low budget deficit therefore reduces the possibility of default on these bonds (which have to be ultimately financed from domestic taxation). The 60% ratio of the *stock* of outstanding debt is also a rather arbitrary figure, but is supposed to ensure that an individual country's bonds (denominated in euros) will be accepted by the capital markets because the overall level of debt is capable of ultimately being paid off by that country's taxpayers. These latter two budgetary conditions lessen the likelihood that a country in Euroland could default on its government debt and try and get the other Euroland countries to 'bail it out'. We discuss these 'debt issues' more fully in Chapter 16.

In January 1999, 11 EU countries formed an **Economic and Monetary Union, EMU** and irrevocably locked their exchange rates against the euro, with a view to full implementation of euro 'notes and coins' in retail transactions beginning in January 2002. The EU countries which entered 'Euroland' were Austria, Belgium, Finland, France, Germany, Ireland, Italy, Luxembourg, Netherlands, Portugal and Spain. By and large these countries met the inflation and interest rate targets, but meeting the maximum 3% budget deficit criterion took some 'creative accounting'. Most but not all countries met the 'ERM criteria', but a large number failed the debt ratio criterion (e.g. Belgium and Italy had debt–GDP ratios in excess of 100%). So the Maastricht criteria were in the end merely 'guidelines' for entry. The EU countries which stayed out were the UK, Denmark, Greece and Sweden. These can join at a later date if they fulfil the Maastricht criteria.

The euro is currently used amongst the 11 participating European countries for invoicing commercial transactions, and there are many financial assets (e.g. loans, stocks, bonds, futures, swaps and derivatives) which are now denominated in euros. The euro is a rival to the US dollar and it may eventually become an important vehicle and reserve currency. However, it has experienced a continuous fall against the US dollar from 1.17 euros per USD in January 1999 to around 0.83 euros per USD in October 2000, a fall of around 30% in under 2 years.

The interest rate policy in Euroland is determined by the **European System of Central Banks, ESCB** with the primary objective of maintaining price stability. The ESCB also conducts the foreign exchange operations (e.g. intervention) and manages the foreign exchange reserves. Somewhat more nebulous is its objective of supporting the general economic policies of the EU. The decisions of the **European Central**

**Bank, ECB** in Frankfurt are supposed to be made independently of governments of member states and EU institutions. The Governing Council of the ESCB, which consists of the Executive Board of the ECB and the Governors of the national Central Banks of the 11 members, determines EU interest rates at its monthly meetings. Day-to-day operations are under the auspices of the Governor of the ECB, currently Wim Duisenberg. Because of the fall in the euro, the ESCB decided on 22nd September 2000 that it would undertake intervention in the FX market to support the euro if it fell below $0.87. By October it touched a low of $0.833 after Wim Duisenberg's comments that support for the euro would be difficult during the run up to the US presidential elections, and the prospect of conflict in the Middle East. Duisenberg had forgotten the 'First Law of Central Banking' namely, don't reveal any information about FX intervention to speculators—keep them guessing.

Willem Buiter, an ex-member of the UK Monetary Policy Committee of the Bank of England (see Box 2.1), argues that the ECB is less 'independent' and transparent in its policymaking than is the MPC in the UK. He therefore proposes that one should end the rule that each EMU member's national Central Bank has a seat on the Governing Council and that the EU Council of Ministers should not be allowed to give 'general orientations' for exchange rate policy (as probably applied in October 2000 when there was concerted intervention by EMU member states to support the euro). Buiter (1999) would also like to see more transparency in the form of publication of the minutes of the ECB's voting records and an explicit inflation target, as well as more 'teeth' for the European Parliament.

The years 1997–99 saw great currency turmoil in the Far East where banking crises in Thailand, Indonesia, Malaysia and Japan resulted in depreciations of some of these currencies against the US dollar of around 30–40% (see Chapter 1). The immediate reason for the withdrawal of foreign capital appears to be the 'excess' foreign currency borrowing by domestic banks. This foreign currency was then switched into local currency loans (many of which were used in property speculation) and these became 'non-performing'. Hence, it was (correctly) thought that the banks who were unhedged could not pay back the interest and capital on the foreign currency loans and this triggered a general capital outflow.

Also, in 1998 the Russian rouble depreciated sharply against the US dollar, again because bank loans to Russia denominated in foreign currency seemed to be liable to default. Growth in the Russian economy was virtually non-existent, there were massive falls in tax receipts (and a disintegration of the tax collecting system) and hence many public sector workers had wage arrears in excess of 6 months. The Brazilian 'real' became the next victim in 1999 when Brazil too had to devalue in the face of speculative pressure, which the IMF and the granting of loans from the US were unable to stem. This set of events has led for calls in the G10 for a 'new economic order' or a **'new financial architecture'** which involves a more pro-active role for the IMF in trying to avert currency crises (or at least mitigate their adverse impact on countries—see Chapter 16).

Having delt with the broad issues surrounding alternative exchange rate regimes we now turn to the detailed workings of the spot and forward FX markets.

## 15.2 SPOT FX DEALS

When a bank purchases foreign currency in the spot market it does not receive the funds that day. The foreign exchange (FX) is delivered in two working days time on what is known as the **spot value date**. Hence a spot deal done on Wednesday will be settled on Friday (the 'spot value date'). A deal done on Thursday will normally be settled on Monday (unless this is also a holiday).

Settlement actually takes place in the two separate countries, even though the deal may be done in a third country. Trading the French franc against Swiss francs would be FRF for CHF in terms of the currencies' SWIFT codes or 'Paris–Swissy' over the phone. If the trade is with a bank in London, the funds are not transferred in London. Instead, the accounts of the two parties to the deal will be held in their (correspondent) banks in the settlement countries, namely France and Switzerland, and there will be a payment of French francs in France against Swiss francs in Switzerland. Generally, currencies are almost always quoted against the US dollar. Other SWIFT codes and 'shorthands' for these FX trades are:

| Currencies | SWIFT codes | Shorthand |
|---|---|---|
| Sterling–US dollar | USD/GBP | Cable |
| French franc–US dollar | USD/FRF | Paris |
| Swiss franc–US dollar | USD/CHF | Swissy |
| Euro–US dollar | USD/EURO | Euros |
| Deutschmark–US dollar | USD/DEM | Dollar–Mark |
| Japanese yen–US dollar | USD/JPY | Bill and Ben |

The use of 'Bill and Ben' for the Japanese yen is Cockney rhyming slang and is used in the London market. Of course, with the advent of the euro then 'Paris' and 'Dollar–Mark' will soon be a thing of the past. Note that the 'slash /' here does not mean 'divide by', it is merely a convention used to separate 'base' (the currency on the left) from 'quoted' (the currency on the right). In fact 'USD/GBP' would be a quote in terms of 'Great Britain pounds per US dollar'.

Settlement will be on the same 'working day' in both countries, but because of time zone differences, settlement will take place earlier in the Far East, followed by Europe and then in the USA. So, for example, a bank in London selling Swiss francs may deliver them in Zurich before receiving USDs from New York. If the Swiss bank goes bankrupt before delivering the USDs from its New York correspondent bank, then the London bank will face default losses. This happened when the Herstatt Bank in Germany went bankrupt in 1974 and failed to deliver the foreign currency it owed to counterparties. Hence this settlement risk is sometimes referred to as 'Herstatt risk'.

### BASE/QUOTED CURRENCY

Dealing with exchange rate quotes can be difficult to grasp at first, since two currencies are always involved (e.g. EURO and USD), and the quote could in principal be either EURO per

USD or USD per EURO. There are various conventions which we now illustrate with specific examples:

| **If the quote is written** | 'EURO 1 = USD 0.85' (or in words '0.85 dollars per euro') |
| | then |
| **Base currency** | is the EURO = 'fixed number' = 'one' |
| **Quoted currency** | is the USD = 'variable number' = 0.85 (in this case) |

If the quote is 'written' as 'base/quoted', then the above would be denoted 'USD 0.85'. A change from USD 0.8500 to 0.8501 is an increase of 0.0001 or 1 tick or 1 point or 1 pip.

## DIRECT (NORMAL) AND INDIRECT (RECIPROCAL) QUOTES

> **Direct quote is 'domestic per unit of foreign currency'**
> **Indirect quote is 'foreign per unit of domestic currency'**

Most international markets (e.g. USA, Australia, Japan) use direct quotes for most currencies, while London uses indirect quotes. For example, a quote by a Swiss bank would be a direct quote such as CHF 160 per EURO 100. Dealers normally trade the base currency (here the euro) in round amounts of the base currency (e.g. 5m euros). Dealers make money from the **bid–ask spread**, the difference between the buying price and selling price of a currency. The 'bid price' is the 'buying price' but we need to make it clear which currency is being bought and which sold by the market maker. The quote by the dealer (market maker) might be as follows:

**Bid–ask spread: Quote is USD 1 = EURO 0.8550/60**

In the above quote 0.85 is the **big figure**, and the bid–ask spread = 10 **points**. The rule of thumb to obtain the correct buy or sell outcome is the 'three B's rule', namely:

> **The market maker Buys the Base currency at the Bid**
> **rate—which is the 'low' figure (usually the figure which**
> **comes first in the quote)**

Hence the market maker:

Buys $1 and pays out ('low') EURO 0.8550—bid rate
Sells $1 and receives ('high') EURO 0.8560—offer rate

making a net profit on the round trip of EURO 0.0010 (= 10 points). This rule retains the 'buy low, sell high' convention. Note that it is the dealer 'making' the quote who buys $1 at

EURO 0.8550, the counterparty must therefore be selling $1 and receiving EURO 0.8550. There are two sides to every deal.

## TELEPHONE DEALS

In the above quote '0.85' is the **'big figure'** and the quote over the telephone at 0.8550/0.8560 (EURO per $) where bank M is the market maker would go something like this (on Monday 1st March):

**Bank A:** 'Hi guys. Spot dollar–euro please'
**Bank M:** '50/60'
**Bank A:** 'OK, at 50 I sell 10 dollars'
**Bank M:** 'Done. I buy $10m dollars at 0.8550 for 3rd March and sell you euro 8.55m. My dollars to Merrill's, New York'
**Bank A:** 'OK, my euros to Deutsche Bank, Frankfurt. Thanks and bye'

Note that it is bank M who *gives* the quote and hence is the market maker. Therefore bank M buys the base currency (USD) at the bid ('low') rate of '50', so that bank A, the counterparty, is selling $10m and receiving EURO 8.55m (= $10m × 0.8550 euro/$).

## MARKET MAKING

If you are a market maker you can use the bid–ask spread to help achieve your desired holdings of currencies. For example, suppose the 'big figure' is 0.85 EURO per $ and the average market spread is 06/16. Suppose you are **'square'**, that is happy with the dollar and euro inventory you are holding. You now receive a (telephone) call for a price but you don't know whether it's a buy or sell order, what do you do? You don't really want to deal, so you need to discourage both buyers and sellers. You do this by widening your spread to 04/18. If you are given dollars at 04 you might be able to immediately sell them in the market at 06 (euro per $) making 2 points profit and squaring your position. Alternatively, if you sell dollars at 18 (euro per $) you might be able to buy them back at 16, again locking in a 2 point profit. However, trying to reverse such deals is dangerous since you may not be able to act quickly enough before rates change against you. This is particularly relevant in thin markets where sufficient liquidity may not be available to absorb your reverse trade (at going rates). The greater your fears on these two counts the wider your spread will be.

Consider a different scenario where you would rather be long than short dollars and the current market spread is again 06/16. Again you don't know if the caller wants to buy or sell USDs. To increase the chances of getting a deal where you receive dollars you would **shade the rate upwards** to 10/18. You will therefore pay 10 (euro per $) to buy dollars, which is better than the market rate of 06. But if the caller is actually trying to buy dollars from you then she faces having to pay 18 (euro per $) to you, rather than the market's 16. Hence, overall, she will be less inclined to buy dollars from you and more inclined to sell dollars to you.

## CROSS-RATES

Calculation of cross-rates depends on the way the two currencies are quoted against the dollar. The best way to proceed is to use a simple example.

### CASE A: BASE (UNIT) CURRENCY DIFFERS

Quotes are written base/quoted and are GBP/USD and USD/CHF. Note again that the 'slash' here merely separates 'base' from 'quoted' and 'GBP/USD' would be a quote in terms of 'USD per GBP' (Table 15.1). Suppose we require quotes for the cross-rate CHF per GBP:

[15.1] $$\text{Cross-rate} = \frac{\text{CHF}}{\text{GBP}} = \left(\frac{\text{USD}}{\text{GBP}}\right)\left(\frac{\text{CHF}}{\text{USD}}\right)$$

> **Rule for cross-rates when the base currency is different is 'bid × bid' and 'offer × offer'. You 'multiply down' the columns**

The market maker quoting the above cross-rates therefore effectively 'buys the base currency at the bid rate'. The 'big figure' is 2.9 and therefore the market maker:

- Buys £1 and pays out '797' SFr's.
- Sells £1 and receives '822' SFr's.
- Makes a profit of 25 points (in SFr's) on the bid–ask spread.

### CASE B: BASE (UNIT) CURRENCY THE SAME

Quotes are written base/quoted and we take the Swiss franc and the South African Rand as our required cross-rates (Table 15.2). The dollar quotes are SFr per $ and Rand per $.

*Cross-rates*

[15.2a] $$\text{Cross-rate} = \frac{\text{SFr}}{\text{Rand}} = \left(\frac{\text{SFr}}{\text{USD}}\right)\Big/\left(\frac{\text{Rand}}{\text{USD}}\right)$$

### TABLE 15.1: Cross-rate: base (unit) currency differs

| Spot | Bid | Offer |
|---|---|---|
| **GBP/USD** | 1.9720 | 1.9730 ($/£) |
| **USD/CHF** | 1.5110 | 1.5115 (SFr/$) |
| | | |
| **Cross-rate:** | | |
| **GBP/CHF** | 2.9797 | 2.9822 (SFr/£) |

## TABLE 15.2: Cross-rate: base (unit) currency the same

| Spot | Bid | Offer |
|---|---|---|
| USD/SFr | 1.5110 | 1.5115 (SFr/$) |
| USD/rand | 5.7050 | 5.7065 (Rand/$) |
| Cross-rate: | | |
| SFr/rand | 3.7744 | 3.7766 (Rand/SFr) |
| Rand/SFr | 0.2648 | 0.2649 (SFr/Rand) |

**[15.2b]** $$\text{Cross-rate} = \frac{\text{Rand}}{\text{SFr}} = \left(\frac{\text{Rand}}{\text{USD}}\right) \Big/ \left(\frac{\text{SFr}}{\text{USD}}\right)$$

Consider the cross-rate 0.2648 SFr per rand (**bid**) in Table 15.2. How is this figure arrived at? If market maker-A is quoting this cross-rate to a corporate then the base currency is the rand. Hence, as a market maker bank-A is buying Rand and selling SFr. To fulfil the cross-rate deal bank-A has to go via the USD, hence:

Bank-A must first buy SFr for USDs from market maker bank-B
Bank-A must also sell Rand for USDs to market maker bank-B

It is convenient here to assume that 'B' is the counterparty on both sides of the deal, although in practice it would normally be two *different* market makers. It follows from the above that:

Market maker bank-B must buy the base currency (USD) and sell SFr's at 1.5110 (bid)
and
Market maker bank-B must sell the base currency (USD) and buy Rand at 5.7065 (offer)

Hence the cross-rate is:

1.5110 (bid)/5.7065 (offer) = 0.2648 SFr per Rand (bid)

(SFr/USD)/(Rand/USD)  = (SFr per Rand)

Therefore the figure of 0.2648 SFr per Rand (**bid**) is obtained from:

**[15.3a]** $$\left(\frac{\text{SFr}}{\text{Rand}}\right)_b = \left(\frac{\text{SFr}}{\text{USD}}\right)_b \Big/ \left(\frac{\text{Rand}}{\text{USD}}\right)_o \quad \text{(i.e. 'Cross' bid rate} = \text{bid/offer)}$$

Similarly, the figure 0.2649 SFr per Rand (**offer**) in Table 15.2 is obtained from:

**[15.3b]**     $\left(\dfrac{\text{SFr}}{\text{Rand}}\right)_o = \left(\dfrac{\text{SFr}}{\text{USD}}\right)_o \Big/ \left(\dfrac{\text{Rand}}{\text{USD}}\right)_b$     (i.e. 'Cross' offer rate = offer/bid)

Hence:

0.2649(SFr per Rand offer) = 1.5115 (offer)/5.7050 (bid)

---

**Rule for cross-rates when base currency is the same is therefore, 'divide across' either (a) bid cross-rate = bid/offer or (b) offer cross-rate = offer/bid**

---

Faced with the cross-rate 0.2648/0.2649 SFr/Rand (bid/offer), market maker bank-A:

- Buys the base currency of 1 Rand and pays out 0.2648 SFr's.
- Sells the base currency of 1 Rand and receives 0.2649 SFr's.
- Makes a spread on the round trip of 1 point.

## 15.3  FORWARD RATE AND COVERED INTEREST PARITY

The purpose of this section is to explain the detailed workings of the forward market and its relationship to the spot market. There are two main types of 'deal' on the FX market. The first is the 'spot' rate, which is the exchange rate quoted for immediate delivery of the currency to the buyer (actually the delivery is two working days later). The second is the forward rate, which is the guaranteed price agreed today at which the buyer will take delivery of the currency on a specific future date. For most major currencies, the most liquid forward contracts are in the 1–6 month maturities, although forward deals in some currencies are available for 3 to 5 years ahead. Use of the forward market eliminates risk from possible future changes in the spot exchange rate as the forward rate is agreed today, even though the cash transaction takes place in (say) 1 years time. The market makers in the FX market are mainly the large banks (e.g. Merrill Lynch, Citibank, etc.).

The pricing of a forward contract involves a relationship between the forward rate and three other variables, the spot rate and the money market interest rates in the two countries, and is known as **covered interest parity, CIP**. We shall see that in an efficient market, the quoted forward rate ensures that no riskless arbitrage profits can be made by transacting between the spot currency market, the two money markets and the forward market. Hence, CIP is an equilibrium 'no arbitrage' condition.

The relationship between spot and forward rates can be derived as follows. Assume that a UK Corporate Treasurer has a sum of money £$A$, which he can invest in the UK or the USA for 1 year, after which time the returns must be paid in the domestic currency, sterling. We assume the transaction must have zero market risk (and we also assume zero credit/default risk). For the UK Treasurer to be indifferent as to where the money is invested, it has to be the case that the riskless return from investing in the UK equals the return *in sterling* from investing in the USA. Assume interest rates in the 'domestic' (sterling) money market and the 'foreign' (US) money market and the exchange rates are:

$r_d = 0.11$ (11%)          $r_f = 0.10$ (10%)
$S = 0.666666$ £/$       (equivalent to 1.5 $/£)
$F = 0.67272726$ £/$    (equivalent to 1.486486 $/£)

Note that the forward rate $F$ and the spot rate $S$ are measured as 'domestic per unit of foreign currency', that is £'s per $. We can show that the above figures give equal returns to investing in either the UK or the USA. Also, the two investments involve no (market) risk and therefore the Corporate Treasurer will be indifferent to placing his funds in either the US or the UK—this is **covered interest parity**.

### *Investment Strategy 1: Invest in UK*
In 1 year receive (terminal value)

$$\mathbf{TV_{UK}} = £100(1.11) = \mathbf{£111} = £A(1 + r_d)$$

### *Investment Strategy 2: Invest in US*

(a) Convert £100 to $150 (= £100/0.6666 £/$) in the spot market *today* then
(b) Invest in dollar deposits and dollar receipts at end-year are:

$$\$150(1.10) = \$(A/S)(1 + r_f) = \$165$$

(c) Enter into a forward contract *today* for delivery of sterling in 1 years time and be certain of receiving a terminal value TV (in £'s):

$$\mathbf{TV_{US}} = [(£100/0.6666 \ (£/\$))(1.10)]0.6727 \ (£/\$) = \mathbf{£111}$$

$$= £[(A/S)(1 + r_f)]F$$

All of the above transactions (a)–(c) are undertaken today at known 'prices', hence there is no (market) risk. Since both investment strategies are riskless, arbitrage will ensure that they give the same terminal value:

[**15.4**]          $TV_{UK} = TV_{US}$

$$£A(1 + r_d) = £[(A/S)(1 + r_f)]F$$

Hence, **covered interest parity** can be expressed as:

[**15.5**]        $F/S = (1 + r_d)/(1 + r_f)$

Subtract '1' from each side of equation [15.5]:

[15.6]     $(F - S)/S = (r_d - r_f)/(1 + r_f)$

The above CIP formulae are exact, but if $r_f$ is small (e.g. 0.03) then $(1 + r_f)$ is approximately equal to 1 and we have:

> **Forward premium/discount = interest rate differential**
> $$(F - S)/S \approx (r_d - r_f)$$

In practice, outright forward rates do not usually appear on dealer's screens, but instead the **forward points** are quoted where:

Forward points $= F - S = 0.6727 - 0.6667 = 0.0060$ (+60 points)

Given the forward points of +60 from the dealer's screen, he would quote:

'Outright' forward rate $F = S +$ 'forward points'

$$= 0.6667 + 0.0060 = 0.6727 \ (£/\$)$$

This method of quoting forward rates is discussed further below. Two other rearrangements of the CIP condition are worth mentioning, which are:

[15.7a]     $F = S(1 + CC)$     where   $CC = (r_d - r_f)/(1 + r_f)$

and

[15.7b]     $F = S + \chi$     where   $\chi = S(r_d - r_f)/(1 + r_f)$

CC is known as the *percentage* **cost of forward cover** and $\chi$ is the *dollar* cost of forward cover (both terms are also frequently used in the discussion of FX *futures* contracts—Cuthbertson and Nitzsche, 2001). The cost of forward cover clearly depends on the interest differential between the two countries. The logical sequence is that observed quotes for $r_d$, $r_f$ and $S$ are used to calculate CC or $\chi$ and using equation [15.7] we then obtain the 'no arbitrage' quoted forward rate $F$. Alternatively, once we know $F$ we could then calculate the percent cost of cover as $CC = (F - S)/S$ and the dollar cost of forward cover as $\chi = F - S$. The dollar cost of forward cover is also usually referred to as **forward points** or **swap points**—this is discussed further below. It is easy to check that the above data are consistent with the (exact) algebraic CIP condition of equation [15.6]:

[15.8a]     Interest differential $= (r_d - r_f)/(1 + r_f) = (0.11 - 0.10)/1.10 = 0.0091$ (0.91%)

and

[15.8b]     Forward discount on sterling $= (F - S)/S = 0.0091$ (0.91%)

One further 'trick' to note is that the CIP formula [15.5] looks slightly different if $S$ and $F$

are measured as 'foreign per unit of domestic currency'. However, the following 'rule of thumb' always holds:

> **If $S$ and $F$ are measured as 'currency X *per unit* of currency Y' then in equation [15.5] the interest rates are $r_x$ in the numerator and $r_y$ in the denominator**

For example, if $S$ and $F$ are measured as Swiss francs per US dollar then the CIP condition is:

[15.9]     $$F/S = (1 + r_{SF})/(1 + r_{\$})$$

where $r_{SF}$ and $r_{\$}$ are the Swiss and USD interest rates, respectively. The above equations represent the CIP condition, which is an equilibrium condition based on riskless arbitrage. If CIP doesn't hold then there are forces which will restore equilibrium. For example, if $r_{SF} > r_{\$}$ and $F = S$ then the equality in [15.9] does not hold and arbitrage profits can be made. A US resident would purchase Swiss bills, pushing their price up and their interest rate down. (Alternatively US residents would all want to invest in Swiss franc deposits and the banks would lower their deposit rates.) To purchase the Swiss bills, US residents would have to buy Swiss francs spot and simultaneously sell Swiss francs forward (in return for USDs). Hence spot Swiss francs would appreciate (i.e. $S$ falls) and forward Swiss francs would depreciate (i.e. $F$ rises). These changes would therefore tend to restore equality in [15.9].

## WHAT FORWARD RATE TO QUOTE?

We show below that a Corporate Treasurer can create a 'synthetic forward'. If the *quoted* forward rate does not equal this 'synthetic forward' rate then the bank will be giving the Corporate Treasurer a riskless profit opportunity. Such riskless profits are quickly eliminated (in an efficient market) and this is what determines the equilibrium forward rate in equation [15.5]. We demonstrate this proposition by first considering the cash flows in an **actual** forward contract. We then reproduce these cash flows using 'other assets', that is the money markets in each country and the spot exchange rate: this is the synthetic forward contract. Since the two sets of cash flows are identical, the *actual* forward contract must have a 'value' or 'price' equal to the *synthetic* forward contract. Otherwise riskless arbitrage (e.g. buy low, sell high) is possible.

For example, if you are a UK resident, then you can create a 'sythnetic forward' by:

- borrowing sterling at a cost of $r_{UK}$;
- switching the sterling funds into US dollars in the spot market;
- placing the US dollars on deposit for 1 year in a US account at $r_{US}$.

You have therefore promised to pay out sterling but you will also receive dollars, both at *the end of the year.* This is a *synthetic* forward contract to receive dollars in exchange for sterling (in 1 years time). Let us look at this in more detail.

## CASH FLOWS IN ACTUAL AND SYNTHETIC FORWARD CONTRACT

If the quoted forward rate is $F = 1.50$ ($\$/\pounds$) then the cash flows in the actual forward contract are shown in Figure 15.1. Note that no cash changes hands today. Now let us deal with the 'synthetic'. Suppose money market interest rates and the spot rate are:

$$r_{UK} = 11\% \qquad r_{US} = 10\% \qquad S = 1.513636 \ (\$/\pounds)$$

Now we create cash flows equivalent to those in the actual forward contract. First, 'create' the cash outflow of £100 at $t = 1$, by borrowing $\pounds100/(1 + r_{UK})$ at $t = 0$, and convert this to US dollars in the spot FX market. Place these dollars on deposit in the US at $t = 0$ from which you will receive dollars at $t = 1$. By investing all the borrowed sterling funds in the US, we reproduce a zero net cash flow at $t = 0$ (which mimics that of the actual forward contract). The cash flows for the synthetic forward contract are:

- Borrow $\pounds100/(1 + r_{UK})$       $= \pounds90.09$       at $t = 0$
                                        Pay out £100       at $t = 1$
- Convert to USD $= [100/(1 + r_{UK})]S$       $= \$136.36$       at $t = 0$
- Lend in the US and receive USDs       $= [100/(1 + r_{UK})]S(1 + r_{US})$
                                          $= \$150$       at $t = 1$

---

## FIGURE 15.1: Actual FX forward contract: cash flows

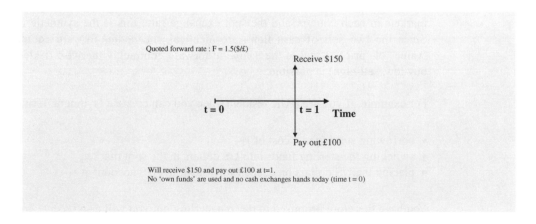

Quoted forward rate : F = 1.5($/£)

Receive $150

t = 0         t = 1   Time

Pay out £100

Will receive $150 and pay out £100 at t=1.
No 'own funds' are used and no cash exchanges hands today (time t = 0)

## FIGURE 15.2: Synthetic FX forward contract

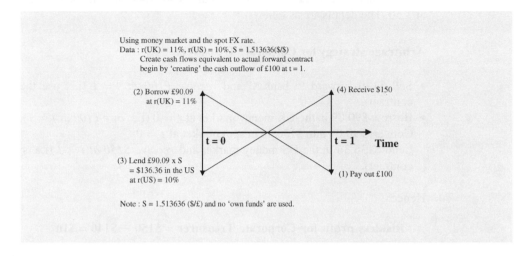

Using money market and the spot FX rate.
Data : r(UK) = 11%, r(US) = 10%, S = 1.513636($/$)
 Create cash flows equivalent to actual forward contract
 begin by 'creating' the cash outflow of £100 at t = 1.

(2) Borrow £90.09
    at r(UK) = 11%

(4) Receive $150

t = 0          t = 1    Time

(3) Lend £90.09 x S
  = $136.36 in the US
  at r(US) = 10%

(1) Pay out £100

Note : S = 1.513636 ($/£) and no 'own funds' are used.

**Synthetic forward rate, *SF*:**

[**15.10**]
$$SF(\$/£) = \frac{\text{receive USD at } t = 1}{\text{pay out GBP at } t = 1} = \frac{\$150}{£100}$$

$$= \frac{\$100}{1 + r_{UK}} \times \frac{S(1 + r_{US})}{£100} = \frac{S(1 + r_{US})}{(1 + r_{UK})}$$

The actual forward rate $F$ must equal this synthetic forward rate $SF$ or riskless arbitrage profits can be made. So, FOREX dealers will calculate and *quote* a forward rate that is equal to $S(1 + r_{US})/(1 + r_{UK})$ to eliminate any arbitrage opportunities.

## POSSIBILITY OF ARBITRAGE PROFITS

If the actual forward quote $F$ by bank-M does not equal the synthetic forward rate $SF$ then a Corporate Treasurer can make riskless arbitrage profits. To demonstrate this possibility suppose the Treasurer is faced with the following data.

***Actual forward quote (from bank M)***:
**$F =$ 1.40 ($/£)**
Here, this implies that the Treasurer *pays out* $140 and *receives* £100 at $t = 1$.

***Synthetic forward (money market)***:
Data: $r_{UK} = 11\%$, $r_{US} = 10\%$, $S = 1.513636$ ($/£)

Hence, we know that the synthetic forward rate (see above) is **$SF = 1.50$ ($/£)**
This implies that the Treasurer can *receive* $150 and has to *pay out* £100 (both at $t = 1$).

Since $SF > F$ (i.e. $1.50 > 1.40$), the Treasurer would sell dollars to bank-M in the actual forward market at a cost of 1.40 and use the synthetic money market route to receive dollars at 1.50. The details are as follows.

**Arbitrage strategy for Corporate Treasurer:**

- Sell $140 forward to bank-M and *receive £100 at $t = 1$* (i.e. use the actual forward contract).
- Borrow £90.09 in the UK money market at $t = 0$ (i.e. *owe £100 at $t = 1$*).
  Convert £90.09 into $136.36 in spot market at $t = 0$.
  Lend $136.36 in the US money market and *receive $150 at $t = 1$* (i.e. synthetic forward contract).

Hence:

**Riskless profit for Corporate Treasurer = \$150 − \$140 = \$10**

As we shall see below, this also means that bank-M which quoted $F = 1.4$ ($/£) will be losing $10 on the deal and would go bankrupt pretty quickly (since the illustrative $10 profit for the Corporate Treasurer is riskless and could easily be $1bn and emulated by other Corporate Treasurers). Given this riskless profit opportunity, everyone (except bank-M!) would try and implement this strategy, but this would result in:

- Buying £'s in the actual forward market which raises $F$ ($/£).
- Borrowing in the sterling money market which raises $r_{UK}$ while lending dollars causes downward pressure on $r_{US}$.
- Buying dollars spot which raises $S$ ($/£), thus lowering $SF$ (see equation [15.10]).

The above scenario tends to raise $F$ and lower $SF$ and hence bring them into equality. Later in this chapter we examine whether such arbitrage opportunities exist in the real world, when we also take into account bid–ask spreads and other transactions costs of creating the synthetic forward. It is sometimes useful to express the CIP condition in linear form by taking logarithms of equation [15.5]:

[15.11]     $f - s = r_d - r_f$

where $f = \ln F$, the logarithm of the forward *price*, and similiarly $s = \ln S$ and we have used the approximation $\ln(1 + r) = r$, where $r$ is measured as a decimal. (Alternatively, equation [15.11] is exact if we use continuously compounded interest rates.)

## BID–ASK SPREAD

The next few sections consider some detailed practical issues concerning the mechanisms of forward quotes such as the bid–ask spread, swap points and FX swaps. They are of interest to those who require an insight into how FX dealers actually operate in the market, but these concepts are not central issues in later chapters and some readers might wish to skip to Section 15.4.

When we derived the forward quote above by *exactly replicating* the cash flows in the actual forward contract we were being a little disingenuous. What is important when a bank gives a customer a forward quote is that the bank can (if it wishes) *exactly offset* the cash flows in the forward deal by using the spot market and the two money markets—then the bank will be perfectly hedged. It is also the case in practice that the bank giving the forward quote to the customer must take into account the bid–ask spread on borrowing and lending money. Let us now incorporate these complexities into a forward quote on the euro against the USD:

$S = 0.85$ (Euro/$)

$r_{US} = 7\ 5/16 - 3/16$   offer–bid (LIBOR–LIBID)

$r_{EU} = 9\ 7/16 - 3/8$   offer–bid

What will be the forward bid–ask quotes and the forward points $F - S$, quoted to a customer if bank H covers its forward deal in the money markets?

## CASE A: FORWARD BID RATE

Bank-H acting as a market maker in the forward market agrees to receive $1 from a customer and sell (i.e. pay out) a certain amount of euros, both at $t = 1$. Hence we are calculating the forward *bid rate* quoted by bank-H. At the outset it is easiest to assume that bank-H covers the deal by hedging in the money markets, although in practice as we see below an FX swap would be used. Bank-H will receive $1 in the forward deal but also needs to pay out euros at $t = 1$ (Figure 15.3a).

To hedge the forward deal, bank-H must 'engineer' cash flows so that it has a zero net postion at '$t = 1$' (i.e. 'be square'). Hence, at $t = 1$ it must generate cash flows which result in paying out $1 at $t = 1$ and receiving euros (Figure 15.3b). Borrowing $1/(1 + r_{US,o})$ at the offer rate $r_{US,o}$ at $t = 0$ implies a cash outflow of $1 at $t = 1$. Bank-H therefore:

(i) borrows $1/(1 + r_{US,o})$ dollars at $t = 0$;
(ii) sells these USDs spot and buys EUROs $= S/(1 + r_{US,o})$;
(iii) lends these euros at the *bid rate*, $r_{EU,b}$.

Bank-H will receive EURO $= [S/(1 + r_{US,o})](1 + r_{EU,b})$ at $t = 1$ (Figure 15.3b). The forward bid rate is therefore:

[15.12a]     $F(\textbf{bid, euros per \$}) = S(1 + r_{EU,b})/(1 + r_{US,o})$

There is a 'rule of thumb' in the above equation, namely if $F$ is the bid rate then the interest rate in the *numerator* on the right is also the bid rate. In practice, if the forward contract was for 90 days and the day count convention is actual/360 then:

$$F(\textbf{bid, euros per \$}) = \frac{0.85[1 + 0.09375(90/360)]}{[1 + 0.073215(90/360)]} = \textbf{0.85428 (euro/\$)}$$

Forward points (**bid**) $= 0.85428 - 0.85000 = \textbf{+428 points}$

## FIGURE 15.3: Calculating bid rate for forward deal

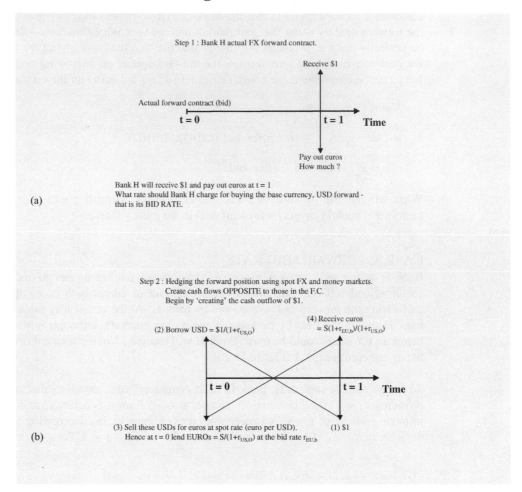

Step 1 : Bank H actual FX forward contract.

Receive $1

Actual forward contract (bid)

t = 0          t = 1     Time

Pay out euros
How much ?

Bank H will receive $1 and pay out euros at t = 1
What rate should Bank H charge for buying the base currency, USD forward -
that is its BID RATE.

(a)

Step 2 : Hedging the forward position using spot FX and money markets.
Create cash flows OPPOSITE to those in the F.C.
Begin by 'creating' the cash outflow of $1.

(4) Receive euros
= $S(1+r_{EU,b})/(1+r_{US,o})$

(2) Borrow USD = $\$1/(1+r_{US,o})$

t = 0          t = 1     Time

(3) Sell these USDs for euros at spot rate (euro per USD).          (1) $1
Hence at t = 0 lend EUROs = $S/(1+r_{US,o})$ at the bid rate $r_{EU,b}$

(b)

It may seem strange that we have not mentioned either the bid or offer rate for $S$, the spot exchange rate. As we see below, this is because in practice the forward position is hedged using an FX swap and this requires only that we always use the same spot rate in the above calculations and usually this is the mid-point spot rate.

## CASE B: FORWARD OFFER RATE

A similar expression can be worked out for the offer rate in the forward contract. Suppose bank-H acts as a market maker in the forward market and agrees to pay out $1 and receive euros in 1 year (Figure 15.4a), then the rate it quotes will be the offer rate. It can hedge its forward position by creating an opposite cash flow at $t = 1$ using the money markets.

## FIGURE 15.4: Calculating offer rate for forward deal

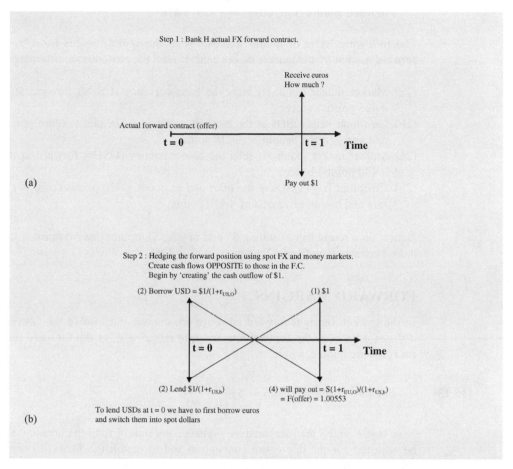

To create a cash inflow of \$1 at $t = 1$ using the money market, bank-H must lend $\$1/(1 + r_{US,b})$ dollars at the *bid rate* (Figure 15.4b). To be able to lend these dollars at $t = 0$ without using any 'own funds', bank-H must borrow euros equal to $S/(1 + r_{US,b})$ at $t = 0$. This loan in euros will incur interest at the offer rate and will involve a cash outflow at $t = 1$ equal to $S(1 + r_{EU,o})/(1 + r_{US,b})$. The hedge therefore implies that bank H will quote a 90-day forward (offer) rate of:

[15.12b]   $F(\textbf{offer, euros per \$}) = S(1 + r_{EU,o})/(1 + r_{US,b})$

$$F(\textbf{offer, euros per \$}) = \frac{0.85[1 + 0.094375(90/360)]}{[1 + 0.071875(90/360)]} = \textbf{0.85470 (euro/\$)}$$

Forward points (**offer**) = 0.85470 − 0.85000 = **+470 points**

Hence the forward points bid–offer quote would be:

**Forward points (bid/offer) = +428/+470**

The following 'rules of thumb' indicate what this quote implies for a 'round trip' on the forward market by the market maker bank-H (and the customer/counterparty):

(1a) Market maker (bank-H) buys the base currency (USDs) forward at the bid rate (of +428 points) hence:

(1b) Customer sells USDs at the bid and receives +428 points (euro per \$) over the spot rate and gets the benefit of +428 points.

(2a) Market maker (bank-H) sells the base currency (USDs) forward at the offer rate (of +470 points) hence:

(2b) Customer buys USDs at the offer and pays out +470 points (euro per \$) over the spot rate and has an extra cost of +470 points.

Hence, on a round trip of selling \$1 and buying \$1 in the forward market, the market maker bank-H makes a profit of 42 points ($= 470 - 428$).

## FORWARD MARGINS

In the market, outright forward rates are not quoted, but instead the convention is that the *difference* between the forward rate and spot rate $F - S$, or the **forward points** or **forward margins** are quoted, where:

[15.13]     $$\text{Forward points} = F - S = S\left[\frac{(r_d - r_f)}{(1 + r_f)}\right]$$

Note that $F$ and $S$ are measured as 'domestic per unit of foreign currency' and $r_d$, $r_f$ have to be adjusted for the day count convention and to match the forward contract period. The forward points would usually be quoted on FX screens for 1, 2, 3, 6 and 12 months and the value dates for the forward contract would coincide with maturity dates for Eurocurrency deposits and loans. The forward points equal $F - S$, but by covered arbitrage this is the same as an interest differential (multiplied by the spot rate). For example, if $r_d = 5\%$ and $r_f = 6\%$ then if you transfer from the domestic to the foreign currency you will earn 1% more interest. Whatever the spot rate, the only way you *cannot* earn a riskless profit is if the forward domestic currency you receive after 1 year is 1% less than the spot domestic currency you gave up at $t = 0$. That is, if $(F - S)/S$ equals $-1\%$. It is the *difference* between the spot and forward rates that is important, rather than the outright spot rate, $S$ (at which the initial exchange of currencies took place). This point becomes important when we discus FX swaps, below.

The 'forward points' are calculated from the RHS of equation [15.13] using $S$, $r_d$, $r_f$. The **outright forward rate** is then calculated as:

[15.14]     $F = S +$ 'quoted forward points'

where the forward points could be positive or negative (depending on whether $r_d$ is greater or less than $r_f$). A further practical complication is that the forward rate calculated from the money market rates will have a bid–ask spread (as noted above) depending on which currency is being borrowed or placed on deposit in the money markets. Because of this, the easiest way to calculate the outright forward rate $F$ from the quoted forward points is to use the following rules of thumb. Below, the spot rates ($/£) and forward points are given as bid/offer (and conventions are based on the 'Reuters 3000 system').

## RULES OF THUMB FOR OUTRIGHT FORWARD RATES

1. Subtract forward points from spot rates if the LHS forward points is numerically greater than the RHS:

   | **Spot** | **2-month forward points** | **outright forward rate** |
   |---|---|---|
   | 1.6000/10 | 0.0120/0.0115 | 1.5880/95 (bid/offer) |

   Hence: 'high/low' (120/115) implies SUBTRACT the forward points.

2. Add the forward points if the RHS margin numerically exceeds the LHS margin:

   | **Spot** | **3-month forward margin** | **outright forward rate** |
   |---|---|---|
   | 1.6000/10 | 0.0180/0.0190 | 1.6180/1.6200 (bid/offer) |

   Hence: 'low/high' (180/190) implies ADD the forward points.

3. A minus sign on the LHS and a plus sign on the RHS of the forward points implies subtract the left-hand forward points and add the right-hand forward points:

   | **Spot** | **2-month forward points** | **outright forward rate** |
   |---|---|---|
   | 1.6000/10 | −0.0002/+0.0003 | 1.5998/1.6013 (bid/offer) |

   Hence: 'minus/plus' implies 'SUBTRACT/ADD'.

An outright 3-month forward deal over the telephone with market maker bank-M on 10th March might go something like the following:

| | |
|---|---|
| **Customer:** | 'What's your 3-month Cable for $10m?' |
| | (Bank M will now check the forward points with the forward trader and also get a quote from the spot desk.) |
| **Bank M:** | 'Rates are 1.6000/1.6010 with forward points 180/190' |
| **Customer:** | 'OK at 1.6200, I sell $10m' |
| **Bank M:** | 'OK at 1.6200, I buy $10m for value date 11th June and sell £6,172,839. 'Thanks, bye' |

Note that the forward points '180/190' follow the 'low/high' of rule 2 above, so we add the forward points to get the outright forward quote. Bank-M is the market maker and therefore 'buys the base (£) at the bid', and simultaneously *sells dollars at the bid*. Hence the market maker *must buy dollars at the offer rate*. So when the customer sells dollars she does so at the offer rate 1.6200 and delivery is on the forward value date of 11th June. (The exact forward value date of 11th June will also coincide with a working day for the expiration of the appropriate Eurocurrency deposits.)

## COVERING A FORWARD TRANSACTION WITH AN FX SWAP

Suppose a bank has agreed to receive USDs, 1-year forward (i.e. for value 12 months forward) at a rate $F = 0.625$ (£/$) (or 1.60 ($/£)). The cash flow for the bank is given in Figure 15.5 and the bank now has an open forward position.

If the dollar strengthens to $S_T = 0.630$ (£/$), that is $S_T > F$, the bank can take the forward dollars and pay $F = 0.625$ (£/$) but can then sell each dollar for say $S_T = 0.630$ (£/$), making a profit. However, if the dollar falls the bank will lose out. How can bank H avoid (hedge) this exchange risk?

First, as we have seen above, bank H could cover its position with a synthetic forward using the spot and money markets. Bank H will receive $10m and pay £6.25m in the forward contract. To be sure of having the sterling it could borrow dollars, switch them into sterling in the spot market and lend for 1 year using a Eurosterling deposit. On maturity these money market sterling receipts are used to pay the forward sterling and the forward USDs received are used to pay off the USD money market loan. However, in practice this strategy has two weaknesses. First, some Eurocurrency markets may not be liquid enough to accommodate large trades without moving the rates. Second, and more important, the money market transactions appear on the balance sheet of the bank and are therefore subject to capital charges for credit risk. To avoid the latter, the bank in practice covers its forward position using an FX swap. (Note that an FX swap is very different from a 'foreign currency swap'— see Cuthbertson and Nitzsche, 2001.) The FX swap keeps the whole of the hedging transaction 'off' the bank's balance sheet.

## FIGURE 15.5: Hedging a forward deal with an FX swap

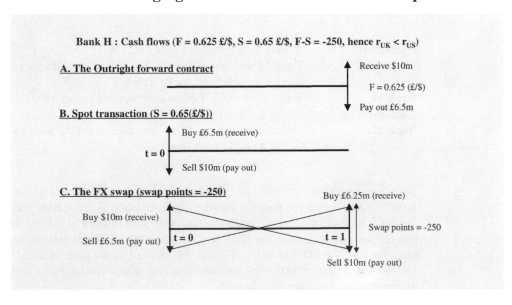

> **DATA FOR FX SWAP**
> $S = 0.6500$ (£/\$)   $F = 0.6250$ (£/\$)
> Forward points $F - S = -250$

It follows from equation [15.13] that $r_{UK} < r_{US}$. Bank H is long \$10m and short £6.25m 'in the 12 months'. It covers (hedges) this position in two stages, using the spot market and an FX swap. In the spot market bank H covers its forward position by selling \$10m spot at $S = 0.6500$ (£/\$) and receives £6.5m spot. It now has £6.5m spot which it could 'carry' for 1 year and deliver against the actual forward contract (Figure 15.5A). But the bank doesn't want to use the money market. Instead it now undertakes an FX swap (Figure 15.5B) which is rather like a repo, except that two currencies are involved and the difference in the buying and selling rates for a currency is equivalent to an implicit interest rate.

> **FX SWAP**
> An agreement **to buy** a fixed amount of currency at an agreed exchange rate and for a fixed value date and ***simultaneously*** **sell** the same amount of currency for a later value date at an agreed exchange rate.
> The **difference between the two exchange rates** in the swap is known as the **swap points** and is the implicit cost of the FX swap

The FX swap is shown in Figure 15.5C. Bank-H has to finance the \$10m sales in the spot market (Figure 15.5B) described above. The first leg of the FX swap involves bank H buying \$10m spot at $S = 0.6500$ (i.e. pays £6.5m). The second leg involves simultaneously selling \$10m at $F = 0.6250$ (£/\$) (i.e. receives £6.25m) for value date in 12 months. The first leg of the swap finances the earlier *spot* sale of USDs and the second leg produces the sterling required at $t = 1$ for the original forward deal. The swap 'carries' the spot sterling over the 'time gap' of 1 year. Note, however, that the swap costs bank-H 250 points since it pays £6.5m spot and receives only £6.25m in 12 months. This is equivalent to the implicit 'interest cost' in the CIP formula:

[15.15]
$$\frac{F - S}{S} = \frac{(r_£ - r_\$)}{(1 + r_\$)}$$

The right-hand side is an interest differential (e.g. % p.a.), hence so is the left-hand side. However 'On the Street', it is the outright forward points $F - S$ rather than the percentage $(F - S)/S$ which is quoted. It is clear from panel B and panel C of Figure 15.5 that hedging the initial forward contract involves no use of own funds at $t = 0$ and hence no change in bank H's balance sheet.

Over the telephone, bank-H who requires the swap on 10th March will deal with bank M, the market maker who facilitates the swap in the following fashion. (The dollar is the base currency and the rates are £ per $.)

| Bank H: | 'What's your forward 12-month Cable, please?' |
| Bank M: | 'We deal 250/245' |
| Bank H: | 'OK, at 250 I buy and sell $10m' |
| Bank M: | 'Fine, I sell $10m for value 12th March at 0.6500 and buy $10m value 12th March *in 1 year* at 0.6250. My sterling to Barclays, London and dollars at maturity to Chase, New York' |
| Bank H: | 'OK, my sterling to Lloyds, London and my dollars at Citibank, New York' |

Note that the value date for the spot leg of the swap at $S = 0.6500$ is in 2 days time on 12th March. In an FX swap, the convention is that the market maker bank M always sells the base currency *spot* and buys the base currency *forward* at the rate on the left (of the 250/245 quote). Alternatively, for the counterparty bank H, the larger figure '250' represents the points it pays and the smaller figure the points it earns. The hedger bank H bought USDs spot at 0.6500, but it is the *swap points* of 250 that are important, and this is established at the outset. Using the bid or offer for the actual spot rate does not affect the cost of the swap, and often the quoted spot rate used will be the mid-point rate.

Finally, from Figure 15.5C, the swap can be seen to be equivalent to one party borrowing a currency (i.e. receiving a currency) for 1 year and simultaneously lending (i.e. paying out) another currency also for 1 year. Because the rates of exchange differ at $t = 0$ and $t = 1$, the FX swap is like a repo and the swap points represent the interest cost. Bank H at $t = 0$ receives USDs which earn a higher interest rate than the sterling that bank H gives, since $r_{UK} < r_{US}$. At $t = 1$ this 'interest rate gain' has to be offset by bank H receiving less sterling (£6.25m) in the forward deal than it gave up at $t = 0$ in the spot deal (i.e. £6.5m). The forward (swap) points $(F - S)$ of $-250$ for bank H are therefore equivalent to the interest differential between the US and UK. To summarise, the sequence of events when bank H hedges its initial *outright forward* deal to receive $10m and pay out £6.25m at $t = 1$ is therefore (see Figure 15.5):

---

**Hedge forward receipts of $10m (and pay out £6.5m) at $t = 1$**
- At $t = 0$, buy £6.5m *spot* sterling at $S = 0.6500$ (£/$) and pay $10m dollars.
- At $t = 0$, use an FX swap to finance the above spot dollar payment (first leg) and carry the sterling forward 12 months (second leg).
- **First leg**: buy $10m spot and sell £6.5m spot.
- **Second leg**: sell $10m and buy £6.25m for a 12-month value date.

---

The above considerations are of crucial importance to FX dealers in the market and even more complex deals are possible. For example, a dealer might wish to execute an FX swap over the coming month and a reverse FX swap over the next year. This enables the dealer to take a speculative position on the change in domestic–foreign interest rate differential over the next month, without using her own capital. This is a forward–forward swap and is rather like an FRA except that it is interest differentials rather than the absolute level of interest rates which are important in the forward–forward swap. The cash transactions in the forward–forward swap net out at $t = 0$, but each separate transaction appears on the balance sheet and attracts capital charges. To avoid the latter the OTC market packages the two back-to-back FX swaps into a **SAFE—synthetic agreement for forward exchange**.

SAFEs come in two main types, the **exchange rate agreement (ERA)** and the **forward exchange agreement (FXA)**. The payoff to an ERA depends only on the *change* in the swap points between two time periods (in the future), which is equivalent to change in the domestic–foreign interest differential. The payoff to an FXA not only depends on the evolution of the swap points, but also on the change in the absolute level of the exchange rate. An ERA would therefore be useful for someone exposed solely to movements in interest rate differentials, while a dealer wishing to hedge a book of FX swaps would use an FXA. Both types of deal are based on a notional principal in the SAFE, and as the payoffs are based on 'differences' there is less credit risk and hence lower capital charges. (For further details on SAFEs see Galitz, 1996.)

The refinements discussed in this section are not particularly important when discussing exchange rates in general. Hence, for the most part, we now dispense with bid–ask spreads and present the remainder of our analysis using a single spot or forward FX rate (e.g. the mid-point quote).

## 15.4 HEDGING AND SPECULATION

### LONG FORWARD HEDGE

Suppose a US importer on 1st April will, in 6 months time (on 1st October), have *to pay* SFr 500,000 (Swiss francs) for imports from Switzerland. She has a liability in Swiss francs and hence is short Swiss francs. The US importer fears a strengthening of the Swiss franc against the US dollar. If the Swiss franc appreciates (i.e. the dollar depreciates) over the next 6 months then she *will have to pay out more dollars* (than at the current spot rate). To hedge this position she takes a long position in a Swiss franc forward contract. If the quoted forward rate for delivery on 1st October is $F_0 = 0.6620$ ($/SFr) then she knows today that she will have to pay $331,000 on 1st October. She has removed the uncertainty. The same principle would apply for a US investor who had other types of Swiss franc liabilities (e.g. had issued bonds or had a bank loan denominated in Swiss francs) and was facing coupon (or bank interest) payments in the future.

### SHORT FORWARD HEDGE

An example of a short hedge using a forward contract requires the US resident to have a long position in the cash market. The latter might arise if on 1st April a US multinational expects *to receive* Swiss franc payments on 1st October either from sales of goods in Switzerland or from Swiss investments. Hence the US multinational is 'long' Swiss francs in the cash market and may fear a fall in the Swiss franc, thus receiving fewer US dollars in the future. The US exporter or investor would hedge by selling Swiss francs in the forward market.

Ex-post, whether it was better to hedge or not depends on the spot rate on 1st October relative to the forward rate $F_0 = 0.6620$ ($/SFr) she has locked into. Suppose the spot rate in October is $S_T = 0.6600$ ($/SFr). With hindsight, for the US importer it would have been better not to have hedged, since she can obtain more Swiss francs per US dollar in the spot market $S_T$ (relative to the forward market $F_0$). But the crucial point here is that the spot rate for October is not known in April. If you choose to hedge then you remove risk, so you forego any potential gains or losses which might accrue if you do not hedge. In Chapter 18 we take up the issue of whether it is optimal to hedge a *portfolio* of foreign assets (e.g. stocks and bonds) using the forward market.

## SPECULATION IN THE FORWARD MARKET

Now consider the US dollar–pound sterling exchange rate. Suppose the current (1st April) quoted forward rate is $F_0 = 1.50$ ($/£) for delivery on 1st October. Suppose on 1st April you believe that the spot rate on 1st October will be $S_T = 1.52$ ($/£). Hence, you believe that sterling will be worth more in the cash market in October than indicated by the current forward rate. If your guess about $S_T$ turns out to be correct then you can make a speculative profit by 'buying low and selling high' (i.e. $F_0 < S_T$):

**Today 1st April**

- Agree to receive £1 forward and to supply (sell) $1.50 on 1st October then:

**1st October**

- In the spot market, pay out £1 and receive $S_T = 1.52$ USDs and also
- receive £1 from the forward deal and pay out $F_0 = 1.50$ USDs.
- Profit $= \$1.52 - \$1.50 = \$0.02$ per £1.

If the principal amount in the transaction is $Q = £100,000$ then:

[**15.16**]     Total $ profit $= \$(S_T - F_0)Q = \$2000$

Note that this is a highly risky transaction since if the spot rate on 1st October is below 1.50 ($/£) then the speculator will make a loss (which could be very large). This is also a levered transaction since the speculator uses none of her own funds on 1st April or on the round trip transaction on 1st October.

## TESTING COVERED INTEREST PARITY

Let us consider whether it is possible, in practice, to earn riskless profits via covered interest arbitrage. In the real world the distinction between bid and offer rates both for interest rates and for forward and spot rates is important when assessing potential profit opportunities. In the strictest definition an arbitrage transaction requires no capital: the agent borrows the funds. Consider a UK investor who borrows £$A$ in the euro–sterling market at an offer rate $r_{£,o}$. At the end of the period the cost in sterling, $C$ will be:

[15.17]     Cost $C = A[1 + r_{£,o}(D/365)]$

where $A$ = amount borrowed (£'s), $C$ = amount owed at the end of the period (£'s), $r_{£,o}$ = offer rate on a Eurosterling loan, $D$ = number of days the funds are borrowed. Now consider the following set of transactions. The investor takes his £$A$ and buys USDs from the market maker at the offer rate, $S_o$ (£/$). He invests these dollars in a Eurodollar deposit which pays the bid rate, $r_{$,b}$. He simultaneously sells the USDs forward at a rate $F_b$ (on the bid side). All these transactions take place instantaneously. The amount of sterling he will receive with certainty at the end of $D$ days is given by:

[15.18]     Sterling receipts $SR = \dfrac{AF_b\lfloor 1 + r_{$,b}(D/360)\rfloor}{S_o}$

Note that day count convention in the US is to define '1 year' as 360 days. The *percentage excess return ER* to investing £$A$ in US assets and switching back into sterling using the forward market is therefore given by:

[15.19]     $ER(£ \rightarrow $) = 100(SR - C)/A$

$$= \left[\frac{F_b}{S_o}(1 + $r_b D/360) - (1 + £r_o D/365)\right] \times 100\%$$

Now look at the covered arbitrage transaction from the point of view of a US resident. She moves out of dollars into sterling assets at the spot rate, invests in the UK and switches back into dollars at the current forward rate. This must be compared with the rate of return she can obtain by investing in dollar denominated assets in the US. A similar formula to that given above ensues and is given by:

[15.20]     $ER($ \rightarrow £) = \left[\frac{S_b}{F_o}(1 + $r_b D/365) - (1 + $r_o D/360)\right] \times 100\%$

Given riskless arbitrage one would expect $ER(£ \rightarrow $)$ and $ER($ \rightarrow £)$ to both equal zero. Covered arbitrage involves no 'price risk', the only risk is credit risk due to failure of the counterparty to provide either the interest income or deliver the forward currency. If we are to adequately test the CIP hypothesis we need to obtain absolutely simultaneous 'dealing' quotes on the spot and forward rates and the two interest rates. There have been many studies looking at possible profitable opportunities due to covered interest arbitrage, but not all use simultaneous dealing rates. However, Taylor (1987, 1989) has looked at the CIP relationship in periods of 'tranquility' and 'turbulence' in the foreign exchange market and he uses simultaneous quotes provided by foreign exchange and money market brokers. We will therefore focus on this study. The rates used by Taylor represent firm offers to buy and sell and as such they ought to represent the best rates (highest bid, lowest offer) available in the market, at any point in time. In contrast, rates quoted on the Reuters screen are normally 'for information only' and may not be actual trading rates. Taylor uses Eurocurrency rates and these have very little credit counterparty risk and therefore differ only in respect of their currency of denomination.

Taylor also considers brokerage fees and recalculates the above returns under the assumption that brokerage fees on Eurocurrency transactions represent about $1/50$ of 1%. For example, the percent interest cost in borrowing Eurodollars taking account of brokerage charges is $r_{\$,o} + 1/50$, while the rate earned on any Eurodollar deposits is reduced by a similar amount $r_{\$,b} - 1/50$. Taylor estimates that brokerage fees on spot and forward transactions are so small that they can be ignored.

In his 1987 study Taylor looked at data collected every 10 minutes on the trading days of 11th, 12th and 13th November 1985. This yielded 3500 potential arbitrage opportunities and he found that after allowing for brokerage costs there were no profitable covered arbitrage opportunities. The results therefore strongly support covered interest parity and the efficient markets hypothesis. In his second study, Taylor (1989) re-examined the same covered interest arbitrage relationships, but this time in periods of 'market turbulence' in the FOREX market. The historic periods chosen were the 1967 devaluation of sterling in November of that year, the 1972 floatation of sterling in June of that year, as well as some periods around the General Elections in both the UK and the US in the 1980s. The covered interest arbitrage returns were calculated for maturities of 1, 2, 3, 6 and 12 months. The general thrust of the results are as follows:

- In periods of 'turbulence' there were some profitable opportunities to be made.
- The size of the profits tends to be smaller in the floating rate period than in the fixed rate period of the 1960s, and became smaller as participants gained experience of floating rates, post-1972.
- The frequency, size and persistence over successive time periods of profitable arbitrage opportunities increase as the time to maturity of the contract is lengthened. That is to say, there tended to be larger and more frequent profit opportunities when considering a 12-month arbitrage transaction than when considering a 1-month covered arbitrage transaction.

Let us take a specific example. In November 1967, £1m arbitraged into dollars would have produced only £473 profit. However, just after the devaluation of sterling (i.e. a period of turbulence) there were sizeable riskless returns of about £4000 and £8000 on riskless arbitrage at the 3-month and 6-month maturities, respectively. Capital controls (on UK sterling outflows) which were in force in the 1960s cannot account for these results, since Eurosterling deposits/loans were not subject to such controls. Clearly the market is not always perfectly efficient, in that riskless profitable opportunities are not immediately arbitraged away. In periods of turbulence, returns are relatively large and sometimes persist over a number of days at the long end of the maturity spectrum, while at the short end of the maturity spectrum profits are much smaller.

The reason for small yet persistent returns over a 1-month horizon may well be due to the fact that the opportunity cost of traders' time is positive. There may not be enough traders in the market who think it is worth their time and effort to take advantage of very small profitable opportunities. Given the constraint of how much time they can devote to one particular segment of the market, they may prefer to investigate and execute trades with larger expected returns, even if the latter are risky (e.g. speculation on the future spot rate by taking positions in specific currencies). It may even be more worthwhile for them to fill in their dealers' pads and communicate with other traders rather than take advantage of very small profitable opportunities.

The riskless returns available at the longer end of the market are quite large and represent a clear violation of market efficiency. Taylor puts forward several hypotheses as to why this may occur, all of which are basically due to limitations on the credit positions dealers can take in the foreign exchange market. Market makers are generally not free to deal in any amount with any counterparty that they choose. Usually the management of a bank will stipulate which other banks it is willing to trade with (i.e. engage in credit risk), together with the maximum size of liabilities which the management of the bank consider it is prudent to have outstanding with any other bank, at any point in time. Hence there is a kind of liquidity constraint on covered arbitrage. Once the credit limit is 'full', no further business can be conducted with that bank (until outstanding liabilities have been unwound). This tends to create a preference for covered arbitrage at the short end of the market, since funds are 'freed up' relatively frequently.

Banks are also often unwilling to allow their foreign exchange dealers to borrow substantial amounts from other banks at long maturities (e.g. 1 year). For example, consider a UK foreign exchange dealer who borrows a large amount of dollars from a New York bank for covered arbitrage transactions over an annual period. If the UK bank wants dollar loans from this same New York bank for its business customers it may be thwarted from doing so because it has reached its credit limits with the New York bank. If so, foreign exchange dealers will retain a certain degree of slackness in their credit limits with other banks, and this may limit covered arbitrage at the longer end of the maturity spectrum.

Another reason for self-imposed credit limits on dealers is that Central Banks often require periodic financial statements from banks, and the Central Bank may consider the short-term gearing position of the commercial bank when assessing its 'soundness'. If foreign exchange dealers have borrowed a large amount of funds for covered arbitrage transactions, this will show up in higher short-term gearing. Taylor also notes that some of the larger banks are willing to pay up to $1/16$ of 1% above the market rate for Eurodollar deposits as long as these are in blocks of over $100m. They do so largely in order to save on the 'transactions costs' of the time and effort of bank staff. Hence Taylor recognises that there may be some mismeasurement in the Eurodollar rates he uses, and hence profitable opportunities may be more or less than found in his study.

Taylor finds relatively large covered arbitrage returns in the fixed exchange rate period of the 1960s, however, in the floating exchange rate period these were far less frequent and much smaller. For example, in Table 15.3 we see that in 1987 there were effectively no profitable opportunities in the 1-month maturities from sterling to dollars. However, at the 1-year maturity there are riskless arbitrage opportunities from dollars into sterling on both the Monday and Tuesday. Here $1m would yield a profit of around $1500 at the 1-year maturity.

Taylor's study does not take account of any differential taxation on interest receipts from domestic and foreign investments, and this may also account for the existence of persistent profitable covered arbitrage at maturities of 1 year. It is unlikely that market participants are

## TABLE 15.3: Covered arbitrage (% excess returns)

| Test date | 1 month | | 6 month | | 1 year | |
|---|---|---|---|---|---|---|
| | $(£ \rightarrow \$)$ | $(\$ \rightarrow £)$ | $(£ \rightarrow \$)$ | $(\$ \rightarrow £)$ | $(£ \rightarrow \$)$ | $(\$ \rightarrow £)$ |
| Monday 8/6/87 (12 noon) | −0.043 | −0.016 | −0.097 | −0.035 | −0.117 | −0.162 |
| Tuesday 9/6/87 (12 noon) | −0.075 | −0.064 | −0.247 | 0.032 | −0.192 | 0.15 |

Source: Taylor, 1989, table 3

influenced by the perceived relative risks of default between say Eurosterling and Eurodollar investments, and hence this is unlikely to account for arbitrage profits even at the 1-year maturities. Note that one cannot adequately test CIP between assets with different risk characteristics (either 'market price risk' or 'credit risk'). For example, studies that compare covered transactions between Eurosterling deposits and US corporate bonds are unlikely to be very informative about market efficiency in the forward market. Hence our overall conclusion is:

> **Riskless arbitrage opportunities in the FOREX market sometimes do appear at relatively long horizons (1 year), but for the most part there are no large persistent profitable opportunities and covered interest parity holds**

# 15.5 UNCOVERED INTEREST PARITY

We can repeat our analysis whereby the UK Corporate Treasurer is considering whether to invest in the UK or the US for 1 year, but this time we assume the Treasurer is willing to take a guess on the exchange rate that will prevail in 1 years time, $S_{t+1}^e$ (domestic per unit of foreign, i.e. £/$) when she converts her dollar investments back into sterling. The UK Treasurer is therefore undertaking a *speculative* spot transaction since she does not know what the exchange rate will be in 1 years time. What is the relationship between the spot rate today, the expected spot rate in 1 years time and the two money market interest rates that will just make the Treasurer indifferent as to which country the money is invested? If the Corporate Treasurer is **risk neutral**, she is concerned only with the *expected* return from the two alternative investments and she will continue to invest in the US rather than the UK until *expected returns* are equalised:

[15.21]     $S_{t+1}^e / S_t = (1 + r_{d,t})/(1 + r_{f,t})$

This is the **uncovered interest parity condition (UIP)** which can also be written:

**[15.22a]** $$\frac{(S_{t+1}^e - S_t)}{S_t} = \frac{r_{d,t} - r_{f,t}}{(1 + r_{f,t})}$$

or

**[15.22b]** $$\frac{(S_{t+1}^e - S_t)}{S_t} \approx r_{d,t} - r_{f,t}$$

> *Expected depreciation* of domestic currency = *interest differential* (in favour of the domestic currency)

Equation [15.22b] holds as an approximation if $r_f$ is small and hence $1/(1 + r_f) \approx 1$. The Corporate Treasurer knows that she is making a risky investment decision because the value of the exchange rate in 1 years time is uncertain. However, UIP assumes she ignores this risk when undertaking her portfolio allocation decision. The UIP relationship is the condition for equilibrium on the capital account under the assumption of risk neutrality. Note that the only 'algebraic difference' between the UIP and CIP condition is that for UIP $S_{t+1}^e$ 'replaces' the forward rate $F$ used in the CIP relationship—this is because the same sequence of transactions is involved, except one uses the forward market to remove risk and the other takes a speculative guess as to the future spot rate.

You may remember in Chapter 2 we talked about how the Monetary Policy Committee (MPC) of the Bank of England determines a path for the exchange rate, when it is working out the likely impact of its interest rate decisions on the exchange rate (and hence on future inflation). For its baseline case, the MPC assumes that the future course of the exchange rate is set according to UIP. Suppose that the MPC is contemplating raising UK interest rates by 1% above foreign interest rate, and it believes this is also the view of market participants (i.e. the rise in interest rates is *anticipated*). UIP then implies that the exchange rate will fall by around 1% over the coming year, and this is the assumed future path the MPC will use in its projections for future inflation. This depreciation in the exchange rate will imply a contribution to higher inflation of 1% over the next 3 years or so—see Section 15.6 and Chapter 16.

Let us examine the UIP condition in a little more detail. Suppose interest rates in the UK and US are both currently 10%. Assume now that the MPC of the Bank of England announces an *unexpected* 2% rise in UK interest rates. There is now a 2% interest differential in favour of the UK. If FX dealers believed that the spot rate for sterling would remain constant (i.e. zero expected depreciation of sterling) over the coming year, then they would all want to invest in UK assets. This is because they get a 2% higher rate than in the US and this translates into an *expected* 2% higher rate *in dollars* at the end of the year. Hence UIP does not at present hold, and there would be many US dealers buying spot sterling (and selling spot dollars). This demand for spot sterling would cause sterling to appreciate *today*. This might be exactly the result the MPC wants if it is trying to reduce inflation, since the higher UK interest rate will reduce domestic demand and the higher exchange rate will in time reduce UK exports, both of which put downward pressure on UK prices (see Chapter 2).

How high will spot sterling rise? Well, the only thing that will stop US dealers buying spot sterling is if they think they will lose *dollar payments by the end of the year* on their UK investments. If spot sterling *today* rises so high that FX dealers believe that *in the future* it can only fall, their sterling investments, when converted into dollars at the *end-year* spot rate, will be worth less dollars. If spot sterling today has risen so high that US dealers expect that over the coming year sterling will fall by 2%, this will just wipe out their extra 2% sterling interest payments when they are converted into dollars. Now UIP has been restored.

Note the paradox here. For UIP to hold then spot sterling *today* must *rise*, so that dealers *expect a fall* (depreciation) of sterling in the future. All in all, if there is a 2% interest differential in favour of the UK then this implies that FX dealers believe that sterling will depreciate by 2% over the coming year. Of course, this is nothing more than FX dealers' 'best guess' of what will happen. What will actually happen to the spot FX rate over the coming year will depend on a whole host of economic factors that may affect interest rates in the two countries over the year ahead (e.g. fiscal policy, direct investment flows). What is important here is expectations. It is obvious that if UIP does *not* hold, then there is an incentive for speculators to switch funds between countries. But if the latter happens very quickly (or the threat of it happening is prevalent) *and if speculators are risk neutral*, then UIP will be maintained at all times.

Note that the UIP condition assumes that the market is *dominated* (at the margin) by risk neutral speculators. Put another way, it is assumed that neither *risk averse* 'rational speculators' nor 'irrational' **noise traders** (who follow 'fads and fashion' and may induce herding behaviour) influence movements in the spot rate. We certainly cannot rule out that at certain times such noise traders may have an influence on the exchange rate and hence create additional uncertainty (risk) for the 'rational traders', particularly in 'crisis periods'. If so any 'central projection' for the future path of the exchange rate by the monetary authorities is likely to be extremely uncertain, thus complicating their efforts to set an appropriate interest rate to achieve their inflation target. In the presence of noise traders, the expected change in the exchange rate can be viewed as a weighted average of the behaviour of the rational UIP traders and the noise traders:

[15.23]    Expected change in the exchange rate $= w_C(r_d - r_f) + w_{NT} NT$

where $w_{NT} = 1 - w_C$ is the relative influence of the noise traders on the change in the exchange rate. The difficulty lies in modelling '$NT$', the influence of the noise traders. Models of noise trader behaviour in the FX market are discussed in the next chapter.

## SOME VARIANTS

We can express UIP in a linear form by taking logarithms of equation [15.21]:

[15.24]    $s_{t+1}^e - s_t = r_{d,t} - r_{f,t}$

where $s_{t+1} = \ln S_{t+1}$ and if $r_{d,t}$ and $r_{f,t}$ are continuously compounded rates then the relationship is exact. (If interest rates are measured as discrete rates then equation [15.24] is an approximation.) We could of course relax the risk neutrality assumption by invoking the CAPM. For the UK Treasurer the risk free rate is $r_d$ and the expected return on the 'round trip' risky investment in the US capital market is:

[15.25]     $1 + E_t R_{t+1} = E_t S_{t+1}^e (1 + r_{f,t})/S_t$

The CAPM predicts:

[15.26]     $E_t R_{t+1} - r_t = \beta_i (E_t R_{t+1}^m - r_t)$

where $\beta$ is the beta of the foreign investment, which depends on the covariance between the (world) market portfolio and the UK portfolio. $(E_t R_{t+1}^m - r_t)$ is the expected return on the 'world' portfolio of assets held in all the different currencies and assets. The RHS of equation [15.26] is a measure of the risk premium as given by the CAPM. Relationships like [15.26] are known as the International CAPM (see Cuthbertson and Nitzsche, 2001). For the moment notice that in the context of UIP and the CAPM, if we assume $\beta_i = 0$, then the above equation reduces to UIP.

# 15.6 PURCHASING POWER PARITY

Purchasing power parity PPP is an equilibrium condition in the market for tradeable goods and forms a basic building block for several models of the exchange rate based on economic fundamentals. It is a 'goods arbitrage' relationship. For example, if applied solely to the US economy it implies that a 'Lincoln Continental' should sell for the same price in New York City as in Washington, DC (ignoring transport costs between the two cities). If prices are lower in New York then demand would be relatively high in New York and low in Washington, DC. This would cause prices to rise in New York and fall in Washington, DC, hence equalising prices. In fact, the threat of switch in demand would be sufficient for well-informed traders to make sure that prices in the two cities were equal. PPP applies the same arbitrage argument across countries. The only difference being that one must convert one of the prices to a 'common currency' for comparative purposes.

If domestic tradeable goods are perfect substitutes for foreign goods and the goods market is 'perfect' (i.e. there are low transactions costs, perfect information, perfectly flexible prices, no artificial or government restrictions on trading, etc.), then 'middlemen' or arbitrageurs will act to ensure that the price is equalised in a common currency.

---

**PURCHASING POWER PARITY (PPP)**

Implies:

- Same prices in a common currency.
- Price competitiveness (or the 'real exchange rate') is constant.
- Equilibrium on the current account of the balance of payments.

---

The final condition, 'equilibrium on the current account' refers to the contribution to trade flows due to the effect of relative prices. Imports are also influenced by the level of domestic demand (GDP) and exports by the level of world trade. These two variables can lead to changes in the current account independent of relative prices. For industrial economies, if domestic demand and world trade grow at the same rate, then one might expect their effect on imports and exports to broadly cancel out. Algebraically PPP can be expressed as:

[15.27]     $S = P_d/P_f$

where $S$ = exchange rate (domestic per unit of foreign currency), $P_d$ = domestic price index, $P_f$ = foreign price index. In logarithms:

[15.28]     $s = p_d - p_f$

To show that PPP implies the same price in a common currency, consider the following simple example, where the UK is the 'domestic' country and $S$ is defined as ($£/\$$). We take $P_f = \$200$ (e.g. Sak's Hamper) and the spot rate $S = 0.5$ $£/\$$ (or $\$2$ per $£$). Hence the UK import price of a Sak's Hamper is £100 (= $P_f S = \$200 \times 0.5$ $£/\$$). If PPP holds then the price of a Harrods' Hamper $P_d$ will also *be set equal to the price of the Sak's Hamper at* £100, that is:

[15.29]     $P_d = P_f S$

If the price of the Harrods' Hamper $P_d$ was higher than $P_f S$, then Harrods would be priced out of the 'hamper market'. Alternatively, if Harrods sold at a price lower than $SP_f$ they would be losing profits, since they believe they can (eventually) sell all they put on display, at a price just equal to the imported Sak's Hamper. This is the usual perfect competition assumption, here applied to domestic and foreign firms. Absolute equality of prices is known as the **strong form of PPP**.

How does goods arbitrage restore PPP? For example, if $P_d$ rose to £110 then the equality in [15.29] would not hold. However, a UK resident would now want to purchase the cheaper Sak's Hamper. The subsequent purchase of spot dollars would lead to an appreciation of the dollar. Also, the increased demand for Sak's Hampers and the reduced demand for Harrods' Hampers would raise $P_f$ and lower $P_d$. All of these changes would tend to restore price competitiveness and equalise prices in a common currency (thus restoring the equality in [15.29]).

If goods arbitrage were the only factor influencing the exchange rate then the exchange rate *should always* obey PPP. Let us define the 'PPP exchange rate' as:

[15.30]     $S_{ppp} = P_d/P_f$     (or in logs: $s_{ppp} = p_d - p_f$)

We can think of the above equation as giving us the value for the exchange rate that will just preserve price competitiveness (i.e. the same price for a Harrods' Hamper as for a Sak's Hamper). For example, if a Harrods' Hamper cost £100 in London and a Sak's Hamper cost $\$200$ in New York, then $S_{ppp} = £100/\$200 = 0.5$ $£/\$$. The *actual* exchange rate $S$ that would just make you indifferent as to which (identical) hamper you puchased would be $\$2$ per $£$ (or equivalently $S = 0.5$ $£/\$$). If the actual exchange rate $S$ does not equal the PPP exchange rate then one of the currencies will be either over or undervalued and the price of each of the hampers will be different in a common currency. Again suppose $P_d = £100$ and $P_{US} = \$200$ so that $S_{ppp} = £100/\$200 = 0.5\ £/\$$. If the actual spot rate is $S = 0.55\ £/\$$ then the pound is undervalued since you can get more pounds per dollar than is warranted by the relative prices of 0.5. A US resident can take \$200, the price of a Sak's Hamper, and exchange it for £110 $(= \$200 \times 0.55\ \$/£)$, which will enable her to purchase more than one (identical) Harrods' Hamper.

Now the 'strong form' might not hold because of transport costs or slight mismeasurement of the price of the 'identical' basket of goods in each country. There might be a fixed 'gap' between the sterling import price of US goods (i.e. Sak's Hamper) and the UK pound sterling price of an equivalent 'basket' (e.g. Harrods' Hamper). However, if this 'gap' remains fixed over time then PPP (in equation [15.30]) implies that the *inflation rate* of the Harrods' Hamper will equal that of the Sak's Hamper (expressed in terms of its sterling import price). Hence, in general, for the 'basket' of all tradeable goods we might expect that over a run of years:

> **% Inflation of UK tradeable goods = % US inflation rate + % depreciation of pound sterling**

This is the so-called **weak form of PPP**, which algebraically is:

[15.31] $\qquad \dot{P}_{UK} = \dot{S} + \dot{P}_{US}$

where the 'dot' indicates a percentage change in the variable. In logarithms this becomes:

[15.32] $\qquad \Delta p_{UK} = \Delta s + \Delta p_{US}$

where $p_{UK} = \ln P_{UK}$, etc. PPP may also be viewed as an equilibrium condition for the current account of the balance of payments (for given levels of domestic demand and world trade). This is simply because if PPP holds over time then it means that there are no profitable opportunities for domestic residents to switch demand from tradeable goods of the foreign country (i.e. imports) to domestically produced substitutes (or vice versa). Hence, the current account (or more accurately the visible trade account) should remain in balance. So, if export receipts initially equalled import payments and the weak form of PPP holds, then the current account should remain in balance (assuming no net effects from world trade growth on exports and the growth of domestic output on imports).

The *real exchange rate* is an alternative way of representing the PPP condition and hence price competitiveness. For example, stylistically:

> **REAL EXCHANGE RATE**
> **= £ price of Sak's Hamper/£ price of Harrods'**
> **Hamper = $(S\ P_{US})/P_{UK}$**

If the real exchange rate remains constant then you are neither gaining nor losing price competitiveness. It follows from the definition of the real exchange rate that if PPP holds then the real exchange rate or price competitiveness remains constant.

There is no causality implied by the PPP relationship per se. Any one of the three variables can be considered as the 'left-hand side' variable. PPP is a relationship which must hold if price competitiveness is to be maintained, but any (or all) of the three variables can change to bring about this equality. Often, however, the PPP condition is used to analyse changes in the exchange rate. If PPP holds then the exchange rate should be determined by relative inflation rates:

> **% Depreciation of £ = % UK inflation rate − % US inflation rate**

Hence movements in the exchange rate would *immediately* reflect differential rates of inflation and the latter is often found to be the case in countries suffering from hyperinflation (e.g. some Latin American countries in the 1980s, economies in transition in Eastern Europe and Russia in the 1990s). In contrast, one might expect goods arbitrage to work rather imperfectly in moderate inflationary periods in complex industrial economies with a wide variety of heterogeneous tradeable goods. Hence PPP may hold only in the very long run in such economies.

There have been a vast number of empirical tests of PPP, but only recent ones use the 'latest' statistical technique (e.g. cointegration using panel data). We do not have time to examine these studies in detail, but refer the reader to a recent comprehensive study by Ardeni and Lubian (1991) who examine PPP for a wide range of currencies of industrialised nations (e.g. USA, Canada, UK, France, Italy). They find no evidence that relative prices and the exchange rate are 'linked' when using monthly data over the post-1945 period. However, for annual data over the longer time span of 1878–1985 they do find that PPP holds, although deviations from PPP (i.e. changes in the real exchange rate) can persist for considerable time. Hence if we were to plot the PPP exchange rate $S_{ppp,t}$ against the actual exchange rate $S_t$—see equation [15.30]—then although there is some evidence that $S_t$ and $S_{ppp,t}$ move together in the long run (for most currencies), nevertheless they can also deviate substantially from each other over a number of years. It follows that the real exchange rate (i.e. price competitiveness) is far from constant over time spans of several years.

This can clearly be seen in Figure 15.6, where we plot $S_{ppp} = P_{US}/P_{UK}$, the PPP exchange rate against the actual USD–sterling spot rate $S$ (USD per £). For example, if we assume (not unreasonably) that just before 1979 the UK was price competitive against the USD, so that $S_{ppp} = S = 2$ ($/£). In 1979 the then Prime Minister, Margaret Thatcher embarked on a 'tight' monetary policy and raised UK interest rates from 12% to 15%. Over the next few years there was a massive appreciation in the actual exchange rate by over 30%, while the PPP exchange rate (i.e. relative prices) remained largely unchanged. This resulted in a loss of UK competitiveness, a fall in exports and a rise in unemployment. By 1982/3 competitiveness was back at its 1979 level (i.e. $S_{ppp} = S$) but it looks as if there was exchange rate

## FIGURE 15.6: Actual and PPP exchange rate

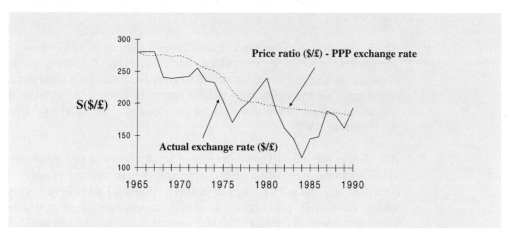

'overshooting' between 1979 and 1981—an issue we take up in the next chapter. What is clearly obvious from Figure 15.6 is that with a freely floating exchange rate there can be large movements in the nominal and real exchange rate, and hence in price competitiveness.

The evidence found by Ardeni and Lubian (1991) reflects the difficulties in testing for long run equilibrium relationships in aggregate economic time series, even with a very long span of data, given measurement problems in forming a 'representative' index of tradeable goods. One's view might therefore be that the forces tending to produce PPP are rather weak, although in the very long term there is a tendency for PPP to hold (see Grilli and Kaminsky, 1991; Fisher and Park, 1991). The very long run here could be 5–10 years. Another somewhat lighthearted way of looking at PPP is *The Economist's* BigMac Index (see Box 15.2).

Box 15.2    BigMac INDEX

A lighthearted suggestion by *The Economist* magazine is that rather than using aggregate price indices (e.g. RPI, CPI) we might examine PPP by looking at the price of a BigMac in different countries. Some of you might remember the minimal research on this topic carried out by Vincent Vega at the beginning of Quentin Tarrantino's film *Pulp Fiction,* where Vincent was explaining to his partner Jules the differences between a BigMac in the USA and in Amsterdam.

Each BigMac is in a sense a homogeneous basket of goods (e.g. bun, meat, ketchup, girkin), produced locally in about 70 countries. There are no acute measurement problems here, a BigMac is a BigMac wherever you purchase it. In contrast, aggregate price indices cover a whole host of 'goods and services' which may not be perceived as being equivalent in different countries (e.g. a restaurant meal in China, the USA and France).

*The Economist's* BigMac Index demonstrates the strengths and weaknesses of the PPP approach to measuring 'overvalued' and 'undervalued' currencies (so vital when choosing an appropriate rate at which to enter the ERM, or a common currency such as the euro, for example). How are the figures in Table B15.1 related? If you were a US citizen, where would you visit for an 'expensive' and a 'cheap' BigMac? Do the figures refute PPP?

Bill Clinton was a well-known devotee of hamburgers and as a result, after a gruelling election campaign, he was a little overweight when he became President in 1992. (The American term for a lover of junk food is a 'Bubba', I do believe.) So let us examine where 'Bubba Bill' could obtain a value for money hamburger or whether hamburger prices in a common currency in 1992 were the same around the world. First, take the UK relative to the US. Calculate the BigMac PPP-exchange rate and compare it with the actual exchange rate $(S, £/\$)$:

PPP exchange rate $S_{ppp} = £P/\$P = £1.74/\$2.19$     $= \mathbf{0.79}$ $(£/\$)$
Actual exchange rate $S$     $= \mathbf{0.57}$ $(£/\$)$
Percentage difference $= (0.57 - 0.79)/0.79$     $= \mathbf{-28}$

## TABLE B15.1: The BigMac Index 1992

| Country | Price in local currency | Implied PPP of the dollar | Actual exchange rate (10.04.92) foreign currency per $ | % Over (+) or under (−) valuation of $ |
|---------|------------------------|---------------------------|-------------------------------------------------------|----------------------------------------|
| Canada | Can $2.76 | 1.26 | 1.19 | − 6 |
| China | Yuan 6.30 | 2.88 | 5.44 | + 89 |
| Germany | DM 4.50 | 2.05 | 1.64 | − 20 |
| Hong Kong | HK $8.90 | 4.06 | 7.73 | + 91 |
| Ireland | I £1.45 | 0.66 | 0.61 | − 8 |
| Russia | Rouble 58 | 26.48 | 98.95 | + 273 |
| Singapore | S $4.75 | 2.17 | 1.65 | − 24 |
| UK | £1.74 | 0.79 | 0.57 | − 28 |
| USA | $2.19 | – | – | – |

Source: 'BigMac Currencies', *The Economist*, 18th April 1992, p. 81. © The Economist Newpaper Limited, London. Reproduced with permission

Thus, the sterling price of a BigMac is 0.79 of the USD price. If you are Bill Clinton and you could get more than 0.79 £'s for every $, then you would buy your BigMac in the UK (as it would be cheaper than buying it in the US). Unfortunately, you only get $S = 0.57$ £'s per $ so it's cheaper for Bill Clinton to buy his BigMac in the US.

Looked at another way, for a 'Piccadilly Circus BigMac' Bill Clinton would have to pay £1.74/0.57 (£/$) = $3.05. So instead he will send for a take-out from Georgetown costing $2.19. Actually, if Bill Clinton had really wanted to save money (see Table B15.1) he should have got Boris Yeltsin to send over a cruise missile, replacing the nuclear warhead with BigMacs from Moscow. (We are ignoring transport costs here.)

Of course there are problems in using the BigMac Index as a measure of competitiveness. Transport costs, differences in sales taxes, possible subsidies to cattle farmers and possible differences in profit margins in different countries. Also, one major problem with Table B15.1 is that it is a 'snapshot' at a point in time. Maybe *over time* the two prices and the exchange rate will move towards equality. Then PPP would hold and Bill Clinton would pay the same price (in USD) for his BigMac wherever he happens to take his holidays (after standing down as President in 2000). So, the reader might like to look at a recent issue of *The Economist* to see whether certain countries in Table B15.1 have come closer to equalising their BigMac prices.

The above empirical results, where it takes a long time to restore price competitiveness, can be explained not only by 'goods arbitrage' but by assuming PPP is ultimately re-established via the wage–price mechanism. We show in Appendix 15.1 that a rise in foreign (import) prices or a depreciation of the domestic currency raises production costs for the domestic industry and hence domestic prices and wages. The resulting equation, which explains domestic inflation over the long term (i.e. averaged over several years) is:

[15.33]
$$\Delta p = \frac{b_1}{1 - b_1}[f + b_1(\chi_w - \chi_p) + a_2(y - \bar{y})] + \Delta(pm + s)$$

where $p = \ln P$, the logarithm of the domestic aggregate price level (e.g. consumer price index, CPI); $w = \ln W$, the logarithm of aggregate wage index; $pm = \ln PM$, the logarithm of import prices measured in foreign currency; $(y - \bar{y}) = $ the deviation of output from its natural (or trend) rate; $f = $ exogenous 'wage push' factors; $\chi_w = $ exogenous growth in real wages and $\chi_p$ is the growth in labour productivity. It follows that PPP will hold if:

[15.34]
$$[b_1(\chi_w - \chi_p) + f + a_2(y - \bar{y})] = 0$$

Hence PPP holds when output is at its natural rate and 'wage push' factors are zero and when real wages grow at the rate of labour productivity. One can see that the factors in equation [15.34] involve rather complex, slowly varying long-term economic and socio-political forces, and this may account for the fact that PPP will only hold approximately even over a long time horizon (e.g. 5–10 years).

## 15.7 INTERRELATIONSHIPS BETWEEN CIP, UIP AND PPP

### FORWARD RATE UNBIASEDNESS

The CIP and UIP relationships are:

$$F/S = (1 + r_d)/(1 + r_f) \quad \text{and} \quad S^e_{t+1}/S_t = (1 + r_{d,t})/(1 + r_{f,t})$$

Hence, if CIP and UIP hold simultaneously, this implies that the forward rate is an unbiased predictor of the future spot rate, that is $F = S^e_{t+1}$. We refer to the latter condition as the **forward rate unbiasedness, FRU**. From the above (using logarithms):

[**15.35**]     $f_t = E_t s_{t+1}$

Note that unbiasedness holds regardless of the expectations formation process for $E_t s_{t+1}$ but it does require risk neutrality (so that UIP holds). However, for the market to be informationally efficient, agents must use all avaliable information in forecasting $E_t s_{t+1}$ in the UIP relationship, and hence we need to assume rational expectations, RE. If any two of the relationships from the set UIP, CIP and FRU are true then the third will also be true.

We could have started directly with the FRU relationship. Under risk neutrality, if equation [15.35] did not hold there would be (risky) profitable opportunities available by speculating in the forward market. In an efficient market (with risk neutrality) such profits should be instantaneously eliminated, so that equation [15.35] holds at all times. Tests of the FRU condition usually assume RE, so that the forecast error for the future spot rate $\varepsilon_{t+1}$ is zero on average (and independent of any information available at time $t$):

**Forecast error = actual spot rate − forecast of the spot rate**

[**15.36**]     $\varepsilon_{t+1} = s_{t+1} - E_t s_{t+1}$

Hence equation [15.35] becomes:

[**15.37**]     $s_{t+1} = f_t + \varepsilon_{t+1}$

Initial tests of the FRU condition consisted of a regression of $s_{t+1}$ on $f_t$ where we expect the intercept in this regression to be zero and the slope coeffficient to be unity. Unfortunately, even though these tests appeared to support FRU it was later found that there were statistical problems with the test (because the spot and forward rates are random walks and hence have a 'unit root'—see Cuthbertson, 1996). To get round this statistical problem we subtract $s_t$ from both sides of equation [15.37] so an equivalent form of the FRU condition is:

[**15.38**]     $s_{t+1} - s_t = f_t - s_t$

---

**Change in the spot rate = forward premium/discount**

---

When this regression is run for almost any pair of bilateral exchange rates it is found that the regression coefficient on the forward premium is closer to *minus one* than the theoretically expected value of *plus one.* This implies that there is something amiss with either the CIP or UIP condition. Given our observation that CIP holds, then it is the UIP condition that appears to be at fault. Either all FX market players do not use RE (i.e. they make systematic under or overpredictions of the future spot rate) or there is a time varying risk premium which 'breaks' the risk neutrality assumption implicit in the UIP condition. However, there is one further explanation of why FRU is empirically refuted, yet the EMH and RE still hold. This is the Peso problem (already discussed as an explanation of excess volatility in stock prices, in Chapter 13).

## PESO PROBLEM

You may recall that the Peso problem leads the researcher to measure expectations incorrectly, hence forecasts may appear biased. The Peso problem original arose from the behaviour of the Mexican peso in the mid-1970s. Although the peso was on a notionally fixed exchange rate against the US dollar, it traded consistently at a forward discount for many years, in anticipation of a devaluation, which did not actually occur until as late as 1976. So, was it the case that FX traders made systematic forecast errors every day over several years? Prima facie, the fact that the forward rate for the peso was persistently below the out-turn value for the spot rate implies persistent profitable arbitrage opportunities for risk neutral speculators.

The Peso problem arises from the fact that there could be unobservable events which *may* occur in the future, but in our *sample of data* never actually do occur. It is therefore a 'small sample problem'. Suppose we had a longer data set which included a period when the Mexican Government announced a fixed exchange rate but that agents then believed this announced rate might be abandoned in favour of a *revaluation* of the peso. Hence with a long enough data set where 'unfavourable' and 'favourable' unobserved 'regimes' occur, our data set would conform to the rational expectations postulate of unbiased forecast errors, on average. (Afficionados of RE will note that even with this extended data set the forecast errors are autocorrelated, so the RE assumption is still invalid.) One way to circumvent the Peso problem when investigating FRU is to use accurate **survey data** on expectations to measure $E_t s_{t+1}$ and hence to test whether $E_t s_{t+1} = f_t$. However, in practice, analysing survey data has its own problems.

It is possible that Peso problems are fairly prevalent in any actual data set we have, because of the frequency of possible 'regime changes' in a world where the future is not always like the past (with some random noise) regime switching technique. So far, researchers who have tried to take account of the Peso problems in FX data have found that FRU is still refuted (Evans, 1997). Research has now moved away from 'rational expectations' to models where agents learn slowly about regime changes. Also, agents are not assumed to be 'optimising' all the time, but they look for some 'robust' rules of thumb that can minimise adverse outcomes if the 'regime' turns out to be different from the one they anticipated (see Chapters 16 and 17 for further details). There has been a lot of 'academic blood' spilled over the FRU issue, and it is still not resolved. (For other reasons why the FRU condition might break down, see Cuthbertson, 1996.)

### REAL INTEREST PARITY: INTERNATIONAL FISHER EFFECT

If both UIP *and* the weak form of PPP hold then:

[15.39a] $\qquad \Delta s^e_{t+1} = s^e_{t+1} - s_t = (r_d - r_f)_t$

[15.39b] $\qquad \Delta s^e_{t+1} = (\Delta p^e_d - \Delta p^{*e}_f)_{t+1}$

It follows that:

[15.40] $\qquad r_{d,t} - \Delta p^e_{d,t+1} = r_{f,t} - \Delta p^e_{f,t+1}$

---

**INTERNATIONAL FISHER EFFECT**
**PPP + UIP $\Rightarrow$ real interest rate parity (RIP) $\Rightarrow$**
**Expected real return in domestic economy = expected real**
**return in foreign economy**

---

The RIP condition also goes under the name of the International Fisher Hypothesis. It implies that capital flows (e.g. direct investment in land and buildings and in takeovers of domestic firms by foreign firms) will be from those countries with a low expected real return (i.e. high cost countries) to those with high real returns (i.e. low cost countries). This process will tend to push up inflation in the recipient countries (and lower inflation in those countries with a capital outflow). Hence one might expect real interest rate parity to come about, but only very slowly. If there is changing 'political and economic risk' to international investment (e.g. a fear that the 'foreign' government may nationalise or financially penalise multinationals in their countries, or undertake deflationary economic policy measures) then the international Fisher effect will at best provide a crude approximation. In short, we might expect real interest rate convergence only between reasonably homogeneous 'developed capitalist countries' that are relatively free of large changes in political and economic risk.

Let's push this argument a little further. Instead of thinking of 'interest rates' let us apply the Fisher equation to rates of return on capital (ROC), where ROC = (average long run profit/capital employed). If exchange rate risk is removed by entering a common currency area (e.g. the euro zone) then there is only one 'safe' interest rate and one currency. *Within this 'zone'* there are no exchange rate changes. But, interest rates on corporate bonds of firms registered in different countries could differ slightly because of differing default probabilities of these firms. Prices are perhaps more likely to be equalised (i.e. ignoring differences in indirect tax regimes) because of the 'transparency' provided by prices being expressed in a single unit of account. It is then argued that firms within the euro zone will more easily be able to plan their long run production decisions based on relative profitability in different countries (e.g. because of low wage costs or a highly educated work force, good infrastructure, good legal system, etc.). This will tend to equalise 'returns' more quickly than under a flexible exchange rate system. Hence actually entering a common currency area *could of itself* speed up 'convergence' of different economies and add to overall economic growth. If correct, this is a major positive reason for joining a common currency area like the euro zone, even before economies have fully 'converged'. This is part of the reason why the December 1991 Maastricht Treaty conditions for entry to the euro zone (see Box 15.1) were treated as *guidelines*, not strict conditions of entry.

Real interest parity is an arbitrage relationship based on the view that 'capital' (i.e. investment funds) will flow between countries to equalise the *expected* real return in each country and hence that investors ignore the riskiness of these investments. (This is risk neutrality again.) One also assumes that a representative basket of goods (with prices $P_d$ and $P_f$) in each country gives equality satisfaction (or utility) to the international investor (e.g. a 'Harrods' Hamper' in the UK is perceived as equivalent to a 'Sak's Hamper' in New York). International investors then switch funds via purchases of financial assets (or by direct investment) to where these funds are expected to yield the highest expected return in real terms. This arbitrage leads to an equalisation of expected real rates of return. Note that the investor's returns initially accrue in terms of the consumption goods of one particular country (currency). For example, if a US investor's real returns accrue in the UK but she wishes to consume US goods (e.g. a Ford Mustang produced in the US), then she will have to exchange sterling for dollars at the end of the investment period. However, if PPP holds over her investment horizon then she can obtain the same purchasing power (or set of goods) in the US as she can in the UK.

## OVERVIEW

All of these arbitrage relationships we have been discussing are summarised in Table 15.4. In the real world one would accept that CIP holds, as here arbitrage is riskless. One might *tentatively* accept that UIP holds in all time periods since financial capital is highly mobile and speculators (i.e. FX dealers in large banks) may act as if they are risk neutral (after all it's not their money they are gambling with, but the bank's). Hence one would then expect FRU to hold in all periods. However, UIP and FRU do not hold empirically. Investors also appear to be concerned about time varying risk premia, and this then invalidates the risk neutrality assumption at certain times (e.g. particularly in currency crises).

From what has been said above and one's own casual empiricism about the real world it would seem highly likely that CIP holds at most, if not all, times. Agents in the FX market are unlikely to 'miss' any *riskless* arbitrage opportunities. On UIP one might accept that this is the best *approximation* one can get of behaviour in the spot market. We know that FX dealers take quite large open speculative positions, at least in the main currencies, almost minute by minute. Hence, FX dealers who are 'on the margin' and actively making the market may mimic risk neutral behaviour. However, this assumption may break down in the frequent 'crisis periods' which occur in the spot market when 'riskiness' obviously increases (hence the risk neutrality assumption may break down) and forecasting becomes extremely hazardous.

Given relatively high information and adjustment costs in goods markets one might expect PPP to hold only over a relatively long time period (say 5–10 years). Indeed we know that, in the short run, movements in the real exchange rate are substantial. Hence, even under risk neutrality (i.e. UIP holds) one might take the view that *expected* real interest rate parity would only hold (if at all) over a rather long horizon and in countries where there is little or no political risk. Note that it is *expected* real interest rates that are equalised. However, if

## TABLE 15.4: Relationships between CIP, UIP, RIP and PPP

**COVERED INTEREST PARITY (CIP)**

$$\frac{F}{S} = \frac{1 + r_d}{1 + r_f} \quad \text{or} \quad \frac{F - S}{S} = \frac{r_d - r_f}{1 + r_f}$$

where $S$ and $F$ are measured as domestic per unit of foreign currency. If $r_f$ is small:

$$\frac{F - S}{S} \approx r_d - r_f$$

**Forward premium/discount = interest differential**

**UNCOVERED INTEREST PARITY (UIP)**

$$\frac{S_{t+1}^e}{S_t} = \frac{1 = r_{d,t}}{1 + r_{f,t}} \quad \text{or} \quad \frac{S_{t+1}^e - S_t}{S_t} = \frac{r_{d,t} - r_{f,t}}{1 + r_{f,t}}$$

Again if $r_f$ is small:

$$\frac{S_{t+1}^e - S_t}{S_t} = r_{d,t} - r_{f,t}$$

***Expected* depreciation of domestic currency = interest differential (in favour of the domestic currency)**

**PURCHASING POWER PARITY (PPP)**

Let sterling be the domestic currency and the US dollar be the foreign currency

**(1) STRONG FORM**

**DOMESTIC PRICE = FOREIGN PRICE IN STERLING (i.e. sterling import price)**

$$P_d = S \times P_f$$

**Equivalently:**

**ACTUAL EXCHANGE RATE = PPP EXCHANGE RATE**

$$S = S_{ppp}(\equiv P_d / P_f)$$

*continued overleaf*

## TABLE 15.4: (*Continued*)

**(2) WEAK FORM**

**DEPRECIATION OF £ = UK INFLATION RATE − US INFLATION RATE**

$$\dot{S} = \dot{P}_{UK} - \dot{P}_{US}$$

**REAL INTEREST RATE PARITY (RIP)**

$$r_t - \Delta p^e_{t+1} = r^*_t - \Delta p^{*e}_{t+1}$$

**Real interest rates are equalised across countries**

over a run of years agents are assumed *not* to make systematic errors when forecasting price and exchange rate changes, then on average measured (ex-post) real interest rates should also be equalised.

It is worth emphasising that all the relationships given in Table 15.4 are arbitrage conditions. There is no direction of causality implicit in any of these relationships. They are merely 'no profit' conditions under the assumption of risk neutrality. Thus in the case of UIP we cannot say that interest differentials 'cause' expectations of changes in the exchange rate (or vice versa). Of course we can expand our model to include other equations where we explicitly assume some causal chain. For example, suppose we assert (on the basis of economic theory and evidence about government behaviour) that exogenous (unanticipated) changes in the money supply by the Central Bank 'cause' changes in domestic interest rates. Then, given the UIP condition, the money supply also 'causes' a change in the expected rate of appreciation or depreciation in the exchange rate. The exogenous change in the money supply influences both domestic interest rates and the expected change in the exchange rate. Here 'money' is causal (by assumption) and the variables in the UIP relationship are jointly and simultaneously determined.

In principle, when testing the validity of the three relationships UIP, CIP and FRU or the three conditions UIP, PPP and RIP we need only test any two (out of three), since if any two hold, the third will also hold. However, because of data availability and the different quality of data for the alternative variables (e.g. $F_t$ is observable/published frequently, but $P_d$ and $P_f$ are available only infrequently and may be subject to index number measurement problems), evidence on all these relationships has been investigated by researchers.

# 15.8 SUMMARY

- In most spot FX transactions the **US dollar is the vehicle currency**. Rates are usually quoted with respect to the US dollar and **cross-currency transactions**, for example Brazilian real to Swiss francs involves going from 'real' to US dollars and then to Swiss francs. In the future, the euro may come to rival the US dollar as a vehicle and reserve currency in international transactions.

- **Currency forwards are OTC contracts** which can be designed to exactly fit the client's requirements as to amount, delivery dates and currencies. Currency forwards can be used for hedging and speculation. Both types of transaction require the forward contract to be honoured on its maturity date.

- The cash flows from an actual forward contract can be 'engineered' by using the spot rate and two money market interest rates—this is the **synthetic forward**. Riskless arbitrage then ensures that the quoted forward rate equals the synthetic forward rate. This is the **covered interest parity CIP relationship**, which for actively traded currencies is likely to hold at all times.

- **Forward quotes** are usually given in terms of the **forward points (or swap points)** rather than as outright forward quotes. An outright **forward position** held by a bank will usually be **hedged using an FX swap**.

- **Uncovered interest parity UIP** requires the assumption of risk neutrality. The UIP relationship is difficult to test and may not hold at all times because a time varying risk premium may invalidate the risk neutrality assumption (e.g. during banking or currency crises which frequently occur around the world).

- It follows that the **forward rate unbiasedness FRU property may not hold** (since this requires both CIP and UIP to hold). There is strong empirical evidence that FRU is invalid (see Cuthbertson 1996 for a summary).

- The existence of '**noise traders**' in the spot FX market who **follow 'fads and fashions'** may also invalidate the UIP relationship. This is because the noise traders create *extra* risk for the 'rational' traders (whose behaviour would normally be consistent with the UIP relationship)—see Chapter 17 for further discussion.

- Given the relatively high information and adjustment costs in goods markets then **purchasing power parity** PPP will hold only over a relatively long time period (say 5–10 years). Hence under freely floating exchange rates there may be **substantial swings in price competitiveness**, and this will affect imports and exports and hence result in booms and recessions.

- For the **general level of domestic prices** (e.g. consumer price index, CPI) it is likely that the PPP relationship arises from the interaction between price setting by firms and workers attempting to obtain 'cost of living' increases, rather than from 'goods arbitrage'. This would explain why PPP (and hence price competitiveness) does not hold in the short run but may be restored over the long run (e.g. over a 5–10 year horizon).

- Since under flexible exchange rates PPP only holds over long periods of time, then **real interest parity, RIP (or the international Fisher effect)** between countries will also be a long run phenomenon. Indeed RIP may not hold even in the long run because of changing perceptions of 'political and economic risk' between different countries.

# END OF CHAPTER EXERCISES

**Q1** What are the key differences between the spot and forward FX markets? Can you use both for speculation?

**Q2**  What is the key difference between the uncovered interest parity UIP and the covered interest parity CIP relationship?

**Q3**  Dealers are quoting the following rates for 'Cable' (i.e. GBP/USD, 'base/quoted'):

Dealer A       1.5205/15
Dealer B       1.5207/17
Dealer C       1.5200/10
Dealer D       1.5202/12

   (i)   To which dealer would you sell GBP?
   (ii)  From which dealer would you buy GBP?

**Q4**  The current exchange rate is 0.90 (euros per \$); the price of Californian wine is \$10 (per bottle) and the price of Europlonk is 10 euros (per bottle). The exchange rate now moves to 0.85 euros per \$ but the local currency price of the Californian wine and the Europlonk remains the same. What are the likely consequences for the US economy and the Euroland economy?

**Q5**  A UK firm knows it will receive \$10m in 1 years time (from the sale of goods in the USA). Current interest rates are $r_{UK} = 10\%$, $r_{US} = 12\%$ and the spot rate is $S = 1.6$ (\$/£). Carefully explain the steps the UK firm would take to hedge this inflow of dollars, using the money markets (and the spot FX market).

**Q6**  Interest rates in the UK and USA are $r_{UK} = 12\%$ p.a., $r_{US} = 10\%$ p.a. and the current spot rate is $S = 1.6$ (\$/£). If you are a speculator, what is the expected value of the exchange rate in 1 years time that will just make you indifferent between investing in the UK or the USA?

**Q7**  Given the following information:

   Spot rate of US dollar and pound sterling is 1.65 (\$/£)
   3-month UK interest rates are at 7.5% p.a. (actual/365 day count basis)
   3-month US interest rates are at 6% p.a. (actual/365 day count basis)

   Assume there are 30 days in each month, then:

   (i)  Calculate the 30-day forward rate and the forward margin.
   (ii) Is sterling at a forward discount or forward premium?

# APPENDIX 15.1  PPP AND THE WAGE–PRICE SPIRAL

In the wages version of the expectations augmented Phillips curve, wage inflation $\Delta w$ is determined by domestic price inflation $\Delta p$ and excess demand $(y - \bar{y})$. To this we can add the possibility that workers may push for a particular growth in real wages $\chi_w$ based *on their perceptions* of productivity growth. There may also be other exogenous forces $f$ (e.g. minimum wage laws, socio-economic forces) which may influence wages. We assume firms set prices as a fixed mark-up on total unit costs (which comprise unit wage costs and domestic import prices of raw materials, $pm$). Hence our wage–price model is:

[A15.1] $\qquad \Delta w = \chi_w + a_1 \Delta p + a_2(y - \bar{y}) + f$

[A15.2] $\qquad \Delta p = b_1(\Delta w - \chi_p) + b_2 \Delta pm$

where $w$, $p$ and $pm$ are in logarithms and hence $\Delta w$, $\Delta p$ and $\Delta pm$ are percentage (proportionate) changes. The term $\chi_p$ is the trend growth rate of labour productivity (i.e. output per man). Imports are assumed to be predominantly homogeneous tradeable goods (e.g. agricultural produce, oil, iron ore, coal) or imported capital goods. Their foreign price $p_f$ is set in world markets and translated into domestic (sterling) prices by the following (identity):

[A15.3] $\qquad \Delta pm = \Delta p_f + \Delta s$

Hence, we are assuming that world commodities or 'raw materials' are priced on world markets in say dollars and that PPP does hold for these homogeneous traded commodities. What we are concerned with is the implication of these relationships for the *general level* of prices (e.g. CPI) in the domestic economy. Will the general level of 'domestic prices' also obey PPP? That is, does a 1% rise in world (US dollar) prices or a 1% fall in the exchange rate of the domestic economy (e.g. sterling) eventually lead to a 1% rise in the general level of domestic (UK) prices. Substituting equation [A15.1] into equation [A15.2] we obtain:

[A15.4] $\qquad \Delta p = (1 - a_1 b_1)^{-1}[b_1(\chi_w - \chi_p) + b_2 \Delta pm + a_2 b_1(y - \bar{y}) + b_1 f]$

Equation [A15.4] is the price expectations augmented Phillips curve (PEAPC) which relates price inflation to excess demand $(y - \bar{y})$ and other variables. If we now make the reasonable assumption that in the long run workers eventually obtain full cost of living increases (i.e. there is no money illusion) then $a_1 = 1$ (that is a vertical long run PEAPC). Next we make the reasonable assumption that in the long run firms have a constant profit margin (over costs) and hence firms ultimately raise prices one for one with an increase in total costs. This implies $b_1 + b_2 = 1$. Hence equation [A15.4] becomes:

[A15.5] $\qquad \Delta p = [b_1/(1 - b_1)][f + b_1(\chi_w - \chi_p) + a_2(y - \bar{y})] + (\Delta p_f + \Delta s)$

For the moment assume that over a long run of years the terms in square brackets are approximately zero. Then the long run secular influences on domestic prices are $\Delta p_f$ and $\Delta s$:

[A15.6] $\qquad \Delta p = \Delta p_f + \Delta s$

and it follows that the general level of domestic prices will obey PPP. The implication is that a 1% rise in foreign prices $p_f$ or a 1% depreciation of the domestic currency (i.e. $s$ rises) leads to a rise in domestic prices (via equation [A15.2]) which in turn leads to higher wage inflation (via equation [A15.1]). The strength of this wage–price feedback as wage rises lead to further price rises depends on the size of $a_1$ and $b_1$. Under the assumptions $a_1 = 1$ and $b_1 + b_2 = 1$, the strength of the feedback is such that domestic prices rise one for one with either a rise in foreign prices or a fall in the domestic exchange rate. In short, PPP holds in the long run. Of course, PPP will not hold in the short run in this model either because of money illusion $a_1 < 1$, or less than full mark up of costs $b_1 + b_2 < 1$, or because of the influence of the terms in square brackets in equation [A15.4]. Taking the last, output can deviate from its 'natural' or trend growth rate for several years and this is a major additional cause of short run deviations in price competitiveness.

# CHAPTER 16

# Spot FX: Fundamentals and Noise Traders

## LEARNING OBJECTIVES

- To analyse various **'fundamentals models'** in which movements in the spot exchange rate are largely determined by monetary policy variables (e.g. interest rates or the money supply).
- Fundamentals models include the **flex-price monetary model (FPMM)**, the **sticky price monetary models (SPMM)** (e.g. the Dornbusch overshooting model and the Frankel real interest rate model) and the **portfolio balance model (PBM)**.
- To examine how **chaos models** can be used to mimic the stylised facts of changes in spot exchange rates.
- Chaos models usually rely on the presence of two types of traders, rational FX speculators (or **'smart money'**) who base their foreign investment decisions on uncovered interest parity and **'noise traders'** who follow 'rules of thumb' or trends in the exchange rate. The outcome for the actual spot rate in these models depends on the relative influence of these two types of trader.
- In the light of the above models, to analyse the reasons for entering into a **common currency area**, such as 'Euroland'.

One of our main tasks in this part of the book is to examine why there is such confusion and widespread debate about the desirability of floating exchange rates. It is something of a paradox that economists are usually in favour of 'the unfettered market' in setting 'prices', but in the case of the exchange rate, perhaps the key 'price' in the economy, there are such divergent views.

There are a large number of alternative models based on **'economic fundamentals'** that have been used to analyse movements in the spot exchange rate. We can do no more than sketch the main ideas in this chapter. It is probably correct to say that monetary models in their various forms have dominated the theoretical and empirical exchange rate literature, and we discuss a number of these, such as the flex-price and sticky price monetary models and the Frankel real interest rate model. As we shall see, these models have been far from successful in explaining movements in exchange rates. Indeed, there is no consensus amongst economists on the appropriate set of economic fundamentals that influence exchange rates and this, in part, is why policy makers have sought to limit exchange rate movements by co-operative arrangements such as Bretton Woods and the ERM in Europe (and in the latter case to implement proposals for a move towards a common currency).

Milton Friedman, the famous US advocate of money supply targets, suggested as early as the 1950s (along with a number of other eminent economists) a move from the Bretton Woods fixed exchange rate system to a freely floating exchange rate. It was argued that 'market forces' would determine the 'correct' or equilibrium exchange rate, and that in practice the actual exchange rate would move smoothly to correct for any price differentials between countries and hence 'effortlessly' ensure price competitiveness at all times (i.e. the actual exchange rate would never be far from the PPP exchange rate). Indeed, control of the money supply would be the macro-policy instrument that would ensure both price stability (i.e. moderate or zero inflation) and via PPP a stable (or slowly changing) exchange rate. These ideas were developed and became what is known as the **flex-price monetary model (FPMM)** of the exchange rate.

Because the centrepiece of this model is maintaining PPP (and it ignores the capital account), it is also often referred to as the 'current account' model of the exchange rate. The model assumes prices are flexible and output is exogenously determined by the supply side of the economy. Under floating rates the FPMM model predicts a close relationship between rapid monetary growth and a depreciating exchange rate (and vice versa)—which, for example, is broadly consistent with events in Italy, the UK, Germany and Japan in the first half of the 1970s, and in some 'high inflation' Latin American countries in the 1970s and 1980s. (In fact, in terms of its predictions the textbook Mundell–Fleming model under the assumption of a full-employment level of output yields similar results to the FPMM.)

Unfortunately, the FPMM failed to adequately explain the large swings in the *real* exchange rate (or competitiveness) that occurred in a number of small open economies, such as those of the UK, the Netherlands and Italy in the second half of the 1970s and early 1980s. The FPMM takes 'money' as the only asset of importance, and hence ignores other asset flows in the capital account of the balance of payments. Once we recognise the importance of capital flows, which have obviously increased due to the gradual dismantling of exchange controls, we have to address the question of expectations. Speculative short-term capital flows respond to relative interest rates between the domestic and foreign country, but also depend upon expectations about exchange rate movements (i.e. uncovered interest parity is assumed to hold at all times and there is a 'high' level of capital mobility between countries). The **sticky price monetary models (SPMM)** invoke the rational expectations hypothesis to deal with exchange rate expectations, and it is usually assumed that capital account flows are perfectly mobile. Price adjustment in the goods market is slow, and is determined by excess demand working via the price expectations augmented Phillips curve, PEAPC. The combination of 'sticky prices and smart speculators' implies that changes in monetary (and fiscal) policy can cause 'large' swings in the nominal and real exchange rate, and possibly lead to exchange rate overshooting.

Finally, a defect in the SPMM is its implicit assumption of the perfect substitutability of domestic and foreign assets, and failure to analyse explicitly the stock-flow interactions arising from current account imbalances. This is remedied in the **portfolio balance model (PBM)** of exchange rates.

# 16.1 FLEX-PRICE MONETARY MODEL

The FPMM model relies on the PPP condition (and the existence of a stable demand for money function depending on output, the price level and interest rates—we largely ignore this aspect here). In the FPMM model the domestic interest rate is exogenous—a rather peculiar property. This assumption implies that the domestic interest rate is rigidly linked to the exogenous world interest rate because of the assumption of 'perfect capital mobility' and a *zero* expected change in the exchange rate. Given that output is also assumed fixed at the full-employment level (the neoclassical supply curve), then any excess money can only influence the 'perfectly flexible' domestic price level, one for one. Hence the 'neutrality of money' holds.

Equilibrium in the traded goods 'market' (i.e. the current account) ensues when prices in a common currency are equalised: in short when PPP holds. Using lowercase letters to denote logarithms, the PPP condition is:

[**16.1**]    $s = p_d - p_f$

where $s$ is the log of the exchange rate, $p_d$ is the log of the domestic price level, $p_f$ is the log of the foreign price level. The world price $p_f$ is exogenous to the domestic economy (being determined by the world money supply). The domestic money supply determines the domestic price level and hence the exchange rate is determined by *relative* money supplies as shown in equation [16.2]:

[**16.2**]    $s = (m_d - m_f) + $ 'other variables'

where 'other variables' in this model are usually taken to be output and interest rates in the two countries. Possible transmission mechanisms from the money supply to the exchange rate are:

- An increase in the domestic money supply leading to an increased demand for *foreign* goods (and assets), an excess demand for foreign currency, and a depreciation in the domestic currency Producers then 'arbitrage' domestic prices upwards to match the new level of import prices of tradeable goods.
- Excess money balances causing an excess demand for *domestic* goods, followed by a rise in domestic prices via the Phillips curve. This is followed by a switch to relatively cheap foreign goods, causing downward pressure on the domestic exchange rate.

It is probably the first transition mechanism that is closest to the spirit of the FPMM price arbitrage approach. The FPMM as presented here may be tested by estimating equations of the form [16.2] for the exchange rate or by investigating the stability of the PPP relationship (and the demand for money functions). As far as equation [16.2] is concerned, it worked reasonably well empirically in the early 1970s floating period for a number of bilateral exchange rates (see Bilson, 1978), but in the late 1970s the relationship performed badly other than for countries with high inflation (e.g. Argentina and Brazil).

By way of illustration, consider a 'high inflation' country like Russia after it introduced a market economy. Figure 16.1 shows the exchange rate in roubles per USD so that a rise in this variable represents a *devaluation of the rouble*. The figure also shows the relative money supply ($M_{\text{rouble}}/M_{\text{USD}}$), which indicates that the Russian money supply was growing much faster than the US money supply. The figure is broadly consistent with the FPMM, since there is a positive correlation between the rapid money supply growth in Russia and the massive depreciation of the rouble from around 6 roubles per USD in June 1998 to about 27 roubles per USD in June 2000. Some caveats are in order. The initial sharp fall in the rouble in August 1998 is almost certainly due to the loss of confidence when Russia defaulted on its rouble denominated debts (e.g. bank loans and bonds). But note that it did not default on its foreign currency denominated debts. After December 1998 the exchange rate fall and rise in relative money supply is quite closely correlated (although there are difficult 'unit root' problems here), even though, with increasing 'dollarisation', the rouble money supply figures understate the true level of 'transactions money' in the Russian economy. Thus, while the FPMM has some relevance in hyperinflation countries it does not explain exchange rate behaviour in economies with relatively moderate inflation rates. An increase in *capital* mobility in the 1970s may account for this failure of the FPMM, as well as the fact that PPP only holds over relatively long horizons.

## FIGURE 16.1: Russian crisis. Rouble–dollar exchange rate and relative money supply

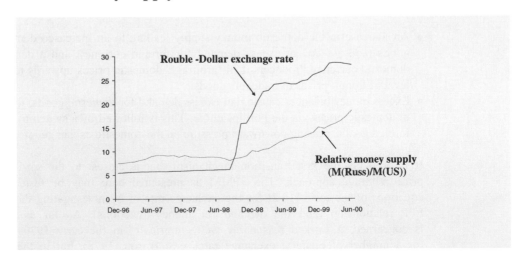

## 16.2 STICKY PRICE MONETARY MODELS

In the latter half of the 1970s the FPMM ceased to provide an accurate description of the behaviour of exchange rates for a number of small open economies. For example, in the UK over the period 1979–81 the sterling *nominal* effective exchange rate (i.e. the rate against a basket of currencies) *appreciated* substantially, even though the UK money supply grew rapidly relative to the growth in the 'world' money supply. However, more startling, the *real* exchange rate (i.e. price competitiveness or the terms of trade) appreciated by about 40% over this period, and this was followed by an equally sharp fall over the 1981–84 period. The FPMM can only explain changes in the real exchange rate by *differential short run* lags in the response of the nominal exchange rate and the domestic (and foreign) price level to changes in relative money supplies. Faced with the kind of evidence cited above, these lags appeared to be highly variable or, in other words, the FPMM failed to explain this phenomenon adequately. Large volatile swings in the real exchange rate may lead to large swings in net trade (i.e. real exports less real imports), with consequent multiplier effects on domestic output and employment. The SPMM provides an explanation of exchange rate overshooting (Dornbusch, 1976) and short run changes in real output, as for example occurred in the very severe recession of 1979–82 in the UK.

Like the FPMM, the SPMM is 'monetarist' in the sense that the neutrality of money is preserved *but only in the long run*—so (nominal) money supply only affects the price level and does not affect real variables such as output and employment (in terms of economic concepts). This arises because of a vertical neoclassical supply curve for output, or equivalently a vertical long run Phillips curve. However, PPP holds only in the long run, and hence short run changes in competitiveness are allowed.

Key elements in the SPMM are the assumption that uncovered interest parity (UIP) holds at all times while prices are 'sticky' in the short run. (The model also assumes a 'conventional', stable demand for money function.) Hence speculators in the foreign exchange market are assumed to form 'rational' expectations about the future path of the exchange rate: they immediately act on any new information or 'news' and this is what makes the exchange rate 'jump' and undergo frequent changes. It is this combination of 'perfectly flexible price response' by FX speculators and 'sticky' goods prices that produces exchange rate overshooting.

The uncovered interest parity relationship expresses the condition for equilibrium in the capital account. Foreign exchange speculators investing abroad *expect* a return of $r_f + (S_{t+1}^e - S_t)/S_t$, where $r_f$ is the foreign interest rate and $(S_{t+1}^e - S_t)/S_t$ is the expected *appreciation* of the *foreign* currency (depreciation in the domestic currency) over the coming year, say. With perfect capital mobility and risk neutrality, there will be no (expected) financial gain to FX speculators from switching funds between countries when the domestic interest rate $r_d$ equals the return (in domestic currency) from investing abroad, that is UIP holds:

[16.3] $$r_{d,t} = r_{f,t} + \frac{S_{t+1}^e - S_t}{S_t}$$

or, equivalently, with the UK as the domestic economy and the US as the foreign economy and $S$ measured as (£/$):

[16.4]
$$\frac{(S^e_{t+1} - S_t)}{S_t} = r_{d,t} - r_{f,t}$$

> **_Expected_ depreciation of sterling**
> **= interest rate differential (in favour of the UK)**

## DORNBUSCH OVERSHOOTING

We present a simplified account of the Dornbusch (1976) model by considering the possible impact on the UK economy of a tight monetary stance. (For a detailed account see Cuthbertson, 1996.) Suppose the economy is initially in (short run and long run) equilibrium, so there is initially price competitiveness (i.e. PPP) and UIP holds:

- $r_{UK} = r_{US} = 10\%$ p.a. and since UIP holds then the expected depreciation of sterling is 0%, that is speculators currently believe the spot rate will remain constant over the coming year.
- $P_{UK} = £100$ (for a basket of UK goods).
- $P_{US} = \$100$ (for an identical basket of US goods) and $S = 1.0$ (£/$), so we have PPP.

**Scenario:**
Suppose now there is a 'shock' whereby the UK Central Bank announces a new lower target for the money supply which is 1% below the previous target and, to implement this policy, UK interest rates are increased by 2% to 12%. We deal first with the 'long run' implications and then the 'short run'.

**Long run:**
- Since the UK money supply has been cut by 1%, the UK price level will ultimately fall by 1% (move from point A to C in Figure 16.2a) as the higher interest rates lead to downward pressure on wages and prices. (We are invoking the long run neutrality of money here.)
- Since UK prices are lower, then to preserve price competitiveness (i.e. PPP) _sterling must appreciate by 1% in the long run (to 1.01 $/£)._

**Short run:**
- If speculators initially believe that sterling will remain constant, then US investors want to buy UK bonds and hence they buy sterling, pushing up the sterling spot rate _today_.
- Sterling will appreciate _today_ until it gets so high that US investors _think it will fall by 2% over the coming year_ (move from point A to B in Figure 16.2b). Now UIP is restored and capital inflows into the UK will cease.
- As UK prices slowly fall by 1% then both the exchange rate and the interest rate fall, and

## FIGURE 16.2: Overshooting: (a) long run, (b) short run

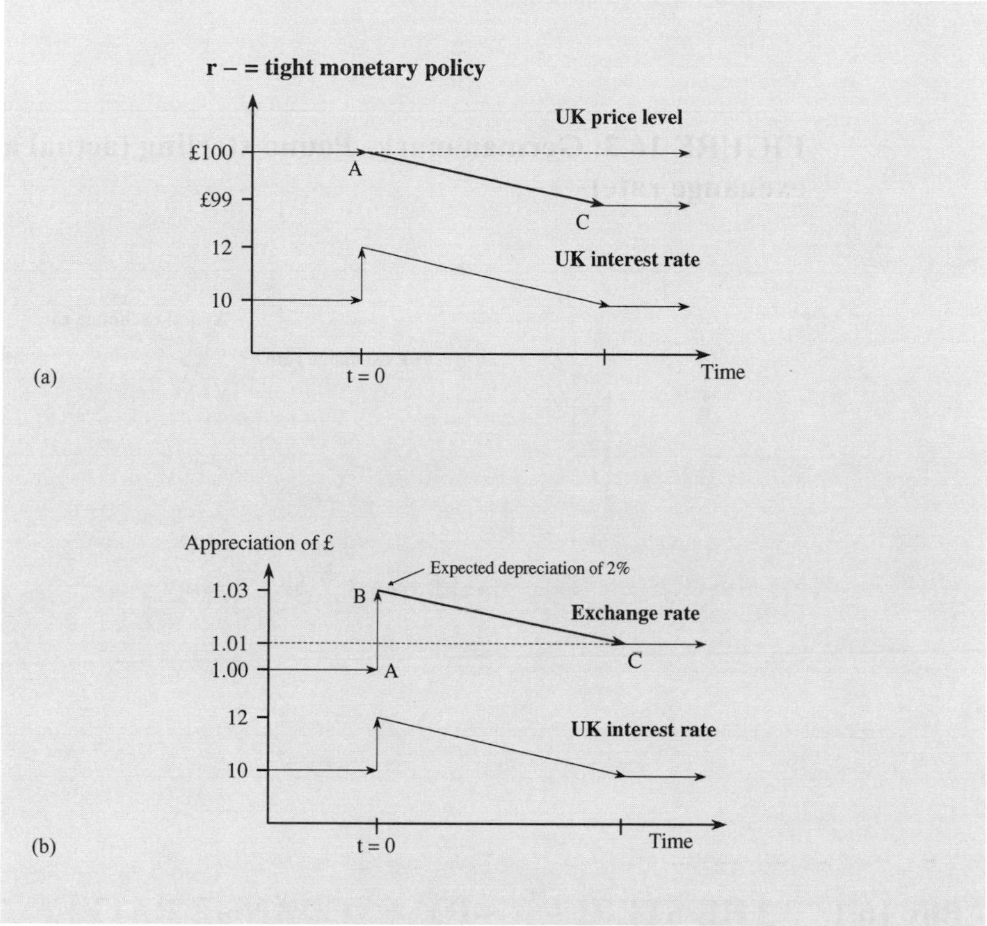

(a)

(b)

the exchange rate eventually ends up at 1% above its initial value, which restores price competitiveness (move from point B to C in Figure 16.2b).

The Dornbusch model implies that the 'market mechanism' that is, smart rational FX speculators coupled with sticky goods prices, could lead to overshooting of the nominal exchange rate. Hence there could be large changes in price competitiveness in the short run, where the short run could be anything between 3 and 10 years depending on how long it takes goods prices to fully adjust. This loss of competitiveness could severely exacerbate the recession caused by the higher UK interest rates because it would lead to a fall in UK exports and a rise in UK imports, thus reducing demand for UK goods and increasing the level of unemployment. The free market therefore produces a less than desirable *short run* outcome when trying to reduce inflation using a contractionary monetary policy. Add to this the possibility that once you have lost export markets and lost domestic sales to cheap imports you might never fully recover your competitive position, then clearly the maxim 'there is no gain without the pain' certainly applies here. An example of the difficulties of being in an exchange rate band and of the volatility of freely floating exchange rates is illustrated in Box 16.1 and the accompanying Figure 16.3.

### FIGURE 16.3: German mark–Pound sterling (actual and PPP exchange rate)

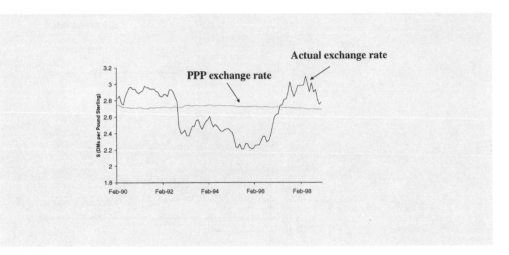

| Box 16.1 | THE STERLING–DM EXCHANGE RATE: A ROLLERCOASTER RIDE |
|---|---|

Consider the sterling–Deutsche Mark exchange rate and relative prices (i.e. the PPP exchange rate) in Figure 16.3. The UK entered the ERM in the early 1990s at a rate of 2.95 DMs to the pound (sterling), a rate widely regarded by economists as 'uncompetitive'. Let us assume that a competitive rate would have been 2.75 DMs, which is where we have anchored the relative price graph in 1990, implying a substantial overvaluation of sterling.

In September 1992, with unemployment having risen substantially (in part because of a loss of export markets due to the overvalued pound), there was a speculative attack on sterling. The UK Government raised interest rates from 10 to 15% and intervened heavily in the FX market, selling DMs and buying sterling. But this did not stem the attack and sterling left the ERM on 16th September and the exchange rate fell substantially to around 2.40 DMs. The UK Government lost £7bn in reserves trying to defend the pound and it was reported that George Soros made $1bn successfully betting against sterling remaining in the ERM (i.e. he sold sterling and purchased other currencies prior to 16th September and then could buy back sterling at a lower price).

Sterling was now under a 'free float' and the UK gained competitiveness over the period 1992–96. The corresponding boost to exports meant that the real economy by 1996 was expanding. However, between the end of 1996 and 1998 sterling rose against the DM and became overvalued. This led to a slower growth in exports (primarily by manufacturers) while the service sector continued to boom. The Monetary Policy Committee of the Bank of England then had a major dilemma in 1990/2000 in setting interest rates. It needed to increase interest rates to offset the boom in the service sector and the rise in house price inflation, both of which threatened to lead to increased consumer price inflation after a lag of up to 2 years—see Chapter 2).

However, an increase in interest rates could have led to a higher level of sterling and hence an even greater level of price uncompetitiveness. There was also a 'regional dimension' to the decision, since most of the manufacturing sector is located in the North while the boom in the service sector was mainly in the 'prosperous' South East. Who would the MPC favour? It increased interest rates on a number of occasions. Probably because it felt it had a better idea of how higher rates might affect the service sector but was less certain about their impact on the exchange rate. Anyway, this just goes to show that 'one size fits all' in terms of setting interest rates often does not apply within a single country, let alone across a number of countries (as when setting the interest rate in the euro area). The key fact of this analysis is that even with a 'sensible' or 'reasonable' economic policy, that occurred in the UK over 1994 to 2000, the exchange rate can be extremely volatile and there can be large changes in price competitiveness.

Whether or not 'real world' economies suffer from exchange rate overshooting in practice is not clearly established. The classic case of the large UK appreciation in 1979–82 could have been partly due to the rise in world oil prices (when the UK North Sea oil fields were coming on stream), coupled with speculative capital inflows by 'noise traders'. However, it is difficult to know why there has been such a massive change in competitiveness of sterling versus the DM over the 1994–2000 period, and this is the danger in having a freely floating exchange rate.

## FRANKEL REAL INTEREST DIFFERENTIAL MODEL

Frankel (1979) modified the Dornbusch model by allowing long run views about the underlying rate of inflation (in two countries) to influence FX dealers' *expectations* of exchange rate changes. The idea is that expected rate of depreciation of the domestic currency will be higher if the underlying domestic inflation rate is higher than the rate of inflation in the foreign country. This allows Frankel's model to reproduce all the

Dornbusch-type results, but also to provide a route whereby inflation rates influence the spot rate. This is a fairly complex model and results in an exchange rate equation:

[16.5]     $s = \bar{m}_d - \bar{m}_f - (1/\theta)(r_d - r_f) + [(1/\theta + \lambda)(\pi_d - \pi_f)] + \text{other variables}$

where $s$ is the exchange rate (defined as domestic per unit of foreign currency)
   $\bar{m}_d - \bar{m}_f$ is the relative secular or 'long run' money supply in the two countries
   $\pi_d - \pi_f$ is the relative expected inflation in the two countries.

The Frankel model allows us to separate out the effects of changes in nominal and changes in real interest rates on movements in the spot rate. For example, if there is a 'surprise' or *unanticipated* increase in domestic interest rates with no change in inflationary expectations (i.e. an increase in the *real* interest rate) then equation [16.5] predicts that 's' will fall, that is sterling will appreciate. This is what we would intuitively expect from a Central Bank which had a credible anti-inflationary stance (e.g. the Bundesbank in Germany and the Federal Reserve under Alan Greenspan). On the other hand, an increase in inflationary expectations $\pi_d$, which is accompanied by an *equal* increase in the domestic interest rate $r_d$ (i.e. an unchanged *real* interest rate) causes a depreciation in the domestic exchange rate (i.e. 's' increases). This is the kind of result we might expect when a Central Bank in a high inflation country (and with a low reputation for combating inflation) raises interest rates, as happened in certain Latin American countries in the 1970s and 1980s. Hence, the Frankel model highlights the possible differential response of the exchange rate to changes in interest rates, the key factor being whether the rise in interest rates by the Central Bank is seen as a strong anti-inflationary stance (i.e. a rise in real interest rates) or merely as a rise in interest rates to reflect continuing high inflation (i.e. keeping interest rates constant).

## THE PORTFOLIO BALANCE MODEL

The current account 'flex-price' and capital account 'sticky price' monetary models which have been the subject matter of the preceding sections make at least two important simplifying assumptions: domestic and foreign assets are perfect substitutes (this is the UIP condition) and any wealth effects of a current account surplus or deficits are negligible. The portfolio balance model of exchange rates explores the consequences of explicitly relaxing these assumptions (see Branson, 1977; Isard, 1978; Dornbusch and Fischer, 1980). The level of the exchange rate in the portfolio balance model PBM is determined, at least in the short run, by supply and demand in the markets for all financial assets (i.e. money, domestic and foreign bonds). In the PBM a surplus (deficit) on the current account represents a rise (fall) in net domestic holdings of foreign assets. The latter affects the level of wealth and hence the desired demand for assets, which then affects the exchange rate. Thus, the PBM is an inherently dynamic model of exchange rate adjustment which includes behavioural inter-actions in asset markets, the current account, the price level and the rate of asset accumulation. The reduced form equations used in testing the PBM therefore include stocks of assets other than money. For example, equations to test the PBM might include the ratio of domestic to foreign bonds (or equities, or equities + bonds) in the exchange rate equation. Often the *net* foreign asset position (i.e. the stock of foreign assets minus foreign liabilities) of domestic residents is included in the exchange rate equation, and this is measured by the *cumulative* current account position.

## A RISK PREMIUM?

The UIP condition assumes that FX speculators ignore any (market) risk that is present when investing in the foreign currency—that is, they 'put all their eggs in one basket and watch the basket very carefully'. This is the complete antithesis of the (mean–variance) portfolio approach, where there is an explicit risk premium (i.e. the foreign investment's 'beta' with the return on 'the market' being the 'world portfolio' of stocks and other risky assets). Monetary models of the spot rate cannot easily incorporate the portfolio model as a description of the behaviour of the expected spot rate. Instead, for analytic tractability they tend to amend the UIP condition and merely include a relative risk premium (*rp*). Suppose the UK is the domestic economy, then there will be no incentive for any net capital flows between the UK and the US when:

> **Interest rate in the UK**
> **= foreign interest rate + expected appreciation of the**
> **foreign currency *less* the additional risk from investing**
> **in the US by the UK resident**

[16.6]
$$r_{d,t} = r_{f,t} + \frac{(S^e_{t+1} - S_t)}{S_t} - \text{increased riskiness of investing in the US}$$

This approach implicitly assumes there are possible macroeconomic variables that affect risk that have not already been assimilated, by dealers in the money and FX spot market, into their views about interest rates and expected changes in the spot rate. This is rather ad hoc and variables which have been used to 'model' the risk premium include the value of oil reserves (which are closely related to oil prices), the cumulative current account deficit and the government debt to GDP ratio, but none have been particularly illuminating. This difficulty in modelling the FX 'risk premium' and hence getting a 'handle' on determinants of movements in the exchange rate, led some countries to consider an exchange rate band, such as the Exchange Rate Mechanism (ERM) of the European Monetary System (EMS). In this arrangement countries agree to adopt macroeconomic policies to ensure price competitiveness (e.g. raising interest rates to reduce inflation down to the level of the other members of the 'club'). There is also an agreement to undertake co-ordinated intervention in the FX market to support a 'temporarily' weak currency, until macroeconomic measures have time to correct any price uncompetitiveness.

France and Germany were enthusiastic members of the ERM in the 1990s and the French franc–DM exchange rate is shown in Figure 16.4, together with the PPP exchange rate. The nominal rate in early 1990 was about 3.4 FRF/DM. This rate varied hardly at all from 1990 to the latter part of 1993 when the FRF came under speculative attack. Even then, it did not fall below about 3.5 FRF/DM and remained at about 3.4 FRF/DM until entry into the euro in January 1999. Hence price competitiveness was preserved over this period. However, this was at a cost, since in order to bring down the French inflation rate to the lower German rate (and hence via PPP help keep the exchange rate at an unchanged level), unemployment in France rose substantially (although it began falling in 2000). Since France and Germany

## FIGURE 16.4: French franc–German mark (actual and PPP exchange rate)

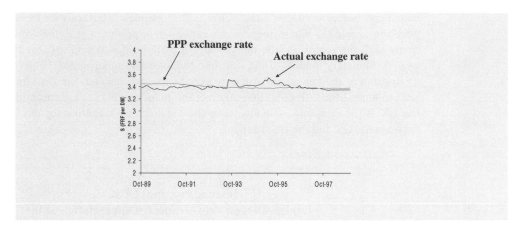

joined the EMU and adopted the euro in January 1999, any divergence in price competitiveness between the two countries will not come from unforeseen changes in their exchange rate (since it is 'one for one') but from changes in wage rates and labour productivity.

## TESTING THE MODELS

As one can see from the above analysis, tests of SPMM involve regressions of the spot rate on relative money stocks, interest rates, etc., while tests of the PBM would also include some measure of the *total* net foreign assets held (i.e. money + bonds + equities). If we ignore hyperinflation periods, then these models have not proved successful in predicting movements in bilateral spot rates, particularly in post-1945 data. Some of the models do work reasonably well over short subperiods, but not over the whole period. Meese (1990) provides a useful 'summary table' of the performance of such models. He estimates a general equation which, in the main, subsumes all of the above theories:

[16.7]
$$s_t = a_0 + a_1(L)(m_{\mathrm{d}} - m_{\mathrm{f}})_t + a_2(L)(y_{\mathrm{d}} - y_{\mathrm{f}})_t + a_3(L)(r_{\mathrm{d}} - r_{\mathrm{f}})_t$$
$$+ a_4(L)(\pi_{\mathrm{d}} - \pi_{\mathrm{f}})_t + a_5(L)(F_{\mathrm{d}} - F_{\mathrm{f}})_t + e_t$$

where $a(L)$ is a lag operator and implies that several lagged values of the variable are included in the equation

$F_{\mathrm{d}}$ is the stock of domestic assets held by foreign residents

$F_{\mathrm{f}}$ is the stock of foreign assets held by domestic residents.

Meese (1990) repeats the earlier tests of Meese and Roghoff (1983) by estimating equation [16.7] up to time period $t$ and then using it to forecast out-of-sample for horizons of 1, 6 and 12 months. New data is then added and the estimation and forecasting process is repeated.

The forecasts based on the structural equations use actual future values of the RHS variables. He then compares the root mean square forecast errors from equation [16.7] with those from a benchmark provided by the 'no change' prediction of the random walk model of the exchange rate. It is clear from Table 16.1 that the forecasts using the economic fundamentals in equation [16.7] are in all cases worse than those of the random walk hypothesis.

Meese (1990) dismisses the reasons for the failure of these models based on fundamentals as mismeasurement of variables, inappropriate estimation techniques or even omitted variables (since so many alternatives have been tried). He suggests that the failure of such models may be due to weakness in their underlying relationships such as the PPP condition, and the instability found in money demand functions and the mounting evidence from survey data on expectations that agents' forecasts do not obey the axioms of rational expectations. He notes that non-linear models (e.g. chaotic models) that involve regime changes (e.g. Peso problem) and models that involve noise traders may provide some insights into the determination of movements in the spot rate, but research in these areas is only just beginning.

A novel approach to testing monetary models of the exchange rate is provided by Flood and Rose (1993). They compare the volatility in the exchange rate and in economic fundamentals for periods of 'fixed rates' (e.g. Bretton Woods, where permitted exchange rate fluctuations were ±1%) and 'floating rates'. Not surprisingly, exchange rates are far more volatile in the floating rate periods. If the monetary models are correct then one should also observe a dramatic increase in volatility in some of the economic fundamentals (e.g. relative money supplies) when a previously fixed exchange rate is floated. For nine industrialised

## TABLE 16.1: Root mean square error (RMSE) out-of-sample forecast statistics (November 1980 through June 1984 (44 months))

| | | | Model | |
|---|---|---|---|---|
| Exchange rate | Horizon (months) | Random walk | 1 | 2 |
| log(DM/$) | 1 | 3.1 | 3.1 | 3.2 |
| | 6 | 7.9 | 8.4 | 8.5 |
| | 12 | 8.7 | 11.1 | 11.4 |
| log(yen/$) | 1 | 3.5 | 3.3 | 3.5 |
| | 6 | 7.8 | 7.0 | 7.7 |
| | 12 | 9.0 | 7.5 | 8.7 |

(OECD) countries, Flood and Rose find that although the conditional volatility of bilateral *exchange rates* against the dollar alters dramatically across these exchange rate regimes, none of the economic fundamentals experiences a marked change in volatility. Hence one can legitimately conclude that the economic fundamentals in the monetary models (e.g. money supply, interest rates, inflation rates, output) do not explain the volatility in exchange rates. (It is worth noting however that the latter conclusion may not hold in the case of extreme hyperinflation where the variability in relative inflation rates (i.e. fundamentals) across regimes might alter substantially.)

Flood and Rose argue that since few macroeconomic variables undergo dramatic changes in volatility when there are dramatic changes in the volatility of the exchange (e.g. in a move from 'fixed' to floating rates), then it is unlikely that *any* exchange rate model based only on economic fundamentals will prove adequate. For nine OECD countries, they also correlate the average monthly variance of the exchange rate $\sigma^2(S)$ over successive 2-year horizons against the variance of various macroeconomic variables. They find that there is no relationship between the change in $\sigma^2(S)$ and either the (change in the) variability in the money supply or interest rates or FOREX reserves or stock prices, and only a rather weak negative relationship with the variance of output. Hence in moving from a floating exchange rate regime to a fixed rate regime, the reduced volatility in the exchange rate is *not* reflected in an increase in volatility of other macroeconomic variables. (A similar result is found by Artis and Taylor, 1994 for European countries who moved from a floating rate into the ERM in the 1980s.)

In a recent study Mark (1995) has re-examined the usefulness of 'fundamentals' in explaining changes in the (log) exchange rate over short and long horizons. Mark (1995) takes the monetary model as determining the long run exchange rate $z_t = (m_d - m_f)$ $-\alpha(y_d - y_f)$ (where $y_d$ and $y_f$ represent real output in the two countries). Changes in the spot rate depend on how far the actual spot rate $s_t$ currently is from its long run equilibrium level $z_t$ that is on the current 'disequilibrium' $(s_t - z_t)$. If the exchange rate adjusts slowly to disequilibrium in the fundamentals then:

[16.8]
$$s_{t+k} - s_t = \delta_k + \beta_k(s_t - z_t)$$

Mark (1995) finds that the $R^2$ in the above regression and the value of $\beta_k$ increase as the horizon $k$ increases from 1 to 16 quarters. (He uses quarterly data on the US dollar against the Canadian dollar, Deutsche Mark, Japanese yen and Swiss franc from 1973–91.) Also, out-of-sample forecasts at long horizons ($k = 16$) outperform the random walk for the DM, yen and Swiss franc. The above analysis is not a test of a 'fully specified' monetary model but demonstrates that 'monetary fundamentals' may provide a useful predictor of the exchange rate over long horizons (although not necessarily over short horizons). Clearly, if one is looking for a purely statistical representation one may also consider non-linear models (e.g. Engel and Hamilton, 1990), neural networks (e.g. Trippi and Turban, 1993) and chaos models of the exchange rate. Below we briefly discuss the latter.

The above evidence also suggests that there is some change in the trading behaviour of FX dealers when there is a move from flexible to fixed rates (e.g. Do noise traders transfer to other 'unrestricted' speculative markets? Does the credibility of the fixed rate policy play an important role in influencing expectations and hence trading activity?).

The balance of the argument on **fixed versus floating exchange rates** based on the above evidence would not seem to unequivocally favour either regime, and this is why governments and some economists advocate either:

(i) trying to keep the exchange rate with pre-announced target bands (as in the ERM in Europe in the 1980s and 1990s), or
(ii) forming common currency blocs (e.g. the 11 European countries that have agreed to adopt the euro as their common currency).

The main arguments surrounding entry into a common currency area come under the heading of **optimal currency areas** or, more succinctly, **monetary union**. The pro's and con's of the UK entering 'Euroland' are outlined in Box 16.2.

## Box 16.2    EUROLAND: 'WANNA BE IN MY GANG?'

The United Kingdom is currently not among the 11 countries who joined 'Euroland' and adopted the euro in January 1999, even though over 50% of its overseas trade is with the Euroland countries. The key economic factors which will determine whether it is beneficial for the UK (or other countries) to enter Euroland are as follows.

- If you believe that FX traders are rational but goods prices are sticky, then you are more likely to want to join Euroland to avoid exchange rate overshooting and subsequent destabilising movements (primarily) in manufacturing output but also in the tourism industry.
- If you believe 'noise traders' in the FX market cause changes in the exchange rate unrelated to economic fundamentals (i.e. currency crises), then you are more likely to enter Euroland.
- If you prefer the independent yet unelected Monetary Policy Committee (MPC) of the Bank of England to set UK interest rates rather than the independent, unelected MPC at the European Central Bank (ECB) in Frankfurt, then you will wish to remain outside Euroland.
- If you believe that 'one size (approximately) fits all' (in terms of one interest rate being set for the whole of the euro area) rather than the alternative of possibly a volatile exchange rate (if you keep your own currency and interest rate policy), then you will enter Euroland.
- If you believe that economic 'shocks' (e.g. a fall in the *world* demand for manufacturers) are relatively evenly spread across the countries within Euroland, then this will not discourage you from joining. This is because the interest rate set by the ECB for the whole of Euroland will be broadly correct for *individual countries* in Euroland. For this we require a fairly homogeneous industrial structure across Euroland countries.
- If economic 'shocks' are asymmetric then you would not favour joining Euroland. To take an extreme example, if the UK 'produced' only fish and the fish died (e.g. environmental pollution) then unemployment in the UK would rise. The interest rate in Euroland would not be changed because only the UK 'region' is affected. Hence UK unemployment requires either a fall in real wages, which would lead to

increased direct investment and higher employment, or migration of UK workers to jobs in the rest of Euroland. Both of these are very slow processes. With an independent currency the UK Government could *attempt* to engineer a lower exchange rate by reducing UK interest rates, in order to boost investment and employment. But note that the interest rate policy of the MPC is not usually directed at 'real' variables like employment but only towards influencing the inflation rate.

- With the euro money supply fixed by the ECB, the UK Government could only finance cyclical increases in welfare payments (e.g. in times of high unemployment) by additional issues of UK government bonds (denominated in euros), since it cannot rely on any fiscal transfers from other euro countries. Being in Euroland therefore limits welfare payments if 'shocks' are asymmetric. (Note that if adverse 'shocks' are symmetric and influence *all* Euroland countries approximately equally, then the ECB would lower euro interest rates to stimulate the whole euro economy.) Indeed, the **stability pact** agreed at the EU meeting in Dublin in December 1996 set stringent financial penalties on running excess deficits. For budget deficits above 3%, 4%, 5% and 6% of GDP the fines (as a percentage of GDP) are 0.2%, 0.3%, 0.4% and 0.5%. (Over the past 30 years the average budget deficit in the UK has been about 3% of GDP, but it has exceeded 3% in more than half the years.)

- Having a common currency set by the ECB also requires some restrictions on the *long run* fiscal position of member countries. This is most evident with pensions policy where state pension provisions in Italy, Germany and France are relatively high. If these countries honour their current state pensions commitments, then they will have to issue a large amount of bonds to finance future pension payments. Ultimately the interest and principal on these bonds needs to be repaid from taxation. Given a limit to tax rises (because of possible political unrest), these governments could default on bond interest payments. Then other countries' citizens holding these bonds would lose out or there might be a strong temptation for other Euroland governments to bail-out the 'pension countries' by transferring funds from their taxpayers. Hence, because countries can default on their bonds, some limits on budget deficits are required, in the common currency area. This is an intertemporal fiscal problem.

- If you simply just like the idea of your 'own currency' even though it involves transactions costs of changing currency when purchasing goods from Euroland, and even though your domestic MPC may not have a predictable influence on the exchange rate, you will favour 'staying out' (for sentimental reasons).

- If you believe that the euro will fluctuate wildly against non-euro countries (e.g. US dollar, Japanese yen) with whom you also have substantial trade, then you will be less inclined to join Euroland.

- If you believe that direct investment (e.g. by US and Japanese firms) into the UK will increase because of reduced currency uncertainty, then you will favour the euro. This is because it is highly likely that Japanese firms which want to sell in the European market will want to locate in countries where their costs are largely determined in euros, so as to hedge any currency mismatch between sales receipts and costs).

Of course, there are political arguments about the desirability of increased 'integration' in general (e.g. common defence, immigration, environmental policies, etc.), but these are largely independent of accepting a common currency. So 'it's your call' (and if you are a UK resident you are likely to vote on the issue in a referendum before 2005).

## RANDOM WALK REAPPEARS

The failure of 'fundamentals models' of the spot rate to explain *short run* movements in the spot rate (e.g. changes over 1 day, 1 month or up to 1 year) led practitioners in the real world to look for ways of mitigating the adverse consequences by using forwards, futures, options and swaps. Researchers on the other hand investigated purely parsimonious *statistical* representations of movements in the spot rate. For example, to a reasonable approximation, daily bilateral (logarithms of) exchange rates follow a random walk (strictly speaking a 'martingale') $E_{t-1}s_t = s_{t-1}$ where the forecast error $\eta_t = s_t - E_{t-1}s_t$ has a non-constant variance (see Baillie and Bollerslev, 1989; Baillie and Mahon, 1989). Hence the model is:

[16.9] $$s_t = s_{t-1} + \eta_t$$

and the time varying variance of $\eta_t$ denoted $\sigma_t^2$ seems to be well approximated by an autoregressive structure of the form:

[16.10] $$\sigma_t^2 = \alpha_0 + \alpha_1\sigma_{t-1}^2 + \alpha_2\eta_{t-1}^2$$

which is known as a GARCH(1, 1) process. The GARCH process simply implies that there are periods of 'calm' and 'turbulence' in the FX market. So, if the market was turbulent yesterday it is likely to remain turbulent for several more days, before eventually switching to a sustained period of calm. (This is the autoregressive property of volatility.) The simple statistical model represented by the above two equations can be used to provide a forecast of exchange rate volatility which is needed to price foreign currency options (see Cuthbertson and Nitzsche, 2001).

# 16.3 CHAOS AND FUNDAMENTALS

So-called rational expectations RE models of the exchange rate attribute the volatility in the spot rate to the arrival of new information or news. However, using high-frequency data the study by Goodhart and O'Hara (1997) finds that most exchange rate movements appear to occur in the absence of observable news. Add to this, evidence from cointegration studies where for many currencies there is no long run (cointegrating) relationship between the spot rate and economic fundamentals (e.g. Boothe and Glassman, 1987; Baillie and Selover, 1987), then models based on fundamentals begin to look rather weak. There is also evidence that at short horizons (e.g. 1 month) the spot rate is positively autocorrelated whereas at longer horizons there is significant negative serial correlation (Cutler *et al.*, 1989), which is indicative of noise traders with extrapolative predictions at short horizons and with fundamentals more predominant at longer horizons. Finally, there is evidence using survey data that expectations are not rational, and may exhibit bandwagon effects at short horizons with mean reversion at longer horizons (e.g. Frankel and Froot, 1990; Takagi, 1991).

An eclectic view of the evidence on exchange rate behaviour therefore provides a number of anomalies relative to the central paradigm of a model based on economic fundamentals in which *all* agents use RE. Models of chaos suggest that apparent random behaviour may not be due solely to 'shocks' or noise, and point to the possibility that *non-linear deterministic* dynamic models may lie behind observed movements in exchange rates. The spirit in which we approach models of chaos is one where we hope they can begin to provide alternative insights into the somewhat anomalous behaviour of the exchange rate (and other asset prices) rather than provide a complete theory of such movements.

In this section we examine the contribution that chaos theory can make in accounting for the empirical results discussed earlier, which seem to indicate a failure of fundamentals in explaining movements in the spot rate and for an apparent failure of RE and market efficiency.

Here, we draw heavily on the work of DeGrauwe *et al.* (1993) to show how a specific illustrative chaotic model can provide a starting point, at least into the apparent anomalous behaviour of the FOREX market. We do so by using the sticky price monetary model SPMM to determine the equilibrium exchange rate as viewed by the smart money. We combine this with a model of heterogeneous expectations by noise traders and smart money, and it is this which provides the main source of non-linearity in the model.

The model gives rise (under certain parameter values) to chaotic behaviour of the exchange rate. We are then able to show that the *simulated* exchange rate series from this chaos model:

- approximates a random walk;
- yields a regression in which the forward premium is a biased predictor of the future change in the exchange rate;
- yields a regression of the exchange rate on fundamentals (i.e. money supply) in which the economic fundamentals provide a poor predictor of future movements in the exchange rate (i.e. consistent with the Meese and Roghoff results) and yet the spot rate and the money supply are linked in the long run (i.e. consistent with Mark's results).

All of the above empirical results are observed in the real world data and hence the chaotic model is at least capable of mimicking the behaviour of real world data in the FOREX market. In the final part of this section we briefly outline the results of some tests for chaos and for the presence of non-linearity in relationships in the FOREX market.

## STICKY PRICE MONETARY MODEL

The DeGrauwe *et al.* chaos model, just like the Dornbusch overshooting model, has PPP holding in the long run but not in the short run and for *the market as a whole* (i.e. smart money and noise traders), the expected change in the exchange rate is determined by UIP:

[16.11] $\qquad E_t(S_{t+1}/S_t) = (1 + r_{d,t})/(1 + r_{f,t})$

The smart money forecast the exchange rate using 'rational expectations' and hence do not make systematic forecast errors (i.e. they sometimes overestimate and sometimes under-estimate next period's spot rate but *on average* they guess correctly). However, the noise traders forecast the change in the exchange rate by extrapolation of past movements in the spot rate (i.e. their forecasts are based on a chartist-type analysis). The exact 'trend extrapolation' technique assumed is based on the cross-over point where the so-called 'short moving average' crosses the 'long moving average' (see next chapter). However, the details need not concern us here, all we need to know is that the noise traders' forecasting behaviour is represented by a highly non-linear function of past levels of the exchange rate (which represent past trend movements in the data), which we simply denote as $f(S_{t-1}, S_{t-2}, \ldots)$.

We turn now to the *market's* expectation of the change in the spot rate. This is a weighted average of the behaviour of the noise traders and the smart money and provides an important non-linearity in the model:

[16.12] $\qquad E_t(S_{t+1}/S_t) = f(S_{t-1}, S_{t-2}, \ldots)^{m_t}(S^*_{t-1}/S_{t-1})^{(1-m_t)}$

where $S^*$ is *the long run* equilibrium level of the exchange rate determined by PPP.

The *weight* given to noise traders in determining the overall market expectation is also a non-linear function of the spot rate:

[16.13] $\qquad m_t = 1/(1 + \beta(S_{t-1} - S^*_{t-1})^2)$

The above equations can be solved for the equilibrium exchange rate and, not surprisingly, this is a highly non-linear dynamic equation of the general form:

[16.14] $\qquad S_t = (X_t)^{\theta_1}(S_{t-1})^{\phi_1}(S_{t\ 2})^{\phi_2}(S_{t\ 3})^{\phi_3}(S_{t\ 4})^{\phi_4}$

where $X_t$ is a set of 'fundamentals' such as relative money supplies in the two countries.

The model can then be simulated for different assumptions about the path of the 'fundamentals'. For example, that the money supply in the domestic economy is adjusted as domestic interest rates rise and fall—that is an 'accommodating' or interest rate smoothing policy. The simulated path of the exchange rate for a given chaotic solution has the general random pattern that we associate with real world exchange rate data.

DeGrauwe *et al.* then take this simulated data from a 'manufactured' known chaotic monetary model and perform various tests on this data to see if the model reproduces the 'stylised facts' found in the real world exchange rate data. First there is a test for a random walk (strictly, a unit root):

[16.15] $\qquad S_t = \alpha S_{t-1} + \varepsilon_t$

and they find that one cannot reject $\alpha = 1$ (for a wide variety of parameters of the 'manufactured' model which result in chaotic solutions). Hence a purely deterministic 'fundamentals model' can produce data for the spot rate which looks like a stochastic process with a unit root.

As covered interest parity holds, then the forward premium $(F/S)_t$ is equal to the interest differential $(1 + r_d)/(1 + r_f)$. DeGrauwe *et al.* use the simulated values of the interest rate differential as a measure of $(F/S)_t$ and regress the latter on the simulated values of $S_{t+1}/S_t$:

[**16**.16]   $S_{t+1}/S_t = a + b(F/S)_t$

They find $b < 0$ which is also the case with actual real world data. Hence in a chaotic model the forward premium is a biased forecast of the change in the spot rate even when we have risk neutrality *at the level of the market* (i.e. UIP holds). This is because the presence of the noise trader behaviour 'distorts' the movement in $S_{t+1}/S_t$.

DeGrauwe *et al.* also simulate the model when *stochastic shocks* (i.e. zero mean random shocks) are allowed to influence the money supply. The money supply is assumed to follow a random walk and the error term therefore represents this 'news' or random shock. Over a long time period the simulated data for $S_t$ broadly moves with that for the money supply, as our fundamentals model would indicate, and a simple (OLS cointegration) regression confirms this:

[**16**.17]   $S_t = \underset{(0.5)}{0.02} + \underset{(32.8)}{0.99 M_t}$

The variability in $S_t$ is much greater than that for $M_t$. The simulated data is then split into several subperiods of 50 observations each and the regression $S_t = \alpha + \beta M_t$ is run. DeGrauwe *et al.* find that the parameters $\alpha$ and $\beta$ are highly unstable, the equation forecasts badly out-of-sample and has a RMSE that exceeds that for a random walk. Therefore over a short period the simulated 'chaotic data' mimics the results found using actual data by Meese (1990).

However, the chaotic data still exhibits some predictive features. For example, a purely autoregressive model of order three (AR(3)), when estimated on the simulated data using 50 data points, forecasts better than either the random walk or the structural model. Thus, data from a chaotic system can be modelled and may yield reasonable forecasts over short horizons. These results provide a prima facie case for the statistical success of so-called error correction or threshold and asymmetric error correction models over static models or purely AR models, if the real world exhibits chaotic behaviour. Of course, the (linear) error correction model is not the correct representation of the true non-linear chaotic model, but it may provide a reasonably useful approximation for any finite set of data.

Chaotic models applied to economic phenomena are in their infancy, so one cannot expect definitive results at present. However, they do suggest that non-linearities in economic relationships might be important, and the latter may yield chaotic behaviour. In addition one can always add stochastic shocks to any non-linear system which will tend to increase the noise in the system. Hence, although much of economic theory has been founded on linear models or linear approximations to non-linear models to ensure tractability and closed-form solutions, it may be that such approximations can mask important non-linearities in behavioural responses (see Pesaran and Potter, 1993).

A key question that we have not yet tackled is whether *actual* data on exchange rates exhibit chaotic behaviour. We have already remarked on the obvious difficulty in discriminating between a chaotic deterministic process and a purely linear stochastic process. There are several tests available to detect chaotic behaviour, but they require large amounts of data (i.e. say 20,000 data points) to yield reasonably unambiguous and clear results. DeGrauwe *et al.* (1993) use several tests on daily exchange rate data, but find only weak evidence of chaotic behaviour for the yen/dollar and pound sterling/dollar exchange rates and no evidence at all for chaotic behaviour in the DM/dollar exchange rate over the 1972–90 period. This may be due to insufficient data or because the presence of any stochastic 'noise' masks the detection of chaos. They then test for the presence of non-linearities in this exchange rate data. Using two complementary test statistics (Brock *et al.*, 1990; Hinich, 1982) they find that for six major bilateral rates they could not reject the existence of non-linear structures for any of the bilateral rates using daily and weekly *returns* (i.e. the percentage change in the exchange rate) and for monthly data they only reject non-linearity in one case, namely the pound sterling/yen exchange rate.

Of course, non-linearity is necessary for chaotic behaviour, but it is not sufficient: the presence or otherwise of chaotic behaviour depends on the precise parameterisation of the non-linear relationship. Also the above tests do not tell us the precise form of the non-linearity in the dynamics of the exchange rate, merely that some form or other of non-linearity appears to be present. We are still left with the somewhat Herculean task of specifying and estimating a non-linear structural model of the exchange rate.

'Fundamentals' models of the exchange rate have largely failed to explain, let alone predict, movements in exchange rates. In addition, because the exchange rate (in a small open economy) is a key determinant of inflation, output and unemployment, this has led finance ministers of the G10 and other countries to suggest new international monetary arrangements to try and reduce the frequency and size of large unexpected exchange rate changes, and also to mitigate any adverse effects of such changes. This decision is also influenced by the fact that changes in the exchange rate may be partly due to irrational noise traders. The recent policy emphasis has been on 'pro-active' measures to try and avoid currency crises, and these proposals have been given the grandiose title of the 'new financial architecture' (see Box 16.3).

| Box 16.3 | A NEW INTERNATIONAL FINANCIAL ARCHITECTURE? |
|---|---|

Over the last 20 years there have been many major international financial crises. In the 1980s, we had the Latin debt crisis, in 1994–96 the Mexican crisis and more recently some of the 'Tiger Economies' such as Thailand, Malaysia, Korea and Indonesia experienced large devaluations in 1997/8. Also in 1998, Brazil experienced speculative capital outflows and a devaluation of the Brazilian 'real' followed. This has led to criticisms of the role of the International Monetary Fund (IMF) and suggestions for a new 'Bretton Woods'. Proposals for reform, of which there are many, tend to fall under the snappy title of 'new international financial architecture'.

In the past, the IMF has given loans to countries, *conditional* on them adopting specific macroeconomic policies. These policies were not designed to stem a *current* capital outflow during a financial panic. That is, the IMF has not acted as an international lender of last resort ILLR, but has given conditional 'debtor-in-possession loans' to improve matters in the future. However, in 1998, in the wake of the crisis in the Far East, the IMF did set up a Supplemental Reserve Facility to channel funds to (solvent) countries suffering a speculative currency attack. However, it is debatable whether this fund is sufficient to deter international speculators.

Currency speculation has, of course, been made easier by the liberalisation of capital flows (and removal of exchange controls) which began with the UK and USA in the early 1970s and was followed by Europe and much of the rest of the world in the early 1990s. In this era of high capital mobility, some countries tried to achieve the 'Holy Trinity' of fixed exchange rates, free capital flows and an independent monetary policy. However, it soon became apparent that a country cannot simultaneously achieve all three objectives, and it is usually the 'fixed' exchange rate which comes under downward pressure in financial crises. When the latter occurs, as in Asia in 1997/8, the devaluation can cause a severe fall in output (e.g. of around 5% in many of the Far Eastern countries in 1998) and a cut in the standard of living (as import and domestic prices rise) and sometimes civil unrest (e.g. in Indonesia and, to a lesser extent, Korea and Malaysia).

The problem with the IMF acting as an ILLR is moral hazard: private investors have less incentive to assess the soundness of the economic fundamentals of a country, since they will be bailed out (in part) by the IMF. On the other hand, without an ILLR, speculators may 'herd' and precipitate crises in otherwise 'sound' economies.

Policy proposals to mitigate currency crises are many and varied. They include more transparency on macro-policies, more regulation of the banking system in vulnerable countries, better accounting standards and corporate governance. Also, collective action clauses in bond contracts and taxes on foreign borrowing by developing countries, have been suggested. These proposals, although eminently sensible, seem unlikely to radically reduce the number or severity of currency crises.

Considering the wider picture, economists have no firm empirical evidence on whether fixed exchange rates, floating rates or currency boards provide the 'best' exchange rate policy. They all have drawbacks. In the long run, it seems more likely that individual countries will seek to become part of large currency blocs (e.g. as we have seen with the move to a common currency by 11 European states). This common currency model 'pushes' the adjustment process in the economy onto labour markets, rather than the exchange rate. But given the wild gyrations in the latter, countries may feel it is the lesser of two evils.

# 16.4 SUMMARY

It is important that the reader is aware of the attempts that have been made to explain movements in spot exchange rates in terms of economic fundamentals, not least because these models have to some extent helped to shape key economic policy decisions as we noted in our opening remarks. However, the concepts and ideas which underlie these fundamentals models (e.g. PPP, UIP, relative money supplies) do still play a role in guiding policy makers, not least because they have little else to go on other than their 'hunch' about the appropriate interest rate–exchange rate nexus to apply in particular circumstances. The absence of firm policy implications which arise because of the statistical inadequacy of these fundamentals models, has resulted in policy makers trying to mitigate the severity of wide swings in the real exchange rate by co-ordinated Central Bank intervention, a move towards currency zones and in Europe the proposal to adopt a common currency, the euro. Market practitioners have largely accepted that it is not possible to predict the large changes in the spot rate which are frequently observed, and hence have developed a wide range of derivative securities to hedge this uncertainty.

It would seem unlikely that any minor refinements to the traditional monetary models discussed above would lead to dramatic improvements in their statistical performance. At present it would appear to be the case that *formal* tests of the various models lead one to reject them. Hence our conclusions about these **fundamentals models** of the spot rate are:

- **Over short horizons**, say up to about 2 to 3 years, monetary fundamentals generally do not help predict changes in the spot rate. **Over longer horizons** of 4 years fundamentals do provide a modicum of predictive power for some currencies (Mark, 1995).
- In terms of economic theory, the above is consistent with the view that **purchasing power parity** and the (demand for) money–income nexus hold in the long run (i.e. the relevant variables are cointegrated). However, on balance we must recognise that we are still very unsure of the underlying determinants of the spot exchange rate in industrialised countries with moderate inflation.

The lack of success of 'pure fundamentals' models in explaining movements in the spot exchange rate has recently led researchers to consider non-linear models that may result in chaotic behaviour. The underlying theory in these models usually involves both rational traders and some form of noise trader behaviour. They are not models that involve all agents being rational and maximising some well-defined objective function. Nevertheless, their ad hoc assumptions are usually plausible. The main conclusions to emerge from this literature as applied to exchange rates are:

- **Deterministic non-linear** models are capable of generating apparently persistent random and irregular time series (i.e. **chaotic behaviour**) which broadly resemble real world movements in the exchange rate. The addition of 'news' or random 'shocks' provides additional random impulses.

- The **empirical evidence on exchange rates** is ambivalent concerning the presence of chaotic behaviour, however, it does quite strongly indicate the **presence of non-linearities** in the data generation process for exchange rates.
- The challenge now is to produce coherent non-linear theoretical models. Non-linear (fundamentals) models need not necessarily rule out the use of expectations. Models involving the **interaction of noise traders and smart money,** which are not fully (Muth) rational, also seem worthy of further analysis. Non-linear theoretical models will need to be tested against the data, and this may provide further econometric challenges.
- The problem with **chaotic models** and indeed **non-linear stochastic models** is that often small changes in parameter values can lead to radically different behaviour or forecasts for the exchange rate. Given that econometric parameter estimates from non-linear models are frequently subject to some uncertainty, the range of possible forecasts from such models becomes potentially quite large. If such models are not firmly rooted in economic theory then their predictions and policy implications might not carry great weight. However, on purely academic grounds there may be further insights to be obtained from such models.
- Because of the uncertainty concerning the determinants of the spot exchange rate market practitioners have gone in two directions. Those that want to try and improve on their predictions of the exchange rate (e.g. speculators), particularly over short forecast horizons of several minutes up to (say) 1 year, have moved towards largely **statistical models (e.g. neural networks)** or **judgmental approaches (e.g. charts and candlesticks)**. Others accept the uncertainty inherent in the volatile spot rate and look to **FX derivatives** to minimise this risk.

# END OF CHAPTER EXERCISES

**Q1** Why might a rapid growth in the domestic money supply lead to a depreciating exchange rate? Do you know of any instances where this has occurred?

**Q2** If exchange rates are fixed, then what determines the rate of price inflation in a small open economy?

**Q3** Why might the economy take a long time to achieve PPP?

**Q4** Suppose that the 1-year spot interest rate in Euroland is $r = 8\%$ and in USA is $r^* = 5\%$ and (rather stupidly) FOREX dealers (who are risk neutral) expect the euro–USD exchange rate over the next year to remain unchanged?

(a) What will happen to the spot exchange rate today and why?

(b) At what point will the spot exchange rate stop rising or falling? (i.e. equilibrium is restored on the capital account).

(c) What are the likely consequences for Euroland's exports and imports in the short term and in the longer term?

Q5    In practice what do you think determines 'short run' and 'long run' changes in the exchange rate?

Q6    Do monetary models of the exchange rate explain past movements in spot FX rates?

Q7    What are the principal mechanisms that produce exchange rate overshooting?

# Technical Trading Rules

Technical trading methods are often applied in practice to predict stock prices and spot FX rates. We will concentrate on their use in FX markets. If one were to read the popular press then one would think that foreign exchange dealers were speculators par excellence. Particularly in the 1980s, young men in striped shirts wearing primary coloured braces were frequently seen on television, shouting simultaneously into two telephones in order to quickly execute buy and sell orders for foreign currencies. The obvious question which arises is, are these individuals purchasing and selling foreign exchange on the basis of news about fundamentals or do they in fact 'chase trends'? If the latter is true, the question then arises as to whether they can have a pervasive influence on the price of foreign exchange and introduce 'excess volatility' into the market.

As we have seen, there have been a large number of technically sophisticated tests of market efficiency in the foreign exchange market, including ones based on covered interest parity (CIP), spot speculation (i.e. UIP), speculation in the forward market (i.e. FRU) as well as many tests of whether certain economic variables (e.g. PPP or money supply) explain the behaviour of spot exchange rates. In all of these approaches, 'rational investors' base their forecasts of the spot FX rate on a specific set of **economic fundamentals** (e.g. interest rates, prices, money supplied). Not surprisingly therefore, these approaches come under the heading of 'economic fundamentals'. In contrast, so-called **technical traders** study only past price movements in the market and base their view of the future solely on past price changes. For example, chartists believe that they can isolate patterns in past price movements which can be used to predict future movements and hence generate profitable trading strategies, even after correcting for the riskiness of the position. (This, of course, would not be possible in an efficient market.) **Chartists** may use graphs based on very high-frequency data (e.g. tick-by-tick) and they attempt to infer systematic patterns in these graphs. The term **technical analysis** is a generic term which includes chartists (graphs), candlesticks (bar charts), filter rules, moving averages and momentum indices.

Regression techniques, based on estimating statistical regularities using only past prices as independent variables, also provide a specific quantitative method of capturing possible regularities. But generally speaking, these would not come under the heading of 'technical trading rules'. However, in this chapter we also discuss **neural networks** which are a kind of non-linear regression/estimation technique, although the data inputs usually include variables other than past prices.

# 17.1 CHARTISTS

Over short horizons (e.g. intra-day, overnight, weekly), FX traders use forecasts based on some form of technical trading rules, rather than on fundamentals (see Allen and Taylor, 1989a,b). In fact, about 75% of FX spot trades are between brokers/dealers and are closed out within the day (Bank for International Settlements, 1996). With more than 1trn US dollars per day traded on the spot FX market, one might think that the market is efficient and there are no unexploitable profit opportunities to be made. However, if technical analysts chase trends then they could make money, particularly if the 'fundamentals traders' do not bet against them. Trading on the basis of economic fundamentals in the spot FX market could be relatively weak because the fundamentals–exchange rate link is very imprecise (over all but the longest horizons of several years). Fundamentals traders may also have a limited impact on the spot rate because they face liquidity constraints and may have to close out all (or most of) their positions by the end of the trading day (otherwise they would incur overnight interest payments as well as risky overnight positions).

To illustrate some aspects of this approach, consider the idealised pattern given in Figure 17.1 which is known as the **'head and shoulders reversal pattern'**. On this graph is drawn a horizontal line called 'the shoulder'. Points A and B are the top of the shoulders and B is the 'head'. Once the pattern reaches point D, that is a peak below the shoulder, the chartist would assume this signals a full trend reversal. She would then sell the currency believing that it would fall in the future and she could buy it back at a lower price. As another example, consider Figure 17.2, the so-called **'symmetric triangle'** indicated by the oscillations converging on the point at A. To some chartists this pattern would signal a future upward movement as the upward trend in the price series 'breaks out' of its restrictive (narrowing) triangle. Clearly the interpretation of such graphs is subjective.

## FIGURE 17.1: Head and shoulders

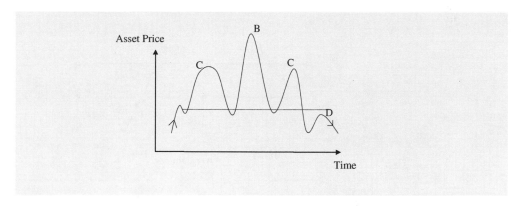

## FIGURE 17.2: Symmetric triangle

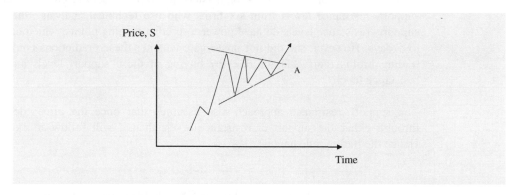

It is well known that some chartists also complement their graphical approach with the use of survey data on 'market sentiment'. For example, if 'sentiment' is reported to be optimistic about the German economy, then chartists may well try and step in early and buy euros. For chartists as a group to influence the market, most chartists must interpret the charts in roughly the same way, otherwise all the chartists would do would be to introduce some random noise into prices but no trends.

## SUPPORT–RESISTANCE LEVELS

Another variant on chartism is the use of support–resistance levels. If, in the past, the spot rate had repeatedly hit an upper level without breaking through it, this is designated as the current **resistance level** (R–R in Figure 17.3). Similarly, the lower limit is known as the **support level**, S–S. These support–resistance levels can change daily and, for example, Reuters FXNL screens give these levels at the beginning of the trading day, based on a sample of FX dealers' views of the trading range expected over the coming day.

One way of interpreting these support–resistance levels is to assume they impart information about possible breaks in trend. So if the exchange rate hits the support level (from

## FIGURE 17.3: Resistance and support levels

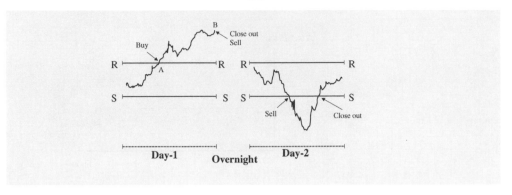

above) or the resistance level (from below) we can expect a 'bounce' back off these levels (i.e. a form of intra-day mean reversion). Osler (2000) uses intra-day spot FX data on (US) dollar–yen, dollar–mark and dollar–sterling over January 1996 to March 1998 and support–resistance levels from six firms who use technical analysis. She found that the support–resistance levels do have power to predict turning points, which can persist for up to 5 days. However, she did not investigate whether these predictions could lead to actual trading profits (corrected for risk) by buying at these support levels and selling at the resistance level.

The support–resistance approach also assumes that once the price 'decisively' breaks through either the support or resistance levels then it will follow an extrapolative path. Hence the trading rule here is:

> **Buy spot FX when the FX rate 'decisively' crosses the**
> **resistance level from below**
> **Sell spot FX when the FX rate 'decisively' crosses the**
> **support level from above**

After a 'buy' decision, the trader is assumed to close out her position either when the spot rate falls back to the R-level (making no profit over this period) or at the close of trading (e.g. by midnight if we assume traders are not allowed to hold an open position overnight). In Figure 17.3 the trader makes a profit on day 1 but not on day 2. It is also possible to lose money. For example, buying on day 1 at A would cause a loss if the spot rate subsequently *fell* throughout the day, being closed out at the lower closing price.

Using tick data and hourly checks on whether to trade, Curcio *et al.* (1996) find that for DM, yen and sterling against the US dollar, intra-day trading leads to some small positive returns (relative to buy and hold) but only when exchange rates are trending (up or down). The support–resistance levels were those supplied daily by Reuters, and they adjusted the returns for the bid–ask spread. For example, a buy signal would be executed at the bid rate and the subsequent 'sell' at the ask rate (and vice versa for a 'sell–buy' sequence).

However, the Curcio *et al*. (1996) study cannot indicate what 'dollar bets' were placed for each trade and the (small) profits are not corrected for any measure of the riskiness of the transaction (in contrast to the Pesaran and Timmermann, 1994 study for stock returns). Also, it is always possible that either different trading rules (e.g. moving averages) or another technical trading strategy involving a portfolio of currencies might yield substantial profits net of transactions costs and corrected for risk (e.g. Surajas and Sweeney, 1992). Brock *et al*. (1992) and Levich and Thomas (1993), using other types of technical rules, find profits can be made on *inter*-day trading in the FX market, although these 'profits' do not take account of transactions costs and the profitable trading horizons were much longer than over 1 day.

Overall, these results suggest that it is very difficult to make profits (net of transactions costs) in the spot FX market by using chartist methods. However, this does not appear to prevent traders making continued use of these techniques.

## CANDLE CHARTS

These are Japanese in origin and are used to indicate 'buy' or 'sell' decisions largely based on the direction of movement between the opening and closing prices (relative to the degree of underlying volatility in the market over the trading day). To get the ball rolling consider the 'candles' in Figure 17.4. Any price fall between open and close is designated by black 'bars' and price rises by grey 'bars'. The maximum and minimum intra-day prices are indicated by a thin black line. Thus each day's high–low and open–close prices resemble a candle with a wick at both ends.

Candle A indicates that the market fell considerably between open and close and is known as a *Major Yin*. The latter is usually taken to indicate that a further fall (bearish) is expected and hence is a strong signal to sell. Candle B is the opposite (i.e. a *Major Yang*) and is a strongly bullish signal (i.e. buy). Candle C is a *Yang with Upper Shadow*, showing a small rise from open to close but a much larger rise during the day's trading: the signal here is

## FIGURE 17.4: Candle patterns

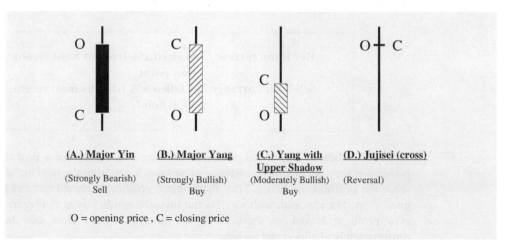

**(A.) Major Yin**

(Strongly Bearish)
Sell

**(B.) Major Yang**

(Strongly Bullish)
Buy

**(C.) Yang with Upper Shadow**

(Moderately Bullish)
Buy

**(D.) Jujisei (cross)**

(Reversal)

O = opening price , C = closing price

mildly bullish. Candle D is a *Jujisei* (cross) where the market opened and closed at the same price but there was substantial movement during the day. This indicates that a reversal of the recent trend (either up or down) is likely. Clearly, a large amount of judgement is required when interpreting candle patterns, and this subjective element means that there are no formal tests of their effectiveness in predicting changes in spot FX rates.

# 17.2 OTHER 'CHARTIST' FORECASTING METHODS

Some other trading strategies based on past price behaviour but not explicitly on charts include 'high–low extremes', 'filter rules', 'momentum indices' and 'cross-over methods', and we now discuss these methods.

## HIGH–LOW EXTREMES

In a high–low (HL) strategy, buy and sell decisions are determined by a movement outside recent highs or lows. Suppose the highest and lowest closing prices for dollar–sterling over the last $T = 10$ trading days are 1.65 $/£ and 1.60 $/£, respectively. If on the next trading day (i.e. $T + 1$) the *closing price* is 1.70 $/£ ($> 1.65$ $/£) then we buy sterling at *the opening* of trading on the next day (i.e. $T + 2$). Similarly, if the closing price on day $T + 1$ had been 1.55 $/£ ($< 1.60$ $/£) then we sell sterling. This trading rule is based on a breakout from a previous high or low. If the breakout is in the upward direction we buy, believing that the upward movement will continue (the upper breakout is like a moving 'resistance level'). This is a trend extrapolation strategy. Only one position is signalled each day and we are either long or short, we are never 'square'. When a new buy/sell signal arrives we just close out the old position. If the high and low prices on day $T + 1$ are equal then the market is 'locked limit' and nothing is done on that day.

## FILTER RULES

This approach is also a trend following strategy. Suppose we have an $x\%$ filter rule, then the strategy is:

> **Buy if the currency has risen $x\%$ from its most recent low point**
> **Sell if the currency has fallen $x\%$ from its most recent high point**

If $x = 2\%$, then we buy if the price increases by 2%, hoping for a further price rise. The position is then held until the currency moves down $x\%$ from the next highest level reached, since the position was taken. Then the original position is closed out and the investor also goes short. For example, with $x = 2\%$ the investor would buy at A (Figure 17.5), close out at a profit at B and go short. At C the investor would close out the short position (unfortunately at a loss) and go long.

## FIGURE 17.5: Filter rule, $x = 2\%$

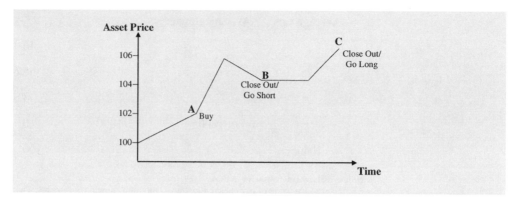

## MOMENTUM MODELS

These models provide a measure of the relative strength or 'momentum' of 'up' and 'down' *movements* in the spot FX rate. The relative change in direction of the spot rate is measured by the 'momentum':

[17.1]
$$M_{t+1} = \frac{(1/n) \sum_{i=1}^{n} u_{it}}{(1/n) \sum_{i=1}^{n} d_{it}} = \frac{\text{average of 'ups'}}{\text{average of 'downs'}}$$

where
$$u_{it} = S_{t-i+1} - S_{t-i} \quad \text{if } S_{t-i+1} > S_{t-i}$$
$$d_{it} = |S_{t-i+1} - S_{t-i}| \quad \text{if } S_{t-i-1} < S_{t-i}$$

So $u_{it}$ is the 'up' change and $d_{it}$ is the (absolute) 'down' change in the spot rate, each of which is measured over the previous $n$ periods in calculating $M_t$. The index can be normalised to lie between 0 and 100 and is known as the **relative strength index RSI**:

[17.2]
$$\text{RSI}_t = 100 - \frac{100}{(1 + M_t)}$$

As can be seen from Table 17.1 for 'average ups' equal to 'average downs', $M_t = 1$ and $\text{RSI}_t = 50$, which is a neutral position. If 'average ups' have been twice the size of 'average downs', $M_t = 2$ and $\text{RSI}_t = 66.6$, indicating a substantial recent upward momentum. The RSI index might be implemented as follows. $\text{RSI}_t = 70$ would indicate recent substantial upward momentum, which cannot be sustained, and hence the decision would be to sell (i.e. close out existing long positions). Similarly, if the 'average downs' have been twice the size of 'average ups', $M_t = 0.5$ and $\text{RSI}_t = 33.3$. $\text{RSI}_t = 30$ is usually taken to mean the recent downward momentum is at an end and should be reversed in the future, hence the signal is to buy (or keep the existing position). In summary:

## TABLE 17.1: Calculation of relative strength index

| Average ups | Average downs | $M_t$ | $RSI_t$ |
|:---:|:---:|:---:|:---:|
| z | z | 1 | 50 |
| 2z | z | 2 | 66.6 |
| z | 2z | 1/2 | 33.3 |
| z | 1000z | 1/1000 | 0 |
| 1000z | z | 1000 | 100 |

Notes: $RSI_t = 100 - 100/(1 + M_t)$

$z$ = the absolute value of our chosen illustrative 'up' and 'down' movements. This allows us to calculate the corresponding values for the momentum index $M$ and the relative strength index RSI

---

**$RSI_t > 70$ then sell**
**$RSI_t < 30$ then buy**

---

Thus the RSI assumes some mean reversion in the spot rate: rapid rises are expected to be followed by a fall in the future (and vice versa).

## CROSS-OVER (MOVING AVERAGE) METHODS

This method is based on the relationship between a 'short' and 'long' moving average of *the level* of the exchange rate. A moving average (MA) is a weighted average of past values of the exchange rate $S$ which can either use equal weights or declining weights (i.e. more recent values of $S$ are given greater weight than more distant values of $S$).

*Equally weighted moving average (MA):*

[17.3a]     $MA_{t+1} = (S_t + S_{t-1} + \ldots + S_{t-n+1})n$

*Exponentially weighted moving average (EWMA):*

[17.3b]     $EWMA_{t+1} = (1 - \alpha) \sum_{i=0}^{\infty} \alpha^i S_{t-i}$

In the EWMA scheme [17.3b] the weights decline geometrically and add to unity. If $\alpha = 0.9$ then successive weights $\alpha^i$ decline as follows: 0.9, 0.81, 0.73, etc. If we just wish to use '$n$' past observations in calculating $EWMA_t$ the formula is:

[17.4]     $EWMA_{t+1} = k \sum_{i=0}^{n-1} \alpha^i S_{t-i}$

where $k = (1 - \alpha)/(1 - \alpha^n)$. The adjustment '$k$' is required because the $\alpha^i$ terms sum to $[(1 - \alpha^n)/(1 - \alpha)]$ and hence '$k$' ensures that if all '$n$' past levels of $S_{t-i}$ were constant ($= S$) then the moving average $MA_t$ would also be equal to $S$. Alternatively it can be shown that (for $n$ reasonably large, that is $\alpha^n \to 0$):

[17.5]     $$EWMA_{t+1} = \alpha EWMA_t + kS_t$$

So that given an arbitrary starting value for $EWMA_1$ ($= S_1$ for example) equation [17.5] can be used to continually update the calculation of $EWMA_t$ as each successive value of $S_t$ becomes available. (The forecast value of $EWMA_{t+1}$ is independent of the starting value for $EWMA_1$ after about 50 data points have been used.) Hence equation [17.5] provides a useful recursive computational device for calculating the EWMA forecast (which can be easily programmed).

The cross-over method works like this. First construct a 'short' EWMA from $n_1$ past data points and a 'long' EWMA from $n_2$ data points, based on the closing prices for the spot exchange rate (with $n_2 > n_1$). For example, $n_1 = 5$ days and $n_2 = 15$ days or $n_1 = 15$ days and $n_2 = 20$ days are frequently used. The trading rule is based on the **cross-over point** in the trend in the short EWMA relative to the long EWMA, hence (see Figure 17.6):

> **Buy, if short MA crosses long MA from below**
> **Sell, if short MA crosses long MA from above**

Hence at point A (Figure 17.6) you would buy at the opening of the next trading day and at B you would close out the old position and sell (or go short).

## FIGURE 17.6: Cross-over strategy

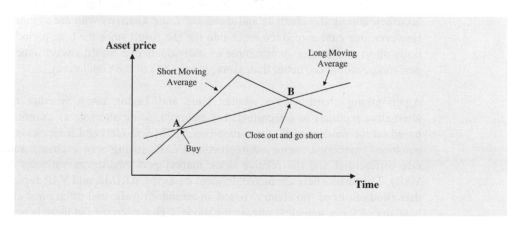

## 17.3 EVIDENCE ON CHARTISTS

Allen and Taylor (1989a) have undertaken a study of the behaviour of chartists, although the sample of data on which the study is based is rather small. The survey was conducted on a panel of chartists (between 10 and 20 responded every week) over the period June 1988– March 1989. They were telephoned every Thursday and asked for their expectations with respect to the sterling–dollar, dollar–mark and dollar–yen exchange rates for 1 and 4 weeks ahead, yielding about 36 observations per chartist per currency. The survey also asked the chartists about the kind of information they used in making their forecasts and who the information was passed on to (e.g. actual traders).

It was found that at the shortest horizons (say intra-day to 1 week) as many as 90% of the respondents used some chartist input in forming their exchange rate expectations. As the time horizon lengthens to 3 months, 6 months or 1 year the weight given to fundamentals increases and 85% of the respondents judged that over these longer horizons 'fundamentals' were more important than chart analysis. However, the chart analysis was always seen as complementary to the analysis based on fundamentals, and therefore it is possible that chart analysis influences exchange rates even at these longer horizons.

If one looks ex-post at the accuracy of the chartists' forecasts (taken as a group) for the dollar–mark spot rate, the 4-week ahead forecasts are fairly typical of the results for other currencies. In general Allen and Taylor find:

- There is a tendency for the forecasts to miss turning points. On a rising or falling market the chartists' expectations underestimate the extent of the rise or fall.
- Prediction errors are noticeably greater at the 4-week horizon than at the 1-week horizon. Also individual chartist's forecasts for 4-week ahead predictions are generally unbiased, but they are biased for the 1-week ahead predictions.
- For all the chartists taken as a whole, they correctly predict the change in the exchange rate over 1 week and 4 week horizons approximately 50% of the time. This is what one would expect if their forecasts were purely due to chance.

The above result for all chartists neglects the possibility that individual chartists might in fact do well and do consistently well over time. In fact there are differences in forecast accuracy among the chartists and there are some chartists who are systematically 'good'. However, one cannot read too much into the last result since the time period of the survey is fairly short and in a random sample of individuals one would always expect that a certain percentage would do 'better than average' (e.g. 5% of the population).

Again taking chartists as a whole, Allen and Taylor assess whether they outperform alternative methods of forecasting. For example, some alternatives examined are forecasts based on the random walk, those based on ARIMA models and forecasts using a system of equations, namely a vector autoregression (VAR) (using spot exchange rates, the interest rate differential and the relative stock market performance as variables included in the VAR). The results here are mixed. In most cases the ARIMA and VAR forecasts were worse than predictions of 'no change' based on a random walk, and often most chartists failed to beat any of these statistical forecasting models. However, overall there is not much in it. All of the statistical forecasting methods and the chartists' forecasts had approximately the same RMS errors for 1-week and 4-week ahead forecasts with, on balance, the random walk probably doing best. However, there were some individual chartists who consistently outperformed all other forecasting methods.

Since Allen and Taylor have data on expectations, they can correlate changes in expectations with past changes in the actual exchange rate. We are particularly interested in whether chartists have bandwagon or extrapolative expectations. That is to say, when the exchange rate increases between $t-1$ and $t$, does this lead all chartists to revise their expectations upwards. Allen and Taylor tested this hypothesis but found that for all chartists as a group, bandwagon expectations did not apply.

Thus chartist advice does not appear to be intrinsically destabilising in that they do not overreact to recent changes in the exchange rate. In fact Allen and Taylor find that chartists tend to have either 'adaptive' or 'regressive' expectations. These two types of expectation formation are essentially *mean reverting*, which means that if expectations of the spot rate are currently above some 'long run level' then they believe the spot rate will, in subsequent time periods, tend to fall back towards this long run level. Overall the results seem to suggest there are agents in the market who make systematic forecasting errors, but there appears to be no bandwagon or explosive effect from this behaviour, and at most chartists might influence short run deviations of the exchange rate from fundamentals.

The Allen and Taylor study did not examine whether chartists' forecasts actually resulted in profitable trades. They merely looked at the accuracy of chartists' forecasts. However, a number of studies have been done (Goodman, 1979, 1980; Levich, 1980; Bilson, 1981) which have looked at ex-post evaluations of exchange rate forecasting services, some of which were provided by technical analysts (e.g. chartists). A major finding of these studies is that certain foreign exchange advisory services do consistently outperform the forward rate as a predictor of the future spot rate. In particular, Goodman (1980) finds that 'technical advice' is consistently superior to both the forward rate and other econometric models based on fundamentals in forecasting the future spot rate.

# 17.4 NEURAL NETWORKS

Neural networks have wide applicability in many areas of finance and we can only present an introductory overview here. Much of finance theory is used to guide us towards a possibly 'true' description of the way a variable such as the expected return on a stock, $ER_i$, is determined. For example, the CAPM implies that $ER_i$ depends linearly on the excess return on the market, that is $ER_i - r = \beta_i(ER_m - r)$. In contrast, a neural network is a statistical way of discovering 'patterns' in data and representing these relationships mathematically. A neural network is a 'black-box' forecasting system. Given inputs $X_i$ ($i = 1, 2, \ldots, n$) the neural network works out the best method of predicting the outputs $Y_j$, but it is impossible to put an interpretation or 'story' as to how particular values of the $X_i$ give rise to a particular forecast of $Y_j$. The term **artificial neural network ANN** arises because the 'neural net' mimics the behaviour of the neurons in the brain as it 'learns about' the patterns in the data and then represents this pattern mathematically.

There are many situations in finance where an accurate forecast would be useful. For example, suppose we are trying to predict whether or not an individual, financial institution or country will default on a debt obligation. Then the output of our model $Y$ might be dichotomous, that is $Y = 1$ implies 'default' and $Y = 0$ implies 'no default'. The neural network uses a set of input variables $X_i$ such as income level, age and marital status of the individual and will 'train itself' to yield the best forecast. Take chartism as another example. Maybe a neural network can be trained to recognise chartist patterns and hence produce a forecast of the stock price (or the FX rate) based on a highly non-linear relationship between current stock prices, past movements in the stock price and other asset prices. Because ANNs are non-linear models they are clearly consistent with the non-linearities found in empirical studies of financial asset returns. Key features of this approach are:

- the functional form used is highly non-linear and is primarily based on past movements in the data and not on any particular economic theory of the spot rate;
- the network is 'trained' on past data from which it 'learns' about the past behaviour of the (spot FX rate) data and updates the parameters in an attempt to minimise the forecast errors of the equation.

Note that, conceptually, this is not an entirely novel approach. Indeed, as a first approximation, a neural network can be considered as a 'normal' non-linear regression equation, with time varying parameters that are updated as new information about the spot rate arises. Neural nets are popular for short run predictions (e.g. predicting tick-by-tick data or for say predictions up to 1 week ahead) and may be used as an independent check on a trader's 'gut feelings'.

Alternatively, the method can be used relatively mechanically to trigger buy and sell orders. For example, the neural net would be 'trained' on data up to time $t$ (the 'training period') and then would give a series of predictions for each of the next 15 minutes (the 'testing period'). If these lay outside the 'error band' for the forecast (calculated from the 'training period' data) then this would lead to the parameter of the ANN being updated. Having obtained the 'best equation' it would then be used in a 'genuine prediction'. If the ANN forecasts a rise in the spot rate which lies above the upper error band then this would be a 'buy signal'. After say 15 minutes any 'new' data would be added and the parameters re-estimated. The 'updated equation' is then used to provide a further prediction for the next 15 minutes (along with the new error bands).

There are now quite a number of software companies which provide neural net programmes that are easy to use (i.e. menu driven) yet allow the user some flexibility in how she chooses to 'train the network' (e.g. 'Neuralist' by *Palisade Corporation*). More sophisticated systems are used by banks and securities houses and *Olsen and Associates* in Zurich were early advocates of using this approach to forecast very short run changes in the spot rate. The method is now becoming more widely used amongst a relatively small number of 'quant jocks' for predicting other financial time series (see Trippi and Turban, 1993). The method is clearly a useful one, as it is merely a highly sophisticated statistical technique for fitting non-linear functions to time series data.

A slightly different way of looking at neural networks is that it is a method that can be used to 'statistically explain' the movement in financial asset returns that is not explained by 'conventional' economic models. For example, if the risk premium in the uncovered interest parity (UIP) relationship has a highly non-linear functional form this could be 'statistically modelled' using a neural network while still allowing the change in the spot rate to be partly influenced by interest differentials.

## BUILDING BLOCKS

The key elements in a neural network are the inputs $X_i$, the outputs $Y_j$ and the weights $w_i$ which represent the relative strength of each of the $X_i$'s in its effect on the $Y_j$. Suppose we have three inputs $X_i$ and one output $Y$ (Figure 17.7). If the $w_i$ are the weights then the *summation function* is:

[17.6] $$Y = w_1 X_1 + w_2 X_2 + w_3 X_3$$

Based on the level of $Y$ from the above equation, the ANN may or may not produce an output (i.e. the neuron may or may not be activated). For example, a **threshold detector** might give an output $y$ as follows:

$Y > 0.5$     then     $y = 1$

$Y < 0.5$     then     $y = 0$

This is the kind of output from the ANN we would use in predicting a default/no default outcome on outstanding debt contracts. Alternatively the output $y$ might be a non-linear *transfer function* of $Y$, a popular one being the sigmoid function:

[17.7] $$y = \frac{1}{1 + e^{-Y}}$$

## FIGURE 17.7: Neural network (No hidden layers)

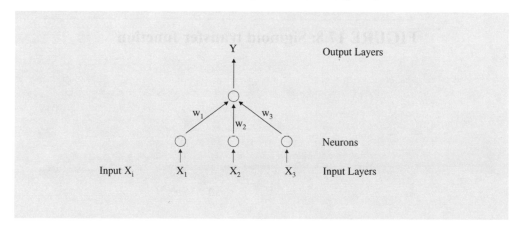

No matter how large or small $Y$ turns out to be, the output $y$ always lies between 0 and 1 (Figure 17.8). For example, if $X_1 = 6$, $X_2 = 2$, $X_3 = 3$ and $w_1 = 0.2$, $w_2 = 0.3$, $w_3 = 0.1$ then $Y = 2.1$ and:

[17.8]
$$y = \frac{1}{1 + e^{-2.1}} = 0.89$$

The so-called hyperbolic tangent (transformation) allows somewhat greater variability since the output $y$ then lies between $-1$ and $+1$. (This would be useful for a model of stock picking where 'good stock return' $= +1$ and 'bad stock return' $= -1$.)

How does the ANN determine the values for $w_i$? An ANN cannot be fitted to *all* of the available data because in principle it can 'fit' the data with 100% accuracy (because of the flexible non-linear relationship between the $X_i$ and $Y$). This is known as **overfitting** and is illustrated in Figure 17.9. Suppose for simplicity the true model is linear but we have only three data points {A, B, C}. A quadratic equation (i.e. one containing terms in $X_i$ and $X_i^2$) can fit these three points exactly, whereas a linear relationship fits worse. An ANN based on a within-sample 'best fit' criterion (e.g. minimising the residual sum of squares) would search over many non-linear (and linear) relationships and would end up fitting a quadratic function exactly. This is **overfitting**. The forecast with the ANN equation from C is worse than that with the linear equation from C'.

Remember that an equation that is *designed* to fit well 'in-sample' may not necessarily forecast 'well' out-of-sample. The choice of the non-linear functional form has to be reasonably flexible, since the relationship under study may be extremely non-linear. It also follows that one will need a large amount of data if the method is to be of practical use, since it is well known that the parameters of non-linear models are very sensitive to alternative small samples of data (and the estimation algorithm may not converge).

The overfitting problem can be mitigated by splitting the data into two sets: a *training set* and a *testing set*. (In econometrics these are usually referred to as 'within-sample' and 'out-of-sample' data sets.) We then choose the weights $w_i$ to minimise the forecast errors in the

---

## FIGURE 17.8: Sigmoid transfer function

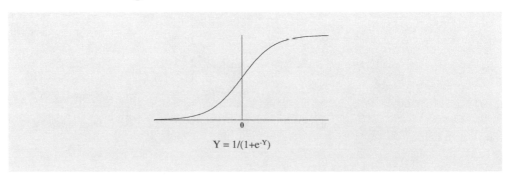

$$Y = 1/(1+e^{-Y})$$

## FIGURE 17.9: ANN and overfitting

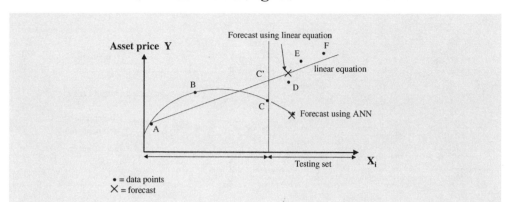

testing set of data. Thus with A, B and C in the training set the ANN 'fits' a quadratic but this leads to a poor forecast of points D, E and F (Figure 17.9). Hence, the ANN recalculates the weights $w_i$ on the $X_i$ to minimise these forecast errors and hence will 'learn' that the best weights are given by the linear relationship. This is known as **training the network** and is how the network learns and adjusts the weights as new data is incorporated.

Let us extend this 'overfitting example' to the prediction of the FX rate where the criterion used in choosing the appropriate neural network is minimising the out-of-sample forecast error. So 'M/s Neural Network' proceeds as follows. She takes the last $T = 1$ year of 15 minute (or even tick-by-tick) data on the spot FX rate. Initially she uses only the first 9 months of data to 'fit' her neural network. She then uses this model to predict the next 50 data points (i.e. 50 of the next 15 minute data points) and clearly the existing neural net will make forecast errors. The 'parameter estimates' are then altered to minimise these out-of-sample prediction errors (e.g. minimising the RMS forecast error). This process is repeated after adding the next 50 data points to the training set and the 'parameters' of the neural net are again updated. In this way the neural net is 'trained' on the existing data on the basis of the prediction errors which ensure (rather than using all the data at one go to 'fit' the best model). Apart from the non-linear aspect however, it is worth noting that this emphasis on model design, based on the out-of-sample prediction, is now common in standard econometric modelling (see Hendry, 1995). Of course, for any model the only 'true forecast' is when the model is used to predict *beyond* the existing complete data set.

There are many different objective functions (or learning algorithms) we could put forward for choosing the optimal values for the $w_i$ (e.g. minimising the sum of squared errors, the sum of absolute errors, the proportion of correct 'up' or 'down' predictions, etc.) and each arbitrary choice will give different optimal weights.

The flexibility and highly non-linear relationships that can be produced by an ANN are facilitated by adding *hidden layers* (Figure 17.10). From each 'input neuron' $X_i$ there is an output $Y_j$ which is then linked to all the other neurons in the 'hidden layer' and these in turn

## FIGURE 17.10: ANN (One hidden layer)

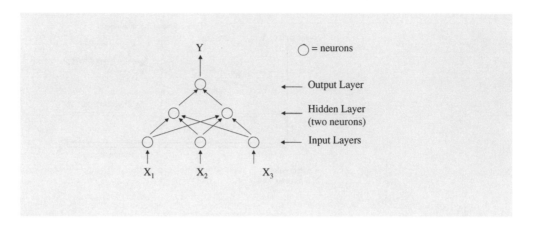

are linked to the output layer. (In Figure 17.10 we show only one output layer.) At each neuron the transfer function is operational, making the relationship between the inputs $X_i$ and the output $Y$ potentially highly non-linear. The *network configuration* in Figure 17.10 is an example of what is called a **multilayer perceptron**. In principal you can have many hidden layers, although in practice one or two are usual.

From the standpoint of a financial economist (or market analyst) the biggest drawback of neural networks is that they are a 'black-box'. The inputs (e.g. current and past values for the spot rate) are 'popped' into the 'box', the algorithm 'whurrs' around and out 'pops' the optimal forecast at the other end, but without any explanation whatsoever. If the neural network is given to another technician who chooses to train it in a slightly different way then a different forecast will be produced. Quite rightly, managers of the FX trading desk do like to be able to 'tell a story' to justify their actions (particularly if they have to justify why they lost a lot of money). Hence in practice, neural networks are only ever likely to provide a complementary technique to the traders' gut feelings. On an academic level, neural networks are a way of modelling our ignorance of the behavioural mechanisms behind decisions in the FX market. Neural networks may, at the margin, improve the forecasts from more 'theory' or 'fundamentals' based models and their strengths and weaknesses are summarised in Box 17.1.

## Box 17.1   ARTIFICIAL NEURAL NETWORKS: PRO'S AND CON'S

- ANNs are a useful method of obtaining **'pattern recognition'** which can then be used in forecasting, particularly where our theoretical or intuitive knowledge is very weak and the underlying relationships are highly **non-linear** (and possibly with time varying parameters). However, it remains a 'black-box' (and unlike the black-box on an aircraft we usually cannot 'look inside'). In contrast, models based on **'economic fundamentals'** (e.g. money supply, interest rates, competitiveness) usually allow some kind of optimal or 'reasonable' behavioural assumptions and this helps in explaining the working of the economy and gives credence to the model (assuming it performs reasonably well on statistical grounds).

- ANNs require considerable **judgement** in choosing the inputs $X_i$, the transfer function, the number of hidden layers and the objective function, in order to determine the optimal weights. 'Fundamentals models' also require judgement, for example which variables are most important, which functional form to use (linear or non-linear), what statistical tests are crucial, etc.

- For some situations (e.g. forecasting bankruptcies) ANNs do not necessarily provide significantly better forecasts than 'simpler' or more conventional methods (e.g. non-linear time series regressions based on 'fundamentals' such as accounting ratios, discriminant analysis, logit and probit models, etc.), yet they have significantly higher costs in terms of complexity, data requirements and implementation.

- ANNs may prove useful in explaining (in a statistical sense) movements in a variable which 'remain' after using a more conventional model. For example, a great deal of the behaviour of monthly spot FX or stock return volatility may be explained using a simple EWMA or GARCH model. However, there may be some unexplained 'regularities' (e.g. skewness, fat tails) which can then be modelled by applying an ANN in addition to the GARCH model. (Strictly, ANN is applied to the residuals from the GARCH model.)

At this point it is worth briefly mentioning another artificial intelligence based forecasting system, known as an **expert system ES**. To calibrate an ES, a fund manager will respond to a set of questions which are then programmed into a computer. For example, she may be asked: 'If GDP rises by 1% p.a. and interest rates also rise by 50 bp would you buy or sell the S&P500?'. Having programmed the responses to a whole host of scenarios, we check to see if these decisions were correct or incorrect in the past and hence 'fine tune' our ES. Then when one of these thousands of scenarios occur in the future, the computer can produce a buy or sell decision based on the expert's past decisions. Clearly, ES requires detailed structured interviewing techniques and a tremendous number of scenarios which need to be coded into a programme. It is very labour and computer intensive and for this reason is not widely used.

In summary, we note that ANNs are being used in all areas of financial forecasting but their success over rival methods has yet to be clearly demonstrated (see Trippi and Turban, 1993). It seems most likely that they will be used extensively in credit scoring where there is plentiful data on which to 'train' the system and test the genuine forecast out-turns. Another possible fruitful area is in modelling 'tick-by-tick' data on asset prices such as FX rates and stock prices. Forecasts can then be produced over say each successive 10-minute horizon, together with error bands and 'buy and sell' decisions if the forecasts lie outside the error bands. However, probably the greatest weakness of ANNs is that they are a black-box and hence you cannot tell a 'plausible story' of why a particular combination of inputs will lead to a particular forecast output value.

## 17.5 NOISE TRADERS VERSUS FUNDAMENTALS

It is generally agreed that there are two broad types of trader present in financial markets, often referred to as 'smart money', those who base their predictions on 'rational funda- mentals' (i.e. some economic theory) and those that use informal forecasting schemes, who are generically referred to as 'noise traders'. Note, however, that it is always possible that the 'noise traders' make more money (even corrected for risk) than do the 'smart money', so the 'smart money' may not be so smart after all! Even when there are only 'rational smart money' traders operating in the market, asset prices can still be highly volatile (e.g. as we saw in the case of the Dornbusch FX overshooting model and the Gordon growth model for stocks).

It is very difficult to give a balanced view of the behaviour and influence of 'noise traders' because (a) theoretical models of noise trader behaviour are relatively new, (b) we have little hard empirical evidence on noise trader behaviour and (c) conclusions must be based on evidence from several asset markets (e.g. stocks, bonds, spot and forward FX). So the views we express below would undoubtedly be fiercely contested by a large number of our colleagues.

In our view, evidence from the anomalies literature, variance bounds tests and general tests of asset market returns (e.g. CAPM, consumption CAPM, APT—see earlier chapters and Cuthbertson, 1996) provide reasonable evidence that all is not well with theories based on only 'smart money' traders. We state this even though there have been many ingenious attempts to 'resurrect' these theories. In addition, there is much circumstantial evidence from psychological studies (see Shiller, 2000) that often individuals do not behave in a rational manner—they may suffer from 'irrational overexuberance'.

However, the key question is how much influence do these noise traders have in practice. This is much more difficult to answer. Certainly, the lack of any substantial new information or 'news' about fundamentals at times of currency (or stock market) crises suggests that there can be acute herding behaviour by noise traders over short periods of time (e.g. over a matter of days) and that in the FX market this can have serious repercussions for the economy in general (e.g. sudden changes in price competitiveness after the Asian crisis of 1997/8 and the Russian 'bond crisis' of 1998). In more tranquil periods, it is hard to discern any herding behaviour (and indeed this is entirely consistent with some theoretical models of noise traders' behaviour—e.g. Kirman's 1993 'Ants model'), but this does not mean that these noise traders do not cause additional uncertainty in the market and some 'excess volatility' (e.g. as in the model of DeLong et al., 1990). It is just that the evidence is not clear-cut on this issue.

It is also true that there is not much one can do (or might wish to do) from a public policy point of view, even if one believes these noise traders do create excess volatility and occasional currency (or stock market) crises. One would hardly advocate closing down these markets. The growth of derivatives markets (i.e. forwards, futures, options and swaps) has enabled much of the short run volatility in spot markets to be hedged and hence the risk largely removed at fairly low cost (at least over horizons of up to 1 year).

Trading halts at times of herding behaviour particularly for stock (and stock index futures) markets are sometimes implemented (e.g. in the stock market crash of 1987). For spot FX markets, which operate 24 hours a day around the globe, it is clearly almost impossible to implement a trading halt during a currency crisis. There have been schemes to 'throw sand in the wheels' of the FX market, most notably the 'Tobin tax' which involves a tax on FX deals, to try and mitigate some of the perceived excess volatility of the spot rate. But to date, these have met with little enthusiasm from 'practitioners' (e.g. within the IMF) and instead Central Bankers have tried to combat this problem in a variety of ways. Most obvious is the (threat of) concerted intervention in favour of one particular currency as set out, for example, in the Plaza and Louvre accords of 1985 and 1987 on the US dollar and more recently during the Asia and Japan crises of 1997/8. Some countries embed their mutual support for each other's currencies in a legalistic framework, such as the European Exchange Rate Mechanism (ERM) which has culminated in the recent historic move for 11 European countries to be in the 'first wave' to use a common currency, the euro. Other methods of trying to gain 'credibility' for your exchange rate include announcing a 'fixed parity' against a key trading partner and sometimes this is accompanied by the introduction of a currency board (e.g. as in Hong Kong and Latvia).

## 17.6 SUMMARY

- There are a large number of **alternative statistical methods** used to forecast the spot FX rate, most of which rely on predictions based on past movements in the exchange rate. In broad terms, these are **technical trading methods**.
- **Chartists** base their forecasts on time series graphs of the spot rate. Either they recognise patterns in the data that they think will repeat themselves or they use simple quantitative rules. **Other forms of technical trading** include the use of high–low extremes, moving average cross-over points, support–resistance levels and momentum indices.
- '**Candlesticks**' are based on the pattern of spot FX prices during the day, namely the opening and closing prices and the 'high' and 'low' during the day. Again specific 'candlestick patterns' signal buy or sell decisions.
- **Artificial neural networks (ANNs)** link an asset price (e.g. the spot FX rate) to other variables (e.g. past spot rates, interest rates, etc.) in a highly **non-linear relationship**. The network is first fitted to a 'training data set' and then tested on additional data. The parameters of the ANN are updated so as to minimise out-of-sample forecast errors. In time series analysis ANNs are mainly used for forecasting over very short horizons (e.g. tick-by-tick data).
- The **spot exchange** rate is close to a **random walk** over short horizons (e.g. up to a 1-month horizon), but it also **exhibits some non-linear behaviour** (most obviously the persistence in the volatility of the spot rate as evidenced in ARCH models) which may be modelled with the help of a (non-linear) neural network.
- **Over very long horizons** (e.g. in excess of 3–5 years) the spot rate does have some (rather tenuous) links to '**fundamentals**' (e.g. relative money supplies as shown in the Mark's 1995 study and the PPP relationship found in other studies), but noise traders also appear to influence the spot rate. Opinion is divided on the relative impact on the spot FX rate of these two types of trader.

# END OF CHAPTER EXERCISES

**Q1** Broadly speaking, how do 'technical traders' differ from 'fundamentals traders'? Use the issue of predicting the spot FX rate as an example.

**Q2** What is a 'support level' for spot FX and how is it used by speculators?

**Q3** What is an exponentially weighted moving average (EWMA) forecast? If the current spot rate $S_0 = 100$ and the previous day's EWMA forecast had been 90, the 'weight' is $\alpha = 0.9$ and h = 20, what would be your forecast for the spot rate tomorrow? Briefly comment.

**Q4** Does the presence of noise traders automatically imply that asset prices will exhibit trends?

**Q5** What is the purpose of a 'transfer function' in an artificial neural network, ANN?

**Q6** What is 'overfitting' applied to artificial neural networks (ANNs). Why is it a problem?

**Q7** What is a momentum strategy?

# International Portfolio Diversification

In this chapter we analyse the theoretical and practical issues when mean–variance portfolio theory is applied to international asset allocation. First, let us briefly review some results on portfolio diversification and consider the additional issues when adding foreign assets. First we know that if you *randomly* select stocks from a large set of stocks (e.g. those in the FTSE100) then it is found that the risk of the portfolio (i.e. measured by the standard deviation) quickly falls to a near minimum value when only about 25 stocks are included. Some risk nevertheless remains—this is known as systematic or undiversifiable risk. A question arises as to whether this minimum level of systematic risk can be reduced by widening the choice of stocks in the portfolio to include foreign stocks (or assets).

Second, can we do better than a *random* selection of stocks. In general we are interested in trading off 'risk against return'. The efficient frontier gives this trade-off for a given set of assets once we know the variances and covariances (correlations) of returns (and a forecast of expected returns). If we can widen the set of assets (e.g. include foreign as well as domestic assets) then it may be possible to substantially move the efficient frontier 'to the left', giving a better risk–return trade off to the investor. Table 18.1 shows the mean monthly return, standard deviation and correlations on a number of country indices over the period January 1990 to August 1999 (these are the figures used to construct the graphs in Chapter 1). The mean monthly returns differ substantially, being 1.35% p.m. for the Hang Seng index and *minus* 0.46% p.m. for the Nikkei 500. The Nikkei also has a standard deviation of 6.83%, which is marginally lower than that on the Hang Seng at 8.57%. Some of the correlations are quite low, particularly between the Nikkei and the other indices. A key issue for the benefits of portfolio diversification is whether these *historic* low correlations will persist in the future and whether the estimates of the volatilities and (particularly) the average returns are constant over time.

Third, if we include foreign assets in the portfolio then the investor will usually be interested in the return (and risk) measured in terms of her 'home currency'. If the investor does not hedge these risks then we need estimates of variances and correlations for bilateral exchange rates. If the investor hedges these risks then, broadly speaking, exchange rate risk can be ignored and it is the 'local currency' statistics discussed above (e.g. volatility of the Hang Seng, etc.) that are relevant. However, there is still the issue of what instruments to use for the hedge, forwards, futures or options?

Fourth, suppose we base our international portfolio decisions on the efficient frontier using variances and correlations *between broad market indices* (e.g. FTSE100, S&P500, DAX, CAC, Nikkei, etc.). If we then '*mechanically*' allocate across industries in each country according to existing market capitalisation weights in each index, we will obtain a particular industry weighting in each country. Alternatively, we could base our initial efficient frontier on the variances and correlations between returns across *all* the major *industries* in the world. This would result in a different set of optimal 'industry weights' and we can then examine which efficient frontier gives the best risk–return trade off.

## TABLE 18.1: Monthly stock market returns (January 1990 to August 1999)

|  | FTSE | S&P500 | Nikkei 500 | Hang Seng | DAX |
|---|---|---|---|---|---|
| **Mean return** | 0.83 | 1.15 | −0.49 | 1.35 | 0.74 |
| **Standard deviation** | 4.27 | 3.66 | 6.83 | 8.57 | 5.66 |
| **Correlation matrix** | | | | | |
| **FTSE** | 1 | | | | |
| **S&P500** | 0.6368 | 1 | | | |
| **Nikkei 500** | 0.3386 | 0.3778 | 1 | | |
| **Hang Seng** | 0.5015 | 0.5232 | 0.2527 | 1 | |
| **DAX** | 0.6482 | 0.6134 | 0.2818 | 0.4333 | 1 |

Fifth, if we allow the investor to borrow and lend at a risk free rate, and we have the individual's forecasts of expected returns and covariances, then we can determine the optimal portfolio weights for this particular investor. We can then compare the efficiency of alternative international investment strategies (e.g. an equally weighted world portfolio) using performance indicators such as the Sharpe ratio.

Finally, the optimal portfolio weights clearly depend on our estimates of the future values of the expected returns, variances and covariances between the assets. We need to know how sensitive our optimal weights are to minor changes in these crucial inputs (since they are invariably measured with error) and whether constraining these weights (e.g. no short sales) can improve matters.

# 18.1 THE BASICS

The benefits of portfolio diversification depend upon finding 'new' assets which have a 'low' correlation with existing assets in the portfolio. For $n$ assets the expected return and variance of the portfolio are:

[18.1] $$ER_p = \sum_{i=1}^{n} w_i ER_i$$

[18.2] $$\sigma_p^2 = \sum_{i}^{n} w_i^2 \sigma_i^2 + \sum_{i}^{n} \sum_{j}^{n} w_i w_j \rho_{ij} \sigma_i \sigma_j \qquad i \neq j$$

In an early study of international diversification Solnik (1974) concentrated on the possible *risk reducing benefits* of international diversification (and ignored the expected returns from the portfolio). He asked the questions:

- How many *domestic* securities must be held to ensure a reasonable level of diversification?
- Does *international* diversification lead to less risk?

Using equation [18.2] his inputs were firstly equal weights ($w_i = 1/n$) for each asset and secondly estimates of the $\sigma_{ij}$ based on simple (arithmetic) historic sample averages (using weekly returns from 1966–71). The steps in the analysis were:

1. Generate portfolios by randomly choosing from a large set of possible stocks.
2. Form a portfolio of $n = 1$ stocks and repeat this $m$ times. Calculate the average standard deviation $\sigma_p^{(1)}$ for a '1-stock portfolio' (i.e. $\sigma_p^{(1)}$ is averaged over the $m$ '1-asset' portfolios). This averaging prevents the calculation being dominated by 'outliers'.
3. Repeat step 2 for $n = 2$, $n = 3$, ..., etc., 'size' portfolios to obtain a sequence of average values for $\sigma_p^{(i)}$.
4. Scale each of the estimated 'size based' standard deviations using $\sigma_p^{(1)}$:

   $$V_p^{(n)} = (\sigma_p^{(n)} / \sigma_p^{(1)})^2$$

and plot $V_p^{(n)}$ against '$n$', the number of securities in the portfolio. (Note that $V_p^{(1)} = 100\%$.)

5. Repeat steps 1 to 4 for different countries.

Solnik's key results were that about 20 randomly selected 'domestic securities' achieve the minimum level of systematic (market) risk within any one country. For example, for the USA and Germany the minimum values of $V_p^{(n)}$ are 27% and 44%, respectively, implying Germany has a higher level of systematic risk.

How effective was international diversification in reducing risk? Solnik assumes perfect hedging of foreign currency returns (at zero cost of forward cover) so that any prospective foreign currency receipts from the foreign asset are sold in the forward market (or you borrow foreign currency to purchase the shares). Note that in practice the above does not guarantee that you are fully hedged, since you do not know *exactly* what the shares will be worth in say 1 months time. For a US resident (we take the USA as the 'domestic country') investing in the German all share index, the DAX, the dollar hedged return is:

> **Hedged return = $R_{DAX}$ + forward premium on the euro**
>
> $$R_{US}^h = R_{DAX} + (F-S)/S$$

where $R_{DAX}$ = return on DAX (proportionate)

$(F - S)/S$ = forward premium on the euro (exchange rates measured as \$/euro).

(In the above we have used the euro as the foreign currency, although when Solnik's study was done this would have been the Deutsche Mark.) For a US based investor an **unhedged portfolio** in German securities provides a return in dollar terms of:

> **Unhedged return = return on the DAX + appreciation of the euro**
>
> $$R_{US}^u = R_{DAX} + R_S$$

where $R_S$ = return on \$/euro (i.e. proportionate change in the \$/euro spot rate).

Solnik (1974) takes nine countries (stock indices) and randomly selects stocks from these countries, forming different size based *international* portfolios. For the unhedged portfolio the standard deviation of 'returns' and the correlation coefficients are derived using the *unhedged* return. For the hedged returns, the forward premium is assumed to be small relative to $R_{DAX}$ and is set to zero. Therefore unhedged returns are equal to 'local currency' returns. Solnik then calculates the statistic $V_p^{(n)}$ for the hedged and unhedged portfolios.

The hedged international diversification strategy will reduce portfolio risk $\sigma_p$ if correlations between returns in different 'local currencies' are low, relative to those within a single country. We briefly looked at these 'local currency' indices (e.g. the S&P500, the FTSE100) in Chapter 10. Solnik finds that for a US based investor the statistic $V_p^{(n)}$ falls to about 11% for the internationally diversified portfolio (*whether hedged or unhedged*), which is well below that for the domestic (US) portfolio of about 27%. The reason the unhedged portfolio does nearly as well as the hedged portfolio is that, in the former, movements in the set of bilateral exchange rates (against the dollar) will be offsetting in such a well-diversified portfolio. Also, changes in most exchange rates against the dollar were not large up to 1974 (when Solnik's study ends) because the quasi-fixed exchange rate regime of Bretton Woods was in existence until about 1973. The Solnik study was pioneering in this area but has obvious limitations, namely:

- Historical averages are used for $\sigma_{ij}$.
- It takes no account of the expected returns from the portfolios.
- It assumes perfect hedging of foreign currency receipts.

## INDUSTRY BASED INTERNATIONAL DIVERSIFICATION

Cavaglia *et al.* (1994) and Cavaglia and Cuthbertson (1995) extend the Solnik analysis in a number of ways, and in particular their analysis considers both risk and return. The aim is to see if one can obtain a better risk–return trade off from international diversification (i.e. optimal $w_i$'s) by one of the following scenarios:

- Diversify by optimal allocation *across countries* based on aggregate 'broad market' indices (e.g. FTSE100, DAX, S&P500, etc.) and *then* use index tracking for the industrial allocation. The latter implies allocating industry stocks based on their existing weights in the broad market index. Call this the **'broad indexing market portfolio'**.
- Diversify by choosing the optimal weights ($w_i$) across *all* industry sectors in *all* the countries (in the study). Call this the **'cross-industry portfolio'**.

The above scenarios assume:

- All prospective foreign currency receipts are 100% hedged in the forward market at cost equal to the known forward premium (so only the variation in local currency returns determines the variation in the total return to foreign investment).
- Expected returns, variances and covariances are based on historic (monthly) sample averages.
- The optimal weights for each scenario are based on maximising the Sharpe ratio ($S = R_p/\sigma_p$ where $R_p$ and $\sigma_p$ have their usual definitions), although no short sales (i.e. $w_i > 0$) are allowed in their base case.

The intuition behind this approach is as follows. The 'cross-industry portfolio' will tend to have a lower variance than the 'broad market indexing portfolio' if the correlation between *industry returns in different countries* is lower than the correlation between the returns on *the broad market indices* (e.g. FTSE100, DAX, S&P500). For example, for UK and US broad market return indices and the direct industry correlations we have:

$\rho$(FTSE, S&P) $\approx 0.35$–$0.7$
$\rho$(UK industry $i$, US industry $j$) $\approx 0.1$–$0.4$ (approximately and on average)

Not surprisingly perhaps the 'cross-industry strategy' is found to give a better risk–return efficiency frontier than simply allocating funds based on the broad market indices, the respective Sharpe ratios being 1.12 and 1.94 (see table 4, Cavaglia *et al.*, 1994). Of course, if one adopts the 'cross-industry strategy' the final allocation of funds across different countries (i.e. the sum of the optimal industry weights in each country) will in general be very different from 'the optimal country weights' obtained with the 'broad market indexing portfolio'. For example, the US allocation of funds in the cross-industry strategy is $w_{US} = 27\%$ whereas for the broad market strategy 62% of the total portfolio is held in US denominated assets (see table 5, Cavaglia et al., 1994).

Cavaglia and Cuthbertson (1995) extend the above analysis to include *rolling forecasts* of the expected returns and variances and covariances as inputs to the maximal Sharpe ratio and then calculate optimal portfolio weights. The results are qualitatively similar to those reported above.

## HEDGING FOREIGN CURRENCY RECEIPTS

Up to now we have largely ignored the hedging issue. Filatov and Rappoport (1992) address this issue of whether an investor who holds domestic and foreign assets should *always* fully hedge the prospective foreign currency receipts in the forward market. The answer lies in the correlations between returns on domestic and foreign stock markets and their correlation with the return on the spot currency. An unhedged position 'adds' an extra element of risk, namely the variance of the spot rate. But it also gives rise to the possibility of low (or negative) correlations between the spot rate and either the domestic stock market or the foreign stock market or both. These correlations may offset the variance of the spot rate and hence reduce overall portfolio variance of the *unhedged portfolio*.

Let us develop this argument more formally using the following notation:

$R_d$ = return on the domestic asset
$R_f$ = return on the foreign asset (in local currency)
$R_s$ = appreciation of the foreign currency
$FP$ = forward premium on the foreign currency (i.e. $(F - S)/S$).

For a domestic US resident the hedged and unhedged returns to foreign investment are:

[18.3]      $R^h_{US} = R_f + FP$

[18.4]      $R^u_{US} = R_f + R_s$

The total return to the internationally diversified portfolio is:

[18.5]      $R_p = w_d R_d + w_u(R_f + R_s) + w_h(R_f + FP)$

where $w_d$ is the proportion held in the domestic portfolio
$w_u$ is the proportion held in the *unhedged* foreign assets
$w_h$ is the proportion held in the *hedged* foreign assets
$w_d + w_u + w_h = 1.$

The hedge ratio ($h$) is defined as:

[18.6] $$h = \frac{\text{proportion in hedged foreign assets}}{\text{proportion in hedged plus unhedged foreign assets}}$$

$$= \frac{w_h}{w_h + w_u} = \frac{w_h}{1 - w_d}$$

It follows from equation [18.6] that:

[18.7a] $$w_h = h(1 - w_d)$$

[18.7b] $$w_u = (1 - w_d)(1 - h)$$

and hence:

[18.8] $$R_p = w_d R_d + (1 - w_d)[R_f + h(FP) + (1 - h)R_s]$$

Once $w_d$ has been fixed by the investor then the variance of the portfolio return depends on the variances and covariances and the choice of the hedge ratio $h$. With no short sales allowed $h$ will be greater than or equal to zero. It also follows that $h = 0$ implies zero hedging while $h = 1$ implies 100% hedging.

The variance of $R_p$ is easily obtained from equation [18.8], and note that Var($FP$) and all covariances with respect to $FP$ are zero (since $FP$ is known at the outset of the investment decision). Hence, heuristically:

[18.9] $$\sigma_p = f(\sigma_d, \sigma_f, \sigma_s; \sigma_{df}, \sigma_{ds}, \sigma_{fs}; h w_d)$$

where '$f$' indicates 'function of'. Setting $\partial \sigma_p / \partial h = 0$, we obtain the optimal hedge ratio:

[18.10] $$h^* = 1 + \left[ \frac{w_d \sigma_{ds} + (1 - w_d)\sigma_{fs}}{(1 - w_d)\sigma_s^2} \right]$$

From equation [18.10], we can see that:

- If at least one of $\sigma_{ds}$ or $\sigma_{fs}$ is sufficiently negative, then $h^*$ can be less than 1. That means some proportion of the portfolio should be *unhedged*.
- If $\sigma_{ds}$ and $\sigma_{fs} > 0$, then $h^* > 1$ (i.e. 'overhedged', you hedge more than your *total of foreign assets*).

A key result of this analysis is the somewhat paradoxical result that if it is optimal to hedge more than 100% for say a US resident investing in the UK, then the UK resident investing in the USA *must* have an optimal hedge ratio which is less than 100%. This follows because if $(\sigma_{ds}, \sigma_{fs})^{US} > (0, 0)$ for a US resident then:

$$(\sigma_{ds})^{US} = -(\sigma_{fs})^{UK} \quad \text{and} \quad (\sigma_{fs})^{US} = -(\sigma_{ds})^{UK}$$

Hence we must have $(\sigma_{ds}, \sigma_{fs})^{UK} < (0, 0)$ and the latter implies $(h^*)^{UK} < 1$. Filatov and Rappoport (1992) find that for a US based investor $\sigma_{ds}$ and $\sigma_{fs}$ are both positive with respect to an investment in UK shares. Hence the US resident should be overhedged ($h^* > 1$), but it then follows that the UK resident should be less than 100% hedged. The overall conclusion is that it is not necessarily the case that one should always hedge *all* of the foreign currency receipts—it depends on one's view about the size of the variances and covariances.

## KEY FACTORS IN INTERNATIONAL PORTFOLIO ALLOCATION

It is clear from the above studies that there are many potential factors to consider in evaluating alternative portfolio allocation decisions. These include:

- How many countries to include in the study and how many assets within each country (e.g. stocks only, bonds only or both, or an even wider set of assets—such as including property).
- What will be the numeraire currency (i.e. home country) in which we measure returns and risk. Results are not invariant to the choice of 'home currency' or the time horizon (e.g. 1 month or 1 year) over which returns are measured.
- We must consider expected returns as well as risk and provide a measure of portfolio performance which includes both (e.g. Sharpe ratio, Treynor index).
- It may be just as beneficial in practice if we use some simple method of international portfolio diversification (e.g. an equally weighted allocation between alternative countries or an allocation based on a set of existing weights, as in *Morgan Stanley's Capital International World Index).*
- Whether to hedge or not hedge prospective foreign currency receipts. The practical and important detail is that any foreign currency receipts may be uncertain (e.g. the next dividend payments are not known with certainty) and hence it may be worth hedging using options as well as futures/forwards.
- Alternative forecasts of changes in the exchange rate (e.g. historic arithmetic averages, random walk model, use of the forward rate as a predictor of next period's spot rate) give rise to different unhedged optimal portfolio weights, as do different forecasts of variances and covariances (correlations).
- The different optimal portfolio weights using different forecasting schemes may not be statistically different from each other, if the alternative forecasting schemes have wide margins of error.

We can only briefly deal with these issues in this chapter, but it is worth noting the results in Eun and Resnick (1997), who consider a number of these crucial issues. They consider the home country as the USA, use a monthly return horizon for stocks (only) for six foreign country indices (Canada, France, Germany, Japan, Switzerland and the UK). They use simple historic arithmetic averages to measure the variances and covariances of returns, but because the optimal portfolio weights are rather sensitive to changes in expected returns they consider a number of alternative forecasting schemes. They measure these variables using 'in-sample' data and then calculate the optimal portfolio weights, but they then compare the outcome for the return and standard deviation of these ex-ante portfolios over a 12 month 'out-of-sample' period (using a 'bootstrapping method'). The Sharpe ratio is one measure they use to compare results from alternative methods of choosing the optimal portfolio weights. In broad terms they find that for a US based investor:

- For an unhedged portfolio it is found that investing in an internationally diversified portfolio gives results that are superior (in terms of the Sharpe ratio or 'stochastic dominance analysis') to investing solely in US stocks. This result applies irrespective of whether the international portfolio comprises an equally weighted portfolio or weights equal to those in *Morgan Stanley's Capital International World Index* or the 'optimal weights' given by mean−variance analysis. However, the gains to an unhedged internationally diversified strategy are only *marginally better* than a solely domestic investment, at least for a US investor. (Clearly this result may not hold for an investor based in a 'small' country where international diversification, even if unhedged, may be a substantial improvement on a purely domestic strategy.)

- When considering the hedging decision, fully hedging using forward contracts nearly always produces superior results than not hedging (e.g. this applies whether one uses the 'optimal' portfolio weights or the equally weighted portfolio or the weights in *Morgan Stanley's Capital International World Index*). Also, the use of the forward market is usually superior to using a protective put to hedge foreign currency receipts. Hence there is reasonably strong evidence that for the US investor, if she diversifies internationally, then it pays to fully hedge the foreign currency receipts in some way.

- It was also found that assuming the spot rate next month equals this month's spot rate (i.e. a random walk) provides a better forecast than that based on the current forward rate. Of course the latter is consistent with the 'poor' results found in testing the forward rate unbiasedness FRU proposition. (i.e. where a regression of the change in the spot rate on the lagged forward premium, invariably gives a *negative* coefficient).

It appears from the above evidence that there is a gain to be had by investing internationally, even for a US resident. It is therefore something of a puzzle why, in practice, there is so little international diversification. This 'home bias puzzle' is outlined in Box 18.1.

## Box 18.1    THE HOME BIAS PROBLEM

Portfolio theory highlights the possible gains from international diversification when domestic and foreign returns have lower correlations than those between purely domestic securities, or if exchange rate movements lower these correlations. It has been estimated that a US resident would have been 10–50% better off investing internationally (in the G7 counties) than purely domestically. However, somewhat paradoxically US residents keep over 90% of their assets 'at home'. This also applies to investors in other countries, although the figure for other countries is usually less than this 90%—for example UK pension funds currently have about a 30:70 split in favour of the home country. The problem is so pervasive that it is known as the **home bias problem**. It appears as if neither the risk of imposition of capital controls nor high taxes on capital can explain why these apparent gains from holding foreign equity are not exploited.

One reason for this 'home bias' may be a perceived **lack of information** about the detailed performance of many foreign based companies (e.g. small 'foreign' firms). Sometimes there are legal restrictions on foreign investments. For example, currently UK pension funds have to meet the minimum funding requirement (MFR) which is a type of solvency test, encouraging investment in domestic government bonds and to a lesser extent UK equities. Another reason for 'home bias' is that a 'proven gain' using past data does not necessarily imply a gain in the (uncertain) future.

Yet another reason why investors might not diversify internationally is that they wish to consume mainly **home country goods and services** with the proceeds from their investments. This would imply that they have to hedge their foreign investments to be sure of getting the purchasing power they expected in terms of the domestic goods. However, if **purchasing power parity (PPP)** holds, the return from foreign investment in terms of purchasing power in the US could be met without hedging.

In practice, **hedging costs money** (e.g. the forward discount) and you would need a rolling hedge (see Cuthbertson and Nitzsche, 2001) for horizons over 1 year, which entails risks. Also, deviations from PPP can be large (e.g. plus or minus 20%) over say a 5–10 year horizon, and this introduces uncertainty since you may wish to cash in your foreign investments just when the exchange rate is least favourable. With increasing globalisation, equity returns across different countries have become more positively correlated, although in principle they still allow for mean–variance gains (at least ex-ante). With the cost of information flows becoming lower (e.g. the prospect of increased information on foreign companies and real time stock price quotes and dealing over the internet), it is always possible that the home bias problem may attenuate and investors may become more willing to diversify internationally.

On the other hand, some argue that the 'home bias' problem is illusory once one takes into account the fact that the inputs to the mean–variance optimisation problem are **measured with uncertainty**. Although a US investor holding her stocks in the same proportions as in the S&P500 may not hold precisely the mean–variance optimum proportions, nevertheless her S&P500 indexed portfolio may be within a 95% confidence band of this optimum position. This argument may apply with even greater force if we recognise that, in the real world, we need to make a 'genuine' forecast of the inputs (i.e. forecasts of expected returns and the variance–covariance matrix) to the mean–variance optimisation problem. Under these circumstances the S&P500 indexed portfolio may actually outperform the optimum mean–variance portfolio.

There is also the technical issue addressed in the text, that an 'industry allocation' rather than a 'country allocation' is the correct focus for the application of mean–variance analysis, and there is no reason why the former may not give a higher weight to domestic assets. So, there are plenty of practical reasons why the 'theoretical optimum' from mean–variance theory can be overruled.

## 18.2 MEAN–VARIANCE OPTIMISATION IN PRACTICE

It is probably true to say that a large proportion of investment funds are not allocated on the basis of mean–variance optimisation. Usually, a wide variety of criteria such as political risk, business risk and the state of the economic cycle are used in a relatively informal way, by the investment policy committee of an investment bank to determine asset allocation, across different countries. What are the problems associated with the 'pure application' of mean–variance optimisation as espoused in the textbooks and which make it difficult to apply in practice? Most obviously it only deals with risk as measured by the variance–covariance matrix and not other forms of risk (e.g. political risk) and (in its simplest form) it only covers one specific time horizon (e.g. 1 month or 1 year, etc.). However, the main reason it is not widely used is that it is somewhat of a 'black-box' and the results are subject to potentially large estimation errors.

### ESTIMATION ERRORS

Consider possible estimation errors. If (continuously compounded) returns are normally, identically and independently distributed (*niid*), with a constant population mean $\mu$ and variance $\sigma^2$, then (unbiased) estimates of the mean and standard deviation are given by:

**[18.11a]**
$$\bar{R} = \frac{\sum_{i=1}^{n} R_i}{n}$$

**[18.11b]**
$$s = \sqrt{\frac{\sum_{i=1}^{n}(R_i - \bar{R})^2}{n - 1}}$$

The above formulae can be applied to any chosen frequency for the data (e.g. daily, weekly, monthly) to obtain the appropriate mean return and standard deviation for any particular horizon. (We ignore complexities due to the use of overlapping data.) For example, using monthly returns data we might find that $\bar{R} = 1\%$ p.m. and $\sigma = 4\%$ p.m. It can be shown that the standard deviation of the estimate of $\bar{R}$ is:

**[18.12]**
$$\text{Std. dev.}(\bar{R}) = \frac{\sigma}{\sqrt{n}}$$

Suppose we wanted to obtain an estimate of the population mean return that was accurate to $\pm 0.1\%$, given that $\sigma = 4\%$ p.m. This would require $n = 4^2/(0.1)^2 = 1600$ monthly observations, that is 133 years of monthly data! Clearly the accuracy of our estimate of the mean return obtained from a 'moderate sample' of say 60 monthly observations (i.e. 5 years) will be very poor. For example, for $n = 60$, Std. dev.$(\bar{R}) = \sigma/\sqrt{n} = 0.52\%$, so the error is more than half of the estimated mean value for $\bar{R}$ of 1% p.m. There is an additional problem. If the population mean is not constant over time then even using a lot of past data will not provide an accurate estimate, as data from the beginning of the period will not provide an accurate representation of the changing population mean. Hence, analysts tend to use other methods to estimate expected returns. They might use an estimate from the security market line (SML) and the asset's beta to predict expected returns or even use predictions from the APT or a more general regression model, where returns are assumed to depend on a set of 'fundamental variables' (e.g. dividend or price–earnings ratio, yield spreads, etc.). They will also combine these estimates with ancillary information on the firm or sector's company reports.

What about the accuracy of our estimate of the standard deviation $\sigma = 4\%$ p.m.? The standard deviation (for normally distributed returns) of $s^2$ is given by:

[18.13]
$$\text{Std. dev.}(s^2) = \frac{\sqrt{2}\sigma^2}{\sqrt{n-1}}$$

Suppose we used 5 years ($n = 60$ monthly observations) of data to estimate $s^2$. Using the above equation, we get Std. dev.$(s^2) = \sqrt{2}\, 4^2/\sqrt{60-1} = 2.94\%$ p.m. Hence the accuracy of $\sigma^2 = 16\%$ p.m. is relatively small at 2.94% p.m. Estimates of variances (and covariances) using historic data are subject to much less error (relatively speaking) than estimates of the expected return.

It might be thought that the precision in estimating the expected return could be enhanced by keeping the same 'length' of data, say 5 years, but increasing the frequency of data from say monthly to daily. However, this does not in fact help—you can't get something for nothing out of your fixed data set. This arises because if say *monthly returns* are statistically independent then it can be shown that the expected *daily* return and standard deviation are given by $\mu_d = T\mu_m$ and $\sigma_d = \sqrt{T}\sigma_m$ where $T$ is the *fraction* of a month (and here $T = 1/30$ approximately). Hence $\sigma_d/\mu_d = \sqrt{T}\sigma_m/(T\mu_m) = \sqrt{30}\,\sigma_m/\mu_m$, which implies that the daily standard deviation relative to the daily mean is about 5.5 times the monthly value (i.e. $\sigma_m/\mu_m$).

## BLACK-BOX?

The 'black-box' element in mean–variance portfolio analysis arises because the optimal weights $w_i^*$ simply 'pop-out' of the maximisation procedure and it is often difficult (especially with many assets) to undertake a sensitivity analysis that is tractable and easy to understand. Estimation error arises because the inputs, that is the forecast of expected returns $(ER_i)$ and of the elements of the variance–covariance matrix $\{\sigma_{ij}\}$, may provide poor predictions of what actually happens in the future. The 'optimiser' will significantly overweight (underweight) those securities that have large (small) forecast expected returns, negative (positive) estimated covariances and small (large) variances. Generally, it is the bias in forecasts of expected returns that is the major source of error: by comparison forecasts of the $\sigma_{ij}$ are reasonably good.

Generally, historic averages of past returns (e.g. the sample mean return over a given 'window' of recent data) are used to measure future expected returns. These methods can be improved upon, for example, using more sophisticated recursive multivariate regressions, time varying parameter models, or pure time series models (e.g. ARIMA and the stochastic trend model), Bayesian estimators and most recently, predictions based on neural networks. Forecasts of the variances and covariances can be based on exponentially weighted moving averages EWMA or even simple ARCH and GARCH models (see Cuthbertson, 1996 for a survey). Essentially these methods assume that the variance (or covariance) is a weighted average of past *squared* returns. Of course, they involve increased computing costs and more importantly costs in interpreting the results for higher management, who may be somewhat sceptical and lack technical expertise. However, we have little or no evidence on how these more sophisticated alternatives might reduce the 'estimation error' in the mean–variance optimisation problem. But Simons (1999) provides a simple yet revealing sensitivity analysis. She uses historic sample averages for *ER* and the variance–covariances and calculates the optimal weights (from a US perspective) on the efficient frontier (with no short sales) taking US equities, US bonds, US money market assets, European stocks and Pacific stocks as the set of assets in the portfolio. She then repeats the exercise using EWMA forecasts for variances and covariances and finds a dramatic change in the optimal weights, thus showing the extreme sensitivity of mean–variance analysis to seemingly innocuous changes in the inputs.

What evidence we do have (e.g. Jobson and Korkie, 1980, 1981; Frost and Savarino, 1988) on the 'estimation error' from mean–variance optimisation uses simple 'historic' sample averages for forecasts of $R_i$ and $\sigma_{ij}$. As we shall see, in general, these studies suggest that the best strategy is to constrain the weight attached to any single 'security' to a relatively small value, possibly in the range 2–5% of portfolio value, and one should also disallow short sales or buying on margin.

The technique known as **Monte Carlo simulation** allows one to measure the 'estimation error' implicit in using the M–V optimiser. Monte Carlo simulation allows 'repeated samples' of asset returns and the variance–covariance matrix to be generated. For each 'run' of simulated data we can calculate the estimated optimal portfolio return $R_p$ and its standard deviation $\sigma_p$ and hence the Sharpe ratio $(R_p - r)/\sigma$. We then compare these simulated outcomes with the known 'true' values given from the underlying known distribution. The procedure involves the following steps, where:

$n =$ number of assets in the chosen portfolio (e.g. 20)
$m =$ number of simulation runs in the Monte Carlo analysis
$q =$ length of data sample used in calculating mean returns and the variances and covariances.

1. Assume returns are multivariate normal with true mean returns $\mu_i$ and variance–covariance matrix $\boldsymbol{\Sigma} = \{\sigma_{ij}\}$. In the two-asset case the 'true values' of $\mu_1$, $\mu_2$, $\sigma_1$, $\sigma_2$ and $\sigma_{12}$ will be based on historic sample averages using $q = 60$ data points (say). But from this point on we assume these values are known *constants*. We therefore know the true 'population parameters' $\mu_i$, $\boldsymbol{\Sigma}$ and hence can calculate the true optimal weights $w_i^*$ and hence the true optimal portfolio returns $R_p^*$ and standard deviation $\sigma_p^*$ that maximise the Sharpe ratio $S = (ER_p^* - r)/\sigma_p^*$.

2. Assume asset returns are generated from a multivariate normal distribution which encapsulates the correlation structure between the asset returns:

$$R_i = \mu_i + \varepsilon_i$$

where $\varepsilon_i$ is drawn from a multivariate normal distribution, with known variance–covariance matrix $\Sigma$, calculated as noted above. Now generate $q = 60$ simulated returns $(R_i)$ for each of the $i = 1, 2, \ldots, n$ assets. This is our first Monte Carlo 'run' (i.e. $m = 1$).

3. With the $q = 60$ data points for each return series, calculate the sample average returns $E\hat{R}_i^{(1)} = \sum_{i=1}^{q} R_i^{(1)}/q$ and variance–covariance matrix $\Sigma^{(1)}$. Then use these as inputs to solve the portfolio maximisation problem to give our 'first run' values for the *simulated* optimal portfolio weights $\hat{w}_i$, portfolio return and its variance $(\hat{R}_p, \hat{\sigma}_p)^{(1)}$.

4. Repeat steps 2 and 3, $m$-times and use the $m$ generated values of $(\hat{R}_p, \hat{\sigma}_p)$ to obtain their average values (over '$m$ runs') which we denote $(\bar{R}_p, \bar{\sigma}_p)$ together with the average Sharpe ratio $\hat{S} = (\bar{R}_p - r)/\bar{\sigma}_p$. We can compare these averages from the Monte Carlo simulation with the known true values $(R_p^*, \sigma_p^*$ and $S^*)$ to provide a measure of the 'bias' produced by our estimation method for expected returns and covariances.

Some empirical results from Jobson and Korkie (1980) for monthly returns on 20 stocks generated from a known multivariate distribution show that the Sharpe ratios for the simulated data $(\bar{R}_p, \bar{\sigma}_p)$, the known population parameters $(R_p^*, \sigma_p^*)$ and an equally weighted portfolio were vastly different at 0.08, 0.34 and 0.27, respectively. Hence, 'estimation error' can be substantial and radically alters the risk–return trade off.

Frost and Savarino (1988) in a similar experiment found that the 'biases' $\bar{R}_p - R_p^*$ and $\bar{\sigma} - \sigma_p^*$ (particularly the former) fall dramatically as the portfolio weights in any one asset are restricted to a small positive value and if no short sales are allowed. In addition, for investors who are either twice or half as risk averse as the market investor (i.e. where the latter holds a 'market portfolio' of 25 equities say), the best outcome (in terms of certainty equivalent returns) occurs if the M–V optimisation is undertaken under the restriction that no more than about 3–5% is held in any one security. Also, note that either short selling or buying on margin considerably worsens performance. Thus it appears that mean–variance optimisation can provide some improvement (albeit not large) on holding the 'market portfolio' as long as some restrictions are placed on the optimisation problem.

**Index tracking** in equity markets using market value weights $(w_{im})$ is fairly commonplace. One constrained optimisation strategy is to maximise the Sharpe ratio subject to the optimal weights $(w_i^*)$ not being more than say 2% from the current market weights for that stock. Cavaglia *et al.* (1994) find that the Sharpe ratio can be improved for an international equity portfolio (i.e. one which includes equity held in a large number of countries) as one moves a small amount away from the current market value weights. It is also the case in practice that no investment manager would believe the optimal weights if these are not close to her intuitive notions of what is 'reasonable'. Indeed UK pension funds rarely invest more than 5% of their equity portfolio in a single stock (even though an indexing strategy on the FTSE100 would involve holding about 15% in Vodaphone–Mannesmann and a Finish pension fund would have to hold over 50% in Nokia!).

Some constraints need to be placed on the weights obtained from the M–V optimiser if 'unrestricted weighting' means that the investor holds a significant percentage of any one firm or industry sector (e.g. as might be the case when holding 90% of your wealth in small cap stocks or a large proportion of stocks in emerging markets). Unconstrained optimisation which allows short selling often results in weights which imply that you should short sell large amounts of one stock and use the proceeds to invest long in another stock. Practitioners would simply not believe that such a strategy would be successful, ex-post.

There have been attempts to see if a given portfolio is 'close to' in a statistical sense the M–V optimal portfolio (e.g. Jobson and Korkie, 1980). However, such tests appear to have low power (i.e. tend not to reject mean–variance efficiency when it is false) and do not allow for inequality constraints (e.g. no short selling), so this approach is not often used in practice.

It is also worth noting that there are some technical problems in calculating the optimal weights. If the covariance matrix is large, there may be problems in inverting it and then the optimal weights may be very sensitive to slight changes in the estimated covariances.

It remains the case that, for all its elegance, mean–variance optimisation is in practice merely one method of deciding on portfolio allocation. Other judgmental factors, such as an assessment of political risk and the state of the economic cycle in different countries or industries, play as important a role as 'pure' mean–variance analysis. Current market value proportions as embodied in the S&P index (for example) would not be the same as those given by an unconstrained mean–variance analysis (e.g. one which uses sample averages as forecasts of the mean return and the covariance matrix). Therefore, in practice, mean–variance analysis tends to be used to see if 'new forecasts' of $R_i$ and $\sigma_{ij}$ provide some improvement in the Sharpe ratio. Sensitivity analysis of the Sharpe ratio is also usually conducted with 'user imposed' changes in key returns and covariances rather than basing them on historic averages. As the scenarios change, if the optimal weights $w_i^*$ vary greatly in the unconstrained optimisation problem, then some constraints will be placed on the $w_i^*$ (e.g. that the new optimal proportions do not vary greatly from the current market value 'index tracking' weights and also perhaps that no short selling is allowed).

In summary, our overall conclusions might be that mean–variance optimisation is useful if:

- Portfolio weights are constrained to a certain extent (e.g. hold less than 5% of value in any one asset, or do not move more than 2% away from the 'market index weight' or do not allow short sales).
- Better forecasts of returns $R_i$ and covariances $\{\sigma_{ij}\}$ are used in place of historic averages.
- A small number of assets are used (e.g. using mean–variance optimisation for allocation between say 10 country indices) so that transparency and sensitivity analysis is possible.

# 18.3  PASSIVE AND ACTIVE PORTFOLIO ALLOCATION IN PRACTICE

There are billions under management in open and closed-end funds (in the UK these are known as unit trusts and investment trusts) and in insurance and pension funds worldwide. These funds are often managed by independent advisors such as Fidelity Investments and Mercury Asset Management and offshoots of large international banks (e.g. Schroder Asset Management, Morgan Grenfell Asset Management, Nomura Securities, etc.). How do they decide on their optimal asset allocation and changes in this allocation? First, they will have an existing position which they, along with their clients (e.g. the trustees of a pension fund) are broadly happy with. This initial allocation will almost certainly not be the result of unconstrained mean–variance analysis as outlined in the textbooks. It will involve the following key considerations:

- Can we get most of our diversification benefits from purely domestic investment? Clearly the answer will be broadly 'yes' if the domestic economy is large as in the USA or in the countries covered by the new single currency, the euro. The answer may be 'no' for small open economies—those in the Far East (Singapore, Thailand, Malaysia, etc.), in Eastern Europe (Czech Republic, Hungary, Poland, etc.) and even for the economies of South America.
- How far should we diversify internationally, given the 'domestic currency' base of our investors (i.e. at present the bulk of pension recipients usually want to spend most of their pension in the domestic economy)? If we do invest abroad, should we hedge or not hedge the foreign currency receipts?

It is likely that most of the funds allocated domestically and internationally will be 'index trackers', that is the proportions will mimic those of some broad market index (e.g. FTSE100, S&P500). The domestic/international allocation will probably be decided largely on 'ad hoc' grounds with most allocated to 'domestic currency' assets. (There is much empirical evidence that there is a 'home bias' in international asset allocation.) Allocation to specific foreign countries may mimic the proportions in some world index (e.g. Morgan Stanley's World Index excluding the domestic economy) or be tempered by perceptions of 'political risk' and perhaps a general 'gut feeling' about the future performance of these economies.

There are good reasons for pursuing such a strategy. First, no fund wants to underperform an index tracking strategy and by placing most of their funds into 'trackers' they ensure they will not be far from this 'industry baseline'. Second, the weights in the 'tracker fund' may not be far from the 'optimal weights' given by mean–variance analysis once account is taken of the (statistical) uncertainty attached to the latter. Finally, index tracking is transparent—the pension fund trustees are clear about the benchmark adopted. Index tracking is a **passive asset allocation strategy**. This does not mean that no effort is required! The investment manager still has to decide on the subset of assets in the broad market index (e.g. S&P500) which will best track the index.

For those interested in index tracking the concept of **cointegration** is useful here, since the investment manager has to choose say 20 assets which 'best' cointegrate with the aggregate index. From time to time the portfolio has to be rebalanced as the weights in the aggregate index change. Often the optimal mean–variance asset allocation will be judged against this baseline index tracker position. Hence, the optimal mean–variance weights might be calculated (based on forecasts of expected returns and covariances), but these would be highly constrained so that the final weights produced by the optimiser do not move more than 10% from their current index tracker values (e.g. from 20% to 22%).

Asset managers also use a proportion of funds to undertake **active portfolio management**. (Indeed some funds are advertised as 'actively managed funds' as opposed to index trackers.) The possible variants here are numerous. If the asset manager 'places bets' on the direction of say stock and bond prices and switches between these two assets and a safe asset (e.g. bank deposit or T-bill) based on her view of the future state of the macroeconomy, this is generally known as **market timing**. Gambling on the *longer term* behaviour of economies (e.g. the Asian 'Tiger' economies, the emerging markets of Eastern Europe, countries in South America) is often referred to as **strategic asset allocation**. Switching funds between countries based on 'short run' views about the state of the economic cycle (e.g. US is entering an expansionary phase and Japan a contractionary one) is often referred to as **tactical asset allocation**. Clearly the use of these terms is far from precise. **Hedge funds** use active portfolio management techniques and often 'lever' their exposure to certain assets (i.e. increase their exposure at low cost) by using derivatives. Because of this leverage, hedge funds can often produce high returns on 'own capital' invested but they can also be extremely risky investments (see Box 18.2).

## Box 18.2    HEDGE FUNDS

Hedge funds (e.g. George Soros' Quantum Fund) are actively managed funds which usually use highly leveraged transactions such as short sales and borrowing in the repo market to finance their investments. They take large open positions in the underlying cash market assets (e.g. stocks, bonds, spot FX) and also in derivative assets (e.g. futures and options). The initial capital tends to be provided by very wealthy individuals. Their investment decisions are often (but not always) aided by some form of quantitative model (e.g. using neural networks, chartism or complex non-linear models based on fundamentals or models of derivatives prices based on stochastic calculus).

There is probably in excess of $50bn in hedge funds and management fees are usually high (say a minimum 10% of total profits). George Soros' Quantum Fund essentially places directional bets on asset prices (especially currencies), and this is a market timing strategy. Most notable events where hedge funds were heavily involved include the selling of sterling in the ERM crisis of September 1992 (profits were made by the Quantum Fund selling sterling), the Asian currency crisis of 1997/8 and the devaluation of the Russian rouble in August 1998.

As we have seen, the hedge fund **Long Term Capital Management (LTCM)** lost over $3bn in 1999 by taking bets on the direction that domestic and foreign interest rates would take. They levered their speculative positions by using interest rate options. LTCM was 'bailed out' under the auspices of the Federal Reserve in the US on the grounds that no intervention by the regulator may have resulted in widespread failures of other financial institutions, who held outstanding positions with LTCM. The issue of whether and how to regulate hedge funds will be of increasing importance in the future.

We do not have enough space here to fully explain the basis of 'macroeconomic models' (or fundamental models) of forecasting expected returns for use in active portfolio management. Indeed different analysts will have different models. In practice the model will usually remain in the analyst's head since then the veracity of the model cannot be verified against past events and she can change her 'story' (i.e. the model in her head) to accommodate any 'new facts', which do not fit in with her previous investment pronouncements. Of course, it may be that the economy is far too complex to model in a formal way, although this does not excuse active portfolio managers whose investment decisions result in a Sharpe ratio below that given by a broad market index. Since the latter outcome appears to occur with remarkable frequency (see for example Timmermann and Blake, 1997) we can most charitably view these active portfolio managers as satisfying the human craving for a story to 'explain' recent events. These stories often lack coherence and consistency and are no help whatsoever in predicting what will actually happen in the future—but soothsayers are alive and well and earning good money in the major financial centres around the world!

Mainly for illustrative purposes we now sketch out *one possible* 'macroeconomic model' to explain movements in some broad market index such as the FTSE100. Analysts use such models to get a broad picture of what might happen in the macroeconomy, from which they then derive industry forecasts and eventually forecasts of *individual company* profits and earnings. (The latter forecasts are then used as inputs to stock valuation formulae such as Gordon's growth model.) Think first of a stylised 'long run static equilibrium', where all variables are constant. Here the 'long run' stock price $\hat{P}$ would be determined by the DPV formula:

[18.14] $$\hat{P} = \frac{D}{R}$$

where $D$ is the level of dividends and $R$ is the 'required return' on the broad market index. It follows that at any time $t$, the *actual* stock price might differ from this long run value, but if it did it would slowly adjust towards the 'long run', hence:

[18.15] Disequilibrium stock price = actual stock price − long run equilibrium stock price

$$= P_t - \hat{P}_t$$

The change in the stock price is then given by:

[18.16] $$\Delta P_{t+1} = \gamma - \alpha(P_t - \hat{P}_t) + \varepsilon_{t+1}$$

so that when the actual stock price $P_t$ is above its 'long run' value $\hat{P}_t$ then on average the price will fall tomorrow (i.e. at $t+1$) giving a negative stock return. This is an **error correction model**. The macroeconomic model then needs to explain the 'required rate of return' $R$ and the future path of dividends $D$, since $\hat{P}_t$ is not directly observable. Two useful 'definitional relationships' for the required rate of return and the nominal interest rate are:

$R$ = nominal rate of interest + risk premium = $r + rp$
$r$ = expected inflation rate + real rate of return = $\Delta p^e + rr$

The system of ('behavioural') equations (in schematic form) to forecast these variables might be:

$rr = f$(growth of real output, debt to GDP ratio)

$\Delta p^e = f$(change in the exchange rate, change in interest rates)

$rp = f$(volatility of real output and real interest rates)

where $f(.)$ stands for 'depends upon' or mathematically 'is a function of'. The real rate of interest is assumed to increase if either the growth of real output increases or the debt to GDP ratio rises (see Martin, 1997). The rate of inflation rises if the domestic currency is devalued or if interest rates fall, since the latter usually implies an expansionary monetary policy. The equity risk premium is assumed to increase if either the *volatility* of real output or of the real interest rate increases. The volatility of these variables can be forecast by using so-called ARCH models of volatility persistence. Finally, we might assume that (nominal) dividend growth depends directly on real output growth (i.e. company profits will be higher) and on expected inflation:

[18.17]     $\Delta D = f$ (real output growth, expected inflation)

To forecast the exchange rate in such models is extremely difficult and here one might simply assume random walk behaviour or alternatively some form of UIP relationship (perhaps with a time varying risk premium depending on the cumulative deviation from PPP).

Clearly even this rather 'sketchy' model is quite complex, which is why in practice such macro-models are not often constructed, let alone used by analysts. Their main advantage is as a 'check' on some of the more bizarre claims of 'back of the envelope' analysts and indeed some of the relationships (e.g. that for inflation or dividend growth) may have reasonable predictive power. In any case, the usefulness of such models is not just whether they forecast well in absolute terms, but whether they forecast better than the 'analyst's hunch' or some other method (e.g. chartists or neural networks). Also, there is no reason in principle why an economic model like the one outlined above cannot form the basis of one's forecast of the expected return and (conditional) covariances of these returns, to use as inputs to the mean–variance optimisation problem.

# 18.4 MATHEMATICS OF MEAN–VARIANCE PORTFOLIO THEORY

So far we have side-stepped the details of the mathematical calculations needed to obtain the optimal portfolio weights. It turns out that this is not too difficult if there are no constraints put on the optimal weights (e.g. we allow a solution with some $w_i < 0$, that is short selling) since we then have a standard quadratic programming problem with an analytic solution. Even in this case, however, some readers might prefer to skip the details in this section, except perhaps for the numerical examples given. If we want to solve the portfolio allocation problem with constraints (e.g. no short selling) then in general there is no analytic solution and a numerical optimisation routine is needed, but these are now commonplace (e.g. as an Excel add-on or in programmes such as RATS and GAUSS) and mathematical software such as Mathematica.

In this section we demonstrate the mathematics behind various portfolio problems for an investor who is only concerned about the expected return and the variance of portfolio returns. We cover the following:

- How to calculate the proportions $w_i$ to hold in each risky asset, so that the investor is at a point on the efficient frontier. This is the famous **Markowitz problem**.
- To demonstrate that any two points on the Markowitz efficient frontier can be used to map out the whole of the efficient frontier. This is often referred to as the **two-fund theorem**.
- How to combine riskless borrowing or lending, together with the choice amongst $n$ risky assets to determine the optimal proportions $w_i$ held in the **market portfolio**. This is the point of tangency between the capital market line CML and the efficient frontier.
- To demonstrate the applicability of the two-fund theorem by showing that the *market portfolio* is a particular combination of two efficient portfolios.
- To show that the capital asset pricing model CAPM is a direct consequence of mean–variance optimisation (when we also allow riskless borrowing and lending).
- To interpret an asset's beta ($\beta_i$) in terms of the incremental risk of the portfolio.

The reader should be warned that although the mathematics used does not go beyond simple calculus, the various models discussed have rather subtle differences, in terms of maximands and constraints. These differences should be carefully noted and are summarised at the end of the section.

## THE EFFICIENT FRONTIER: MARKOWITZ MODEL

To find a point on the efficient frontier such as 'A' in Figure 18.1 the investor solves the following constrained minimisation problem:

[18.18] $$\text{Min}\,\frac{1}{2}\sigma_p^2 = \frac{1}{2}\sum_{i,j=1}^{n} w_{ij}\sigma_{ij} = \frac{1}{2}(\mathbf{w}'\mathbf{\Omega}\mathbf{w})$$

where $\mathbf{w}' = (w_1, w_2, \ldots, w_n)$ and $\mathbf{\Omega}$ is the $n \times n$ covariance matrix $\{\sigma_{ij}\}$. The constraints are:

## FIGURE 18.1: Efficient frontier

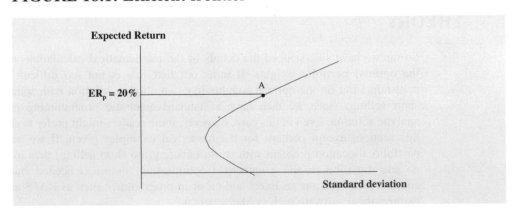

**[18.19a]**
$$\sum_{i=1}^{n} w_i ER_i = ER_p$$

**[18.19b]**
$$\sum_{i=1}^{n} w_i = 1$$

The use of $1/2$ in equation [18.18] just makes the algebra neater. Note that the investor has estimates of $\sigma_{ij}$ and $ER_i$ and can only invest her own wealth, so that $\sum w_i = 1$. In the minimisation, we obtain point A in Figure 18.1 for $ER_p$ fixed at 20%. Choosing $w_i$ to minimise equation [18.18] subject to an arbitrarily chosen 'known value' of $ER_p$ provides portfolio weights $w_i$ which correspond to a single point 'A' on the efficient frontier. Note that the $w_i$ are not constrained in any way and some of the optimal values for $w_i$ may be less than zero ($w_i < 0$), so that **short selling** is allowed. The solution to this optimisation problem is fairly standard and involves the use of two unknown **Lagrange multipliers**, $\lambda$ and $\mu$ for the two constraints:

**[18.20]**
$$\text{Min } L = (1/2) \sum_{i,j=1}^{n} w_i w_j \sigma_{ij} - \lambda \left( \sum_{i=1}^{n} w_i ER_i - ER_p \right) - \mu \left( \sum_{i=1}^{n} w_i - 1 \right)$$

This type of problem is most easily solved by setting it up in matrix notation, but there is a pedagogic advantage in considering the algebra of the three-variable case:

**[18.21]**
$$L = (1/2)[w_1^2 \sigma_{11} + w_1 w_2 \sigma_{12} + w_1 w_3 \sigma_{13} + w_2 w_1 \sigma_{21} + w_2^2 \sigma_{22}$$
$$+ w_2 w_3 \sigma_{23} + w_3 w_1 \sigma_{31} + w_3 w_2 \sigma_{32} + w_3^2 \sigma_{33}]$$
$$- \lambda(w_1 ER_1 + w_2 ER_2 + w_3 ER_3 - ER_p) - \mu(w_1 + w_2 + w_3 - 1)$$

Differentiating equation [18.21] with respect to $w_i$, $\lambda$ and $\mu$ gives us the following first-order conditions (FOCs):

**[18.22a]**
$$\frac{\partial L}{\partial w_1} = (1/2)[2w_1 \sigma_{11} + w_2 \sigma_{12} + w_3 \sigma_{13} + w_2 \sigma_{21} + w_3 \sigma_{31}] - \lambda ER_1 - \mu = 0$$

**[18.22b]**
$$\frac{\partial L}{\partial w_2} = (1/2)[w_1 \sigma_{12} + w_1 \sigma_{21} + 2w_2 \sigma_{22} + w_3 \sigma_{23} + w_3 \sigma_{32}] - \lambda ER_2 - \mu = 0$$

**[18.22c]**
$$\frac{\partial L}{\partial w_3} = (1/2)[w_1 \sigma_{13} + w_2 \sigma_{23} + w_1 \sigma_{31} + w_2 \sigma_{32} + 2w_3 \sigma_{33}] - \lambda ER_3 - \mu = 0$$

**[18.22d]**
$$\frac{\partial L}{\partial \lambda} - \sum_{i=1}^{3} w_i ER_i - ER_p = 0$$

**[18.22e]**
$$\frac{\partial L}{\partial \mu} = \sum_{i=1}^{3} w_i - 1 = 0$$

## EQUATIONS FOR THE MINIMUM VARIANCE SET

The last two equations merely reproduce the constraints. However, there is a pattern in the first three equations. Noting that $\sigma_{ij} = \sigma_{ji}$, the above equations, generalised to the $n$ asset case, can be written:

[18.23a]
$$\sum_{j=1}^{n} \sigma_{ij} w_j - \lambda ER_i - \mu = 0$$

or

[18.23b]
$$\Omega w - \lambda ER_i - \mu = 0$$

[18.23c]
$$\sum_{j=1}^{n} w_i ER_i = ER_p$$

and

[18.23d]
$$\sum_{i=1}^{n} w_i = 1$$

where $\Omega$ is an $n \times n$ covariance matrix, and $ER_i$ and $\mu$ are $(n \times 1)$ vectors. In equation [18.23a] we know the $\sigma_{ij}$ and $ER_i$ and in [18.23c] we arbitrarily set $ER_p$ to any fixed value. We have $(n + 2)$ linear equations and $(n + 2)$ unknowns, the $w_i$'s, $\lambda$ and $\mu$. These linear equations are easily solved using spreadsheet programmes (e.g. in Excel) to give the optimal weights for one point on the minimum-variance set. We have illustrated this in Table 18.2, using five asset prices and a 'step-by-step' procedure. First we would calculate the asset returns and use this historic data to calculate our basic inputs, namely the means $ER_i$ (i.e. our estimate of expected returns), the standard deviations and covariances $\sigma_{ij}$ for each asset. The latter appear in the covariance matrix in Table 18.2.

We then use the Excel 'add in' called SOLVER to minimise the portfolio standard deviation subject to a specific (but arbitrary) level of (expected) portfolio return which we 'input' (e.g. $ER_p = \bar{R}_p = 15\%$. We provide SOLVER with some starting values for 'weights' which must sum to unity (e.g. 0, 0, 0, 0, 1 will do) and SOLVER then calculates 'new' values for the weights $w_i$ which minimise $\sigma_p$ and also provides us with this optimal value of $\sigma_p$ (e.g. 0.75%). We can then plot our first point on the efficient frontier, namely the pair $\bar{R} = 15\%$, $\sigma_p = 0.75$. We now choose a new (arbitrary) value for $\bar{R}p$, say 0.08 (or 8%), and repeat the exercise until we have enough points to plot out the efficient frontier which is shown in Table 18.2. (This Excel worksheet is on our web site.)

Because the optimal weights are totally unconstrained they can take on any value. A negative value indicates short selling of the stock. Any funds obtained from short selling can be used to invest in other assets and hence for some assets $w_i$ may exceed unity (i.e. you hold more than your initial 'own wealth' in this asset). The only restriction on the optimal weights is that they sum to unity, which implies all of your initial wealth is held in the risky

## TABLE 18.2: Calculating the Efficient Frontier—using Solver in Excel

**Variance–covariance matrix (of asset returns)**

|     | 1     | 2     | 3     | 4    | 5     |
| --- | ----- | ----- | ----- | ---- | ----- |
| 1   | **2.2**   | 0.9   | −0.3  | 0.65 | −0.42 |
| 2   | 0.9   | **1.5**   | −0.39 | 0.2  | 0.47  |
| 3   | −0.3  | −0.39 | **1.8**   | 0.8  | 0.27  |
| 4   | 0.65  | 0.2   | 0.8   | **1.5**  | −0.5  |
| 5   | −0.42 | 0.47  | 0.27  | −0.5 | **1.7**   |
| *ER* | 8.5  | 18.3  | 12.7  | 10.8 | 9.5   |

**Correlation matrix (of asset returns)**

|     | 1       | 2       | 3       | 4       | 5       |
| --- | ------- | ------- | ------- | ------- | ------- |
| 1   | **1**       | 0.4954  | −0.1508 | 0.3578  | −0.2172 |
| 2   | 0.4954  | **1**       | −0.2373 | 0.1333  | 0.2943  |
| 3   | −0.1508 | −0.2373 | **1**       | 0.4869  | 0.1543  |
| 4   | 0.3578  | 0.1333  | 0.4869  | **1**       | −0.3131 |
| 5   | −0.2172 | 0.2943  | 0.1543  | −0.3131 | **1**       |

**Portfolio risk and return calculations**

| Portfolio return   | 15       |
| ------------------ | -------- |
| Portfolio variance | 0.570691 |
| Portfolio Std. dev. | 0.755441 |

|                   | $w_1$    | $w_2$    | $w_3$    | $w_4$    | $w_5$    |
| ----------------- | -------- | -------- | -------- | -------- | -------- |
| Portfolio weights | 0.016595 | 0.490336 | 0.347744 | 0.068348 | 0.076976 |

**Sum of weights 1**

Solver determines optimum portfolio weights (minimises portfolio Std. dev. for fixed return)

*continued overleaf*

## TABLE 18.2: (*Continued*)

| Efficient frontier | |
|---|---|
| Portfolio | |
| Risk | Return |
| 2.12 | 35 |
| 1.93 | 32.5 |
| 1.73 | 30 |
| 1.54 | 27.5 |
| 1.36 | 25 |
| 1.18 | 22.5 |
| 1.02 | 20 |
| 0.87 | 17.5 |
| 0.76 | 15 |
| 0.69 | 12.5 |
| 0.68 | 10 |
| 0.73 | 7.5 |
| 0.84 | 5 |
| 0.98 | 2.5 |
| 1.14 | 0 |

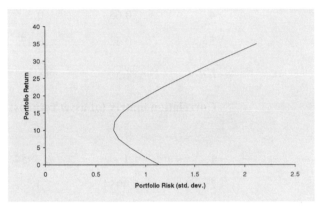

Note: Repeated use of Solver for different expected portfolio returns

assets. Clearly the above is an instructive way of demonstrating how the efficient frontier can be constructed, but it is hardly an 'efficient' computational method. However, the solution we require can be obtained in a simpler fashion by using a special property of the solution to equations [18.23a]–[18.23d] known as the two-fund theorem.

## TWO-FUND THEOREM

Suppose we find two optimal solutions to the Markowitz FOCs (equations [18.23a]–[18.23d]) for arbitrary values of $ER_p^{(1)}$ and $ER_p^{(2)}$.

> **Solution 1:** $\mathbf{w}^{(1)} = \{w_1^{(1)}, w_2^{(1)}, \ldots, w_n^{(1)}\}$ and $\lambda^{(1)}, \mu^{(1)}$
> **Solution 2:** $\mathbf{w}^{(2)} = \{w_1^{(2)}, w_2^{(2)}, \ldots, w_n^{(2)}\}$ and $\lambda^{(2)}, \mu^{(2)}$

where $\mathbf{w}^{(1)}$ and $\mathbf{w}^{(2)}$ are column vectors. Then any linear combination of $\mathbf{w}^{(1)}$ and $\mathbf{w}^{(2)}$ is also a solution to the FOCs. Hence another solution to equations [18.23a]–[18.23d] is $\mathbf{w}^{(q)} = \alpha\mathbf{w}^{(1)} + (1 - \alpha)\mathbf{w}^{(2)}$ where $-\infty < \alpha < +\infty$ and it is easy to see that $\sum w_i^{(q)} = 1$. Since both solutions $\mathbf{w}^{(1)}$ and $\mathbf{w}^{(2)}$ make the left-hand side of equation [18.23a] equal to zero, their linear combination also satisfies equation [18.23a]. Since we have already solved for $\mathbf{w}^{(1)}$ and $\mathbf{w}^{(2)}$ then by altering $\alpha$ we can map out the entire minimum variance set (which will include all points on the efficient set, the upper portion of the curve). The **two-fund-theorem** means that if an investor can find two 'mutual funds' (i.e. portfolios of securities which have asset proportions $\mathbf{w}^{(1)}$ and $\mathbf{w}^{(2)}$ which satisfy the Markowitz equations and are on the efficient set) then she can combine these two mutual funds in proportions $\alpha$ and $1 - \alpha$ to construct a portfolio which lies anywhere along the mean–variance efficient frontier. In short:

> **The two-fund theorem implies that we only require two points on the efficient frontier (often referred to as two mutual funds) in order to map out the whole of the efficient frontier**

The expected return and variance of the portfolio $q$ are:

[18.24a]
$$\mathbf{ER}^{(q)} = \sum_{i=1}^{5} w_i^{(q)}\mathbf{ER}_i = \mathbf{w}^{(q)\prime}\mathbf{ER}_i$$

[18.24b]
$$[\sigma^{(q)}]^2 = \mathbf{w}^{(q)\prime}\mathbf{\Omega}\mathbf{w}^{(q)} = \sum_{i,j}^{5} w_i^{(q)}w_j^{(q)}\sigma_{ij}$$

As $\mathbf{w}^{(q)}$ is a function of $\alpha$ then each value chosen (arbitrarily) for $\alpha$ gives us a point on the mean–variance efficient frontier. By altering $\alpha$ we map out the whole of the efficient frontier. At a purely mathematical level the two-fund theorem allows us to simplify the solution procedure for the Markowitz equations [18.23a]–[18.23d]. To solve equations [18.23a]–[18.23d] for *all* values of $ER_p$ we need only to find two arbitrary solutions and then form linear combinations of these two solutions. Obvious choices to simplify the problem are:

a) $\lambda = 0, \qquad \mu = 1$

b) $\mu = 0, \qquad \lambda = 1$

In '(a)' the constraint $\sum w_i ER_i = ER_p$ is ignored so this gives the $\mathbf{w}^{(1)}$ corresponding to the minimum variance point. Imposing (a) and (b) may lead to a violation of the constraint $\sum w_i = 1$, but the solutions can be rescaled to allow for this. Setting $\lambda = 0$ and $\mu = 1$, in equation [18.23a] or [18.23b] gives $n$ equations in the $n$ unknowns $z_i^{(1)}$ (for $i = 1, 2, \ldots, n$).

[18.25a] $\quad \displaystyle\sum_{j=1}^{n} \sigma_{ij} z_j^{(1)} = 1 \quad$ or $\quad \boldsymbol{\Omega}\mathbf{z}^{(1)} = \mathbf{1}$

which is easily solved for $\mathbf{z}^{(1)} = \{z_1^{(1)}, z_2^{(1)}, \ldots, z_n^{(1)}\}$. We then normalise the $z_j$'s so they sum to one, giving:

[18.25b] $\quad w_i^{(1)} = \dfrac{z_i^{(1)}}{\displaystyle\sum_{j=1}^{n} z_j^{(1)}}$

The vector $\mathbf{w}^{(1)} = \{w_1^{(1)}, w_2^{(1)}, \ldots, w_n^{(1)}\}$ is then the minimum variance point on the efficient frontier. The second (arbitrary) solution has $\mu = 0$ and $\lambda = 1$ and equation [18.23a] becomes:

[18.26] $\quad \displaystyle\sum_{j=1}^{n} \sigma_{ij} z_j^{(2)} = ER_i \quad$ or $\quad \boldsymbol{\Omega}\mathbf{z}^{(2)} = \mathbf{ER}_i$

giving a solution $\mathbf{z}^{(2)} = \{z_1^{(2)}, z_2^{(2)}, \ldots, z_n^{(2)}\}$ and associated $\mathbf{w}^{(2)} = \{w_1^{(2)}, w_2^{(2)}, \ldots, w_n^{(2)}\}$. Having obtained these two solutions $\mathbf{w}^{(1)}$ and $\mathbf{w}^{(2)}$ we can calculate the values of $ER_p = \sum w_i ER_i$ and $\sigma_p = \sum\sum w_i w_j \sigma_{ij}$ at these *two* points on the efficient frontier. We then calculate $\mathbf{w}^{(q)} = \alpha \mathbf{w}^{(1)} + (1 - \alpha)\mathbf{w}^{(2)}$ for any arbitrary $\alpha$ and alter $\alpha$ to map all the combinations of $\mathbf{ER}^{(q)}$ and $\boldsymbol{\sigma}^{(q)}$ using equation [18.24].

## SIMPLE 2 × 2 EXAMPLE
Calculation of the optimal weights for the market portfolio is illustrated for the simple two variable case in Table 18.3. The optimal market portfolio weights are $w_1 = 2/3$ and $w_2 = 1/3$, which gives a 'market portfolio' with $ER_p = 12\%$ and $\sigma_p = 4.58\%$.

## FURTHER EXAMPLE
Let us move to a 5 × 5 assets case and use matrix algebra, with the aid of Excel. Suppose (using sample averages of historic returns data) we find the following values of $\sigma_{ij}$ and $ER_i$ for the 5 × 5 case (see Table 18.4):

[18.27a] $\quad \boldsymbol{\Omega}_{(5\times 5)} = \{\sigma_{ij}\} = \begin{bmatrix} 2.2 & 0.9 & -0.3 & 0.65 & -0.42 \\ 0.9 & 1.5 & -0.39 & 0.2 & 0.47 \\ -0.3 & -0.39 & 1.8 & 0.8 & 0.27 \\ 0.65 & 0.2 & 0.8 & 1.5 & -0.5 \\ -0.42 & 0.47 & 0.27 & -0.5 & 1.7 \end{bmatrix}$

[18.27b] $\quad \mathbf{ER}_i = [ER_1, \ ER_2, \ ER_3, \ ER_4, \ ER_5] = [8.5, \ 18.3, \ 12.7, \ 10.8, \ 9.5]$

In matrix notation, the $n = 5$ equations in [18.25a] can be written as:

[18.28] $\quad \mathbf{z}^{(1)} = \boldsymbol{\Omega}^{-1}\mathbf{e}$

## TABLE 18.3: Optimum portfolio weights

**Data:**  The expected returns and variances of a two-asset portfolio are $ER_1 = 14\%$, $ER_2 = 8\%$, $\sigma_{11} = 36$, $\sigma_{22} = 9$, $\rho = 0.5$ and the risk free rate is $r = 5\%$

**Question:**  Calculate the optimal portfolio weights and hence the market portfolio, its expected return and variance

**Answer:**  We have $\sigma_{12} = \rho\sigma_1\sigma_2 = 9$. Hence, the optimum is given by:

[1]  $(\mathbf{ER} - \mathbf{r}) = \mathbf{\Omega z}$  or  $(ER_i - r) = \displaystyle\sum_{i=1}^{n} \sigma_{ki}z_i$  $(k = 1, 2 \text{ and } n = 2)$

Hence:

[2a]  $9 = 36z_1 + 9z_2$

[2b]  $3 = 9z_1 + 9z_2$

The solution using [1] is given by $\mathbf{z} = \mathbf{\Omega}^{-1}(\mathbf{ER} - \mathbf{r})$, which is:

[3]  $\begin{pmatrix} z_1 \\ z_2 \end{pmatrix} = \begin{bmatrix} 36 & 9 \\ 9 & 9 \end{bmatrix}^{-1} \begin{pmatrix} 9 \\ 3 \end{pmatrix}$

Alternatively by substitution from [2a] we get:

[4]  $z_1 = (1/4) - (1/4)z_2$

Substituting for $z_1$ in [2b] gives us:

[5]  $z_2 = (1/3) - z_1 = 1/9$

Substituting [5] in [4]:

$z_1 = (1/4) - (1/4)(1/9) = 2/9$

Also

$z_1 + z_2 = 2/9 + 1/9 = 1/3$

Hence:

[6a]  $w_1 = \dfrac{z_1}{\sum z_i} = \dfrac{(2/9)}{(1/3)} = \dfrac{2}{3}$

[6b]  $w_2 = \dfrac{z_2}{\sum z_i} = \dfrac{(1/9)}{(1/3)} = \dfrac{1}{3}$

*continued overleaf*

## TABLE 18.3: (*Continued*)

Expected return:

[7]   $ER_p = (2/3)14\% + (1/3)8\% = 12\%$

Standard deviation of the optimal portfolio:

[8]   $\sigma_p = [(2/3)^2(36) + (1/3)^2(9) + 2(2/3)(1/3)9]^{1/2} = \sqrt{21} = 4.58\%$

where **e** is a $5 \times 1$ column vector of ones and hence:

[18.29a]   $\mathbf{z}^{(1)} = \mathbf{\Omega}^{-1}\mathbf{e} = \{0.3902, 0.2073, 0.3091, 0.5519, 0.7406\}$

[18.29b]   $\sum_{i=1}^{5} z_i^{(1)} = 2.1991$

[18.29c]   $w_i^{(1)} = z_i^{(1)} / \sum z_i^{(1)} = \{w_1, w_2, w_3, w_4, w_5\}$

$= \{0.1774, 0.0942, 0.1406, 0.2510, 0.3368\}$

The weights $\mathbf{w}^{(1)}$ are actually the weights required to achieve the minimum variance point (since we set $\lambda = 0$ in equation [18.20]). The second solution using equation [18.26] in matrix notation is:

[18.30a]   $\mathbf{\Omega}\mathbf{z}^{(2)} = \mathbf{ER}_i$

[18.30b]   $\mathbf{z}^{(2)} = \mathbf{\Omega}^{-1}\mathbf{ER} = \{-1.3839, 16.1736, 10.6532, -0.3818, -1.0294\}$

with $\mathbf{w}^{(2)} = \{-0.0576, 0.6730, 0.4433, -0.0159, -0.0428\}$. The above results are shown in Table 18.4. We can then map out the whole of the mean–variance set (and hence the efficient frontier) by taking linear combinations $\mathbf{w}^{(q)} = \alpha\mathbf{w}^{(1)} + (1 - \alpha)\mathbf{w}^{(2)}$ with $\alpha$ varying between $-\infty$ and $+\infty$ and each time calculate $\mathbf{ER}^{(q)}$ and $\boldsymbol{\sigma}^{(q)}$ (which are functions of $\alpha$). This gives the expected return and standard deviation combinations shown in Table 18.4 and the accompanying graph of the efficient frontier. Unrestricted minimisation of portfolio variance can often give portfolio weights $w_i < 0$ (i.e. short selling) and $w_i > 1$ (i.e. more than one's own wealth held in one asset). Some financial institutions do not allow short selling (e.g. UK pension funds). Hence we need to derive the efficient frontier with all $w_i > 0$.

## NO SHORT SALES

In this case the minimisation problem is exactly the same as in equations [18.18] and [18.19] but with an additional constraint, namely $w_i \geqslant 0$ ($i = 1, 2, \ldots, n$). In this case we cannot use the two-fund theorem to simplify the solution procedure, and indeed a special form of programming in which the first-order conditions are known as the **Kuhn–Tucker**

# TABLE 18.4: Calculating the efficient frontier—using the 'two-fund theorem'

**Variance–covariance matrix (of asset returns)**

|  | 1 | 2 | 3 | 4 | 5 |
|---|---|---|---|---|---|
| 1 | 2.2 | 0.9 | −0.3 | 0.65 | −0.42 |
| 2 | 0.9 | 1.5 | −0.39 | 0.2 | 0.47 |
| 3 | −0.3 | −0.39 | 1.8 | 0.8 | 0.27 |
| 4 | 0.65 | 0.2 | 0.8 | 1.5 | −0.5 |
| 5 | −0.42 | 0.47 | 0.27 | −0.5 | 1.7 |
| ER | 8.5 | 18.3 | 12.7 | 10.8 | 9.5 |

**Correlation matrix (of asset returns)**

|  | 1 | 2 | 3 | 4 | 5 |
|---|---|---|---|---|---|
| 1 | 1 | 0.4954 | −0.1508 | 0.3578 | −0.2172 |
| 2 | 0.4954 | 1 | −0.2373 | 0.1333 | 0.2943 |
| 3 | −0.1508 | −0.2373 | 1 | 0.4869 | 0.1543 |
| 4 | 0.3578 | 0.1333 | 0.4869 | 1 | −0.3131 |
| 5 | −0.2172 | 0.2943 | 0.1543 | −0.3131 | 1 |

**Determining the portfolio weights for two portfolios on the efficient frontier**

| Ones | Return | $z_1$ | $z_2$ | $w_1$ | $w_2$ |
|---|---|---|---|---|---|
| 1 | 8.5 | 0.3902 | −1.3839 | 0.1774 | −0.0576 |
| 1 | 18.3 | 0.2073 | 16.1736 | 0.0942 | 0.6730 |
| 1 | 12.7 | 0.3091 | 10.6532 | 0.1406 | 0.4433 |
| 1 | 10.8 | 0.5519 | −0.3817 | 0.2510 | −0.0159 |
| 1 | 9.5 | 0.7406 | −1.0294 | 0.3368 | −0.0428 |
| Sum | | 2.1991 | 24.0319 | 1 | 1 |

continued overleaf

573

## TABLE 18.4: (Continued)

| | Portfolio | |
| --- | --- | --- |
| | Portfolio-1 | Portfolio-2 |
| **Portfolio variance** | 0.45473 | 0.702316 |
| **Portfolio Std. dev.** | 0.674336 | 0.838043 |
| **Portfolio return** | 10.928 | 16.87796 |

**Portfolio weights for alternative portfolios on the efficient frontier (linear combination of portfolios 1 and 2)**

| | | | | | | Alternative values for alpha | | | | | | | |
| --- | --- | --- | --- | --- | --- | --- | --- | --- | --- | --- | --- | --- | --- |
| | $-3$ | $-2.5$ | $-2$ | $-1.5$ | $-1$ | $-0.5$ | $0$ | $0.5$ | $1$ | $1.5$ | $2$ | $2.5$ | $3$ |
| $w_1$ | −0.7627 | −0.6452 | −0.5276 | −0.4101 | −0.2926 | −0.1751 | −0.0576 | 0.0599 | 0.1774 | 0.2950 | 0.4125 | 0.5300 | 0.6475 |
| $w_2$ | 2.4093 | 2.1199 | 1.8305 | 1.5411 | 1.2518 | 0.9624 | 0.6730 | 0.3836 | 0.0942 | −0.1951 | −0.4845 | −0.7739 | −1.0633 |
| $w_3$ | 1.3515 | 1.2001 | 1.0488 | 0.8974 | 0.7460 | 0.5947 | 0.4433 | 0.2919 | 0.1406 | −0.0108 | −0.1622 | −0.3136 | −0.4649 |
| $w_4$ | −0.8165 | −0.6831 | −0.5496 | −0.4162 | −0.2827 | −0.1493 | −0.0159 | 0.1176 | 0.2510 | 0.3844 | 0.5179 | 0.6513 | 0.7847 |
| $w_5$ | −1.1816 | −0.9918 | −0.8020 | −0.6122 | −0.4224 | −0.2326 | −0.0428 | 0.1470 | 0.3368 | 0.5266 | 0.7164 | 0.9062 | 1.0960 |
| **Sum of $w$** | 1 | 1 | 1 | 1 | 1 | 1 | 1 | 1 | 1 | 1 | 1 | 1 | 1 |

*continued overleaf*

## TABLE 18.4: (*Continued*)

| | Alternative values for alpha | | | | | | | | | | | | |
|---|---|---|---|---|---|---|---|---|---|---|---|---|---|
| | -3 | -2.5 | -2 | -1.5 | -1 | -0.5 | 0 | 0.5 | 1 | 1.5 | 2 | 2.5 | 3 |
| **Portfolio Std. dev.** | 2.101 | 1.867 | 1.637 | 1.414 | 1.202 | 1.005 | 0.838 | 0.718 | 0.674 | 0.718 | 0.838 | 1.005 | 1.202 |
| **Portfolio return** | 34.72 | 31.75 | 28.77 | 25.8 | 22.82 | 19.85 | 16.87 | 13.90 | 10.92 | 7.95 | 4.97 | 2.00 | -0.97 |

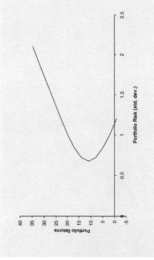

Note: The efficient frontier is the graph of 'portfolio mean' against 'portfolio standard deviation'

### Determining the weights for the (optimum) market portfolio, $w^*$

Market portfolio $z^*$ = (inverse of the variance–covariance matrix × excess return vector)

Market portfolio $w^*$ = normalised $z^*$ values

| | Asset 1 | Asset 2 | Asset 3 | Asset 4 | Asset 5 | Risk free |
|---|---|---|---|---|---|---|
| *ER* | 8.5 | 18.3 | 12.7 | 10.8 | 9.5 | 5 |
| **Excess R** | 3.5 | 13.3 | 7.7 | 5.8 | 4.5 | |

*continued overleaf*

## TABLE 18.4: (Continued)

First approach: $z^* = z_2 - rf z_1$

Second approach: $z^* = \text{Inv(Var–Cov)} \times \text{excess return}$

| | | 1st approach | 2nd approach | |
| | | $z^*$ | $z^*$ | |
| $z_1$ | $z_2$ | | | $w^*$ |
|---|---|---|---|---|
| 0.3902 | −1.3839 | −3.33498 | −3.33498 | −0.2558 |
| 0.2073 | 16.1736 | 15.13733 | 15.13733 | 1.1612 |
| 0.3091 | 10.6532 | 9.10774 | 9.10774 | 0.6982 |
| 0.5519 | −0.3817 | −3.1414 | −3.1414 | −0.2410 |
| 0.7406 | −1.0294 | −4.7324 | −4.7324 | −0.3630 |
| Sum 2.1991 | 24.0319 | 13.0363 | 13.0363 | 1.0000 |

conditions. Some readers may be familiar with this type of solution procedure. It is usually the case that when short selling *is* allowed nearly all of the $w_i$ are non-zero (i.e. either positive or negative—see Table 18.4) but when short sales are *not* allowed many of the optimal $w_i$'s are set to zero and hence only a subset of the total assets is held by the investor.

## THE MARKET PORTFOLIO

When we allow the investor to borrow or lend at the risk free rate and also to invest in $n$ risky securities, the optimal solution is the market portfolio (if all investors have the same view of expected returns, variances and covariances). The optimal proportions are determined by the tangency of the transformation line with the efficient frontier (short sales are permitted). Mathematically, to obtain the **market portfolio** we choose the proportions $w_i$ to:

[**18.31**] $$\text{Max } \theta = \frac{ER_p - r}{\sigma_p}$$

Subject to constraints:

[**18.32a**] $$ER_p = \sum w_i ER_i$$

[**18.32b**] $$\sum w_i = 1$$

[**18.32c**] $$\sigma_p = \left( \sum_{i=1}^{n} w_i^2 \sigma_i^2 + \sum_{i \neq j} w_i w_j \sigma_{ij} \right)^{1/2} = \left( \sum_{i,j=1}^{n} w_i w_j \sigma_{ij} \right)^{1/2}$$

$ER_i$ is the *expected* return on asset $i$, $ER_p$ and $\sigma_p$ are the expected return on the portfolio and its standard deviation, respectively. The constraint [18.32b] can be directly incorporated in the maximand [18.31] by writing $\theta$ as:

[**18.33**] $$\theta = \frac{\sum w_i(ER_i - r)}{\sigma_p}$$

It can be shown (see Appendix 18.1) that the FOCs are of the form:

[**18.34**] $$z_1 \sigma_{11} + z_2 \sigma_{12} + \ldots + z_n \sigma_{1n} = ER_1 - r$$

$$z_1 \sigma_{12} + z_2 \sigma_{22} + \ldots + z_n \sigma_{2n} = ER_2 - r$$

$$\ldots$$

$$z_1 \sigma_{1n} + z_2 \sigma_{2n} + \ldots + z_n \sigma_{nn} = ER_n - r$$

where $z_i = \lambda w_i$ and $\lambda$ is a constant. The constant $\lambda$ does not affect the solution since if $w_i$ is a solution to equation [18.33] then so is $\lambda w_i$, since the $\lambda$ cancels from the numerator and denominator. Having solved equation [18.34] for $z_i$ then we can determine the optimal values for $w_i$ from:

**[18.35]**
$$\sum_{i=1}^{n} w_i = 1 = \lambda^{-1} \sum_{i=1}^{n} z_i$$

Hence:

$$\lambda = \sum_{i=1}^{n} z_i \quad \text{and} \quad w_i = \frac{z_i}{\lambda} = \frac{z_i}{\sum_{i=1}^{n} z_i}$$

Since $ER_i$, $r$, $\sigma_i^2$ and $\sigma_{ij}$ are known, then equation [18.34] is an $n$-equation system, which can be solved for the $n$ unknowns $z_1$ to $z_n$. Equation [18.34] can be written (for $k = 1, 2, \ldots, n$):

**[18.36]**
$$\sum_{i=1}^{n} \sigma_{ki} z_i = (ER_k - r) \qquad \Omega\mathbf{z} = \mathbf{ER} - \mathbf{r}$$

where $\mathbf{z} = (z_1, z_2, \ldots, z_n)$, $\mathbf{ER} - \mathbf{r} = E(R_1 - r, R_2 - r, \ldots, R_n - r)'$ and $\Omega$ is the $(n \times n)$ variance–covariance matrix. It follows that:

**[18.37]**
$$\mathbf{z}^* = \Omega^{-1}(\mathbf{ER} - \mathbf{r})$$

The above solution is easily obtained and is shown in Table 18.4. Again, we have placed no restrictions on the values that the optimal weights can take, and some may be negative, implying that the stock is sold short. If short sales are prohibited then $w_i > 0$ (for all $i$), and the optimisation involves application of the Kuhn–Tucker conditions. In practice, software for a variety of optimisation procedures of this type is available as 'add ons' to commonly used spreadsheet programmes like Lotus 1-2-3 and Excel. As the number of assets increases or the type of restrictions on the $w_i$ become more complex, then the analysis will require more flexible (and speedy) software packages such as **Gauss**, Excel–Visual Basic, C++, etc.

In the general case of $n$ assets (plus the risk free asset) we have to solve the $n$ equations in [18.36]. This is relatively straightforward in Excel once we are given the covariance matrix $\Omega$ and the forecast of expected returns $ER_i$. This is done in Table 18.4 for $n = 5$ assets. The solution is $\mathbf{z}^* = \{-3.33, 15.14, 9.11, -3.14, -4.73\}$ and $\mathbf{w}^* = \{-0.26, 1.16, 0.70, -0.24, -0.36\}$.

There is a nice connection between our earlier Markovitz mean–variance problem and that for the market portfolio weights. The set of FOCs in equation [18.34] for the market portfolio is rather similar to the FOCs in the Markowitz two-fund problem (equations [18.25a] and [18.26]) which are rewritten here:

**[18.25a]**
$$\sum_{j=1}^{n} \sigma_{ij} z_j^{(1)} = 1 \quad \text{or} \quad \Omega\mathbf{z}^{(1)} = \mathbf{e}$$

**[18.26]**     $\sum_{j=1}^{n} \sigma_{ij} z_j^{(2)} = ER_k$     or     $\mathbf{\Omega z}^{(2)} = \mathbf{ER}_k$

with solutions $\mathbf{z}^{(1)}$ and $\mathbf{z}^{(2)}$. The right-hand side of equation [18.36] is $ER_k - r$ and the left-hand side is identical to that in equations [18.25a] and [18.26]. Hence if $\mathbf{z}^{(1)}$ and $\mathbf{z}^{(2)}$ are solutions to the FOCs for the Markovitz efficient frontier, then $\mathbf{z}^* = \mathbf{z}^{(2)} - r\mathbf{z}^{(1)}$ is a solution for the market portfolio problem in equation [18.36]. This should not be too surprising. Earlier we found that any linear combination of the Markovitz solutions also lies on the efficient frontier. But clearly the market portfolio lies on the efficient frontier, so it too is a linear combination of $\mathbf{z}^{(1)}$ and $\mathbf{z}^{(2)}$. We have already calculated $\mathbf{z}^{(1)}$ and $\mathbf{z}^{(2)}$, so given $r = 5\%$, the solution for the market portfolio is:

**[18.38]**     $\mathbf{z}^* = \mathbf{z}^{(2)} - 0.05\mathbf{z}^{(1)} = \{-3.33, 15.14, 9.11, -3.14, -4.73\}$

which gives market portfolio weights of $\mathbf{w}^* = \{-0.26, 1.16, 0.70, -0.24, -0.36\}$. The latter is, of course, the same solution as that from direct application of $\mathbf{z}^* = \mathbf{\Omega}^{-1}(\mathbf{ER} - \mathbf{r})$ from equation [18.34]. The solution $\mathbf{z}^*$ in equation [18.34] is another consequence of the two-fund theorem.

Notice that equation [18.38] is only the market portfolio if all investors have homogeneous expectations about the $ER_i$ and the $\sigma_{ij}$'s. If the investor has her own expectations about the aforementioned variables then $\mathbf{z}^*$ still gives the optimum weights but only for that single investor. Different investors will then have different optimal portfolio weights. One can also introduce additional constraints such as no short selling (i.e. $w_i > 0$), but then we can no longer use the simplified solution method above and the optimal weights do not constitute the 'market portfolio'. All the above calculations require as inputs expected returns (and the current risk free rate $r = 5\%$ say), variances and covariances (correlations), which we have assumed are constant in the above examples. In practice we need to estimate these variables over the appropriate horizon (e.g. a day, month or year) and recalculate the optimal portfolio proportions, as our forecasts of these variables alter.

A rather neat (and, as it turns out, intuitive) way of obtaining the optimal (unrestricted) mean–variance weights from a simple regression is given in Britten-Jones (1999). You simply take as dependent variable $\mathbf{Y}$ a $(T \times 1)$ column of ones. The independent variable $\mathbf{X}$ is a $(T \times k)$ matrix of $k$ asset *excess* returns and the regression has no intercept:

**[18.39]**     $\mathbf{Y} = \mathbf{X}\beta + \mathbf{u}$

The optimum weight is $\mathbf{w} = \mathbf{b}/\sum_{i=1}^{k} b_i$ where $\mathbf{b}$ is the OLS estimator. This procedure also yields the standard error of $\mathbf{b}$, so we can test hypotheses about these optimal weights. In particular Britten-Jones considers an optimal (unhedged) internationally diversified portfolio (from a US investor perspective) and then tests to see if the weights $w_i$ on all the *non-US* countries are jointly statistically zero. He finds that they are, with the conclusion that a US investor should not diversify internationally. This is really an alternative manifestation of the result that the optimal weights are very sensitive to assumptions about mean returns and the latter are measured with great uncertainty. Also, note that the 'invest at home' conclusion has only been tested for a US based investor and the analysis only holds true if volatilities and correlations are constant (in the population). But the optimal weights (for the US investor) are found to be time varying (e.g. that for Denmark changes from a short position of 29% to a long position of 69% when the data sample is split). Finally, the analysis does not apply if weights are restricted a priori (e.g. no short sales).

## THE CAPM

The market portfolio is held by all investors and all assets in the market portfolio have a particular expected return. What is the relationship between these expected returns and what factors determine any particular expected return? The link between the market portfolio and expected asset returns is given by the CAPM. The CAPM assumes all investors have homogeneous expectations and decide on the proportions of risky assets to hold by maximising $\theta$ in equation [18.31] (i.e. at the point of tangency between the CML and the efficient frontier). When all assets are held, the equilibrium expected return on any asset $k$ is:

[18.40]       $ER_k = r + \beta_k(ER_m - r)$

where $\beta_k = \text{Cov}(R_k, R_m)/\sigma_m^2$.

The above relationship must be implicit in the FOC of the market portfolio. Taking the $k$ th equation in [18.34] we have:

[18.41]       $ER_k - r = \lambda[w_1\sigma_{1k} + w_2\sigma_{2k} + \ldots + w_n\sigma_{nk}]$

The term in square brackets is $\text{Cov}(R_k, R_m)$ since at the optimal values for $w_i$ we have:

[18.42]       $\text{Cov}(R_k, R_m) = \text{Cov}\left[R_k, \left(\sum_{j=1}^{n} w_jR_j\right)\right] = \sum_{j=1}^{n} w_j \, \text{Cov}(R_j, R_k) = \sum_{j=1}^{n} w_j\sigma_{jk}$

Hence equation [18.41] can be written as:

[18.43]       $ER_k - r = \lambda \, \text{Cov}(R_k, R_m)$

Since equation [18.43] holds for all assets it must also hold for the market portfolio, hence:

[18.44]       $ER_m - r = \lambda\sigma_m^2$

Substituting for $\lambda$ from equation [18.44] in equation [18.41] we obtain the CAPM:

[18.45]       $ER_k - r = [(ER_m - r)/\sigma_m^2]\text{Cov}(R_k, R_m) = \beta_k(ER_m - r)$

The expected return on any asset is determined by the asset's beta and the excess market return. In a diversified portfolio the *relative* riskiness of any two assets is determined by the relative size of their betas.

## 18.5 SUMMARY

We have discussed a wide range of practical and theoretical issues in this chapter concerning international portfolio diversification. The key elements are listed below.

---

- There appear to be substantial gains in **reducing portfolio risk by diversification** with only a small number of assets (about 25). A greater risk reduction can be obtained if we diversify internationally, even if we *randomly* choose the diversified set of stocks.
- When we consider both expected return and risk then **international diversification** generally improves the risk–return trade off (i.e. pushes the efficient frontier to the left), particularly if the **foreign returns are hedged** either with forwards, futures or options. The improvement from international diversification is more debatable when **returns are unhedged** and must be examined on a case-by-case basis for a particular 'home currency' investor.
- Diversification can proceed on the basis of either **random selection of stocks,** or an **equally weighted portfolio** or **tracking a broad market index** (e.g. Morgan Stanley World Index) or using a **mean–variance optimiser**.
- The main problem in accepting the results from a totally unconstrained mean–variance analysis is that the **optimal proportions (weights) are very sensitive** to forecasts of expected returns and to assets which have either very high or very low forecast variances. In practice therefore the **optimal proportions are constrained** in some way (e.g. that they must not differ from the current proportions by more than 2%).
- The **mathematics of mean–variance optimisation** forms the basis for other more complex portfolio optimisation techniques (e.g. those which impose constraints on the portfolio weights) and provides the basic mathematical and conceptual ideas that are used in analysing asset returns (e.g. the CAPM).
- In general, **active international portfolio management** involving investments in broad market indices for different countries uses either implicit or explicit macro-economic models coupled with a view about 'political risk'.

---

## END OF CHAPTER EXERCISES

**Q1**    Why might portfolio variance fall as we add foreign assets to our domestic portfolio?

**Q2**    What does 'hedging foreign currency receipts' mean? Is it possible to perfectly hedge receipts from a portfolio of foreign stocks?

**Q3**    If you impose short sales constraints, then in practice, does this improve or worsen the Sharpe ratio?

**Q4**    Why might an (unhedged) internationally diversified portfolio have a lower standard deviation than a purely domestic portfolio even though exchange rates are themselves highly volatile?

**Q5** What is the 'home bias problem' and why is it difficult to ascertain whether this really is a genuine puzzle (or anomaly)?

**Q6** Show how the (uncovered) return in US dollars to a US investor from investing in the DAX (i.e. the German stock index) is given by:

$$R_{US} = R_{DAX} + R_{\$/E}$$

where $R_{\$/E}$ is the annual return on the USD/EURO exchange rate.

**Q7** What are the key issues in whether to hedge an internationally diversified portfolio using the forward currency markets?

# APPENDIX 18.1 OPTIMUM PORTFOLIO WEIGHTS: THE MARKET PORTFOLIO

We assume short selling is permitted. Since $\sum w_i = 1$ then we can write the maximand, incorporating this constraint:

[A18.1] $$\text{Max } \theta = \frac{ER_p - r}{\sigma_p} = \frac{\sum w_i(ER_i - r)}{\sigma_p}$$

where

[A18.2] $$\sigma_p = \left( \sum_{i,j=1}^{n} w_i w_j \sigma_{ij} \right)^{1/2}$$

We will first illustrate the solution without using matrix algebra. Since $ER_p$ and $\sigma_p$ depend on the $w_i$, then differentiating equation [A18.1] requires the use of the 'product rule' of differentiation (i.e. $d(uv) = u\,dv + v\,du$):

[A18.3] $$\frac{\partial \theta}{\partial w_i} = \sum w_i(R_i - r)\left[ \frac{\partial}{\partial w_i}\left( \sum_{i,j=1}^{n} w_i w_j \sigma_{ij} \right) \right] + \frac{1}{\sigma_p}\frac{\partial}{\partial w_i}\left[ \sum_{i=1}^{n} w_i(ER_i - r) \right]$$

$$= \sum w_i(ER_i - r)\left[ \left(\frac{1}{2}\right)\left(\sigma_p^{-3/2}\right)\sum_{j=1}^{n}(2w_j\sigma_{ij}) \right] + \frac{1}{\sigma_p}(ER_i - r) = 0$$

Multiplying through by $\sigma_p$ and noting $\sum w_i ER_i = ER_p$:

[A18.4] $$\left[ \frac{ER_p - r}{\sigma_p^2} \right]\sum_{j=1}^{n} w_j \sigma_{ij} = (ER_i - r) \quad \text{for } i = 1, 2, \ldots, n$$

At the maximum, the term in square brackets is a constant which we denote:

[A18.5] $$\lambda = \left[\frac{ER_p - r}{\sigma_p^2}\right]$$

where $\lambda$ is often referred to as the **market price of risk**. Substituting equation [A18.5] into equation [A18.4] we obtain the FOC for the market portfolio (equation [18.36] in the text):

[18.36] $$\sum_{j=1}^{n} \sigma_{ij}z_j = ER_i - r \text{ for } i = 1, 2, \ldots, n$$

where $z_j = \lambda w_j$.

## SOLUTION: MATRIX NOTATION

We now repeat the above solution using matrix notation:

[A18.6] $$\boldsymbol{\theta} = \frac{\mathbf{w}'(\mathbf{ER} - \mathbf{r})}{(\mathbf{w}'\boldsymbol{\Omega}\mathbf{w})^{1/2}} = \frac{\sum w_i(ER_i - r)}{\sigma_p}$$

where $\mathbf{w}' = (w_1, w_2, \ldots, w_n)$, $\mathbf{ER} - \mathbf{r} = (ER_1 - r, ER_2 - r, \ldots, ER_n - r)$, $\sigma_p = (\mathbf{w}'\boldsymbol{\Omega}\mathbf{w})^{1/2}$ and $\boldsymbol{\Omega}_{(n\times n)} = \{\sigma_{ij}\}$. Using the product rule and chain rule of differentiation:

[A18.7] $$\frac{d\boldsymbol{\theta}}{d\mathbf{w}} = (\mathbf{ER} - \mathbf{r})(\mathbf{w}'\boldsymbol{\Omega}\mathbf{w})^{-1/2} - (1/2)\mathbf{w}'(\mathbf{ER} - \mathbf{r})(\mathbf{w}'\boldsymbol{\Omega}\mathbf{w})^{-3/2}(2\boldsymbol{\Omega}\mathbf{w}) = 0$$

where $d(\mathbf{w}'\boldsymbol{\Omega}\mathbf{w})/d\mathbf{w} = 2\boldsymbol{\Omega}\mathbf{w}$. Multiplying through by the *scalar* $(\mathbf{w}'\boldsymbol{\Omega}\mathbf{w})^{1/2}$:

[A18.8] $$\mathbf{ER} - \mathbf{r} = [\mathbf{w}'(\mathbf{ER} - \mathbf{r})/(\mathbf{w}'\boldsymbol{\Omega}\mathbf{w})]\boldsymbol{\Omega}\mathbf{w}$$

The term in square brackets, a scalar, is the excess return on the portfolio $(\mathbf{ER_p} - \mathbf{r})$ divided by the variance of the portfolio $\sigma_p^2 = \mathbf{w}'\boldsymbol{\Omega}\mathbf{w}$ and is constant for any set of $w_i$'s. We denote this constant as $\lambda$ (see equation [A18.5]) and equation [A18.8] becomes:

[A18.9] $$\mathbf{ER} - \mathbf{r} = \boldsymbol{\Omega}(\lambda\mathbf{w}) = \boldsymbol{\Omega}\mathbf{z}$$

where $\mathbf{z} = \lambda\mathbf{w}$. The solution for $\mathbf{z}$, an $(n \times 1)$ vector, is therefore given by:

[A18.10] $$\mathbf{z} = \boldsymbol{\Omega}^{-1}(\mathbf{ER} - \mathbf{r})$$

As noted in the text, $\sum w_i = 1$ implies $w_i = z_i/\sum z_i$. This completes the derivation of the optional market portfolio weights $\mathbf{z}$ or (strictly) $\mathbf{w}$.

# PART 7

# DERIVATIVE SECURITIES

# Derivative Securities: An Overview

There are three main types of derivative securities, namely futures, options and swaps. Derivative securities are assets whose value depends on the value of some other (underlying) asset, and their value is *derived* from the value of this underlying asset. For example, a futures contract on a stock such as AT&T would not be traded if AT&T went bankrupt. These derivative securities can be used by hedgers, speculators and arbitrageurs. Derivatives often receive a 'bad press', partly because there have been some quite spectacular derivatives losses. Perhaps the most famous are the losses of Nick Leeson, who worked for Barings Bank in Singapore and who lost $1.4bn when trading futures and options on the Nikkei 225, the Japanese stock index. This led to Barings going bust. More recently, in 1998, Long Term Capital Management (LTCM), a hedge fund which levered its trades using derivatives, had to be rescued by a consortium of banks under the imprimator of the Federal Reserve Board. This was all the more galling since Myron Scholes and Robert Merton, two academics who received the Nobel prize for their work on derivatives, were key players in the LTCM debacle. The theory of derivatives is a bit like nuclear physics. The derivative products that they have spawned can be used for 'good' but they can also be dangerous, if used incorrectly. Let's see how these products can be used, so that you can make up your own mind on this issue.

## 19.1 FORWARDS AND FUTURES

Except where explicitly noted we will use 'forward' and 'futures' interchangeably, since analytically they are very similar, even though the way the contracts are traded differ in some respects. A holder of a long (short) forward contract has an agreement to buy (sell) an asset at a certain time in the future for a certain price which is fixed today.

> **The buyer (seller or short position) in a forward/futures contract:**
>
> - acquires a legal obligation to buy (sell) an asset (**the underlying**)
> - at some specific future date (**maturity/expiry date**)
> - in an amount (**contract size**)
> - and at a price (**the forward/futures price**) which is fixed today.

A futures contract is similar to a forward contract. The **forward contract** is an over-the-counter (OTC) instrument, and trades take place directly (usually over the telephone) for a specific amount and specific delivery date as negotiated between the two parties. In contrast, **futures contracts** are standardised (in terms of contract size and delivery dates), trades take place on an organised exchange and the contracts are revalued (marked to market) daily. When you buy or sell a futures contract, on say cocoa, it is the **'legal right'** to the terms in the contract that is being purchased or sold, not the cocoa itself (which is actually bought and sold in the spot market for cocoa). As we shall see in the next chapter, there is a close link between the futures price and the spot price (for cocoa), but they are not the same thing!

Futures contracts are traded between market makers in a 'pit' on the floor of the exchange, of which the largest are the Chicago Board of Trade (CBOT), the Chicago Mercantile Exchange (CME) and Philadelphia Stock Exchange (PHSE). However, in recent years there has been a move away from trading by 'open outcry' in a 'pit', towards electronic trading between market makers (and even more recently over the internet). For example, the London International Financial Futures Exchange (LIFFE) is now an electronic trading system, as are the European derivatives markets, such as the French MATIF and the German DTB. Some of the futures contracts traded on various exchanges are shown in Table 19.1.

Originally, futures markets were introduced to eliminate risk for commodities. For example, a farmer might know in April that he is to harvest 5000 bushels of wheat in September. A wholesaler who purchases grain for the food industry might know their requirements as early as April. The two participants can eliminate (or hedge) risk by negotiating a contract to supply grain in September at a price which is agreed in April. This is a type of forward contract and eliminates risk for each side of the bargain. Similar considerations to the above apply to an agent who stores grain which has already been harvested. He can hold on to the grain for a number of months in the hope that the spot price for grain will increase. Alternatively, he can negotiate a price today for delivery of the grain at some time in the future. Both the merchant who holds the grain and the purchaser are 'locked in' to the forward price quoted today and thereby reduce to zero any risks due to future *spot* price fluctuations.

## TABLE 19.1: Selected futures contracts

| Contract | Exchange | Contract size |
|---|---|---|
| **1.   Grains and oilseed** | | |
|      Corn | CBOT | 5000 bu |
|      Corn | MCE | 1000 bu |
|      Wheat | CBOT | 5000 bu |
|      Wheat | MCE | 1000 bu |
| **2.   Food** | | |
|      Cocoa | CSCE | 10 metric tons |
|      Orange juice | NYCTN | 15,000 lbs |
| **3.   Metals and petroleum** | | |
|      Gold | MCE | 33.2 troy oz |
|      Gold—1 kilo | CBOT | 32.15 troy oz |
|      Silver | CBOT | 5000 troy oz |
| **4.   Livestock and meat** | | |
|      Hogs | CME | 50,000 lbs |
|      Pork bellies | CME | 40,000 lbs |
| **5.   Foreign currency** | | |
|      British pound | IMM | £62,500 |
|      Swiss franc | CME | SFr125,000 |
|      Euro | CME | euro 125,000 |
|      Japanese yen | CME | yen 12.5m |
| **6.   Stock indices** | | |
|      S&P500 | IOM | $250 × index |
|      Value Line | KCBT | $500 × index |
|      FTSE100 | LIFFE | £10 × index |
|      Eurotop100 | LIFFE | euro 20 × index |
|      Nikkei 225 | IOM | $5 × index |

*continued overleaf*

## TABLE 19.1: (*Continued*)

| | Contract | Exchange | Contract size |
|---|---|---|---|
| 7. | **Interest rates** | | |
| | Eurodollar—90 day | IMM | $1,000,000 |
| | Eurodollar—30 day | IMM | $3,000,000 |
| | Euromark | IMM | DM1,000,000 |
| | US T-bills | IMM | $1,000,000 |
| | US T-bonds | CBOT | $100,000 |
| | US T-bonds | MCE | $50,000 |
| | UK 3m sterling interest rate | LIFFE | £500,000 |
| | UK 3m euro-LIBOR | LIFFE | euro 1m |
| | UK long gilt future | LIFFE | £100,000 |

Notes: CBOT = Chicago Board of Trade
CME = Chicago Mercantile Exchange
NYCE = New York Cotton Exchange
IMM = International Money Market (Chicago)
IOM = Index and Option Market
KCBT = Kansas City Board of Trade
MCE = Mid America Commodity Exchange
LIFFE = London International Financial Futures Exchange

## MARKET CLASSIFICATION

A key feature of futures and options is that the contract calls for *deferred delivery* of the underlying asset (e.g. AT&T shares), whereas spot assets are for *immediate delivery* (although in practice, there is usually a delay of a few days). To distinguish between purchases and sales of derivatives and the underlying (spot) asset the latter are often referred to as transactions in the **cash** or **spot market**. A primary use of derivative securities is to minimise price uncertainty. Therefore, where the underlying assets (e.g. currencies, shares) are widely traded and yet exhibit great volatility, there is likely to be a large active derivatives market.

Trading in derivative securities can be on a trading floor (or 'pit') or via an electronic network of traders, within a well-established organised market (e.g. with a clearing house, membership rules, etc.). Some derivatives markets, for example all FX forward contracts and swap contracts, are OTC markets where the contract details are not standardised but individually negotiated between clients and dealers. Options are traded widely on exchanges, but the OTC market in options (particularly 'complex' or 'exotic' options) is also very large.

Today there are a large number of exchanges which deal in futures contracts, and most can be categorised as either agricultural futures contracts (where the underlying 'asset' is, for example, pork bellies, live hogs or wheat), metallurgical futures (e.g. silver) or financial futures contracts (where the underlying asset could be a portfolio of stocks represented by the S&P500, currencies, T-bills, T-bonds, Eurodollar deposits, etc.). Futures contracts in agricultural commodities have been traded (e.g. on CBOT) for over 100 years. In 1972 the CME began to trade currency futures, while the introduction of interest rate futures occurred in 1975 and in 1982 stock index futures (colloquially known as 'pinstripe pork bellies') were introduced. The CBOT introduced a clearing house in 1925, where each party to the contract had to place 'deposits' into a margin account. This provides insurance if one of the parties defaults on the contract. The growth in the volume of futures trading since 1972 has been astounding: from 20m contracts per year in 1972 to over 200m contracts in the 1990s on the US markets alone.

Analytically, forwards and futures can be treated in a similar fashion. However, they differ in some practical details (see Table 19.2). Forward contracts (usually) involve no 'up front' payment and 'cash' only changes hands at the expiry of the contract. A forward contract is negotiated between two parties and (generally) is not marketable. In contrast, a futures contract is traded in the market and it involves a 'down payment' known as the **initial margin**. However, the initial margin is primarily a deposit to ensure both parties to the contract do not default. It is not a payment for the futures contract itself. The margin usually earns a competitive interest rate so it is not a 'cost'. As the futures price changes then 'payments' (i.e. debits and credits) are made into (or out of) the margin account. Hence a futures contract is a forward contract that is 'marked to market' daily.

Because the futures contract is marketable, the contracts have to be standardised, for example by having a set of fixed expiry (delivery) dates and a fixed contract size (e.g. $100,000 for the US T-bond futures on IMM in Chicago). In contrast, a forward contract can be 'tailor made' between the two parties to the contract, in terms of size and delivery date.

## TABLE 19.2: Forwards and futures contracts

| Forwards | Futures |
|---|---|
| • Private (non-marketable) contract between two parties | • Traded on an exchange |
| • (Large) trades are not communicated to other market participants | • Trades are immediately known by other market participants |
| • Delivery or cash settlement at expiry | • Contract is usually closed out prior to maturity |
| • Usually one delivery date | • Range of delivery dates |
| • No cash paid until expiry | • Cash payments into (out of) margin account, daily |
| • Negotiable choice of delivery dates and size of contract | • Standardised contracts |

Finally, forward contracts almost invariably involve the delivery of the underlying asset (e.g. currency), whereas futures contracts can be (and usually are) closed out by selling the contract prior to maturity. Hence with futures delivery of the underlying asset rarely takes place.

A forward or futures contract can be used for speculation, even if the contract is held to maturity. The speculator (e.g. holder of a forward or futures contract) makes her gain or loss *at the time the contract matures*. For example, suppose the futures price on a commodity (e.g. silver) at $t = 0$ is $F_0 = \$100$ per ton, with maturity date in September. If the spot price in September ($= T$) turns out to be $S_T = \$105$ per ton, then the holder of the ('long') futures contract can accept delivery of the commodity in the futures contract (and pay out \$100 at $T$) and then sell it onwards in the spot market for $S_T = \$105$, giving an overall profit of \$5 per ton ($= S_T - F_0$). Hence speculators are active in forward futures markets.

As mentioned above, most futures contracts are closed out prior to maturity. When they are, the clearing house sends out a cash payment which reflects the amount remaining in your margin account after all the daily adjustments have been made for gains and losses over the time you have held the contract. Therefore futures contracts can be used for speculation even when they are closed out prior to maturity. Because the price of a futures contract is derived from the price of the underlying asset, then the changes in the futures price usually move (nearly) one-for-one with changes in the price of the underlying spot asset. Speculation with futures is straightforward. Suppose you purchased a 3-month futures contract at a price $F_0 = \$100$ and 1 month later you closed out the contract by selling it at the market price of $F_1 = \$110$. Then the clearing house 'effectively' sends you a cheque for \$10 and it obtains this \$10 from the 'short', that is, from a person who initially sold the contract. (The institutional details differ from this as we shall see in the next chapter, but the principle is correct.) It also follows that you would earn a \$10 profit if you initially sold a contract at $F_0 = \$100$ and later closed out the contract by buying it back at $F_1 = \$90$ (i.e. 'sell high buy low'). The possible types of futures contracts that can be traded are almost limitless, but only those which are useful for hedging and speculation will survive. The exchange will remove any futures contract where trading volume is low.

## 19.2 OPTIONS

While futures markets in commodities have existed since the middle of the 1800s, options contracts (see Table 19.3) have been traded for a far shorter period of time.

> **The holder of an option has the right to buy or sell an 'asset' (the underlying) at some time in the future at a fixed price, but she does not have to exercise this right and this is a key distinction between options and forward/futures contracts**

Note again that it is the **legal right** to buy or sell the underlying asset in the contract which

## TABLE 19.3: Selected options contracts

| | Contract | Exchange | Contract size |
|---|---|---|---|
| 1. | **Individual stocks** | CBOE, NYSE, AMEX, | Usually for 100 stocks |
| | | PHSE, LIFFE, SIMEX | |
| 2. | **Index options** | | |
| | S&P500 index | CBOE | $500 × index |
| | FTSE100 index | LIFFE | £10 per index point |
| | (European and American) | | |
| | NYSE index | NYSE | $500 × index |
| | Gold/silver index | PHSE | |
| | **Foreign currency options** | | |
| | Sterling | PHSE | GBP31,250 |
| | Deutsche Mark | PHSE | DEM62,500 |
| | Japanese yen | PHSE | JPY6.25m |
| | Canadian dollar | PHSE | CND50,000 |
| | Swiss franc | PHSE | CHF62,500 |
| 3. | **Options on futures contracts** | | |
| | **Options on interest rate futures:** | | |
| | Eurodollars | IMM | $1m |
| | 1-month LIBOR | IMM | $3m |
| | US T-bills | IMM | $1m |
| | US T-bond and 5-year T-note | CBOT | $100,000 |
| | 3-month euro-LIBOR | LIFFE | as for futures |
| | UK long gilt | LIFFE | as for futures |
| | **Options on index futures:** | | |
| | S&P500 index | IOM | $500 × premium |
| | NYSE Composite | IOM | $500 × premium |
| | Nikkei 225 | IOM | $5 × premium |

*continued overleaf*

## TABLE 19.3: (*Continued*)

| Contract | Exchange | Contract size |
|---|---|---|
| **Most commodities** (agriculture and metals) on which there are futures contracts (see above) | CBOT, CME, KCBT, COMEX, CTN | The same as in the futures contract (see above) |
| **Options on foreign currency futures** | | |
| British pound | IMM | £62,500 |
| German mark | IMM | DM125,000 |
| Japanese yen | IMM | yen 12.5m |
| Swiss franc | IMM | CHF125,000 |

Notes: CBOT = Chicago Board of Trade
CME = Chicago Mercantile Exchange
NYCE = New York Cotton Exchange
IMM = International Money Market (Chicago)
IOM = Index and Option Market
KCBT = Kansas City Board of Trade
MCE = Mid America Commodity Exchange
LIFFE = London International Financial Futures Exchange

is being bought and sold, not the asset itself. The holder of a long futures contract commits herself to buy or sell an asset at a certain price at a certain time in the future, *and if she does nothing before expiration,* she will have to take delivery of the underlying in the contract, at the agreed delivery price. In contrast, the holder of a **call option** can simply 'walk away' from the contract. She has the choice as to whether or not she exercises the option and buy the asset at a fixed price, at a certain time in the future. As we see below, this 'right without the obligation' allows the holder of an option to benefit from any 'upside' while also providing insurance in the form of a maximum 'downside loss'. For this privilege, an investor must pay an up front, non-returnable fee in order to purchase an option contract, that is the option price or premium. Partly because a futures contract does not confer the privilege of 'walking away' from the contract, it costs nothing to purchase a futures.

The holder of a **European** option can buy or sell the underlying asset only on the expiry date, but the holder of an **American** option can also exercise the option before the expiry date (as well as sell it on to a third party). But, *all* option contracts can be resold to a third party, at any time prior to expiration—this is known as **closing out** or **reversing** the contract.

There are two basic types of options: calls and puts (which can either be American or European).

## CALL OPTIONS

> A ***European call option*** gives the holder (the long) the right (but not an obligation):
>
> - to **purchase** the **underlying asset**
> - at a specified future date (known as the ***expiration, expiry*** or ***maturity date***)
> - for a certain price (the ***exercise*** or ***strike price***)
> - and in an amount (**contract size**) which is fixed in advance.
> - For this privilege you pay today the **call premium/price**.

If you are a speculator and you think that stock prices will increase in the future then you should purchase a call option. Alternatively, if you are a pension fund manager and know that you will receive money in the future but fear a rise in stock prices, then you can 'lock in' the price you will pay for the stock in the future by purchasing a call option today. Here you use the call to reduce risk, given your existing position in the cash market.

LONG CALL

Consider for example the purchase in July of a (European) call option on the shares of XYZ. Let us assume that one stock option contract is a contract to buy or sell 100 shares. If the quoted call premium in July is $C = \$3$ per share then the contract will cost $300 to purchase. Let us suppose that the strike price in the contract is $K = \$80$ and that the expiry date $T$ is in 3 months time, in October (Figure 19.1).

If a pension fund purchases the call option in July, it has locked into a *minimum purchase price* of $80, if it decides to exercise the contract in October—this is a form of **insurance**. Clearly, if in October $S_T = \$88 > K = \$80$ then the pension fund will exercise the option and pay $80 per share (which is cheaper than purchasing them on the NYSE at $88). On the other hand, if the share price in October is $S_T = \$77$ (i.e. below the strike price of $K = \$80$) then the pension fund will not exercise the call option since it can purchase the shares at lower cost in the spot market. Hence, for the pension fund the call option provides insurance

## FIGURE 19.1: Buy one European call option

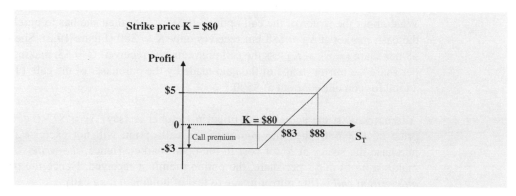

in the form of a maximum price payable of $K = \$80$, but also allows the pension fund to 'walk away' from the contract and benefit from lower prices if $S_T < K$.

Now consider the **speculative motive** for purchasing the call option. If the actual price of the stock in October turns out to be $S_T = \$88$, then the holder of the call option can take delivery at $K = \$80$ and sell each share in the spot market at $88. She will make a profit of $8 per share (i.e. $S_T - K = \$88 - \$80$) less $C = \$3$ for the option premium, giving a net profit of $5 per share (Figure 19.1). Hence the payoff to holding one long call is:

[19.1]     $\Pi = (+1)[\max(0, S_T - K) - C]$

          $= S_T - K - C \qquad$ for $S_T > K$

          $= -C \qquad\qquad$ for $S_T < K$

The breakeven stock price occurs when $\Pi = 0$ and hence is:

[19.2]     $S_{BE} = K + C = \$80 + \$3 = \$83$

Since the contract is for 100 shares, if $S_T = \$88$ the speculator makes an overall profit of $500. On the other hand if at expiry $S_T = \$78$ ($< K$) the speculator would not exercise the option, which expires worthless, but she has only lost the call premium of $300, which was paid when she initially purchased the option.

Thus the person who holds (i.e. is long) a call option limits downside risk to the call premium (here $C = \$3$) but can benefit from any upside potential. Her return is asymmetric and non-linear. Hence, the long call option provides **insurance** since it provides a lower bound for the speculator of $C = \$3$ but allows 'upside capture' if stock prices rise (above the strike price). For the pension fund, the insurance is the knowledge that the maximum price it will have to pay in 3 months time for the stock is $K = \$80$ and the 'insurance premium' is the call premium of $C = \$3$. Suppose the actual stock price, when you purchased the call *in July*, had been $S_0 = \$78$. Note that this is *not* the minimum purchase price you 'lock into', which is the strike price $K = \$80$.

## WRITE (SELL) A CALL

What about the writer of the call option? If $S_T = \$88$, then she has to purchase the stock in the cash market at $S_T = \$88$ but receives only $K = \$80$ (Figure 19.2). She makes a loss of $8 per share ($= S_T - K$) less the call premium she received $C = \$3$, making a net loss of $5 per share—a mirror image of the gain made by the purchaser of the call. (The writer makes a total loss on one contract of $500.)

Alternatively, if the actual share price in October is (say) $S_T = \$77$ (i.e. below the strike price of $K = \$80$) then the *holder* of the call option will not exercise it, since she can purchase the shares at lower cost in the open market. Hence, *the writer* of the call option makes a profit of $3 per share, the option premium received. Hence the payoff to holding *one written call* is (the mirror image to that of holding a long call):

## FIGURE 19.2: Sell (write) a European call option

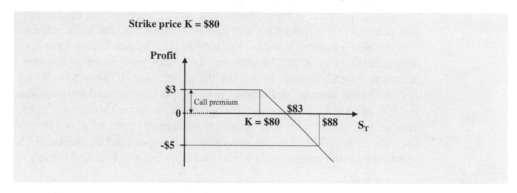

[19.3]

$$\Pi = (-1)[\max(0, S_T - K) - C]$$

$$= -[(S_T - K) - C] \qquad \text{for } S_T > K$$

$$= +C \qquad\qquad \text{for } S_T \leq K$$

### CLOSING OUT

Usually options are not held to expiration. Instead, the speculator holding the long call reaps a profit by closing out (or 'reversing') her long position, by shorting (selling) the call option prior to expiration. As we shall see, if there has been a rise in the price of the underlying stock $S$ since the option was initially purchased then the call premium $C$ will also have increased from say $C_0 = \$3$ to $C_1 = \$4$. Hence when she closes out (i.e. sells) her option prior to expiry, she will receive $C_1 = \$4$ from the counterparty to the deal (i.e. the purchaser). She therefore makes a speculative profit of \$1 ($= \$4 - \$3$), the difference between the buying and selling price of the call. 'The long' obtains her cash payment via the clearing house. Conversely, if the stock price falls after she has purchased the call for $C_0 = \$3$, then the call premium will now be below \$3 and when she sells it (i.e. closes out) she will make a loss on the deal. Thus a **naked position** in a long call, held over a short horizon, can be very risky (although the most you can lose is still only the call premium, which here is $C_0 = \$3$).

## PUT OPTIONS

> A *European put option* gives the holder the right (but not an obligation):
>
> - to **sell** the **underlying asset**
> - at a specified future date (**expiration/expiry date**)
> - for a certain price (**strike/exercise price**)
> - and in an amount (**contract size**) which is fixed in advance.
> - For this privilege you pay the **put premium/price**.

## LONG PUT

For example, suppose you are a pension fund manager and you hold 100 shares of ABC and the current spot price of these shares is $S_0 = \$72$. Suppose you have to pay someone's lump-sum pension in 3 months time and you are worried that the stock price will fall *below* $70 over the next 3 months. You can eliminate this risk by purchasing a put option on 100 shares, with a strike price $K = \$70$ with an expiry date in 3 months. For this you pay the put premium $P = \$2$ (Figure 19.3). On the other hand, if $S_T = \$75$, which is greater than $K = \$70$, then you can 'walk away' from the put contract and sell your shares on the NYSE for $75 per share. This means that whatever happens to the spot price over the next 3 months, you can either sell the shares at a minimum price of $K = \$70$ or, if the stock price rises above $K = \$70$, you can sell them in the spot market. Hence the long put provides **insurance** for the pension fund whilst also allowing it to benefit from any 'upside potential'.

There are also opportunities for **speculation** with put options. If the spot price at expiry is $S_T = \$65$ (i.e. below $K = \$70$) then a speculator who is long the put option could buy 100 shares in the market for $S_T = \$65$ per share and receive $K = \$70$ per share on exercising the put option. Thus she will have made a profit of $5 ($= K - S_T$) per share and a net profit of $3 after paying the put premium. Hence the payoff to holding one long put is:

[19.4]
$$\Pi = (+1)[\max(0, K - S_T) - P]$$

$$= K - S_T - P \qquad \text{for } S_T < K$$

$$= -P \qquad \text{for } S_T \geqslant K$$

The breakeven stock price occurs when $\Pi = 0$ and hence is:

[19.5]
$$S_{BE} = K - P = \$70 - \$2 = \$68$$

If $S_T > K$ then the speculator does not exercise the put (which expires worthless) but the most she loses is the put premium, $P = \$2$.

---

## FIGURE 19.3: Buy (long) a European put

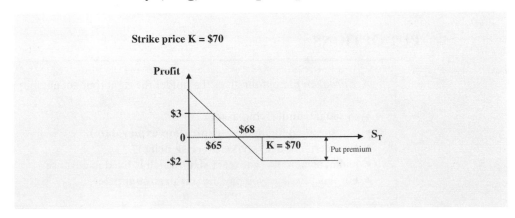

### WRITE (SELL) A PUT

The writer of the put option at a strike price $K = \$70$ and $S_T = \$65$ will lose $5 per share since she has to purchase the share from the long at $K = \$70$ when it is only worth $65 (Figure 19.4). However, this loss is reduced to $3 after allowing for the receipt of the put premium of $2. Hence the payoff to holding one written put is (the mirror image to that of holding a long put):

[19.6]
$$\Pi = (-1)[\max(0, K - S_T) - P]$$
$$= -[(K - S_T) - P] \qquad \text{for } S_T < K$$
$$= +P \qquad\qquad \text{for } S_T \geqslant K$$

There are now many markets on which options contracts are traded, the largest exchange for trading (individual) *stock* options is the Chicago Board of Trade (CBOT). The growth in the use of options markets since 1973 has been quite phenomenal. In the 1970s, markets for options developed in foreign currencies and by the 1980s there were also options markets on stock indices (such as the S&P500 and the FTSE100), on T-bonds and interest rates, as well as options on futures contracts and options on swaps.

## 19.3 SWAPS

Swaps first appeared in the early 1980s and are primarily used for hedging interest rate and exchange rate risk.

> **A swap is a negotiated (OTC) agreement between two parties to exchange cash flows at a set of prespecified future dates**

## FIGURE 19.4: Sell (write) a European put

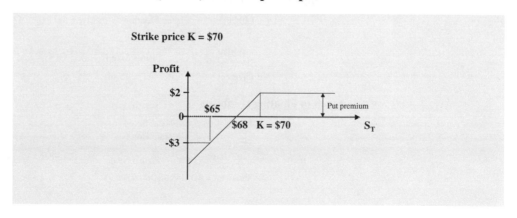

A **plain vanilla interest rate swap** involves a periodic exchange of fixed payments for payments at a floating rate (usually LIBOR), based on a notional principal amount. For example, M's A might agree to receive annual interest at whatever the US dollar (USD) LIBOR rate turns out to be at the end of each year, in exchange for payments (from M's B) at a fixed rate of 5% p.a., based on a notional principal amount of $100m. M's B is the counterparty and has the opposite cash flows to M's A. The payments are based on a stated notional principal, *but only the interest payments are exchanged.* The payment dates and the floating rate to be used (usually LIBOR) are determined at the outset of the contract. In a plain vanilla swap 'the fixed rate payer' knows exactly what the interest rate payments will be on every payment date, but the floating rate payer does not.

The intermediaries in a swap transaction are usually banks who act as dealers. They are usually members of the *International Swaps and Derivatives Association* (ISDA), which provides some standardisation in swap agreements via its **master swap agreement**, which can then be adapted where necessary to accommodate most customer requirements. Dealers make profits via the bid–ask spread and might also charge a small brokerage fee. If swap dealers take on one side of a swap but cannot find a counterparty, then they have an open position (i.e. either net payments or receipts at a fixed or floating rate). They usually hedge this position in futures (and sometimes options) markets until they find a suitable counterparty.

## INTEREST RATE SWAPS

A swap can be used to alter series of floating rate payments (or receipts) into fixed rate payments (or receipts). Consider a firm that has issued a floating rate bond and has to pay LIBOR + 0.5% (Figure 19.5, top). If it enters a swap to receive LIBOR and pay 6% fixed, then its net payments are 6% + 0.5% = 6.5% fixed. It has transformed a floating rate liability into a fixed rate liability. Next, Figure 19.5, (bottom) shows that if a firm issues a 6.2% fixed rate bond but later decides it wants to pay a floating rate then it can do this by

## FIGURE 19.5: Liabilities: using swaps

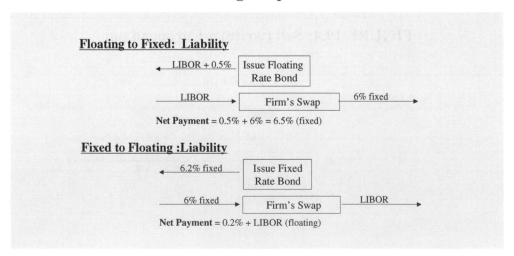

entering into a 'receive 6% fixed, pay LIBOR floating' swap, which has the net effect of being equivalent to the firm having a floating rate liability at LIBOR + 0.2%.

Similarly, if the firm or financial institution holds a 5.7% fixed rate bond (Figure 19.6, bottom) and enters a 'pay 6% fixed, receive LIBOR floating' swap then the net result is an 'asset' which pays floating at LIBOR − 0.3%. Finally, if the financial institution holds a floating rate bond paying LIBOR − 0.5% (Figure 19.6, top) and enters a 'receive LIBOR floating, pay 6% fixed' then the net result is a receipt of 5.5% fixed. Hence a swap can be used to engineer a change in interest receipts (payments) from floating to fixed (or vice versa).

Now let us see how a swap can be used to reduce overall interest rate risk. The normal commercial operation of some firms naturally implies that they are subject to interest rate risk. A commercial bank or Savings and Loan (S&L) in the US (building society in the UK) usually has fixed rate receipts in the form of loans or housing mortgages, at say 12%, but raises much of its finance in the form of short-term floating rate deposits, at say LIBOR − 1% (Figure 19.7). If LIBOR currently equals 11% the bank earns a profit on the spread of 2% p.a. However, if LIBOR rises by more than 2% the S&L will be making a loss. The financial institution is therefore subject to interest rate risk. If it enters into a swap to receive LIBOR and pay 11% fixed, then it is protected from rises in the general level of interest rates since it now effectively has fixed rate receipts of 2%, which are independent of what happens to floating rates in the future.

Another reason for undertaking a swap is that some firms can borrow relatively cheaply in either the fixed or floating rate market. Suppose firm A finds it *relatively cheap* to borrow at a fixed rate but would prefer *to ultimately borrow* at a floating rate (so as to match its floating rate receipts). Firm A does not go directly and borrow at a floating rate because it is relatively expensive. Instead it borrows (cheaply) at a fixed rate and enters into a swap where it pays floating and receives fixed. This is a 'cost saving', known as the **comparative**

## FIGURE 19.6: Assets: using swaps

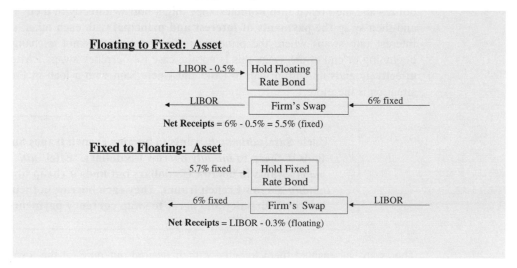

**Floating to Fixed: Asset**

LIBOR - 0.5% → Hold Floating Rate Bond

← LIBOR — Firm's Swap — 6% fixed

Net Receipts = 6% - 0.5% = 5.5% (fixed)

**Fixed to Floating: Asset**

5.7% fixed → Hold Fixed Rate Bond

← 6% fixed — Firm's Swap ← LIBOR

Net Receipts = LIBOR - 0.3% (floating)

## FIGURE 19.7: Swap: financial intermediary

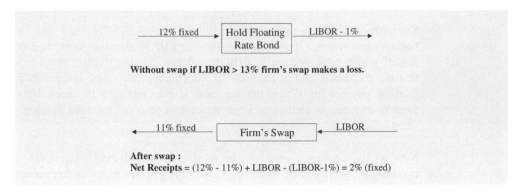

advantage motive for a swap and is the financial incentive mechanism behind the expansion of the swaps business.

## CURRENCY SWAPS

A **currency swap** in its simplest form involves two parties exchanging debt denominated in different currencies. Nowadays, one reason for undertaking a swap might be that a US firm ('Uncle Sam') with a subsidiary in France wishes to raise say 50m in French francs to finance expansion in France. The French francs receipts from the subsidiary in France will be used to pay off the debt. Similarly a French firm ('Effel') with a subsidiary in the US might wish to issue 100m in US dollar denominated debt and eventually pay off the interest and principle with dollar revenues from its subsidiary. This reduces foreign exchange exposure.

But it might be relatively expensive for Uncle Sam to raise finance directly from French banks, and similarly for Effel from US banks, as neither might be 'well established' in these foreign loan markets. However, if the US firm can raise finance (relatively) cheaply in dollars and the French firm in francs, they might borrow directly in their 'home currencies' and then swap **the payments of interest and principal** with each other. (Note that unlike interest rate swaps where the principal is 'notional' and is not exchanged either at the beginning or end of the swap, this is not the case for currency swaps.) After the swap Effel effectively ends up with a loan in USD and Uncle Sam with a loan in French francs. The situation is therefore:

> 'Uncle Sam' *ultimately* wants to borrow French francs but finds it cheap to *initially* borrow US dollars. 'Effel' *ultimately* wants to borrow US dollars but finds it cheap to *initially* borrow French francs. They each borrow in their 'low cost' currency and agree to swap currency payments

The swap has enabled them to achieve their desired outcome (at the lowest interest cost).

Let's see how this works out in detail. Suppose, for simplicity, the current exchange rate is $2 per FRF. Uncle Sam's US dollar loan is from Wells Fargo bank for $100m at 8% interest. Effel's French franc loan is from Crédit Agricole for FRF50m at 9% interest. The following stages take place in the swap.

**At $t = 0$**

- Effel borrows FRF50m from Crédit Agricole and passes the money to Uncle Sam.
- Uncle Sam borrows $100m from Wells Fargo and passes the money to Effel.

**At $t > 0$**

- Effel's revenues from its US subsidiary are used to pay Uncle Sam $8m p.a. (8% of $100m) who passes this on to Wells Fargo.
- Uncle Sam's revenues from its French subsidiary are used to pay Effel FRF4.5m p.a. (9% of FRF50m) who then passes this on to Crédit Agricole.

**At $t = T$ (maturity of the loan)**

- Effel pays ($100m + $8m) back to Uncle Sam, who then pays off the loan plus the last interest instalment to Wells Fargo.
- Uncle Sam pays (FRF50m + FRF4.5m) back to Effel, who then pays Crédit Agricole.

So even though Uncle Sam *initially* borrows US dollars and Effel *initially* borrows French francs, nevertheless after the swap it is as if Uncle Sam has a French franc loan and Effel has a USD loan. A more light-hearted, but we hope instructive, analogy for a currency swap is given in Box 19.1.

---

**Box 19.1     SWAPS: KEN AND BARBIE**

Consider Sharon and Darren, two 9-year olds from Essex. Darren is genetically predisposed to choose the best (i.e. lowest cost, highest quality) 'Ken Doll' around and he purchases the best one from his local shop. Sharon, on the other hand, is predisposed to choose the best 'Barbie Doll' around, which she duly does. Some years pass and Sharon decides that what she would really like is a Ken Doll, while Darren decides he would now really like a Barbie Doll.

Sharon knows that Darren is good at buying Ken Dolls and his 'accessories' and Darren knows that Sharon is good at buying Barbie Dolls and her accessories. So at $t = 0$ (today) Sharon and Darren swap dolls. However, they also agree to swap the annual 'replacement outfits' required for each doll, so each remains 'well dressed'. Therefore, every year Darren receives from Sharon a replacement outfit for Barbie and Sharon receives from Darren a replacement outfit for Ken. If the maturity of the swap is 4 years, then at this point they swap dolls back again (since by this time both prefer the 'real thing').

Thus, although Sharon initially purchased a Barbie Doll, the swap enables her to effectively have a Ken Doll together with his annual update of clothes. Similarly, Darren effectively has a Barbie Doll, over the life of the swap. Our 'Ken and Barbie' example is therefore like a plain vanilla currency swap.

Indeed, we can push our analogy a little further. Suppose the swap had involved the *same* 'replacement outfit' for Ken every year (e.g. a John Travolta disco outfit), but the type and cost of Barbie's outfits had been uncertain each year (e.g. in some years second-hand retro outfits and in others 'designer labels'). Then Darren's annual receipt of clothes for Barbie would be 'variable', while his annual payments for Ken's clothes would be fixed. Darren is a 'receive variable–pay fixed' leg of the swap. Sharon's annual 'clothes parcel' would be the mirror image of Darren's. Sharon is therefore the 'receive fixed–pay variable' leg of the (clothes) swap. The latter scenario is equivalent to one leg of the currency swap being at a variable (or 'floating') interest rate and the other at a fixed interest rate. Swaps? Just child's play.

## 19.4 HEDGERS, SPECULATORS AND ARBITRAGEURS

Part of the reason for the success of both futures and options is that they provide opportunities for hedging, speculation and arbitrage.

### HEDGERS

Examples of hedging using the forward market in foreign exchange are perhaps most common to the lay person. Using the futures market is, for the hedger, very similar in principle to using the forward market. If an exporter based in the US expects to receive £3000 in 3 months time, then the Corporate Treasurer can buy dollars today in the forward market or buy dollar futures contracts. There are of course differences in practice. A futures contract for foreign exchange is for fixed amounts and therefore the hedger has to buy that number of contracts which most closely matches the amount of currency required. However, the key element in both cases is that the US company fixes the price today that they will receive when the money is delivered. Alternatively, the US exporter can 'insure' (i.e. set a lower limit) for her US dollar receipts by buying a put option on sterling at a strike price of $1.5 per £. She is then assured of receiving a minimum of $1.5 per £, but if in 3 months time the spot exchange rate is $1.6 per £ she can 'walk away' from the option contract and exchange her £3000 at the higher spot rate. For the privilege of having this 'option' she has to pay an option premium at the outset.

Futures contracts, if held to maturity, neutralise risk by exactly fixing the price that the hedger will pay or receive in the future. Even if the futures contract is not held to maturity, much of the risk can be hedged, but some does remain (this is known as **basis risk**). Although payments in the form of margin requirements are required on futures contracts, these funds usually pay a competitive interest rate and therefore are not a 'cost'. Options contracts are slightly different in that they provide insurance. Investors in options can protect themselves against adverse price movements in the future, but they still retain the possibility of benefiting from any favourable price movements. For this insurance 'the long' has to pay an option premium.

## SPECULATORS AND LEVERAGE

In our example above the purchaser of the call option on XYZ had the right to purchase 100 shares in 3 months at a strike price of $K = \$80$. For this she paid $300 ($3 premium $\times$ 100 shares in the options contract)—see Figure 19.1. Alternatively, she could have purchased 100 shares in the spot market at $S_0 = \$78$ (a total cost of $7800 today) and held on to these shares for 3 months. Note that here the amount of capital she has to put up is much larger, at $7800, than for the option which is $300.

By October the stock price has risen to $S_1 = \$80$. The profit from these two strategies is given in Figure 19.8. The dollar amount of profit from buying the shares is larger at $1000 ($= \$10 \times 100$ shares) than the net profit from exercising the call of $500 = (S_1 - K - P) \times 100$. However, the long call only has to pay the option premium of $3 per share, whereas the transaction in the cash market requires $78 per share. The call option involves far less capital and hence earns a higher percentage return of 167% compared with 12.8% on the outright share purchase. Options therefore provide a form of **leverage**.

Leverage also applies to futures contracts where (if we ignore margin requirements) the speculator would not have to provide any funds for 3 months. Suppose the spot price in 3 months time, $S_T$, turns out to be above the futures price $F_0$. Then a speculator who is long the futures can pay $F_0$ and take delivery of the shares from the futures contract. She can then immediately sell the shares at a profit in the open market at $S_T (> F_0)$. The profit is $\Pi = S_T - F_0$. In principle, she has provided no capital herself and hence the leverage is infinite. If (as is usual) the long future is not held to maturity but closed out, then the speculative profit depends on the increase in the futures price.

By using futures, speculators can make very large losses as well as very large gains.

## FIGURE 19.8: Leverage from option. P

| OPTIONS MARKET (JULY) | CASH MARKET (JULY) |
|---|---|
| Call premium, C = $3<br>Premium paid = $300<br>Strike price, K = $80 | Spot price, S = $78<br>Cash paid = $7800 |

| OPTIONS MARKET (OCT.) | CASH MARKET (OCT.) |
|---|---|
| Profit = $8 = ($88 - $80)<br>Net profit = $800 - $300<br>Return = $500/$300 = 167% | Profit = $10 = ($88 - $78)<br>Total profit = $1000<br>Return = $1000/$7800 = 12.8% |

However, there is a difference between futures and options. In the case of futures the potential loss equals the potential gain (assuming equal probabilities of a fall or rise). In the options example our speculator, who is long in the call option, makes a profit if the spot price $S_T$ at expiry is above the strike price $K$. However, if the spot price falls below the strike price, say even to zero, the speculator's loss is limited to the option premium payment of \$300 (\$3 × 100): her downside risk is limited. Note, however, that the writer of the call does have (virtually) unlimited downside risk.

## ARBITRAGEURS

Arbitrage involves locking in a *riskless* profit by entering into transactions in two or more markets simultaneously. Usually 'arbitrage' implies that the investor does not use any of his own capital when making the trade. Arbitrage plays a very important role in the determination of both futures and options prices, as we shall discuss later. Arbitrage is often loosely referred to as the 'law of one price' for financial assets. Simply expressed, this implies that identical assets must sell for the same price. We have seen in earlier chapters that it is possible to use combinations of some assets (e.g. B and C) which provide the same payoffs as another asset A. Asset 'B + C' is known as a synthetic security. Arbitrage then ensures that the quoted market price of asset A equals the price of the synthetic version of asset A. Before we illustrate this let us consider a very straightforward example of arbitrage which implies that the 'law of one price' should hold.

Suppose the price of XYZ's shares in New York is \$100 while in London they are trading at £120 and the spot exchange rate is £1 for \$1. Clearly there is a riskless profit to be made here by 'buying low and selling high'. A UK resident buying company XYZ on the New York Stock Exchange (NYSE) for \$100 (at a cost of £100) and *simultaneously* selling it on the London Stock Exchange (LSE) for £120 locks in a riskless profit of £20 (or \$20) per share. Clearly, in a fully informed market one would not expect such riskless arbitrage opportunities to persist for very long. In fact, the forces of supply and demand (or even just the price information on dealers' screens) would bring these two prices quickly into equality. Large purchases in New York would push the dollar price of the shares up, while sales in London would push the sterling share price down, and at an unchanged exchange rate this would bring the two prices nearer to equality. In addition, in order to purchase the shares on the NYSE, UK residents would have to purchase dollars and sell sterling and hence the dollar would appreciate relative to sterling.

Suppose that the exchange rate moved to £1.20 per \$1. In this case a UK resident would have to give up £120 in order to purchase \$100 spot, to buy XYZ on the NYSE. This is exactly the amount he would need to purchase it on the LSE. Of course, in practice, how much the two stock prices or the exchange rate move to achieve equality of prices is indeterminate. It is just that all three 'prices' will quickly move to eliminate any (riskless) arbitrage opportunities. This is the 'law of one price', again applied to assets (rather than to traded goods).

Fairly simple examples of where arbitrage is used to establish the price of assets are the determination of the forward rate of exchange in the FX market (see Chapter 15) and determination of the quoted forward (interest) rate on an FRA (see Chapter 8). In the case of covered interest arbitrage, riskless profits can be made unless the forward rate is determined by:

$$[19.7] \qquad F = S \frac{(1 + r_d)}{(1 + r_f)}$$

where $S$ is the spot exchange rate (domestic per unit of foreign currency), $F$ is the forward exchange rate, $r_d$ is the domestic interest rate and $r_f$ is the foreign interest rate. As can be seen from the above equation, arbitrage provides a 'strong link' (or correlation) between the spot price and the forward/futures price. As we shall see this 'link' is exploited by hedgers.

Similarly, the equilibrium forward rate on an FRA, quoted by a bank, is determined by riskless arbitrage, since we can create a synthetic FRA by borrowing and lending in the spot market. Suppose in the money market we can borrow $100 for 2 years at $r_2$ and use these funds to invest for 1 year at $r_1$. This gives rise to receipts of $100(1 + r_1)$ at $t = 1$ and an amount owed at $t = 2$ of $100(1 + r_2)^2$. This is equivalent to a synthetic forward–forward contract, namely receipts at $t = 1$ and payments at $t = 2$ (see Chapter 8). The synthetic forward rate is given by $(1 + sf_{12}) = (1 + r_2)^2/(1 + r_1)$. If a bank offers an FRA, namely borrowing at the end of year-1 and paying back at the end of year-2, then the *quoted* rate it must charge has to be $f_{12} = sf_{12}$. Otherwise riskless arbitrage would ensue. Riskless arbitrage therefore determines the fair forward–forward rate, $f_{12}$. As we shall see in the next chapter, establishing a 'synthetic' forward/futures contract and invoking riskless arbitrage is the method used to price the actual futures contract.

By way of an analogy consider 'Dolly' the sheep. You will remember that Dolly was cloned by scientists at Edinburgh University and was an exact replica of a 'real' sheep. Clearly Dolly was a form of genetic engineering. Suppose we could create 'Dollys' at a cost of $200 per sheep, which was below the current market price of the real sheep, at say $250. Then arbitrage would ensure that the price of the real sheep would fall to $200. Dolly is like our 'synthetic' or 'replication' portfolios in finance, which allow us to undertake *financial engineering*. Indeed Larry Summers, a prominent US economist (and now US Treasury Secretary) has rather impishly characterised the difference between economists and traditional finance specialists, with the following analogy. He says that economists are interested in why, for example, the price of a bottle of ketchup moves up and down (e.g. because of changes in income, production processes, etc.), while finance specialists are only interested in whether a 16oz bottle of ketchup sells for the same price as two 8oz bottles. Luckily, given the material in this text, we can justifiably call ourselves *financial economists* and avoid this somewhat pejorative analogy.

## 19.5 SUMMARY

- **Forward contracts are over-the-counter (OTC)** agreements whose terms (e.g. 'size', delivery date and price) are negotiated between two counterparties. In contrast, **futures contracts are standardised agreements** which are traded on exchanges and their daily change in value is reflected in payments into and out of a margin account.

- Both **forwards and futures can be used for speculation and hedging**. The hedge 'locks in' the quoted forward/futures price (not the spot price) at time $t = 0$, when the contract is purchased/sold.
- **Options contracts can provide insurance** in that they can be used to limit downside risk while allowing 'upside capture'. Hence the payoff to an option at expiration, is non-linear or asymmetric.
- Options can also be used for **speculation** without having to put up much capital (i.e. you only pay the option premium). That is they provide **leverage**.
- **Interest rate swaps** allow you to convert floating rate (variable) interest payments into fixed rate payments (or vice versa). **Swap dealers** act as intermediaries and try to match those who want to make fixed rate payments and receive floating rate payments, with a counterparty who wishes to do exactly the opposite.
- **Currency swaps** allow you to swap payments/receipts of principal and interest in one currency for payments/receipts in a different currency.
- **Risk free arbitrage** allows one to determine the 'fair price' of derivative securities.

## END OF CHAPTER EXERCISES

Q1   Why are futures and options contracts generically referred to as 'derivatives'?

Q2   In what ways is an agreement to marry Vito Corleone's daughter in 1 years time a type of futures or a forward contract? Which one does it most closely resemble?

Q3   What is the difference between a European and an American option, as far as the buyer and the writer are concerned?

Q4   If $K = 150$ and the put premium is $P = 5$ should you exercise the option if the spot price at expiry is $S_T = 148$? What is your profit?

Q5   The strike price for a put is $K = 100$ and the put premium is $P = 2$. Why is the put payoff (for the long) at expiration $T$, equal to $5$, if the stock price at expiry is $95$?

Q6   Under what circumstances would you make a profit at maturity from a long position in a futures contract on 'live hogs'?

Q7   How does going long a futures contract give you 'leverage' compared with going long in the spot market. Take stocks as an example and use $F_0 = \$101$ and $S_0 = \$100$, with out-turn values (3 months later) of $F_1 = \$111$ and $S_1 = \$110$.

# Futures Markets

## 20.1 TRADING ON FUTURES MARKETS

We have already discussed the basic principles behind a forward or futures contract. Forward contracts are analytically easier to deal with than futures contracts, and so we often apply mathematical results from forwards (e.g. pricing forward contracts) to futures contracts. However, there are differences in practice between the two types of contract, and we discuss the mechanics of these contracts in this section.

Forward contracts are traded over-the-counter (OTC), whereas most futures are traded on an exchange, and the differences between these two approaches are summarised in Figure 20.1. The range of assets on which futures contracts are written is very wide and they are traded on a large number of exchanges around the world (Figure 20.2). The basic requirements in buying and selling different types of futures contracts and in using them for hedging and speculation are very similar, even though futures contracts are written on a diverse set of underlying assets. The growth in futures and forward contracts is primarily due to the increased volatility of the underlying assets and the need to hedge this risk. However, except for the forward market for foreign exchange (and for swaps as these can be viewed as a series of forward contracts), forward contracts are used far less than futures contracts, which are available on a wide variety of underlying assets. Indeed, some traders who have agreed to deliver euros *forward* and receive US dollars may well hedge by taking an offsetting position in *a futures* contract.

A futures exchange is usually a corporate entity whose members elect a Board of Directors

## FIGURE 20.1: Types of derivative markets

| OVER-THE-COUNTER | EXCHANGE TRADED |
|---|---|
| • Supplied by intermediaries (banks)<br>• Customise4d to suit buyer<br>• Can be done for any amount, any settlement date<br>• Credit risk of counterparty and expensive to unwind<br>• Allows anonymity - important for large deals<br>• New contracts do not need approval of regulator | • Traded on exchanges (e.g. LIFFE, CBOT, CME)<br>• Available for restricted set of assets<br>• Fixed contract sizes and settlement dates<br>• Easy to reverse the position<br>• Credit risk eliminated by clearing house margining system ('marking to market') |

## FIGURE 20.2: Financial futures markets

| INSTRUMENTS | EXCHANGES |
|---|---|
| • Money Market Instruments<br>  3 month Eurodollar deposit,<br>  90 day US T-bills,<br>  3 month Sterling or Euro deposits | CBOT<br>CME<br>NY Futures Exchange<br>Philadelphia Exchange<br>Pacific Stock Exchange |
| • Bonds<br>  US T-bond, German Bund | |
| • Stock Indices<br>  S&P500, FTSE100 | LIFFE (London)<br>MATIF (Paris)<br>Eurex (Frankfurt) |
| • Currencies<br>  Euro, Sterling, Yen, etc. | Singapore, Hong Kong, Tokyo, Osaka |
| • Mortgage Pools (GNMA) | Sydney Futures Exchange |

who decide on the terms and conditions under which existing contracts are traded and whether to introduce new contracts (subject usually to the regulatory authority which in the US is the Commodity Futures Trading Commission, CFTC and in the UK is the Financial Services Authority, FSA).

The market price of the futures contract is known as the futures price and each contract specifies a delivery month. *When the contract is first negotiated* the quoted futures price is the **delivery price** for the underlying asset. The quoted futures price then varies continuously until the expiry date, when the futures price must equal the spot price (since the futures is then for immediate delivery):

[20.1]     $$F_T = S_T$$

For pedagogic purposes we assume futures contracts are traded on individual stocks (even though such contracts are not available). A buyer of a futures contract is said to be *long* and agrees to purchase the **underlying asset** (e.g. AT&T share). The writer or seller of the futures is said to be *short* and agrees to supply the underlying asset. *Financial futures* are written on financial assets (e.g. stock indices, currencies, T-bills or T-bonds), whereas agricultural or metallurgical futures are written on say wheat or silver (respectively). The underlying asset (e.g. AT&T share) is traded at a spot price in the cash market (which in this case is the NYSE). The futures price is closely linked to the *current* spot price, hence the generic term **derivative security**.

Futures markets can be used for speculation, hedging or arbitrage. Because there is always a counterparty to a futures contract (i.e. M's A is long, M's B is short), then any gains by M's A are met by M's B—overall it is a zero sum game (ignoring transactions costs). However, for any individual trader on one side of the market (i.e. either long or short) there are potential cash gains and losses to be made. Alternatively, futures can be used to reduce risk (i.e. hedging).

Since futures contracts (unlike forward contracts) are traded on an exchange, there needs to be some standardisation of the contracts and price quotes. Also, to minimise default risk, a clearing house and some collateral are required to compensate a trader if another trader defaults (this is taken care of with the margin requirement).

## STANDARDISATION

The futures exchange sets the size of each contract, the units of price quotation, minimum price fluctuations, the 'grade' and place for delivery, any daily price limits and margin requirements as well as opening hours for trading. For agricultural commodities, the type or grade is fixed in the futures contract (e.g. wheat of a particular quality or variety). The futures exchange sets the minimum contract size (e.g. $y$ bushels of wheat), delivery dates (e.g. March, May, June, July, September and December for wheat) and delivery arrangements (e.g. only in towns A, B and C).

For futures on financial assets such standardisation is easier. For example, an FX futures contract on the pound sterling is rather a homogeneous product and only delivery dates, settlement price and contract size need to be set by the exchange. Some examples of the contractual arrangements on futures contracts for US T-bonds, the sterling–dollar FX rate and the S&P500 equity index are shown in Table 20.1. Some contracts have expirations only out to a year or two, but others can be for a much longer period. It depends primarily on the demand for such contracts by hedgers. For example, Eurodollar futures contracts have

## TABLE 20.1: Futures (contract specification)

| Commodity | Delivery | Contract | Minimum price change | Daily limit |
|---|---|---|---|---|
| **1) US T-bonds** | Mar/June | $100,000 | 1/32 (of 1%) | 2% |
| **(CBOT)** | Sept/Dec | 8% coupon bond | =$31.25 | =$2000 |
| **2) £-Sterling** | Jan/Mar | £125,000 | 0.00005 £/$ | None |
| **(CME–IMM)** | Apr/June | | (=1/2 tick) | |
| | Jul/Sept | | =$6.25 | |
| | Oct/Dec | | | |
| **3) S&P500** | Next 4 months + | $250×(S&P500) | 10 points | None |
| **(CBOT)** | Mar/Jun | | (0.1) = $25 | |
| | Sept/Dec | | | |

maturities out to 10 years because these contracts are used by swap dealers to hedge their interest rate swap positions.

The **size of the contract** is important. If too small, speculators will not trade the contract because the transactions costs per contract will be relatively high, but if the 'size' is too large then hedgers will not be able to hedge relatively small amounts (e.g. Eurodollar futures have a contract size of $1m and you cannot hedge $500,000 using half a contract). The **tick size** and **tick value** should be easily understood, yet relatively small for obvious reasons. For example, the US T-bond futures contract has a contract size of $100,000 and a quotation unit of 1/32 of 1% (of the contract size). Hence the minimum price change is $31.25 $(= 0.0003125(\$100,000))$.

The total number of futures contracts outstanding is called the **open interest**. As each contract has both a long and a short position, this counts as 'one' open interest. Looked at another way, the open interest is the number of deals outstanding which could either be closed out before maturity or result in delivery of the underlying.

## FUTURES EXCHANGES AND TRADERS

In some futures markets traders meet face-to-face in a pit, such as on the International Money Market (IMM) in Chicago and on the trading floor of the Chicago Board of Trade (CBOT, or CBT) and until 1999 on the London International Financial Futures Exchange (LIFFE, pronounced 'life'). Prices and deals are indicated by hand signals and the system is known as **open outcry**. All exchanges *settle* trades using computers, but now more exchanges are moving away from open outcry and *trades* are conducted electronically. Some of these systems are 'order driven' whereby the buyers and sellers are 'matched' via the computer as, for example, on EUREX in Frankfurt and the Marché à Terme International de France (MATIF) in Paris. In fact, by fully automating trades in the German Bund (bond) futures contract, the EUREX captured all of this business, which used to take place by open outcry on LIFFE. LIFFE has also now moved to a screen based system. It claims it now has around double the trade (in value terms) compared with Frankfurt's EUREX exchange on the Euribor (interest rate) futures contract and LIFFE also has permission to put its screens into the US. The old LIFFE self-employed floor traders (i.e. locals) have now gravitated to 'arcades' where they can sit together and play the electronic market, with presumably less 'buzz' than in the pit.

Futures trading is becoming more 'global'. For example, GLOBEX which is owned by the CBOT and Reuters plc (UK) provides an *after-hours* electronic futures trading system— 'after-hours' being from a US perspective. Note, however, that GLOBEX does not automatically match buyers and sellers and then automate the trades. It merely provides price information to traders.

## FUTURES TRADING

Public orders must be placed through a broker who will then contact a floor broker in the exchange. Trades are monitored by the **clearing house** (e.g. Chicago Board of Trade Clearing Corporation, BOTCC) and all floor traders must have an account with a member clearing firm. If your floor broker purchases a futures contract on your behalf then you will have to pay the initial margin to the floor broker who will then pay this into her clearing firm ABC, say. The seller may be a local or a broker acting on behalf of a customer 'off the floor'. The seller also deposits the initial margin with her clearing firm XYZ. Both clearing firms ABC and XYZ each aggregate up their net positions from their customers and deposit a margin payment with the BOTCC, who then guarantees both sides of the contract.

## MARGINS AND MARKING TO MARKET

Margin payments provide financial protection in case one of the counterparties to the futures contract defaults. Suppose you purchase one US T-bond futures contract at noon on day 1 when the current futures price $F_0 = \$98$ (per $100 nominal) and one contract is for $100,000 nominal (see Table 20.2). Let us act as the clearing house and define 'one tick' as a change in $F$ of 1 unit. The **tick value** of a *change* in $F$ of 1 point is therefore $1000 = (1/100) \times \$100,000$. (In reality, for the US T-bond futures contract the tick value is $32.50—but forget this for now and use our 'simpler' tick value.)

The **initial margin** we take as $5000 and the **maintenance margin** is $4000. The initial margin is not a payment for the futures contract. It is a 'good faith' deposit to ensure that the terms of the futures contract are honoured. Some large active traders can in fact post Treasury bills for margin calls. Note that if the balance in the margin account falls below the maintenance margin of $4000 then the trader has to deposit extra funds, known as **variation margin**, to restore the balance to the *initial margin* (of $5000).

When you purchase the contract at $98 you deposit your initial margin of $5000. Suppose that by the end of day 1 the futures price falls dramatically, from $F_0 = \$98$ to $F_1 = \$94$.

## TABLE 20.2: Marking to market

| Day | Settlement (price) | Mark to market | Margin payment | Balance |
|---|---|---|---|---|
| 1 | $94,000 (94.0) | −$4000 | $5000 | $1000 |
| 2 | $93,500 (93.5) | −$500 | $4000 | $4500 |
| 3 | $98,500 (98.5) | +$5000 | | $9500 |

Contract size = $1000,000

Initial margin = $5000

Maintenance margin = $4000

Buy at $F_0$ = $98 (noon, day 0)

The investor has a loss of $4000 since at the end of day 1 she can now only sell her futures contract for $94,000. The balance on the margin account is therefore reduced to $1000 (see Table 20.2). This is **marking to market**. The balance at the end of day 1 of $1000 is below the maintenance margin. Hence, the next morning, the investor must immediately pay a **variation margin** of $4000 (so that the balance in the margin account at the *beginning* of day 2 is back to $5000). Suppose now that the futures price at *the close* of day 2 falls to $F_2 = $93.50 and there is an additional loss of $500 which brings the balance in the margin account to $4500. On day 3, the investor reverses his position and closes out at $F_3 = $98.50 (i.e. an increase of 5 points) and $5000 is added to the margin account which now stands at $9500, which is paid to the 'long' by the clearing house. Since the long has previously paid in $5000 + $4000 then the net profit over the 3 days is $500. Of course, this equals the change in the futures price $(F_3 - F_0)$ grossed up by the tick value: (= 98.50 −$98.00)$1000 = $500.

Thus, in the case of a price fall, the long pays into the margin account and the exchange credits the margin account of someone who has a short position (i.e. who has previously sold one futures contract). The opposite occurs for a rise in the futures price. The investor can withdraw (if she wishes) any excess in the margin account, over and above her initial margin.

Clearly it is possible for the futures price to fall dramatically and the loss may exceed the amount in the margin account. To ensure the balance never becomes negative a *variation margin* is payable. (This is lower than the initial margin and is usually about 75% of the initial margin.) If the balance falls below the maintenance margin, then the investor must top-up his account (i.e. pay variation margin) so that it equals the *initial margin* by the next day. (If the investor doesn't do this, the broker closes out the position by selling the contract.) In addition, the exchange sets *daily price limits* (e.g. for oil futures this equals $1). If the price falls (or rises) in 1 day by as much as the 'limit down' ('limit up'), then trading (usually) ceases for that day. These **circuit breakers** limit the daily payments/

receipts to and from the margin accounts, so that the balance in the margin account does not fall below zero before the broker can close out the position. This is why the initial margin can be relatively small (which allows speculators and hedgers to obtain leverage). Often the initial margin is set equal to the value of the contract's daily price limit.

## CLOSING OUT POSITIONS

In practice most traders (about 99%) close out their positions before the expiration of the futures contract. They therefore make a gain or loss depending on the difference between the initial futures price $F_1 = \$100$ and the futures price at which they close out the contract, say $F_2 = \$110$ (Figure 20.3). If you are long the futures, then when the futures price *increases,* the profit from your futures position also *increases*—this is a positive relationship.

Of course, if you are long the futures and *F falls* then your profit also *falls* (i.e. you make losses), but this too is a positive relationship. **Closing out** the contract merely involves shorting (i.e. selling) the contract. The profit on the futures position is equal to the *cumulative gain* or loss incurred day-by-day as the contract is marked to market, but this is simply equal to $F_2 - F_1$. The profit accrues in daily instalments over the life of the futures contract. Although most futures contracts are closed out via reversing trades, it is the possibility of delivery (and the method of actual delivery) which links the futures price to the underlying spot price—see below.

Now consider an investor who has initially sold (shorted) a futures contract at $F_1 = \$100$ (Figure 20.3). She obtains an *increase* in profit of $10 if the futures price *falls* to $F_2 = \$90$ since she can then buy back the contract (and hence close out her position) at a lower price than she initially sold it. Conversely, if the futures price *rises* to $F_2 = \$110$, her profit falls (i.e. she makes a loss).

## DELIVERY AND SETTLEMENT

The seller of the futures makes the choice of whether to deliver and usually delivery can take place on any of several days in the delivery month (and sometimes on any day during

## FIGURE 20.3: Speculation with futures

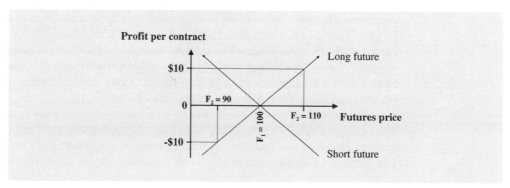

the delivery month). So the person holding a short September wheat futures might notify the clearing house that she intends to deliver. The clearing house then selects (usually in a random fashion) someone with a long position in September wheat futures and lets them know they must accept delivery within the next few days. So, for 'commodities', delivery is usually in the form of a warehouse receipt and the precise time and place for delivery is determined by the party with the short position. The recipient is then responsible for any warehousing costs or, for livestock futures, for the care of the animals.

Some financial futures contracts involve the delivery of the underlying asset (e.g. T-bills, T-bonds) while others, such as stock index futures, are settled in cash. Often cash settled contracts use the settlement price on the last trading day and the positions of the long and the short are then 'closed' by the clearing house and the contract no longer exists. Often the **settlement price** is determined by a settlement committee and is an average of the spot prices of the previous session's last few trades.

One of the key differences between forwards and futures is that forward contracts cannot be easily closed out. Usually M's A can only close out her long *forward contract* (with counterparty B) by selling her contract to M's C. In general, M's B will have to agree the 'new' contract between M's A and M's C because of the credit risk to M's B who is short the contract. However, if M's A has a long position in a 'live hogs' *futures* contract then she can easily offset it by selling a *new* futures contract *with the same delivery date*. This may involve a cash gain or loss, but she is then under no obligation to receive any live hogs at maturity. For a light-hearted view of delivery and settlement of forward and futures contracts see Box 20.1.

| Box 20.1 | HEDGING WITH FORWARDS AND FUTURES: KEN AND BARBIE |
|---|---|

If you still find forwards and futures a little bewildering perhaps the following analogy will help. Just think of a forward or futures contract in terms of engagement or marriage to a 'partner'. A 'partner' here is a homogeneous commodity. For example, this might include the market in 'Sloane Rangers' (of a given age range but of either sex) who parade up and down the Kings Road and around Peter Jones in London in their designer sunglasses and clothes. Other reasonably homogeneous markets include 'Essex man and woman' (e.g. Sharon and Darren), Royalty, Hollywood celebs, and the occupants of many 'clubs' in big cities and on holiday islands (Ibiza comes to mind). In somewhat disparaging terms, these spot markets are colloquially known as 'cattle markets'. To financial economists, markets are impersonal: 'it's the price that matters, stupid!'. We will make our market impersonal but interpersonal. Assume there is a market in a homogeneous class of men called 'Ken'. The spot price of Kens varies with their earning power and their general demeanour.

Now, Barbie might be quite willing to pay the spot price $S = \$100$ in January, to take delivery of a Ken and immediately marry him (e.g. at Gretna Green in Scotland or in Las Vegas). Using the spot market is all very well if you know you want a partner immediately. But what if you knew you definitely wanted to be married to a Ken, but not until after you had sown some 'wild oats' over the coming year. The problem you have is that if Kens do very well in the job market over the next year, their spot price will then be high and you might not be able to afford one. You currently have a 'naked' position in spot Kens. As a hedger what you require is a contract which fixes the price of the 'underlying' Ken today, for delivery in 1 years time. This is a forward contract on Ken. So a **forward contract** is like a 'traditional engagement'.

Unfortunately a forward contract has one major drawback. It is very difficult and expensive to 'get out' of the contract and hence delivery invariably takes place. Do you remember the film Godfather I with Marlon Brando as Vito Corleone? Well, in terms of our analogy, a forward contract is like agreeing an engagement with Vito Corleone's daughter, Connie. Since the costs of reneging on such a contract are prohibitively high (e.g. horses' heads in people's beds) the marriage to Connie went ahead. This is the case with forward contracts on financial assets, they nearly all go to delivery.

The key difference between a forward and a **futures contract** is that the latter is easily 'reversed' or 'closed out' prior to maturity. A futures contract is therefore like an engagement between Hollywood stars or a more typical 'Western engagement'. In terms of our analogy, all Barbie has to do to 'close out' her long position in a December Ken futures contract is to phone up the futures exchange (in June say) and sell one Ken futures contract. Then, no delivery (i.e. marriage) will take place at the end of the year. (Of course, Barbie may have made a loss or gain on her futures position if she closes out in June before maturity, but this may be preferable to delivery in December, if she has changed her mind about the desirability of a Ken.)

## TABLE 20.3: Futures: Newspaper Quote (*Wall Street Journals* 25th July 2000)

**Corn (CBT) 5000 bu (cents per bushel)**

| Month | Open | High | Low | Settle | Change | Lifetime high | Lifetime low | Open interest |
|---|---|---|---|---|---|---|---|---|
| September | $247\frac{1}{4}$ | $249\frac{1}{2}$ | $242\frac{1}{2}$ | $245\frac{1}{2}$ | $1\frac{3}{4}$ | 335 | 239 | 62,411 |
| December | 265 | 267 | 260 | $262\frac{3}{4}$ | $1\frac{3}{4}$ | 345 | 258 | 52,499 |
| March 01 | 281 | $282\frac{1}{2}$ | 276 | $278\frac{3}{4}$ | 2 | 327 | $274\frac{1}{2}$ | 17,588 |
| May | $286\frac{1}{2}$ | $288\frac{1}{2}$ | $286\frac{1}{2}$ | $288\frac{1}{2}$ | 2 | 326 | $284\frac{1}{2}$ | 964 |
| July | 299 | 299 | 294 | 297 | $1\frac{3}{4}$ | 350 | $293\frac{1}{2}$ | 8064 |
| December | 314 | 315 | 313 | 315 | 1 | 343 | 312 | 461 |

Notes: Est. vol. 16,000
Vol. Fri. 12,738
Open int. 141,997 + 534
Source: *Wall Street Journal*, Tuesday 25th July 2000

## FIGURE 20.4: Futures prices: Agricultural commodities (*Wall Street Journal*). Reproduced with permission

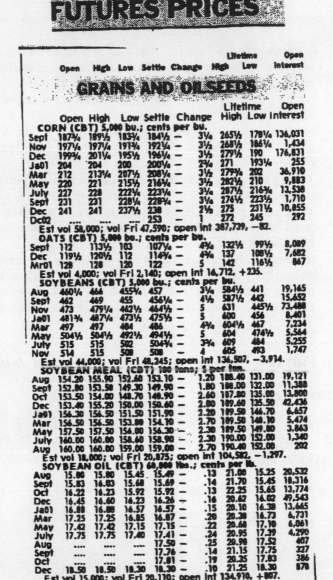

### NEWSPAPER QUOTES

A stylised example from the *Wall Street Journal* for 25th July on the CBOT for corn futures is given in Table 20.3. The size of the contract is for 5000 bushels and the price is in cents per bushel with (only) six maturity dates, namely September, December, March, May, July and December, illustrated.

The price quotes in the *Wall Street Journal* of 25th July are those pertaining to the trades on 24th July. The opening futures price (for the trade immediately after the opening bell) and the 'high' and 'low' daily futures prices during the trading day are given in columns 2 to 4. The fifth column gives the settlement price which is an average of prices just before the closing bell and the sixth column shows the *change* in the settlement price. The latter is used to calculate daily changes in margin requirements. Thus between the previous two trading days the settlement price for September futures increased by $1\frac{3}{4}$ cents and an investor long in one contract would have his margin account credited by \$87.50 ($= 5,000 \times 1\frac{3}{4}$ cents).

The 'lifetime high' and 'low' prices are self-explanatory, while the open interest is the number of futures contracts currently outstanding. Underneath each contract is given each day's volume of trading, the volume on the previous day, the *total* open interest at the beginning of the day and the change in the open interest from the previous day. Futures prices on other agricultural commodities are given in Figure 20.4.

## 20.2 FORWARD AND FUTURES PRICES

In this section we analyse how forward and futures prices are determined as functions of known variables such as the current market price of the underlying asset and the risk free interest rate. We will consider a simple case, without entering into the details of contract specifications. Forward contracts are easier to analyse than futures contracts, since the latter have the added complication of daily settlement (i.e. marking to market), whereas for the forward contract there is one payment at the expiry date. However, it can be shown that the futures price of an asset closely follows that of the forward price, for any given maturity. Therefore, in general, we will use forward and futures prices interchangeably. In general we shall assume:

- zero transactions costs;
- zero tax rates;
- agents can borrow or lend unlimited amounts at the 'safe' rate of interest;
- riskless arbitrage opportunities are instantaneously eliminated.

We will in the main use riskless arbitrage arguments when valuing futures contracts and this method is also referred to as the **carrying-charge** or **cost of carry** determination of futures prices. Riskless arbitrage arises because it is possible to create a 'synthetic forward'.

## NON-INCOME PAYING SECURITY

Consider the determination of the futures price on a contract for a non-income paying security (i.e. the share pays no dividends). The contract is for the delivery of a single share in 3 months time (Figure 20.5).

where $F = \$102$ is the *quoted* futures price (on the underlying share)

$S = \$100$ is the spot price of the share

$r = 0.04$ is the interest rate, 4% p.a. (simple interest)

$T = 1/4$ is the time to maturity (fraction of a year).

With the above figures it is possible to earn a riskless profit. The arbitrageur borrows $100 today and purchases the share. She therefore can deliver the share in 3 months. She has created a synthetic future by 'borrowing plus spot purchase'. This strategy involves no 'own capital', since the money is borrowed. The arbitrageur at $t = 0$ also sells a futures contract at $F_0 = \$102$, although no cash is received at $t = 0$.

The cost of the synthetic future $SF$ in 3 months time is $101 $(= \$100(1 + 0.04/4) = S(1 + rT))$. After 3 months the arbitrageur receives $F = \$102$ from the sale of the futures contract (and delivers one share) and therefore makes a riskless profit of $1 $(= \$102 - \$101)$. The strategy is riskless since the arbitrageur knows $S$, $F$ and $r$ at $t = 0$. The synthetic future has a cost of $SF = S(1 + rT)$ which is lower than the quoted futures price $F$.

Market participants will therefore take advantage of the riskless profit opportunity by 'buying low' and 'selling high'. Buying the share in the cash market and borrowing tends to increase $S$ and $r$ (and hence $SF$), while selling futures contracts will push $F$ down. Profitable riskless arbitrage opportunities will only be eliminated when the quoted futures price equals the 'price' of the synthetic future, $SF$:

---

## FIGURE 20.5: Arbitrage with futures

| | |
|---|---|
| **Stock price** | **S = $100** |
| **Safe rate** | **r = 4% p.a.** |
| **Quoted futures price** | **F = $102** |

**Strategy today**

Sell futures contract at $102 (receive nothing today)

Borrow $100, but stock (= synthetic future)

Use no 'own funds'

**3 months time (T = 1/4)**

Loan outstanding = $100 (1+0.04/4) = $101

Deliver stocks and receipts from F.C. = $102

Riskless profit = $1

[20.2]     $F = SF = S(1 + rT)$

Alternatively we can write the above as:

Forward price = spot price + dollar cost of carry

[20.3a]     $F = S + \chi$     where the *dollar* cost of carry $\chi = SrT$

Forward price = spot price(1 + percent cost of carry)

[20.3b]     $F = S\,(1 + \text{CC})$     where the *percent* cost of carry $\text{CC} = rT$

The **dollar** (interest) **cost of carry** equals $SrT$ and the **percent cost of carry** equals $rT$, over the horizon $T$. Note that CC also equals $(F - S)/S$, if the contract is fairly priced.

While the futures contract is being held, the spot price will change, and because of the possibility of riskless arbitrage profits, this will cause the price of the futures contract to alter. It is immediately apparent from equation [20.2] that the futures price and the stock price will move closely together, if $r$ stays constant. If $r$ changes before closing out the contract then $F$ and $S$ will change by different amounts. This is known as **basis risk**.

At expiry of the futures contract (i.e. at $T$) the futures price must equal the then spot price, $F_T = S_T$. This is because the person with a long futures position can obtain immediate delivery of one stock at a price of $F_T = \$98$ say. If the spot price at $T$ were say $S_T = \$103$, then the person holding the long futures can take the stock and immediately sell it in the cash market for \$103, making a riskless profit of \$5. At expiration, unless the *price* of a futures contract equals the spot price ($F_T = S_T$), then riskless arbitrage profits are possible. This can be seen in equation [20.2] by setting $S = S_T$ and $F = F_T$ and $T = 0$. (Note that for some contracts where delivery costs are high, the basis might not be exactly zero at expiry and $F_T$ would exceed $S_T$ by the amount of delivery costs.)

If $r$ is measured as a discrete compound rate or as a continuously compounded rate then the above formula (equation [20.2]) becomes:

[20.4a]     $F = S(1 + r)^T$     (discrete compounded rates)

or

[20.4b]     $F = S\,e^{rT}$     (continuously compounded rates)

In practice market makers would use equation [20.2] to determine their 'quote' for $F$, thus ensuring equality. It is possible for equation [20.2] not to hold at absolutely every instant of time and, providing a trader can act quickly enough, he may make a small arbitrage profit: this is known as **index arbitrage** if the underlying is a stock index future. Note that from equation [20.2] the futures price $F$ is the 'future value of the spot price'. This is due to the fact that the futures contract (which delivers one share in 3 months time) is equivalent to the synthetic future, namely 'borrowing today plus purchasing one share today'. Equivalently the spot price is the PV of the futures price (e.g. $S = F/(1 + rT)$).

# 20.3 HEDGING USING FUTURES CONTRACTS

Futures contracts are often used for hedging a position. For example, an oil producer might have a large amount of oil coming 'on stream' in 3 months time and may fear a fall in the spot price, or a US exporter might be receiving sterling from the sale of goods in 3 months time but fears a fall in the spot rate for sterling (which implies receiving less dollars). In these cases the investor doesn't know what the spot price will be in 3 months time, and future receipts are subject to risk. Hedging can be used to reduce such risk to a minimum. In practice, a perfect hedge is often not possible, hence the phrase: 'The only perfect hedge is in a Japanese garden'.

The basic idea behind hedging is very simple. If you are holding (i.e. long) the underlying asset then you need to take a futures position such that the gain on the futures contract offsets any losses in the spot market. Futures and spot prices tend to rise and fall together because $F = S(1 + rT)$. Hence, if you are long in the underlying asset you need to short the futures contract. Alternatively, if the investor wishes to purchase a spot asset in the future (i.e. she is currently short the underlying) but is worried about a rise in the spot price, she should purchase (go long) in the futures contract.

A hedged position *by design* is (nearly) risk free and therefore it will only earn the risk free rate of return. You therefore forego any big gains (or losses) if you take up a hedged position using futures. Put another way, the 'stocks + futures' hedged position can be shown to be equivalent to holding a risk free asset such as a bank deposit (which will also earn the risk free rate of interest)—this is a form of **financial engineering** because 'stocks + futures' = 'risk free asset'.

## HEDGING USING STOCK INDEX FUTURES

Suppose that on 2nd January a portfolio manager wishes to hedge her diversified stock portfolio, as she is worried about a *general fall* in the stock market over the next 2 months. She can hedge by using a March futures contract on a stock index (such as the S&P500). Alternatively, she could of course sell all or some of her stocks if she believes their prices will fall, but a more cost effective method of hedging is to use stock index futures. Stock index futures are cash settled. Each index point ('tick') is assigned a value, and for the S&P500 it is $250 per index point.

Since she is long the underlying stock portfolio she takes a **short futures hedge** (i.e. she sells March index futures). An effective hedge position requires a calculation of the number of futures contracts she needs to short. The simplest way to consider this issue is to assume a spot ('cash') position of $1.4m in a portfolio of *stocks which exactly mirrors the composition of the S&P500 index*. Hence we are assuming **perfect correlation** between the underlying index $S$ and the futures index $F$ (i.e. correlation coefficient of $+1$) and that both indices move by the same amount. If the S&P500 index in January is $S_0 = 1400$, then it seems intuitively obvious that the required number of futures contracts should be:

[20.5] $$N_f = -\left(\frac{\$1.4m}{\$250(1400)}\right) = -4 \text{ (i.e. short four contracts)}$$

Suppose the initial futures price in January is $F_0 = 1417$. The hedger sells four futures contracts. Over the next 2 months the portfolio manager's worse fears are met and the S&P500 falls by 10% to $S_1 = 1260$, so the loss on the stock portfolio is \$140,000. Since the March index futures is close to maturity, then it too will have a value very close to 1260 and we take this to be $F_1 = 1263$. The futures contract is closed out (i.e. sold) and in March the fall in the futures price is 154 ($= 1417 - 1263$). The outcome of the hedged position in March is therefore:

Loss on stock portfolio $=$ **\$140,000**

Gain on futures $=$ change in futures index $\times$ tick value $\times$ 4 contracts

$$= 154 \times \$250 \times 4 = \mathbf{\$154,000}$$

Hence the hedge position has produced a small profit, but most importantly it has averted a possible large loss of \$140,000 had the position remained unhedged. The reader can verify for herself that a similar hedged outcome would ensue if the stock price (and hence futures price) had risen by 10%. The gain on the stocks would then be offset by the *loss* on the short futures position. In this case, with hindsight it would have been better not to hedge. But 'hindsight' is not 'available' in January and the whole idea of the hedge is to remove risk and in doing so, you also forego any favourable outcomes. You can't have your cake and eat it—you can be a hedger or a speculator in any given deal, but not both.

---

### USING INDEX FUTURES FOR HEDGING

- If you are **long** (i.e. own) the spot asset (e.g. stocks) then undertake a **short** futures hedge (i.e. sell futures). If you are **planning to purchase** the underlying asset in the future (i.e. you are short in the cash market) then **go long** (i.e. purchase) in futures. This gives a negative correlation for the hedged portfolio of 'spot + future'.
- Note that any losses on the futures contract may involve **additional margin calls** and it is usually inconvenient (or impossible) to use any profits that may have *accrued* from the cash market assets (e.g. stocks held) to pay these margin calls. Hence a hedger must have lines of credit or other assets available to meet possible margin calls.

---

## HEDGING USING INTEREST RATE FUTURES

The following illustrate how interest rate futures allow investors to hedge spot positions in money market assets, such as T-bills and (Eurodollar) deposits and loans. Interest rate futures can be used to 'lock in' an interest rate or the price of an interest sensitive asset (such as a T-bill or commercial bill). Consider the following situations:

- You hold \$10m worth of 91-day T-bills which you will sell in 1 months time (i.e. before the bills mature) because you will then need cash to pay your creditors. You fear a rise in interest rates over the next month which will cause a fall in value of your T-bills. You can hedge your spot position in T-bills by shorting (selling) T-bill futures contracts at $F_0$. This guarantees that you can sell your T-bills for $F_0$ in 1 months time.

- You will receive $10m in 6 months time which you will then want to invest in a Eurodollar bank deposit for 90 days. You fear a fall in interest rates over the next 6 months, which means you will earn less interest on your deposits. You can hedge this risk by going long (i.e. buying) a Eurodollar futures contract.
- You hope to issue $10m of 180-day commercial paper in 3 months time (i.e. to borrow money). You fear that interest rates will rise over the next 3 months (i.e. bill prices will fall) so your borrowing costs will increase. You can hedge your borrowing costs by shorting (i.e. selling) T-bill futures contracts. This is an example of a cross-hedge since there is no commercial bill futures contract, so you have to use T-bill futures.

The key feature to remember when hedging using interest rate futures is that when interest rates (or yields) fall, the futures *price* will rise (and vice versa). However, we have not been precise about what interest rates we are referring to. At this point, to simplify matters, we assume rates (yields) for all maturities and all forward rates move together and by the same amount.

Interest rate futures contracts can be used to hedge the interest rate payments/receipts on future cash flows. Suppose on 15th April an investor is to take out a loan of £1m in 2 months time on 15th June and the loan is for a further 3 months. The exposure period is 2 months and the protection period in the futures contract is 3 months. Suppose she fears a rise in interest rates over the next 2 months, so her loan will then cost more. Since futures prices fall when interest rates rise, if she hedges by going short in interest rate futures she makes a gain on the futures. The latter offsets the higher interest rate she has to pay on the loan in 2 months time.

To illustrate the above consider the 'short sterling' interest rate futures contract but note that the mechanics of using interest rate futures is a little more complex than for stock index futures. The contract size for the short sterling contract is £500,000. The futures price $F$ is quoted on an index basis and is linked to the futures interest rate $f$ by:

[20.6] $$F = 100 - f$$

For example, on 15th April a futures interest rate $f_0$ of 7% on the contract maturing in June implies that the holder of the June futures has 'locked in' an interest rate of 7%. This interest rate will apply between June and September (i.e. for 3 months) on a notional amount of £500,000. Hence, the cost of borrowing at this rate is:

[20.7] Cost of borrowing at $f_0 = 7\%$ over 3 months $= £1m(0.07/4) = $ **£17,500**

Note also that $f_0$ ($= 7\%$) corresponds to a quoted futures price of $F_0 = 93$. However, note that the futures price does not mean '£93', it is merely a device for keeping the inverse relationship between $F$ and $f$. For convenience we also assume that the spot interest rate is also $r_0 = 7\%$ on 15th April.

The next issue to consider is the tick size and tick value. LIFFE sets the tick size of the futures at 1/100 of 1% and hence the tick value (over the 3-month interest period) is:

[**20.8**]      Tick value $= £500,000 \times (0.01/100) \times (3/12) = £12.50$

Hence traders know that a change in $F$ of 1 unit (i.e. 100 ticks) corresponds to a change in value of £1250. We are now in a position to hedge our future 3-month loan (beginning in 2 months time) with the 3-month short sterling futures contract. On 15th April we fear a rise in interest rates over the next 2 months so we *go short* the futures contract. If 3-month interest rates do rise over the next 2 months then the futures *price* will fall. Hence the short futures position will offset some or all of the higher costs of the loan, when it is taken out in June. With a contract size of £500,000 and a loan of £1m the number of June futures contracts *to short* on 15th April is:

[**20.9**]      $N_{\mathrm{f}} = £1\mathrm{m}/£500,000 = 2$

Suppose 3-month spot interest rates in June rise to $r_1 = 9\%$. Since the June futures is now close to maturity then $f_1$ will also equal 9% and therefore $F_1 = 91$. The change in the futures price is 200 ticks. The hedged outcome in June is:

| | |
|---|---|
| Cost of borrowing (June–September) in spot market | $= £1\mathrm{m}\,(0.09/4) = £22,500$ |
| Gain on futures $= 200$ ticks $\times £12.50 \times$ two contracts | $= £5000$ |
| Net cost of the hedged position | $= \mathbf{£17,500}$ |

Therefore even though the futures have been closed out (immediately) prior to maturity for a 'cash profit', the latter just offsets the higher interest cost in the spot market in June and hence the hedge 'locks in' the initial futures rate of $f_0 = 7\%$ as expected (which is equivalent to £17,500 over 3 months).

---

### USING INTEREST RATE FUTURES FOR HEDGING

- If you are **taking out a loan** in the future and hence you fear a rise in interest rates then **hedge by going short** an interest rate futures contract.
- If you are going to **place some money on deposit** in the future and you fear a fall in interest rates then **hedge by going long** an interest rate futures contract.

---

## 20.4 SPECULATION

Speculation with futures is relatively straightforward. First consider stock index futures. Since $S$ and $F$ move together, then if you think $S$ will rise (fall) in the future you will go long (short) in index futures. Compared to speculation by purchasing the underlying stocks, the long futures position provides leverage, since you do not have the cost of buying (and later selling) the underlying stocks. You merely have to provide a relatively small 'good faith deposit' for your margin account. Of course, if the futures price initially falls (before hopefully it ultimately rises) then you may have to be prepared to 'top up' your margin account, and you therefore need cash or collateral (e.g. T-bills) available.

Speculation with interest rate futures is also not particularly difficult. If you want to speculate on a future fall in interest rates then you would go long an interest rate futures contract (e.g.

either a T-bill or 'short-sterling' or Eurodollar futures). For *any* interest rate futures contract the key feature is the inverse relationship between interest rates and the futures *price*, and it is the latter which determines your profit (or loss). Hence if interest rates fall the futures price rises and hence you make a profit from your long position. Clearly, to bet on a future rise in interest rates you would short an interest rate futures contract. Of course any naked position in a futures contract is highly risky, since futures prices can fall and rise as rapidly as the 'prices' of their underlying assets (i.e. including interest rates).

## 20.5 SUMMARY

- **A futures contract is marked to market**, so its value is reset to zero at the end of each day (by payments into or out of the margin account). The clearing house keeps track of the margin account and if it falls below the maintenance margin additional payments have to be made. This minimises counterparty (credit) risk.
- The **Clearing House sets the terms for each contract**, such as the contract size, tick value, delivery dates, settlement prices and margin requirements. Trading is sometimes via **open outcry** in a trading pit, but recently there has been a move towards **electronic trading**.
- **Riskless arbitrage** ensures that the **futures price equals the spot price plus the 'cost of carry'**.
- **Hedging** requires that if the investor is **long the underlying asset** (e.g. a portfolio of shares) she should **short the futures contract** (and vice versa). Since $F$ and $S$ tend to move together this strategy creates a (near perfect) **negative correlation** between the return on the underlying asset and the futures contract. However, there is always some **basis risk** in the hedge.
- **Hedging future changes in interest rates** is based on the inverse relationship between the interest rate and the futures *price*. If you are **planning to take out a loan** in the future then you hedge any future rise in the cost of borrowing by going **short an interest rate futures contract**. Conversely, if you are **planning to lend money** in the future then you should hedge by going **long an interest rate futures contract**.
- **Speculation (i.e. a naked position) in futures** allows almost **unlimited leverage** (since any margin payments usually earn interest). A speculator buys (sells) a **stock index futures contract** if she expects the underlying asset price (and hence the futures price) to rise (fall) in the future. A person who speculates on interest rate changes would buy (sell) an **interest rate futures contract** if she expects interest rates in the future to fall (rise).

## END OF CHAPTER EXERCISES

**Q1** Explain how a forward/futures contract can be used for hedging and speculation.

**Q2** Briefly explain 'open interest' and 'trading volume' for a futures contract. What is a 'margin account' and how do margin payments on futures contracts reduce counterparty risk?

**Q3** What is basis risk in a hedge and is it ever zero?

**Q4** You are *already long* 100 contracts at a settlement price of $50,000 per contract. Next day at 11 a.m. you acquire an additional 20 contracts at a price of $51,000 per contract. The initial margin is $2000 per contract. The settlement price at the end of the day is $50,200 per contract. What happens to the margin account on day 2?

**Q5** You enter into a forward contract on a non-dividend paying stock with maturity of 1 year, with $S_0 = \$40$ and $r = 10\%$ p.a.

(a) What is the 'no arbitrage' (synthetic) futures price of the contract?
(b) If the *actual* futures price is $F = 46$ how can you make a riskless arbitrage profit?
(c) If the *actual* futures price is $F = 42$ how can you make a riskless arbitrage profit?

**Q6** When are a 'long hedge' and a 'short hedge' appropriate? Use the examples of an oil producer and an oil consumer.

**Q7** A *forward* contract is usually held to maturity (at $T$), when delivery then takes place in exchange for a payment of the forward price initially agreed, $F_0$. Why then does the *value* of the forward contract vary between $t = 0$ and $t = T$?

# Options Markets

## 21.1 OPTIONS

Options contracts are extensively traded on a large number of exchanges, with the underlying assets being individual stocks, stock indices, interest rates, currencies, commodities and futures contracts. There is also a large OTC market in options. The mechanics of trading options and the terminology used are common across a wide range of option contracts.

## CALL OPTIONS

> A *European call option* gives the holder the right (but not an obligation):
> - to **purchase the underlying asset**
> - at a specified future date (known as the ***expiration***, ***expiry*** or ***maturity date***)
> - for a certain price (**the *exercise* or *strike price***)
> - and in an amount (**contract size**) which is fixed in advance.
> - For this privilege you pay today the **call premium/price**.

A **European option** can only be exercised on the expiry date itself, whereas an **American option** can be *exercised* any time up to the expiry date. Note, however, that European (and American) options can be *sold* to another market participant at any time. Most options traded on exchanges are American, but as European options are easier to analyse we deal mainly with the latter. Note that in this chapter we concentrate on the payoff profiles *at expiry*, and only briefly mention the change in the value of options prior to expiry.

Table 21.1 summarises the issues involved in the purchase of a **call option**. The investor purchases one call option which involves 100 shares of XYZ at a cost of $300 ($3 × 100 shares). The strike price is $K = \$80$.

At time $T$ the investor could exercise the option and purchase the 100 shares at $K = \$80$ and then sell them in the market for $S_T = \$88$ (see Figure 21.1). At expiry she makes a profit of $8 per share which, net of the call premium of $3, gives a net profit of $5 per share ($500 in total). (In fact, the net profit *at expiry* will be less, as we have ignored the foregone interest on the initial premium of $300 paid at $t = 0$.) If the share price at expiration had turned out to be $82

---

## TABLE 21.1: Buy (long) call option current

**Current share price $S = \$78$**

*Trader's desk (today, time t)*

Contract size = 100 shares

Strike price $K = \$80$

Call premium (price) $C = \$3$

Premium paid = 100($3) = $300

*Outcome (3 months later at time T)*

Share price at expiry = $S_T = \$88$

Profit from exercise:     $(S_T - K)100 = (\$88 - \$80)100 = \mathbf{\$800}$

Profit net of call premium:  $(S_T - K - C)100 = (\$8 - \$3)100 = \mathbf{\$500}$

then the net profit would have been $-\$100$ ($=$ [($82 - $80)100] $-$ $300), that is a loss of $100. However, it is still worth exercising the option if $S_T > K$, since if the investor does not do so, her net loss is the whole option premium of $300. In fact, if the share price exceeds the strike price ($S_T > K$) at the expiration date, it always pays to exercise the option. If $S_T < K$, then the option will not be exercised since it is cheaper to purchase the shares in the spot market at time $T$—this is the 'insurance' provided by the call option, you can 'walk away' from the contract if the out-turn is not favourable. The decision to exercise depends on $S_T$ relative to $K$, hence options are **contingent claims**.

The relationship between the terminal price of the stock $S_T$ and the profit from exercising the long call is given in Figure 21.1. It is clear that the downside risk for the investor who is long in the call option is limited to $3 (per share), while she also has the opportunity to make very large profits if the stock price on the expiry date is high. It is useful to designate the profit profile from options in terms of direction vectors. Hence the payoff from a long call is $\{0, +1\}$, since the option earns profits which rise one for one with the price of the underlying, once $S_T$ exceeds $K$ (see insert in Figure 21.1)

## FIGURE 21.1: Buy one European call option

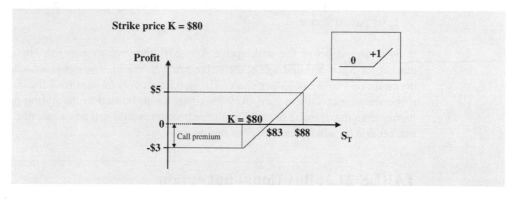

For the **writer (seller) of the call option** the profit profile is the mirror image of that for the investor who is long in the call option. The writer of the call has a profit profile $\{0, -1\}$ since she *loses* money when the stock price *rises*—hence the 'minus 1' (see insert in Figure 21.2) signifying this negative relationship.

## PUT OPTIONS

A **European put option** gives the holder the right (but not an obligation):

- to sell the underlying asset
- at a specified future date (**the expiration/expiry date**)
- for a certain price (**strike/exercise price**)
- and in an amount (**contract size**) which is fixed in advance.
- For this privilege you pay the **put premium/price**.

## FIGURE 21.2: Sell (write) a european call option

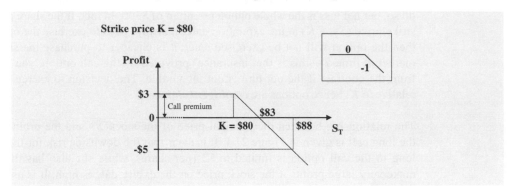

Since a holder of an option contract can choose whether to exercise the option, the contract provides a form of insurance. An example of a put option in which the investor makes a profit is given in Table 21.2. In contrast to the holder of a call option, the holder of a put option will exercise the option if the share price $S_T$ at the expiry date is below the strike price $K = \$70$. The profit from the exercise of a long put is shown in Figure 21.3. It has a $\{-1, 0\}$ payoff vector.

If $S_T = \$65$ is below the strike price $K = \$70$, the investor can buy the share in the cash market for $S_T = \$65$ and sell at the strike price $K = \$70$. The net profit after paying the put premium of $P = \$2$ is \$3 per share. The maximum (yet finite) profit for the long put occurs if the share price falls to zero. Any losses are again limited to the option premium. If $S_T$ is *higher* than the exercise price $K$, then the investor would sell any shares he owns in the cash market and he will not exercise the option.

## TABLE 21.2: Buy (long) put option

**Current share price $S = \$78$**

*Trader's desk (today, time t)*

Contract size $= 100$ shares

Strike price $K = \$70$

Put premium (price) $P = \$2$

Premium paid $= 100(\$2) = \$200$

*Outcome (3 months later at time T)*

Share price at expiry $S_T = \$65$

Profit from exercise:        $(K - S_T)100 = (\$70 - \$65)100 = \mathbf{\$500}$

Profit net of put premium:   $(K - S_T - P)100 = (\$5 - \$2)100 = \mathbf{\$300}$

## FIGURE 21.3: Buy (long): European put

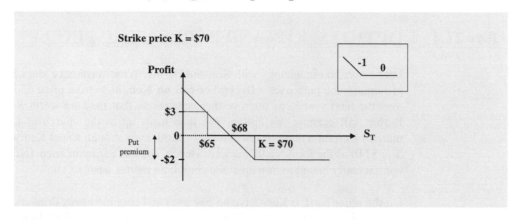

Consider the **writer (seller) of the put option** whose profit profile is the mirror image of that for the long (Figure 21.4). If you hold a short put then your downside risk could be large but it is limited to $K = \$70$ per share (i.e. if the share price falls to zero). The payoff profile is $\{+1, 0\}$ because as the stock price rises the profits for the writer of the put also rise—this is a positive relationship.

## POSITIONS IN OPTIONS

It should now be clear that there are two sides of the market for calls and puts. The two parties to each option contract are classified as follows:

> **Long call** = buy a call option
> **Long put** = buy a put option
> **Short call** = sell (or write) a call option
> **Short put** = sell (or write) a put option

## FIGURE 21.4: Sell (write): European put

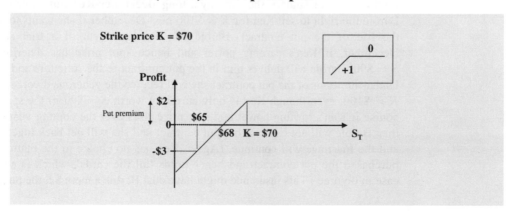

For a light-hearted analysis of the payoffs to calls and puts you can take a look at Box 21.1.

| Box 21.1 | OPTIONS: KEN AND BARBIE, THE FINALE |
|---|---|

Let's return to our analogy with Ken and Barbie. What 'insurance' does Barbie have if in January she purchases a **December-call on Ken**, at a strike price of $K = \$100$? If, over the next year Kens improve their salaries so that they are worth $S = \$110$, then Barbie will exercise her option. She then turns up at the church in December and marries Ken for a mere payment of $K = \$100$, even though a spot Ken would cost her $S = \$110$ at the local 'cattle market'. Hence, she has her **insurance**. (Note that Ken is contractually bound to turn up at the church no matter what.)

On the other hand, if Kens have no pay rises and become heavy drinkers over the next year, their spot price might fall below $K = \$100$, to say $S = \$90$. In this case Barbie would **not exercise her option** and would simply not turn up at the church. Under the terms of the option contract, she does not even have to tell Ken she will not be turning up. This is why Ken received the call premium the previous January, as monetary compensation for his possible subsequent embarrassment at the altar. So we can also infer that although Hugh Grant's character 'Charles', in *Four Weddings and a Funeral*, did turn up at the church with the intention of marrying 'Duck Face', he really could have saved himself the trouble and embarrassment if he had simply purchased a long call on her earlier in the year. (Those of you who are familiar with the film will know that what 'Duck Face' actually had was a down-and-out option on 'Charles' which she executed with a right hook once she realised Charles' true worth that day.)

Now suppose the 'fair' or market price for a Ken in the spot market in December turns out to be $S = \$90$, reflecting his lower earning potential. Then, Barbie could if she wished purchase a Ken in the spot market at her local club, and take immediate delivery. So the option contract really did give her the insurance of a maximum price of $K = \$100$ for a Ken, yet she can take advantage of the lower spot price for Kens in 1 years time, if she so wishes.

Suppose Barbie has been married to Ken for some time but feels she is getting rather tired of him. In January she can buy a **long December-Ken put** contract. This gives Barbie the right to sell Ken for $K = \$100$ next December if she wants to. Hence, over the life of the put contract, Barbie has the equivalent of a trial separation. In December, if Ken's earning power and hence spot price has deteriorated to say $S = \$90$, Barbie will deliver him in the put contract to the solicitors and get divorced. Under the terms of the put contract she will receive the generous divorce settlement of $K = \$100$, even though Ken is only currently worth $S = \$90$ in the spot market. Of course if Ken's earning power and spot price rises over the coming year to $S = \$110$ then Barbie will not exercise her put contract and she will get back together with Ken and the marriage will continue. (Again, Ken has no choice in the matter, Barbie has purchased the put contract and hence holds 'all the cards', which is sometimes the case in divorce.) This insurance might have cost Barbie a mere $2, the put premium.

Again those of you who know the ending of *Four Weddings and a Funeral* will realise that what 'Charles' probably held was an embedded **rainbow option** (or **alternative option**). With this type of option the payoff can be based on the better performance of *two* underlying 'assets' (i.e. 'Duck Face' and Andie MacDowell's character).

I hope the above has whetted your appetite for options contracts, whether applied to financial assets or more light-heartedly about the issues behind your decisions on engagement, marriage and divorce. Your new enthusiasm might lead you to investigate the practical uses of straddles, straps, condors, butterfly spreads, lookbacks, caps, floors, collars and other 'exotic' derivatives. Who said finance wasn't sexy? Not me. So if you agree why not hedge your future success in this area today, by taking out a futures contract on *'Financial Engineering: Derivatives and Risk Management'* by Cuthbertson and Nitzsche, so the future price you will pay is fixed. Alternatively, you could take out an options contract which sets an upper limit on the price you will pay for the book in the future, but also allows you to 'walk away' from the contract should you hear that the book is a vacuous load of garbage.

## OPTION STRATEGIES PRIOR TO EXPIRATION

Speculation with options will usually not involve holding the option to maturity but buying and selling (closing out) over a very short period of time. Prior to maturity it can be shown that the option premium varies minute-by-minute as the stock price, interest rate and volatility of the stock change.

Let us develop some intuitive arguments which help us to explain the determination of option prices prior to maturity, since any option, whether it be American or European, can be *traded* prior to maturity. We consider each factor in turn, holding all the other factors constant. In each case we assume the investor has a long position (i.e. has purchased a call or a put) and we only consider European stock options (where the stock pays no dividend).

### TIME TO EXPIRATION ($T$)
**Calls:**   In general, a European call option will increase in value with time to maturity since the option has more time to end up well in-the-money (and the downside is limited to the call premium, should it end up out-of-the-money).

**Puts:**   The put premium on a European option increases with time to maturity for the same reason as for the call.

### STRIKE PRICE ($K$) AND CURRENT STOCK PRICE ($S$)
**Calls:**   European call options have a larger payoff the higher is the stock price $S_T$ at expiry relative to the strike price $K$. However, if stock price movements are random then the higher the *current* stock price $S$ relative to the strike price, the more likely it is that the stock price *at expiry* will also be above the strike price. Hence the purchaser of a long European call option will be willing to pay a higher price for the option the higher is ($S/K$).

**Puts:** It should be obvious that the value (price) of a put option varies with $S$ and $K$ in the opposite direction to that for a call. Hence the value of a long position in a European or American put option depends negatively on $(S/K)$.

## VOLATILITY ($\sigma$)

**Calls:** The greater the volatility of the return on the share $\sigma$, the greater the possible range of share prices that might exist at the expiry date. But the owner of a long call option has limited downside risk. Hence, increased volatility increases the chance of a high share price and hence high payoff for the call option (at the expiry date), while downside risk is limited. The *current* value of a long position in a call option therefore increases with volatility.

**Puts:** The owner of a long put benefits from price decreases but also has limited downside risk from price increases. Hence the put premium increases with an increase in volatility.

## RISK FREE INTEREST RATE ($R$)

**Calls:** Firstly, an increase in interest rates reduces the present value of any future profits from the option. This tends to directly reduce the value of a long call. Secondly, to the extent that a general rise in interest rates increases the expected growth rate of stock prices, this tends to increase the value of a long call. It can be shown that the second effect dominates and the value of the long position in a call, increases with $r$.

**Puts:** As a higher interest rate leads to a higher growth in the stock price this increases the chance that the put will be out-of-the-money at expiry. A higher interest rate also reduces the present value of any profits from the put. Hence a rise in interest rates reduces the value of a put option.

It would be extremely useful if all of the above factors could be included in a single equation to determine the call ($C$) or put premium ($P$). This 'closed-form' solution is the **Black–Scholes equation** for option premia and has the general form:

$$C \,(\text{or } P) = f(S,\ K,\ T,\ r,\ \sigma)$$

To work out the exact functional form for the Black–Scholes equation is rather difficult, but it does result in a 'curved' or 'non-linear' relationship between the call (or put) premium and the price of the underlying stock, $S$. This positive relationship for a long call is shown as the curved line A–B in Figure 21.5. In fact, as the option approaches maturity the 'curved line' moves towards the 'kinked line' which represents the payoff at maturity. If the current stock price was $S_t$ then the current call premium would be $C_t$ (point B in Figure 21.5). However, if the stock price remained at $S_t$ the call premium would fall towards point C and the option is said to 'lose time value' as it approaches maturity (see below).

Figure 21.5 shows how we can speculate over short horizons using call options. For example, suppose that immediately after purchasing a call option (on a stock) for a market price of $C_0 = \$3$ the stock price increases. New call options coming on to the market with the same strike price (and expiry date) will sell for more, say $C_1 = \$3.1$. Hence the 'old' call option is also more valuable and can be sold at a higher price, $C_1 = \$3.1$. If the speculator paid the

## FIGURE 21.5: Black–Scholes

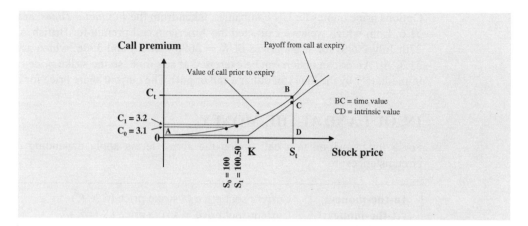

$3 to the clearing house at $t = 0$, then at $t = 1$ when she closes out her initial long position by selling the call at $3.1, the clearing house sends the speculator $3.1. Thus there is no need to wait until expiry to carn a speculative profit.

A speculator would purchase a call option if she expected a bull market (i.e. a rise in stock prices). She would gain leverage (because the call premium is a small proportion of the value of the underlying stocks in the option contract) and her downside loss would be limited to the initial call premium paid (since the lowest price the call can fall to is zero, if the stock price falls to zero).

Prior to maturity the relationship between the put premium and the stock price is also a 'curved line', but for a put, the put premium $P$ and the stock price $S$ are negatively related. Hence, a speculator would purchase a put option if she felt that stock prices would fall in the near future. She would pay the put premium $P_0 = \$2$ at $t = 0$. If the stock price fell, at $t = 1$ then the put premium would increase, to say $P_1 = \$2.1$, and if she then closes out her initial position by selling the put, she will receive $2.1 from the clearing house.

We also noted above that the Black–Scholes formula (and our intuition) show that the price of both calls and puts are positively related to the volatility of the stock, as perceived by the 'players' in the market. Suppose the *perceived* volatility of a stock increased (e.g. because the firm had factories overseas in the emerging economies of Asia and forecasts for these economies had suddenly become more uncertain). Then both call and put premia would increase and, had the speculator been long either calls or puts, she could now close out her position at a profit. Options therefore allow speculators to make a profit (or loss) by predicting changes in volatility. This is sometimes referred to as **trading volatility**.

Finally, note that riskless arbitrage ensures the 'fair pricing' of options contracts, but we cannot deal with this more advanced issue here (see Cuthbertson and Nitzsche, 2001).

## 21.2 INTRINSIC VALUE AND TIME VALUE

Options price quotes for UK companies, taken from the *Financial Times*, are shown in Figure 21.6, from which we have extracted the American call premia for British Airways (BA) (for 27th July 2000) for strike prices of $K = 360$p (pence) and 390p, which are shown in Table 21.3. An American option can be exercised at any time, so the strike price could be obtained immediately by the long (for either a call or put). The current share price for BA is $S = 376$p.

### IN, OUT AND AT-THE-MONEY

For a long position in a call option the above terms apply depending on the following circumstances:

| | |
|---|---|
| **In-the-money:** | Current spot price > strike price $(S > K)$ |
| **At-the-money:** | Current spot price = strike price $(S = K)$ |
| **Out-of-the-money:** | Current spot price < strike price $(S < K)$ |

Strictly speaking an option is in-the-money if $S_t$ exceeds the discounted present value of the strike price (i.e. $S_t > K \exp(-rT)$), but the simpler definitions above are used 'On the Street'.

### NEWSPAPER QUOTES: BRITISH AIRWAYS CALLS

For example the BA-360 calls (Table 21.3) must be worth at least 16p because the long has the right to buy BA immediately at $K = 360$p and she could then sell the share for $S = 376$p. The possibility of immediate exercise places a minimum intrinsic value on the option:

[21.1]      **Intrinsic value** $= S - K = 376\text{p} - 360\text{p} = 16\text{p}$

The BA-360 call for October expiry has a call premium of $36\frac{1}{2}$p, which is greater than the intrinsic value of 16p. The reason for this is that there is a chance that between 27th July and the October expiry date, the share price will increase even further (thus increasing the value of owning the call). This extra amount is known as the time value of the option:

[21.2]      **Time value** (October call) $=$ **call premium** $-$ **intrinsic value**

$$= 36\tfrac{1}{2} - 16\text{p} = 20\tfrac{1}{2}\text{p}$$

Now consider the BA-390 call. This has an intrinsic value of zero since you would not wish to buy at $K = 390$p and then sell in the cash market at $S = 376$p. However, there is a chance that on or before expiry the spot price will rise beyond $K = 390$p. For the BA-390 October call, the longs are willing to pay $21\frac{1}{2}$p for that chance. Notice that for either of the calls $(K = 360\text{p}$ or $K = 390\text{p})$ the longs are willing to pay higher call premia the longer the time to expiry, and hence these options have time values that increase with time to maturity (look along the rows). This is because there is a longer time over which the spot price might rise above (or well above) the strike price. In summary we have:

FIGURE 21.6: Newspaper quotes (*Financial Times*). Reproduced with permission

| Option | | Calls Oct | Calls Jan | Calls Apr | Puts Oct | Puts Jan | Puts Apr |
|---|---|---|---|---|---|---|---|
| Abbey Natl | 700 | 68½ | 96½ | 112½ | 34½ | 53 | 77½ |
| (*740) | 750 | 44 | 72½ | 86½ | 59½ | 78½ | 101 |
| Ald Domecq | 330 | 27½ | 42 | 52½ | 23½ | 34 | 40½ |
| (*333½) | 360 | 16½ | 29½ | 39½ | 41½ | 51½ | 57½ |
| Allied Zurich | 800 | 88 | 91½ | 109 | 20½ | 33 | 40½ |
| (*836½) | 850 | 39½ | 64½ | 83 | 42½ | 56 | 64 |
| AstraZeneca | 2800 | 235½ | 346 | 402 | 120½ | 193½ | 268 |
| (*2894) | 2900 | 186½ | 297 | 345½ | 170 | 243 | 283 |
| BAA | 500 | 54½ | 66 | 79 | 17 | 27 | 34 |
| (*530½) | 550 | 27½ | 41 | 54½ | 40½ | 52 | 59 |
| BAT | 390 | 34½ | 51½ | 59½ | 34 | 46 | 59½ |
| (*390) | 420 | 23 | 38 | 48½ | 52½ | 83½ | 78½ |
| Barclays | 1450 | 129½ | 186½ | 217½ | 79 | 116 | 152½ |
| (*1499) | 1500 | 104½ | 162 | 193 | 104 | 142 | 177½ |
| Bass | 650 | 78½ | 95 | 112½ | 21½ | 41½ | 58½ |
| (*698½) | 700 | 50 | 68 | 86½ | 42½ | 65½ | 81 |
| Boots | 500 | 34½ | 47 | 61½ | 28 | 41 | 49½ |
| (*500) | 550 | 15 | 27½ | 41½ | 59 | 71½ | 79½ |
| Br Airways | 360 | 38½ | 50 | 57½ | 16 | 25 | 27½ |
| (*376) | 390 | 21½ | 35½ | 44 | 31 | 40 | 43½ |
| BP Amoco | 550 | 52 | 67½ | 84 | 21½ | 31½ | 42 |
| (*576) | 600 | 27½ | 41 | 58½ | 47½ | 58½ | 66 |
| Option | | Oct | Dec | Mar | Oct | Dec | Mar |
| Cable & Wire | 1200 | 140½ | 181½ | 226 | 105 | 135 | 167½ |
| (*1220) | 1250 | 117 | 159 | 202 | 131 | 161½ | 193 |
| Option | | Oct | Jan | Apr | Oct | Jan | Apr |

| Option | | Calls Oct | Calls Dec | Calls Mar | Puts Oct | Puts Dec | Puts Mar |
|---|---|---|---|---|---|---|---|
| Reed Intl | 500 | 56 | 69½ | 80½ | 29½ | 39 | 50½ |
| (*524) | 550 | 33½ | 48½ | 66½ | 57 | 65½ | 76½ |
| Option | | Oct | Jan | Apr | Oct | Jan | Apr |
| Reuters | 1250 | 167 | 221½ | 275½ | 99½ | 148 | 185½ |
| (*1295) | 1300 | 133½ | 197½ | 254 | 125½ | 171 | 212½ |
| Royal Bk Scot | 1019 | 94 | 130½ | - | 50½ | 73 | - |
| (*1059) | 1065 | 71½ | 108½ | - | 73½ | 96 | - |
| Royal/Sun Al | 390 | 43½ | 57½ | 66½ | 21½ | 31 | 44 |
| (*414½) | 420 | 28 | 43½ | 52 | 37 | 46½ | 59½ |
| Safeway | 260 | 24½ | 33 | 43½ | 12½ | 20 | 27½ |
| (*269) | 280 | 16 | 22½ | 34½ | 22½ | 30 | 37½ |
| Sainsbury | 300 | 34 | 43½ | 52½ | 15 | 23½ | 29½ |
| (*315) | 330 | 16½ | 28 | 36½ | 30½ | 39½ | 44½ |
| Sema | 1050 | 133½ | 186 | 221 | 102½ | 141 | 163½ |
| (*1068½) | 1100 | 111 | 164 | 190½ | 129½ | 168 | 191 |
| Shell Trans | 500 | 46½ | 62½ | 73½ | 19 | 28½ | 36½ |
| (*525) | 550 | 21½ | 38 | 48 | 45½ | 55 | 62 |
| SmKl Bchm | 800 | 70 | 98 | 117½ | 38½ | 58½ | 71 |
| (*824) | 850 | 45½ | 73 | 94 | 64 | 82½ | 97½ |
| Std Chartd | 900 | 88½ | 126½ | 147½ | 50½ | 76 | 95½ |
| (*934) | 950 | 64 | 102½ | 122 | 76 | 101½ | 119½ |
| Thames Wtr | 800 | 64 | 89½ | 75½ | 47 | 61 | 57½ |
| (*820) | 850 | 24½ | 49 | 53½ | 78½ | 91 | 87 |
| Vodafone | 300 | 31 | 46½ | 56½ | 23½ | 34½ | 40½ |
| (*304) | 330 | 19 | 33 | 42½ | 41 | 51 | 57 |

| Option | | Calls Aug | Calls Nov | Calls Feb | Puts Aug | Puts Nov | Puts Feb |
|---|---|---|---|---|---|---|---|
| Gallaher | 380 | 15 | 32½ | 48 | 14 | 33 | 44 |
| (*360) | 390 | 5 | 21 | 38 | 34 | 51½ | 62 |
| Hanson | 420 | 29 | 65 | 72½ | 13½ | 35½ | 46½ |
| (*436½) | 460 | 10½ | 37 | 54 | 36 | 57 | 68 |
| Hilton | 220 | 17 | 28 | 37½ | 5 | 17½ | 22½ |
| (*231) | 240 | 7 | 19½ | 28 | 15 | 28 | 33 |
| Impl Tobacco | 650 | 29 | 64½ | 80½ | 20½ | 47½ | 71½ |
| (*656) | 700 | 10 | 42½ | 59½ | 52 | 76 | 101 |
| Invensys | 220 | 19½ | 33 | 41½ | 4½ | 15½ | 23 |
| (*234) | 240 | 8½ | 23½ | 32 | 13½ | 25½ | 33½ |
| Kingfisher | 550 | 22 | 60½ | 70½ | 15½ | 40½ | 53 |
| (*554½) | 600 | 5 | 30 | 49 | 49 | 70½ | 81½ |
| Lasmo | 130 | 6 | 13 | 18 | 6 | 10½ | 14 |
| (*130) | 140 | 2½ | 8½ | 13½ | 12 | 16½ | 19½ |
| Legal & Gen | 160 | 10½ | 16 | 25 | 3½ | 11 | 15 |
| (*166½) | 180 | 2 | 10½ | 16½ | 15 | 22½ | 26 |
| Logica | 1700 | 136½ | 280½ | 309½ | 86½ | 211 | 276½ |
| (*1743) | 1800 | 88 | 230½ | 327½ | 139 | 265½ | 332 |
| Marconi | 1050 | 78 | 149 | 191½ | 34½ | 90 | 122½ |
| (*1088) | 1100 | 50 | 122½ | 160 | 58 | 116½ | 149 |
| P & O | 500 | 38½ | 62 | 67½ | 6½ | 25½ | 35 |
| (*530) | 550 | 12 | 28½ | 44 | 30 | 53 | 61½ |
| Prudential | 950 | 48½ | 88½ | 127½ | 36 | 77 | 100 |
| (*956) | 1000 | 24½ | 68½ | 103½ | 65 | 104½ | 126 |
| Rentokil Intl | 140 | 12½ | 20½ | 24½ | 3 | 10 | 12 |

| Option | | Calls Sep | Calls Dec | Calls Mar | Puts Sep | Puts Dec | Puts Mar |
|---|---|---|---|---|---|---|---|
| CMG | 1100 | 128 | 180½ | 238½ | 70½ | 121 | 155 |
| (*1148) | 1150 | 104½ | 180 | 217 | 96½ | 147½ | 182 |
| Celltech | 1200 | 148½ | 228½ | 283 | 88½ | 149½ | 191½ |
| (*1250) | 1250 | 125½ | 204½ | 262 | 115 | 177 | 219 |
| Centrica | 220 | 20½ | 31 | 39 | 11 | 19 | 24 |
| (*227½) | 240 | 11½ | 21½ | 29½ | 22 | 29½ | 34½ |
| Colt Tel | 2400 | 298 | 390½ | 508 | 205½ | 316 | 395 |
| (*2430) | 2500 | 210 | 365 | 486½ | 258½ | 370½ | 450½ |
| Dixons | 263 | 31 | - | - | 19½ | - | - |
| (*275½) | 276 | 24½ | - | - | 28½ | - | - |
| EMI | 600 | 68½ | 85 | 108 | 35 | 57½ | 74½ |
| (*625½) | 650 | 33 | 62 | 83½ | 63 | 84½ | 101 |
| Energis | 580 | 63½ | 97½ | 120½ | 48½ | 74½ | 90½ |
| (*590) | 600 | 54 | 88½ | 112 | 59 | 85½ | 101½ |
| Freeserve | 300 | 48 | 64½ | 73 | 24½ | 39 | 43½ |
| (*319) | 330 | 32 | 51½ | 60½ | 40½ | 55½ | 60 |
| Granada | 796 | 60½ | 95½ | 118 | 51 | 76 | 92 |
| (*790) | 862 | 33½ | 67 | 80 | 91 | 113½ | 129 |
| Granada Media | 600 | 45½ | 71½ | 92½ | 40½ | 58 | 71½ |
| (*600) | 650 | 28 | 50 | 70½ | 70½ | 87 | 99½ |
| GUS | 420 | 20½ | 40½ | 49½ | 27 | 40½ | 49½ |
| (*424½) | 480 | 8½ | 25½ | 36 | 55½ | 60 | 74½ |
| LloydsTSB | 600 | 37½ | 63 | 79 | 37 | 54 | 74½ |
| (*603) | 650 | 14½ | 44 | 58 | 68½ | 85½ | 104½ |
| Option | | Sep | Jan | Apr | Sep | Jan | Apr |
| Lonmin | 800 | 98½ | 98 | 166½ | 23½ | 49 | 61½ |
| (*820) | 850 | 28½ | 65 | 80 | 49½ | 74 | 85½ |

## TABLE 21.3: Call premium on BA: 27th July 2000

| | Expiry month | | |
| --- | --- | --- | --- |
| **Strike price $K$** | October | January | April |
| **360p** | $36\frac{1}{2}(16/20\frac{1}{2})$ | $50(16/34)$ | $57\frac{1}{2}(16/41\frac{1}{2})$ |
| **390p** | $21\frac{1}{2}(0/21\frac{1}{2})$ | $35\frac{1}{2}(0/35\frac{1}{2})$ | $44(0/44)$ |

Current share price $S = 376$p

Note: Prices denoted in pence. (./.) gives (intrinsic/time value)
Source: *Financial Times*, 27th July 2000

$$\textit{For long calls:} \quad \textbf{Intrinsic value} = \max[S - K, 0]$$
$$\textbf{Time value} = C - \max[S - K, 0]$$

Note that with an American option you can exercise at any time. However, if you exercise the option you only receive the intrinsic value. If you *trade* the option by selling your existing long position then you receive the market price, which is the sum of the intrinsic and time values. Hence, for a plain vanilla American *call* you will always *trade* the option rather than exercise it. (Note, however, that the latter result does not apply to all types of American options.)

Let us briefly return to Figure 21.5 above. As the option approaches maturity the current value of the call, which is represented by the curved line A–B, 'collapses' on to the 'kinked line' that shows the payoff at maturity. The intrinsic value $\max[S_t - K, 0]$ at stock price $S_t$ is the distance CD in Figure 21.5. The quoted call premium for stock price $S_t$ is $C_t$, and therefore the time value of the option is ($C_t$ − intrinsic value), that is the distance BC. The longer the time to maturity of an option the higher the call premium (for any given stock price) and the higher is the curved line at B. This would also imply a higher time value (i.e. the distance BC would be greater). It is also worth noting at this point that the time value BC falls rather slowly at first, but very sharply when the option is just a few weeks from expiry.

## NEWSPAPER QUOTES: BRITISH AIRWAYS PUTS

Let us undertake a similar analysis for the BA puts in Table 21.4. The BA-390 puts must be worth at least 14p as the long put could buy the shares spot for $S = 376$p and sell them immediately for $K = 390$p by exercising the long put. The BA-360 puts have no intrinsic value.

The BA-390 puts have intrinsic value of 14p, but the BA-390 October put premium is 31p. The time value is therefore 17p ($= 31$p $-$ 14p). This reflects the possibility that between the

## TABLE 21.4: Put premium on BA: 27th July 2000

|  | Expiry month | | |
|---|---|---|---|
| Strike price $K$ | October | January | April |
| 360p | 16 (0/16) | 25 (0/25) | $27\frac{1}{2}(0/27\frac{1}{2})$ |
| 390p | 31 (14/17) | 40 (14/26) | $43\frac{1}{2}(14/29\frac{1}{2})$ |

Current share price $S = 376$p

Note: Prices denoted in pence. (./.) gives (intrinsic/time value)
Source: *Financial Times*, 27th July 2000

27th July and the October settlement, the spot price of BA might fall, thus increasing the value of the put option with a right to sell at a strike price of $K = 390$.

> *For long puts*:  **Intrinsic value** $= \max[K - S, 0]$
> **Time value** $= C - \max[K - S, 0]$

Again put premia (and intrinsic values) increase as the time to expiry increases (look along the rows in Table 21.4), since there is an increased chance that the spot price will be below the strike price over a longer horizon.

### In/out-of-the-money

Note that the 360 calls (Table 21.3) are in-the-money ($S - K > 0$) while the 390 calls are out-of-the-money. Hence the 360 calls have relatively high intrinsic values and relatively low time values. The converse applies for the 390 calls, which are out-of-the-money and hence have zero intrinsic value and relatively high time values. Similar considerations apply to the puts.

# 21.3 ORGANISATION OF OPTIONS MARKETS

Options are traded on individual stocks, stock indices, foreign currencies, futures contracts and to a much lesser extent on Treasury notes and Treasury bonds. The major exchanges are the Chicago Board Options Exchange (CBOE), New York Stock Exchange (NYSE), the Philadelphia Stock Exchange (PHLX), the Pacific Stock Exchange (PSE in San Francisco), the London International Financial Futures and Options Exchange (LIFFE) and EUREX in Frankfurt. The CBOE was established in 1973, initially trading stock options. It is the largest organised options market trading standardised contracts and has a deep secondary market.

The **over-the-counter** (OTC) options market tailors the option contract to the buyer's specifications and is now very large and probably over 10 times larger than the traded options market, although often the secondary OTC market is thin. However, active secondary OTC markets do exist, particularly the interbank market in European options on foreign exchange negotiated for commercial customers. The advantage of OTC markets can be illustrated by considering a portfolio manager who wishes to hedge her particular portfolio of stocks (which we assume does not match any available stock index on which options are available) by buying a put option (often known as a *basket option*).

---

### ADVANTAGES OF 'INSURANCE' USING AN OTC PUT OPTION

- To exactly match her portfolio composition with the underlying in the tailor made OTC put option.
- The expiry date of the put can be tailored to her investment horizon.
- To maintain anonymity, so that the fact that she believes the market will fall is not communicated to other traders.
- Also, new options contracts do not need the approval of regulatory authorities.
- However, drawbacks to using the OTC market are possibly higher transactions costs and credit counterparty risk.

---

There are about 100 stocks on LIFFE (UK) and about 500 stocks on the CBOT (US) on which options are traded. We will take the example of US stock options to illustrate some of the administrative procedures which operate in this market.

## US STOCK OPTIONS

### CONTRACT SIZES
Options on individual stocks are usually for 'delivery' of 100 stocks. Contract sizes for other options usually involve a contract multiple. For example, for the S&P500, the multiple is $100 times the index.

### EXPIRY DATES
These are fixed by the exchange and options are traded for expiration up to 4.30 p.m. (Central Time) on the third Friday of the expiry month. Some index options expire on the last day of each quarter.

Expiry dates for options on individual stocks usually extend to about 9 months, but with some exceptions. For example, *LEAPS (long-term equity anticipation shares)*, which are primarily options on individual stocks (but some are also on stock indices) have expiration dates of up to 3 years ahead. Similarly, *FLEX options* on stock indices can have any expiration date up to 5 years and in addition they permit the purchaser to set any exercise price.

### STRIKE/EXERCISE PRICES
These, for example, might be set at a $2.50 spacing when the underlying stock price is less than $25, a $5 spacing when the stock price is between $25 and $200, and at $10 intervals

for a stock price over $200. Strike prices are set either side of the current stock price and as the stock price moves up or down, new strike prices are added.

## TRADING

An individual who has purchased (or rents) a seat on the CBOE can be either a market maker or a floor broker or both (but not on the same day!). The latter is known as **dual trading**. The **market maker** must stand ready to quote both bid and ask prices on the option. The 'bid' price is the price the market maker is prepared to buy and the 'ask' price is the price at which he is prepared to sell. Market makers must stand ready to trade with investors. An investor who has purchased an option can close out her position by selling (writing) the same option. If investors as a whole are not offsetting existing positions, then the number of contracts (i.e. the 'open interest') increases by one.

**Floor brokers** who have a seat on the exchange merely buy and sell options on behalf of their customers and usually earn a commission on each trade. They do not hold a book and they are not obliged to 'make a market' in the options. There appears to be an accelerating trend away from 'open outcry' in derivatives markets towards screen based trading, as well as increased use of computers for matching buyers and sellers and in settling trades.

## OPTIONS CLEARING CORPORATION

For US options markets (except those trading futures options) the Options Clearing Corporation (OCC) standardises contracts and acts as an intermediary, effectively creating two separate contracts. For example, if a trader buys a call option the OCC guarantees that the writer will honour the contract. An option *writer* represents a credit risk to the OCC since she may not have funds to purchase the underlying in the spot market to effect delivery. The OCC therefore requires the writer to post a margin payment (usually in cash and equal to at least 30% of the value of the stocks underlying the option plus the call premium). There is also a maintenance margin which might be set at a minimum of 15–25% of the value of the stocks underlying the option. An option *buyer* has no margin requirement with the OCC since the most she can lose is the option premium, which is paid at the outset of the contract.

Initial margins vary depending on whether one has a naked position (i.e. no offsetting holding in the underlying stocks) or a covered/hedged position. The latter is less risky and involves less initial margin.

## OFFSETTING ORDER

If you originally purchased a call option on a stock at $4.10 at a cost of $410 then you can sell the contract by placing an **offsetting order**. If the price is now $4.50 and your broker finds a purchaser at this price then $450 will be passed to your clearing firm ABC (and then on to you) and the OCC will cancel your position in this contract. The purchaser will generally not be the person from whom you initially purchased the contract, but if she initially had a short position then the open interest will fall by one. About 55% of stock option contracts are closed in this manner.

## EXERCISING AN OPTION

If the buyer of the call exercises the option then your broker notifies the clearing firm (XYZ) through which the original trade was cleared. XYZ then places an exercise order with the OCC who **'assigns'** a trader who has written a similar contract. (This may be a random

**FIGURE 21.7: Newspaper quotes (*Wall Street Journal*). Reproduced with permission**

| Option | Strike | Exp. | -Call- Vol. | -Call- 3 pm | -Put- Vol. | -Put- 3pm |
|---|---|---|---|---|---|---|
| ADC Tel | 45 | Aug | 903 | 5 | 604 | 2 1/4 |
| 46 3/4 | 50 | Aug | 532 | 2 1/2 | 27 | 4 5/8 |
| ATT Wrls | 30 | Aug | 715 | 1 1/8 | ... | ... |
| 29 | 30 | Sep | 3132 | 2 | ... | ... |
| AT&T | 30 | Aug | 436 | 3 | 989 | 9/16 |
| 32 5/8 | 35 | Aug | 6538 | 9/16 | 619 | 3 |
| 32 5/8 | 40 | Aug | 737 | 1/16 | 43 | 7 1/4 |
| Abgenix | 60 | Aug | 713 | 6 | 2 | 11 7/8 |
| A M D | 65 | Aug | 64 | 11 3/4 | 527 | 2 1/8 |
| 74 3/8 | 70 | Aug | 1273 | 8 1/2 | 273 | 3 1/2 |
| 74 3/8 | 80 | Aug | 918 | 3 7/8 | 352 | 8 1/4 |
| 74 3/8 | 80 | Sep | 623 | 6 1/2 | 10 | 11 5/8 |
| 74 3/8 | 85 | Aug | 930 | 2 3/4 | 25 | 12 5/8 |
| 74 3/8 | 90 | Aug | 663 | 1 5/8 | 75 | 17 1/8 |
| 74 3/8 | 95 | Aug | 1308 | 1 | 22 | 20 3/4 |
| 74 3/8 | 100 | Sep | 4821 | 1 7/8 | ... | ... |
| 74 3/8 | 105 | Aug | 609 | 1/4 | 8 | 30 1/4 |
| Aetna | 50 | Jan | ... | ... | 1780 | 2 |
| 54 9/16 | 60 | Oct | ... | ... | 500 | 7 1/8 |
| 54 9/16 | 60 | Jan | 1759 | 3 | ... | ... |
| Affymet | 170 | Aug | 511 | 9 | 2 | 24 1/4 |
| Alcoa | 30 | Aug | 1277 | 1 13/16 | 65 | 15/16 |
| 31 | 35 | Aug | 506 | 1/8 | ... | ... |
| Alergn | 70 | Aug | 1275 | 4 | 70 | 1 3/4 |
| Allstte | 22 1/2 | Aug | 752 | 4 | 10 | 3/16 |
| 26 3/4 | 25 | Aug | 510 | 2 1/2 | 55 | 1/2 |
| 26 3/4 | 27 1/2 | Aug | 690 | 1 1/8 | 10 | 1 3/8 |
| Alteon | 135 | Sep | 1 | 29 7/8 | 500 | 14 1/2 |
| Altera | 110 | Aug | 496 | 4 1/4 | 3 | 14 |
| Alza | 55 | Aug | 490 | 8 1/8 | 45 | 7/8 |
| 61 1/4 | 60 | Aug | 625 | 4 3/8 | 31 | 2 3/16 |
| Amazon | 40 | Aug | 1675 | 2 1/4 | 447 | 7 |
| 34 1/4 | 45 | Aug | 4273 | 1 1/8 | 263 | 11 1/4 |
| 34 1/4 | 50 | Aug | 803 | 9/16 | 10 | 15 |
| AmOnline | 45 | Oct | 22 | 11 1/8 | 429 | 1 7/16 |
| 53 11/16 | 47 1/2 | Oct | 50 | 9 | 709 | 2 1/8 |
| 53 11/16 | 50 | Aug | 799 | 5 1/8 | 573 | 15/16 |
| 53 11/16 | 50 | Oct | 33 | 7 3/8 | 565 | 3 |
| 53 11/16 | 55 | Aug | 2093 | 2 1/8 | 1331 | 3 |
| 53 11/16 | 55 | Sep | 464 | 3 1/2 | 78 | 4 1/8 |
| 53 11/16 | 55 | Oct | 370 | 4 3/4 | 9828 | 5 1/4 |
| 53 11/16 | 60 | Aug | 2089 | 11/16 | 185 | 6 3/4 |
| 53 11/16 | 60 | Sep | 482 | 1 5/8 | 95 | 7 3/8 |
| 53 11/16 | 60 | Oct | 642 | 3 | 107 | 8 1/4 |
| 53 11/16 | 60 | Jan | 1948 | 5 3/8 | 149 | 10 1/8 |
| 53 11/16 | 65 | Aug | 1337 | 1/4 | 5 | 11 1/8 |
| 53 11/16 | 65 | Oct | 450 | 1 3/4 | 11 | 12 |
| 53 11/16 | 65 | Jan | 438 | 4 | 10 | 13 1/8 |

| Option | Strike | Exp. | -Call- Vol. | -Call- 3 pm | -Put- Vol. | -Put- 3pm |
|---|---|---|---|---|---|---|
| Finova | 15 | Aug | 1294 | 13/16 | 704 | 3 7/8 |
| 12 5/8 | 17 1/2 | Aug | 518 | 5/8 | 30 | 4 1/2 |
| Flextrn | 85 | Aug | 829 | 4 1/4 | 13 | 7 3/4 |
| Gap | 40 | Aug | 460 | 11/16 | 10 | 4 1/2 |
| Gemstar-TV | 50 | Aug | 1501 | 12 | 254 | 2 1/16 |
| 60 5/8 | 60 | Aug | 3117 | 7 | 13 | 5 7/8 |
| 60 5/8 | 70 | Aug | 461 | 3 1/2 | ... | ... |
| Gen El | 50 | Aug | 138 | 3 5/8 | 1049 | 5/8 |
| 52 15/16 | 50 | Dec | ... | ... | 861 | 2 5/16 |
| 52 15/16 | 55 | Aug | 726 | 3/4 | 5284 | 2 11/16 |
| GnMills | 35 | Oct | ... | ... | 2020 | 1 5/8 |
| GenMotr | 60 | Aug | 1181 | 1 3/8 | 105 | 3 1/4 |
| 58 1/4 | 65 | Aug | 1023 | 1/4 | 100 | 7 1/2 |
| GaPcGP | 35 | Oct | 550 | 7/16 | ... | ... |
| Gillet | 30 | Sep | 505 | 2 | 12 | 1 5/8 |
| GlblCrss | 25 | Aug | 535 | 4 1/4 | 65 | 7/8 |
| 27 15/16 | 30 | Aug | 696 | 1 5/8 | 12 | 3 1/8 |
| Globalstr | 7 1/2 | Aug | 338 | 15/16 | 428 | 1 1/16 |
| GuilfrdPh | 17 1/2 | Sep | ... | ... | 520 | 1 3/4 |
| Halbtn | 45 | Aug | 3384 | 1 11/16 | 10 | 3 |
| HlthMgt | 17 1/2 | Aug | ... | ... | 590 | 2 3/4 |
| Hewlet o | 110 | Aug | 4492 | 8 1/8 | 903 | 5 1/2 |
| 109 13/16 | 115 | Aug | 1367 | 5 7/8 | 79 | 9 1/2 |
| BigEnt | 15 | Nov | 600 | 13/16 | ... | ... |
| HomeDp | 55 | Aug | 557 | 2 | 282 | 2 1/8 |
| 54 3/4 | 60 | Aug | 535 | 1/2 | 118 | 5 5/8 |
| IDTCorp | 25 | Sep | ... | ... | 620 | 3/8 |
| IbisTech | 40 | Aug | 504 | 5 1/8 | 335 | 4 1/8 |
| Imclne | 90 | Aug | 854 | 1 1/2 | ... | ... |
| Immunex | 50 | Sep | 111 | 9 1/8 | 2194 | 5 1/8 |
| 52 7/16 | 55 | Aug | 1618 | 4 7/8 | 24 | 6 3/8 |
| InfinityB | 30 | Aug | 500 | 5 5/8 | ... | ... |
| Infocure | 7 1/2 | Aug | 605 | 1/8 | ... | ... |
| InfoSpce | 50 | Aug | 553 | 5 3/8 | 6 | 8 3/4 |
| Insight | 45 | Aug | 58 | 5 1/8 | 1050 | 2 7/8 |
| IntgDv | 65 | Aug | 446 | 5 1/4 | 180 | 5 5/8 |
| 63 31/64 | 70 | Aug | 479 | 3 1/8 | 1028 | 9 3/4 |
| Intel | 115 | Aug | 1002 | 24 3/4 | 45 | 7/16 |
| 137 7/16 | 120 | Aug | ... | ... | 650 | 3/4 |
| 137 7/16 | 120 | Sep | 2 | 21 3/8 | 1054 | 2 7/16 |
| 137 7/16 | 125 | Aug | 2128 | 16 | 292 | 1 1/4 |
| 137 7/16 | 130 | Aug | 111 | 12 3/4 | 586 | 2 3/16 |
| 137 7/16 | 135 | Aug | 699 | 9 1/8 | 659 | 3 7/8 |
| 137 7/16 | 140 | Aug | 2269 | 5 1/2 | 1459 | 5 3/8 |
| 137 7/16 | 145 | Aug | 1442 | 3 1/2 | 64 | 10 |
| 137 7/16 | 155 | Oct | 453 | 5 7/8 | ... | ... |
| 137 7/16 | 170 | Sep | 806 | 7/8 | ... | ... |
| 137 7/16 | 200 | Jan | 1068 | 2 3/8 | ... | ... |

| Option | Strike | Exp. | -Call- Vol. | -Call- 3 pm | -Put- Vol. | -Put- 3pm |
|---|---|---|---|---|---|---|
| Nike | 60 | Jan | 1464 | 3 | ... | ... |
| NokiaA | 50 | Oct | 27 | 9 7/8 | 547 | 3 |
| 55 9/16 | 55 | Aug | 1135 | 3 7/8 | 676 | 3 |
| 55 9/16 | 60 | Aug | 1552 | 1 3/4 | 837 | 6 |
| NortelNwk | 70 | Aug | 182 | 15 1/4 | 1087 | 11/16 |
| 83 7/8 | 72 1/2 | Sep | 543 | 14 1/4 | ... | ... |
| 83 7/8 | 75 | Aug | 1565 | 11 1/2 | 313 | 1 3/16 |
| 83 7/8 | 75 | Sep | 2717 | 12 3/4 | 327 | 2 11/16 |
| 83 7/8 | 80 | Aug | 769 | 7 5/8 | 644 | 2 1/2 |
| 83 7/8 | 85 | Aug | 1788 | 4 3/4 | 384 | 4 3/8 |
| 83 7/8 | 85 | Sep | 1590 | 6 3/4 | 84 | 6 3/8 |
| NoStPw | 22 1/2 | Dec | 750 | 1 9/16 | ... | ... |
| Novlus | 70 | Aug | 57 | 1/2 | 510 | 17 |
| Oracle | 70 | Aug | 9116 | 9 1/4 | 632 | 1 9/16 |
| 75 1/2 | 75 | Aug | 628 | 5 7/8 | 665 | 3 1/8 |
| 75 1/2 | 80 | Aug | 2641 | 3 1/8 | 31 | 6 3/8 |
| 75 1/2 | 85 | Aug | 1696 | 1 1/4 | 19 | 10 |
| 75 1/2 | 100 | Mar | 470 | 6 1/2 | ... | ... |
| OxfdHl | 22 1/2 | Aug | 220 | 2 1/16 | 435 | 1 7/8 |
| 23 1/16 | 25 | Aug | 1490 | 1 1/4 | 210 | 2 1/8 |
| PMC Srra | 170 | Aug | ... | ... | 1004 | 6 1/4 |
| Palm | 25 | Aug | 3 | 10 1/4 | 419 | 3/8 |
| 35 1/8 | 30 | Aug | 899 | 6 7/8 | 785 | 1 1/8 |
| 35 1/8 | 30 | Nov | 2236 | 9 | 20 | 3 |
| 35 1/8 | 35 | Aug | 922 | 3 3/4 | 454 | 2 3/4 |
| 35 1/8 | 40 | Aug | 1128 | 1 5/8 | 121 | 6 1/8 |
| 35 1/8 | 50 | Aug | 459 | 3/8 | 453 | 15 3/8 |
| ParmTc | 10 | Aug | 189 | 1 | 1495 | 7/8 |
| PepsiCo | 45 | Sep | 1035 | 1 15/16 | 1000 | 2 5/16 |
| Pfizer | 45 | Aug | 1530 | 1 3/16 | 320 | 2 1/8 |
| 44 1/2 | 47 1/2 | Aug | 3036 | 1/2 | 10 | 3 1/4 |
| Ph Mor | 25 | Aug | 66 | 1 9/16 | 661 | 13/16 |
| ProtDg | 160 | Aug | 953 | 10 | ... | ... |
| Qualcom | 60 | Aug | 328 | 10 1/4 | 895 | 1 1/2 |
| 68 1/4 | 65 | Aug | 862 | 7 1/4 | 578 | 3 1/4 |
| 68 1/4 | 70 | Aug | 8568 | 4 3/4 | 281 | 5 3/8 |
| 68 1/4 | 75 | Aug | 2109 | 2 11/16 | 22 | 9 7/8 |
| 68 1/4 | 80 | Aug | 934 | 1 1/2 | 13 | 12 7/8 |
| QtmHDD | 10 | Nov | 901 | 1 3/8 | 12 | 2 1/2 |
| RJReyn | 25 | Aug | ... | ... | 1900 | 1/2 |
| Rambus | 60 | Aug | 799 | 18 1/4 | 259 | 2 3/8 |
| 73 11/16 | 70 | Aug | 450 | 11 5/8 | 686 | 6 |
| 73 11/16 | 75 | Aug | 541 | 7 5/8 | 323 | 8 3/8 |
| 73 11/16 | 80 | Aug | 597 | 6 | 370 | 10 3/4 |
| 73 11/16 | 90 | Aug | 536 | 3 5/8 | 403 | 17 1/4 |
| 73 11/16 | 100 | Aug | 763 | 2 | 27 | 26 7/8 |
| 73 11/16 | 115 | Aug | 509 | 7/8 | 3 | 41 |

assignment or a first-in, first-out rule may be used.) Roughly speaking about 10% of calls and puts on the CBOE are exercised and about 30–40% expire out-of-the money.

## NEWSPAPER QUOTES

We have already considered most of the information in newspaper quotes when considering the option quotes for British Airways in the *Financial Times*. Quotes in the *Wall Street Journal* follow a similar pattern and an extract is given in Figure 21.7. Consider the options on *Intel* for the CBOT as quoted in the *Wall Street Journal* (Europe) for 27th July. All prices refer to the previous day (i.e. 26th July). The left-hand column contains only the number 137–7/16 which is the current stock price. The strike prices in the second column are set (by the exchange) above and below the current price. The expiry dates are in the third column. The last four columns show the volume traded as well as the option premium for calls and puts, respectively (for the 3 p.m. trade). Note that the quoted option price for the '3 p.m. trade' might not coincide with the time of recorded price for the underlying stock, especially if the option is rather illiquid and hence infrequently traded. The letter 'r' or a zero entry '. . .' indicates the option was not traded on 26th July.

From Figure 21.7 you can see that the closing price (on NASDAQ) for Intel is $137\frac{1}{2}$ and the alternative exercise (strike) prices range from 115 to 200. The call prices (premiums) are given in the fifth columns for the expiration months August, September, October and January. The quoted option premium is to buy or sell one share (but 100 shares must be purchased for each contract, so the contract price = '100 × quoted price').

By looking at the August contracts (Figure 21.7) with strike prices $K = 125, 130, 135, 140$ you can see that the call premia fall as the strike price increases. The converse applies to the put premia which are positively related to the strike price. By looking at the 120-August and 120-September put contracts you can see that the put premia increase with the time to maturity of the contract. These observations are of course consistent with the Black–Scholes formula for option premia (see Cuthbertson and Nitzsche, 2001) and with our earlier intuitive arguments.

# 21.4 HEDGING USING STOCK INDEX OPTIONS

Stock index options (SIO) are frequently used to hedge the systematic (market) risk of a *diversified portfolio* of shares. A fund manager using index options is therefore hedging the market risk but leaving the portfolio exposed to specific risk, presumably on the grounds that she is a good 'stock picker' (i.e. she can identify those stocks which will perform well relative to others in the same risk class). To understand the hedging process we need to consider the contract specifications of index options and we focus on the S&P100 (American style) contract. The S&P100 index option is often referred to by its ticker symbol, OEX and it is the most actively traded option on CBOE.

SIO are settled in cash. If $z is the value of one index point and the current index level is $S$, then the face value of (stocks underlying) one index option contract is given by FVO = $zS$. For the S&P100 index option, $z = \$100$. Hence, if the index $S_0 = 200$, the contract has a face value FVO = $zS_0 = \$20,000$. Put slightly differently, if FVO = $20,000$ then one SIO option contract relates to a $20,000 position in an underlying portfolio of shares which mimics the S&P100. Call and put premia are also quoted in terms of index points.

Suppose you hold a stock portfolio with total value $TVS_0 = \$400,000$, whose composition mirrors the S&P100 (i.e. your portfolio has $\beta = 1$) and you fear a price fall in the future. You could limit the downside risk by purchasing puts. This is a **protective put**. If the S&P100 index currently stands at $S_0 = 200$, then the whole index is worth $20,000 ($= zS_0 = \$100 \times 200$) and hence it looks as if you should purchase $N_p = \$400,000/\$20,000 = 20$ put contracts. This is correct:

$$N_p = \frac{\text{total value of (spot) portfolio}}{\text{value of index point} \times S_0} = \frac{TVS_0}{zS_0} = \frac{TVS_0}{FVO} = 20$$

Assume the strike price chosen is $K = 200$ (i.e. it is an at-the-money put). If the index falls 20% to $S_T = 160$, then the value of your stock portfolio falls by $80,000. But if you exercise the put (at expiry) you make a profit of 40 points ($= 200 - 160$) per contract, which with 20 contracts gives you a payoff of $80,000 ($= 20$ contracts $\times 40$ points $\times \$100$ per point). Here, the loss on the stock portfolio is exactly offset by the gain on the puts. However, there is the put premium to consider. Suppose the put premium paid was $P = 5$ index points, the 20 put contracts would have cost $10,000 ($= 20 \times \$100 \times 5$ points). Without the puts you would have lost $80,000, with the puts you only lose the put premium of $4000, you have therefore 'insured' most of the portfolio's value.

The put premium paid is like a 'deductible' ('excess') in a normal insurance policy. Of course if the S&P index rose, the put would expire worthless and we would not exercise. But the value of our stock portfolio would have risen and the only loss is from payment of the put premium, for our 'insurance'—which in this case was not needed. All of the options described below can be used to 'insure' a position you hold in the cash market (e.g. bonds, interest rates, etc.).

## 21.5 OTHER OPTIONS

Options can be written on individual stocks, stock indices, currencies, futures contracts, the price of interest bearing assets (e.g. T-bonds) and interest rates (e.g. caps and floors). There is a very large OTC market in options and some options are only available OTC (e.g. for caps and floors).

Simplifying a little, a **caplet** is a call option which pays off max $[r_T - K_{cap}, 0]$ where $r_T$ is the interest rate at the expiration of the option contract and $K_{cap}$ is the strike (interest) rate. Clearly a caplet can be used to speculate on a future rise in interest rates. However, let us consider how it can be used to insure you against interest rate rises. Suppose in January interest rates are currently at 10%. You decide to purchase a caplet with $K_{cap} = 10\%$ which expires in March. Then in March, if interest rates turn out to be 12%, the caplet payoff is 2%. The cap contract also includes a notional principal amount of say $1m and hence the payoff would be $20,000. If in January you know you will be taking out a loan of $1m in March and you are worried that interest rates will rise, then you could 'lock in' a maximum rate of $K_{cap} = 10\%$ by buying the caplet. In March if $r_T = 12\%$ then your loan costs you 2% more as interest rates have risen, but the caplet provides a cash payoff of 2% to compensate for this higher cost. But things can get even better. If in March interest rates have fallen to 8% then you can just 'walk away' (i.e. not exercise) the caplet and simply borrow at the current low spot rate of 8%. Hence, once again options allow you to insure yourself against adverse outcomes (i.e. high interest rates) but allow you to benefit from any 'upside' (i.e. low interest rates). For this privilege you pay a caplet premium 'up front' (i.e. in January).

If your loan has a number of reset dates for the interest rate payable (i.e. it is a floating rate loan) then you can insure your loan costs by buying a series of caplets, each with an expiry date which matches the reset dates on you loan. **A set of caplets is a cap**. Financial institutions will 'design' and sell you a cap in the OTC market. (Caps are not traded on an exchange.)

A **floorlet** has a payoff equal to max $[K_{fl} - r_T, 0]$ and is therefore a long put on interest rates. Clearly, if you are a speculator and you think interest rates are going to fall below $K_{fl}$ in 3 months time, then you can make a profit if you are long the floorlet. Alternatively, if you are going to place money on deposit in say 3 months time and you are worried that interest rates will fall, then a long floorlet will ensure that the minimum you earn on your deposits will be $K_{fl} = 8\%$ say. If interest rates turn out to be $r_T = 7\%$ in 3 months time, you exercise the floorlet and earn a profit of 1%, which when added to the interest on your deposit of $r_T = 7\%$ implies your overall return is 8%. If interest rates turn out to be 9% say, then you would not exercise the floorlet (since it is out-of-the-money) but simply lend your money at the current interest rate of 9%. A **floor** is a series of floorlets, with different maturity dates, and can be used to insure your investment in the deposit account where interest rates on the latter are reset periodically (e.g. every 6 months).

Finally, the combination of a long cap with $K_{cap} = 10\%$ and a long floor with $K_{fl} = 8\%$ is known as a **collar**. This is because if you already have a floating rate loan and you also purchase a collar, the *effective* interest rate payable on the loan cannot go above 10% or fall below 8%—so the effective interest payable is constrained at an upper and lower level.

There is no end to the number of types of option that can be offered in the OTC market, and those with complex payoffs are know as **exotic options**. For example, Asian options have a payoff which is based on the average price over the life of the option. An **Asian (average price) call** option has a payoff which depends on max $[S_{av} - K, 0]$ where $S_{av}$ is the average price over the life of the option. So, an Asian average price *currency* option would be useful for a firm that wants to hedge the average level of its future sales in a foreign currency. The firm's foreign currency monthly sales may fluctuate over the year, so an Asian option is a cheap way to hedge, rather than purchasing options for each of the prospective monthly cash flows.

Other types of exotic options are **barrier options**. These may either expire or come into existence before expiration. For example, in a **knockout option** the option contract may specify that if the stock price rises or falls to the 'barrier level', the option will terminate on that date, and hence cannot be exercised. If options are terminated when the stock price falls to the barrier, then they are referred to as **down-and-out options**, while if they are terminated when the price rises to the barrier, they are **up-and-out options**. These options pay off at maturity just the same as ordinary options, *unless they have already been knocked out.*

As we noted as long ago as Chapter 1, there are also options which are 'embedded' in other securities, and examples of **embedded options** include rights issues, callable bonds, convertible bonds, warrants and executive stock options and share underwriting. (The latter involves the underwriter agreeing to purchase any shares which are not taken up by the public, at an agreed minimum price. The agreed minimum price is equivalent to the strike price in a put contract and the underwriting fee is the put premium. The corporate is long the put and the underwriter has written the put.)

In earlier chapters we spent some considerable time in discussing real investment decisions using the NPV criterion. The latter usually involved an 'all or nothing' decision based on whether the NPV was positive. However, what that analysis lacked was the ability to incorporate the strategic opportunities which *might arise* in the future from a particular real investment project. For example, if you undertake an NPV calculation as to whether you should enter the 'dot.com' sector, based on a forecast of 'average growth', you may find that the NPV is negative. However, entering this sector may provide you with golden opportunities *at some time in the future* (e.g. a global market) which would not be available if you did not undertake your current negative NPV investment. In other words, if you do not invest today the 'lost expertise and knowledge' may imply that it is too late (and prohibitively costly) to enter this market in say 5 years time. Your initial investment therefore has an **'embedded strategic call option'** to expand in the future, should the market show rapid growth. Call options are more valuable when there is greater uncertainty about the future. In fact the 'adjusted' NPV of your project is:

[21.3]     Adjusted NPV = conventional NPV + value of the option to expand

When the premium of the embedded option is added to the conventional NPV then the overall 'adjusted NPV' may be positive, indicating that you should go ahead with the project because of its strategic importance in establishing you in a market which could be very large. Similarly, a firm could either start its investment in plant and machinery today and face uncertain sales, or it could **defer the project** for 18 months by which time the economy *may* have improved. The manager holds the **option to defer**, which is valuable when uncertainty about future revenues is high.

**Real options theory** is an application of option pricing to corporate finance and is used to quantify the value of managerial flexibility—the value of being able to commit to or amend a decision. This is a relatively new and complex area of options theory, but one that could aid managers in making strategic investment decisions.

## 21.6 SUMMARY

The key points made in this chapter are the following.

> • **A long call allows upside gains** to be made as the price of the underlying asset rises (above the strike price), but **limits the downside losses** to the call premium. For a speculator, it provides a $\{0, +1\}$ payoff profile at maturity (which is clearly asymmetric).

- **A long** put provides a positive payoff at maturity if the underlying asset price falls (below the strike price). This is a negative relationship. If the stock price at maturity is above the strike price then the option expires worthless, but the downside loss is limited to the put premium. The payoff profile for the speculator is of the $\{-1, 0\}$ variety.

- In contrast to a long position in either a call or a put, a short position in these options exposes the writer to high levels of risk. A **written (short) call** gives **unlimited downside risk** should the stock price rise, while a **written (short) put** provides **large downside risk** should the price of the underlying asset fall towards zero.

- **Long calls and long puts** can also be used to hedge, or more accurately to **provide a form of insurance**. Suppose you are planning to purchase a stock in the future. Then a **long call** ensures you have the right to purchase the stock in the future, at the known strike price agreed today. If the stock price should fall in the future then you can 'walk away' from the contract (i.e. not exercise the call) and purchase the stocks in the spot market at their current low price.

- **If you already hold stocks then a long put can provide insurance** in the form of a lower bound on the future selling price of the stocks. But it also allows you to 'not exercise' the put, if at expiry the stocks can be sold in the spot market at a higher price.

- **The call (or put) premium** comprise the **intrinsic value** of the option, which is the profit to be made on immediate exercise. But option premia also incorporate **time value**, which reflects the fact that the option may eventually end up in-the-money at (or before) the expiry date.

- **Prior to maturity**, the call premium is positively related to changes in the price of the underlying asset (e.g. stocks), while the put premium is negatively related to the price of the stocks. These relationships are derived from the famous **Black–Scholes formula** which allows us to price (European) options at each point in time. It follows that a **speculator** who thinks that stock prices will rise (fall) in the near future will buy calls (buy puts).

- The **Clearing House** facilitates an active market in traded options by minimising credit (default) risk, as those holding short positions have to post margin payments.

- **Newspaper (and screen) quotes** are available on calls and puts for several different strike prices and expiry dates, for about 100 individual stocks on LIFFE (UK) and over 500 stocks on CBOT. Most traded stock options have **expiry dates** no longer than 1 year, but on some stocks traded options are available with expiry dates out to 3 years. These are know as **LEAPS** and if these longer term options are written on stock indices, they are know as **FLEX options**.

- Options can be written on individual stocks, stock indices, currencies, futures contracts, (the price of) interest bearing assets (e.g. T-bonds) and interest rates (e.g. caps, floors and collars). There is a **very large OTC market in options** and some options are only available OTC (e.g. caps and floors).

- Options with complex payoffs are know as **exotic options**. Examples include **Asian options** and **barrier options**, but there are many more.

- **Some options are 'embedded'** in other securities (e.g. callable bonds, convertible bonds, warrants and executive stock options). Some **decisions to invest in a new business also contain embedded options** to expand or delay production or to abandon the business. These 'options' provide strategic flexibility for the firm and their valuation forms part of **real options theory**.

# END OF CHAPTER EXERCISES

**Q1** Intuitively, would you pay more for a European put option on a stock with a strike price of $K = 100$ when the current stock price was 98 or when it was 99? Briefly explain.

**Q2** Would you make a profit on a long call option or a long put option if the stock price was $S = 100$ when you purchased the option and $S = 120$ when you sold the option (assume no change in other factors that influence the option price)?

**Q3** On 1st March the ordinary shares of *Branson plc* stood at $S = 469p$. In the traded options market April-500p puts have a premium $P = 47p$. If the share price falls to $S_T = 450p$, how much, if any, profit would an investor make? What will the option be worth if the share price moves up to 510p?

**Q4** Frank purchased a call option on 100 shares in *Gizmo plc* 6 months ago at a call premium of $C = 10p$ per share. The share price at the time was $S = 110p$ and the strike price was $K = 120p$. Just prior to expiry the share price rose to $S_T = 135p$.

(a) State whether the option should be exercised.
(b) Calculate the profit or loss on the option.
(c) Would Frank have done better by investing the same amount of cash 6 months ago in a bank offering 10% p.a.?

**Q5** Below are quotes for options on IBM from the *Wall Street Journal*. Explain the key features in the table.

## Listed options quotations (Monday 3rd January 2000)

| IBM | Strike | Exp. | Call Vol. | Call Last | Put Vol. | Put Last |
|-----|--------|------|-----------|-----------|----------|----------|
| $107^{7/8}$ | 105 | Jan | 325 | $6^{1/2}$ | 1679 | $3^{1/2}$ |
| $107^{7/8}$ | 110 | Jan | 1068 | $4^{1/8}$ | 403 | $6^{1/8}$ |
| $107^{7/8}$ | 115 | Jan | 928 | $2^{1/2}$ | 21 | $9^{1/4}$ |
| $107^{7/8}$ | 115 | Feb | 842 | $4^{3/4}$ | 22 | $11^{1/4}$ |
| $107^{7/8}$ | 120 | Jan | 677 | $1^{5/16}$ | 40 | 13 |
| $107^{7/8}$ | 120 | Feb | 165 | $3^{1/4}$ | 2 | $14^{3/4}$ |

**Q6** Using the data in the table above calculate and comment on the intrinsic value and time value of the 115 calls which expire in January and February.

**Q7** If you exercise a position in a long call option on IBM shares on CBOE, who exactly delivers the shares?

# Glossary

| | |
|---|---|
| **Abnormal profits** | The rate of return in excess of the rate of return which reflects the riskiness of the investment |
| **Accrued interest** | See **Gross accrued interest** |
| **Active portfolio management** | Investment strategy which aims to achieve abnormal returns by buying and selling assets |
| **Adjusted present value** | Alternative approach to NPV which takes account of the financial benefits of tax deductibles and certain corporate expenditures, see **Net present value** |
| **Adverse selection** | Economic principle which arises in insurance markets. It describes the problem of pricing insurance products when it is not possible to distinguish between different risk categories of applicants |
| **Agency broker** | Broker–dealer who acts as an intermediary between investors and market |
| **Agency costs** | Costs associated with monitoring contracts |
| **Aggressive stock** | Stock whose beta is greater than 1, which means that its return moves more than the market |
| **Allotment price** | Price at which stock is allotted to successful bidder in a tender offer |
| **American option** | Option which may be exercised at any time up to the expiry date |
| **Anomaly** | Empirical observations which cannot be explained by known asset pricing models |
| **Arbitrage** | Undertaking a trade that enables a risk free profit to be made |
| **Arbitrage pricing model** | Equilibrium asset pricing model which links an asset's return with its sensitivity to economic variables or factors |
| **ARCH/GARCH model** | Measures time varying conditional volatility using historical data |
| **Asian option** | Option whose payoff depends on the average price over the life of the option |
| **Ask (offer) price** | The price at which a market maker offers to sell a primary or derivative security |
| **Asset** | General term for anything with economic value |
| **Asset allocation** | Decision on how to split your wealth into different asset classes, for instance stocks, bonds and cash |

| | |
|---|---|
| **Asymmetric information** | Situation where one party has more information than the other party |
| **At-the-money option** | An option with a strike price equal to, or very close to, the current market price of the underlying security |
| **Auction (gilts)** | Sale of new stock at which successful competitive bidders pay the price bid. Non-competitive bidders pay the weighted average price of successful competitive bids |
| **Backwardation** | A condition in which the forward/futures price is below the current spot price, see **Contango** |
| **Bank bill (acceptance credit)** | Bank buys a bill of exchange from a corporate (at a discount) and the bank then guarantees future payment to any holder of the bill at maturity |
| **Barbell portfolio** | A bond portfolio in which the duration of the individual bonds varies widely |
| **Basis** | The difference between the spot and futures prices |
| **Basis point** | 1/100 of 1% |
| **Basis risk** | The risk associated with variation in the basis over time |
| **Bear market** | Market condition which describes falling prices |
| **Bear spread (with calls)** | Describes the payoff profile of selling a call with a low strike price and buying a call with a higher strike price. Both calls will have the same maturity |
| **Bearer bond** | Bond for which ownership is evidenced by possession of the document rather than entry in a register; title is transferred by delivery of the bearer document |
| **Benchmark portfolio** | Alternative portfolio which an existing investment is being compared against, with respect to its performance and riskiness |
| **Best execution** | Duty of a broker–dealer to provide the lowest available price (when buying stock) or the highest available price (when selling stock) for his customers |
| **Beta** | A measure of the responsiveness of a security's returns to movements in the return on the market portfolio |
| **Bid price** | The price at which a market maker offers to buy a primary or derivative security |
| **Bid–ask (offer) spread** | Difference between the bid and ask (offer) price, see **Bid price**, **Ask (offer) price** |
| **Bill of exchange** | Like a post-dated cheque. The buyer of goods sends a 'note' promising to pay at a future date. Can be sold in the secondary market for cash, prior to maturity. Used to finance overseas trade |
| **Black–Scholes model** | A model for pricing European option contracts |
| **Bond market** | Market where long-term fixed income securities are traded. These instruments usually pay coupons |
| **Bootstrapping** | Specific statistical technique to extract a random sample from a given data set. The sample is generated by repeated resampling of the original observations |
| **BOPM** | Binomial option pricing model |
| **Broker** | Individual or company who executes orders to buy or sell financial assets, see **Discount broker** |

| | |
|---|---|
| **Brownian motion** | A specific stochastic process which describes the random time path of a variable (e.g. stock price) |
| **Bubble** | Rapid increase in share price which indicates an overvaluation of the company relative to fundamentals |
| **Bull market** | Market condition which describes rising prices |
| **Bull spread (with calls)** | Describes the payoff profile from buying a call with a low strike price and selling a call which has the same maturity but with a higher strike price |
| **Bullet portfolio** | Bond portfolio which contains bonds where the durations of the individual bonds are close together |
| **Butterfly** | Payoff profile engineered by either buying and selling calls or buying and selling puts. This payoff profile will be V-shaped 'with wings' |
| **Call option** | A derivative security giving the holder the right to buy an underlying asset on either a specified date (European) or on or before a specified date (American), at a fixed price |
| **Call premium** | Price of a call option |
| **Callable bond** | Bond which can be redeemed by the company that issues it, before its maturity date |
| **Calling the mark** | The process of calling for margin to be reinstated following a mark-to-market revaluation of a repo transaction |
| **Candlesticks** | Method of predicting asset prices based on high–low and open–close prices |
| **Cap** | Set of caplets |
| **Capital asset pricing model (CAPM)** | An equilibrium model where there is a linear relation between the expected return on an asset and the return on the market portfolio |
| **Capital market line (CML)** | The line which combines the market portfolio with the risk free rate. It describes the linear relationship between the expected return and risk, see **Efficient frontier** |
| **Caplet** | Interest rate call option, which pays off if the interest rate at expiry exceeds the strike or cap rate. Caplets can be used for speculating on interest rate rises, or for hedging |
| **Cash flow mapping** | Process of converting actual cash flow maturities into standardised maturity dates in order to simplify the calculation of 'Value at Risk' |
| **Cash flow matching** | Passive bond portfolio strategy which aims to match the actual cash flows of the bond portfolio with the stream of liability payments |
| **Cash settlement** | A procedure applicable to certain futures and options contracts wherein a cash transfer is employed at contract settlement, rather than the actual delivery of the underlying asset in question |
| **Cash-and-carry arbitrage** | A theoretically riskless arbitrage trading strategy involving the underlying asset and a futures contract |
| **Central Gilts Office (CGO)** | The office of the Bank of England which until 1999 ran the computer-based settlement system for gilt-edged securities, and certain other securities (mostly bulldogs) for which the Bank acts as Registrar. Now undertaken by *CrestCo* |

| | |
|---|---|
| **Certificate of deposit** | A time deposit issued by banks and other financial institutions. It is a bearer denominated money market instrument which is quoted on a yield basis |
| **Chaos theory** | Attempts to explain the random pattern observable in asset prices and returns by using deterministic non-linear models |
| **Chartist** | Technical analyst who bases her forecast of price movements on charts or other plots |
| **Cheapest to deliver (CTD)** | Refers to the cheapest bond which can be delivered by the short in a T-bond futures contract. The exchange denotes a set of bonds which can be delivered |
| **Clean price** | Quoted price of a bond which excludes accrued interest or rebate interest |
| **Clearing house** | A firm associated with an options or futures exchange, that guarantees contract performance and otherwise facilitates trading |
| **Closed-end funds** | Managed investment company which is listed on the stock exchange. The price of its shares will be determined according to demand and supply |
| **Closed-form solution** | A mathematical solution of the form $y = f(x, z)$ |
| **Closing out** | Selling a contract you already hold or buying a contract you have previously shorted |
| **Closing price** | Price of the last trade on a particular day for a specific security |
| **Collar** | Combination of a long cap and a long floor |
| **Collateral** | The value of any assest held against borrowed funds |
| **Commercial paper** | A legal document ('paper') setting out loan terms. Maturity 7 days to 2 years. Active secondary market |
| **Condor** | Options trading strategy which involves buying and selling an option with different strike prices |
| **Consol** | See **Perpetuity** |
| **Contango** | A condition in which the forward price is above the (current or) expected future spot price, see **Backwardation** |
| **Contract** | A binding agreement between two parties |
| **Convenience yield** | Return from holding the spot commodity |
| **Conventional 'stocks'** | Bonds on which interest payments and principal repayments are fixed |
| **Conversion factor** | Used in the futures market to adjust the value of a deliverable Treasury note or Treasury bond |
| **Convertible bond** | Bond which may be converted by the holder, into a certain number of stocks of the firm, at a predetermined price at certain times in the future |
| **Convertible stock** | Stock which gives the holder the right but not the obligation to convert all or part of her holding into another stock or stocks, on specified dates and on specified terms |
| **Convexity** | Measures the curvature of the price–yield relationship for bonds |
| **Corporation** | Form of ownership where the company is owned by its shareholders. In the case of bankruptcy the personal assets of the shareholders cannot be used to pay off residual debt |

| | |
|---|---|
| **Correlation** | A measure of the linear dependence between variables |
| **Cost of carry** | The cost of holding a spot asset between two time periods |
| **Counterparty** | The agent on the other side of a contract |
| **Coupon** | Annual interest paid on a bond, usually in two equal semi-annual instalments |
| **Coupon stripping** | Process referring to the separation of the coupons from the principal of the bond. This creates a series of zero coupon assets |
| **Covariance** | A measure of the dependence of two variables (unbounded) |
| **Covered interest rate parity** | Relationship which describes a no arbitrage condition in the foreign exchange market. Relationship between money market rates and the spot and forward exchange rate |
| **Credit derivatives** | Derivatives where the payoff depends on a 'credit event' |
| **Credit risk** | Describes the general risk that the counterparty will default and not honour the contract, see **Default risk** |
| **Credit risk plus** | Methodology proposed by Credit Suisse First Boston to measure credit risk |
| **CreditMetrics$^{TM}$** | Methodology proposed by J.P. Morgan to measure changes in credit risk |
| **Cross-hedge** | A futures hedge in which the asset underlying the futures contract differs from the asset being hedged |
| **Cross-rate** | An exchange rate between two currencies that is implied by their exchange rates with a third currency |
| **Cum-dividend** | A stock purchased cum-dividend gives the purchaser the right to the next interest payment (see **Ex-dividend**) |
| **Currency swap** | Process which swaps payments/receipts of principals and interest in one currency for payments/receipts in a different currency |
| **Daily price limits** | Barriers which indicate the cessation of trading for that day, if those limits are reached |
| **Day count** | Convention about the number of days used for calculating the price of money market instruments. The day count convention determines the use of number of days per month and number of days per year |
| **Day trading** | Buying and selling the same securities within the same day. Closing out the positions before the end of the trading day |
| **Dealer** | See **Market maker** |
| **Debenture (secured loan stock/bond)** | A document entitling the holder to specific interest payments and capital repayments. 'Fixed charge' implies payments are backed by specific assets; 'floating charge' implies the security comprises the present and future assets of the firm. 'Unsecured loan stock' is debt which is low down the pecking order for repayment (including any available after liquidation) |
| **Debt** | Loan which is a liability of the issuer, who has to make cash payments in future periods |
| **Default risk** | The risk that one counterparty will fail to honour its part or the remaining part of an agreed transaction |

| | |
|---|---|
| **Defensive stock** | Asset with a beta of less than 1. If the market falls the return on this stock would fall by less than the market return |
| **Delivery day** | Day when the underlying product has to be delivered and the long pays the short |
| **Delta hedge** | To create a hedged position which takes into account the sensitivity of an option's premium to changes in the price of the security on which the option is based |
| **Delta neutral portfolio** | A portfolio whose value is not affected by changes in the value of the underlying asset |
| **Deposit insurance** | Insured bank deposits. Insurance pays out if the bank goes bankrupt |
| **Derivative security** | A security whose existence is dependent, or contingent, upon the existence of another security |
| **Dirty price** | The price of a bond including accrued interest. Also known as the all-in price |
| **Discount broker** | Firm which offers a limited brokerage service at reduced prices compared to brokers who offer a full range of services |
| **Discount rate (on Treasury bills)** | The annualised difference between the redemption value and the purchase price |
| **Diversification** | A process of adding assets to a portfolio to reduce risk |
| **Dividend yield** | The ratio of the dividend per share to the share price |
| **Dividends** | Cash payments made to shareholders of a firm. They can vary over time and are not guaranteed |
| **Duration** | A measure of the sensitivity of a bond's price to changes in market rates of interest |
| **Dynamic hedging** | A strategy in which an equity portfolio is insured through the continual trading of stock index futures contracts |
| **Economic profit** | Method of determining the profitability of a project, proposed by McKinsey. It is defined as the difference between the *return on capital* and the *weighted average cost of capital*, multiplied by the *capital used* |
| **Economic value added (EVA)** | Method of measuring and monitoring the performance of divisions within a firm and to compare economic performance across firms |
| **Efficient frontier** | = *Efficient set*. Set of efficient risky portfolios. Those portfolios that represent the best possible risk–return trade off |
| **Efficient market** | A market in which asset prices reflect the true intrinsic value of those assets |
| **Efficient set** | See **Efficient frontier** |
| **Embedded option** | The possibility to alter/change the production process of a firm if circumstances change. Concept used in real options theory |
| **Equity** | Ownership interest of shareholders in a company |
| **Equity (value)** | The share capital in a company = number of shares × current price. The shares themselves are also referred to as stock or equities |
| **Equity market** | Market where shares of companies are traded |
| **Equity premium puzzle** | Empirically observed scenario which describes the fact that the average return on equity is higher than that predicted by economic models of the risk premium |

| | |
|---|---|
| **Error correction model** | Specific type of econometric model which can be used for forecasting. This type of model allows one to distinguish between short run and long run effects |
| **Eurobonds** | Bonds sold outside the country of issue and denominated in a foreign currency (e.g. US dollars for a non-US firm or government). Interest is paid before tax and they are usually bearer bonds |
| **Eurodollar** | A dollar denominated deposit in an overseas bank |
| **Eurodollar market** | Marketplace where Eurodollar deposits are traded |
| **'Euroland'** | Countries in Europe who entered into monetary union by adopting a single currency, the euro |
| **European option** | Option which may only be exercised on the expiry date |
| **Excess return** | See **Abnormal profits** |
| **Excess volatility** | The view that asset prices move more than they should if they are determined solely by economic fundamentals |
| **Exchange rate** | The price of one currency relative to another currency |
| **Exchange rate overshooting** | Type of monetary model which predicts that because of sticky goods prices, but fully flexible asset prices, the exchange rate overshoots its long run equilibrium value, see **Sticky price monetary model** |
| **Exchange rate risk** | Uncertainty of asset returns caused by fluctuations of the exchange rate |
| **Ex-dividend (xd)** | A coupon payment will be made to the person who is the registered holder of the stock on the xd date. For most gilts, this is seven working days before the payment day |
| **Ex-dividend date** | Date on which a holder of stock becomes entitled to receive the next dividend, after which the stock trades ex-dividend |
| **Exercise price** | The price at which an option owner may buy or sell the underlying asset, if the option is exercised |
| **Exotic option** | Generic term for options with relatively complex payoffs which can be path dependent. Examples of exotic options are Asian options, lookback, barrier and chooser options |
| **Expectations theory** | A theory of the term structure of interest rates in which forward rates of interest represent the market's unbiased expectation of future interest rates |
| **Expiry date** | Date when an option expires and the underlying asset has to be delivered, if the contract has not been closed out |
| **Exponential weighted moving average** | Statistical method which calculates the variability of a data series, allowing the variability to change over time |
| **Face value** | See **Nominal (value)** |
| **Filter rule** | Method used by technical analysts to earn abnormal profits |
| **Financial engineering** | Generic term which describes a combination of different derivative instruments (e.g. calls, puts, futures) to create certain payoff scenarios, see **Synthetic securities** |
| **Financial futures contract** | A futures contract written on a financial asset such as a bond, stock index, or unit of foreign exchange |
| **Financial instrument** | An umbrella term used to cover all types of securities |
| **Fiscal policy** | Describes the changes in government spending or taxation |

| | |
|---|---|
| **Flat yield** | = **Interest yield** = **Running yield**. Income earned per annum on par value of a bond; calculated by dividing the coupon by the price and multiplying by 100 |
| **Flex-price monetary model** | Exchange rate model which is based on economic fundamentals (i.e. money supply, output, interest rates). It assumes that prices are fully flexible and adjust instantaneously, see **Sticky price monetary model** |
| **Floor** | Set of floorlets |
| **Floorlet** | Interest rate put option whose payoff is the difference between the floor (strike) rate and the actual interest rate at expiry. Floorlets are used to hedge or speculate against falling interest rates |
| **Foreign exchange market** | Market where one currency is exchanged for another currency |
| **Forward contract** | An agreement between two parties to trade foreign currency at a future date and at a prescribed exchange rate, which is determined today |
| **Forward points** | Difference between the forward and spot rate for FX |
| **FRA (forward rate agreement)** | An interest rate agreement where the parties involved agree to pay the difference between the current market rate of interest and the rate of interest agreed in the contract |
| **FRNs (forward rate notes)** | An interest bearing security where the coupon payments vary |
| **Future value** | The amount of money a lump sum will grow to at some future date |
| **Futures contract** | A contract between two parties to trade a specified asset in the future for a prescribed price, determined at contract inception |
| **Garman–Kohlhagen formula** | Valuation formula for European style foreign currency options. Based on the Black–Scholes formula |
| **GEMM prices** | Prices of gilts as at 4.15 p.m. collected from gilt-edged market makers and disseminated by the Bank of England. Participants in gilt repo are likely to use these as the standard basis for marking-to-market gilt collateral |
| **Gilt-edged market maker (GEMM)** | Dealer in gilts required to make continuous two-way prices on request to any member of the London Stock Exchange and to investors known to them directly |
| **Gilts, gilt-edged securities** | Sterling interest bearing securities issued by the United Kingdom Government |
| **Gordon growth model** | Economic model which calculates the value of a firm/stock. It assumes that the value of the firm is determined by the current dividends, the future dividend growth rate and the discount rate |
| **Greeks** | Summary statistics for the change in the price of an option (e.g. option delta, option gamma, option theta, option vega) |
| **Haircut** | See **Initial margin**. It should be noted that 'haircut' has several different meanings |
| **Hedge** | A transaction in which a trader tries to protect a pre-existing position in the spot market, by the trading derivative securities |
| **Hedge fund** | Actively managed funds which usually use highly leveraged transactions to finance their investments |

| | |
|---|---|
| **Hedge ratio** | The expected change in the value of a derivative following a change in the market price of the underlying asset |
| **Herding effect** | Investor following trends in market prices |
| **Historic volatility** | Description of the historic price fluctuations, often measured by the standard deviation, see **Volatility** |
| **Holding period return** | The rate of return over a specific period of time |
| **Immunisation** | Strategy which aims to protect the value of a bond portfolio from changes in yields |
| **Implied volatility** | The variance of the returns of an asset that is derived by equating an observed option price with a 'theoretical' option price |
| **Index linked stock** | Bonds whose coupon payments and redemption value are adjusted according to the rate of inflation |
| **Index tracking** | A form of passive portfolio management aiming to replicate the movements of a selected index |
| **Initial margin** | The excess either of cash over the value of securities, or of the value of securities over cash in a repo transaction at the time it is executed and, subsequently, after margin calls. Also known as the 'haircut'. Also a 'deposit' in futures market |
| **Interbank market** | An informal network of banks that executes transactions in currency, currency forwards and currency options |
| **Intercommodity spread** | A long and short position in two different futures contracts (i.e. different underlying asset) but with the same delivery date |
| **Inter-dealer broker (IDB)** | Firm which the GEMMs may use to deal with other GEMMs via screen trading on a no-names basis |
| **Interest rate caps** | See **Cap** |
| **Interest rate floor** | See **Floor** |
| **Interest rate futures** | Futures contracts written on fixed-income securities such as Treasury bills, notes and bonds |
| **Interest rate parity** | Equilibrium model which describes the relationship between interest rates in different countries and the exchange rate, see **Covered interest rate parity**, **Uncovered interest rate parity** |
| **Interest rate swap** | Process which converts floating rate (variable) interest payments into fixed rate payments (or vice versa) |
| **Interest yield** | See **Flat yield** |
| **Internal rate of return (IRR)** | The constant rate of return which just allows a project/ investment to break even |
| **In-the-money** | A call (put) option where the underlying asset price is greater (less) than the option's strike price |
| **In-the-money option** | An option with a positive intrinsic value |
| **Intracommodity spread** | A long and short position in two futures contracts (on the same underlying asset) but with different delivery dates |
| **Intrinsic value (of an option)** | Difference between the current stock price and the strike price. This represents the profit which could be earned if the option is exercised immediately. If intrinsic value is positive the option is said to be **In-the-money** |
| **Investment trust** | See **Closed-end funds** |

| | |
|---|---|
| **January effect** | An empirical anomaly whereby stock returns seem to be higher in January than in other months of the year, see **Small firm effect**, **Weekend effect** |
| **Jensen index** | Performance measure of portfolios based on regression analysis, see **Sharpe ratio**, **Treynor ratio** |
| **Jump diffusion process** | Random series for asset prices which experience sudden 'jumps' |
| **Leverage** | Increasing the return (or losses) on an investment, relative to that obtained when only 'own funds' are used |
| **Limited company** | See **Corporation** |
| **Liquidity preference hypothesis** | Extension of the expectations hypothesis which assumes that bonds with longer maturities require a term premium which depends on the term to maturity but does not vary over time |
| **Local** | A trader on the floor of a futures exchange who trades on his own account |
| **London Interbank Offer Rate (LIBOR)** | The variable interest rate earned on Eurodollar deposits |
| **Long hedge** | Hedging a long position |
| **Long position** | Denotes the position of one who buys a primary or derivative security |
| **Margin** | Collateral that must be posted to transact in a futures or options contract, in order to insure the clearing house against credit risk |
| **Margin call** | A request following the mark-to-market of a transaction, for the initial margin to be reinstated |
| **Market maker** | A trader on an exchange who is charged with the duty of filling public market orders |
| **Market portfolio** | Portfolio which represents all assets in a particular market with weights according to the market capitalisation |
| **Market risk** | Risk which cannot be diversified away. Proportion of the asset's total risk which relates to movements in the market portfolio, see **Systematic risk** |
| **Market segmentation hypothesis** | Explains the yield on bonds with different maturities, according to variables which influence the demand and supply of bonds |
| **Market timing** | Form of active portfolio management which shifts funds between the market portfolio and risk free assets |
| **Mark-to-market** | The act of revaluing securities to current market values (and taking account of accruals of interest on bonds) |
| **Maturity date** | Date on which a stock is redeemed |
| **Mean return** | Measure of central tendency, defined as the sum of individual returns divided by the number of observations |
| **Mean reversion** | Process which describes the path of a time series which frequently returns to its long run average |
| **Mean–variance portfolio** | Portfolio optimisation technique which only considers expected returns, variances and covariances of the individual assets |
| **Mergers** | Agreement by two companies to join together and operate as one company |

| | |
|---|---|
| **Mezzanine finance** | Hybrid debt often with both debt and equity characteristics. High yield, high risk, often with equity warrants attached. Subordinated debt and junk bonds are counted as mezzanine finance |
| **Middle price** | Average of the bid and offer price of a stock |
| **Monetary policy** | The use of interest rates or changes in the growth rate of the money supply in order to influence inflation |
| **Money market** | The market for 'paper' with less than 1 year to maturity |
| **Moral hazard** | Economic concept often observed in insurance cases where the likelihood of a claim being made increases after the insurance has been taken out |
| **Mutual funds** | See **Closed-end funds** |
| **Naive hedge ratio** | Method of calculating the number of futures contracts required to hedge a position. The naive hedge ratio is calculated by dividing the total value (at time zero) of the contract to be hedged with the face value of the futures contract |
| **Naked position** | Describes a position where a derivative is held but the risk is not offset by holding the underlying security |
| **Net present value (NPV)** | Present value of future cash flows less capital or investment costs, see **Adjusted present value** |
| **Nominal (value)** | = **Face value** = **Par value**. The cash amount agreed in a transaction |
| **Normal distribution** | Bell-shaped, symmetric probability distribution for continuous random variables which is widely used in finance. The distribution can be described by only two parameters, the mean and the standard deviation of the underlying random variable |
| **Off balance sheet items (OBS)** | Specific form of financing which is not shown on the liability side of the bank's balance sheet |
| **Open interest** | Total number of futures or option contracts which have not been closed out or delivered |
| **Option** | Contract which gives the purchaser the right, but not the obligation, to buy (a 'call' option) or to sell (a 'put' option) a specified amount of a commodity or financial asset at a specified price, by or on a specified date |
| **Option premium** | The price to be paid for the option to buy or sell the underlying asset |
| **Options Clearing Corporation (OCC)** | The corporation that serves as the clearing house for all options traded on US markets (except futures options) |
| **Ordinary shares** | Ordinary shares represent a claim on the residual profits of a firm. They are characterised by voting rights and the shareholders are the owners of the firm, see **Preference shares** |
| **Out-of-the-money** | A call (put) option where the underlying asset price is below (above) the option's exercise price |
| **Over-the-counter (OTC) instrument** | Contract which is negotiated between the issuer and purchaser |
| **P–E ratio (price–earnings ratio)** | A company's current share price divided by its earnings per share |
| **Par value** | See **Nominal value** |

| | |
|---|---|
| **Partnership** | Form of ownership where two or more people combine to conduct business |
| **Passive portfolio management** | See **Index tracking** |
| **Performance measures** | A 'statistic' to measure the performance of a portfolio relative to some benchmark portfolio. Differences in the risk of the different portfolios are usually taken into account |
| **Perpetuity** | Fixed income asset which is never redeemed by the issuer and pays coupons for ever |
| **Peso problem** | A situation where forecasts appear biased because the sample of data used is not representative of the complete data set. Initially data applied to the forward rate of the Mexican peso in the 1970s |
| **Pit** | An area on the trading floor of a futures or options exchange where contracts are traded |
| **Plain vanilla swap** | A term which describes a basic 'fixed for floating' interest rate swap |
| **Political risk** | Describes the uncertainty in the returns on foreign assets due to policy changes by the foreign government, which would not be in the interests of the investor |
| **Portfolio** | A 'basket' of different assets |
| **Portfolio balance model** | Model where the exchange rate is determined by the stock of foreign and domestic assets and not just by a single asset, the money supply |
| **Portfolio insurance** | A strategy using combinations of options, futures and/or other securities, designed to ensure a minimum future value of an equity portfolio |
| **Position limit** | The maximum amount held in a particular asset or set of assets. This limit might be set by the individual trader, a broker or the exchange itself (e.g. CBOE) |
| **Position trader** | Trader who holds speculative positions over horizons of 1 day to 1 month or even longer |
| **Preference shares** | Hybrid instrument which has some characteristics of ordinary shares and some characteristics of debt instruments, see **Ordinary shares** |
| **Present value** | Value today of future cash payments |
| **Primary market** | Market where new issues are offered to the public |
| **Principal–agent problem** | Describes a conflict of interest which can arise between different agents (e.g. shareholders and directors) |
| **Program trading** | The use of computers with real time data in order to detect arbitrage opportunities |
| **Project finance** | Borrowing where future interest payments depend on the success of a specific project (e.g. hydroelectic plant) rather than on the overall profits of the borrowing firm |
| **PSBR (public sector borrowing requirement)** | Amount the UK Government requires to borrow in a year to fund any shortfall of revenue against expenditure |
| **Purchasing power parity** | The proposition that prices of traded goods produced in different countries, sell for the same price in a common currency |

| | |
|---|---|
| **Pure discount bond** | See **Zero coupon bond** |
| **Put** | A derivative security giving the buyer the right to sell an underlying asset at a prescribed strike price on or before a specified maturity date |
| **Put premium** | Price of a put option |
| **Put–call parity** | A pricing relation between puts and calls that follows from arbitrage |
| **Random walk (model)** | A model where the changes in a variable (e.g. stock price, exchange rate) are independent and identically distributed. This means the change in the variable is unpredictable |
| **Rational bubble** | See **Bubble** |
| **Rational expectations** | The idea that agents use all relevant information when forecasting a variable and hence do not make systematic forecasting errors |
| **Real option** | Term which describes the value of managerial flexibility and which should be incorporated in NPV calculations |
| **Rebate interest** | Interest paid by the seller of a bond to the purchaser, when the bond is bought without the right to receive the next interest payment |
| **Redemption yield** | Yield required to equate the purchase price of a bond with the present value of the remaining coupon payments and the maturity value. It is the IRR of the bond |
| **Registration** | Process by which ownership of an asset is entered on an official register |
| **Replication portfolio** | See **Synthetic securities** |
| **Repo (repurchase agreement)** | A transaction, carried out under an agreement, in which one party sells securities to another and at the same time and as part of the same transaction, commits to repurchase equivalent securities on a specified future date (or at call), at a specified price |
| **Repo rate** | The return earned on a repo transaction expressed as an interest rate (% p.a.) |
| **Retained earnings** | Company's earnings which are not being distributed to shareholders |
| **Return on capital (ROC)** | Method to evaluate the profitability of a project. It is defined as *earnings after depreciation and taxes* divided by *capital used* |
| **Reverse repo** | A reverse repo is a repo transaction as seen from the point of view of the party who is buying the securities |
| **Rights issue** | The sale of stock, often to existing shareholders, to obtain additional finance |
| **Risk** | Uncertainty associated with the price or return on assets, see **Systematic risk**, **Unsystematic risk** |
| **Risk adjusted return on capital (RAROC)** | Introduced by Bankers Trust, it measures the return on capital in the banking sector, see **Return on capital** |
| **Risk aversion** | Describes the attitude towards risk by investors. Choosing between two investments with the same level of expected return, a risk averse investor would choose the investment with the lower level of risk |

| | |
|---|---|
| **Risk free rate** | The rate on return of an investment which is known with certainty |
| **Risk management** | Set of techniques for measuring and controlling risk |
| **Risk neutral valuation** | Describes the no arbitrage approach to option pricing where the option price today is a weighted average of the value of the option tomorrow. The weights represent risk neutral probabilities, which implies that the stock price grows at the risk free rate |
| **Risk neutrality** | A state in which investors are indifferent towards risk |
| **Risk premium** | The additional return (over the risk free rate) that risk averse investors require to willingly hold speculative assets |
| **RiskGrade™** | Methodology proposed by J.P. Morgan to measure the change in risk of a portfolio relative to a 'market' benchmark |
| **RiskMetrics™** | Methodology proposed by J.P. Morgan to measure market risk of cash market and derivative assets |
| **Running yield** | See **Flat yield** |
| **Scalpers** | Name for options or futures traders who buy at the bid and sell at the ask price, before market prices move. They only hold their position for a few minutes |
| **Script issue** | Denotes when new shares are given to existing shareholders |
| **Secondary market** | Market where securities are traded once they have been issued |
| **Securities and Exchange Commission (SEC)** | A Federal agency charged with the regulation of all US security and option markets |
| **Security market line** | Describes the linear relationship between the expected return on different assets and the riskiness of those assets as measured by their betas, see **Capital market line** |
| **Self-regulating organisation (SRO)** | A body responsible under the Financial Services Act (1986) for the authorisation and regulation of companies providing financial services. (New defunct) |
| **Settlement date** | The date on which the ownership of an instrument passes from one party to the other |
| **Settlement price** | The futures price established at the end of each trading day, upon which daily marking-to-market is based |
| **Sharpe ratio** | = Reward to variability ratio. Risk adjusted measure of portfolio return, where risk is measured by portfolio standard deviation |
| **Short hedge** | Hedging a long position in a cash (spot) market asset |
| **Short position** | Position held by a market maker who has sold more of a stock than she actually holds |
| **Short sale** | A transaction in which a security is borrowed and sold, with the obligation to return the borrowed security at a later date |
| **Single index model (SIM)** | Linear model which describes the relationship between the return on an individual stock using only one 'variable' (factor). If this factor is the return on the market, the single index model is also referred to as the market model |
| **Small firm effect** | An empirical anomaly whereby stock returns of small firms earn a higher return corrected for risk than other possible portfolios (e.g. market portfolio), see **January effect**, **Weekend effect** |

| | |
|---|---|
| **Sole proprietor** | Form of ownership where an individual is the owner of a firm and who has unlimited liabilities |
| **Specific risk** | Component of total risk of a company's stock return which is firm specific. This type of risk can be diversified away, hence specific risk is not priced, see **Market risk** |
| **Speculation** | Investment strategy which has an uncertain outcome |
| **Speculative bubble** | See **Bubble** |
| **Spot (cash) market** | The market for assets that entail immediate (or near immediate) delivery |
| **Spot price** | The current price of an asset traded in the spot (cash) market |
| **Spread (yield spread)** | Difference between a market maker's selling price and buying price. Or the difference in yields on two bonds |
| **Spread trading** | Involves holding different futures contracts so that negative correlation arises which reduces the overall risk exposure |
| **Static hedge** | A strategy in which a (spot) asset is insured using options which are held to expiry/maturity |
| **Sticky price monetary model** | Exchange rate model where asset prices are perfectly flexible but goods prices are 'sticky' and slower to adjust (see **Flex-price monetary model**, **Exchange rate overshooting**) |
| **Stock exchange money broker (SEMB)** | Company which acts as intermediary in borrowing and lending money, gilts and other securities |
| **Stock index futures** | Futures contracts written on stock indices. The contracts are cash settled |
| **Stock index option** | An option giving the owner the right to buy or sell a claim on an aggregate stock index at a known strike price |
| **Stock split** | Refers to the process where the number of stocks held by existing shareholders increases but no additional funds are raised. It implies that the price of the stocks has to fall |
| **Straddle** | Payoff profile of a call and put with the same strike price. 'V-shaped' or 'inverse V-shaped' payoff profile |
| **Strangle** | Option trading strategy which involves the combination of a call and a put with different strike prices. 'Flat bottom' or 'flat top' payoff profile |
| **Strategic asset allocation** | Investment strategy based on the long-term prospects for specific sectors or countries |
| **Strike price** | Price at which the option holder has the right to buy or sell the underlying commodity or financial asset some time in the future, see **Exercise price** |
| **Strips market** | This is the secondary market which trades the individual coupons that have been 'stripped' (i.e. legally separated) from a coupon paying bond |
| **Subordinated debt** | Ranks behind other bondholder claims if the firm goes bankrupt |
| **Swap dealer** | Intermediary who matches fixed rate payer with floating rate payer or who matches anyone who wants to swap principals and interest payments in different currencies |
| **Swaps** | A negotiated agreement between two parties to exchange cash flows at specified future dates |

| | |
|---|---|
| **Synthetic securities** | 'Engineered' product which replicates the same cash flows as another asset, but uses different financial instruments (e.g. synthetic forward using money market assets) |
| **Systematic risk** | The risk of a security that is attributable to general market conditions, see **Market risk** |
| **Tactical asset allocation** | Switching funds between countries based on a 'short run' view about the state of the economic cycle in those countries |
| **Tail** | Difference between average price and lowest price accepted at an auction. Usually expressed in terms of the difference in yield |
| **Tap stock** | Stock held in official portfolios for gradually selling to market makers in the future |
| **Term repo** | Repo trades (of maturity greater than 1 day) with a fixed maturity date |
| **Term structure of interest rates** | Relation between yields and maturities on bonds of a similar risk class |
| **Tick** | Units in which price movements are usually measured. The smallest permissible price fluctuation of a security |
| **Time value (of an option)** | The amount by which the option premium exceeds the intrinsic value |
| **Transformation line** | The relationship between the expected return and the risk of a portfolio where the portfolio comprises only one 'bundle' of risky assets and the risk free asset |
| **Transmission mechanism** | The process which describes the way the economy (e.g. level of output, inflation) is affected in the long and short run by changes in economic policy |
| **Treasury bill** | Instrument of up to 12 months maturity, but normally less, issued by the government at a discount |
| **Treasury bond** | Debt security issued by the government with a term to maturity in excess of 12 months. Treasury bonds usually have periodic coupon payments |
| **Treasury note** | US expression for Treasury bonds with maturity of between 1 and 7 years. Type of Treasury bond |
| **Treynor ratio** | Risk adjusted measure of portfolio return, where risk is measured by the beta (market risk of the portfolio) |
| **Uncovered interest (rate) parity** | Relationship between interest rates in different countries and the expected change in the exchange rate |
| **Underlying (asset)** | Specific asset on which a derivative contract is based (e.g. commodity, T-bond, equity, equity index) |
| **Unit trusts** | Open-end investment fund. Type of portfolio investment for small investors |
| **Unsecured loan stock** | Debt which is low down the pecking order for receipts (including any funds available after liquidation). If 'convertible' then can be exchanged for equity capital (at a known fixed conversion rate) at the option of the holder |
| **Unsystematic risk** | The risk of a security that is not attributable to general market conditions |

| | |
|---|---|
| **Value at risk** | Maximum 'dollar' loss over a specific time horizon at a prespecified probability |
| **Variance** | A measure of the dispersion of a security's return about its expected value. It is the square of the standard deviation |
| **Variation margin** | Profits or losses which occur daily, due to marking-to-market |
| **Vega (also known as lambda, kappa and sigma)** | A measure of the sensitivity of the call/put premium to changes in volatility |
| **Venture capital** | Funds raised from small 'boutique' firms for 'new' growth companies. Usually a mixture of debt and equity finance |
| **Volatility** | Measure of the variability in asset prices, see **Implied volatility, Historic volatility** |
| **Volatility smile** | The relationship between the implied volatility of an option and 'other' variables (e.g. different strike prices, time to maturity) |
| **Warehousing** | Denotes the situation where a financial institution carries an open position on its books until a suitable long-term counterparty can be found |
| **Warrant** | Instrument which gives the holder the right (but not the obligation) to buy shares directly from the company at a fixed price, some time in the future. A type of call option |
| **Weekend effect** | Empirical anomaly which describes the fact that shares have lower returns on Mondays than on other days of the week, ceteris paribus, see **January effect, Small firm effect** |
| **Weighted average cost of capital (WACC)** | Overall cost of capital/financing when a mix of debt and equity finance is be used. Calculated on a before and after tax basis |
| **Wiener process** | See **Brownian motion** |
| **Writer** | The seller of an option contract. The writer of a call or put option has a short position |
| **Yield curve** | See **Term structure of interest rates** |
| **Yield to maturity** | The internal rate of return on a bond |
| **Zero coupon bond** | A bond which does not pay any coupons. It sells at a discount to its face (par) value |

# List of Symbols

| | |
|---|---|
| $f(.)$ | Function (of a set of variables) |
| $a$ | Number of days in the year (for day count convention of money market instruments) |
| Aaa, Aa, A, Baa, etc. | Moody's Corporate Bond Ratings |
| AAA, AA, A, BBB, etc. | Standard & Poor's Corporate Bond Ratings |
| AAR | Annual abnormal returns |
| ADR | American depository receipts |
| AI | Accrued interest |
| AIM | Alternative investment market |
| ANN | Artificial neural network |
| APT | Arbitrage pricing theory |
| APV | Adjusted present value |
| AR | Abnormal returns |
| ARCH | Autoregressive conditional heteroscedasticity |
| ARR | Accounting rate of return |
| AV | Abandonment value |
| $B$ | Basis (on a futures contract) or value of debt |
| BBA | British Bankers Association |
| BCCI | Bank for Credit and Commerce International |
| BD | Bad debt |
| BDT | Black–Derman–Toy model for pricing interest rate derivatives |
| $BF$ | Value of the floating rate bond underlying the swap contract |
| BIS | Bank for International Settlements |
| BOPM | Binomial option pricing model |
| B–S | Black–Scholes option pricing model |
| $BX$ | Value of a fixed rate bond underlying a swap |
| $BY$ | Bond yield equivalent |
| $C$ | Price of call (call premium) or coupon (interest) payment on a bond |
| **C** | Variance–covariance matrix (for value at risk) |
| $C(S, T, K)$ | Price of call option given spot price $S$, time to maturity $T$ and strike price $K$ |
| CAPM | Capital Asset Pricing Model |

| | |
|---|---|
| CC | Cost of carry (for futures contract) |
| CD | Certificate of deposit |
| CF | Conversion factor used for T-bond futures |
| $CF_i$ | Cash flows in period $i$ |
| CML | Capital market line |
| CMR | Cumulative mortality rate |
| CP | Commercial paper |
| $cp_T$ | Coupon swap rate at maturity of a swaption |
| CTD | Cheapest to deliver (bond) |
| $C_u, C_{uu}, C_{ud}$ | Call price sequence in the binomial model |
| CV | Continuing value |
| C-VaR | Credit value at risk |
| $D$ | Duration of a bond or depreciation or 'dollar' discount for money market assets or dividends on a stock or debt or deposits |
| DCF | Discounted cash flow |
| DPV | Discounted present value |
| d$z$ | Standard Wiener process |
| $E$ | Shareholder equity capital or company earnings |
| $E^*$ | Expected value in a risk neutral world |
| EAR | Equity (total) assets ratio |
| EBITD | Earnings before interest, tax and depreciation |
| EDF | Expected default frequency |
| EH | Expectations hypothesis |
| EMH | Efficient markets hypothesis |
| EP | Economic profits |
| ES | Expert system |
| $E_t r_{t+i}$ | Expected value of short-term interest rate for period $t + i$ |
| EV | Extreme value approach |
| EVA | Economic value added |
| EWMA | Exponentially weighted moving average |
| $EX$ | Expected value of $X$ |
| $F$ | Futures/forward price |
| $f_c$ | Continuously compounded futures/forward rate |
| FDIC | Federal Deposit Insurance Corporation |
| FFA | Forward–forward agreement |
| $f_{ij}$ | Forward interest rate from end of $t = i$ to $t = j$ |
| FP | Forward premium (on a currency) |
| FPMM | Flex-price monetary model |
| FRF | French francs (SWIFT code) |
| FRN | Floating rate note |
| FRU | Forward rate unbiasedness |
| FSA | Financial Services Authority |
| FT | *Financial Times* |
| FV | Face value (of a bond) |
| FVF | Face value of one futures contract |
| FVS | Face value of spot position |
| FX | Foreign exchange |

| | |
|---|---|
| $g$ | Growth rate or default rate of bank loans |
| GARCH | Generalised ARCH model |
| GBM | Geometric Brownian motion |
| GDR | Global depository receipts |
| $h$ | Hedge ratio |
| HPR | Holding period return |
| IMRO | Investment Managers Regulatory Organisation |
| IO | Interest only strips |
| IPO | Initial public offering |
| IR | Investment ratio |
| IROC | Incremental return on capital |
| IRR | Internal rate of return |
| $I_t$ | Investment at time $t$ |
| $J$ | Size of the jump in a jump diffusion process |
| $K$ | Strike price of an option |
| $k$ | Number of 'up' movements in BOPM |
| KC | Capital cost |
| LAPF | Life Assurance and Pension Funds |
| LAUTRO | Life Assurance and Unit Trust Regulatory Organisation |
| LBO | Leveraged buyout |
| LIBID | London Interbank Bid Rate |
| LIBOR | London Interbank Offer Rate |
| $M$ | Maturity value or other known future payment |
| $m$ | Number of days until investment matures (for day count convention of money market instruments) or number of payments per year in a swap |
| MA | Moving average |
| MBO | Management buyout |
| MBS | Mortgage-backed security |
| MCS | Monte Carlo simulation |
| MD | Modified duration |
| $m_i$ | Natural log of the money supply of country $i$ |
| $M_i$ | Money supply of country $i$ |
| MM | Modigliani–Miller |
| MMR | Marginal mortality rate |
| MPC | Monetary Policy Committee |
| MSD | Marginal standard deviation |
| $N$ | Number of periods to maturity |
| $N(\mu, \sigma)$ | Normal probability distribution with mean $\mu$ and standard deviation $\sigma$ |
| NCPPS | Non-cumulative perpetual preference shares |
| $N_f$ | Number of futures contracts |
| NPV | Net present value |
| NVA | Net asset value |
| OBS | Off balance sheet items |
| OCC | Options Clearing Corporation |
| OMO | Open market operation |
| OTC | Over-the-counter |

| | |
|---|---|
| $P$ | Price (e.g. put premium) of an asset |
| P&L | Profit and loss figures |
| $P(S, T, K)$ | Put premium given spot price $S$, time to maturity $T$ and strike price $K$ |
| $P^*$ | 'Long run' equilibrium price |
| p.a. | Per annum |
| PBM | Portfolio balance model |
| PCS | Property claim service |
| PDE | Partial differential equation |
| PEAPC | Price expectations augmented Phillips curve |
| %RI | Percentage risk impact |
| PI | Profitability index |
| $p_i$ | Probability of outcome $i$ |
| PO | Principal only strips |
| PPP | Purchasing power parity |
| PSBR | Public sector borrowing requirement |
| $P_t^*$ | Perfect foresight stock price |
| PV | Present value |
| $Q$ | Notional principal value (e.g. par value in a swap agreement) |
| $Q_f$ | Quoted index price of futures contract |
| $R$ | %Return on an asset (i.e. capital gain + per period cash flow) or sales revenue |
| $\overline{R}$ | (Sample) mean return |
| R&D | Research and development |
| $R(S, t)$ | Real option value which is a function of the value of the underlying asset and time $t$ |
| $r$, $r_f$ | Nominal (risk free) interest rate or safe rate between today ($t = 0$) and time $t$ (i.e. spot rate) |
| RADR | Risk adjusted discount rate |
| RAR | Risk adjusted asset ratio |
| $R_c$ | Continuously compounded return |
| $r_{corp}$ | Interest rate charged by a bank to a corporate |
| RE | Rational expectations |
| $RG_i$ | RiskGrade of a portfolio of assets |
| $R_j$ | 'Long-term' interest rate with maturity of $j$ periods |
| $R_m$ | Return on the market portfolio |
| RMSE | Root mean squared error |
| RNV | Risk neutral valuation |
| ROC | Return on capital employed |
| ROI | Return on investment |
| $rp$ | risk premium on a stock |
| $R_r$ | Real return |
| RSI | Relative strength index |
| $r_{t+i}^e$ | Expected future 'short-term' interest rate for period $t + i$ |
| $S$ | Asset price, spot price (e.g. stock price, exchange rate) or the value of the equity (of a firm) |
| S&L | Savings and Loans: financial institutions (USA) |
| $s^2$, $\hat{\sigma}^2$ | Sample variance |

| | |
|---|---|
| $S_{\text{BE}}$ | Breakeven share price |
| SEC | Securities and Exchange Commission |
| $SF$ | Synthetic forward/futures rate |
| SFA | Security and Futures Association |
| $S_i$ | Sharpe ratio for fund $i$ |
| SIM | Single index model |
| SIO | Stock index option |
| SL | Synthetic levered firm |
| SML | Security market line |
| $Sp$ | Interest rate credit spread |
| SPMM | Sticky price monetary model |
| SR | Survival rate |
| SRO | Self-regulatory organisation |
| Std | Standard deviation |
| SV | Scrap value |
| $T$ | Time to expiration/maturity of a derivatives contract/receipts, total tax or transition probability |
| $t$ | Tax rate |
| $T_t^{(n)}$ | Term premium at time $t$ for $n$-period bond |
| TV | Terminal value |
| $U$ | Utility |
| $\text{URG}_{\text{p}}$ | Undiversified RiskGrade of a portfolio |
| USD | US dollars (Swift code) |
| UU, UD, DD, etc. | Movements in a decision tree where U indicates an 'up' move and D refers to a 'down' move |
| $V$ | Value of an asset/portfolio/firm |
| VAR | Vector autoregressive model |
| VaR | Value at risk |
| VLIS | Value Line Investment Survey |
| $V_{\text{p}}$ | Value of a portfolio |
| WACC | Weighted average cost of capital |
| WC | Working capital |
| WCS | Worse case scenario analysis |
| $w_i$ | Weight of asset $i$ in a portfolio |
| $y$ | Yield, current yield, yield to maturity or internal rate of return |
| $y_{\text{f}}$ | Settlement yield on futures contract |
| $z$ | Value of one index point |
| $\Delta$ | Delta of an option (or discrete change in a variable) |
| $\Gamma$ | Gamma of an option |
| $\Lambda$ | Vega of an option |
| $\Pi$ | Profits |
| $\Theta$ | Theta of an option |
| $\alpha, \beta$ | Parameters in a regression model |
| $\beta_i, \beta_{\text{f}}, \beta_{\text{p}}$ | Beta of asset $i$, beta of futures, beta of portfolio |
| $\delta_i$ | Discount rate $= (1 + r_i)^{-1}$ |
| $\varepsilon_{it}$ | Unsystematic or specific risk of asset $i$ |
| $\lambda$ | Instantaneous probability of the arrival of a competitor (used to value real options) or decay factor in EWMA model |

| $\lambda_{\mathrm{m}}$ | Market price of risk |
| $\mu$ | Expected value (e.g. of the exchange rate) |
| $\nu$ | Convenience yield |
| $\pi$ | Rate of inflation (of goods and services) |
| $\rho$ | Correlation coefficient or 'Rho', the change in time value of an option |
| $\sigma$ | (Population) standard deviation or volatility ($\sigma^2$ = variance) |
| $\sigma_{ij}$ | Covariance between asset $i$ and asset $j$ |

# List of 'Topic Boxes'

# Internet Sites

**Credit Rating Agencies**
Moody's  http://www.moody.com
Standard & Poor's  http://www.standardandpoors.com

**Global Investment Banks**
Goldman Sachs  http://www.goldmansachs.com
Morgan Stanley Dean Witter  http://www.morganstanley.com
Merrill Lynch  http://www.merrilllynch.com
J.P. Morgan  http://www.jpmorgan.com
Chase Manhatten  http://www.chase.com
Deutsche Bank (Research)  http://www.dbresearch.de
HSBC  http://www.hsbc.com
Nomura  http://www.nomura.com

**Stock Exchanges**
London Stock Exchange  http://www.londonstockexchange.com
New York Stock Exchange  http://www.nyse.com
Nasdaq Stock Exchange  http://nasdaq.com
Hong Kong Stock Exchange  http://www.hkex.com.hk/index.html
Tokyo Stock Exchange  http://www.tse.or.jp
Australian Stock Exchange  http://www.asx.com.au
Gruppe Deutscher Borse  http://www.exchange.de

**Derivative Exchanges**
Chicago Board Options Exchange  http://www.cboe.com
Chicago Board of Trade  http://www.cbot.com
Chicago Mercentile Exchange  http://www.cme.com
Philadelphia Stock Exchange  http://www.phlx.com
SIMEX (Singapore)  http://www.simex.com.sg
Hong Kong Futures Exchange  http://www.hkfe.com
Sydney Futures Exchange  http://www.sfe.com.au
LIFFE (London)  http://www.liffe.com
Eurex (Frankfurt)  http://www.eurexchange.com

## Central Banks and Regulatory Authorities

| | |
|---|---|
| Bank for International Settlements | http://www.bis.org |
| Bank of England | http://www.bankofengland.co.uk |
| Federal Reserve Board (USA) | http://bog.frb.fed.us |
| Bank of Japan | http://www.boj.or.jp/en/index.htm |
| Reserve Bank of Australia | http://www.rba.gov.au |
| Monetary Authority of Singapore | http://www.mas.gov.sg |
| Securities and Exchange Commission | http://www.sec.gov |
| European Central Bank | http://www.ecb.int |
| Financial Service Authority (FSA) | http://www.fsa.gov.uk |
| HM Treasury | http://www.hm-treasury.gov.uk |

## Federal Reserve Banks in the USA

| | |
|---|---|
| Federal Reserve Bank of Atlanta | http://www.frbatlanta.org |
| Federal Reserve Bank of Boston | http://www.bos.frb.org |
| Federal Reserve Bank of Chichago | http://www.chi.frb.org |
| Federal Reserve Bank of Cleveland | http://www.clev.frb.org |
| Federal Reserve Bank of Dallas | http://www.dallasfed.org |
| Federal Reserve Bank of Kansas City | http://www.kc.frb.org |
| Federal Reserve Bank of Minneapolis (Woodrow) | http://woodrow.mpls.frb.fed.us |
| Federal Reserve Bank of New York | http://www.ny.frb.org |
| Federal Reserve Bank of Philadelphia | http://www.phil.frb.org |
| Federal Reserve Bank of Richmond | http://www.rich.frb.org |
| Federal Reserve Bank of St. Louis | http://www.stls.frb.org |
| Federal Reserve Bank of San Francisco | http://www.frbsf.org |

## Risk Management

| | |
|---|---|
| RiskMetrics | http://www.riskmetrics.com |
| RiskGrade | http://www.riskgrade.com |
| CreditRisk+ | http://www.csfb.com/creditrisk |
| KMV | http://kmv.com |

## Newspapers and News Agencies

| | |
|---|---|
| Bloomberg UK | http://www.bloomberg.co.uk |
| Bloomberg | http://www.bloomberg.com |
| Reuters | http://www.reuters.com |
| *The Economist* | http://www.economist.com |
| *Financial Times* | http://www.ft.com |
| *Wall Street Journal* | http://www.wsj.com |

## Discount Online Brokers

http://www.iii.co.uk
http://www.dljdirect.co.uk
http://www.comdirect.co.uk
http://www.selftrade.com
http://www.charlesschawb.com
http://www.thestreet.com

**Others**

| | |
|---|---|
| Globex | http://www.cme.com/globex2 |
| Handbook of World Stock, Derivatives and Commodity Exchanges | http://www.exchange-handbook.co.uk/sites.cfm |

# References

Allen, H. and Taylor, M.P. (1989a) 'Chart Analysis and the Foreign Exchange Market', **Bank of England Quarterly Bulletin**, Vol. 29, No. 4, pp. 548–551.

Allen, H.L. and Taylor, M.P. (1989b) 'Charts and Fundamentals in the Foreign Exchange Market', **Bank of England Discussion Paper No. 40**.

Anderson, N. and Sleath, J. (1999) 'New Estimates of the UK Real and Nominal Yield Curves', **Bank of England Quarterly Bulletin**, Vol. 39, No. 4, pp. 384–392.

Anderson, N., Breedin, F., Deacon, M., Derry, A. and Murphy, C. (1996) **Estimating and Interpreting the Yield Curve**, J. Wiley, Chichester.

Ang, A., Bekaert, G. and Liu, J. (2000) 'Why Stocks May Disappoint', **NBER Working Paper No. 7783**, July, Cambridge, Massachusetts.

Ardeni, P.G. and Lubian, D. (1991) 'Is There Trend Reversion in Purchasing Power Parity', **European Economic Review**, Vol. 35, No. 5, pp. 1035–1055.

Artis, M.J. and Taylor, M.P. (1994) 'The Stabilizing Effect of the ERM on Exchange Rates and Interest Rates: Some Nonparametric Tests', **IMF Staff Papers**, Vol. 41, No. 1, pp. 123–148.

Asch, S.E. (1952) **Social Psychology**, Prentice Hall, Englewood Cliffs, New Jersey.

Baillie, R.T. and Bollerslev, T. (1989) 'Common Stochastic Trends in a System of Exchange Rates', **Journal of Finance**, Vol. 44, No. 1, pp. 167–181.

Baillie, R.T. and Mahon, P.C. (1989) **The Foreign Exchange Market: Theory and Evidence**, Cambridge University Press, Cambridge.

Baillie, R.T. and Selover, D.D. (1987) 'Cointegration and Models of Exchange Rate Determination', **International Journal of Forecasting**, Vol. 3, pp. 43–52.

Bank for International Settlements (1996) **BIS Annual Report**, June, BIS, Basle.

Bank of England (1995) **Strips and New Instruments in the Gilt Edged Market: A Consultative Paper**, Bank of England, May.

Bank of England (2000) **The Transmission Mechanism of Monetary Policy**, Monetary Policy Committee, Bank of England (also available on Bank of England web site).

Barro, R. and Gordon, D. (1983) 'Rules, Discretion and Reputation in a Model of Monetary Policy', **Journal of Monetary Economics**, Vol. 12. No. 1, pp. 101–121.

Barsky, R.B. and DeLong, J.B. (1993) 'Why Does the Stock Market Fluctuate?', **Quarterly Journal of Economics**, Vol. 108, No. 2, pp. 291–312.

Becker, G.S. (1991) 'A Note on Restaurant Pricing and Other Examples of Social Influences on Price', **Journal of Economic Perspectives**, Vol. 3, No. 1, pp. 77–105.

Bierwag, G.O., Kaufman, G.C., Schweitzer, R. and Toevs, A. (1981) 'The Art of Risk Management in Bond Portfolios', **Journal of Portfolio Management**, Spring, pp. 27–36.

Bilson, J.F.O. (1978) 'The Monetary Approach to the Exchange Rate: Some Empirical Evidence', **IMF Staff Papers**, Vol. 25, pp. 48–77.

Bilson, J.F.O. (1981) 'The Speculative Efficiency Hypothesis', **Journal of Business**, Vol. 54, No. 3, pp. 435–451.

BIS (1988) **Basle Committee of Banking Supervision, Statement on Capital Requirements for Credit Risk**, Bank for International Settlements, Basle, Switzerland.

Boothe, P. and Glassman, P. (1987) 'The Statistical Distribution of Exchange Rates: Empirical Evidence and Economic Implications', **Journal of International Economics**, Vol. 2, pp. 297–319.

Branson, W.H. (1977) 'Asset Markets and Relative Prices in Exchange Rate Determination', *Sozial Wissenschaftliche Annalen*, Band 1.

Brealey, S.A. and Myers, S.C. (2000) *Principles of Corporate Finance*, McGraw-Hill, Boston, Massachusetts.

Bremer, M.A. and Sweeney, R.J. (1991) 'The Reversal of Large Stock Price Decreases', *Journal of Finance*, Vol. 46, No. 2, pp. 747 ff.

Britten-Jones, M. (1999) 'The Sampling Error in Estimates of Mean–Variance Efficient Portfolio Weights', *Journal of Finance*, Vol. 52, No. 2, pp. 637–659.

Brock, W.A., Hsieh, D.A. and LeBaron, B. (1990) *A Test for Non-Linear Dynamics*, MIT, Cambridge, Massachusetts.

Brock, W., Lakovishok, J. and LeBaron, B. (1992) 'Simple Technical Trading Rules and the Stochastic Properties of Stock Returns', *Journal of Financial Literature*, Vol. 47, pp. 1731–1764.

Buiter, W. (1999) 'Alice in Euroland', *Journal of Common Market Studies*, forthcoming.

Cavaglia, S. and Cuthbertson, K. (1995) 'Industrial Action', *Risk*, Vol. 8, No. 5, May, pp. 2–4.

Cavaglia, S., Melas, D. and Miyashita, O. (1994) 'Efficiency Across Frontiers', *Risk*, Vol. 7, No. 10.

Constantinides, G.M., Donaldson, J.B. and Mehra, R. (1988) 'Junior Can't Borrow: A New Perspective on the Equity Premium Puzzle', *NBER Working Paper No. 6617*, June, Cambridge, Massachusetts.

Copeland, T., Koller, T. and Murrin, J. (2000) *Valuation: Measuring and Managing the Value of Companies*, J. Wiley, Chichester (3rd edition).

Cukierman, A. (1992) *Central Bank Strategy, Credibility and Independence: Theory and Evidence*, MIT Press, Cambridge, Massachusetts.

Curcio, R., Goodhart, C.A.E., Guillaume, D. and Payne, R. (1996) 'Do Filter Rules Generate Profits? Conclusions from the Intra-Day Foreign Exchange Market', *FMG Discussion Paper*, London School of Economics.

Cuthbertson, K. (1996) *Quantitative Financial Economics: Stocks, Bonds and Foreign Exchange*, J. Wiley, Chichester.

Cuthbertson, K. and Nitzsche, D. (2001) *Financial Engineering: Derivatives and Risk Management*, J. Wiley, Chichester.

Cutler, D.M., Poterba, J.M. and Summers, L.H. (1989) 'What Moves Stock Prices?', *Journal of Portfolio Management*, Vol. 15, pp. 4–12.

DeBondt, W.F.M. and Thaler, R.H. (1985) Does the Stock Market Overreact?', *Journal of Finance*, Vol. 40, No. 3, pp. 793–805.

DeBondt, W.F.M. and Thaler, R.H. (1989) 'Anomalies: A Mean-Reverting Walk Down Wall Street', *Journal of Economic Perspectives*, Vol. 3, No. 1, pp. 189–202.

DeGrauwe, P., Dewachter, H. and Embrechts, M. (1993) *Exchange Rate Theory: Chaotic Models of Foreign Exchange Markets*, Blackwell, Oxford.

DeLong, J.B., Shleifer, A., Summers, L.H. and Waldmann, R.J. (1990) 'Noise Trader Risk in Financial Markets', *Journal of Political Economy*, Vol. 98, No. 4, pp. 703–738.

Dornbusch, R. (1976) 'Expectations and Exchange Rate Dynamics', *Journal of Political Economy*, Vol. 84, No. 6, pp. 1161–1176.

Dornbusch, R. and Fischer, S. (1980) Exchange Rate and the Current Account', *American Economic Review*, Vol. 70, No. 5, pp. 960–971.

Engel, C. and Hamilton, J.D. (1990) 'Long Swings in the Dollar: Are They in the Data and Do Markets Know It?', *American Economic Review*, Vol. 80, No. 1, pp. 689–713.

Eun, C.S. and Resnick, B.G. (1997) 'International Equity Investment With Selective Hedging Strategies', *Journal of International Financial Markets, Institutions and Money*, Vol. 7, No. 1, pp. 21–42.

Evans, M.D.D. (1997) 'Peso Problems: Theoretical and Empirical Implications', in G.S. Maddala and C.R. Rao (eds.) *Handbook of Statistics: Statistical Methods in Finance*, North Holland, Amsterdam.

Fama, E.F. and Bliss, R.R. (1987) 'The Information in Long Maturity Forward Rates', *American Economic Review*, Vol. 77, No. 4, pp. 680–692.

Fama, E.F. and French, K.R. (1992) 'The Cross-Section of Expected Stock Returns', *Journal of Finance*, Vol. 47, No. 2, pp. 427–465.

Filatov, V.S. and Rappoport, P. (1992) 'Is Complete Hedging Optimal for International Bond Portfolios', *Financial Analysts Journal*, July/August. Vol. 48, No. 3, pp. 37 ff.

Fisher, E.O. and Park, J.Y. (1991) 'Testing Purchasing Power Parity Under the Null Hypothesis of Cointegration', *Economic Journal*, Vol. 101, No. 409, pp. 1476–1484.

Flavin, M.A. (1983) 'Excess Volatility in the Financial Markets: A Reassessment of the Empirical Evidence', *Journal of Political Economy*, Vol. 91, No. 6, pp. 929–956.

Flood, M.D. and Rose, A.K. (1995) 'Fixing Exchange Rates: A Virtual Quest for Fundamentals', *Journal of Monetary Economics*, Vol. 36, No. 1, pp. 3–38.

Fong, H.G. and Vasicek, O. (1984) 'A Risk Minimising Strategy for Multiple Portfolio Immunisation', *Journal of Finance*, December, Vol. 39, No. 5, pp. 1541–1546.

Frankel, J.A. (1979) 'On the Mark: A Theory of Floating Exchange Rates Based on Real Interest Differentials', *American Economic Review*, Vol. 69, No. 4, pp. 610–622.

Frankel, J.A. and Froot, K.A. (1990) 'Chartists Fundamentalists and Trading in the Foreign Exchange Market', *American Economic Review*, Vol. 80, No. 2, pp. 42–48.

French, K.R. (1988) 'Permanent and Temporary Components of Stock Prices', *Journal of Political Economy*, Vol. 96, pp. 246–273.

Frost, P. and Savarino, J. (1988) 'For Better Performance Constrain Portfolio Weights', *Journal of Portfolio Management*, Fall.

Galitz, L. (1996) *Financial Engineering*, Financial Times, Pitman Publishing, London.

Gatev, E. and Ross, S.A. (2000) 'Rebels, Non-Conformists, Contrarians and Momentum Traders', *NBER Working Paper No. 7835*, August, Cambridge, Massachusetts.

Gilles, C. and LeRoy, S.F. (1991) 'Econometric Aspects of the Variance-Bounds Tests: A Survey', *Review of Financial Studies*, Vol. 4, No. 4, pp. 753–792.

Goodhart, C.A.E. and O'Hara, M. (1997) 'High Frequency Data in Financial Markets: Issues and Applications', *Journal of Empirical Finance*, Vol. 4, No. 2/3, pp. 73–114.

Goodman, S.H. (1979) 'Foreign Exchange Rate Forecasting Techniques: Implications for Business and Policy', *Journal of Finance*, Vol. 34, No. 2, pp. 415–427.

Goodman, S.H. (1980) 'Who's Better than the Toss of a Coin?', *Euromoney*, pp. 80–84.

Gordon, M.J. (1962) *The Investment, Financing and Valuation of the Corporation*, Irwin, Homewood, Illinois.

Granger, C.W.J. and Terasvirta, T. (1993) *Modelling Non-Linear Economic Relationships*, Oxford University Press, Oxford.

Grilli, V. and Kaminsky, G. (1991) 'Nominal Exchange Rate Regimes and the Real Exchange Rate: Evidence from the United States and Great Britain, 1885–1986', *Journal of Monetary Economics*, Vol. 27, No. 2, pp. 191–212.

Hamilton (1994) *Time Series Analysis*, Princeton University Press.

Hendry, D.F. (1995) *Dynamic Econometrics*, Oxford University Press, Oxford.

Hinich, M.J. (1982) 'Testing for Gaussianity and Linearity of Stationary Sequence', *Journal of Time Series*, Vol. 3, No. 3, pp. 169–176.

Holloway, C. (1981) 'A Note on Testing an Aggressive Investment Strategy Using Value Line Ranks', *Journal of Finance*, Vol. 36, No. 3, pp. 711–719.

Isard, P. (1978) 'Exchange Rate Determination: A Survey of Popular Views and Recent Models', *Princeton Studies in International Finance, No. 42*.

J.P. Morgan (1997) *CreditMetrics, Technical Document*, J.P. Morgan, *RiskMetrics*.

Jaffe, J., Kein, D.B. and Westerfield, R. (1989) 'Earnings Yields, Market Values and Stock Returns', *Journal of Finance*, Vol. 44, No. 1, pp. 135–148.

Jensen, M.C. (1968) 'The Performance of Mutual Funds in the Period 1945–64', *Journal of Finance*, Vol. 23, pp. 389–416.

Jobson, J.D. and Korkie, B. (1980) 'Estimation for Markowitz Efficient Portfolios', *Journal of American Statistical Association*, September.

Jobson, J.D. and Korkie, B. (1981) 'Putting Markowitz Theory to Work', *Journal of Portfolio Management*, Summer.

Jorion, P. (2000) 'Lessons from Long Term Capital Management', *Graduate School of Management*, University of California (Irvine, mimeo).

Keen, S.M. (1983) *Stock Market Efficiency: Theory, Evidence and Implications*, Philip Alan, Oxford.

Keim, D.B. and Stambaugh, R.F. (1986) 'Predicting Returns in the Stock and Bond Markets', *Journal of Financial Economics*, Vol. 17, No. 2, pp. 357–390.

Kellogg, D. and Chames, J.M. (2000) 'Real-Options Valuation for a Biotechnology Company', *Financial Analysts Journal*, Vol. 56, No. 3, pp. 76–84.

Kirman, A.P. (1991) 'Epidemics of Opinion and Speculative Bubbles in Financial Markets', in M. Taylor (ed.) *Money and Financial Markets*, MacMillan, London.

Kirman, A.P. (1993) 'Ants, Rationality, and Recruitment', *Quarterly Journal of Economics*, Vol. 108, No. 1, pp. 137–156.

Kleidon, A.W. (1986) 'Variance Bounds Tests and Stock Price Valuation Models', *Journal of Political Economy*, Vol. 94, pp. 953–1001.

Lee, C.M.C., Shleifer, A. and Thaler, R.H. (1990) 'Closed-End Mutual Funds', *Journal of Economic Perspectives*, Vol. 4, No. 4, pp. 153–164.

Leibowitz, M.L. and Weinberger, A. (1983) 'Contingent Immunisation. Part II: Problem Areas', *Financial Analyst Journal*, January/February, pp. 35–50.

LeRoy, S.F. (1989) 'Efficient Capital Markets and Martingales', *Journal of Economic Literature*, Vol. 27, December, pp. 1583–1621.

Levich, R.M. (1980) 'Analysing the Accuracy of Foreign Exchange Advisory Services: Theory and Evidence', Chapter 5 in Levich and Wihlborg (eds.) *Exchange Risk and Exposure*, Lexington Books.

Levich, R.M. and Thomas, L. (1993) 'The Significance of Technical Trading-Rule Profits in the Foreign Exchange Market: A Bootstrap Approach', *Journal of International Money and Finance*, Vol. 12, pp. 451–474.

Levis, M. (1993) 'The Long Run Performance of Initial Public Offerings: The UK Experience 1980–88', *Financial Management*, Vol. 22, Spring, pp. 28–41.

Lewellen, J. and Shanken, J. (2000) 'Estimating Risk, Market Efficiency and the Predictability of Returns, *NBER Working Paper No. 7699*, May, Cambridge, Massachusetts.

Lofthouse, S. (1994) *Equity Investment Management*, J. Wiley, Chichester.

Macaulay, F.R. (1938) 'Some Theoretical Problems Suggested by the Movements of Interest Rates, Bond Yields and Stock Prices in the US Since 1856', *National Bureau of Economic Research*, New York.

Malkiel, B.G. (1977) 'The Valuation of Closed-End Investment-Company Shares', *Journal of Finance*, Vol. 32, No. 3, pp. 847–859.

Mankiw, N.G., Romer, D. and Shapiro, M.D. (1991) 'Stock Market Forecastability and Volatility: A Statistical Appraisal', *Review of Economic Studies*, Vol. 58, pp. 455–477.

Mark, N.C. (1995) 'Exchange Rates and Fundamentals: Evidence on Long Horizon Predictability', *American Economic Review*, Vol. 85, No. 1, pp. 201–218.

Martin, B. (1997) 'The Real Yield Puzzle', *Union Bank of Switzerland, London*, December.

Meese, R. (1990) 'Currency Fluctuation in the Post-Bretton Woods Era', *Journal of Economic Perspectives*, Vol. 4, No. 1, pp. 117–134.

Meese, R.A. and Roghoff, K. (1983) 'Empirical Exchange Rate Models of the Seventies: Do They Fit out of Sample?', *Journal of International Economics*, Vol. 14, pp. 3–24.

Miles, A. and Ezzel, J.R. (1980) 'The Weighted Average Cost of Capital, Perfect Capital Markets and Project Life', *Journal of Financial and Quantitative Analysis*, Vol. 15, September, pp. 719–730.

Miles, D. and Timmermann, A. (1996) 'Variation in Expected Stock Returns: Evidence on The Pricing of Equities from a Cross-Section of Companies', *Economica*, Vol. 63, pp. 369–382.

Mishkin, F.S. (1988) 'The Information in the Term Structure: Some Further Results', *Journal of Applied Econometrics*, Vol. 3, No. 4, pp. 307–314.

Modigliani, F. and Miller, M.H. (1958) 'The Cost of Capital, Corporate Finance and the Theory of Investment', *American Economic Review*, Vol. 48, June, pp. 261–297.

Moody's Bond Record (1992)

Osler, C. (2000) 'Support for Resistance: Technical Analysis and Intraday Exchange Rates', *Economic Policy Review (Federal Reserve Bank of New York)*, Vol. 6, No. 2, pp. 53–68.

Pesaran, M.H. and Potter, S.M. (1993) *Nonlinear Dynamics, Chaos and Econometrics*, J. Wiley, Chichester.

Pesaran, M.H. and Timmermann, A. (1994) 'Forecasting Stock Returns: An Examination of Stock Market Trading in the Presence of Transaction Costs', *Journal of Forecasting*, Vol. 13, No. 4, pp. 335–368.

Poterba, J.M. and Summers, L.H. (1988) 'Mean Reversion in Stock Prices: Evidence and Implications', *Journal of Financial Economics*, Vol. 22, pp. 26–59.

Reinganum, M.R. (1983) 'The Anomalous Stock Market Behaviour of Small Firms in January: Empirical Tests for Tax-Loss Selling Effects', *Journal of Financial Economics*, Vol. 12, No. 1, pp. 89–104.

Reitano, P.R. (1992) 'Non-Parallel Yield Curve Shifts and Immunisation', *Journal of Portfolio Management*, Spring, Vol. 18, pp. 36–43.

Roll, R. (1977) 'A Critique of Asset Pricing Theory's Tests', *Journal of Financial Economics*, Vol. 4, pp. 1073–1103.

Ross, R.A., Westerfield, R.W. and Jaffe, J.F. (1996) *Corporate Finance*, Irwin, Boston, Massachusetts (2nd edition).

Schaefer, S.M. (1984) 'Immunisation and Duration: A Review of Theory, Performance and Applications', *Midland Corporate Finance Journal*, Vol. 2, pp. 41–58.

Schwartz, E.S. and Moon, M. (1999) 'Rational Pricing of Internet Companies, *Financial Analysts Journal*, Vol. 56, No. 3, May/June, pp. 62–75.

Seix, C. and Akoury, R. (1986) 'Bond Indexation: The Optimal Quantitative Approach', *Journal of Portfolio Management*, Spring, pp. 50–53.

Shawky, J. (1982) 'An Update on Mutual Funds: Better Grades', *Journal of Portfolio Management*, Winter.

Sherif, M. (1937) 'An Experimental Approach to the Study of Attitudes', *Sociometry*, Vol. 1, pp. 90–98.

Shiller, R.J. (1981) 'Do Stock Prices Move Too Much to be Justified by Subsequent Changes in Dividends?', *American Economic Review*, Vol. 71, pp. 421–436.

Shiller (1989) *Market Volatility*, MIT Press, Cambridge, Massachusetts.

Shiller, R.J. (1990) 'Speculative Prices and Popular Models', *Journal of Economic Perspectives*, Vol. 4, No. 2, pp. 55–65.

Shiller, R.J. (2000) Irrational Exuberance, Princeton University Press.

Shleifer, A. (2000) *Inefficient Markets: An Introduction to Behavioural Finance*, Oxford University Press, Oxford.

Shleifer, A. and Summers, L.H. (1990) 'The Noise Trader Approach to Finance', *Journal of Economic Perspectives*, Vol. 4, No. 2, pp. 19–33.

Simons, K. (1999) 'Should US Investors Invest Overseas?', *New England Economic Review (Federal Reserve Bank of Boston)*, November/December, pp. 29–39.

Solnik, B. (1974) 'Why Not Diversify Internationally?', *Financial Analysts Journal*, August, pp. 48–54.

Standard & Poor's Bond Guide (1992)

Surajas, P. and Sweeney, R. (1992) *Profitmaking Speculation on Foreign Exchange Markets*, Westview Press Inc., New York.

Svensson, L. (1994) 'Estimating and Interpreting Forward Interest Rates: Sweden 1992–94', *IMF Working Paper No. 114*.

Takagi, S. (1991) 'Exchange Rate Expectations', *IMF Staff Papers*, Vol. 8, No. 1, pp. 156–183.

Taylor, M.P. (1987) 'Covered Interest Parity: A High Frequency, High Quality Data Survey', *Economica*, Vol. 54, pp. 429–438.

Taylor, M.P. (1989) 'Covered Interest Arbitrage and Market Turbulence', *Economic Journal*, Vol. 99, No. 396, pp. 376–391.

Timmermann, A. and Blake, D. (1997) 'Home Country Bias and Institutional Investors Foreign Equity Holdings', Birkbeck College, University of London (mimeo).

Tornell, A. (2000) 'Robust-$H_\infty$ Forecasting and Asset Pricing Anomalies', *NBER Working Paper No. 7753*, June, Cambridge, Massachusetts.

Trippi, R.R. and Turban, E. (1993) *Neural Networks in Finance and Investing*, Irwin, Burr Ridge, Illinois.

Wright, S. (1995) 'Forecasting the Bond Market', *Manchester School*, Vol. LXIII, Supplement, pp. 1–21.

# Authors Index

# Subject Index

Working Capital 86–92
Writer (of an Option) (see Option)

Yankee Bonds 17
Yield 161, 162, 188
    Dividend 107, 401

Instrument 166, 167
Redemption 187
Running/Flat/Interest 185
to Maturity 106, 107, 186–189, 193,
    194
Yield Curve 218, 223–225, 229–233,

236–240, 244, 245, 257–259, 263,
382, 383

Zero Coupon Bond (see Bond)